# Lecture Notes in Computer Science    3133

Commenced Publication in 1973
Founding and Former Series Editors:
Gerhard Goos, Juris Hartmanis, and Jan van Leeuwen

Andy D. Pimentel   Stamatis Vassiliadis (Eds.)

# Computer Systems: Architectures, Modeling, and Simulation

Third and Fourth International Workshops
SAMOS 2003 and SAMOS 2004
Samos, Greece, July 21-23, 2003 and July 19-21, 2004
Proceedings

 Springer

Volume Editors

Andy D. Pimentel
University of Amsterdam, Department of Computer Science
Kruislaan 403, 1098 SJ Amsterdam, The Netherlands
E-mail: andy@science.uva.nl

Stamatis Vassiliadis
TU Delft, Department of Computer Engineering
Mathematics and Computer Science Faculty
Mekelweg 4, 2628 CD Delft, The Netherlands
E-mail: stamatis@dutepp0.et.tudelft.nl

Library of Congress Control Number: 2004109047

CR Subject Classification (1998): C, B

ISSN 0302-9743
ISBN 3-540-22377-0 Springer-Verlag Berlin Heidelberg New York

Springer-Verlag is a part of Springer Science+Business Media

springeronline.com

© Springer-Verlag Berlin Heidelberg 2004
Printed in Germany

Typesetting: Camera-ready by author, data conversion by Olgun Computergrafik
Printed on acid-free paper     SPIN: 11018575     06/3142     5 4 3 2 1 0

# Preface

The SAMOS workshop is an international gathering of highly qualified researchers from academia and industry, sharing in a 3-day lively discussion on the quiet and inspiring northern mountainside of the Mediterranean island of Samos. As a tradition, the workshop features plenary presentations in the morning, while after lunch all kinds of informal discussions and nut cracking gatherings take place. The workshop is unique in the sense that not only solved research problems are presented and discussed, but also (partly) unsolved problems and in-depth topical reviews can be unleashed in the scientific arena. Consequently, the workshop provides the participants with an environment where collaboration rather than competition is fostered.

This fourth edition of the SAMOS workshop developed into a highly interesting event with a program that consisted of 36 paper presentations as well as a keynote speech by Kees Vissers from Xilinx Research. The paper authors represented 12 different countries, the USA, UK, Canada, Brazil, Germany, France, Spain, Finland, Belgium, Portugal, Greece and The Netherlands. The presentations were divided into three tracks: reconfigurable computing, architecture and implementation, and system modeling and simulation. We believe that all three tracks showed high-quality, state-of-the-art research in their respective fields.

Besides the papers from SAMOS IV, this proceedings also features numerous papers from the SAMOS III workshop. As the SAMOS III edition did not have a well-established proceedings mechanism, we decided to give the authors from last year's edition the opportunity to formally publish their papers in this proceedings.

A workshop like this cannot be organized without the help of many other people. We therefore want to thank the members of the Steering and Program Committees as well as the General Chair for their assistance in the organization and the review process for both the SAMOS III and IV papers that are included in this proceedings. Furthermore, we would like to express our sincere gratitude to Iosif Antochi who prepared the proceedings and to Lidwina Tromp for her support in organizing both the SAMOS III and IV workshops.

We hope that the attendees enjoyed the SAMOS IV workshop in all its aspects, including its many informal discussions and gatherings.

July 2004

Andy Pimentel
Stamatis Vassiliadis

# Organization

The workshop SAMOS IV took place during July 19–21, 2004 at the Research and Teaching Institute of East Aegean (INEAG) in Agios Konstantinos on the island of Samos, Greece.

## General Chair

Shuvra Bhattacharyya    University of Maryland, USA

## Program Chair

Andy Pimentel    University of Amsterdam, The Netherlands

## Steering Committee

Shuvra Bhattacharyya    University of Maryland, USA
Ed Deprettere    Leiden University, The Netherlands
Patrice Quinton    Irisa, France
Stamatis Vassiliadis    Delft University of Technology, The Netherlands
Jürgen Teich    University of Erlangen-Nuremberg, Germany

## Program Committee

Nikitas Dimopoulos    University of Victoria, Canada
Gerhard Fettweis    TU Dresden, Germany
Georgi Gaydadijev    Delft University of Technology, The Netherlands
John Glossner    Sandbridge Technologies, USA
Wayne Luk    Imperial College London, UK
Andy Pimentel    University of Amsterdam, The Netherlands
Bernard Pottier    Université de Bretagne Occidentale, France
Jarmo Takala    Tampere University of Technology, Finland
Serge Vernalde    IMEC, Belgium
Jens Peter Wittenburg    Thomson Corporate Research, Germany

## Local Organizers

Lidwina Tromp    Delft University of Technology, The Netherlands
Yiasmin Kioulafa    Research and Training Institute of East Aegean, Greece

# Table of Contents

## SAMOS III – Reconfigurable Computing

## SAMOS III – Architectures and Implementation

## SAMOS III –
## Compilers, System Modeling, and Simulation

## Systems, Architectures, Modeling, and Simulation 2004
## (SAMOS IV)

## SAMOS IV – Reconfigurable Computing

## SAMOS IV – Architectures and Implementation

## SAMOS IV – System Modeling, and Simulation

# The Molen Programming Paradigm

Stamatis Vassiliadis, Georgi Gaydadjiev,
Koen Bertels, and Elena Moscu Panainte

Computer Engineering Laboratory,
Electrical Engineering Dept., EEMCS, TU Delft, The Netherlands
{stamatis,georgi,koen,elena}@ET.TUDelft.NL
http://ce.et.tudelft.nl/

**Abstract.** In this paper we present the Molen programming paradigm, which is a sequential consistency paradigm for programming Custom Computing Machines (CCM). The programming paradigm allows for modularity and provides mechanisms for explicit parallel execution. Furthermore it requires only few instructions to be added in an architectural instruction set while allowing an almost arbitrary number of op-codes per user to be used in a CCM. A number of programming examples and discussion is provided in order to clarify the operation, sequence control and parallelism of the proposed programming paradigm.

## 1 Introduction

Programming *Custom Computing Machines* (CCMs) usually implies the introduction in the software design flow of detailed knowledge about the reconfigurable hardware. The compiler plays a significant role in the software design flow as it has to integrate most of this information. Computational-intensive operations are usually implemented on the reconfigurable hardware provided by different vendors and the challenge is to integrate them – whenever possible – in new or existing applications. Such integration is only possible when application developers as well as hardware providers adopt a common programming paradigm.

In this paper we present such a programming paradigm. The main contributions of the paper are:

- The presentation of a programming model for reconfigurable computing that allows modularity, general "function like" code execution and parallelism in a sequential consistency computational model,
- The definition of a minimal ISA extension to support the programming paradigm. Such an extension allows the mapping of an arbitrary function on the reconfigurable hardware with no additional instruction requirements,
- The introduction of a mechanism allowing multiple operations to be loaded and executed in parallel on the reconfigurable hardware,
- Support for the application portability to multiple reconfigurable platforms.

A. Pimentel and S. Vassiliadis (Eds.): SAMOS 2004, LNCS 3133, pp. 1–10, 2004.

This paper is organized as follows: Section 2 introduces the Molen programming paradigm and shows its advantages compared to related work. Section 3 discusses the sequence control of the programming paradigm. The discussion is supported by a wide range of examples. Section 4 concludes the discussion.

## 2   The Molen Programming Paradigm

In this section first the Molen machine organization [1] is briefly introduced. Consequently the Molen programming paradigm is described. This paradigm addresses a number of fundamental shortcomings of other approaches being: (i) the opcode space explosion [2–4], (ii) the limitation in the number of parameters [5,6], (iii) the lack of support for parallel execution (as shown in [7]) and (iv) no support for modular and portable design. To clarify the discussion, a variety of examples will be supplemented.

The main Molen components as depicted in Figure 1 are: the Core Processor – which is a GPP, and the reconfigurable processor (PR) – implemented in the FPGA. The Arbiter performs a partial decoding and issuing of memory fetched instructions. The *Custom Computing Unit* (CCU) is performing the reconfigurable execution. The conceptual idea of how a Molen application looks like is presented in Figure 2. First, there are clear boundaries between the software execution and the RP noted by **input** and **output**. One should think of predefined parameters (or pointers to parameters) to be passed to and back from the hardware CCU engine. Second, the CCU configuration file is to be loaded into the configuration memory in order to prepare the hardware (the CCU part on Figure 1). This

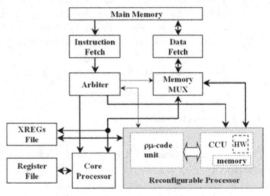

**Fig. 1.** The Molen machine organization

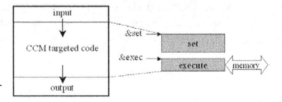

**Fig. 2.** Molen interface

is performed by the SET instruction. The SET instruction requires single parameter – the beginning address of the *configuration microcode* as explained in [8]. When a SET instruction is detected, the Arbiter will read the reconfigurable code until the termination condition is met, e.g. *end_op* microinstruction is detected. The $\rho\mu$ code unit ensures that the data fetched from memory is redirected to the reconfiguration support unit, e.g. FPGA configuration memory. After completion of the SET phase, the EXECUTE instruction invokes the execution microcode which performs the real CCU operations, reading the input parameters, performing the targeted computation and writing the results to the output registers. The majority of the CCUs will additionally access the system memory while running (depicted with horizontal arrow in Figure 2). The input/output and SET/EXECUTE parameters (and information about the memory segments used by the CCU) are made available to the compiler through a CCU *description file*. This description file and the binary images of the configuration and the execution microcode are sufficient for the compiler / linker to create adequate Molen binaries.

The above two generic phases SET/EXECUTE are emulated as an instruction is substituted by a sequence of micro-operations using an extension of microcode (referred also as *reconfigurable microcode*). In addition, Exchange Registers (XR) are used for passing operation parameters to and from the reconfigurable hardware at the beginning and the end of the operation execution. The XRs can receive their data directly from the GPP register bank. Therefore, the corresponding move instructions have to be provided. The number of XRs is implementation dependent.

The Molen programming paradigm is a sequential consistency paradigm for programming CCMs (reconfigurable processors) possibly including a general purpose computational engine(s). The paradigm allows for parallel and concurrent hardware execution and it is intended (currently) for single program execution. It requires only a one-time architectural extension of few instructions to provide a large user reconfigurable operation space. The complete list of eight required instructions is as follows:

**A.** Six instructions are required to control the reconfigurable hardware, as follows:

- Two SET < *address* > instructions: they initiate the CCU configuration. This operation can be additionally split into two sub-phases (accounting for the two set instructions):

  - partial SET (P-SET) to cover common and often used functions of an application or set of applications and to diminish time expensive reconfigurations, and
  - complete SET (C-SET) to deal with the remaining blocks (not covered by the p-set sub-phase) in order to *complete* the CCU functionality by enabling it to perform the less frequent functions.

- EXECUTE < *address* >: for controlling the executions of the operations on the reconfigurable hardware. The address sequence referred by this instruction contains the microcode to be executed on the CCU configured in the SET phase. The microcode sequence is terminated by an *end_op* micro operation.

- BREAK: this instruction may be needed in implementing explicit parallel execution between GPP and CCU if it is found to gain substantial performance with simultaneous execution. This operation is used for synchronization to indicate the parallel execution and setting boundaries. In addition BREAK can be used to express parallelism between two or more concurrent CCU units.

- SET PREFETCH < *address* >: In implementations with a reconfigurable hardware of limited size, this instruction can be used by the compiler to pre fetch the SET microcode from main memory to a local (much faster) on chip cache or the $\rho\mu$ control store in order to minimize the reconfiguration time penalty.
- EXECUTE PREFETCH < *address* >: the same reasoning as for the SET PREFETCH holding for the EXECUTE microcode.

**B.** Two move instructions for passing of values to and from the GPP register file and the reconfigurable hardware. More specially:

- MOVTX $XR_a \leftarrow R_b$: (move to X-REG) used to move the content of general purpose register $R_b$ to $XR_a$.
- MOVFX $R_a \leftarrow XR_b$: (move from X-REG) used to move the content of exchange register $XR_b$ to GPP register $R_a$.

## 3  Sequence Control

There are basically three distinctive cases with respect to the Molen instructions introduced earlier – the *minimal*, the *preferred* and the *complete ISA*. In more details they are as follows:

**the minimal ISA:** This is essentially the smallest set of Molen instructions needed to provide a working scenario that supports execution of an arbitrary application (providing there is no shortage of hardware resources). The four basic instructions needed are SET, EXECUTE, MOVTX and MOVFX. By implementing the first two instructions (SET/EXECUTE) any suitable CCU can be loaded and executed in the reconfigurable processor. The MOVTX and MOVFX instructions are needed to provide the input/output interface between the Software (GPP code) and the Hardware (CCU engine) parts of the application. It should be noted that this case does not introduce any restrictions on parallel hardware execution. There can be more than one CCUs configured or running concurrently. The only difference is that in such cases the GPP will be stalled for the time needed for the "slowest" CCU to complete its operation. An example is presented in Figure 3(b) where the block of EXECUTE instructions which can be processed in parallel contains the first three consecutive EXECUTE instructions and it is delimited by a GPP instruction. The situation when a block of EXECUTE-instructions can be executed in parallel on the RP while the GPP is stalled, will most likely be the case for reconfigured "complex" code and GPP code with numerous data dependencies. In addition, it should be noted that the above reasoning holds for the segments consiting of SET instructions or mixture of independent SET and EXECUTE instructions.

**the preferred ISA:** The minimal case provides the basic support but may suffer from the time consuming reconfiguration times that can become prohibitive for some real-time applications. In order to address this issue the two additional SET sub-phases (P-SET) and (C-SET) are introduced for distinction among very often and least often used CCU functions. More specifically in the P-phase the CCU is partially configured to perform the common functions of an application, while the C-phase takes care only of the remaining (much smaller) set of less frequent functions. This allows the compiler to "hide" the time consuming reconfiguration operations better. In addition, for the cases when the P-set and C-set improvements are not sufficient, the two prefetch instructions (SET and EXECUTE PREFETCH) are provided to allow additional freedom to the compiler instruction scheduler and further reduce the reconfiguration penalty.

**the complete ISA:** In addition when it is found that there is a substantial performance to be gained by parallel execution between GPP and RP, then the GPP and the EXECUTE-instructions can be issued and executed in parallel. Since the GPP instructions (for the pertinent discussion see parallelism control discussed later) can not be used for synchronization any longer, the additional BREAK instruction is required. The sequence of instructions performed in parallel is initiated by an EXECUTE instruction. The end of the parallel execution is marked by the BREAK instruction. It indicates where the parallel execution stops (see Figure 3 (a)). The SET instructions are executed in parallel according to the same rules. It is clear that in case of an organization utilizing single GPP, the GPP instructions, present in the parallel areas, can not be executed in parallel. This is the most general Molen case that allows the highest instruction level parallelism (the fastest execution). On the other hand this approach is the most complicated in terms of covering issues such as asynchronous interrupts handling and memory management. These all are the Molen implementor responsibility to address and solve properly.

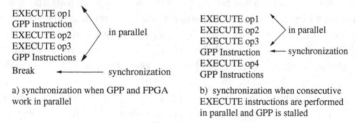

**Fig. 3.** Models of synchronization

**Compilation:** The compiler [9] currently relies on the Stanford SUIF2 (Stanford University Intermediate Format) and the Harvard Machine SUIF back-end framework. The x86 processor has been considered as the GPP in the evaluated Molen organization in [9]. The function implemented in reconfigurable hardware is annotated with a pragma directive named *call_fpga*. The pragma annotation is ignored and a standard function call is included. The function call is replaced with the appropriate instructions for sending parameters to the reconfigurable hardware in XRs, hardware reconfiguration, preparing the fix XR for the microcode of the EXECUTE instruction, execution of the operation and the transfer of the result back to the GPP. The information about the target architecture such as microcode address of SET and EXECUTE instructions for each operation implemented in the reconfigurable hardware, the number of XR, the fix

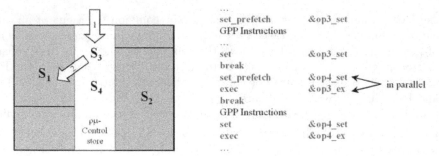

**Fig. 4.** SET PREFETCH instructions flow        **Fig. 5.** Prefetching example

XR associated with each operation, etc needed by the compiler is available in a CCU's description file.

**Prefetching:** The SET PREFETCH instructions behavior is illustrated in Figure 4. The arrow (1) represents the prefetching of microcode $S_3$ from memory to the $\rho\mu$ control store and (2) indicates the actual hardware reconfiguration. The control store area is used to move the prefetched microcode "near by" the reconfigurable hardware long before it is "needed". This instruction allows the compiler to schedule the time demanding load-from-memory operation. In Figure 5 the first *set_prefetch* operation will load the microcode positioned at address &*op3_set* into the $\rho\mu$ control store. When the *set* &*op3_set* instruction is processed, the $S_3$ microcode will be loaded from the control store (instead of the memory) into the hardware configuration memory, e.g. lookup tables, switch boxes and interconnect resources. In such a way the reconfiguration can be performed faster than in the case when loading directly from memory. In case no more hardware resources are available, there should be a replacement strategy applied by the $\rho\mu$ control store, e.g. the least recently used (LRU) configuration will be replaced.

The prefetch instructions, as any other Molen instructions (except of the BREAK) are not limited with respect to concurrency. A Molen instruction initiates the code to be executed in parallel. As shown in Figure 5, the *set_prefetch* &*op4_set* and the $S_3$ execution will be performed in parallel. The first *break* instruction is needed to indicate that *set* and *exec* instructions for $S_3$ cannot be executed in parallel and can be placed before or after the *set_prefetch* instruction for $S_4$. In the *preferred* Molen case the *break* will be a GPP instruction, e.g. NOP.

**Parameter Exchange, Parallelism and Modularity:** As shown earlier, the exchange register bank solves the limitation on the number of parameters as present in other RC approaches. The Molen XR bank can be used for passing parameters by value or by reference. When a limited number of parameters not exceeding the number of XRs is used, a straight forward passed-by-value strategy is applied. In case the number of parameters exceeds the XR bank size, the passing by reference should be used. It is obvious that passing by reference will allow an arbitrary (limited by the hardware) number of parameters to be

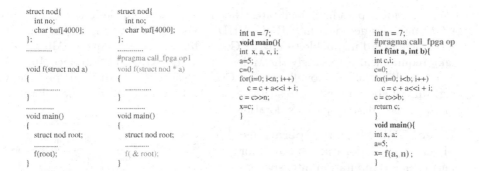

**Fig. 6.** Passing parameters by reference in Molen

**Fig. 7.** Partial function exposing for HW implementation in Molen

exchanged between the calling (software) and called (hardware) functions. An example of how the system designers should modify their code in order to allow this in Molen programming paradigm is given in Figure 6.

It should be noted that the original code passes a copy of the structure to the called function. Since the size of the structure can exceed the XR bank size, e.g. 8, 16 registers, the pass by reference to the structure is used. This introduces, however, an additional feature – this is when the called function (now performed by the CCU in hardware) changes the structure contents, such changes will become "permanent" after the control is returned back to the GPP. Such behavior will differ in functionality from the original software implementation. It is assumed that the system designers utilizing the Molen architecture will be aware about these side effects and will use passing by reference with extreme caution. The description file used as interface between the compiler and the CCU design should be extended with additional information about the structure.

The third shortcoming (parallel execution) indicated in the beginning of this section is addressed as follows. In case that two or more (generalized) functions, appointed for CCU implementation do not have any true dependencies they can be executed in parallel. There is always a physical maximum of how many CCUs can be executed in parallel. This is, however, an implementation dependent issue, e.g. reconfigurable hardware size, CCU sizes, XR bank size etc. and can not be considered as a serious limitation, since it is not limited by the Molen architecture. In addition, it should be emphasized that the Molen Hardware/Software division ability is not limited to functions only. In case the targeted kernel is part of a function, e.g. a highly computational demanding loop, it can be isolated before its transformation to hardware implementation. The only two requirements are: a) to rewrite the kernel as a separate function, and b) to define a clear set of parameters as interface and pass them as values (or references) between the modified "old" and the new function code. All of the communication between the two functions should be done via input/output parameters only since both parts will execute in different contexts. An example of how such division can be done is depicted in Figure 7.

The Molen paradigm facilitates the modular system design. For instance CCM modules designed in a HDL (VHDL, Verilog or System-C) language are straight forward mappable to any FPGA technology, e.g. Xilinx or Altera. The only requirement is to satisfy the Molen SET and EXECUTE interface. In addition a wide set of functionally similar CCUs designs (from different providers), e.g. sum of absolute differences (SAD) or IDCT, can be collected in a database allowing easy design space exploration.

### Direct CCU Memory Operations:

Molen organizations are suitable for performing computation intensive operations in hardware while the data needed for the operations remains in main memory. A simple example of this is how vector addition calculation $(\mathbf{c} = \mathbf{a} + \mathbf{b})$ can be moved to CCU implementation is presented in Figure 8.

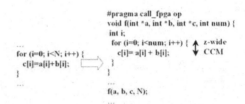

**Fig. 8.** Vector code CCU example

The three vectors $\mathbf{a}$, $\mathbf{b}$ and $\mathbf{c}$ are contiguous vectors with the same length. In the beginning the original code needs to be restructured as introduced earlier to a separate function with usage of pointers. This process is shown by the right block arrow and prepares the input/output interfaces between the software and the CCU. More precisely in this case they are: the addresses of the first vector elements (for each vector), the number of elements to be processed and possibly the stride. The information on how the memory locations are accessed and the type of each vector element, e.g. integer, floating etc. should be taken into consideration in the CCU design. In essence, in this case, the CCU is an augmented vector architecture to include what is not performed (e.g. address generators) in the GPP. It is clear that function $\mathbf{f}$ can be parallelized in the hardware. Lets assume that the memory architecture allows access of $2 * z$ locations for read and $z$ locations for write in parallel. This will allow $z$ elements of the vector addition to be performed in parallel, hence speeding up the calculation by at least $N/z$. This is presented by the sliding window shown in Figure 9. It is clear that in this example the output interface of the CCU is just operation termination (execution of $end\_op$). The result of the CCU is stored in the output vector $\mathbf{c}$ and can be used directly by the subsequent (hardware or software) modules.

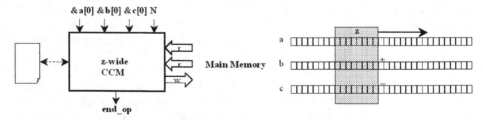

**Fig. 9.** Vector execution CCU example

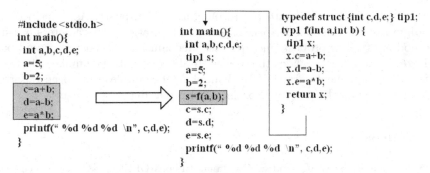

**Fig. 10.** Multiple parameters from CCU example

For efficiency reasons, some operations that compute more than one value may require to return the results in the XRs (instead of memory, which is the straightforward way). These operations represent contiguous statements (in high-level programming languages) where more variables are modified. In order to accommodate to the current approach the associated code has to be isolated in a function. The problem of returning more parameters from a function in XRs can be solved as illustrated in Figure 10. The computed values (for variables c, d, e in Figure 10(a)) are packed in a structure (in Figure 10(b)) in the new function body and unpacked after the new function call. We have to mention here that the CCU designer must be aware of the alignment and packed/unpacked conventions for structures assumed by the compiler.

**Interrupts and Miscellaneous Considerations:** In order to support GPP interrupts properly, the following parts are essential for any Molen implementation: 1) Hardware to detect interrupts and terminate the execution before the state of the machine is changed are assumed to be implemented in both GPP and CCU. 2) Hardware to communicate interrupts to GPP is implemented in CCU. 3) Initialization (via the GPP) of the appropriate routines for interrupt handling.

The compiler assumption is that the implementor of a reconfigurable hardware follows a co-processor type of configuration. The FPGA co-processor facility can be viewed as an extension of the GPP architecture. For examples of conventional architectural extensions that resemble the approach taken here see [10–12]. The above is a recommendation to the FPGA developer. If such an aproach is not followed and no "clean" architecture is implemented some complications may arise. Furthermore, the unconstrained memory access of the CCUs in Molen as in any other architectural or programming paradigm can lead to memory violation problems. For example, a CCU can overwrite memory locations used by other (software or hardware) modules unintentionally.

## 4   Conclusions

In this paper we presented the Molen programming paradigm that addresses a number of previously unresolved issues such as parameter passing and parallel execution of operations into the reconfigurable hardware. As described the paradigm resolves the opcode space expansion, limitation of parameters passing and modularity. The proposal incorporates mechanisms for concurrent and parallel execution and it provides the user with almost arbitrary number of "functions" to be implemented in a CCU. A number of examples have been reported in order to explain the presented programming paradigm.

# References

1. S. Vassiliadis, S. Wong, and S. Cotofana, "The MOLEN $\rho\mu$-Coded Processor," in *11th International Conference on Field Programmable Logic and Applications (FPL)*, vol. 2147. Belfast, UK: Springer-Verlag Lecture Notes in Computer Science (LNCS), Aug 2001, pp. 275–285.
2. S. Hauck, T. W. Fry, M. M. Hosler, and J. P. Kao, "The Chimaera Reconfigurable Functional Unit," in *Proc. IEEE Symp. on Field-Programmable Custom Computing Machines*, Napa, California, 1997, pp. 87–96.
3. A. L. Rosa, L. Lavagno, and C. Passerone, "Hardware/Software Design Space Exploration for a Reconfigurable Processor," in *Proc. of the DATE 2003*, 2003, pp. 570–575.
4. M. Gokhale and J. Stone, "Napa C: Compiling for a Hybrid RISC/FPGA Architecture," in *Proc. IEEE Symp. on Field-Programmable Custom Computing Machines*, Napa, California, April 1998, pp. 126–137.
5. F. Campi, R. Canegallo, and R. Guerrieri, "IP-Reusable 32-Bit VLIW Risc Core," in *Proc. of the 27th European Solid-State Circuits Conference*, Villah, Austria, Sep 2001, pp. 456–459.
6. Z. Ye, N. Shenoy, and P. Banerjee, "A C Compiler for a Processor with a Reconfigurable Functional Unit," in *ACM/SIGDA Symposium on FPGAs*, Montery, California, USA, 2000, pp. 95–100.
7. M. Sima, S. Vassiliadis, S.Cotofana, J. van Eijndhoven, and K. Vissers, "Field-Programmable Custom Computing Machines - A Taxonomy," in *12th International Conference on Field Programmable Logic and Applications (FPL)*, vol. 2438. Montpellier, France: Springer-Verlag Lecture Notes in Computer Science (LNCS), Sep 2002, pp. 79–88.
8. G. Kuzmanov, G. Gaydadjiev, and S. Vassiliadis, "Loading $\rho\mu$-code: Design Considerations," in *International Workshop on Systems, Architecture, Modeling and Simulation (SAMOS)*, Samos, Greece, Jul 2003.
9. E. Moscu Panainte, K. Bertels, and S. Vassiliadis, "Compiling for the Molen Programming Paradigm," in *13th International Conference on Field Programmable Logic and Applications (FPL)*, Lissabon, Portugal, Sep 2003.
10. A. Peleg and U. Weiser, "MMX Technology Extension to the Intel Architecture," *IEEE Micro*, vol. 16, no. 4, pp. 42–50, August 1996.
11. A. Padegs, B. B. Moore, R. M. Smith, and W. Buchholz, "The IBM System/370 vector architecture: Design considerations," *IEEE Transactions on Computers*, vol. 37, pp. 509–520, 1988.
12. W. Buchholz, "The IBM System/370 vector architecture," *IBM Systems Journal*, vol. 25, no. 1, pp. 51–62, 1986.

# Loading $\rho\mu$-Code: Design Considerations

Georgi Kuzmanov, Georgi Gaydadjiev, and Stamatis Vassiliadis

Computer Engineering Laboratory,
Electrical Engineering Dept., EEMCS, TU Delft, The Netherlands
{G.Kuzmanov,G.N.Gaydadjiev,S.Vassiliadis}@ET.TUDelft.NL
http://ce.et.tudelft.nl/

**Abstract.** This article investigates microcode generation, finalization and loading in MOLEN $\rho\mu$ processors. In addition, general solutions for these issues are presented and implementation for Xilinx Virtex-II Pro platform FPGA is introduced.

**Keywords:** Reconfigurable architectures, MOLEN, implementation, loading microcode.

## 1 Introduction

Reconfigurable hardware extensions of general purpose processors (GPP) have indicated considerable potentials for speed-ups of computationally demanding algorithms. Numerous design concepts and organizations have been proposed to support the Custom Computing Machine (CCM) paradigm from different prospectives [2–4, 6]. An example of a detailed classification of CCMs can be found in [5]. Recently, the MOLEN $\rho\mu-$ processors for CCM organizations have been proposed [7]. The MOLEN concept provides a flexible and easily extendable framework for hardware/software co-design of complex computing systems by extending the traditional microcode. The presented paper addresses some specific issues related to the microcode design and maintenance within the MOLEN processors. More specifically, we investigate the problems related to the generation, memory alignment and loading of configuration microcodes.

Hereafter, the discussion is organized as follows. Section 2 gives a brief background on the MOLEN organization. Section 3 introduces the FPGA configuration format for the targeted Xilinx technology. In Section 4, problems related to generation, alignment and loading of reconfigurable microcodes are discussed. Section 5 proposes solutions to different problems with respect to efficient hardware implementations. Finally, the discussion is concluded in Section 6.

## 2 The MOLEN Organization

This section presents the MOLEN $\rho\mu$-coded Custom Computing Machine organization, introduced in [7] and illustrated in Figure 1. The ARBITER performs a partial decoding on the input instructions flow in order to determine where they should be issued. The arbiter controls the proper co-processing of the GPP and the reconfigurable units. Figure 2 depicts a general design of a MOLEN arbiter. It is closely connected to three major components of the CCM: the GPP,

A. Pimentel and S. Vassiliadis (Eds.): SAMOS 2004, LNCS 3133, pp. 11–19, 2004.

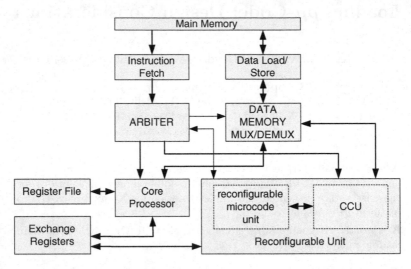

**Fig. 1.** The MOLEN machine organization

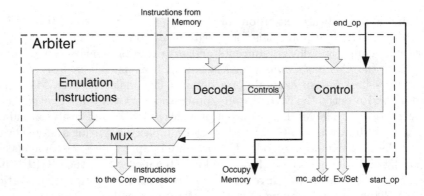

**Fig. 2.** General view of the Arbiter

the memory and the $\rho\mu$-unit. Instructions implemented in fixed hardware are issued to the core processor (GPP). Instructions for custom execution are redirected to the *reconfigurable unit*, referred to as *$\rho\mu$-unit*. The reconfigurable unit consists of a custom computing unit (CCU) and the $\rho\mu$-code unit. An operation, executed by the reconfigurable unit, is divided into two distinct phases: **set** and **execute**. The **set** phase is responsible for reconfiguring the CCU hardware enabling the execution of the operation. This phase may be divided into two subphases - partial set (**pset**) and complete set (**cset**). In the **pset** phase the CCU is partially configured to perform common functions of an application (or group of applications). Later, the **cset** sub-phase only reconfigures those blocks in the CCU, which are not covered in the **pset** sub-phase in order to *complete* the functionality of the CCU.

To perform the actual reconfiguration of the CCU, reconfiguration microcode is loaded into the $\rho\mu$-code unit and then executed. The **execute** phase is responsible for the actual operation execution on the CCU, performed by running the *execution microcode*. It is important to emphasize that both the **set** and **execute** phases do not specify a certain operation to be performed. Instead, the **pset**, **cset** and **execute** instructions (*reconfigurable instructions*) directly point to the memory location where the reconfiguration or execution microcode is stored. The microcode engine is extended with mechanisms that allow permanent and pageable reconfiguration and execution code to coexist.

## 3   FPGA Configuration Microcode

The reconfiguration files generated after synthesis, contain random bit patterns and will highly depend on the targeted FPGA technology. They contain the configuration commands and configuration data needed to configure the different FPGA resources, e.g., switch boxes, interconnect resources, look-up tables and any additional technology dependent information. Usually a configuration file can be considered as a stream of bits and is often referred to as *configuration bitstream* in the literature. Such bit streams are produced by the FPGA synthesis tool, e.g. Synopsis, Xilinx, Altera or Lattice. As it can be assumed, a pre-defined and widely accepted standard for such binary streams does not exists and different vendors use the most convenient format for their technology. It is very important to understand that the same high-level hardware description file will result in complete different configuration bitstreams when different technologies are targeted.

The first target for MOLEN implementation is the Virtex-II Pro [8] FPGA from Xilinx. Virtex II Pro devices incorporate one up to four PowerPC 405 GPP cores, FPGA reconfigurable hardware, dedicated RAM blocks and dedicated high-speed I/O blocks. The FPGA fabric is similar to Virtex II. Although the Virtex II and Virtex II Pro devices are not bitstream compatible, the same considerations hold true for both types and will be referred to as *V2* from now on. V2 devices are organized in columns corresponding to the column organization of the FPGA's logic resources [1]. In other words the V2 configuration memory can be visualized as a rectangular array of bits, grouped in vertical *frames* that are one-bit wide and go from the top of the array to the bottom. The frame is the atomic unit of configuration, this is the smallest piece of the configuration memory that can be written (or read). Such organization allows partial reconfiguration that can be performed with or without shutting down the device. The partial reconfiguration is a very important option, since configuration stream size, and hence the loading time, strongly depends on the targeted device, e.g XC2V1000 incorporates 1104 configuration frames, 3392 bits per frame or 3,744,768 configuration bits in total, while XC2V10000 has 3212 configuration frames, 10432 bits per frame (33,507,584 bits). It is obvious that full reconfiguration of XC2V10000 will be ten times longer than XC2V1000 using identical programming conditions (interface type and clock). Vitrex II Pro sizes and down-

**Table 1.** Virtex II Pro Sizes and Programming times (50MHz Par. mode)

| Device | No. of Frames | No. of bits | Config. time |
|--------|--------------:|------------:|-------------:|
| XC2VP2  |   884 |  1,305,440 |  3.26 ms |
| XC2VP7  | 1,320 |  4.484,472 | 11.21 ms |
| XC2VP20 | 1,756 |  8,214,624 | 20.54 ms |
| XC2VP50 | 2,628 | 19,005,696 | 47.55 ms |

load times for the parallel slave mode assuming a programming clock frequency of 50MHz are depicted in Table 1. A full reconfiguration that takes roughly 48 milliseconds (as for XC2VP50) may be prohibitive in many real-time applications. A reconfiguration of a single frame (a very likely scenario), however, takes about 18 microseconds that would be acceptable.

An example configuration bitstream looks as follows:

```
Dummy word                                    FFFF FFFFh
Synchronization word                          AA99 5566h
Packet Header: Write to CMD register          3000 8001h
Packet Data: RCRC                             0000 0007h
Packet Header: Write to FLR register          3001 6001h
Packet Data: Frame Length                     0000 00--h
Packet Header: Write to COR                   3001 2001h
Packet Data: Configuration options            ---- ----h
Packet Header: Write to MASK                  3000 C001h
Packet Data: CTL mask                         0000 0000h
Packet Header: Write to CMD register          3000 8001h
Packet Data: SWITCH                           0000 0009h
Packet Header: Write to FAR register          3000 2001h
Packet Data: Frame address                    0000 0000h
Packet Header: Write to CMD register          3000 8001h
Packet Data: WCFG                             0000 0001h
```

In the above example the first set of commands will prepare the configuration logic for rewriting the memory frames. All commands are described as 32-bit words, since configuration data is internally processed from a common 32-bit bus. From this data sequence, the first dummy word pads the front of the bitstream to provide the clock cycles necessary for initialization of the configuration logic. No actual processing takes place until the synchronization word is loaded. Since the V2 configuration logic processes data as 32-bit words, but can be configured from arbitrary data sources, e.g. a serial or 8-bit source, the synchronization word is used to define the 32-bit word boundaries. That is, the first bit after the synchronization word is the first bit of the next 32-bit word. The frame length indicates how many 32-bit words of configuration data, depicted as - - - -  - - - -h, will be sent from the configuration controller and will contain "random" data.

## 4   Loading Microcode: Problems and Solutions

In the original MOLEN architectural description, the end of reconfiguration microcode is marked by an *end_op* microinstruction. Conceptually, this is correct, however it creates some implementation drawbacks with respect to whether the reconfigurable operation is *set* or *execute*. That is, whether the microcode, stored into memory is a sequence of microinstructions (*execute*), or a configuration bitstream (*set*).

**Microcode Termination.** In case of *execute* microcode, *end_op* instruction at the end of the microcode segment is sufficient for the proper termination of the reconfigurable operation, provided the microcode is properly aligned into memory. This technique, however, would not work in cases of the *set* microcode, because the reconfiguration bitstreams are an arbitrary bit sequence as discussed in Section 3. It is almost impossible to find a unique bit pattern, which can not be extracted from the reconfiguration bitstreams, thus used as *end_op* microinstruction. Therefore, it is possible, that a reconfiguration microcode loading is terminated earlier. Obviously, other techniques should be utilized for proper microcode segment termination. Figure 3 depicts three possible solutions that can be utilized to solve the pointed problem. On Figure 3a) a flag bit is utilized, to indicate whether the memory word is an *end_op* (1), or any other microinstruction/reconfiguration bit pattern (0). This approach is applicable for both *set* and *execute* microcodes, but it is costly in terms of memory space. Microprogram (resp. reconfigurable bitstream) alignment into the main memory is also severe, since the *end_op* microcode should be strictly aligned in the end of the microprogram segment/block. The examples in Figure 3 b) and c) are functionally equivalent to each other in terms of memory space and differ only in the potential hardware implementations. In both cases, an additional microcode word is aligned at the starting address of the microprogram segment. This word may contain either the length of the microprogram (Figure 3 b) or its final address (Figure 3 c). The latter two techniques are more efficient in terms of memory space since a single extra microinstruction word is required.

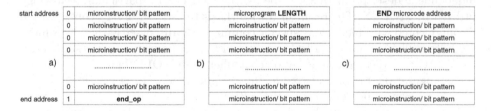

**Fig. 3.** Microcode termination techniques

**Microcode Finalization.** *The process of preparing the microcode for its final alignment into the targeted main memory is called microcode finalization.* In all three cases of microcode termination, extra termination information should be explicitly added to the microprogramable configuration code. In the case of *end_op* attached in the end, additional flag bit fields should be inserted into the microcode. The expanded *set* microcode bit patterns should be properly aligned to fit in the targeted memory. There is a variety of different design

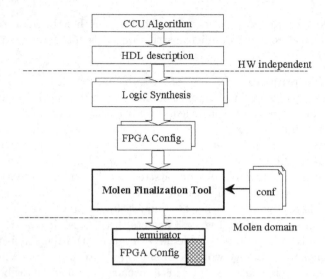

**Fig. 4.** MOLEN Finalization

tools that can potentially be used for *set* microcode generation, e.g., Xilinx or Altera. There is also a number of GPPs, which can be used in the MOLEN organization framework. Therefore, an automated process that will perform the transformation from "raw" configuration stream to *set* microcode is required.

The automated process of microcode finalization for MOLEN is depicted in Figure 4. This figure shows the place of the finalization tool in the MOLEN CCU design process. The CCU algorithm described in any hardware description language, can be targeted to different FPGA technologies. This allows technology independent description that can be synthesized to any particular technology utilized by MOLEN. The result of the synthesis tool is the binary configuration file augmented with technology specific commands as discussed earlier. This file is ready to be loaded into the FPGA via any of the configuration paths supported, e.g. JTAG or dedicated configuration controller. The MOLEN paradigm requires the configuration stream, referred as the *set* microcode, to be positioned in the system main memory (similar to the software modules) and be loaded via the $\rho\mu$ unit. The later $\rho\mu$ unit should know where is the end of the *set* microcode as discussed earlier. In addition the *set* microcode should "fit" nicely in the targeted memory architecture. For example if the targeted MOLEN organization consists of ARM7 processor with 16-bit wide external memory and Xilinx Virtex II FPGA utilizes the CCM part, every configuration word will use two subsequent address places.

It should be stated that such issues as the *set* code endianess are transparent to the proposed approach and do not require special consideration. All of the above is performed by the Finalization tool automatically. The configuration file (indicated as *conf*) contains information about the MOLEN organization needed for the *set* microcode finalization. The product of the Finalization tool is a binary file ready to be used inside the MOLEN paradigm, and can be a linkable object, or a high-level data structure, incorporating the binary information, that can be included directly in a C project before compilation.

## 5  Loading Microcode: $\rho\mu$-Unit Implementation

In addition to the finalization process it is required that the $\rho\mu$-coded unit manages the format of the *set* microcode and transforms it, to the used hardware configuration channel. The loading hardware of the *set* microcodes as described in this section is the major part of the complete data path between the main memory and the particular configuration controller.

**FPGA Implementation.** We have designed an $\rho\mu$-coded unit utilizing the microcode termination mechanism with the end microprogram address value stored at the starting microcode location. A general view of the design is depicted in Figure 5. The load/execute control block is responsible for loading micropro-

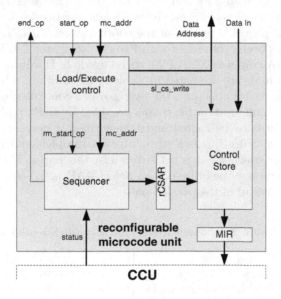

**Fig. 5.** General view of the $\rho\mu$-code unit

grams from the external memory. It generates the starting signal *rm_start_op* to the sequencer once the desired microprogram (at address *mc_addr*) is already transferred or available in the control store. The *start_op* signal is generated by the Arbiter and initiates a reconfigurable operation. The load/execute block sequentially generates the addresses of the microprogram in the main (external) memory with starting address *mc_addr*. During this address generation, the *sl_cs_write* signal is active thus, the desired microprogram is loaded into the control store via the write-only port *Data_In*. Once the desired microprogram is available in the control store, i.e., the end address of the microprogram in the external memory is reached, signal *rm_start_op* is activated and the sequencer starts generating the microcode addresses towards the rCSAR (reconfigurable Control Store Address Register). The microinstruction to be executed is transferred to the CCU via the Microinsruction Register (MIR). *Status* signals from the CCU are directed to the sequencer to determine next microcode address. Once the CCU completes its task, the sequencer generates signal *end_op* to the arbiter. The arbiter initiates the execution of the next instruction from the application program, which can be either a reconfigurable or a fixed one from the core processor ISA.

We assumed a microcode word length of 32 bits and external (off-chip) memory segment of 4Mx32-bit (22-bit address) for microprograms. Virtex II Pro, has been used as a target reconfigurable technology. The (on-chip) control store has been designed to handle up-to 8K 32-bit microcode words. As primary microcode storage units (the control store), we have used the BRAM blocks of the FPGA fabrics, configured as a single dual port memory. Each of the ports is unidirectional - one read-only and one write only. The read-only port is used to feed the MIR, while the write-only one loads microcodes from the external memory into the pageable section of the control store. The VHDL code of the $\rho\mu$-code unit has been synthesized with Project Navigator ISE 5.1 S3 of Xilinx. The target FPGA chip was XC2VP20, speed grade 5. Hardware costs reported by the synthesis tools are presented in Table 2. In addition, a hardware link to the configuration device pins (e.g., the byte-parallel controller, of Virtex II Pro) is required. The configuration bitstream provided by our implementation in a byte wide fashion is to be routed and transformed if necessary to the device configuration pins. Since this is a straightforward implementation issue with a minimal hardware overhead, it is not covered by this paper. Moreover, different configuration paths may be utilized, e.g., SelectMAP, serial (master or slave) or boundary-scan, instead of the parallel path.

**Table 2.** Synthesis Results for xc2vp20, Speed -5

| | | |
|---|---|---|
| Number of Slices | 173 out of 10304 | 1% |
| Number of Slice Flip Flops | 96 out of 20608 | < 1% |
| Number of 4 input LUTs | 315 out of 20608 | 1% |
| Number of BRAMs: | 15 out of 112 | 13% |
| Minimum clock period | 8.160ns | |
| Maximum Frequency | 122.549MHz | |

# 6   Conclusions

In this paper, we addressed several specific problems related to the microcodes management in the MOLEN reconfigurable computing paradigm. More precisely, the generation, memory alignment and loading of configuration microcodes were investigated. The microcode termination issue was discussed in more details and alternative design considerations were proposed. Some specific features of a new microcode finalization tool were outlined after a detailed description of the *set* microcode finalization process. An analysis of several possible solutions of the discussed problems with respect to optimal hardware complexity and memory usage were presented. The described design considerations had been taken into account for an FPGA implementation of the $\rho\mu$-unit, presented in the end. Synthesis results indicate a very low hardware resources utilization of the targeted reconfigurable technology, selected to be Virtex II Pro of Xilinx (XC2VP20 device).

# References

1. Virtex Series Configuration Architecture User Guide. (XAPP151), Sept. 2000.
2. S. C. Goldstein, H. Schmit, M. Moe, M. Bidiu, S. Cadambi, R. Taylor, and R. Laufer. PipeRench: A coprocessor for Streaming Multimedia Acceleration. *The 26-th International Symposium on Computer Architecture*, pages 28–39, May 1999.
3. M.Wazlowski, L.Agarwal, T.Lee, A.Smith, E.Lam, H.Silverman, and S.Ghosh. PRISM-II Compiler and Architecture. In *Proc.IEEE Workshop on FPGAs for Custom Computing Machines*, pages 9–16, Napa Valley,CA, April 5-7, 1993.
4. R.W.Hartenstein, R.Kress, and H.Reining. A new FPGA Architecture for Word-Oriented Datapaths. In *4th International Workshop on Field Programmable Logic and Applications:Architectures, Synthesis and Applications*, pages 144–155, September 1994.
5. M. Sima, S. Vassiliadis, S.Cotofana, J. van Eijndhoven, and K. Vissers. Field-Programmable Custom Computing Machines - A Taxonomy. In *12th International Conference on Field Programmable Logic and Applications (FPL)*, pages 79–88, Montpellier, France, Sep 2002.
6. S.M.Trimberger. *Reprogramable Instruction Set Accelerator.*
7. S. Vassiliadis, S. Wong, and S. Cotofana. The MOLEN $\rho\mu$-Coded Processor. In *11th International Conference on Field Programmable Logic and Applications (FPL)*, volume 2147, pages 275–285, Belfast, UK, Aug 2001. Springer-Verlag Lecture Notes in Computer Science (LNCS).
8. Xilinx Corporation. *Virtex-II Pro Platform FPGA handbook v1.0*, 2002.

# RAMPASS: Reconfigurable and Advanced Multi-processing Architecture for Future Silicon Systems

Stéphane Chevobbe, Nicolas Ventroux, Frédéric Blanc, and Thierry Collette

CEA-List DRT/DTSI/SARC/LCEI , F-91191 Gif/Yvette, France
{stephane.chevobbe,nicolas.ventroux}@cea.fr
{frederic.fblanc,thierry.collette}@cea.fr

**Abstract.** Reconfigurable devices are used to map different kinds of applications that exploit virtual hardware concepts. A more efficient utilization of such circuits is to adapt application at the run-time. During the process of an application, computing methods can change. Therefore, the next generation of reconfigurable architectures should provide many computing methods such as MIMD, SIMD, VLIW or multi-threading.

Any application is composed of two parts: a control part for operation scheduling and a computation part required for operators. Existing reconfigurable architectures use the same structure to implement these two parts. The solution presented in this paper is based on two reconfigurable resources. The first is suitable for control processes and the second for computation purposes.

## 1 Introduction

Reconfigurable devices are composed of functional and interconnect resources. These resources can be arranged to implement a specific application. Semiconductor roadmaps indicate that integration density of regular structures (like memories) increase more quickly than irregular ones (Tab. 1). So, reconfigurable architectures are suitable for future technology evolutions.

**Table 1.** Integration density for futur vlsi devices [1]

| Year | 1999 | 2001 | 2003 | 2005 | 2009 | 2012 |
|---|---|---|---|---|---|---|
| **Process (nm)** | 180 | 150 | 130 | 100 | 70 | 50 |
| **DRAM (bit/chip)** | 1,07 G | 1,7 G | 4,29 G | 17,2 G | 68,7 G | 275 G |
| **MPU (transistors/chip)** | 21 M | 40 M | 76 M | 200 M | 520 M | 1,4 G |

The key feature of reconfigurable architectures is the ability to perform hardware computations to increase performances, while retaining much of the flexibility of a software solution [2]. These architectures are very heterogeneous because their characteristics are adapted for many domains of applications (Co-processing acceleration [3], Hardware emulation [4], Fault tolerance [5], etc.). A classification based on the available resources of reconfigurable architectures, is presented below:

A. Pimentel and S. Vassiliadis (Eds.): SAMOS 2004, LNCS 3133, pp. 20–29, 2004.

- The most famous fine grain reconfigurable architectures are FPGA (Field Programmable Grid Array). These devices merge two kinds of resources: the first one is an interconnection network and the second one is composed of processing blocks, based on special memories called LUT (Look Up Table). Reconfiguration process consists in using the interconnection network to connect processing elements. Furthermore, each LUT is configured to perform the required operation.
- Some coarse grain architecture [5,6] has a reconfigurable network of interconnectors and an array of static processing elements. Processing methods depends on the network topology. For instance the RAPID architecture [6] is adapted for dataflow processing even though SYNTOL [5] is designed to perform SIMD (Single-Instruction Multiple Data) processes.
- Some others architectures use a static network with reconfigurable processing blocks. These architectures [7,8] have been developed to merge together a processor with reconfigurable units. Reconfigurable is used like extra ALUs. These architectures require powerful tools, which are able to manage HW/SW (HardWare/SoftWare) partitioning [9].
- Besides, the DISC [10] architecture focuses on the duality between reconfigurations and instructions. Indeed, it is very hard to define the frontier between reconfigurable architectures and static ones. For instance, an instruction of a processor can be considered as a reconfiguration because it changes the data path for performing the required operation.

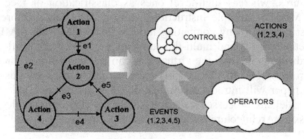

**Fig. 1.** Partitioning of an application in Control / Computation (a) Example of application – (b) partitionning

The main goal of all reconfigurable architectures consists in mapping a large set of applications. As shown in Fig.1, any application can be composed of two different parts: a control part for operations scheduling; and a computation part for computing support. These two parts have quite different characteristics for implementations. Indeed, the first one handles small data but requires global communications. On the contrary, the second one processes large data and uses local communications.

The reconfiguration frequency of these two parts are also different. In a processor, the control part is managed at each cycle whereas operators are fixed. Hybrid architectures like ONECHIP[7] or CHIMAERA[8] are based on a processor with extra reconfigurable operators. The instruction set is then adapted for a specific application. The reconfiguration frequency is quite low because the control is managed by the processor.

All existing architectures use the same structure to implement these two parts. Fine grain architectures are better adapted for performing control tasks than arithmetic tasks, which are well adapted to coarse grain architectures. In order to solve these drawbacks, some commercial architectures [11, 12] provide mechanisms that make arithmetic implementation more efficient. For instance, some multipliers are implemented in the VIRTEX [11] architecture. It might be advantageous to split reconfigurable resources into two parts. The first would deal with control processes, the second with computation purposes.

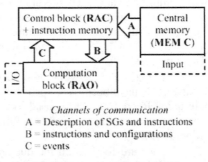

Channels of communication
A = Description of SGs and instructions
B = instructions and configurations
C = events

**Fig. 2.** Synoptic of RAMPASS

Within a given application, it is common to find different level of algorithms. For example, low-level image processing like convolution or filtering will often run on SIMD structures, whereas high-level ones as classification or face recognition are suitable for MIMD (Multiple Instruction Multiple Data) architectures. Future architectures must provide many computing modes such as MIMD, SIMD, VLIW (Very Long Instruction Word) and multi-threading in a complex application. Although the physical hardware is limited, the virtual one can be much larger thanks to the reconfiguration process. The MATRIX [14] architecture focuses on this concept. In the respect, this paper will introduce new paradigm of architecture able to manage such kinds of parallelism processes called RAMPASS (Reconfigurable And Advanced Multi-Processing Architecture for future Silicon System).

## 2  Functional Description of RAMPASS

In this section, the global functionality of RAMPASS is described. It is composed of two main reconfigurable parts (Fig. 2): one dedicated to the control of applications called Reconfigurable Array of Control (RAC); and an other dedicated to the computation named Reconfigurable Array of Operators (RAO). In the first part, these two main elements are presented. In the second part, the working of the architecture is more detailed. Finally, the end of this section underlines the strong points of RAMPASS.

### Overview

A State Graph (SG) is a classical model, which describes the control part of an application. This powerful model permits to represent complex computation concepts such as SIMD, MIMD, VLIW and multi-threading. Thus, the first block can describe and store an application as a SG. These SGs are composed of states and transitions. States drive the computation elements in the RAO, and events coming from the RAO validate transitions in the SG. In order to allow SG implementations, this structure needs boolean logic and a powerful connection network.

RAC block can be seen as a cache memory instruction for reconfigurable elements. As in classical one, the efficiency of this block is ensured by code redundancies. Whole SGs can obviously not be mapped in the RAC, so a mechanism as a dynamic reconfiguration has been introduced in order to permit to increase the virtual size of the architecture. Moreover, auto-routing mechanisms have been introduced in the RAC block to simplify SG configuration. Because the parallelism flexibility is ensured by the RAC part, we will focus on it and not discussed about the second block where computations elements are implemented.

## Mapping and Running an Application with RAMPASS

In this part, the configuration and the execution of an application in RAMPASS are described. The application is stored in an external memory. A boot address must be defined to permit the boot of RAMPASS. Then, the SG is loaded in the RAC from this address. As soon as the SG begins to be stored in the RAC, its execution starts. Indeed, the configuration and the execution are simultaneously performed. During the execution, the SG stored in the RAC is continuously updated. The reconfiguration of the RAC is self-managed and depends on the application progress. This concept is called auto-reconfiguration and allows the architecture to self-manage its configurations.

The execution is based on few steps, which are initiated by the activation of a state stored in the RAC. When a state is activated (when a token is received), the associated instruction is sent to the RAO (Fig. 3(b)). According to the instruction, the RAO returns an event to the RAC. This event corresponds to a transition in the SG mapped in the RAC. These transitions permit the propagation of tokens in SGs.

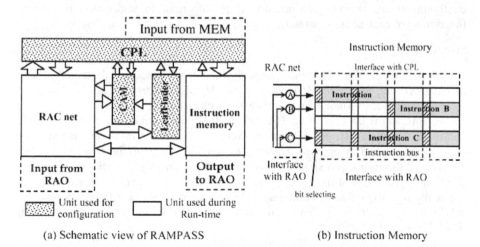

(a) Schematic view of RAMPASS               (b) Instruction Memory

**Fig. 3.** RAC block

The architecture is globally asynchronous. Each block has its own mechanism of synchronization. Blocks are synchronized by acknowledgement protocols. The main protocol is between RAC and RAO because it controls the course of the application. RAC sends instructions and configurations to the RAO, which generates events.

**Strong Points of RAMPASS**

Lastly, we focus on the main advantages of this new architecture. According to the application, computation grain is easily scalable. For example, a filter can be realized in at least two different ways. In the first place, the filter can be completely loaded and controlled by only one state, if the physical resources allow it. In the second place, simple operators as multiplier and adder can be physically stored in the computation block and driven by state graphs, stored in the control block. Trade off between computation grain and control has to be found for each application.

RAMPASS is especially dedicated to parallel algorithms. Because of the structure of the architecture, different kinds of parallel architectures can be loaded in RAMPASS as SIMD, MIMD, VLIW or multi-threading. Moreover, different kinds of reconfiguration allowed by RAMPASS decrease the resource limitation.

## 3   Functional Description of the Control Block: RAC Block

In this third paragraph, more details of the control block are given. First, the different elements composing the RAC block are described. Then, the configuration and the execution of the RAC block are explained.

As previously introduced, the RAC is a reconfigurable block dedicated to the control of an application. It is composed of five units (Fig. 3(a)): the *Configuration Protocol Layer* (*CPL*), the *Content Addressable Memory* (*CAM*) and the *LeafFinder* are used to configure the *RAC net* and the *instruction memory*. Although execution and configuration are running concurrently, it is important to understand the inner-functioning of each phase separately.

**Overview**

In this section, the five elements composing the RAC block are presented. These blocks (*RAC net, Instruction Memory, CPL, CAM, Leaf Finder*) are involved in auto-reconfiguration, auto-routing, and parallelism mechanisms.

The *RAC net* is the core of the RAC block. It is composed of two resources: cells and interconnectors. The geometry of the SG is loaded in the *RAC net*. One state of SGs is implemented by one cell. The *RAC net* applies signals to the *instruction memory* to send the instruction stream to the RAO. The main characteristic of this unit is to physically implement the control of the application. The *RAC net* is partially dynamically reconfigurable. Configuration and execution of SGs are fully independent. *RAC net* owns primitives to ensure the auto-routing. (*RAC net* will be developed in more details in the part 4).

The *Instruction Memory* contains instructions, which are loaded by the *CPL* for the RAO. To ensure parallel working, the *instruction memory* is scalable according to the length of the instruction. The memory line is split in several words (Fig. 3(b)). Each line is separately driven by a state. The position in the line is given by the *CPL* during the storage (bit selecting).

The *CPL* allows the connection between cells. It sends all the useful information to connect cells in the *RAC net,* which can auto-route itself. It can manage two kinds of connections between states: a new connection (the next state is not mapped in the *RAC net*); and connection between two states already mapped in the *RAC net*. It also releases resources when the *RAC net* is full.

The *CAM* associates each cell of the *RAC net* used to map a state of a SG with its address in the external memory. It is used by the *CPL* to check if a cell is already mapped in the *RAC net*. The *CAM* can select a cell in the *RAC net* when its address is presented at the input of the *CAM*.

The *Leaf Finder* identifies all the last cells of the active *SGs* mapped in the *RAC net*, which are called "leaf cells". It is a semi-mapped state which does not yet have an associated instruction.

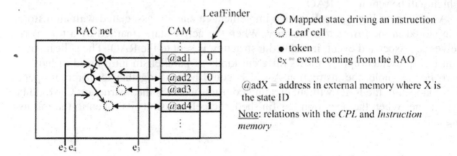

**Fig. 4.** Relation between *RAC net / CAM* & *LeafFinder*

## Configuration

In this section, the operations of the different blocks involved in the implementation of a SG are presented. All the application is stored in the external memory as a SG description. Each state description contains two kinds of information: the future instructions sent to the RAO and the descriptions of SGs. These future instructions will be loaded in the *instruction memory* by the *CPL*, and descriptions of SGs will be also loaded in the *RAC net* by the *CPL*.

Fig. 5 shows the relations between *RAC net* and *CAM* & *LeafFinder* during the configuration of the *RAC net*. A simple OR divergence and convergence graph (Fig. 5) have been chosen as an example. At this time of the course of the application, only a part of the SG is mapped in the *RAC net*: two fully states (state 1 and state 2), and two leaf cells (state 3 and state 4) are mapped. The *CPL* scans continuously the *LeafFinder* to detect a leaf cell in the *RAC net* (for example either state 3 or state 4). As soon as one is detected, the *LeafFinder* selects in the *CAM* its address in the external memory (for example either @ad3 or @ad4). This address is sent to the *CPL*, which reads the description of the corresponding state in the external memory. This description contains the configuration of the state and the addresses of its following states. In order to know whether the cell is already mapped in the *RAC net*, it supplies this address to the *CAM*. According to the result, the *CPL* sends the appropriate primitive to the *RAC net* to realize the connection (either a new connection, between state 4 and state 5, or a connection between two states already mapped, between state 3 and state 4). The *RAC net* notifies the *CPL* when the connection has succeeded. Then, the *CPL* ensures the update of the *CAM* with the address of the new mapped state; the *LeafFinder* to define the new cell as a leaf cell; and the *instruction memory* with the correct instruction.

When a connection fails, the *RAC net* indicates an error to the *CPL*. The *CPL* deallocates resources in the *RAC net* and searches the next leaf cell with the *LeafFinder*. These two operations are repeated until a connection succeeds.

**Run-Time**

The two elements implied in the run-time are the *RAC net* and the *instruction memory*. As a cache memory, the *RAC net* "decodes" the address of the next instructions which will be sent to the RAO.

As shown on Fig. 4, a cell, which implements a state, is associated with an instruction stored in the *instruction memory*. When the active state (marked by a token) receives its associated event, its related instruction is sent to the RAO. The split instruction bus, presented upper, allows different kinds of parallelism introduced in the first part. For example, the instruction A and B could be sent together to different operators mapped in the RAO without creating conflict, whereas the instruction C would be sent alone. When the operation has finished, the cell transmits its token to the following cells.

## 4   Description of the RAC Net

In this section, more details of the core of the RAC block are presented. The *RAC net* works as an address decoder in implementing SGs. This network permits to map physically the control of an application using connections of cells. Its structure is a network based on the duplication of two basic elements: cell and interconnectors.

Elementary connections, which can be mapped in the *RAC net*, are presented in Tab. 2. Linear connections and divergences (AND and OR) are simple to realize. These kinds of connections do not require additional cell to be implemented. Divergent and linear connections are initiated by one cell to find paths to new cells, whereas convergences are initiated by several cells in order to connect one cell. So, the convergent cell must be at the intersection of the different initiating paths. That is why convergences are complex to map in the *RAC net*.

As presented upper, the *RAC net* is auto-routed and can map the different kinds of simple graph elements introduced in the Tab. 2, since six modes have been defined inside cells.

Two kinds of networks have been also introduced: one dedicated to the token propagation which connects cells together; and an other one dedicated to events propagation coming from the RAO.

So, the network for tokens must allow boolean operations in order to implement OR and AND divergences. Reliability and flexibility of the *RAC net* depend on the number of allowed connections. Indeed, the higher the number of connections are allowed, the better the architecture can adapt itself to a large variety of SGs. This network is able to find and create paths between states already mapped (Fig. 4 between states @ad3 and @ad4), or create paths between leaf cells and free cells to implement new connections between states (Fig. 4 between state @ad4 and a future state – not represented). This is an important characteristic of our network. The user has just to describe the geometry of SG without taking care of the routing in the *RAC net*. This routing is automatically done by the network itself. The *CPL* only gives the description of the geometry of SGs, since protocols between cells make possible the auto-routing. Upon a *CPL* request, a cell is able to find a free connectable neighbour and establish a connection. Only three signals are required to perform these operations.

**Table 2.** Elementary implementable part of SGs

| Possible geometry | Cost in RAC cell vs. real graph | Interconnection complexity |
| --- | --- | --- |
| O—O | add none | very simple |
|  | add none | simple |
|  | add n cells for n convergences (OR/AND) | complex |

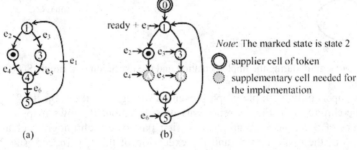

(a)                          (b)

*Note*: The marked state is state 2

O  supplier cell of token

○  supplementary cell needed for the implementation

**Fig. 5.** (a) State graph – (b) implantation of the state graph in the RAC net

Besides, the network for events is a little less constraint. But it must be sufficiently flexible to allow connections from events coming from the computation block to each cell of the *RAC net*.

## 5   Simulations and Results

A functional model of the RAC block has been realized with SystemC. In this part, the results of this model are given, and examples of implementations in the RAC block are discussed.

The characteristics of this description language easily allow hierarchical projects. Although SystemC is a hardware description language, it has the flexibility of the C++ language [16] and owns its paradigms.

A lot of different programming structures have been implemented in the RAC block, e.g. exclusion mechanisms, synchronisations between separated graphs, etc.

Moreover, an application of image processing (complex motion detection) has been mapped. These results permit to consider interesting performance improvements for future works in image embedded systems. Furthermore, these simulations have permitted to validate the paradigms of RAMPASS as auto-routability and auto-reconfiguration during execution of SGs.

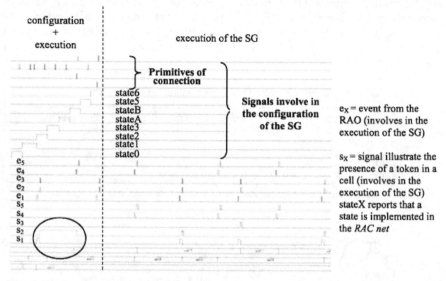

**Fig. 6.** Chronogram during the implementation and the execution of a simple SG (Fig. 5 (b))

In this paper, only a simple graph presented in Fig. 5 is the subject of a particular study. The chronogram (Fig. 6) represents its simulation. It shows mapping and execution steps of a simple state graph. The first part of the chronogram clearly shows the overlap of the configuration and the execution of the SG. Indeed, stateX signals and $s_1$, $s_2$ signals move simultaneously. StateX signals, which indicate the end of the implementation of a state, are involved in the configuration. $s_x$ signals correspond to the presence of the token in a cell. The second part of the chronogram shows the progression of the token in the SG. This propagation through the two branches of the SG is driven by events ($e_x$). The last three lines illustrate the concept of the split bus. Indeed, each part is independently managed and shared between all states.

## 6    Conclusion and Future Works

New architectural concepts are proposed in this paper. A reconfigurable part dedicated to the control of applications is detailed. This control is described using a state graph representation. To perform this control, RAMPASS uses its RAC net as an address decoder. This innovation consists in using a reconfigurable technology to solve drawbacks of cache memory. Thanks to state graph characteristics and the concept of auto-routing, this structure is able to perform many kinds of parallelism processes as SIMD, MIMD, VLIW and multi-threading. The concepts of the RAC block have been successfully checked by simulations.

According to the encouraging results, further works will be performed. To evaluate performances of RAMPASS, a Cmos model and a prototype of the RAC block will be made. But before, the topology of the interconnection network (RAC net) will be optimised. At the same time, a modelisation of the RAO block will be performed.

# References

1. H. Nakada, K. Oguri, N. Imlig, M. Inamori, R. Konishi, H. Ito, K. Nagami et T. Shiozawa, "Plastic Cell Architecture : A Dynamically Reconfigurable Hardware-based Computer", in *IPDPS'99* Apr 1999.
2. K. Compton, S. Hauck, "Reconfigurable Computing : A Survey of Systems and Software" in *ACM Computing Surveys*, Vol. 34, No 2, Jun. 2002.
3. J.R.Hauser, J.Wawrzynek, "Garp: A MIPS Processor with a Reconfigurable Coprocessor" in *Field-Programmable Custom Computing Machines (FCCM)*, Apr 1997.
4. K.S.Oh, S.Y.Yoon, S.I.Chae "Emulator Environement based on an FPGA Prototyping Board" in *Rapid System Prototyping* , 2000.
5. F.Clermidy, T.Collette, M.Nicolaidis, "A new placement algorithm dedicated to parallel computers: Bases and applications", *in Pacific Rim International Symposium on Dependable Computing*, Dec 99.
6. C.Ebeling, D.C.Cronquist, P.Franklin "RaPiD - Reconfigurable Pipelined Datapath" in *Field-Programmable Logic and Applications,* 1996.
7. R.D.Wittig and P.Chow "OneChip: An FPGA processor with reconfigurable logic" in *FCCM*, 1996.
8. S.Hauck, T.W.Fry, M.M.Hosler, J.P.Kao "The Chimarea reconfigurable functional unit" in *FCCM*, 1997.
9. Y.Li, T.Cattahan, E.Darnel, R.Harr, U.Kurkure, J.Stockwood, «Hardware-sofware codesign of *Design Automation Conference.*, Jun. 2000.
10. M.J.Wirthlin, B.L.Hutchings "DISC: the Dynamic Instruction Set Computer" in *FCCM*, Oct. 1995.
11. Virtex II www.xilinx.com
12. Stratix familie www.altera.com
13. S.Copen Goldstein, H.Schmit, M.Budiu, S.Cadambi, M.Moe, and R.Taylor, "PipeRench: A Reconfigurable Architecture and Compiler" in *Computer,* Apr. 2000.
14. E.Mirsky, A.Dehon "MATRIX: A Reconfigurable Computing Architecture with Configurable Instruction Distribution and Deployable Resources", in *FCCM*, Apr. 1996.
15. "The Open SystemC Initiative" www.systemc.org/overview.htm
16. S. Y. Liao, "Towards a new standard for system-level design", in *International Conference on Hardware Software Codesign*, 2000.

# Basic OS Support
# for Distributed Reconfigurable Hardware

Christian Haubelt, Dirk Koch, and Jürgen Teich

Department of Computer Science 12, University of Erlangen-Nuremberg, Germany

**Abstract.** While recent research is mainly focused on the OS support for a single reconfigurable node, this paper presents a general approach to manage distributed reconfigurable hardware. The most outstanding properties of these systems are the ability of reconfiguration, hardware task migration, and fault tolerance. This paper presents first ideas of an operating system (OS) for such architectures. Furthermore, a prototype implementation consisting of four fully connected FPGAs will be presented.

## 1 Introduction

Distributed reconfigurable hardware platforms [1, 2] are becoming more and more important for applications in the area of automotive, body area networks, ambient intelligence, etc. The most outstanding property of these systems is the ability of hardware reconfiguration. In terms of system synthesis, this means that the binding of tasks to resources is not static, i.e., the binding changes over time. In the context of FPGAs, recent research focuses on OS support [3] by dynamically assigning hardware tasks to an FPGA.

In a network of connected FPGAs, it becomes possible to migrate hardware tasks from one node to another during the system operation. Thus, resource faults can be compensated by *rebinding* tasks to fully functional nodes of the network. The task of rebinding is also called *repartitioning* or *online partitioning*. A network of reconfigurable nodes that implements repartitioning will be termed *ReCoNet* in the following (see Figure 2(a) for an example of a ReCoNet).

This paper describes the basic problems to be solved for the implementation of a ReCoNet. The first two features that are provided by the OS of the nodes in a ReCoNet are 1) *rerouting* and 2) *repartitioning*. They deal with erroneous resources. Thus, we are able to compensate line errors by computing a new routing for broken communications and we can migrate tasks from one node in the network to another during the system operation. These two tasks are also necessary in all distributed systems, not only in reconfigurable hardware systems. However, based on these two problems, we define feature 3) *partial reconfiguration* as the process of merging different hardware tasks together on a single FPGA. Here, the reconfiguration of a single node, also called *ReCoNode*, is done partially for the whole network. One outstanding objective in this third process is to deliver a generous approach that is not necessary bounded to a

A. Pimentel and S. Vassiliadis (Eds.): SAMOS 2004, LNCS 3133, pp. 30–38, 2004.

specific FPGA architecture. In the context of our paper, we consider only small networks in the sense that the whole state of the ReCoNet is known and stored in each ReCoNode.

A lot of related work has been published in the area of routing and computer networks [4]. The novelty of our approach is to combine these approaches with the paradigm of hardware reconfigurability.

To the best of our knowledge, there is no implementation of a ReCoNet as described above. Reconfigurable Architectures like PACT [5] and Chameleon [6] are first approaches for coarse grained, networked processing units without providing support for online reconfiguration and optimization.

This paper is organized as follows: Section 2 discusses the three basic OS features needed to provide the necessary support for distributed reconfigurable hardware platforms. Section 3 focuses on the issue how to configure a single node in such a network while section 4 presents our first simple prototype implementation of a ReCoNet. This prototype consists of four connected Altera FPGA boards.

## 2    The Basic OS Features

This section describes the basic features needed for running a distributed reconfigurable system. Before defining these features, we will take a closer look on the underlying architecture. In this paper, we consider "small" networks of hardware reconfigurable embedded systems. The main aspects of the hardware are:

- small: Each node in the network can store the current state of the whole network. The state of a network is given by its actually typology consisting of all available nodes, of available links, and of the distribution of the tasks in the network. In order to store the available connections in the ReCoNet, we use a so-called *incidence matrix* (see Figure 1). This matrix is of dimension $|V| \times |V|$, where $|V|$ is the number of nodes in the network. An element of the incidence matrix is non-zero if there is a direct connection between the two corresponding nodes.
- hardware reconfiguration: Allows the implementation of arbitrary functions in hardware. Thus, it accelerates the computation of the corresponding functions required in the network.
- embedded: Requires the optimization of different objectives, like power consumption, cost, etc. simultaneously.

These are the fundamental properties of a distributed reconfigurable system that we call a *ReCoNet*. Furthermore, a ReCoNet must support repartitioning of tasks in the network. Therefore, we have to implement three OS features. In order to compensate errors in the hardware infrastructure, we implemented the two OS features *rerouting* and *repartitioning*. Network connectivity faults are compensated by the computation of a new routing. And further, the fault of a complete node is compensated by migrating tasks to other nodes. Finally we implemented a third OS feature named *partial reconfiguration*.

In order to describe these OS Features mathematically, we need an appropriate model. The behavior of the system is given by $n$ tasks $T = \{t_1, t_2, \ldots, t_n\}$ running on $m$ possible nodes $V = \{v_1, v_2, \ldots, v_m\}$. Furthermore, the ReCoNet structure is given by $l$ links $C\{c_1, c_2, \ldots, c_l\}$ between the nodes with:

$$C \subseteq V \times V.$$

Each task $t_i \in T$ can be mapped onto an arbitrary set of resources. Therefore, we model all possible bindings as a set $\beta$, where:

$$\beta \subseteq T \times V.$$

The OS features are triggered if a resource fault is detected or a new task becomes ready to run. In the following we reveal the basic OS features rerouting, repartitioning and partial reconfiguration in detail.

### 2.1  Rerouting

The first OS feature to be defined is the task of rerouting. Rerouting is required if a connection ($c_f \in C$) in the network fails. All communications done over this connection has to be rerouted. There are several publications dealing with this issue. Recent work was mainly focused on probabilistic approaches [7].

Here, we consider a high-level fault tolerant approach. Rerouting itself can be decomposed in three subproblems:

1. Line detection: Is a link $c_i = (v_j, v_k)$ between two nodes $v_j$ and $v_k$ available or not?
2. Network state distribution: If a connection between two nodes $(v_j, v_k)$ fails, all nodes $v \in V \backslash \{v_j, v_k\}$ in the network not incident to connection $c_f$ must be informed.
3. Routing of broken communications.

The first subproblem can be solved in several ways. The easiest implementation is to periodically send some predefined data over each connection. If we do not detect any signal changes at the end of this connection, either the line or the sending node may be defect. In both cases, we cannot use this connection any longer.

The second subproblem, the distribution of the network state, could also be solved in many ways. Again, we just mention the simplest one, the broadcast. The detecting node $v_j$ just sends this new information to all its neighbors. These neighbors will relay this message until all nodes in the network are notified. The main problem in this solution is to keep track of already known messages which should not be relayed. Another problem is the time needed for the distribution. If an error is intermittent, there may be several different messages are on their ways through the network all representing a different state of the network. Thus, also if we limit ourselves to applications without any time constraints, we need some time base in the network [8].

The last subproblem, the computation of a new routing can be done with any routing algorithm. Since we only consider small networks, we are able to store the state of all connections of the network in an incidence matrix. Based on this matrix, we can calculate the new routes using for example the shortest path algorithm (see [4]).

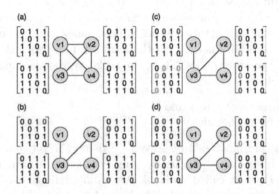

**Fig. 1.** Example of a ReCoNet. (a) The ReCoNet consisting of four ReCoNodes and the corresponding incidence matrices. (b) Two connections failed. (c) All directed neighbors are notified. (d) All indirect neighbors are notified.

Figure 1 shows an example of the first two steps in the process of rerouting. Figure 1(a) shows a ReCoNet consisting of four fully connected ReCoNodes. The corresponding incidence matrices are also shown near each node. In Figure 1(b) the situation is shown where two connections fail. Each incident node detects this error and updates its incidence matrix.

In the next step (Figure 1(c)) all direct neighbors are informed about the topology change of the network. Note, that all nodes store different information of the state of the network. Finally, in Figure 1(d), all nodes have the same information about the state of the network. Based on this information, each node computes the new routing.

On every node this procedure of rerouting can be implemented in the following fashion:

```
if (line_state[i] != next_line_state[i])
   {  Update_Incidence_Matrix( );
      Notify_all_Neighbours(line_fail);
      reroute( )
   };
if(Receive_net_state! = net_state)
   {  Update_Incidence_Matrix( );
      Notify_other_Neighbours(line_fail);
      reroute( )
   }
```

## 2.2   Repartitioning

*Rebinding* describes the migration of hardware tasks $t_i \in T$ from one node $v_j$ in the network to another $v_k$. Thus we need $\{(t_i, v_j), (t_i, v_k)\} \in \beta$. Note, that if we configure the reconfigurable nodes $v_i, v_k$ with a processor, it may be possible to migrate a hardware task $(t_i^{hw})$ to a software task $(t_i^{sw})$ and vice versa, too. For a node $v_k$ this will further need $\{(t_i^{hw}, v_k), (t_i^{sw}, v_k)\} \in \beta$. The task of rebinding is also called *repartitioning* or *online partitioning* in the following.

But when should we migrate a task? In this paper, we just focus on the case of resource faults, i.e., if a node $v_f$ in the network fails, all tasks running on $v_f$ must be migrated to other nodes. Thus, the task of repartitioning can be divided into two subproblems:

1. Detection of resource errors and
2. rebinding of tasks to nodes.

The first subproblem again can be solved by using the incidence matrix of the actual network. If a node $v_f$ has no working connection to any of its neighbors ($\{v_f, v_i\} \in C, \forall i$), it is called *isolated*. An isolated node cannot be used for process execution any more and all tasks bound to this node must be migrated.

An important question is how to perform a save task migration, i.e., how to keep track on the current state of a task. Here, we limit ourselves to stateless tasks which can be started in an appropriate state after a system failure. It is explained in [8] how to handle non-stateless tasks.

Furthermore, we must consider the question of on which node $v_j$ should a task $t_i$ be restarted. Again, there are several well-known approaches and the simplest one is to use a priority binding list $P : \beta \to \mathbb{N}$ for each task $t \in T$, i.e., each task is bounded to the node with highest priority in its priority list. If this node fails, it rebounds to the next available node with the highest remaining priority. Note that when rebinding tasks, we must recompute the routing as well.

## 2.3   Reconfiguration

In order to be as general as possible, we do not require partial reconfiguration as provided by some Xilinx FPGAs [9]. By disconnecting a single node $v_i$, the remaining network $V \backslash \{v_i\}$ should not be affected. Thus, we can reconfigure a disconnected node completely.

If we allow only fully hardware reconfiguration, we must ensure that all tasks $(t_j \in T \quad \forall (t_j, v_i) \in \beta)$, that are implemented on the given node $v_i$ are not needed for the time of the reconfiguration. If we are not sure about this, we first have to migrate these tasks to other nodes in the network. A simple implementation of this algorithm will be presented in Section 4.

Figure 2 shows a scenario where an additional hardware task is loaded into the system. The initial state of the network is shown in Figure 2(a). Each of the four nodes executes software (circles) and hardware (rectangles) tasks. Also, the configuration memory of each node is shown. Next, an additional hardware task $(t_9)$ should be loaded into the system. Here, we assume that $t_9$ should be

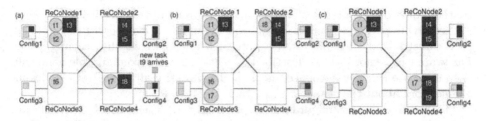

**Fig. 2.** Example of Repartitioning. (a) shows the original ReCoNet configuration. There are four ReCoNodes. Each node is configured with software (circles) and hardware (rectangles) tasks. The configuration memory for each node is also displayed. (b) To configure ReCoNode4 with an additional hardware task ($t_9$), we must move all running tasks of this node to other nodes in the network. At the same time the configuration memory (Config4) is updated with the additional task. (c) After reseting ReCoNode4 the new configuration is loaded.

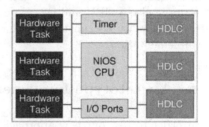

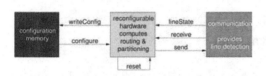

**Fig. 3.** Example of a ReCoNode. The reconfigurable hardware computes the routing and partitioning of the distributed application. The communication module provides information about local connections.

**Fig. 4.** Configuration of a single ReCoNode. Beside the communication modules (HDLC) and the hardware tasks, there is a NIOS CPU with additional timers and I/O ports.

loaded on node ReCoNode4. Therefore, all tasks ($t_7$, $t_8$) running on ReCoNode4 are suspended and restarted on ReCoNode2 and ReCoNode3, respectively (see Figure 2(b)). Note, that task $t_8$ is implemented in software. Furthermore, the new configuration for ReCoNode4 is stored into the configuration memory.

In a last step (Figure 2(c)), the reset signal is issued on ReCoNode4. ReCoNode4 starts with the new configuration. The task $t_7$ and $t_8$ on ReCoNode2 and ReCoNode3 are suspended.

## 3   Configuration of a ReCoNode

A ReCoNode should implement the three basic functions as described in Section 2. Figure 3 shows a simple example of a ReCoNode.

The reconfigurable hardware computes the actual routing and partitioning based on its information about the state of the network. Note, that the hardware could be configured with a processor (as will be presented in the next section) to do the required computation. The communication module is needed for sending and receiving packages over the network. Furthermore, it observes the state of each directly connected line. If the state of a line changes, the reconfigurable hardware will be notified. As described in Section 2, the reconfigurable node will then compute the new incidence matrix and will notify all other ReCoNodes in the network about the change.

To perform the reconfiguration of the hardware, the ReCoNode itself can write the configuration memory and generate a self reset on the FPGA. That way, our solution does not require any partial reconfiguration of the FPGAs. In the simplest scenario, we just migrate all tasks to other nodes of the network, write the desired configuration into the configuration memory, and trigger a reset on the FPGA (see also Figure 2). For non-stateless tasks, additional work is needed to ensure a proper migration of such tasks inside the ReCoNets. Figure 4 shows the configuration of a single ReCoNode as used in the sample implementation described in the next section. Beside the communication modules (HDLC), there is also a CPU and user-defined hardware. By using a CPU core, we have the possibility to run tasks in hardware as well as in software or any mixed implementation.

## 4   A Prototype Implementation

In order to test our new approach, we have constructed a distributed reconfigurable prototype consisting of four Altera Excalibur development boards [10]. With a single Excalibur board, the user has the ability to build a hardware-software-system by using Altera's SoPC-builder [11]. Such a systems is composed of Altera's NIOS processor [12], user-specified hardware, and user-specified software. The user-specified software is given in C/C++. The user-specified hardware and the NIOS-processor are connected by using a hardware description language like VHDL or Verilog. After synthesis of the hardware design, it is downloaded to the FPGA on the Excalibur board.

A single node of the prototype implementation is configured as described in section 3 with a NIOS processor and three communication modules (see also Figure 4). For the communication we have chosen the standard HDLC (High-level Data Link Control) protocol. In order to detect line errors, we have implemented the physical layer with a Manchester encoding. See Figure 4 for the configuration of a single ReCoNode.

The prototype implementation of the ReCoNet is shown in Figure 5. Several automotive applications are implemented on this ReCoNet. The three basic OS features as described in section 2 are implemented as follows:

– Rerouting: Each node stores the current state of the network in an incidence matrix. If a line error is detected the incidence matrices are updated as shown in Figure 1. In a last step, a new routing for all applications is computed by the use of Dijkstra's shortest-path-algorithm. The routing itself is done by the NIOS CPU on each node.

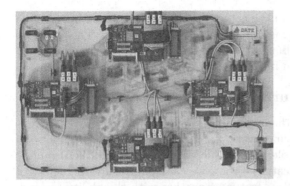

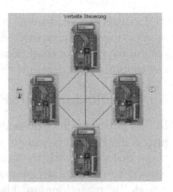

**Fig. 5.** A prototype implementation of a distributed reconfigurable system that supports repartitioning. The prototype is composed of four Altera Excalibur development boards.

**Fig. 6.** Monitoring tool; One can see the active connections as well as the distribution of the processes.

– Repartitioning: Each ReCoNode stores the binding priority list of each task. If a ReCoNode fails, all tasks currently executed on this node are migrated to the next available ReCoNode with the highest remaining priority. If there is no copy of the migrating task available on this ReCoNode, we must perform a reconfiguration step by either copying a software implementation or a complete configuration file to this node. Therefore, the ReCoNode has to know where to find this configurations. In our prototype, only the two nodes ReCoNode2 and ReCoNode3 switch between two different configurations. These configurations are stored in the configurations memory of ReCoNode1 and ReCoNode4. Again, the selection of a configurations file is statically programmed. The transfer of the configuration streams is done over the network.

– Reconfiguration: Reconfiguration is established by writing a configuration stream to the configuration memory. The copying of the configuration file is again done by the NIOS CPU. It requests the configuration from one of its neighbors and stores the data in the configuration memory. The error free transfer of the reconfiguration content is guaranteed by the utilized HDLC protocol. Further, a special bit inside the configuration bitstream is used to indicate valid configurations in the memory. This bit is analyzed by an additional PLD that controls the reconfiguration process after the triggered reset. By writing this bit as the last one to the configuration memory, we can ensure that only valid configurations are transferred to the FPGA. This mechanism is archived by the *configurator* PLD that loads a default configuration on determining an invalid configuration memory content. When all data is written correctly to the configuration memory, the NIOS CPU issues the reset signal to itself. The ReCoNode that sends the reconfiguration bitstream remembers the last read request until a proper reconfiguration has been achieved. This allows the default configuration to initialize a broken reconfiguration process again (e.g. during a power failure in the reconfiguration download phase).

In order to visualize the state of the network as well as the distribution of the applications, we have written a small monitoring JAVA program. This program communicates to a single Excalibur board over the debug port. A screenshot of the monitoring program is shown in Figure 6.

## 5  Conclusions and Future Work

In this paper, we have presented the implementation of basic OS features for running a distributed reconfigurable hardware system, a so-called *ReCoNet*. Two of these tasks deal with the fault tolerance of such a system. While the *rerouting* is used to compensate communication errors, we can compensate the defect of a node by *repartitioning*. These two features together with the ability of *hardware reconfiguration* allows us to build dynamical hardware-software systems. A first implementation of these basic tasks in distributed reconfigurable system consisting of four Altera FPGAs was presented here.

Important issues in the future are to provide support for real-time and non-stateless applications. Furthermore the optimization (online/offline) of distributed reconfigurable systems must be considered in future work.

## References

1. R. Dick and N. Jha, "CORDS: Hardware-Software Co-Synthesis of Reconfigurable Real-Time Distributed Embedded Systems," in *Proceedigns of ICCAD'98*, 1998, pp. 62–68.
2. I. Ouaiss, S. Govindarajan, V. Srinivasan, M. Kaul, and R. Vemuri, "An Integrated Partitioning and Synthesis System for Dynamically Reconfigurable Multi-FPGA Architectures," in *IPPS/SPDP Workshops*, 1998, pp. 31–36.
3. H. Walder and M. Platzner, "Online Scheduling for Block-partitioned Reconfigurable Devices," in *Proceedings of Design, Automation and Test in Europe (DATE03)*, Mar. 2003, pp. 290–295.
4. A. Tanenbaum, *Computer Networks*.  Prentice Hall PTR, 2002.
5. V. Baumgarte, F. May, A. Nückel, M. Vorbach, and M. Weinhardt, "PACT XPP – A Self-Reconfigurable Data Processing Architecture," in *ERSA*, Las Vegas, Nevada, June 2001.
6. Chameleon Systems, *CS2000 Reconfigurable Communications Processor, Family Product Brief*, 2000.
7. T. Dumitraş, S. Kerner, and R. Mărculescu, "Towards On-Chip Fault-Tolerant Communication," in *Proceedings of the Asia and South Pacific Design Automation Conference 2003*, Kitakyushu, Japan, Jan. 2003.
8. H. Kopetz, *Real-Time Systems – Design Principles for Distributed Embedded Applications*. Norwell, Massachusetts 02061 USA: Kluwer Academic Publishers, 1997.
9. Xilinx, 2003, http://www.xilinx.com.
10. Altera, "Excalibur development kit data sheet," June 2000, http://www.altera.com.
11. Altera, "Quartus programmable logic development system & software data sheet," May 1999. [Online]. Available: http://www.altera.com
12. Altera, "Nios soft core embedded processor data sheet," June 2000. [Online]. Available: http://www.altera.com

# A Cost-Efficient RISC Processor Platform for Real Time Audio Applications

Jens Peter Wittenburg, Ulrich Schreiber, Ulrich Gries,
Markus Schneider, and Tim Niggemeier

Deutsche Thomson Brandt GmbH
Thomson Corporate Research
Hannover, Germany
`jens-peter.wittenburg@thomson.net`

**Abstract.** A platform architecture for real time audio applications based on the open source LEON RISC processor and an audio development board based on an FPGA implementation of this platform are presented. Emphasis is on audio-specific extensions of the LEON architecture. In particular, a Floating Point Unit (FPU) for the LEON CPU and a multi-standard audio interface block were implemented. Innovative aspects, as a scoreboard based superscalar scheduler for the FPU and a new flexible approach to the interface block, unifying major parts of the required logic for all relevant interface standards are described. The extended LEON architecture is running on an Altera Stratix EP1S30-5 at more than 50 MHz. This already allows to run an mp3 decoder at up to 128 kbit/s in real-time. Porting of additional decoders as mp3PRO and AAC has been started.

## 1 Introduction

By enabling distribution of digital music over the internet, the MPEG-1 Layer 3 (mp3) [1] audio compression scheme has caused one of the biggest paradigm shifts ever in consumer attitude regarding digital media and consumer electronics products. Today mp3 support is a prerequisite for the acceptance of products ranging from smallest flash memory based portable players to DVD recorders. However, the mp3 standard dates back to 1992, while newer standards offer significantly improved coding efficiency, enable the support for multiple channels (e.g. 5+1) or offer better opportunities to tackle the still unsolved problem of content and copyright protection. Hence, development in audio coding technology is still underway, while there is already a large number of established proprietary and open standards (mp3PRO, AC3, WMA, AAC to name a few). Respective hardware architectures have to be able to support several if not all of these standards – which calls for software programmable solutions.

Since typical tasks of an audio coding scheme include FIR-filtering and discrete Fourier or cosine transforms, such schemes heavily profit from DSP typical architectural features as Multiply & Accumulate (MAC) units of sufficient word-width and separate address generation units. As a coarse figure of merit, a typical audio decoder for stereo signals requires a processing power of about 20 to 25 Million instructions per second (MIPS) based on the instruction set of such a state of the art DSP. This number turned out to be surprisingly stable for the various standards. Furthermore, employment

A. Pimentel and S. Vassiliadis (Eds.): SAMOS 2004, LNCS 3133, pp. 39–48, 2004.

of multi-channel standards as AAC or AC3 leads to linearly scaled performance requirements (e.g. 30-40 MIPS for a 5+1 decoder). The span for encoders is a little bit wider and ranges from about 20 to 70 MIPS.

All major applications of audio coding schemes are in the consumer domain, where cost reduction is usually the major design goal. Considering the advances in silicon technologies and the complexity of embedded DSPs or RISC architectures, the influence of area costs is becoming negligible. Instead costs for licensing – especially royalties payable per manufactured device – and software development costs became important.

To target these shifting cost criteria, a novel audio coding platform based on a royalty free open source RISC architecture called *LEON* [2] has been developed. The LEON is a SPARC V8 [3] compatible RISC-CPU that is distributed under the Lesser GNU Public License (LGPL). The goal of this platform development is twofold: On one hand tailored versions of the platform shall be employed as embedded audio cores in different SoC-designs to be used in various applications as DVD-players, set top boxes or portable disc players. On the other hand, a flexible development platform based on an FPGA-implementation of the LEON architecture shall be implemented to be employed for further algorithm and system development.

To cope with the requirements implied by these goals, the LEON system architecture needs to be extended:

- Audio coding schemes are usually programmed using floating point data types. The 32bit integer arithmetic, as provided by the LEON architecture, is insufficient to provide the required dynamic range of audio applications. It is important to understand, that the dynamic range and not the accuracy of audio application imposes to employ data types larger than 32bit integer. This implies that such algorithms can be ported to integer by tracking the dynamic range in a separate data word (block floating point). Such implementations of some of the coding schemes are available. However, earlier developments in this area have shown, that the development costs for porting of several coding standards will definitely exceed those for development of an appropriate floating point unit. A floating point unit for the LEON architecture capable to provide the required processing power is not available and hence, had to be developed.
- Employment of an audio platform for multiple applications and for algorithm development requires a flexible and customizable media interfacing scheme. At least four different interface standards at even more sample rates are commonly found in typical audio applications (SPDIF [4], ADAT [5], AC'97 [6] and $I^2S$). While all standards are basically serial, they differ significantly in their frame formats and synchronization modes. Respective interface IP-blocks had to be developed that are appropriate to be plugged into the LEON system architecture. To provide better efficiency of these IP-blocks and to allow easier adaptation to specific applications, these IP-blocks feature a common internal format to allow shared use of major modules within a common audio-interface block.

The main part of this paper is organized as follows: The following section (section 2) provides a brief introduction to the LEON CPU and system architecture. Section 3 describes the architecture of the newly implemented floating point unit and its superscalar interface. Section 4 introduces the audio interface block and its concept using a common intermediate format. Finally, section 5 gives an overview of the FPGA based system development board used to implement the audio platform. Section 6 concludes the paper.

## 2 The LEON SPARC V8 Architecture

According to the SPARC V8 standard (aka IEEE-1754), the LEON architecture is a 32bit scalar RISC architecture. Originally developed in a redundant version for space applications at the European Space Agency, the processor is now maintained and distributed under LGPL by a company named *Gaisler Research*. The recent version of the LEON architecture is targeted towards employment as embedded processor in a system on chip environment. Hence, the LEON features several optional peripheral blocks including UARTs, timers, a watchdog, a parallel interface, an interrupt controller and a flexible memory interface (see Fig. 1). The processor and all the peripherals are connected via an AMBA 2.0 AHB respectively APB bus [7]. Due to this fact, the system is compliant to industry standards and hence, is easily extendible by further customized units.

Core of the LEON processor is the integer unit implementing all control and integer instructions of the SPARC V8 instruction set. The architecture features a 5-stage instruction pipeline and 32 bit data and address busses. In addition to an ALU featuring single cycle latency, the arithmetic can be extended by configurable multiply and divide units. In maximum configuration (32 x 32), the multiplier also requires just one cycle to generate the 64bit result. The radix-2 non-restoring divider requires 35 cycles per result. Most load/store and branch instructions have a latency of 2 cycles.

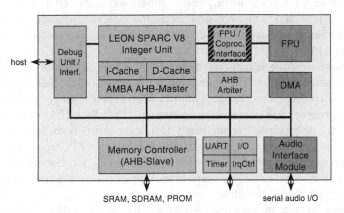

**Fig. 1.** Block Diagram of LEON platform. The darker grey blocks are custom extensions for the audio platform

The cache subsystem features a Harvard architecture i.e. separate data and instruction caches. The caches can be separately configured between 1 and 64 kBytes per set. Both, direct mapped and set-associative organizations are possible. However, it is important to note, that both caches are connected to the memory controller via a single

32bit AHB-bus that is also shared by the other peripherals. The memory controller offers glueless access to PROMs, generic I/O, SRAM, and PC133 SDRAM on a 8, 16 or 32 bit wide memory bus.

The LEON processors comes with a software development package consisting of a GNU-based cross compilation system (called LECCS) featuring GCC C/C++ compiler, linker, assembler and source level debugger. A cycle true simulator with GDB debugger interface and access to all processor registers is the only tool commercially sold by Gaisler Research. An on-chip debug support unit (DSU) and trace buffer offer an efficient way to debug the processor in circuit. The DSU can interrupt the normal processing triggered by breakpoints or software watchdogs. It can be configured as AHB-master and hence has access to all caches and configuration registers. The DSU connects to a monitor program and debugger running on a host computer via a UART using the RS232 protocol at 115 kB/s.

## 3   FPU-Extension

The processing power requirements given in section 1 are based on a DSP instruction set. Hence, they do not translate directly to a RISC architecture. In the particular case of the LEON architecture, the multi-cycle latency of several commonly used instructions (e.g. load/store, branch) will expand this gap even more. However, clock rates of more than 50 MHz are realistic even in an FPGA implementation, which offers more than twice the number of instructions per second than required on a DSP. Hence, regarding integer performance, the processing power should be sufficient at least for stereo decoding.

On the other hand, since floating point support was identified as a requirement, the floating point arithmetic must not slow down the integer processing and the floating point calculations must not be significantly slower than integer – which calls for a high performance FPU.

While the instruction scheduling of the LEON is basically scalar and in order, there is one important exception: The instruction set is defined such, that coprocessors and FPUs have to operate on independent register files. Data exchange can only take place via external memory using load/store operations. Therefore, FPU or coprocessor instructions may be processed concurrently to integer instructions and may also complete out-of-order. However, to ensure coherency between FPU/coprocessor and integer data, the respective interfaces provide an interlocking mechanism to prevent out-of-order memory access and to ensure branch processing on actually corresponding FPU/coprocessor condition codes.

Originally this feature was intended for unpipelined low throughput FPUs requiring several cycles to process an instruction. SUN employed such a FPU (designed by MEIKO) in its MicroSPARC II processor. This type of FPU is of course unacceptable regarding the processing power requirements as stated above. On the other hand, such concurrent interface is basically capable to handle a separate *superscalar-like* floating point instruction scheduler resolving the data dependencies (pipeline hazards) of a fully pipelined FPU with a throughput of (up to) one instruction per cycle.

from Instruction Cache

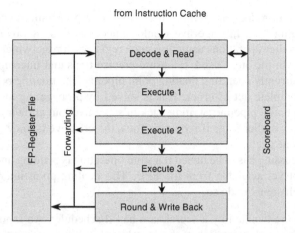

**Fig. 2.** Block Diagram of FPU-pipeline

Such a fully pipelined FPU and a respective instruction scheduler have been designed. The FPU (see Fig. 2) is based on earlier work by Martin Kasprzyk [8], who did a partial and only weakly verified implementation of a SPARC V8 FPU. The concept of this CPU is based on a five stage pipeline with clear separation of the individual tasks of floating point arithmetic. In the existing implementation only ALU instructions were supported, but modularity and very conservative timing constraints made it a good starting point for enhancements.

The pipeline structure is shown in Fig. 2. Stage one is used for instruction decode and register read, stage five is used exclusively for rounding and write back. In case of additions or subtractions, stage two is used for prenormalization, stage three for the actual arithmetic operation on mantissa and exponent, while stage four performs the postnormalization step. Since a floating point multiplication does not require prenormalization, the critical multiplication of the mantissa can be distributed among pipeline stages two and three. In particular, stage two contains the product term generation and the carry save array of a (booth encoded) wallace tree multiplier [9], while stage three contains the carry propagate adder. Synthesis results have shown, that in an ASIC implementation this structure allows multiplications in double precision without slowing down the integer unit. Quad-precision, floating-point division and square-root instructions are not supported, because they are not found in performance critical subtasks and very rarely in audio applications at all. Hence, software emulation of such instructions (which can be performed automatically by the compiler) is fully sufficient.

A special handling was required for the floating point load/store operations. All address calculations for the LEON architecture are handled by the integer unit. This implies, that in case of a load operation, opcode and operands are handed over from the integer unit to the floating point unit via the floating point interface at a fixed number of cycles after the integer unit has issued the respective instruction. The exact opposite applies to store instructions: The operand from the floating point register file is expected at a certain number of cycles after the instruction has been issued. This has several implications:

- A load operation does not require more than one processing cycle to complete. Hence, writing back in stage five would unnecessarily slow down processing of subsequent other operations using the same register address (which is a very common case). On the other hand, to ensure precise traps and interrupts with respect to the concurrently operating floating point pipeline, the floating point instructions must not complete out-of-order. This is solved by propagating the load operands through the entire pipeline (writing back in stage five) but allowing to forward the data from any earlier stage if required. Thus, the effective latency of a load operation is just one cycle.
- Integer processing has to be halted if a store operation is pending and the respective result is not yet available from the FPU. The floating point interface features a selective halt signal to do so.

Both issues are handled by a scoreboard based scheduler. An innovative detail in this context is the implementation of the scoreboard. While a conventional scoreboard would just store a flag per register address, stating that an instruction within the pipeline intends to write its result to this address, the implemented scoreboard stores the type (= latency) of the instruction and keeps track of the pipeline stage carrying the result-generating instruction by implementing individual counters per register address. This allows direct calculation of:

1. The number of stall cycles in case of not yet available results (RAW hazards)
2. The number of the pipeline stage that carries the result required for forwarding

Using such implementation, no further communication between scheduler and pipeline stages (result snooping) is required, which saves significant wiring overhead especially because quite a large number of pipeline stages (4) are able to forward results. This is of special importance in FPGA implementations, where wiring is comparably costly.

## 4   Audio Interface Block

The twofold employment – on one hand as a customizable IP-platform, on the other hand as a software and algorithm development platform – requires an especially flexible and powerful audio interface module. Following are the specific requirements for such an interface block:

- Support for $I^2S$, IEC958 (SPDIF), ADAT and AC'97 standards.
- Support for multiple concurrent input and/or output streams of differing standards.
- Connection to embedded processor via AMBA AHB bus. Support for interrupt triggered DMA transfer and provision of an appropriate FIFO to buffer incoming/outgoing data while DMA is inactive.
- Provision of flexible opportunities for customization and parameterization.
- Support for timestamp mechanism to synchronize various data streams.

The most obvious challenge of this list is the need for support of various standards. Table 1 provides a comparison of the most important features of those standards. It can be seen, that sample rates, channel codes and frame formats are quite heterogeneous. To offer a maximum flexibility while concurrently saving resources, an interface module architecture based on a unified internal format for all interface standards was chosen.

**Table 1.** Comparison of main features of important consumer and professional audio interface standards

| feature | IEC 958 | ADAT | AC'97 | I²S |
|---|---|---|---|---|
| channels | 2 | 8 | max 12 | 2 |
| PCM bits | 24 | 24 | 20 | max 24 |
| subcode bits | 4 per channel | 4 per sample | - | - |
| sample rate | 32/44.1/48 kHz | 44.1/48 kHz | 48 kHz / var. | var. |
| channel clock rate | $64 \cdot F_S$ | $256 \cdot F_S$ | $256 \cdot F_S$ | $64 \cdot F_S$ |
| channel code | biphase-mark | NRZI | - | - |
| clock | self-timed | self-timed | clock net | clock net |

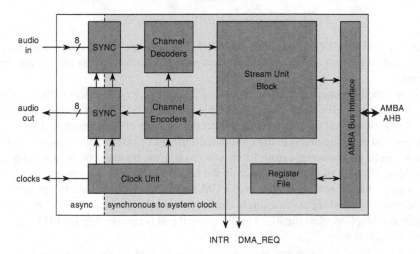

**Fig. 3.** Block diagram of audio interface module

The resulting architecture is shown in Fig. 3. The external interface data first has to be synchronized to system clock respectively internally or externally generated audio clock(s). It has to be mentioned that due to the requirement for concurrent support of multiple standards, also multiple external clock rates have to be supported simultaneously. The synchronizer blocks in collaboration with a clock unit even support switching between differing audio sample rates during operation.

After being synchronized, incoming data streams are converted to the common internal format by so called *channel decoders*. Outgoing streams are converted vice versa from the internal format to the respective interface standard by *channel encoders*. A separate set of channel en-/decoder exist for each of the supported interface standard. The common internal format consist of a serial data stream containing PCM and subcode data and enable/valid signals separated for frame, PCM data and subcode data. Hence, the main purpose of the channel en/decoders is the clock recovery and handling

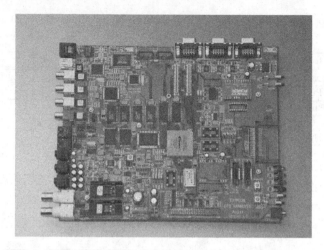

**Fig. 4.** Photograph of *AUDIX* Development Board

of the channel codes (biphase-mark or NRZ). Furthermore, the frame is split respectively packed to/from separate PCM and subcode data according to its specific frame format.

A so called *stream unit block* connects the channel coders/decoders with the AMBA bus. It contains a FIFO (size parameterizable from 4 to 512 32bit words) and a number of generic stream units corresponding to the number of data streams. The number of supported data streams (i.e. the cumulated number of connected audio sources and drains) can be parameterized from 1 to 8, where each stream may contain up to 16 channels. Main purpose of the stream units is the serial to parallel conversion (respectively vice versa) and the actual separation of PCM and subcode data. The stream units may also combine several inputs to a single stream (*channel aggregation*). Furthermore, the stream unit block handles the FIFO buffer control and is responsible for IRQ and DMA request generation.

The benefit of the proposed approach is the separation of the relatively simple and specific channel en-/decoders from the complex and generic stream unit block. This allows more flexible customization regarding number and type of supported data streams, while saving otherwise redundant resources in the serial to parallel conversion process.

## 5  *Audix* Development Board

A development board for the proposed audio platform based on an Altera Stratix EP1S30-5 FPGA has been developed (see Fig. 4). In addition to the physical interfaces (level shifters, optical couplers etc.) for the described audio interface standards, the board contains 64MB SDRAM as well as 2MB SRAM, several debug facilities and additional general purpose peripheral interfaces e.g. IEEE 1394, Ethernet, RS232 or a flash card connector.

The entire audio platform – this means LEON processor including FPU and audio interface block – have been successfully mapped to the Stratix FPGA. The chosen configuration is described by table 2.

**Table 2.** Implemented configuration of LEON-architecture and audio interface module

| Debug Unit | implemented |
|---|---|
| Fixt poit multiplier | 32 x 32 bit |
| FPU-multiplier | single precision only |
| I-Cache size | 8 kB |
| I-Cache organization | 2-way set associative, LRU |
| D-Cache size | 8 kB |
| D-Cache organization | 2-way set associative, LRU |
| number of channel en-/decoders | 4/4 |
| number of stream units | 4 |
| FIFO size | 1 kB |

**Table 3.** Resulting complexity for Altera Stratix implementation. The EP1S30-5 device offers slightly more than 30000 logic elements

| LEON Integer Unit | 4600 logic elements |
|---|---|
| LEON Controller | 3900 logic elements |
| FPU | 5900 logic elements |
| I-Cache | 800 logic elements |
| D-Cache size | 3200 logic elements |
| DMA | 1500 logic elements |
| debug support unit | 1100 logic elements |
| memory controller | 1200 logic elements |
| audio interface block | 7500 logic elements |
| $\Sigma$ | **29700 logic elements** |

An overview of the resulting complexity is provided in table 3. While the complexity of the FPU was to be expected, it can be seen that the audio interface block is also comparably complex.

The entire system reaches a clock rate of more than 50 MHz. It has to be mentioned, that support for double precision multiplication had to be dropped to reach this performance. The reason for this is, that the custom multiplier that are provided by the Stratix FPGA offer an excellent performance but do not fit well with the two pipeline stage approach as implemented in the FPU. However, this is no actual drawback, since audio algorithms do not require double precision anyway.

As first application a mp3 decoder has been successfully ported to the LEON architecture and is successfully running on the Audix development board using real world data streams. The mp3 decoder has also passed the mp3-part of the MPEG compliance test. First synthesis results for an $0.18\mu m$ ASIC technology indicate, that the entire system will operate at clock rates beyond 200 MHz.

## 6   Conclusion

An audio platform based on the LEON open source RISC architecture has been developed. To be appropriate for audio applications, the LEON-processor had to be extendedby a fully pipelined high performance floating point unit featuring a maximum throughput of one instruction per cycle and a flexible audio interface unit supporting all relevant audio interface standards.

A development board providing the required environment for application development and testing has been developed. Extended LEON architecture and audio interface module have been mapped to this board. An mp3 decoder has been successfully ported and tested using real-world and synthetic worst-case data-streams.

The platform will be used both, as a flexibly customizable IP block in future SoCs for audiovisual applications and – mapped to an FPGA based development board – as universal audio development platform. The development board is also an excellent starting point for research on novel reconfigurable architectures offering further increase in efficiency and costs savings for audio applications.

## Acknowledgment

The authors would like to thank Andre Begau, Andreas Wend and Hauke Neumann for valuable contributions to this project.

## References

1. ISO/IEC 11172-3 Information Technology, *Coding of moving pictures and associated audio for digital storage media at up to about 1.5 Mbit/s, Audio*, 1993.
2. Jiri Gaisler, *The LEON-2 Processor User's Manual*, Version 1.0.14, Gaisler Research March 2003, http://www.gaisler.com
3. SPARC International Inc., *The SPARC Architecture Manual – Version 8*, Revision SAV080S19308.
4. IEC 60958-1/2/3, *Digital audio interface* Part 1-3, General / Software information delivery mode / Consumer Applications, 1999
5. Keith Barr et. al., *Method and apparatus for providing a digital audio interface protocol*, US Patent No. 5,297,181; 1994.
6. Intel Corporation, *Audio Codec 97 Component Specification*, Revision 2.3, April 2002.
7. ARM Limited, *AMBA specification*, Rev. 2.0, 1999.
8. Martin Kasprzyk, *Floating Point Unit Digital IC Project*, e00mk, Januar 2002, http://www.gaisler.com
9. Peter Pirsch, *Architectures for Digital Signal Processing*, John Wiley & Sons, 1998

# Customising Processors:
# Design-Time and Run-Time Opportunities

Wayne Luk

Department of Computing, Imperial College,
180 Queen's Gate, London, England

**Abstract.** This paper reviews techniques and tools for customising processors at design time and at run time. We use several examples to illustrate customisation for particular application domains, and explore the use of declarative and imperative languages for describing and customising data processors. We then consider run-time customisation, which necessitates additional work at compile time such as production of multiple configurations for downloading at run time. The customisation of instruction processors and design tools is also discussed.

## 1  Introduction

Customisation is the process of optimising a design to meet application and implementation constraints. It can take place at design time and at run time. We regard design time to have two components: fabrication time and compile time. During fabrication time, a physical computing device is constructed. If this device is programmable, then it is customised by a program produced at compile time and executed at run time.

Three popular means of implementing computations are Application-Specific Integrated Circuits (ASICs), instruction processors such as those from Intel and AMD, and reconfigurable hardware such as Field-Programmable Gate Array (FPGA) devices.

- For ASICs, much of the customisation to perform application functions takes place at fabrication time; hence the high efficiency but low flexibility, since new functions not planned before fabrication cannot be added.
- For instruction processors, fabrication-time customisation produces a device supporting a fixed instruction set architecture, and compile-time customisation produces instructions for that architecture; run-time customisation corresponds to switching between different program executions at run time.
- For reconfigurable hardware, fabrication-time customisation produces a device with a particular structure, typically containing reconfigurable elements joined together by reconfigurable interconnections. At compile time, configuration information is produced for customising the device at appropriate instants at run time.

As we shall see later, many of the customisation techniques can be applied either to ASICs at fabrication time, or to reconfigurable hardware at compile time, hence we use the term 'design time' to cover both possibilities. Also we shall distinguish between instruction processors and data processors; the latter correspond to processors that do not need to process instructions.

A. Pimentel and S. Vassiliadis (Eds.): SAMOS 2004, LNCS 3133, pp. 49–58, 2004.

The purpose of this paper is to review recent design-time and run-time customisation techniques developed mainly at Imperial College. Five areas will be covered. First, domain-specific customisation (Section 2), second, design-time customisation for data processors (Section 3 and 4), third, run-time customisation for data processors (Section 5), fourth, instruction processor customisation (Section 6), fifth, design tool customisation (Section 7). Our review aims to provide a summary of some current research directions, but it is not intended to be an extensive survey.

## 2   Customise Designs: Domain-Specific Issues

This section describes domain-specific customisation using examples in network firewalls and digital signal processing. The purpose is to illustrate: (a) the opportunities for customising designs for various applications, and (b) the design flow from application-specific descriptions to customised hardware implementations.

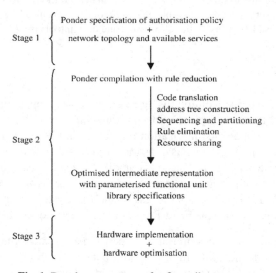

**Fig. 1.** Development stages for firewall processors.

Our first example concerns application customisation for producing network firewalls [19], which involves three stages (Figure 1). In the first stage, an authorisation policy is specified in the Ponder language [6] together with the information about the organisation's network topology and services. In the second stage, this specification is translated into a platform-independent intermediate representation. A series of customisations, including construction of IP address trees, sequencing, rule elimination, and resource sharing, are then performed to optimise the representation. In the third stage, this optimised representation is used to target a specific hardware platform. Hardware packet filter designs are captured using the Handel-C language (see Section 4). Optimisations can be applied to improve performance or resource usage. One advantage of this approach is that multiple levels of customisation, based on various platform-independent and platform-specific criteria, can improve performance, portability and design reuse, since platform-independent customisations are applicable to a large variety of designs.

Our second example involves signal processing applications. Descriptions of such applications are often expressed as signal flow graphs using tools such as Simulink, and can be mapped directly into optimised FPGA libraries using, for instance, Xilinx's System Generator tool [15]. Both analytical and simulation-based techniques have been developed to automate the analysis of bit-widths for all the components in a floating-point [1] or a fixed-point [5] design. While bit-width analysis can also be conducted for a general-purpose program [24], the availability of application-specific information enables more efficient optimisation by trading off design size and performance against accuracy which can be described in terms of, for instance, the signal-to-noise ratio at the output. In particular, it has been shown that a small reduction in accuracy can result in a large improvement in performance and resource usage [1]. This kind of result can help in comparing, for a given precision and range, the design tradeoffs between a customised fixed-point data format and a customised floating-point data format.

Other application domains that have been shown to benefit from customisation include graphics [33] and video [35]. Such customisations usually take place at design time. For loop computations, improved performance can sometimes be obtained by adjusting bit-widths at run time to match the precision of the operands [3].

## 3   Customise Declarative Programs: Design Time

A declarative program consists of a collection of definitions and relations describing what needs to be computed. Declarative style descriptions, including functional expressions and applicative programs, provide a natural way of capturing dataflow computations. Such descriptions have been used to develop various word-level and bit-level designs, particularly those with a regular structure. Examples include linear [20] and non-linear filters [11], systolic data structures [21], and butterfly networks [23]; parametric versions of these designs can be placed in a library to facilitate design re-use [25].

One feature that distinguishes different declarative languages is the treatment of iterative computation. There are two main approaches. The first approach involves affine recurrence equations on sets of indices on which variables are defined [10]; there exist automatic methods for mapping such equations into recurrence equations with explicit space-time coordinates, which can then be used for generating hardware. Design customisation can take place at several steps: during uniformisation, where broadcast circuits are pipelined; during scheduling, where independent computations can be organised into the same time step; and during mapping, where computations are allocated to processors. An example of this approach is the Alpha system [10], which has produced many array-based circuits and regular arithmetic designs.

The second approach involves functional abstractions for common patterns of composing designs, and temporal abstraction for describing stream-processing architectures. These abstractions simplify re-use of existing parts, and designs can be customised by algebraic transformations such as serialisation [20], pipelining [21], and hardware-software partitioning [23]. This approach also supports: (a) optimisation of component placement by partial evaluation [25], (b) production of run-time reconfigurable designs [8] (also see Section 5), and (c) interface to formal verification tools [2].

Figure 2 shows a block diagram of a design tool under development for the Ruby [11] and Pebble [25] declarative languages. The system consists of facilities for opti-

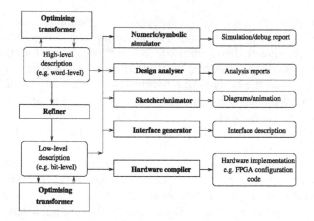

**Fig. 2.** Block diagram of the Ruby/Pebble tool.

mising, simulating, analysing, refining, sketching and animating designs, and for generating interface information and compiling designs into hardware. The optimising transformer provides assistance to optimise a high-level or low-level design by correctness-preserving transformations. The simulator provides support for testing and debugging in the symbolic, numerical and gate-level domains. The design analyser assesses design characteristics, such as the instance count of a specific component, the critical path delay, and the latency. The refiner produces a bit-level design from a high-level design, given the constraints on the input and output of a design; it also supports bit-width optimisation and various arithmetic representations, depending on the availability of suitable hardware libraries and domain-specific information. The sketcher produces design diagrams from a high-level or low-level description. The animator supports visualisation of both design behaviour and its structure by combining the facilities of the simulator and the sketcher. The interface generator produces information to control the run-time environment of the design. Finally, the hardware compiler maps a low-level program into device-specific data format for FPGAs and other hardware technology. Notice that, although not explicitly indicated, the optimising transformers can be driven from the design analyser to facilitate exploration of the design space. Further details of a prototype version of this system can be found in [11].

## 4    Customise Imperative Programs: Design Time

Imperative programs describe computation as a collection of operations, incurring state change by assignment, conditional and iterative statements. Such programs are usually based on a familiar software language such as C or Java. These languages are especially appropriate for control-flow computations.

Some languages, such as StReAm [26], provide annotations to facilitate identification of concurrency and other properties. Other languages, such as Handel-C [4], include statements for user control of parallelism and communication; such languages are often based on process algebras such as CSP [14], and can be compiled into hardware following a syntax-directed scheme [28]. Customising the amount of parallelism by systematic use of such statements can benefit many application domains, including medical imaging [16], channel code evaluation [18], network firewalls [19], and computer graphics [33].

Loops have long been recognised as a rich source of parallelism. It has been found that a loop can be automatically transformed into a hardware pipeline by adapting the vectorisation process in compilers for vector computers [38]. The design flow associated with this method, known as pipeline vectorisation, also includes a step to partition the design into hardware and software to target systems where coprocessor calls in a software program are trapped and executed by the hardware pipeline. This technique is especially effective when combined with customising transformations such as loop tiling, run-time specialisation, and memory access optimisation. Similar methods have been advocated by other researchers [13], [29].

A design which has been customised for one platform could require a different customisation for another platform. Porting designs to different platforms is a tedious and error-prone task. A recent project [7] tackles this problem by introducing a flexible timing model that supports high-level transformations and automatic scheduling. In addition, techniques are developed for unscheduling parallel designs so that they can be rescheduled to meet new performance and hardware constraints. Manual development and computerised customisation can be interleaved to achieve the best effect. The approach is illustrated by a pipelined convolver which is ported to a different platform, achieving a speed resource trade-off from 300% faster to 50% lower resource usage.

This section has focused on the use of imperative languages to produce data processors; Section 6 highlights the use of such languages for producing instruction processors. Note that some optimisations for declarative programs discussed in Section 3 are also applicable to imperative programs. Examples include bit-width optimisation and choice of arithmetic representations. Moreover, it is possible to combine imperative and declarative descriptions within a single framework [36].

## 5   Customise Programs: Run Time

The preceding sections have focused on design-time customisation. This section is dedicated to run-time customisation. One should, however, note that effective run-time customisation hinges on appropriate design-time preparation for such customisation.

To illustrate this point, consider a run-time customisable system that supports partial reconfiguration: one part of the system continues to be operational, while another part is being reconfigured. As FPGAs are getting larger, partial reconfiguration is becoming increasingly important as a means of reducing reconfiguration time. To support partial reconfiguration, appropriate circuits must be built at fabrication time as part of the FPGA fabric. Then at compile time, an initial configuration bitstream and incremental bitstreams have to be produced, together with run-time customisation facilities which can be executed, for instance, on a microprocessor serving as part of the run-time system [32]. Run-time customisation facilities can include support for condition monitoring, design optimisation and reconfiguration control.

Figure 3 shows the possible interactions between compile-time customisation and run-time customisation. Two compilers operate at compile time: one maps high-level descriptions into low-level hardware descriptions, while the other – the RTC (for Run-

Time Customising) compiler – maps the low-level hardware description into appropriate configuration and customisation information, resulting in a run-time system with an efficient, partially evaluated representation of the hardware implementation that incrementally generates customisations at run time. A prototype system based on the RTPebble language and JBits tool is reported in [8].

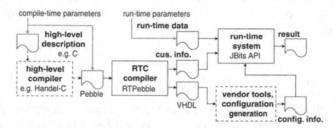

**Fig. 3.** Interactions between compile-time and run-time customisation.

Various opportunities exist for run-time design optimisation; two examples will be considered here. The first example is run-time constant propagation [8], which produces a smaller circuit with higher performance by treating run-time data as constant, and optimising them principally by boolean algebra. However, often modification of both logic and routing can result in long reconfiguration time, so a possible compromise is to modify just the logic but not the routing.

The second example for run-time design optimisation involves exploiting information about program branch probabilities [34]. The idea is to promote utilisation by dedicating more resources to branches which execute more frequently. A hardware compiler has been developed to produce a collection of designs, each optimised for a particular branch probability; the best can be selected at run time by incorporating observed branch probability information in a queueing network performance model.

## 6    Customise Instruction Processors

Techniques for design-time and run-time customisation of instruction processors are well-known. We shall focus on the case of customising instruction processors at compile time and at run time on a reconfigurable device. FPGA technology can now support multiple instruction processors on a single chip; proprietary instruction processors, like MicroBlaze and Nios, are now available from FPGA vendors.

There are three common methods for compile-time customisation of instruction processors. The first method is to select the most appropriate instruction set architecture for a given application. Different instruction set architectures, such as stack processors and register-based processors, have different trade-offs in code size, performance and resource utilisation. After an instruction set architecture has been chosen, the second customisation method enables the designer to remove unused instructions and resources – the customised design only needs to support the instructions required for a specific application. The third customisation method is to provide additional support for instruction sequences that are frequently executed, for instance those in an intensive inner loop. One way is to augment the instruction set by introducing a custom instruction that corresponds to one of these instruction sequences.

Custom instructions have two main benefits. First, they reduce the time for instruction fetch and decode, provided that each custom instruction replaces one or more regular instructions. Second, additional resources can be assigned to a custom instruction to improve performance. Bit-width optimisation, described in Section 2, can also be applied to customise instruction processors at compile time. This process can be speeded up by having a single-pass simulation for a reference customisation and a model for estimating and evaluating system performance [37].

Since custom instructions are a powerful means of customising instruction processors, it is desirable to automate their production. One way of achieving this is by opcode chaining [31], which aims at parallelising and pipelining the operators associated with a custom instruction. The steps include: (a) form a control-flow graph of basic instruction blocks, (b) reduce register sharing to maximise available parallelism, (c) analyse dependences to collapse related instructions into a single instruction, and (d) schedule a computation when the values of all its dependent variables are known.

A challenge of customising instruction processors is that the tools for producing and analysing instructions would also need to be customised. The *flexible instruction processor* framework [30] has been developed to automate the steps in customising an instruction processor and the corresponding tools. The prototype tools are based on the Handel-C language, which has been used to produce customised processors for the MIPS and the JVM architectures. The main steps in this framework include profiling, analysing, instantiating and selecting appropriate processor templates, and the associated customisation of compilers and other tools. Other researchers have proposed similar approaches [17].

It is interesting to note that one can develop an instruction processor to support a declarative language. For instance, a scalable architecture [9], consisting of multiple P-WAM processors based on the Warren Abstract Machine, has been developed to support the execution of the Progol system [27] which is based on the declarative language Prolog. The architecture, shown in Figure 4, has been optimised for hardware implementation using techniques such as instruction grouping and speculative assignment. Its effectiveness has been demonstrated using the mutagenesis data set containing 12000 facts about chemical compounds.

The discussion above has focused on compile-time customisation of instruction processors. Many techniques discussed in Section 5 on run-time customisation for data processors can also be applied to instruction processors. There is an additional avenue of run-time customisation for instruction processors: instructions can be customised on-the-fly to match any run-time customisation of the processor itself.

# 7   Customise Design Tools

As explained in the preceding section, the customisation of instruction processors requires the corresponding customisation of design tools. As our work covers an increasingly diverse range of applications and implementation technologies, the complexity of a single language or a single tool that attempts to cover everything will become unman-

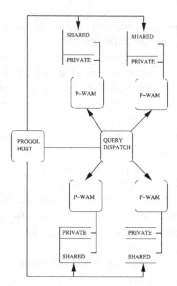

**Fig. 4.** A Progol engine with four P-WAM processors, showing the channels for query dispatching and buses to the various memories. Shared memory is accessible to both the host and the Progol engine, while private memory contains the run-time structure for each processor.

ageable. However, it is also important to be able to re-use and to customise existing tools as much as possible to minimise design effort.

Recent work suggests three promising approaches. The first involves a scripting language [12], which can be used to configure appropriate tools at compile time and at run time for given applications. The second approach involves developing a more closely-coupled tool framework that is customisable and extensible, using a meta-language for easy manipulation of data structures [22]. The third approach involves a multi-layer framework [35] for developing and distributing hardware components, which is designed to separate concerns of application developers from those of hardware library developers. It also includes an application programming interface based on the Component Object Model, providing a well-defined and extensible interface for hardware plug-ins to be incorporated into applications such as Premiere and DirectShow.

## 8   Conclusion

This paper reviews various techniques and tools for customising data processors and instruction processors at design time and at run time. Current and future work includes improving the theory and practice of customisation technology, and exploring new design techniques and tools by composing, extending and generalising current ones.

## Acknowledgments

This paper could not have been written without the support of many colleagues and students, including A.M. Abdul Gaffar, G. Brown, P.Y.K. Cheung, G.A. Constantinides,

G. De Figueiredo Coutinho, A.R.A. Derbyshire, N. Dulay, A.K. Fidjeland, S.R. Guo, P. Haglund, J. Jiang, D.U. Lee, T.K. Lee, E. Lupu, S.W. McKeever, O. Mencer, S.H. Muggleton, I. Page, D. Rueckert, S.P. Seng, N. Shirazi, M.S. Sloman, H.E. Styles, B. Tai, D.B. Thomas, J. Villasenor, M. Weinhardt, T. Wu, and S.O. Yusuf. The support of Celoxica, Xilinx and UK EPSRC (Grant number GR/R 31409, GR/R 55931, GR/N 66599) is gratefully acknowledged.

# References

1. A. Abdul Gaffar et. al., "Floating-point bitwidth analysis via automatic differentiation", *Proc. Int. Conf. on Field-Prog. Tech.*, IEEE, 2002.
2. P. Bjesse, K. Claessen, M. Sheeran and S. Singh, "Lava: Hardware design in Haskell", *Proc. ACM Int. Conf. on Functional Prog.*, ACM Press, 1998.
3. K. Bondalapati and V.K. Prasanna, "Dynamic precision management for loop computations on reconfigurable architectures", *Proc. Symp. on Field-Prog. Custom Computing Machines*, IEEE Computer Society Press, 1999.
4. Celoxica, *Handel-C Language Reference Manual for DK2.0*, Document RM-1003-4.0, 2003.
5. G.A. Constantinides, P.Y.K. Cheung and W. Luk, "The multiple wordlength paradigm", *Proc. Symp. on Field-Program. Custom Computing Machines*, IEEE Computer Society Press, 2001.
6. N. Damianou, N. Dulay, E. Lupu and M. Sloman, "The Ponder policy specification language", *Proc. Workshop on Policies for Distributed Systems and Networks*, LNCS 1995, Springer, 2001.
7. J.G. De Figueiredo Coutinho and W. Luk, "Optimising and adapting high-level hardware designs", *Proc. Int. Conf. on Field-Prog. Tech.*, IEEE, 2002.
8. A. Derbyshire and W. Luk, "Compiling run-time parametrisable designs", *Proc. Int. Conf. on Field-Prog. Tech.*, IEEE, 2002.
9. A. Fidjeland, W. Luk and S. Muggleton, "Scalable acceleration of inductive logic programs", *Proc. Int. Conf. on Field-Prog. Tech.*, IEEE, 2002.
10. A.-C. Guillou, P. Quinton, T. Risset and D. Massicotte, "Automatic design of VLSI pipelined LMS architectures", *Proc. Int. Conf. on Parallel Computing in Elect. Engineering*, 2000.
11. S. Guo and W. Luk, "An Integrated system for developing regular array design", *Journal of Systems Architecture*, Vol. 47, 2001.
12. P. Haglund, O. Mencer, W. Luk and B. Tai, "PyHDL: Hardware scripting with Python", *Proc. Int. Conf. on Engineering of Reconfigurable Systems and Algorithms*, 2003.
13. T. Harriss, R. Walke, B. Kienhuis and E. Deprettere, "Compilation from Matlab to process networks realized in FPGA", *Design Automation of Embedded Systems*, Vol. 7, No. 4, 2002.
14. C.A.R. Hoare, *Communicating Sequential Processes*, Prentice Hall, 1985.
15. J. Hwang, B. Milne, N. Shirazi and J.D. Stroomer, "System level tools for DSP in FPGAs", *Field-Prog. Logic and Applications*, LNCS 2147, Springer, 2001.
16. J. Jiang, W. Luk and D. Rueckert, "FPGA-based free-form deformation", *Proc. Int. Conf. on Field-Prog. Tech.*, IEEE, 2002.
17. V. Kathail et. al., "PICO: automatically designing custom computers", *Computer*, Vol. 35, No. 9, Sept. 2002.
18. D.U. Lee, W. Luk, J. Villasenor and P.Y.K. Cheung, "A hardware Gaussian noise generator for channel code evaluation", *Proc. Symp. on Field-Prog. Custom Computing Machines*, IEEE Computer Society Press, 2003.
19. T.K. Lee et. al., "Compiling policy descriptions into reconfigurable firewall processors", *Proc. Symp. on Field-Programmable Custom Computing Machines*, IEEE Computer Society Press, 2003.

20. W. Luk, "Systematic serialisation of array-based architectures", *Integration*, Vol. 14, No. 3, February 1993.
21. W. Luk and G. Brown, "A systolic LRU processor and its top-down development", *Science of Computer Programming*, Vol. 15, No. 23, December 1990.
22. W. Luk, T. Todman and J.G. De Figueiredo Coutinho, "Customisable hardware compilation", *Proc. Int. Conf. on Engineering of Reconfig. Systems and Algorithms*, 2004.
23. W. Luk and T. Wu, "Towards a declarative framework for hardware-software codesign", *Proc. Int. Workshop on Hardware/Software Codesign*, IEEE Computer Society Press, 1994.
24. S. Mahlke et. al., "Bitwidth cognizant architecture synthesis of custom hardware accelerators", *IEEE Trans. on Computer-Aided Design*, Vol. 20, No. 11, November 2001.
25. S.W. McKeever, W. Luk and A. Derbyshire, "Compiling hardware descriptions with relative placement information for parametrised libraries", *Formal Methods in Computer-Aided Design*, LNCS 2517, Springer, 2002.
26. O. Mencer, H Huebert, M. Morf and M.J. Flynn, "StReAm: Object-oriented programming of stream architectures using PAM-Blox", *Field-Prog. Logic: the Roadmap to Reconfigurable Systems*, LNCS 1896, Springer, 2000.
27. S.H. Muggleton. "Inverse entailment and Progol", *New Generation Computing*, Vol. 13, 1995.
28. I. Page and W. Luk, "Compiling occam into FPGAs", in *FPGAs*, Abingdon EE&CS Books, 1991.
29. R. Schreiber et. al., "PICO-NPA: High-level synthesis of nonprogrammable hardware accelerators", *Journal of VLSI Signal Processing Systems*, Vol. 31, No. 2, June 2002.
30. S.P. Seng, W. Luk and P.Y.K. Cheung, "Flexible instruction processors", *Proc. Int. Conf. on Compilers, Arch. and Syn. for Embedded Systens*, ACM Press, 2000.
31. S.P. Seng, W. Luk and P.Y.K. Cheung, "Run-time adaptive flexible instruction processors", *Field-Prog. Logic and Applications*, LNCS 2438, Springer, 2002.
32. N. Shirazi, W. Luk and P.Y.K. Cheung, "Framework and tools for run-time reconfigurable designs", *IEE Proc.-Comput. Digit. Tech.*, May, 2000.
33. H. Styles and W. Luk, "Customising graphics applications: techniques and programming interface", *Proc. Symp. on Field-Program. Custom Computing Machines*, IEEE, 2000.
34. H. Styles and W. Luk, "Branch optimisation techniques for hardware compilation", *Field-Prog. Logic and Applications*, LNCS 2778, Springer, 2003.
35. D. Thomas and W. Luk, "A framework for development and distribution of hardware acceleration", *Reconfigurable Technology: FPGAs and Reconfigurable Processors for Computing and Communications, Proc. SPIE*, Vol. 4867, 2002.
36. T. Todman and W. Luk, "Combining imperative and declarative hardware descriptions", *Proc. 36th Hawaii Int. Conf. on System Sciences*, IEEE, 2003.
37. M.M. Uddin et. al., "An accelerated datapath width optimization scheme for area reduction of embedded systems", *Proc. Int. Symp. on Systems Synthesis*, ACM Press, 2002.
38. M. Weinhardt and W. Luk, "Pipeline vectorization", *IEEE Trans. on Computer-Aided Design*, Vol. 20, No. 2, 2001.

# Intermediate Level Components
# for Reconfigurable Platforms

Erwan Fabiani, Christophe Gouyen, and Bernard Pottier

Architectures et Systèmes*,
Université de Bretagne Occidentale, Brest, France

**Abstract.** Development productivity is a central point for the acceptance of reconfigurable platforms. Due to the availability of generic low level tools and powerful logic synthesis tools, it becomes possible to define portable components that have both a high level behavior and attributes for physical synthesis. The behavior of a component can be fixed at compile time using concise specifications that will reduce the cost and delays in developments. The method allowing to produce components is illustrated with two case studies.

## 1 Introduction

We are considering a new generation of general purpose circuits allowing to produce applications by field programming or configuration. Following FPGAs, the economic challenge of these circuits is to complement ASIC for markets where the production volume does not balance the cost of a specific SOC design, and where a quick application availability is critical. A consequence of cost and time-to-market constraints is the need to define software production methods with emphasis on designer productivity.

### 1.1 Scope

Among the different architectural options appearing, or likely to appear, we choose a generic architecture shown figure 1.a with the following parts: (1) a dedicated system processor (SP) in charge of tasks and circuit management, (2) a network on chip possibly simple and controlled by SP, (3) several heterogeneous compute units (CU) such as processors, reconfigurable data path or fine grain banks, These units have their own local memories for data, and code or configurations, (4) a memory cache, (5) several input/output units with, possibly, specific support outside the circuit.

There are two main motivations for the choice of such a distributed architecture. One is scalability, with the need to have an evolving choice of off-the-shelf circuits adapted to different kind of applications. A permanent problem with current FPGA technology is the change of scale and the actual difficulty to implement system level communications in an efficient way. The use of a network

---

* http://as.univ-brest.fr

A. Pimentel and S. Vassiliadis (Eds.): SAMOS 2004, LNCS 3133, pp. 59–68, 2004.
© Springer-Verlag Berlin Heidelberg 2004

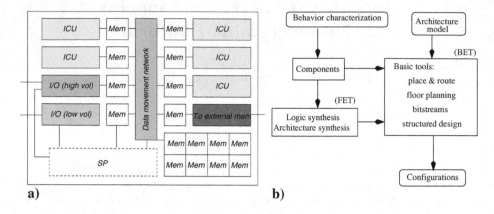

**Fig. 1.** (a) A parallel heterogeneous reconfigurable platform. (b) Position of the component layer related to synthesis tools and basic tools.

on chip allows to merge SOC IPs within the platform, and to control congestion in the routing resources during system activities. The other motivation is heterogeneity, meaning that it will be possible to select a set of reconfigurable or programmable resources suiting the application needs. This implies the development of tools allowing to produce different code or configurations from a single specification, depending on the architecture and execution constraints.

The platform must support compute intensive processes as found in stream, image and signal processing. These processes will use on chip input/output facilities, buffers, memory buffers, and they can spread over several compute units. In this case they need to be prepared as small tasks exchanging data buffers or transactions. Intensive computation tasks will be mapped to reconfigurable units. Other processes needing specific hardware support are controllers having short reaction delays. The operating system decides resource allocation, scheduling, swaps and memory transfers.

During these last years, our research activity has been concentrated on building portable tools for reconfigurable architectures. The MADEO framework is organized in three parts, with the general flow shown figure 1.b.

The lower layer back-end (BET) proposes tools for reconfigurable architecture modeling. Several fine grain FPGA architectures have been described successfully, including commercial circuits. The models are represented using a grammar that enables a set of generic tools to produce the basic functionalities: placing cells on FPGAs, global or point to point routing, floor-planning, regular circuit design[1]. An important property of this framework is its openness allowing synthesis algorithms to build layout of application component under programmer control. Fine control on the geometry and location of components is critical for resource management, as needed in operating systems.

Above these tools, there is a front-end support (FET) for logic synthesis. The second layer uses high level object oriented specifications and produces hierarchical application components for the first layer. The basic flow is based on directed acyclic graph of nodes representing procedure calls that will be translated into look-up tables (LUT) or call of other graphs. The second layer tools can work competitively compared to handwritten hardware implementation because data specifications are required to be richer than usual types. Our data types are based on set of values and intervals. They are automatically produced for each function in the program and propagated downward the hierarchical graph. After type inference, synthesis tools have an exact knowledge of the computation context, and are able to lead very efficient optimizations. These optimizations take place at a symbolic level, by collapsing and simplifying nodes in the LUT graph, and at the encoding level, by exchanging data for indexes, and finally at the logic level using logic synthesis algorithms[2]. Physical mapping for fine grain FPGAs have been described in [3]. Extension for reconfigurable data path code production is currently being investigated from the same set of tools as the type system also provide support for interval description.

Above these levels we are now interested to develop architecture *components* in different ways. This paper will discuss the component status, especially their important position in the design flow and the relation with the physical target.

## 1.2   Component Definition

Components are intermediate in the application design flow. They can be used to define the frontier from software to hardware in a transparent way for application developers. Their main characteristics are described as follow.

**Modularity and reuse:** Components provide a modular behavioral interface usable during application development, either directly or from a compiler. They have an object status grouping a behavioral interface, physical synthesis capabilities, rules for use, and code or configuration to be handled by the operating system. Components provide *software re-usability*, in a way similar as IP modules do in the case of SOC. They are executable in the software development environment.

**Programmability or characterization:** The component behavior can come from a program expressed in a domain specific languages (DSL), or there can be a fixed parametrized behavior. In each case, components carry an implicit execution architecture that will be produced at the physical level.

Software macros as used in the FPGAs environments are components of small complexity whose definitions are hidden to the programmers.

**Physical synthesis:** Components embed algorithms producing a physical description of the application architecture related to a reconfigurable unit target. These algorithms use building blocks in the form of other components, or specific placed and routed primitives. They compute the respective layout of these blocks, and they produce the low level interconnections. Physical synthesis algorithms are portable at least for fine grain architectures.

**Support for compilers:** Some components are explicit structured descriptions of hardware. It is the case for arithmetic operators, regular processing networks, controllers. There are also components representing the necessary transformations enabling a compiler to produce circuits in a restricted context (computation graph, regular networks to be mapped on CUs).

## 2  Productivity Is Concise Specifications

As development productivity is becoming a serious challenge for embedded applications, it is interesting to observe how software has solved this difficulty by the past, then in which way reconfigurable architectures could help in speeding up the development process. An important factor in development productivity is the level of abstraction in which solution specifications are produced. The first benefit of abstraction is the simplicity of the expression obtained due to the meanings of the formalism. Simplicity means speed and security of solution expression, ease to develop and maintain translation and verification tools. Programming languages have achieved a gradual progress in terms of abstraction level and in terms of modularity and reuse.

Software productivity can be evaluated on metrics such as *line of codes*, or may be more accurately on *source statements* implementing equivalent functionalities. According to industrial expert sources, productivity can scale from one to ten for general purpose languages, and it is not necessary to insist on the power of expression of specific languages.

There exists at least two clear demonstrations of the interest of abstraction rising given by *virtual machines* for general purpose languages, and *domain specific languages*. In each case the basic support is provided by a particular virtual architecture or software supports that provide a fixed higher semantic level. The compiler design is usually simple due to the service offered by the underlying support and the language can be ported to different platforms by adapting this support.

*Virtual Machines* can be implemented as a pure software interpreter, or more efficiently in a processor micro-code. Additional supports are required for memory management and OS level primitives. Known examples are Pascal, Smalltalk, or the Transputer[4].

*Domain Specific Languages(DSL)* are largely used in our current software tools, producing the desirable level of abstraction related to a particular domain[5]. Examples of DSL are text processing tools ( sed, awk,. . . ), compilation tools (lex, yacc, . . . ), or more specific domain tools for signal processing, graphics, etc. . . Due to their capability to produce the application architectures, DSL can be implemented on reconfigurable platforms. Drawbacks in using DSL include the excessive specialization of data. Testing can be an issue if the formalism does not support associated execution mechanisms, and finally DSL abstraction does not avoid domain expertise from their programmers but just eases the task.

DSL and Virtual machines are expected to help considerably application module production and control. The last part of the paper will demonstrate the interest of DSL in the case of cellular automata and regular computations.

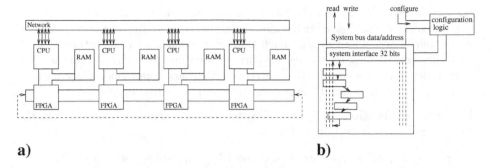

**Fig. 2.** Armen computer: (a)Four interconnected nodes, and (b) physical representation of computation pipelines inside the FPGA.

## 3   Component Design Method

The general approach for component design is bottom-up: (1) Fix the functionality to be addressed by defining what will be explicit in the parameters or program, and what will be implicit, (2) define the internal execution model, (3) define the language, (4) define the synthesis mechanisms related to a support architecture. To help the explanations, this approach will be illustrated on the example of cellular automata on the ArMen computer.

**Platform description:** In this case, the computer is ArMen, a distributed memory architecture whose nodes are fully interconnected using serial links (figure 2.a). Each node processor has an attached FPGA accessed in locked step read or write transactions. The processor has also support in its address space to write and read configurations to the FPGA (figure 2.b). FPGAs are connected together and can exchange data asynchronously, there is no global clock. The interface from the local system bus to the FPGA is fixed and generally used to feed a pipeline. Inside the FPGA, physical synthesis generally proceeds by allocating logic resources along a pipeline using local routes. The pipeline stages are connected to long lines by three-state buffers. Long lines is an internal bus that can bring back results to the interface with short delays. The vertical pipeline advances under processor control while other computations usually take place horizontally in an asynchronous way[6].

**Functionality:** Cellular automata (CA) is a well known paradigm where a discrete space of cells progresses synchronously. To define a CA it is needed to fix: (1) a neighborhood representing the dependencies relative to a cell, (2) a transition function describing the evolution of a cell given its current state and the neighbor states, (3) the geometry of the cell space and its initial value.

A CA specification must *explicit* these three points letting the component implement a massive parallel computation or alternatively observe where new computations are really needed and achieve these computations.

**Execution model:** We use the massive parallel model with a locally parallel, globally sequential approach. The data space is divided in stripes recorded in node memories. The width of the stripes is the bandwidth to the FPGAs (32 bits × number of nodes). One or two nodes are in charge of feeding data dependencies on the slice borders and to read back these dependencies for the future step.

Processors manage two spaces for current state and next state. Their activity is to repetitively transform their current stripe into a new one. They need to exchange values because of the dependencies on the stripe borders.

**Program expression:** Programs are expressed in a simple syntax covering the three definitions given previously:

1. each cell state is described as a C record grouping bit-field variables,
2. the neighborhood is declared as a set of directions (C, for center, N for north, NW for north-west... ),
3. the data space is declared by two integer values for with and height,
4. the transition function is a C function returning the new value of the local cell computed from the neighborhood state.

**Architecture description:** As CAs can be considered as fine grain computations involving a lot of data exchanges, the transition function will be synthesized in hardware [7]. To enable this function to proceed, it is needed to present the neighborhood. Thus, a simple approach for the architecture is to provide a FIFO in which the cells are progressing, and to connect this FIFO to a row of processors. Dependencies can be wired between adjacent nodes. Control is the responsibility of the processors that permanently read their memories, write to the FPGAs, read back the new state from the FPGA to write it to memory. Their coordination is enforced during the accesses by local handshakes. Several time steps can be cascaded along a pipeline.

**Physical synthesis:** Architecture implementation is a fully automatic process leaded by a dedicated synthesizer. The availability of tools described in section 1 allows a constructive approach of the physical synthesis. The constraints that need to be observed are the cell width, the data path width in the FPGA, the size of the processors, the possible saturation of routing resources. Physical layout can be achieved using Madeo tools, following these steps: (1) synthesize, (2) place and route the processor, (3) compute the FIFO size, (4) make an estimation of the routing channel width, (5) place the processors on the FPGA dye, place the FIFO registers, (6) call the point to point router to connect registers together, (7) connect the registers to the processor, connect the processor to the feed back lines, connect the registers to the interface, (8) connect the clock to the interface.

**Stacking components:** Models can be stacked. As an example, we have produced a partial implementation of the Wu and Manber pattern matching algorithm[8, 9] above the CA component. In this case, the program becomes a pattern to be searched and the number of errors that are accepted. Implementation of some low level operators for image processing is also immediate.

**Physical and computational constraints:** Physical synthesis for a component is a determinist approach dealing on one side with the reconfigurable unit

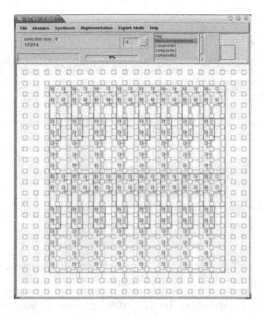

**Fig. 3.** Layout of a cellular automata for fire propagation on an Atmel 40K FPGA. The circuit has small processors which internal state represent the situation on 2 bits at a geographic position. Two stages of automata had been cascaded, and 8 slices are represented.

organization and resources, and on the other side with a characterization of the component. The behavior of the component is fixed by a high level program block processed by the logic synthesizer. Another important issue is the internal development of parallelism during synthesis. Care must be taken not to waste hardware resources by adapting synthesis algorithms to the usable data rate on the unit interface.

## 4    Physical Synthesis: Systolic Array Example

Given a specific applicative model, this part shows what are the advantages of a specific component definition and algorithms for physical synthesis.

**Characterizing a systolic array:** Systolic arrays (SA) represent intensive computations as found in nested loops, in various applicative domains (digital signal processing, DNA comparison, image processing, ...). Basically the corresponding architecture is a regular array of processing elements (PE) performing efficiently the body of the inner loop. All PEs are only connected to their neighbors except for the first and last PEs that are connected to an outside system. Systolic arrays are one of the more structured and regular component and are described by a few number of characteristics (figure 4.a): (1) the inputs, outputs and functionality of one PE, (2) the interconnection pattern between two neigh-

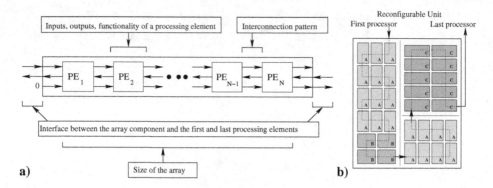

**Fig. 4.** (a) Characterizing a systolic array. (b) Placing a systolic array on a reconfigurable unit using structural properties.

bor PEs, (3) the interface between I/O of the Systolic Array and I/O of the first and last processors, (4) the size of the array.

**Using structural properties in the design flow:** Regularity in a SA occurs in the PE and the interconnection pattern. As all PEs have an identical structure, an implementation pattern for a PE structure can be replicated for all PEs. Depending on limitations related to design tools and target technology, productivity gains could occur in each step of the design flow :

1. *Synthesis, optimizations and mapping:* whether the processor description is behavioral or structural, synthesis, optimization and mapping are just operating on one processor bounding box, reducing drastically the complexity of this step.
2. *Placing:* as for the previous step, complexity is reduced to placing one PE, then simultaneously replicating and floorplanning it for the whole array. Floorplanning complexity is lower than placing a flat design, since it acts on coarser grain component, and that we have the capabilities to constraint the placement of one PE to a geometric shape easier to floorplan. Moreover the floorplanning is automatically deduced from the systolic array topologies (1D or 2D grid).
3. *Routing:* Replicating the routing scheme of a PE and the routing pattern between two neighbor PEs is possible if routing conflicts are overcome.

This design flow induces lot of savings related to classical flow because it takes into account SA properties. All these optimizations decrease the design runtime and increase the productivity. Moreover, by mapping physically the systolic array structure to a reconfigurable unit, savings also include increased clock frequency (by reducing wire length).

**A method to use structural properties for placement:** As an example, we present results of the FRAP tool [10], which aims to put the maximum number of PEs of a linear SA on a reconfigurable unit, given various constraints, by adding placement directives to a structural SA description. Finding such a placement acts in three steps (see figure 4.b for a basic example):

(1) All possible geometric shapes for a PE are generated by combining all shapes of its sub-components, (2) a full snake-like placement is determined using the processing element shapes previously computed, (3) the final internal placement of the processing elements is performed according to their shapes.

Experiments show several savings resulting from the use of this tool. Placement step runtime is divided up to factor of 6. Routing step runtime is divided up to factor of 3. Clock frequency is increased up to a factor of 2. However in some cases results are quite limited and even worst, principally due to lack of control over the vendor design tools that were used.

**Why and how to take care of design structure and regularity?** Given the previous example of using structural properties for physical synthesis, we can extent this principle to all structured components. Once described in a HLL, a circuit structure is deduced from DAG. The structure of a circuit will have different degrees of regularity, occurring at various hierarchical levels, ranging from low (identical slices of an adder) to high (identical PEs of a regular array). It is even possible to extract structure and regularity from a flat design. A distinction must be made between the advantages just induced by knowing the structure, and the advantages induced by having regularity in the structure:

1. *Structure* keeps information about the interconnections (logical optimization, mapping, placement) without needing to recompute it at each design flow step. It principally permits to improve design density and frequency.
2. *Regularity* permits to reduce the design flow runtime, by merging tasks, meaning to find a solution for a structural template and replicate it for all entities assimilated to this template. This method is applied recursively over the component hierarchy, being applied in the steps of synthesis, logical optimization, mapping, placement and routing, if the software or technological environment permits it.

From those two criterion, taking care of design structure increases density, frequency and decreases design flow running time. As applicative design and reconfigurable unit area become larger, using structural properties will allow to deal with the increasing complexity of physical synthesis, although by the past this approach offered limited improvement and big effort to develop specific tools, due to the need to be adapted to closed vendor design environment.

## 5 Conclusion

In the context of reconfigurable heterogeneous platforms, we are proposing a method allowing to produce components from productive development tools. These components can be synthesized for different compute units such as processors or fine grain FPGAs. We are actively working to rise the capabilities of synthesis tools to address mixed grain units and implement transformations such as loop unrolling.

This approach has been made possible by the development of the Madeo open framework in which target reconfigurable architectures can be represented, with the immediate feed-back on basic tools for physical design. The cellular automata example that was actually implemented and executed on the ArMen computer, is now drawn on recent FPGAs without any black-box "support". The new tools created in the object-oriented environment are considerably easing developments, portability, modular assembly of components. The case of systolic arrays is significant in terms of physical design problems since these circuits can be described with simplicity, they produce a lot of computing power, and they are resource hungry.

While there is no reason to restrict the component design method to object-oriented languages and tools, it is expected that such environments will ease the management of run-time exchanges, application development and system activity description.

## Acknowledgements

Parts of this work are supported by the MEFI/STSI and by the Ministry of Research *RNTL*. Thanks are due to T. Ben-Ismail and the AST division of STMicroelectronics for their support and cooperation.

## References

1. Lagadec, L.: Abstraction, modélisation et outils de CAO pour les circuits intégrés reconfigurables. PhD thesis, Université de Rennes 1 (2000)
2. Cong, J., Ding, Y.: Combinational logic synthesis for lut based fpga. ACM transaction on DAES (1996)
3. Lagadec, L., Pottier, B., Villellas-Guillen, O.: An lut-based high level synthesis framework for reconfigurable architectures. In: Domain-Specific Processors : Systems, Architectures, Modeling, and Simulation, Marcel Dekker (2003)
4. Nicoud, J.D., Tyrrell, A.M.: The transputer t414 instruction set. IEEE Micro **9** (1989)
5. Spinellis, D.: Reliable software implementation using domain specific languages. In: ESREL, 10th european conference on safety and reliability. (1999)
6. Dhaussy, P., Filloque, J.M., Pottier, B., Rubini, S.: Global Control Synthesis for an MIMD/FPGA Machine. In: FPGAs for Custom Computing Machines. (1994)
7. Bouazza, K., Champeau, J., Ng, P., Pottier, B., Rubini, S.: Implementing cellular automata on the ArMen machine. In: Algorithms and Parallel VLSI Architectures II, Elseiver (1991)
8. Wu, S., Manber, U.: Fast text searching allowing errors. Communications of the ACM **35** (1992)
9. Champeau, J., Le Pape, L., Pottier, B.: Parallel Grep. In: Algorithms and Parallel VLSI Architectures III, Leuven, Belgium, Elsevier (1994)
10. Fabiani, E., Lavenier, D.: Experimental evaluation of place-and-route of regular arrays on xilinx chips. In: First International Conference on Engineering of Reconfigurable Systems and Algorithms, Las Vegas, USA (2001)

# Performance Estimation of Streaming Media Applications for Reconfigurable Platforms

Carsten Reuter, Javier Martín Langerwerf,
Hans-Joachim Stolberg, and Peter Pirsch

Institute of Microelectronic Systems
University of Hannover
Appelstr.4, 30167 Hannover
Germany
{reuter,jamarlan,stolberg,pirsch}@ims.uni-hannover.de

**Abstract.** A methodology for performance estimation of streaming media applications for different platforms is presented. The methodology derives a complexity profile for an application as a platform-independent metric, and enables performance estimation on potential platforms by correlating the complexity profile with platform-specific data. By example of an MPEG-4 Advanced Simple Profile (ASP) video decoder, performance estimation results are presented. As one particular benefit, the approach can be employed to explore what hardware functions are most suited for the implementation on reconfigurable architectures.

## 1 Introduction

With the introduction of multimedia instruction-set extensions to general-purpose microprocessors, such as MMX/SSE [1], streaming media applications with their special computational characteristics and high processing demands have found their way onto these platforms. Recently, the integration of reconfigurable elements and RISC processors, e.g., Virtex-II-Pro [2], has opened new directions for the design of high-performance and flexible systems. On the other hand, specialized architectures particularly adapted to media processing schemes continue to play an important role, most notably in areas with additional constraints, such as low power or real-time requirements [3]. In total, a large array of implementation alternatives is nowadays available for the implementation of advanced media applications.

Due to continuing advances in algorithmic research, the field of streaming media applications involving complex processing of audio, video, or other media streams to be transmitted on Internet over mobile or stationary channels is rapidly growing, and novel schemes continue to be proposed. In the early implementation stage of a newly emerging scheme, knowledge about the achievable performance of a specific hardware realization is desired in order to take an informed decision about the appropriate target architecture. One way to obtain this knowledge is to fully implement the complete scheme on a candidate platform. The great complexity of today's media processing schemes, however, leads to an unacceptable effort of this approach for target architectures still under development, it is simply not possible. Therefore, it is required to

A. Pimentel and S. Vassiliadis (Eds.): SAMOS 2004, LNCS 3133, pp. 69–77, 2004.

estimate the attainable performance on a candidate platform as precise as possible at low effort.

The traditional approach to performance estimation consists of instruction-level profiling, frequently applied to a non-optimized high-level language software implementation [4]. The result of such profiling is highly platform-dependent and particularly unsuited as an estimate for architectures with special instruction set extensions, subword parallelism, reconfigurable elements, and other non-standard features that are often introduced to speed up exactly the application under investigation.

The approach presented in this paper, by example of an MPEG-4 Advanced Simple Profile (ASP) video decoder [5][6], derives a platform-independent complexity profile for the target application by extracting the execution frequencies of core tasks from bitstream statistics based on real-world data input. By correlating the derived complexity profile with the execution times of the core tasks, the attainable performance of the targeted application on a specific platform realisation can be estimated with high accuracy. The relevant core tasks are usually computation-intensive, but of simple structure; execution times for these tasks can frequently be estimated without much effort or are even available from data sheets for existing platforms.

The complexity profile can be either static or dynamic. While the static profile delivers a compound metric for the entire application, the dynamic profile is repetitively derived for identical structural elements in the input stream, such as video frames, and provides a detailed insight into transient performance requirements that are not visible from the compound estimate.

In the next section, an overview of the methodology is given, and its application to the MPEG-4 ASP example is explained. Section 3 presents static performance estimation results for a specialized processor architecture as well as dynamic estimation results for a core task to be implemented on a reconfigurable device. Also we introduce a possible verification scheme based on HW/SW-coemulation. Section 4 concludes the paper.

## 2    Methodology

### 2.1    Overview

The methodology presented here is based on special processing characteristics observed in streaming media applications. Such applications generally take a continuous data stream as input which is processed in a central processing loop, resulting in a repetitive stream of computations. In complex schemes, a high number of options exists in the main processing loop, leading to a variety of branches to be taken driven by the input data patterns; a good example is the MPEG-4 video coding scheme. Each branch through the main processing loop may involve a different set of subtasks to be executed. By relating the observed input patterns to the core tasks involved, an execution profile of the application can be derived on task level only from analysis of the input data.

As starting point for the implementation of a complex media processing scheme, an unoptimized reference implementation in high-level language is typically available which is used to verify functional correctness. In the case of MPEG-4 video, two verification models written in C/C++ exist [7] [8] that are provenly inefficient in terms of processing performance [9], but include all functionality specified in the MPEG-4 standard.

The performance estimation methodology involves, in the first step, instrumentation of the high-level reference code by inserting counters on those input stream elements that are decisive for the computational flow within the application. Detailed knowledge of the target application is required in order to identify the relevant input stream patterns and their influence on the sequence of core tasks in the execution. Then, by executing the instrumented code with representative test input, statistics on the relevant input stream patterns are obtained, e.g., distribution of coefficients or block types.

In the next step, the platform-independent complexity profile is derived by accumulating the sets of core tasks involved according to the input stream patterns as counted in the previous step, resulting in execution frequencies for the core tasks. The complexity profile only depends on the statistics obtained with the input stream and constitutes an inherent characteristic of the application. Most notably, it is completely independent of the optimization degree of the code used for deriving the profile.

The performance estimate for a specific platform is then obtained by weighting the execution frequencies $F(i)$ of core tasks $i$ with the number of clock cycles $C(i)$ required per task, resulting in an overall performance figure, e.g., in MHz:

$$P_{total} = \sum_i F(i) \cdot C(i) \tag{1}$$

Figure 1 illustrates the flow of the performance estimation methodology. Both, static and dynamic performance estimates can be derived. For a static estimate, the subtask counts are averaged over the entire input stream, resulting in a compound performance figure, e.g., in cycles per second. For a dynamic estimate, a series of complexity profiles is determined consecutively for repetitive structural units in the input data stream, e.g., on frame basis in the case of video decoding. While the static estimate allows to assess the principal eligibility of an architecture for the target application, the dynamic estimate provides insight into transient performance requirements and reveals performance bottlenecks that are not visible from the compound performance figure. The dynamic complexity profile may further be employed for dynamic performance (frequency, voltage) scaling in low-power implementations [10], for dynamic complexity regulation [11] on, e.g., reconfigurable systems.

The presented approach is of particular value in the definition phase of a new architecture or during investigation of extensions to an existing one. The impact of a special architectural measure speeding up a particular subtask on the overall performance becomes instantly visible and can serve as a basis for the decision whether or not to include this feature in the new architecture.

## 2.2 Complexity Profile of MPEG-4 Advanced Simple Profile Decoding

In an MPEG-4 ASP video decoder, the input data stream consists of an encoded video bitstream, and the basic structural element is the video object plane (VOP) or video frame. Each VOP is subdivided into a fixed number of macroblocks (MBs) of $16 \times 16$ pixels, and each MB is further subdivided into six blocks (four luminance, two chrominance) of $8 \times 8$ pixels each. VOPs and MBs can have different types specified in the

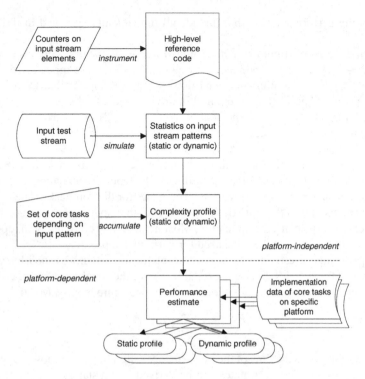

**Fig. 1.** Performance estimation methodology flow.

encoded bitstream (intra (I), bidirectionally predicted (B), and globally motion compensated (S(GMC)), and individual blocks can either be coded or not coded, specified by the block pattern in the bitstream.

The resolution of motion vectors is decisive for the particular interpolation method to be employed in motion compensation, as illustrated in Table 1. In addition to the conventional linear interpolation for half-pel motion vectors in one dimension and bi-linear interpolation for half-pel vectors in two dimensions, an 8-tap FIR filter has to be applied for compensation with motion vectors in quarter-pel resolution.

For bitstream analysis, the C++ reference video decoder software (VM 15 [7]) has been instrumented by inserting counters on the decisive elements of the bitstream, and statistics have been generated during the decoding process. The results have been

**Table 1.** Interpolation method in MPEG-4 ASP motion compensation depending on vector resolution.

| Video data | FF | FH/HF | HH | FQ/QF | HQ/QH | QQ |
|---|---|---|---|---|---|---|
| **Luminance** | - | 1D-FIR | 2D-FIR | 1D-FIR | 2D-FIR | 2D-FIR |
|  |  |  |  | Lin. Interp. | Lin. Interp. | Bilin. Interp. |
| **Chrominance** | - | Lin. Interp. | Bilin. Interp. | Lin. Interp. | Bilin. Interp. | Bilin. Interp. |

**Table 2.** Platform-independent static complexity profile of an MPEG-4 ASP decoder for 1.5 and 3 MBit/s seq. in executions per sec.

| Decoder subtask | 1.5 MBit/s | 3 MBit/s | |
|---|---|---|---|
| **Inverse quant. (IQ)** | 112 k | 282 k | coeffs/s |
| **Inverse DC/AC pred.** | 15 k | 15 k | blocks/s |
| **IDCT** | | | blocks/s |
| DC only | 22 k | 31 k | |
| Horizontal | 8 k | 15 k | |
| Vertical | 12 k | 19 k | |
| 4x4 IDCT | 12 k | 25 k | |
| Full IDCT | 7 k | 24 k | |
| **Motion Compensation** | | | blocks/s |
| Basic mode (full-pel) | 202 k | 202 k | |
| Linear interpolation | 83 k | 83 k | |
| Bilinear interpolation | 43 k | 43 k | |
| 8-tap FIR (QMC) | 162 k | 162 k | |
| Warping (GMC) | 34 k | 34 k | |
| **Reconstruction** | | | blocks/s |
| Copy | 75 k | 49 k | |
| Add | 20 k | 46 k | |
| Average | 96 k | 62 k | |
| Average and add | 38 k | 72 k | |

collected for three test sequences at 1.5 MBit/s, and for one sequence additionally at 3 MBit/s. Further details on relevant bitstream parameters and the sequences used can be found in [12].

As a result, the number of core task executions in units of blocks per second for a real-time ITU-R 601 (720x576@25fps) ASP decoder has been derived. The static complexity profile is shown in Table 2. The results are independent from the target platform and depend only on the application and the input data streams. In the next section, performance estimation results based on this data are presented.

## 3 Performance Estimation Results

Based on platform-independent complexity profiles for the MPEG-4 ASP decoder, a static performance estimate has been derived for a specialized multimedia processor developed at University of Hannover, the macroblock engine (MBE), as well as a dynamic performance estimate for the FIR subtask.

### 3.1 Static Performance Estimation on MBE

The macroblock engine (MBE) is a 64-bit, dual-issue VLIW multimedia processor with SIMD-style subword processing capability and an instruction set adapted to video and multimedia processing applications [13]. The architectural concept of a MBE-based system involves an additional RISC processor for stream processing tasks. Therefore, the results presented here for the MBE only include tasks performed on block or MB level, but not on bit-level.

The required clock cycles per block for implementation of the decoder core tasks on the MBE are given in Table 3. By weighting the cycles per block with the number of executions per second in Table 2 (average of 1.5 and 3 MBit/s streams), the resulting overall performance requirements for real-time MPEG-4 ASP decoding on the MBE amount to about 115 MHz. The results reveal that further optimization should focus on Warping and 8-tap FIR, together consuming about 74% of the total processing requirements. Therefore, in the next section the dynamic performance estimation of a hardware implementation of the FIR subtask on a reconfigurable device is provided.

**Table 3.** Static performance estimate for the MPEG-4 ASP decoder on a specific platform, the MBE.

| Decoder subtask | Cycles/block | MHz | % |
|---|---|---|---|
| **IDCT** | | | |
| DC only | 21 | 0.6 | 0.5 |
| Horizontal | 141 | 1.6 | 1.4 |
| Vertical | 141 | 2.2 | 1.9 |
| 4x4 IDCT | 141 | 2.6 | 2.2 |
| Full IDCT | 190 | 3.0 | 2.5 |
| **Motion Compensation** | | | |
| Basic mode (full-pel) | 71 | 14.3 | 12.4 |
| Linear interpolation | 78 | 6.4 | 5.7 |
| Bilinear interpolation | 139 | 6.0 | 5.3 |
| 8-tap FIR (QMC) | 104 | 16.9 | 14.6 |
| Warping (GMC) | 1,670 | 56.8 | 49 |
| **Reconstruction** | | | |
| Copy | 10 | 0.6 | 0.5 |
| Add | 18 | 0.6 | 0.5 |
| Average | 26 | 2.1 | 1.8 |
| Average and add | 36 | 2.0 | 1.7 |
| **Total** | | 115.7 | 100.0 |

## 3.2   Dynamic Performance Estimation for the 8-Tap 1-D FIR Filter

A platform-independent dynamic profile on VOP basis for the FIR subtask has been created as derived from the bitstream parameters to get deeper insight into transient performance requirements and to reveal potential performance bottlenecks. Figure 2 shows this dynamic profile for one specific MPEG-4 ASP sequence at 1.5 MBit/s (ITU-R 601, 648 VOPs). The average number of FIR executions per VOP is 4735. For B-VOPs there are 2 MVs per blocks and one 1-D FIR per dimension is necessary to

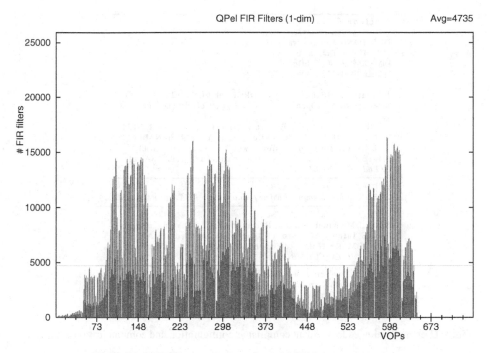

**Fig. 2.** QPel FIR filter executions for 1.5 MBit/s input sequence.

calculate QPel values. Hence, the maximum number of FIR executions per VOP for one $720 \times 576$ ITU-R 601 frame containing $90 \times 72$ blocks is 25920.

To improve the overall system performance we decided to augment the MBE with a reconfigurable element. To estimate its performance we generated a fully parallel implementation of a distributed arithmetic 8-tap FIR filter on a Xilinx XC2V6000 FPGA [14]. In comparison to the FIR realisation on the MBE, 20 cycles per block are achievable, resulting in an overall performance enhancement of about 12% (see Table 4).

**Table 4.** Performance comparison: MBE vs. FPGA for 8-tap FIR filter.

|  | *Cycles/block* | *proc.requirements in %* |
|---|---|---|
| FIR on MBE | 104 | 14.6 |
| FIR on FPGA | 20 | 2.6 |
| **Improvement** |  | 12.0 |

### 3.3 Possible Verification on an Emulation System

To assess the performance of the augmented MBE and to verify the FIR module integration within the whole system, we intend to perform a HW/SW-coemulation on a prototyping platform. This platform comprises a Compact PCI motherboard with onboard FPGA resources [15]. The configuration of the board and the communication

```
#include "dimesdl.h" //contains API functions
//Declare variables
DIME_HANDLE hBenera;
LOCATE_HANDLE hLocate;
DIME_DMAHANDLE hDma;
DIME_MEMHANDLE hMem;

hLocate=DIME_LocateCard(dlPCI,mbtBEN,NULL,dldrDFLT);
hBenera=DIME_OpenCard(hLocate,1,dccOPEN_DFLT);
//Begin of SET-Block
DIME_ConfigDevice(hBenera,"fir8_tag.bit",1,1,NULL);
DIME_CardResetControl(hBenera,drSYSTEM,drENABLE,0);
DIME_SetOscillatorFrequency(hBenera,1,100,NULL);
DIME_CardResetControl(hBenera,drSYSTEM,drDISABLE,0);
//End of SET-Block

//User application code
//Lock down Memory (hMem) and open DMA channel (hDma)

//Begin of EXECUTE-Block
DIME_DMAWriteFromLockedMem(hBenera,1,hMem,,nWords);
DIME_InterruptControl(hBenera,dintALL,dintWAIT);
DIME_DMAReadToLockedMem(hBenera,1,hMem,,nWords);
//End of EXECUTE-Block

//User application code
//Close DMA channel and unlock memory
DIME_CloseCard(hBenera);
DIME_CloseLocate(hLocate);
```

**Fig. 3.** User application code fragment comprising configuration and communication commands.

between the user application and the hardware modules is performed on high level using APIs as shown in Figure 3. Hence it is possible to run the FIR hardware realisation together with the software simulation model of the MBE.

## 4   Conclusion

A platform-independent methodology for performance estimation of streaming media applications has been introduced. The methodology is application-driven and exploits special computational characteristics of media processing schemes. A set of execution frequencies of core tasks can be derived as a platform-independent metric for application complexity. Together with, measured or estimated, implementation data for the core tasks on a specific platform, a performance estimate for the complete streaming media application on this platform is obtained. The methodology can be used in the early implementation stage for selection of a suitable device as well as for informed decisions on how to further optimize an architecture for the target application, or an existing software implementation for a target platform.

The provided methodology has been used to identify the FIR subtask as performance critical for the implementation of the MPEG-4 ASP decoder on a specific platform, the MBE. It was shown that it is possible to enhance the overall system performance by 12%, implementing this subtask onto a reconfigurable device. Furthermore, it was proposed to employ HW/SW-coemulation on a prototyping system to verify the FIR module integration within the system model.

# References

1. Peleg, A., Weiser, U.: MMX Technology Extension to the Intel Architecture. IEEE Micro (1996) 42–50
2. Xilinx, Inc.: Virtex-II Pro Platform FPGA. (2003)
3. Kuroda, I., Nishitani, T.: Multimedia Processors. In: Proc. IEEE. Volume 86. (1998) 1203–1221
4. Kuhn, P.M., Stechele, W.: Complexity Analysis of the Emerging MPEG-4 Standard as a Basis for VLSI Implementation. In: Vol. SPIE 3309 Visual Commun. Image Process, San Jose (1998) 498–509
5. ISO/IEC 14496-2:1999/Amd.1:2000: Coding of Audio-Visual Objects - Part 2: Visual, Amendment 1: Visual Extensions. (1999)
6. ISO/IEC 14496-2:1999/FDAM4: Amendment 4: Streaming Video Profile. (2000)
7. ISO/IEC JTC1/SC29/WG11 N3093: MPEG-4 Video Verification Model Version 15.0. (1999)
8. ISO/IEC JTC1/SC29/WG11 N2918: MoMuSys Implementation of the VM (VM-991029). (1999)
9. Hovden, G., Ling, N.: On Speed Optimization of MPEG-4 Decoder for Real-Time Multimedia Applications. In: Proc. 3rd Int. Conf. Computational Intelligence and Multimedia Applications, New Delhi (1999) 399–402
10. Benini, L., de Micheli, G., Macii, E.: Designing Low-Power Circuits: Practical Recipes. IEEE Circuits and Systems Magazine 1 (2001) 6–25
11. Lan, T., Chen, Y., Zhong, Z.: MPEG2 Decoding Complexity Regulation for a Media Processor. In: Proc. 2001 Workshop on Multimedia Signal Processing. (2001) 193–198
12. Stolberg, H.J., Bereković, M., Pirsch, P., Runge, H.: The MPEG-4 Advanced Simple Profile - A Complexity Study. In: Proc. IEEE 2nd Workshop and Exhibition on MPEG-4. (2001)
13. Stolberg, H.J., Bereković, M., Pirsch, P., Runge, H., Möller, H., Kneip, J.: The M-PIRE MPEG-4 CODEC DSP and its Macroblock Engine. In: Proc. IEEE Int. Symp. Circ. Syst. (ISCAS). Volume II. (2000) 192–195
14. Xilinx, Inc.: CORE Generator Guide. (2002)
15. Nallatech Limited: BenERA User Guide. (2002)

# CoDeL: Automatically Synthesizing Network Interface Controllers

Radhakrishnan Sivakumar[1], Vassilios V. Dimakopulos[2],
and Nikitas J. Dimopoulos[3]

[1] Intel Corporation, Portland, Oregon
[2] University of Ioannina, Greece
[3] University of Victoria, Victoria, B.C, Canada

**Abstract.** In this work we present CoDeL (Controller Description Language), a framework for rapidly prototyping policy specific controllers for routers in interconnection networks. Routing controllers are specified in a high level description and then synthesized automatically.
CoDeL is a general purpose hardware description language for designing sequential machines at the algorithmic level. It is similar to C, and includes a rich library of I/O protocols that simplifies system integration.

## 1  Introduction

Message passing concurrent computers [16, 11, 5, 15] consist of many processing nodes interacting via messages exchanged over communication channels.

Interconnection networks are modeled as graphs; examples include hypercubes [3], Toruses [4], k-ary n-cubes [5], hypercycles [6], etc. Many schemes of routing and flow control have been proposed including store and forward [16] circuit switching [6], virtual channels [4,8], non-minimal routing [12], etc.

The implementation of routing and flow control takes the form of a Network Interface Controller structured as a control module (or controller) and several "helper" modules implementing specific functionality (i.e. cross-bar, routers, buffers, etc.). An example is shown in Fig. 1. The controller imports specific data (e.g. message headers), extracts pertinent information (e.g. destination addresses), performs computations, and elicits appropriate "helper" module(s).

We are interested in developing an environment where a routing engine can be specified and synthesized automatically.

Hardware description languages (HDL), silicon compilation, and automatic synthesis techniques have been investigated intensely. Early attempts in HDLs include AHPL, DDL and ISP [9, 17]. Martin et. al. [13] developed techniques of translating concurrent programs into asynchronous VLSI chips. VHDL [10], and Verilog are considered to be the premier languages for electronic design. Ptolemy [14] describes and simulates systems at a very high level of abstraction. BONeS [2] is a commercial implementation of Ptolemy.

CoDeL (Controller Description Language), targets the specification and design at the behavioral level. It is similar to the C programming language and is

A. Pimentel and S. Vassiliadis (Eds.): SAMOS 2004, LNCS 3133, pp. 78–87, 2004.

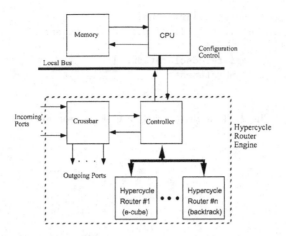

**Fig. 1.** Configuration of routing engine for Hypercycles.

therefore easy to learn. The order of the statements implicitly represents activity sequences. CoDeL extracts data and control flow from the program, assigns the necessary hardware blocks and exploits inherent parallelism. CoDeL introduces the concept of object-oriented hardware design and provides primitives and constructs for manipulating objects at the behavioral/RTL level. It includes a library of I/O protocols that simplify (sub)system interaction. The CoDeL compiler produces synthesizable VHDL code.

This work is organized as follows: Section 2 presents the main language constructs of CoDeL and illustrate their use. Section 3 gives an example of CoDeL's use in designing a routing engine controller, and presents Hardware Synthesis and test results of the implemented controller. Section 4 concludes the paper.

## 2   Controller Description Language (CoDeL)

A controller interacts with a number of "helper" modules. It imports, manipulates and exports data and commands to these modules. This data is embedded in bit-streams of application-specific formats and structure.

CoDeL programs (Fig. 2) comprise i. Structure declarations, ii. Module declaration, iii. Port declarations, iv. Register declarations, and v. CoDeL Statements.

**Structure Declarations.** Analogous to the *struct* definition in C, *bitstruct* in CoDeL defines complex data structures. Data manipulated by the controller are organized into hierarchical structures called frames. Frames represent message headers or specific message types (e.g. connection-setup, -acknowledge etc.). A frame is recursively defined to consist of frames or bitfields. A *bitstruct* therefore is composed of collections of bits or *bitstructs* (see example in Figs. 4 and 3).

**Module Declarations.** A *module* uniquely identifies the top level circuit that is being synthesized. A *module* is declared as follows:

    module module_name ([port_declarations]);

```
[structure declarations]
module   module_name ( port declarations )
{
   [ register declarations ]
   CoDeL Statements
}
```

**Fig. 2.** Basic Structure of a CoDeL program.

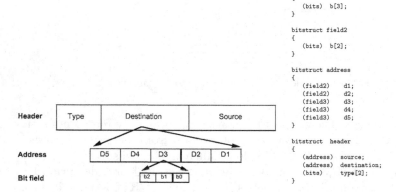

```
bitstruct  field3
{
   (bits)  b[3];
}

bitstruct field2
{
   (bits)  b[2];
}

bitstruct address
{
   (field2)   d1;
   (field2)   d2;
   (field3)   d3;
   (field3)   d4;
   (field3)   d5;
}

bitstruct  header
{
   (address)  source;
   (address)  destination;
   (bits)     type[2];
}
```

**Fig. 3.** A message header frame. Source and destination addresses are expressed as mixed radix numbers.

**Fig. 4.** Example *bitstruct* corresponding to the frame in Fig. 3.

**Port Declarations.** Ports encapsulate both data and protocols in an abstract data type and implement the I/O interaction between modules and external components. Ports are of type *input* or *output*. Bidirectional ports have not yet been introduced in the current implementation of CoDeL.

An example of a fully handshaking protocol is depicted in Fig. 5. The assertion of the *Data_Ready/Strobe* indicates that data is valid. The recipient acknowledges by asserting the *Acknowledge* signal and the sender then negates its *Data_Ready*. The protocol is resolved with the negation of the *Acknowledge*. The inclusion of protocols associated with ports allows abstraction and *hiding* of I/O interaction details.

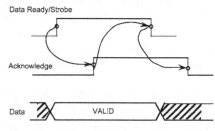

**Fig. 5.** A fully handshaking protocol.

If no protocol (null protocol) is included in the declaration of a port, the designer must explicitly specify the necessary control sequences that will effect the data transfer through the port, enabling thus the development of a library of standard protocols written in CoDeL. Ports are declared in CoDeL as follows:

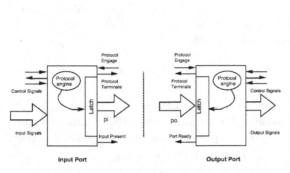

**Fig. 6.** The structure of an I/O port.

```
# Define a 16-bit address
# in 4 dimensions
bitstruct mixed_radix_4
{
    (bits) field1[4];
    (bits) field2[4];
    (bits) field3[4];
    (bits) field4[4];
}

# Define a 36-bit
# message header using
# the above
bitstruct data_frame
{
    (mixed_radix_4) source_address;
    (mixed_radix_4) destn_address;
    (bits) header[4];
}

in  (data_frame) p1 with input_handshake;
out (data_frame) p3 with output_handshake;
```

**Fig. 7.** Port and protocol declarations.

in  (*bitstruct_name*) *port_name* [with *protocol_name* ];
out(*bitstruct_name*) *port_name* [with *protocol_name* ];

The structure of an I/O port is shown in Fig. 6. The protocol engine transfers data to appropriate latches or registers. It interacts with the control path of the controller through the *ProtocolEngage* and *ProtocolTerminate* signals.

**Importing/Exporting Data.** The I/O primitives input (*port_name*) and output (*port_name*), *import/export* data through the declared ports engaging the associated protocols, if any. The *isready* (isready (*port_name*)) primitive is used to check the availability of data at an input port or the readiness of an output port to accept data. The examples shown below use declarations from Fig. 7.

- input(p1) engages the input protocol *input_handshake* which latches valid data to the *p1* latch.
- isready(p3) tests whether the previous output operation has terminated. Useful in asynchronous protocols to test whether the protocol engine has terminated the data transfer and is ready to accept the next set of data.

**Register Declarations.** Registers are declared as having a particular structure.
    register [(*bitstruct_name*)] *register_name*;
The default structure is bits and the components of a register can be addressed at the bitstruct level or at the bit level. We use a dot notation to identify the components under the convention that a sequence of dot separated fields represents a node in the tree representing the structure of the object and it consists of all the bits at the leaf nodes of the sub-tree rooted at the node.

Consider the example of the bit structure header shown in Fig. 4. If we declare
    register (header) r1;
    register r2[4];
then the following are legal names.

- `r1(5:0)` The bits in positions 5 (most significant) to 0 (least significant).
- `r1.destination.d5` The bits from the 25th to the 23rd position (corresponding to the most significant field of the destination) are addressed.
- `register r2` is declared to be of size 4 bits.

## 2.1   CoDeL Statements

**Assignment Statements.** Operations may need to be performed on the bit-fields composing a frame. The assignment statement places the results of a computation to an output port or a register or portions thereof as discussed earlier.

*register_name | output_port_name = computation_expression*

Assignments are implemented as RCR (Register-Combinational Logic- Register) where data is stored in registers, operations are effected by a combinational circuit and the results are stored back in a register.

**CoDeL Operators.** A *computation_expression* can have either input ports or registers as its operands. It is formed using a number of standard C operators, summarized in Table 1, and following the usual C associativity and precedence rules. The use of parentheses defines precedence and can promote parallelism. As an example, the assignments

`r1(7:3) = r1(6:4) + r1(7:5) + r1(8:6) + r1(9:7);`

and

`r1(7:3) = ((r1(6:4) + r1(7:5)) + (r1(8:6) + r1(9:7)));`

represent three adders operating in series as per Fig. 8(a) and a two level network as per Fig. 8(b) respectively.

**Control Statements.** In a sequential environment, the control path is inherently described by the order of the operations in a program. In CoDeL the control path of the design is extracted based on the sequentiality of the algorithm and it includes states which explicitly clock the registers included in the design. The basic control structures in CoDeL include loop, conditional and wait primitives; these are listed below.

> **Loop primitives:** `while` (*condition*)   {
>     *CoDeL statements*
> }
> `for` (*initializer*; *test_condition*; *incr/decr_exprssn*)   {
>     *CoDeL statements*
> }
>
> **Branch primitive:** `if` (*condition*)   {
> *CoDeL statements*
>     }
> [ `else` {
>     *CoDeL statements* } ]

where the else statement is optional.

**Table 1.** List of CoDeL Operators.

| Symbol | Operation | Symbol | Operation | Symbol | Operation |
|---|---|---|---|---|---|
| (,... ,....) | Concatenation | ? : | Conditional | ( : ) | Bit Selector |
| >, >=, <, <= | Relational | << | Left Shift | >> | Right Shift |
| +, - , * | Arithmetic | ! | Logical Negation | \|\| | Logical OR |
| ++ , − | Increment/ Decrement | == | Logical Equality | != | Logical Inequality |
| ~ | Bit-wise Negation | & | Bit-wise AND | && | Logical AND |
| \| | Bit-wise OR | ^ | Bit-wise XOR | ~ \| | Bit-wise NOR |
| ~& | Bit-wise NAND | <@ | Left Rotate | >@ | Right Rotate |

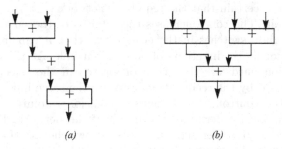

*(a)*                    *(b)*

**Fig. 8.** Altering of the computation structure through the use of parentheses.

**Wait statement:**
wait (*condition*)
wait maintains the current state of the computation until *condition* is satisfied.

## 2.2   CoDeL Compiler

The CoDeL compiler is written in C and it compiles a source CoDeL program to produce a synthesizable VHDL code. The compiler consists of the recursive, descent based [1] with single token lookahead parser and the VHDL builder.

The VHDL builder implements the data path as an RCR (Register Combinational Circuit Register), where operands are in registers, operations are effected by a combinational circuit(s) and the results are stored in registers. The control path is extracted automatically and sequences operations and the storing of results. Optimization includes automatic parallelization of non-dependent assignment statements [7]. This feature schedules multiple register assignments simultaneously improving the efficiency and speed of the resulting hardware.

## 3   A Routing Engine Controller Implementation

In this section, we present the design of an e-cube controller used in a circuit-switched hypercycle network and discuss its implementation using a CoDeL program. The overall architecture of the node is presented in Fig. 9. It is assumed that the communication is bit-serial, and that there are bidirectional serial links between compute-nodes. As the circuit is formed, both links are allocated. One is used for forwarding the message, the other is for acknowledgments. Furthermore, Serial/Parallel (S/P) interfaces at each link present message streams to the controller for a routing decision.

The crossbar is capable of switching the bit-serial streams and is composed of switches which upon detecting a break in the bit-stream disconnect. It is assumed that the switches in the crossbar can be randomly accessed (tested and set) through the crossbar interface. The router component implements a generalized deadlock-free e-cube routing [6] and returns a "network port" through which the circuit is to be extended towards the destination. It is the responsibility of the controller to ascertain that the required "network port" is available and to extend the circuit. The controller uses the address of the "network port" and sets the appropriate switches in the crossbar so that it can inject the header of the message on both directions of the chosen link. At the same time, the collision detection hardware that is incorporated in the injector detects any concurrent attempt by the recipient node to use the same link. Upon detection of a collision, the controller implements a collision resolution strategy based on the lexicographical ordering of the nodes of the network. If no collision is detected, then the controller sets the crossbar switches so that the circuit is extended and marks the "network port" as being used. The cycle continues with the controller sequentially testing all network or host ports for incoming traffic, and the status of the switches that implement the currently active circuits. If a closed switch has been opened because of a break (i.e. termination of the circuit) then the controller updates its internal state of used ports and continues the cycle. It is assumed that the switches at the network part of the crossbar are paired with switches at the controller part so that once the circuit is dissolved, the incoming link is connected to its corresponding port while the outgoing link is disconnected. Any new messages just arriving, will be captured by the ports and initiate a new routing cycle by the controller. The above discussion is summarized in the form of a pseudo code given in Fig. 10.

## 3.1   Hardware Implementation

The control algorithm for the above e-cube routing policy was coded in CoDeL for a 2-dimensional network with a maximum degree 4 and 3 nodes per dimension. The algorithm uses polling to test for availability of data at each of the S/P interfaces in a round-robin fashion. If there is valid data, the header is imported, the destination address is extracted and sent to the router "helper module" and the resulting "network port" through which the route will be extended is read. Fragments of the CoDeL code are included in Figures 11 and 12. The first figure defines some of the data types and ports used while the second one includes CoDeL code at the start of the main loop.

For this example, we assumed a message header consisting of a 1-bit message type and a 4-bit destination address. 5 serial-to-parallel ports (including the host) present messages to the controller for routing decisions. Full handshake protocols

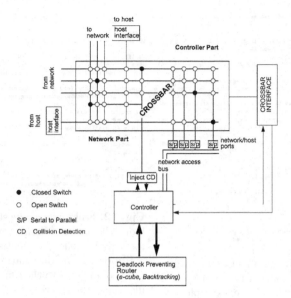

**Fig. 9.** Structure of a circuit switching routing node in a hypercycle network.

– Configuration Phase:
*Initialize and generate appropriate control signals for crossbar and router.*

– Normal Operation:
Repeat for each *input port i, i* = 1 to *maximum_num_available_ports*
  if *input port i* isready then
    -*Import message header*
    -*Extract Destination address, Available ports and send to router.*
    -*Import forwarding port and status signals from router*
    -*Analyze status signal to determine if destination has been reached.*
    if *destination is not reached* then
      -*Configure cross bar and export message header to next node.*
      -*Wait until receiving node acknowledges or a collision signal is generated.*
      if *no collision* then
        -*Clear previous cross bar connection.*
        -*Set crossbar to connect the previous node to the succeeding node for*
        *data transmission.*
      else
        -*Invoke collision resolution strategy.*
      end if
    else
      -*Send message header to local host if it is free since destination has been reached.*
    end if
  end if
end repeat

**Fig. 10.** Pseudo code of the e-cube controller algorithm.

interface the crossbar module and S/P ports. We assume that the injection module/collision detection (CD) circuitry communicated only with the "network ports" connected to outgoing nodes in the cross bar interface and when a collision occurs, messages at either end wait until the polling mechanism services them again. The size of the CoDeL code is 156 lines and was compiled into a 1665 line

```
###############################################################
bitstruct mixed_radix_2  #  2-dimension mixed radix efinitios
{
    (bits) field1[2];        # address in dimension 1
    (bits) field2[2];        # address in dimension 2
}
bitstruct data_frame  # Define header (Msg type, destn address)
{
    (bits)          header;         # message header (1-bit)
    (mixed_radix_2) destn_address;  # dest. address (4-bits)
}
###############################################################
# Protocols associated with various ports              #
#   p1, p3 - full handshake; inport, export dataframes  #
#   p2, p4 - ecube protocol; interfaces to the router   #
#   cf - full handshake; to cross bar and injection modules #
###############################################################
module ecube_controller_new (
    out bus_enable[6],
    in  (data_frame)     p1 with inp_hsk,
    in  (npg_port_frame) p2 with inp_ecube,
    out (data_frame)     p3 with out_hsk,
    out                  p4[11] with out_ecube,
    out (cross_bar_frame) cf with out_hsk,
    out cb_rst,
    in  config,
    in  data_sent,
    in  collision,  # available_ports[0] signifies line
    in  available_ports[5]     # connected to host
                          )
```

**Fig. 11.** CoDeL fragment that defines some of the data structures, ports, modules and protocols of the example controller.

```
#######  Portions of the Main Loop #######

shift_value = 1;
while (i <= 4)  # Loop for scanning the ports
{
    shift_value = shift_value << 1;   # Left Shift by 1
    bus_enable  = shift_value;   # Enable S/P device i
    if (isready(p1))  # test each port for availability of data
    {
        input(p1);  # and read through external inp_hsk protocol
        # extract the destination address from p1
        destn = p1.destn_address;
        # concatenate OD5 with available ports
        # along with 0X0 (hexadecimal 0)
        p4 = (5,available_ports,0X0);
        output(p4);  # send available ports to router via port p4
        # Concatenate and send destination address
        # to router via port p4
        p4 = (0,2,0,0,destn.field2,0,0,destn.field2);
        output(p4);
        input(p2);  # Receive computed forwarding port address
                    # and control signals (from router) in port p2
    ...
```

**Fig. 12.** Fragment of the start of the main loop. Each of the Serial/Parallel (S/P) interfaces is polled sequentially, the header is imported, the destination address is extracted and sent to the router "helper module", and the the resulting "network port" is read.

VHDL code which was synthesized and downloaded to a Xilinx$^{TM}$ 4010PC84-5 chip. The implementation consists of 989 Xilinx primitive cells. The control path for the implementation of the main machine consists of 78 states of which it takes 25 clock cycles for the initialization, 20 cycles for interaction with the router module, 21 cycles for transmitting the message assuming there is no collision or block and 12 cycles to reach the final destination. The protocol engines have a maximum of 9 states.

The chip was tested using an HP16500A Logic Analyzer up to its maximum clock frequency of 25 Mhz. At this clock speed the synthesized design achieves a delay of approximately $3\mu s$ in routing a message from its arrival at an input port, setting up the crossbar and forwarding the message to the next node. We estimate that this design and with the technology used (i.e. Xilinx$^{TM}$ 4010PC84-5) could be clocked at a speed of 30-40 Mhz achieving a sub 2 $\mu s$ delay in routing.

## 4    Conclusion and Discussion

In this work, we have introduced a hardware description language that provides elementary functions, data structures and simplified I/O operations for specifying and automatically synthesizing controllers within NICs.

CoDeL is a compact language which allows us to specify and synthesize systems from the functional description of an algorithm. It has a rich repertoire of operations for efficient data manipulation and its object-oriented features render structured protocols and I/O functions transparent to the user. It automatically extracts the necessary control paths from the algorithm and the compiler does a reasonable job of parallelizing non-dependent assignments.

The most recent version of the CoDeL compiler is V.0.8 and several future improvements are planned to enhance parallelism. In addition the introduction of new operators, bidirectional ports, procedures, asynchronous clocking schemes, and multi-module integration are some of the areas that need further work.

## Acknowledgment

This work was supported by grants from NSERC and by the University of Victoria.

## References

1. A.V. Aho, J.D. Ullman, "Principles of compiler design," Reading, Mass: Addison-Wesley, 1977.
2. *BONeS 3.6 User's Guide,* vol. 1, AltaGroup, CA, 1997
3. E. Chow, H. Madan, J. Peterson, "A Real-Time Adaptive Message Routing Network for the Hypercube Computer," *Proceedings of the Real-Time Systems Symposium,* pp. 88-96, San Jose CA., 1987.
4. W.J. Dally and C. L. Seitz "Deadlock-Free Message Routing in Multiprocessor Interconnection Networks" *IEEE Trans. Comput.* Vol. C-36, No. 5, pp. 547-553, 1987.
5. W. J. Dally, J. A. S. Fiske, J. S. Keen, R. A. Lethin, M. D. Noakes, P. R. Nuth, R. E. Davison, G. Fyler "The Message-Driven Processor: A Multicomputer Processing Node with Efficient Mechanisms" *IEEE Micro* pp. 23-40, April 1992.
6. N.J. Dimopoulos and R. Sivakumar, "Deadlock preventing routing in hypercycles," *Can. J. Elect. Comput. Eng.,* Vol. 19, No. 4, pp. 193-199, 1994.
7. Dimopoulos, N.J., R. Sivakumar and V.V. Dimakopoulos, "A rapid prototyping environment for the specification and automatic synthesis of controllers for interconnection routers", *29th Annual Asilomar Conference on Signals, Systems and Computers,* Pacific Grove, California, pp. 193-198, Oct. 1995
8. J. Duato, "A New Theory of Deadlock-Free Adaptive Routing in Wormhole Networks," *IEEE Trans. Parallel and Distributed Systems,* Vol. 4, No. 12, pp. 1320-1331, Dec. 1993.
9. D.D. Gajski, *Silicon Compilation,* Addison-Wesley, Reading-Mass, 1988.
10. *IEEE Standard VHDL Language Reference Manual,* IEEE Std. 1076-1987, The Institute of Electrical and Electronics Engineers, New York, NY 1988.
11. iPSC User's Guide, No. 17455-3, Intel Corp., Portland, OR, 1985.
12. S. Konstandinidou and L. Snyder, "The Chaos Router," *IEEE Trans. Computers,* Vol. 43, No. 12, pp. 1386-1397, Dec. 1994.
13. A. Martin "Translating Concurrent Programs into VLSI chips" in (D. Etiemble J.C. Syre (Eds). *Lecture Notes in Computer Science No. 605,* Springer Verlag, 1992.
14. *Overview of the Ptolemy Project* Technical Memorandum UCB/ERL M01/11, University of California at Berkeley, CA, March 2001.
15. S. Pakin, M. Lauria, and A. Chien, "High Performance Messaging on Workstation: Illinois Fast Messages (FM) for Myrinet", *Proceedings, Supercomputing95,* Nov. 1995
16. C. L. Seitz, "The cosmic cube", CACM, vol. 28, pp. 22-33, Jan 1989.
17. S. G. Shiva, "Automatic Hardware Synthesis", *Proc. IEEE,* vol. 71, No. 1, 1983.

# Performance and Power Evaluation of Clustered VLIW Processors with Wide Functional Units

Miquel Pericàs, Eduard Ayguadé, Javier Zalamea,
Josep Llosa, and Mateo Valero

Departament d'Arquitectura de Computadors
Universitat Politecnica de Catalunya
Barcelona, Spain
{mpericas,eduard,jzalamea,josepll,mateo}@ac.upc.es

**Abstract.** Architectural resources and program recurrences are the main limitations to the amount of Instruction-Level Parallelism (*ILP*) exploitable from loops. To increase the number of operations per second, current designs use high degrees of *resource replication* for memory ports and functional units. But the high costs in terms of power and cycle time of this technique limit the degree of replication.

*Clustering* is a technique aimed at decentralizing the design of future wide issue cores and enable them to meet the technology constraints in terms of cycle time, area and power. Another way to reduce the complexity of recent cores is using *wide* functional units. This technique only requires minor modifications to the underlying hardware, but also imposes a penalty on the exploitable parallelism.

In this paper we evaluate a broad range of VLIW configurations that make use of these two techniques. From this study we conclude that applying both techniques yields configurations with very good power-performance efficiency.

## 1  Introduction

Technology scaling is allowing computer architects to pack bigger and bigger amounts of logic into a single chip. This allows to increase the exploitable parallelism (ILP), but just increasing resources results in very power–hungry architectures with long wire delays. *Clustering* and *widening* are two techniques with better-than-centralized scaling in terms of power, area and cycle time. The strategy is similar in both cases: reduce the number of functional units connected to the register files and try to limit communications to the local resources only.

### 1.1  Widening

The width of the resources can be increased, exploiting data parallelism at the functional unit level by using the *widening technique* [9]. Using this technique a single operation can be performed over multiple data. This is similar to SIMD, but relies on ILP instead of DLP.

A. Pimentel and S. Vassiliadis (Eds.): SAMOS 2004, LNCS 3133, pp. 88–97, 2004.
© Springer-Verlag Berlin Heidelberg 2004

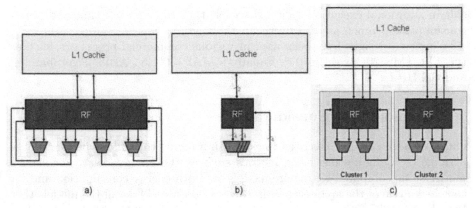

**Fig. 1.** (a) a centralized configuration, (b) a wide–2 configuration and (c) a 2–cluster configuration. All configuration share the same amount of of arithmetic units and memory ports.

Fig. 1b) shows the effects of applying *widening* to a centralizes architecture. As we see, this technique reduces the number of ports that access the register file, while multiplying the width of these ports by the *widening* degree. The same effect happens on the memory ports. Functional units in a wide architecture may execute both simple and wide operations. When simple operations are executed, the functional unit is used only partially and its computational capacity is not fully exploited. This degrades performance in case a program does not contain wide operations.

The *widening technique* has been implemented only in limited quantities in commercial processors. For instance, the IBM POWER2 [11] applies widening to the memory ports. Vector processors like NEC's SX-3 [10] have applied widening to the floating point units (FPUs). Finally, multimedia processor extensions combine sub and superword parallelism, which, in some way, use the basic idea of widening applied to integer and FP operations [15] [16].

Widening requires additional procedures in the VLIW scheduler to detect independent operations that can be compacted into wide operations. In this work we have built an algorithm based on MIRS_C (*Modulo Scheduling with Integrated Register Spilling for Clustered Architectures*) [14] and extended it to handle compaction of operations [9].

## 1.2   Clustering

Another approach for dealing with wire delays is to partition the processor into components that communicate mostly locally. Current trends focus on applying this partitioning to both the register file and the functional units. This type of architecture is named a clustered architecture. Fig. 1c) shows an example of such an architecture. In this case each cluster consists of several functional units connected to a local register file. Data sharing between clusters may result in additional execution cycles. However, the reduced cycle time and power consumption compensate this overhead as shown in [14].

Clustered designs have been used in various commercial processors, such as the TI's TMS320C6x series [17], Equator's MAP1000 [5], ADI's TigerSharc [4] and the HP Lx [3].

## 2   Technological Considerations

Our goal in the project has been to establish a model that allows us to evaluate a range of configurations using metrics such as the energy–delay. For such a metric to be computed we require models for both energy consumption and for the clock cycle of the architecture. In this section we will detail the models that have been used for this purpose.

### 2.1   Clock Cycle

Generated schedules with our scheduling tool allow to make a simple estimation of the number of cycles executed by an application. To complete an execution time estimation we also need knowledge of the clock cycle time. Variations in the clock cycle will also show up in the number of pipeline stages and therefore also in the latency of operations. In a VLIW processor the latency of operations is needed to correctly generate the schedules. Development of a model to determine the maximum frequency of a certain processor configuration is thus a required step.

In superscalar processors the scheduling logic is assumed to be on the critical path. In a VLIW processor this logic is negligible. For our model we will consider that the register file is the critical component. All other structures will be pipelined as a function of the access time of the register file.

Table 1 shows the frequency values for a set of 64–bit register files that correspond to the set of the evaluated configurations in section 3. These values have been obtained using a model for register files based on the CACTI [12] tool. The modeling has been done for a technology parameter of 100nm. We also show how using varying degrees of widening and clustering affects the number of read and write ports.

The use of the *widening technique* requires certain modifications on the structure of the register file so that we can access a wide data word in a single step. If we implement the register file as several replicated 64–bit register files that are accessed in parallel then the paid penalty will be very small. Each of these register files will then store a simple 64–bit word from the wide data word. When simple accesses occur, the decoders of each register file are responsible for determining if they store requested data or if the array can be deactivated.

### 2.2   Energy and Power

The relationship between power and performance is increasingly important in the design of modern processors. Within the same architecture, power scales at a

**Table 1.** Processor frequencies for several configurations of the register file.

| Clusters | Widening Degree | Registers per Cluster | Register Width | Read Ports | Write Ports | Frequency |
|---|---|---|---|---|---|---|
| 1 | 1 | 128 | 64  | 20 | 12 | 873 MHz  |
| 1 | 1 | 64  | 64  | 20 | 12 | 980 MHz  |
| 1 | 1 | 32  | 64  | 20 | 12 | 1461 MHz |
| 2 | 1 | 64  | 64  | 11 | 7  | 1458 MHz |
| 2 | 1 | 32  | 64  | 11 | 7  | 1880 MHz |
| 4 | 1 | 64  | 64  | 6  | 4  | 1884 MHz |
| 4 | 1 | 32  | 64  | 6  | 4  | 2106 MHz |
| 4 | 1 | 16  | 64  | 6  | 4  | 2507 MHz |
| 1 | 2 | 64  | 128 | 10 | 6  | 1558 MHz |
| 1 | 2 | 32  | 128 | 10 | 6  | 1961 MHz |
| 2 | 2 | 32  | 128 | 6  | 4  | 2106 MHz |
| 2 | 2 | 16  | 128 | 6  | 4  | 2507 MHz |
| 1 | 4 | 32  | 256 | 5  | 3  | 2263 MHz |
| 1 | 4 | 16  | 256 | 5  | 3  | 2618 MHz |

higher pace than performance. Future processors may find themselves limited by power requirements instead of delays or other technological limitations. In order to improve the power efficiency of modern processors, alternative architectures are being researched. In this section we explain how power consumption has been modeled for clustering and widening.

For our power evaluation we used the Wattch [2] power modeling infrastructure. To extract power values, Wattch provides parameterized power models of common structures present in modern superscalar microprocessors.

We model led register files, data caches and functional units. For the purposes of this paper we chose to ignore the power consumption of smaller structures such as buses or control units. The remaining structures that have not been evaluated are unaffected by the techniques.

**Conditional Clocking.** Most modern processors are designed with power consumption in mind. *Conditional Clocking* is a technique that disables all or part of a hardware unit to reduce power consumption when it is not being used. Several options exist for estimating the power of multiported structures when they are only partially accessed (*full power* vs *linear scaling*) and when ports are not accessed (*residual power* vs *zero power*). In this work we have used the following conditional clocking style:

- when the unit's ports are only partially accessed, the power is scaled linearly with the port usage.
- ports that are not accessed consume 10%[1] of their maximum power.
- unused ALUs consume 0% of their maximum power[2].

---

[1] 10% is a commonly used turnoff figure for clock gated circuits
[2] The ALUs have very regular access patterns so this election has little impact on the evaluation

# 3   Performance Evaluation

In this section we detail the performance evaluation strategy that has been applied on several processor configurations. The evaluated configurations are the same 14 configurations for which values have been given in table 1. All architectures have a hardware equivalent to 8 floating point units and 4 memory buses, both 64 bits wide. The clustering and widening degrees range from 1 to 4, and the number of registers has been chosen so that configurations have a storage capacity of about 64–128 registers. The memory is assumed to be ideal, meaning that all accesses hit in the cache.

For the evaluation we have constructed a workbench consisting of loops taken from the Perfect Club Benchmark We have only taken loops that are suitable for modulo scheduling and that have executed at least once during a sample execution. A total of 811 loops accounting for 80% of the execution time of the benchmark make up our workbench. Before scheduling, an unrolling degree of 4 has been applied on all loops. Unrolling is required by the compaction algorithm. The chosen number allows us to schedule for all ranges of widening using the same unrolling degree.

A special terminology has been introduced to name each of the fourteen configurations. From now one we will refer to each one as $Cx.Wy.Rz$, where $x$ is the number of clusters, $y$ is the widening degree and $z$ is the number of registers in a single cluster. The total register storage of these configurations can be obtained as the product of these three factors times 64 bits/register. All clustered configurations have two extra ports in the register file to perform intercluster communication using *move* operations.

In Sect. 2 we have presented our methodology for obtaining clock cycle values for our processor configurations. The model obtained depends basically on the number of registers, the number of read/write ports and the technology factor. The analog latency of the operations, on the other hand, depends only on the technology factor $\lambda$. It is thus the same for all configurations. These latencies can be seen in table 2 for a technology of $\lambda = 100nm$ [6]. Once the real latency is known we can compute the number of clock cycles the operation spends in the execution state.

**Table 2.** Execution latencies at 100nm.

| Operation | Execution Latency |
|---|---|
| L1 Cache Access (L/S) | 1.152 ns |
| Division and Modulo | 7.56 ns |
| Square Root (SQRT) | 11.304 ns |
| Others (ADD, MUL, etc..) | 2.52 ns |

The following sections present the results that have been obtained from our workbench.

### 3.1   Execution Time

The schedules generated by our extended MIRS_C algorithm allow us to approximate the number of execution cycles. This number alone carries information on the amount of IPC that is lost by clusterizing our architecture and by having less functional units. Remember that *widening* takes N functional units and generates a single N-wide functional unit. Applications that have no compactible operations effectively see a single 1-wide functional unit. This causes important losses in IPC for those applications. If we combine the number of execution cycles with the clock speed of the processor we will obtain the execution time, our primary performance measurement. The results of this simple calculation are shown in Fig. 2 relative to the base configuration (*C1.W1.R128*). To see the effect of compatibility in loops in the figure we distinguish between execution time contributed to by fully–compactible loops (FC) and the execution time contributed to by all other loops (NFC). The figure shows big gains in terms of speed-up when going from a centralized configuration (like the base configuration *C1.W1.R128*) to clustered or wide architectures. For this test, the best result is obtained with configuration *C4.W1.R16*. This configuration has a clock frequency that is 187% faster than the base configuration. Combined with an exaction cycle degradation of 66% it obtains a speed-up of 1.73.

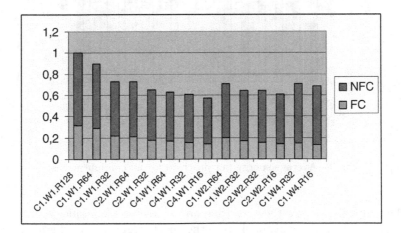

**Fig. 2.** Relative execution time for all configurations. The contribution of fully–compactible and not fully–compactible loops is shown.

Another configuration with very good results is *C2.W2.R16*. This configuration obtains a speed-up of 1.64 but it requires less area compared to configuration *C4.W1.R16*. It is an interesting observation that the best speed-ups are obtained with configurations that have only 16 registers per cluster. This shows that, in this case, having high operating frequencies is more important than ILP when execution time is the principal objective. However, parallelism should not be forgot. The *C1.W4.R16* configuration has the highest clock of all, but due to low ILP extraction in non–compactible loops, the execution time is not particularly good. Note that the contributed executions time of the fully compactible loops is the *smallest* in this case. If our workbench consisted only of fully compactible loops, this configuration would have the best performance. In general, configurations that are based on widening depend very much on the characteristics of the programs.

## 3.2   Energy Consumption

The energy consumption is an important measure that allows us to determine whether a battery will provide enough energy to complete a certain task. The average energy per program is shown in Fig. 3 for each configuration. The contribution of each hardware structure is shown.

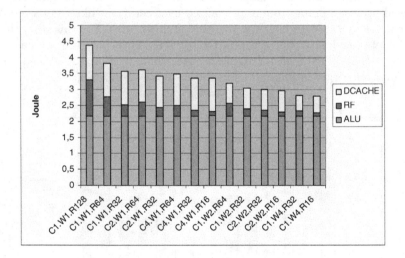

**Fig. 3.** Average energy per program for all configurations.

The figure shows how the clustering and widening techniques reduce the energy consumed in the register file. In the most aggressive configurations, this reduction is over 90%. In the case of wide architectures, the reduction in the number of memory operations also yields big reductions in the energy consumed by the data cache (up to 50%). A completely different image is obtained when looking at the energy spent by the arithmetic functional units. *Clustering* and *widening* do not affect their basic structure and thus the energy consumption is the same. As the *clustering* and *widening* degrees increase, this energy becomes the predominant part of the total energy consumption and further improvements in the register file or memory energy are increasingly irrelevant to the total energy. Adding all three contributions we obtain a maximum 36% energy reduction for configuration *C1.W4.R16*.

### 3.3   Energy–Delay

In the previous sections we have benchmarked the configurations from the point of view of performance and energy consumption. We see that clustering yields better performance but widening is less power–hungry. It would be interesting to have a global metric that takes into account both energy and performance. To evaluate each of the configurations globally we have computed the energy–delay, defined as $ET^n$, where $E$ is the energy dissipated by a certain configuration and $T$ is the execution time. We used $n = 1$, ie., giving energy and delay the same importance. The results are shown in Fig. 4 normalized to $C1.W1.R128$. From this figure we see that the configuration with the best power-performance relation is $C2.W2.R16$ (0.41). If we restrict ourselves to the configurations with a total storage of 128 registers the best configuration is now $C2.W2.R32$ (0.442). So, we confirm that configurations combining *clustering* and *widening* are very interesting structures when power–performance trade-offs need to be taken into account.

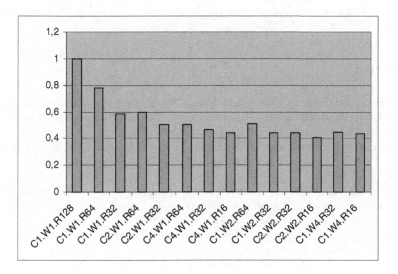

**Fig. 4.** Energy–delay.

## 4   Conclusions and Design Considerations

In order to increase the performance of computers, aggressive processor configurations capable of executing more operations per second are required. The two main strategies that are used to this effect are: 1) increasing the exploitable parallelism (ILP) with more resources and more control logic and 2) increasing the frequency of the processor which normally implies deeper pipelines. On the downside, both of these techniques increase the power consumption of the processor at a faster rate than performance is increased. In this paper we have evaluated two techniques whose goal it is to increase the processor frequency while maintaining high levels of exploitable ILP and with low power consumption. These two techniques are *clustering* and *widening*.

The results show that clustering yields better execution time but widening has lower power dissipation. To establish a global measurement, we computed the energy–delay for each of the configurations. This test yielded two conclusions. First, we saw that the best results were obtained when combining *clustering* and *widening*. And second, we found that the configurations with 16 registers per register file were more efficient than the same configurations with 32, 64 or 128. In our tests, the configuration that obtained the best energy–delay was *C2.W2.R16*.

## Acknowledgment

This work has been supported by Hewlett-Packard and by the Ministry of Science and Technology of Spain and the European Union (FEDER funds) under contract TIC 2001-0995-C02-0.

## References

1. M. Berry, D. Chen, P. Koss and D. Kuck, *The Perfect Club Benchmarks: Effective Performance Evaluation of Supercomputers,* Technical Report 827, CSRD, Univ. of Illinois at Urbana-Champaign, Nov. 1988
2. D. Brooks, V. Tiwari and M .Martsoni, *Wattch: A Framework for Architectural-Level Power Analysis and Optimizations,* Int'l Symp. on Computer Architecture, 2000 (ISCA-00).
3. P. Faraboschi, G. Brown, G. Desoli and F. Homewood. *Lx: A technology platform for customizable VLIW embedded processing,* In Proc. $27^{th}$ Annual Intl. Symp. on Computer Architecture, pages 203-213, June 2000.
4. J. Friedman and Z. Greenfield. *The tigersharc DSP architecture,* IEEE Micro, pages 66-76, January-February 2000.
5. P.N.Glaskowsky. *MAP1000 unfolds at Equator.* Microprocessor Report. 12(16), December 1998
6. M.S. Hrishikesh, N.P. Jouppi, K.I. Farkas, D. Burger, S.W. Keckler and P. Shivakumar, *The Optimal Logic Depth Per Pipeline Stage is 6 to 8 FO4 Inverter Delays,* In Proc. of the $29^{th}$ Symp. on Comp. Arch (ISCA-02), May 2002.
7. J. Llosa, M. Valero, E. Ayguadé and A. González. *Hypernode reduction modulo scheduling,* In Proc. of the $28^{th}$ Annual Int. Symp. on Microarchitecture (MICRO-28),pages 350-360, November 1995.
8. D. Lòpez, J. Llosa, M. Valero and E. Ayguadé. *Cost–Conscious Strategies to Increase Performance of Numerical Programs on Aggressive VLIW Architectures,* IEEE Trans. on Comp., vol 50, no. 10, pp 1033–1051, October 2001.
9. D. Lòpez, J. Llosa, M. Valero and E. Ayguadé. *Cost-Conscious Strategies to Increase Performance of Numerical Programs on Aggressive VLIW Architectures.* IEEE. Trans. on Comp. Vol 50, No. 10, pags 1033-1051, October 2001.

10. T. Watanabe, *The NEC SX-3 Supercomputer System*. Proc. ComCon91, pp. 303-308, 1991
11. S.W. White and S. Dhawan. *POWER2: Next Generation of the RISC System/6000 Family*. IBM J. Research and Development, vol. 38, no. 5, pp, 493-502, Sept. 1994
12. S.J.E. Wilton and N.P. Jouppi. *CACTI: An enhanced Cache Access and Cycle Time Model*, IEEE. J. Solid-State Circuits, vol 31, no. 5, pp. 677-688, May 1996.
13. J. Zalamea, J. Llosa, E. Ayguadé and M. Valero. *MIRS: Modulo Scheduling with integrated register spilling*. In Proc. of 14th Annual Workshop on Languages and Compilers for Parallel Computing (LCPC2001), August 2001.
14. J. Zalamea, J. Llosa, E. Ayguadé and M. Valero. *Modulo Scheduling with integrated register spilling for Clustered VLIW Architectures*, In Proc. 34$^{th}$ annual Int. Symp. on Microarch., December 2001.
15. *AltiVec Vectorizes PowerPC* Microprocessor Report, vol. 12, no. 6, May 1998
16. INTEL, *Pentium III Processor: Developer's Manual,* Intel Technology Report available at http://developer.intel.com/design/PentiumIII, 1999
17. T.I.Inc. *TMS320C62x/67x CPU and Instruction Set Reference Guide*, 1998.
18. S. Rixner, W.J. Dally, B. Khailany, P. Mattson, U.J. Kapasi, J.D. Owens. *Register organization for media processing*, High-Performance Computer Architecture, 2000. HPCA-6. Proceedings. Sixth International Symposium on , 2000.

# An Optimized Flow for Designing High-Speed, Large-Scale CMOS ASIC SoCs

Ulrich Heinkel[1], Claus Mayer[1], Charles Webb[1], Hans Sahm[1],
Werner Haas[2], and Stefan Gossens[2]

[1] Lucent Technologies Network Systems GmbH
{heinkel,clausmayer,cawebb3,hsahm}@lucent.com
[2] University of Erlangen-Nuremberg
wh@lrs.eei.uni-erlangen.de,
stefan.gossens@informatik.uni-erlangen.de

**Abstract.** This paper describes our state-of-the-art design flow used for specification, implementation and verification of a 10 million gates ASIC System-on-Chip (SoC) for a Sonet/SDH application. We present our tools and methodologies currently used and/or being developed for a multisite ASIC design project from the first specification up to the gate level netlist: our multi-site data management environment VHDLDevSys, our multi-use and re-use library ADK-Lib and our multi-platform VHDL/C++ simulation/verification environment PROVerify together with the employment of formal methods.

## 1 Verification Crisis

Not only the complexity of designs increases but also the development costs. [1] describes a new model for the total design costs and shows the impact of different methodologies at RT-level. Major cost savings were made by installing "re-use" at block level and above. Actually industry is introducing an "IC Implementation Toolset" for the automation of the RTL design flow and is moving towards an "Intelligent Testbench" for the automation of the RTL functional verification flow. Future cost savings can be made by moving towards the "Electronic-System Level" and a methodology dealing with hardware, software and mechanical and conceptual level [2]. In this paper we present our approach for automating the RTL flow together with our SONET/SDH specific "Intelligent Testbench" PROVerify.

## 2 Application Field

Our devices mainly doing some kind of mapping/demapping of different client data into a high-speed optical datastream based on SONET/SDH protocols. To allow a long distance transmission with minimal adoption of signal regenerators, State-of-the-Art optical transmission systems perform error correction instead of much simpler error detection. Therefore the traditional SONET/SDH protocol had to be modified in order to allow for additional redundant information. The OTU-3 frame consists of 4

A. Pimentel and S. Vassiliadis (Eds.): SAMOS 2004, LNCS 3133, pp. 98–107, 2004.
© Springer-Verlag Berlin Heidelberg 2004

rows and 4080 columns where the FEC bytes are inserted between column 3825 and 4080. The overhead columns 1 to 6 in row 1 contain a frame alignment word used for the device synchronization to the incoming data stream.The other overhead columns are used for monitoring purposes in the network management. The payload envelope (col. 16 to 3824) holds parts or all of the client data. The data transmission itself is a continuous stream of SONET/SDH frames.

## 3  Device Architecture

The UFEC40G (Figure 1) is a multi-rate multiple forward error correction device supporting SONET/SDH, OTN and Clear Channel applications ([3], [4]). It is divided in 4 major subblocks SB1-4 and can be configured in transceiver and regenerator modes at 43 Gbit/s data rates. In transceiver mode a reduced OTU-3 (only for inter ASIC processing), SONET(OC-768)/SDH or clear channel signals can be mapped into G709V compliant transmission format OTU3 (add functionality) or/and can be extracted from an incoming G709V compliant frame OTU3 (drop functionality). The reduced OTU-3 processing, which is possible on client side, covers framing, SM-BIP8 parity evaluation and de-scrambling for the received data stream (client receive) and SM-BIP8 insertion, scrambling and frame alignment overhead insertion into the transmitted data stream (client transmit). Furthermore, elastic stores, mapper and demapper provide the data rate adoption between different clock domains. Add and drop functionality can be operated independently. The device can be used for FEC code conversion between ULTRA FEC (Proprietary Code) and RS FEC (Reed-Solomon). In such repeater systems the device can be operated in regenerator mode (decode and re-encode). Selected SDH/SONET overhead can be non-intrusively monitored. High speed bipolar multiplexors divide the incoming data frequency to a CMOS compatible one (this results in a data clock rate of e.g. 2.5 GHz per two bytes).

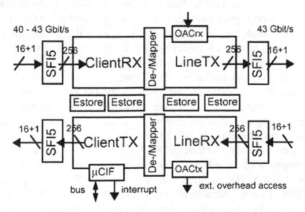

**Fig. 1.** UFEC40G device architecture

The device can be accessed through a control interface (CTLI-D, Control Interface for ASIC Device) for configuring or monitoring the internal state or event/delta registers. An interrupt pin exists for signalling the assertion of an interrupt register. For better handling two types of interrupt registers are implemented: Events indicate special occurrences during device operation, e.g. a buffer overflow. Deltas are used to signal changes of internal device state registers. Every interrupt source is maskable via special bits. If an interrupt occurs it is for example possible to read all the interrupt registers to find the triggering one and then reading the corresponding state bit. It is then possible to reconfigure the device depending on the state, e.g. to change the data transmission mode or to reset the device. Alternatively, it is also possible to poll for a certain event or delta continuously. The design consists of 580.000 loc RT level VHDL written by a team of 10 designers.

### 3.1  The Device Requirements Document

The structure of our device requirements document is quite simple. We have two kinds of requirements, general ones and others dealing with register access. The general requirements are verified in the context together with other requirements. Whereas in principle it is possible to write a testcase per control requirement. The register access description is straight forward and best represented using a tabular notation. First of all the type and name is shown followed by the different possible settings in the description column. This can be a simple condition or a more complex expression if other registers are involved (e.g. alarm indication signal AIS computation over different protocol layers). Although the single requirements are not very complex the over all system complexity is enormous. In total we have more than 800 requirements and they are verifiable in detail only simulating the top level device RT level VHDL description.

## 4  Data Management – VHDL Development System

The design's RT level and verification databases consist of about 900 VHDL files (~600k loc) and related (synthesis/verification) scripts within ~3,000 files. These files have complex dependencies between each other, e.g., the modification of a VHDL package requires re-synthesis of all design blocks that are using this package. In addition, the design imports code from several re-use databases that provide commonly used functional blocks and packages. The design and verification teams were geographically located at three different locations in the USA, Germany and China so the data management system had to provide an efficient and reliable way to support cross-site development between these sites, including support for each sites specific UNIX platform environment (Sun, HP, Linux).

The VHDL Development System (VDS [8], Figure 2) is a commercially available Lucent Technologies tool suite that focuses on two key areas of large VHDL projects: data management and VHDL coding style. For the VHDL coding process itself, VDS provides a *VHDL Coding Standard* (VCS, [9]) document which is enforced by a dedicated VCS checker tool (vlint) and a VHDL formatter (vfmt). In addition, VHDL-sensitive editor modes and auxiliary tools like a pretty-printer for VHDL code are provided. The major part of VDS deals with data management issues. All data management features are provided on command line level (separate shell tools like 'pci' or 'pco') as well as on GUI level. Two GUI applications provide convenient access to the DM functionality: *vguide* visualizes the database and provides access to all related functionality, so its name is often used as a synonym for the entire data management system. In addition, the *pguide* GUI visualizes the inter-project dependencies (project data imports), which is required by the project administrators.

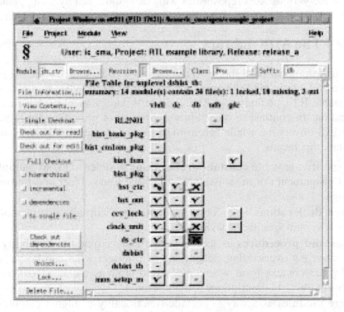

**Fig. 2.** Vguide project window

The key concepts/features of the vguide data management system are as follows:

- The databases are physically isolated from the user's working space. Data access happens on file level, by explicitly checking in/out files.
- The database itself is represented by a plain directory tree, the structure of which is open and configurable. It can be accessed on *file system level* (site-local, just by referring to the project directory path) or on *remote level* (cross-site, by referring to the IPC port/host of a dedicated 'vdspd' project server daemon). In addition, the remote server daemons support *mirror projects*, which significantly improve the performance across slow network links. A *mirror slave* is an identical copy of its *mirror master* and can even be accessed on file system level at the remote site. All update and synchronization issues are automatically handled by the vdspd server daemons of master and slave(s).
- The database 'knows' the design hierarchy and the dependencies between the various files. Based on this information, it provides support for hierarchical tree checkouts, script file generation (e.g., VHDL compile or synthesis). This also includes the detection of '**out-of-date**' conditions on derived files (e.g., vguide detects if a .db file requires a re-synthesis).
- In addition, vguide offers features like project release management, support of various user authorization levels and an email notification that can be bound to certain events within the database.

The base data management features like revision control, branching and locking are provided by the (open source) RCS tools. All vguide-specific configuration files are plain ASCII so there are no binary file formats involved. This ensures that the structure of the entire database directory is open and well-known. In fact, you even could access the various RCS repositories without vguide, just by using plain RCS.

## 5  Reuse – The ADK Library

The ASIC Development Kit Library ADKLIB is a VHDL source code library, providing reusable and configurable library elements for SDH/SONET applications, written in synthesizable RTL coding style. The concept is independent of any particular system application. In contrast to other library approaches providing hardware modules only, ADKLIB covers the whole spectrum of library elements, VHDL is able to support. In detail, this means:

- system specific, reusable **constant declarations** in order to avoid multiple declaration and assignment ('or miss-assignment') of the same object in different locations in a design.
- **data type declarations** in order to guarantee the correct specification of value ranges in a system specific behavior.
- **functions and procedures** as the basic elements providing reusability in a very flexible way, e.g overloading, scheduling of registers what can be partially influenced by the context from where the subprogram is called, avoidance of large numbers of structural descriptions (instantiations).
- **hardware modules** as a way to provide functionality of higher complexity, when e.g. the number of signal parameters is unsuitable for subprogram usage.
- **component declarations** in order to simplify the creation of structural VHDL programs instantiating ADKLIB modules.

The ADKLIB library elements are provided via packages, entities, architectures and configurations. Because ADKLIB is a source code library, it is independent of any VHDL simulation platform. For gate level synthesis, library elements are intended for the current version of Synopsys Design Compiler. All VHDL programs provided are revision controlled using our data management system (see section 4). The same approach is used for maintaining the HTML library documentation which is connected to the vhdl database. Some pages of the present document provide direct access to VHDL source code. This source code is automatically updated, each times the library documentation is checked out from the documentation database (weekly). The ADKLIB elements are classified into four different classes, designated as level I to IV. The library elements of each level are mainly based on elements of levels below. From the lowest level to the highest, the library elements are more and more specialized and complex. Consequently the degree of reusability decreases whereas the expense for modeling, verification and maintenance increases. **Level I and II** are dominated by constant declarations, data types, small functions and procedures, provided by packages. In comparison with it, **level III and IV** are represented by entities, architectures and environment packages. The environment package basically provides composite interface data types and a component declaration for the related design unit. In the current application the elements on **level I and II** are based on small SDH specific functions, procedures, data types and constants with a high degree of reusability. The expense for modeling and verification is small. A high degree of adaptability to different data path architectures and different interfaces is achieved by function and procedure overloading. Procedures of level II are more complex and composed by level I procedures in general. **Level III and IV** are mainly represented by library modules. In this context a module will be defined as a design unit consisting of an entity, architecture and configuration. Additionally each module of the ADKLIB uses a specific environment package. A module is either structural, what means an interconnection of sub modules, or an rt_module, what means a behavioral description on RT-Level composed by processes, functions and procedures. If a module is structural, then the sub modules use the environment package of the top level module. RT_MODULES of the ADKLIB are typically partitioned into a functional part which is independent of the environment and an interface part.

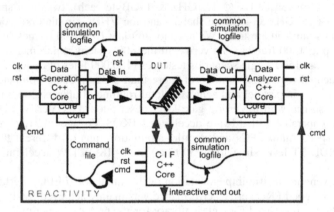

**Fig. 3.** Testbench Overview

# 6  Verification – The PROVerify Simulation Environment

The top level simulation testbench is quite simple. It is only an instantiation of some drivers/monitors, the device and the testbench controller CIF (CPUInterFace). The simulation is set and controlled by the CIF interpreting the main command file and communicating with the device like the software in the "real" world. The CIF command language provides constructs for easily controlling/setting ASIC registers and interacting between all the testbench components. The main parts are the CIF, the DUT (Device Under Test) and the frame generator/analyzer. The generator/analyzer can be reconfigured during simulation by the CIF (see Figure 3). The data flow is very simple: The generator sends the SONET/SDH data input to the DUT which sends the data output to the analyzer. The CIF sends commands to the driver/monitors using a simple string based broadcast mechanism. Each command has a prefix with the name of the recipient at first, e.g. "gen payload 0xab". That means that only the component named "gen" interprets the string. From the next frame on the generator "gen" will fill the payload area with 0xab in every byte. The CIF clock/reset generator can be switched on/off or the clock period can be changed (e.g. to simulate a clock drift). The simulation time is measured in generator frame pulses. All the commands in the main CIF command file are synchronized to either the generator or the analyzer frame pulse. So we are completely time independent and synchronized to frame boundaries. With this event based approach all the testcases (command files) work on every platform and produce the same results. All components write their results in a common simulation log file. The generator frame pulses mark the advance in "frame times". PROVerify testcases can be used on behavioral, RT, gate and board level (we partly "re-use" command files written for RT level simulations on board level for the ASIC validation). The corresponding PROVerify source code consists of approximately 40.000 lines of C++. Its strict object oriented design allows for relatively easy extension towards new protocols. The foreign language interface (FLI) of VHDL is used to offer a seamless integration into the standard simulation flow.

SUN Workstations (2 CPUs @ 900 MHz & 18 GByte), a medium equipped Linux-PC compute farm (36 CPUs @ 1.3 GHz & 1 GByte each), two high speed Linux-PCs(2 CPUs@2.2 GHz & 4 GByte shared) and the VHDL simulators Cadence ncsim 3.2 and MTI vsim 5.5d are used. We need to simulate 10 to 100 frames (in some special cases up to 1000 frames). To verify all the 800 system requirements we have to create more than 1500 single scenarios testcases (120.000 lines of code). This leads to a total sequential regression runtime of more than 5 days. Using compute farms we can start the runs in parallel and achieve a total runtime of approx 2 to 3 days. Some tests were also run with a Verilog gate level description. PROVerify RTL performance was comparable to hardware accelerated IKOS Voyager 3.21, or even better using high-speed Linux- PCs and parallel simulation runs of different testcases (10 frames: VHDL-RT level simulation: 30 to 60 min – IKOS HW accelerator: 20 to 80 min).

Also the vendor specific implementation of the simulators FLI/C-interface is a real bottleneck, the good PROVerify performance was mainly achieved by the decision to develop a highly optimized C++ class library for the protocol generation/verification, the CPU interface and the different simulator/platform dependent C-wrappers. Together with the device the simulation performance of cadence ncsim was the best even with the worst C-interface (the runtimes are very testcase dependent and vary from 30 to 60 min.). The pure C-interface performance depends strongly on the bitwidth of the input signals. A solution of that interface problem could be the usage of SystemC as testbench language with the possibility of integrating foreign VHDL/Verilog modules. With that approach also the debugging problems could be solved if the simulators/debuggers would be able to deal with SystemC/C++/VHDL/Verilog code all in parallel (as they do it today with VHDL/Verilog).

## 6.1  Verification Strategy: Hierarchy

An SoC design is, by definition, too complex to thoroughly verify at the full-chip level. Therefore a hierarchical verification method was adopted, where thorough testing was performed at the block level, and cursory (but still complete) testing was performed at the full-chip level. For example, in block level tests, each state machine must be thoroughly and completely tested. By contrast, for full-chip simulations, it is only necessary to verify that the design meets its requirements, and to be sure to test inter-block connectivity, since that is not tested by block-level tests. The hierarchical

SoC verification strategy we adopted ensures that the design undergoes two independent levels of verification, which substantially reduces the likelihood of an undetected bug and helps to ensure a high quality result.

## 6.2  Verification Strategy: Independent V-Team

It is also important to note that the full-chip verification team was largely independent of the design team, so that the full-chip testcases would not be tainted by prior knowledge of the device's internal design and operation. Each block must pass it's own blocklevel tests prior to integration in a full-chip design release. Then, a simple full-chip "passthrough" testcase was run with the new block as part of the integration to ensure basic functionality. This testcase and it's logfile were part of the handoff package in Vguide so that it can be re-run at any location to ensure successful design transfer. Once the VHDL release is created, the "passthrough" testcase and logfile are in Vguide, and release notes are written, the design can be handed off for full-chip verification.

## 6.3  Verification Principles (Commonality, Compatibility and Self-checking)

Since the verification team comprised 10 verifiers in 3 widely separated locations (Europe, USA, China), communication was a potentially serious challenge which was overcome by adhering to three basic principles for verification. First was commonality of the verification environment across locations. A single common top-level test bench was used at all three locations, which allowed test cases created in one location to be easily re-run and debugged at any of the other locations, and prevented duplicate debugging efforts related to inconsistencies between test benches. In addition, all test cases and simulation log files were shared between locations. The Vguide system made it easy to ensure that each location used the same verification environment.

Second, each major release was backward compatible with previous releases (except, of course, for bugfixes). This allowed test cases created for one release to be easily reused with subsequent releases for regression testing. Since the design is divided into 4 major sub blocks (Figure 1), the plan was to have 4 major releases of the top-level testbench where each release incorporated one new major sub block. One of the things that helped to ensure compatibility between releases was that the UFEC device had more or less the final pinout (data in/out, clocking) in the first functional release. It is also important to note that the "zeroth" release of the top level testbench included only data generators and analyzers, but allowed the verification team to begin developing testcases and automated regression test scripts. As a result, verification and design were fully concurrent activities; while one release was being verified, the next release was being developed.

The third important principle for verification was to write self-checking test cases (at least to the extent that it was feasible). With each major release of the top level testbench a complete regression simulation of all the testcases is done. Such runs needed approx. 3 days (which was typically run over a weekend). The CIF command language (part of ProVerify) made it easy to implement a powerful message passing structure in which failed requirement checks print ERROR messages. These messages are collected at the end of the testcase run – analysis of the regression run is quite simple: no news is good news. The overall verification status was then automatically collected and maintained in an Excel spreadsheet, which acted as a cross reference between the list of design requirements and the verification test cases. Each row of the spreadsheet represented one design requirement to be verified, and contained information such as the affected sub blocks, the design status of the sub block (implemented or not), the name of the verifier, the status (e.g. Pass, Fail, BugTrack), the priority of the requirement (e.g. H, M,L), the name of the testcase(s) that covered the requirement, and a link to a bugtracker entry (if available). By organizing the information this way, it was easy to create pivot tables showing progress by block or by verifier, as well as to create plots showing progress over time, which simplified project management and resource allocation.The overall status report was distributed to team members and also to management on a weekly basis.

### 6.4  Equivalence Checking

In addition to an intensive gate2gate equivalence check we also ran RTL2gate comparisons. We use different checking tools whereas the Infineon toolset CVE ([5]) made the best results (on RT level it is far ahead in runtime and complexity - equivalents to 100 K gates can be checked in minutes of CPU time). Due to tough project plans and milestones RTL2gate checking is of increasing significance (gate level netlist of one sub block is sent to the foundry before the verification is finished). If one "issue" popped up and the code is fixed, a block level RTL2gates check is done together with a regression simulation on top level (re-running all the testcases/requirements of that block which are controllable/viewable on top level).

## 7  Summary

Closing the productivity gap not only means moving to a higher level of abstraction but also means improving the methodology on lower levels and the interworking of tools and flows between the levels. We described our approaches for closing that gap and presented tools and methodologies, some of which were used for the first time in a distributed design project. The foundation of the project was the device requirements document – both the design team and verification team used it to guide their work. It was a comprehensive source of information needed during the project. The VHDL Development System worked excellent, enabling the design and verification teams to easily share and maintain ADK-lib, RTL, testbenches, testcases, scripts and logfiles. Vguide's distributed architecture with "master" and "slave/mirror" servers reduced the overall bandwidth needed for data transmission between locations. Pguide made it easy to create and maintain design releases and formed a very effective project administration tool. The C++-based PROVerify toolsuite is powerful and definitely had a positive impact on the project. The verification environment was common across locations, compatible from release to release and self-checking. Results from the self checking tests were automatically collected and presented using an Excel spreadsheet. Simulation using Linux compute farms was very cost effective and worked well for us especially for running regressions.

# 8  Outlook

Our next steps are going towards a formalization of the specification of our device requirements documents and to introduce model checking techniques at the specification level. This will be an application specific approach based on software cost reduction [6], [7] and we intend to adopt this methodologies to the needs of future hardware specifications. With that approach we would be able to formally verify complex system specifications before the first RT level VHDL code is written. An other research direction goes towards reconfigurable embedded cores, e.g. FPGA/FPFA or processor cores. Using reconfigurable cores for the monitoring and maintenance functionality would lead to shorter over all verification cycles due to an effort shift from RT level to board level. At RT level only the main data path verification must be done but the main verification of the reconfigurable parts could be done in the real hardware environment on board level. Another effect of reconfigurable SoCs are potentially savings in redesign costs when e.g. the protocol standard (SONET/SDH) was reworked and the monitoring/ maintenance needs some feature enhancements or standard adoption.

# References

1. Smith , Kahng: A New Design Cost Model for the 2001 ITRS, Proceedings of ISQED 2002, IEEE 0-7695-1561-4/02
2. Moretti: System Level Design merits a closer look, EDN www.edamag.com, Feb. 21th., 2002
3. ITU-T G.709/Y.1331: Interfaces for the optical transport network
4. ITU-T G.707/Y.1322: Network node interface for the Synchronous Digital Hierarchy (SDH)
5. Drechsler, Höreth: Gatecomp: Equivalence Checking of Digital Circuits in an Industrial Environment, International Workshop on Boolean Problems, pages 195-200, Freiberg, 2002
6. Haas, Heinkel, Gossens: Integration of Formal Specification into the Standard ASIC Design Flow, 7th IEEE/IEICE International Symposium on High Assurance Systems Engineering, Tokio, 2002.
7. Heitmeyer, Jeffords, Labaw: Automated consistency checking of requirements specifications, ACM Transactions on Software Engineering and Methodology, 5(3):231-261, 1996.
8. Sahm, Mayer, Pleickhardt, Schuck: VHDL Development System and Coding Standard, Design Automation Conference Las Vegas 1996
9. Sahm, Mayer, Pleickhardt, Späth: OMI-326 VHDL Coding Standard, Omimo 1996

# Register-Based Permutation Networks
# for Stride Permutations

Tuomas Järvinen and Jarmo Takala

Tampere University of Technology, P.O.Box 553, FIN-33101 Tampere, Finland
{tuomas.jarvinen,jarmo.takala}@tut.fi

**Abstract.** In several digital signal processing algorithms, intermediate results between computational stages are reordered according to stride permutations. If such algorithms are computed in parallel with reduced number of processing elements where one element computes several computational nodes, the permutation, instead of being hardwired, requires a storage of intermediate data elements. In this paper, register-based permutation networks for stride permutations are proposed. The proposed networks are regular and scalable and they support any stride of power-of-two. In addition, the networks reach the minimum of register complexity, i.e., the number of registers, indicating area-efficiency.

## 1 Introduction

Several high-speed implementations of digital signal processing algorithms are based on array processor concept, e.g., Cooley-Tukey radix-$2^s$ fast Fourier transform (FFT) algorithms have been realized with cascaded processing elements computing radix-$2^s$ butterfly operations. Due to the data-dependencies, the data sequences between the processing elements need to be permuted implying need for special interconnection networks. In the derivation of Cooley-Tukey $2^n$-point radix-2 decimation-in-frequency FFT algorithm, the principal method is to interleave the results of two $2^{n-1}$-point FFTs resulting in a perfect shuffle permutation.

In general, the interconnection topologies in Cooley-Tukey radix-$2^s$ FFT algorithms are based on stride-by-$2^s$ permutations. Stride-by-$S$ permutation of a $N$-point sequence reorders the elements of a vector $X = (x_0, x_1, \ldots, x_{N-1})$ as $Y = (x_0, x_S, x_{2S}, \ldots, x_{N-S+1}, x_1, x_{S+1} \ldots, x_{N-1})^T$. Therefore, the perfect shuffle is a special case of stride permutations. Another special case is the matrix transpose which can also be interpreted as a stride permutation. Such stride permutations can be found in discrete cosine, wavelet, sine, and Hartley transforms. The same topology is found also in trellis diagrams of $k/n$ code rate convolutional encoders.

In radix-$2^s$ algorithms, the computation of the basic operational node requires $2^s$ operands implying need for a multi-port reordering unit if several nodes are allocated to one processing element. As an example, a 16-point FFT computed with various levels of parallelism is illustrated in Fig. 1 where permutation

A. Pimentel and S. Vassiliadis (Eds.): SAMOS 2004, LNCS 3133, pp. 108–117, 2004.
© Springer-Verlag Berlin Heidelberg 2004

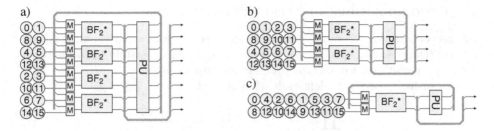

**Fig. 1.** 16-point FFT computation with: a) four butterflies b) two butterflies, and c) one butterfly. $BF_2^*$: Radix-2 FFT butterfly computation. PU: Permutation unit.

unit (PU) is used to permute, i.e., reorder the intermediate data elements. Such an unit can be realized with multi-port memories or multiple parallel memory modules. However, if the sequence length is short, the memory-based realizations are not area-efficient and, therefore, register-based realizations are preferred.

The traditional approach to perform the stride-by-$S$ permutation in cascaded FFT structures is a multi-port commutator, e.g., in [1], which consists of skewed delay lines and a multi-port switch performing complex periodic switching patterns. The drawback of this approach is the complexity of the switching element. In [2], a Viterbi decoder is described where the stride permutations are realized with the aid of parallel tapped first-in, first-out (FIFO) buffers; several data elements are written into consecutive FIFO locations, shift of several elements is performed, and the data elements are read from the tapped outputs. Such an approach requires complex write, shift, and read schemes and the system is actually a multi-rate system requiring FIFOs to operate at higher frequency than the sample clock.

In [3], a sequential permutation network is proposed, which performs arbitrary permutations but only for data in sequential form. The permutations can be realized with the data format converters proposed in [4] and the paper also defines the theoretical lower bound for the number of registers in such converters. However, due to their one-dimensional structure, the multiplexer complexity is high. This can be reduced by using two-dimensional structures as described in [5–7]. They all use heuristics in the structural generation which may cause difficulties in automated design procedures. In addition, the irregular connection wiring in such cases may dominate the overall area consumption [6].

In this paper, permutation networks for power-of-two's strides are derived based on the decompositions of stride permutations. The proposed method is based on the parameterized decomposition of stride permutation matrix and the parameters are the sequence length $N$, $N = 2^n$, the number of ports $Q$, $Q = 2^q$, and the stride $S$, $S = 2^s$. The networks have regular topology and their structures are created without heuristics alleviating the automated design procedure. In addition, they result in the minimum number of registers and use less multiplexers than the earlier networks. Finally, the control generation is simple and can be done with synchronous binary counters.

## 2    Decompositions of Stride Permutations

In this section, the decompositions of stride permutations are derived. A square matrix transpose is a special case and will be covered separately from the other stride permutations. First, some preliminaries are given.

For ordinary products, left evaluation is used, i.e.,

$$\prod_{i=0}^{n} A_i = A_0 \cdot A_1 \cdot A_2 \cdot \ldots \cdot A_n . \tag{1}$$

The formulation used here is based on tensor products; tensor product (or Kronecker product) and direct sum are denoted by $\otimes$ and $\oplus$, respectively. The stride-by-$S$ permutation matrix of order $N$ is a square matrix $P_{N,S}$ where the elements of the matrix are defined as

$$P_{N,S}(m,n) = \begin{cases} 1, \text{iff } n = (mS \bmod N) + \lfloor mS/N \rfloor \\ 0, \text{otherwise} \end{cases} . \tag{2}$$

where mod is the modulus operation and $\lfloor \cdot \rfloor$ is the floor function.

**Theorem 1.** *Stride permutations are periodic* [8], *i.e.,*

$$P_{N,S}^{-1} = P_{N,S}^{T} = P_{N,N/S} . \tag{3}$$

Finally, a special permutation matrix $J_K$ of order $K$ is defined as

$$J_K = \left(I_2 \otimes P_{K/2,K/4}\right) P_{K,2} = P_{K,K/2} \left(I_2 \otimes P_{K/2,2}\right) . \tag{4}$$

The permutation $J_K$ exchanges the odd elements in the first half of a vector with the even elements of the last half of the vector.

### 2.1    Square Matrix Transpose

The basis of our approach to stride permutations is the transpose of a square matrix. In [9], an iterative method to transpose an $S \times S$ matrix transpose is proposed as follows: in the first step, the matrix is divided into $2 \times 2$ submatrices which are transposed. Then, in the second step, the matrix is divided into $4 \times 4$ submatrices where the block size is $2 \times 2$ and such submatrices are transposed in block wise. The operation is continued $\log_2 S$ steps till the sizes of the submatrices and blocks are $S$ and $(S/2)^2$, respectively. The operation can also be described that in every step, $2 \times 2$ submatrices are transposed where the block size is multiplied by four after each step. In [9], the described iterative method is used to develop an $S$-port structure for transposing an $S \times S$ matrix.

We have generalized the method to less number of ports, $1 \le Q \le S$, which results in the decomposition of permutation $P_{2^{2s},2^s}$ for $Q$-port network, $Q = 2^q$, as follows:

$$P_{2^{2s},2^s}(2^q) = \prod_{m=s-1}^{q} \left[I_{2^{s-m-1}} \otimes J_{2^{s+1}} \otimes I_{2^m}\right] \left(I_{2^{2s-q}} \otimes P_{2^q,2}\right) \cdot$$

$$\prod_{i=q}^{1} \left[\left(I_{2^{s-i}} \otimes J_{2^{s+i}}\right)\left(I_{2^{2s-i}} \otimes J_{2^i}\right)\right], \quad 0 \le q \le s . \tag{5}$$

The proof for the decomposition can be found in [10].

Since now $Q$ data elements enter the network at a time, $Q \leq S$, the $S^2$ data elements are given in a $Q \times S^2/Q$ matrix of which $Q$ elements are taken in column wise. First, the permutations of type $(I_{2^{s-i-1}} \otimes J_{2^{s+i+1}})(I_{2^{2s-i-1}} \otimes J_{2^{i+1}})$ are made which follows the interpretation in [9], i.e., the recursive transpose of 2-by-2 submatrices, $i = (q-1, q-2, \ldots, 0)$. Then, the rows are reordered with $(I_{2^{2s-q}} \otimes P_{2^q,2})$ which is a spatial permutation since its size equals to the number of ports. The final term, $(I_{2^{s-m-1}} \otimes J_{2^{s+1}} \otimes I_{2^m})$ is a temporal-only permutation which reorders the $Q$-element columns.

## 2.2 Power-of-Two Strides

In [11], the decomposition of stride permutations was proposed for strides $S$, $S > Q$. Such decomposition does not result in the minimum number of registers in all cases. However, it can be utilized for one-dimensional stride permutation networks since, in such case, the minimum number of registers is attained. For the one-dimensional stride permutation network the decomposition derived in [11] is given as

$$P_{2^n,2^s}(1) = \prod_{i=0}^{n-s-1} \prod_{j=0}^{s-1} \left[ I_{2^{s+i-j-1}} \otimes P_{4,2} \otimes I_{2^{n+j-s-i-1}} \right], Q = 1 \wedge S \neq \sqrt{N} . \quad (6)$$

Next, let us focus on the decomposition of stride permutations for two-dimensional permutation networks where the number of ports $Q$ can be varied, $Q = 2^q$, $1 \leq q \leq n$. Before introducing the decompositions, a modified stride $R$,

$$R = \min(S, N/S), \quad (7)$$

is defined. In the following, the decomposition for two-dimensional networks is divided into three cases depending on the parameters $N$, $Q$, and $R$. The $N$ data elements are given in $Q \times N/Q$ matrix where a block of $Q$ data elements is read by the network in column wise at a time. The resulting stride-by-$S$ ordered data elements are given in a similar matrix.

**Case 1: $Q > N/R$.** It can be proved that in this case

**Theorem 2.** *The number of ports $Q$ is always larger than stride $R$, if $Q > N/R$.*

**Theorem 3.** *The number of ports $Q$ is always larger than $N/Q$, if $Q > N/R$.*

The proofs of the theorems are left out. The decomposition in this case is given as

$$P_{2^n,2^r}(2^q) = (I_{2^{n-q}} \otimes P_{2^q,2^r})(I_{2^q} \otimes P_{2^{n-q},2}) \prod_{i=n-q}^{1} [(I_{2^{n-q-i}} \otimes J_{2^{q+i}}) \cdot$$

$$(I_{2^{n-i}} \otimes J_{2^i})](I_{2^{n-r}} \otimes P_{2^r,2^{q+r-n}}), \quad Q > N/R . \quad (8)$$

In the decomposition, the submatrix transposes are made in $n - q$ steps following the iterative method described earlier. Before and after the transposes, however, other permutations are needed. In this case, prior to submatrix transposes, the permutation $(I_{2^{n-r}} \otimes P_{2^r,2^{q+r-n}})$ is made which reorders the rows. Such a permutation is a spatial permutation according to (2) because its size, $R$, is smaller than the number of ports, and thus, it can be hardwired. After the transposes, another hardwired spatial permutation, $(I_{2^q} \otimes P_{2^{n-q},2})$, is made. The permutation is spatial since the size of the permutation, $2^{n-q}$, is smaller than the number of ports according to (3). The final permutation, $(I_{2^{n-q}} \otimes P_{2^q,2^r})$, is again a spatial permutation since its size equals to the number of ports.

**Case 2: $Q \leq N/R \wedge Q \geq R$.** In this case, the decomposition is given as follows

$$P_{2^n,2^r}(2^q) = (P_{2^{n-q},2^r} \otimes I_{2^q})(I_{2^{n-q}} \otimes P_{2^q,2^r})(I_{2^{n-r}} \otimes P_{2^r,2}) \cdot$$
$$\prod_{i=r}^{1}[(I_{2^{n-q-i}} \otimes J_{2^{q+i}})(I_{2^{n-i}} \otimes J_{2^i})], \quad Q \leq N/R \wedge Q \geq R . \quad (9)$$

In the decomposition, the first permutation is the submatrix transposes made in $r$ steps. Then, the permutation of rows $(I_{2^{n-r}} \otimes P_{2^r,2})$ is made which is a spatial permutation since its size $R$ is smaller than the number of ports according to the constraint $Q \geq R$. Similarly, the next permutation $(I_{2^{n-q}} \otimes P_{2^q,2^r})$ is a spatial one since its size equals the number of ports. On the contrary, the last permutation $(P_{2^{n-q},2^r} \otimes I_{2^q})$ is temporal-only because it reorders the columns by picking up every $R$th column.

**Case 3: $Q \leq N/R \wedge Q < R$.** In the third case, the decomposition is given as

$$P_{2^n,2^r}(2^q) = (P_{2^{n-q},2^r} \otimes I_{2^q})(I_{2^{n-q}} \otimes P_{2^q,2}) \prod_{i=q}^{1}[(I_{2^{n-q-i}} \otimes J_{2^{q+i}})$$
$$(I_{2^{n-i}} \otimes J_{2^i})](I_{2^{n-q-r}} \otimes P_{2^r,2^{r-q}} \otimes I_{2^q}), Q \leq N/R \wedge Q < R. \quad (10)$$

Prior to submatrix transposes, the columns of the matrix are reordered according to $(I_{2^{n-q-r}} \otimes P_{2^r,2^{r-q}} \otimes I_{2^q})$. Then, the submatrix transposes are performed in $q$ steps. After the transposes, the rows are reordered with $(I_{2^{n-q}} \otimes P_{2^q,2})$, which is a spatial permutation. In the final permutation $(P_{2^{n-q},2^r} \otimes I_{2^q})$ the columns are reordered by picking every $R$th column.

In the three previous cases, three different decompositions of stride permutation matrices are given based on the design parameters $N$, $Q$, and $R$. However, the proofs are left out due to space limitations. In the decompositions, the modified stride $R$ is used, which relation to stride $S$ is given in (7), and based on that the decomposition of stride-by-$S$ permutation of size $N$ for $Q$-port network, $P_{2^n,2^s}(2^q)$, can be stated as

$$P_{2^n,2^s}(2^q) = \begin{cases} P_{2^n,2^r}(2^q), & S = R \\ P_{2^n,2^r}^T(2^q), & \text{otherwise} \end{cases} . \quad (11)$$

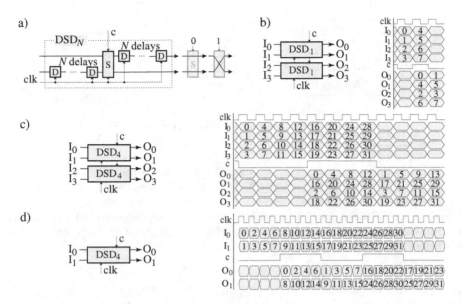

**Fig. 2.** 4-port DSD permutation networks. a) principle block diagram of DSD unit, and block and timing diagrams of b) $J_8$ permutation, c) $J_{32}$ permutation, d) $(I_2 \otimes J_{16})$ permutation. $c$ : control signal. $clk$ : clock signal.

The previous statement can be described as follows: if the stride $S$ is smaller than $N/S$, $R$ equals to $S$ and the decomposition results directly in the stride-by-$S$ permutation network. On the contrary, if the stride $S$ is larger than $N/S$, the resulting stride-by-$R$ permutation network must be reversed for stride-by-$S$ permutations, since $R = N/S$.

## 3  Realizations

In the following, realizations of the previous decompositions are discussed. First, basic switching units are reviewed in short and their capability to perform different permutations is explained. A more detailed review is found in [10]. Finally, the permutation networks based on the given decompositions are given.

**Basic Switching Units.** Two different basic switching units are selected for temporal permutations: a Delay-Switch-Delay (DSD) and a Shift-Exchange-Units (SEU). The principal block diagrams of both units are shown in Fig. 2(a) and Fig. 3(a), respectively. With DSD units, the temporal permutations originated in the folding of the $J$ permutation can be realized; the $J_{2QK}$ permutation over $Q$ ports can be realized with $Q/2$ parallel $DSD_K$ units as illustrated in Fig. 2(b,c). In addition, a 2-port realization of $(I_2 \otimes J_{16})$ with the corresponding timing diagram is shown in Fig. 2(d).

With SEUs, the temporal permutations of type $J$ are realized for sequential data streams. In addition, permutations of type $(I_N \otimes J_K \otimes I_{MQ})$ can be

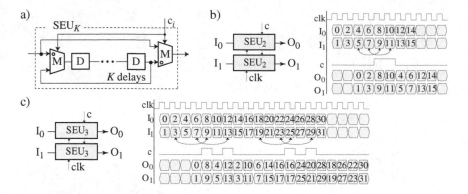

**Fig. 3.** 2-port SEU permutation networks a) principal block diagram of SEU, and block and timing diagrams of b) $(J_{16} \otimes I_2)$ and c) $(P_{4,2} \otimes I_4)$ permutations. $c$ : control signal. $clk$ : clock signal.

realized with $Q$ parallel $\text{SEU}_{M(K/2-1)}$ units, $M = 2^m$, $Q = 2^q$, $K = 2^k$. As an example, a 2-port realization of $(J_{16} \otimes I_2)$ is shown in Fig. 3(b) with the corresponding timing diagram in Fig. 3(d). Furthermore, permutations of type $(I_M \otimes P_{4,2} \otimes I_{QN})$ can be realized with SEUs. As an example, a 2-port realization of $(P_{4,2} \otimes I_4)$ is shown in Fig. 3(c) with corresponding timing diagram in Fig. 3(e). Finally, permutations of type $(I_K \otimes P_{M,S} \otimes I_Q)$ can be realized with $Q$ parallel SEUs by noting that the permutation is temporal only.

**Resulting Stride Permutation Networks.** Next, realizations of stride-by-$S$ permutations are discussed starting from the square matrix transpose, since the submatrix transposes are the basic operations found in all the decompositions of stride permutations for two-dimensional stride permutation networks.

The square matrix transpose is decomposed according to (5) and the block diagram for the general matrix transpose network is given in [10]. A special case is $X \times X$ matrix transpose over $X$ ports, which block diagram is depicted in Fig. 4. It consists of $\log_2 X$ stages of $2^{q-1}$ parallel DSD units which perform temporal permutations of type $(I_M \otimes J_{KQ})$, $M = 2^m$, $Q = 2^q$, $K = 2^k$. Between the DSD stages, there are spatial-only permutations which can be hardwired. The depicted network is referred to as a matrix transpose network $\text{MTN}_X$ and it will be used as a part of the two-dimensional networks.

The decomposition of stride-by-$S$ permutations, $N \neq S^2$, for one-dimensional, i.e., sequential networks is done according to (6), and the resulting network is depicted in Fig. 5(a). When $N = S^2$, the decomposition is done according to (5) and the resulting network is shown in Fig. 5(b). Both the networks consists of cascaded SEUs of various sizes. Such networks are basic units for two-dimensional networks, and thus we call them a sequential permutation network $\text{SPN}_{N,S}$ which performs a stride-by-$S$ permutation of size $N$.

For two-dimensional networks, one of the three different decompositions is selected based on the parameters $N$, $Q$, and $S$. Instead of using the stride $S$ in

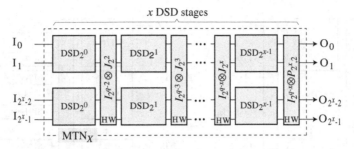

**Fig. 4.** Principal block diagram of $X \times X$ matrix transpose network $\mathrm{MTN}_X$ over $X$ ports. $X = 2^x$. HW: hardwired permutation.

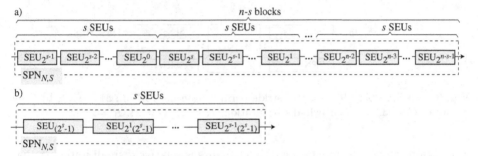

**Fig. 5.** Principal block diagram of sequential stride permutation network $\mathrm{SPN}_{N,S}$ for $P_{N,S}$ permutations when a)$N \neq S^2$ and b) $N = S^2$. $N = 2^n$. $S = 2^s$.

the decompositions, the modified stride $R$ is used. For each three decompositions, the resulting network is different, as illustrated in Fig. 6. However, some commonalities are found including the submatrix transposes and temporal-only permutations, which can be realized with parallel MTN and SPN units, respectively. All the other permutations are spatial-only permutations since their size equals or is less than the number of ports, and thus they can be hardwired.

It can be proved, that the number of registers in the proposed networks equals to the theoretical lower bound given in [4]. Moreover, due to the regular structure of the proposed networks, the wiring area may be reduced compared to [5–7], which all use heuristics in the network generation. In addition, the control of the proposed networks is simpler and can be managed with synchronous binary counters. However, in order to have realistic comparisons, the networks including their control generators should be implemented on silicon.

## 4 Conclusions

In this paper, scalable and regular register-based networks were proposed for stride permutations. The networks can be used in array processors where the intermediate data between processing stages is reordered according to power-of-two stride permutations. Especially, the proposed networks are suitable for

116    Tuomas Järvinen and Jarmo Takala

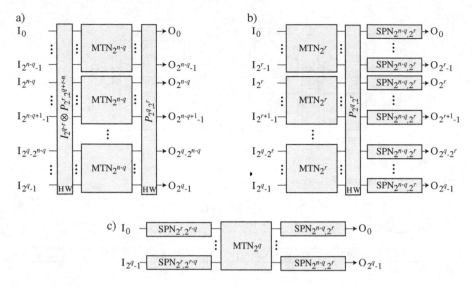

**Fig. 6.** Principal block diagram of stride permutation network in: a) Case 1, b) Case 2, and c) Case 3. HW: hardwired permutation. $N = 2^n$. $Q = 2^q$. $R = 2^r$.

realizations where the number of data elements is relatively small implying that memory-based structures would be expensive solutions.

# References

1. Bidet, E., Castelain, D., Joanblang, C., Senn, P.: A fast single-chip implementation of 8192 complex point FFT. IEEE Journal of Solid-State Circuits. Vol. 30 No. 3 (1995) 300–305
2. Bóo, M., Argüello, F., Bruguera, J., Doallo, R., Zapata, E.: High-performance VLSI architecture for the Viterbi algorithm. IEEE Transactions on Communications. Vol. 45 No. 2 (1997) 168–176
3. Shung, C. B., Lin, H. D., Cypher, R., Siegel, P. H., Thapar, H. K.: Area-efficient architectures for the Viterbi algorithm. Part I: Theory. IEEE Transactions on Communications. Vol. 41 No. 4 (1993) 636–644
4. Parhi, K. K.: Systematic synthesis of DSP data format converters using life-time analysis and forward-backward register allocation. IEEE Transactions on Circuits and Systems – Part II: Analog and Digital Signal Processing. Vol. 39 No. 7 (1992) 423–440
5. Majumdar, M., Parhi, K. K.: Design of data format converters using two-dimensional register allocation. IEEE Transactions on Circuits and Systems – Part II: Analog and Digital Signal Processing. Vol. 45 No. 4 (1998) 504–508
6. Bae, J., Prasanna, V. K.: Synthesis of area-efficient and high-throughput rate data format converters. IEEE Transactions on Very Large Scale Integration (VLSI) Systems. Vol. 6 No. 4 (1998) 697–706
7. Srivatsan, K., Chakrabarti, C., Lucke, L.: A new register allocation scheme for low-power data format converters. IEEE Transactions on Circuits and Systems – Part II: Analog and Digital Signal Processing. Vol. 46 No. 9 (1999) 1250–1253

8. Granata, J., Conner, M., Tolimieri, R.: Recursive fast algorithms and the role of the tensor product. IEEE Transactions on Signal Processing. Vol. 40 No. 12 (1992) 2921–2930
9. Carlach, J. C., Penard, P., Sicre, J. L.: TCAD: a 27 MHz 8 × 8 discrete cosine transform chip. In Proc. IEEE International Conference on Acoustics, Speech, and Signal Processing. Glasgow, UK, May 23–26 (1989) 2429–2432
10. Takala, J., Järvinen, T.: Multi-port interconnection networks for matrix transpose. In Proc. IEEE International Conference on Acoustics, Speech, and Signal Processing, Phoenix, AZ, U.S.A., May 26–29 (2002) 874–877
11. Takala, J., Järvinen, T., Salmela, P., Akopian, D.: Multi-port interconnection networks for radix-$r$ algorithms. In Proc. IEEE International Conference on Acoustics, Speech, and Signal Processing, Salt Lake City, UT, U.S.A., May 7–11 (2001) 1177–1180

# A Family of Accelerators
# for Matrix-Vector Arithmetics
# Based on High-Radix Multiplier Structures

David Guevorkian, Petri Liuha, Aki Launiainen, and Ville Lappalainen

Nokia Research Center
{David.Guevorkian,Petri.Liuha,Aki.Launiainen,Ville.Lappalainen}@nokia.com

**Abstract.** A methodology for designing processor architectures oriented
to matrix-vector operations is proposed in this paper. The methodology is based on high-radix multiplication where first a list of potential
partial products (PPs) of one operand with all possible $t$-bit numbers
($t \in \{2, 3, 4\}$) are computed by simple shifts and additions, then selected
PPs from this list are shifted and added according to $t$-bit slices of the
other operand. Main advantage of the proposed method is that the list
of potential PPs may be reused whenever one multiplicand is to be multiplied with several multipliers. Another advantage is that the hardware
blocks involved for high-radix multiplication may also be used independently to implement other tasks such as parallel addition/subtractions,
accumulations. This allows introducing a group of modifications to high-
radix multiplier structures making them reconfigurable so that single devices having two-fold functionalities of either programmable processors
or reconfigurable hardware accelerators may be designed.

## 1 Introduction

Matrix-vector computations are among the most frequently used computationally intensive operations in many information processing tasks such as digital
signal, image and video processing, numerical analysis, computer graphics and
vision, *etc.* Therefore, in many cases specialized hardware means are used for
different matrix-vector operations (matrix-vector multiplication, convolution (or
FIR filtering), fast orthogonal transforms, *etc.*).

Traditional hardware implementations of matrix vector operations are based
either on programmable Digital Signal Processors (DSPs) or Application-Specific
Integrated Circuits (ASICs) such as systolic arrays, iterative processors, *etc*, or
Field-Programmable-Gate Arrays (FPGAs). As matrix-vector arithmetics extensively involves multiplications and additions, a typical hardware for such
arithmetics involves a number of multipliers or Multiply-Accumulate (MAC)
units and adders-subtractors with fixed or programmable interconnection between them. Exceptions are some early DSPs and microprocessors which did
not include special multiplier units but were implementing multiplication operation as a series of shifts and additions. The underlying multiplication method,

A. Pimentel and S. Vassiliadis (Eds.): SAMOS 2004, LNCS 3133, pp. 118–127, 2004.

however, was the radix-2 multiplication that needs $n$ shift-add operations to get the product $y = ax$ of $n-$bit multiplier $a$ with the multiplicand $x$ [1].

Conventionally, radix-4 Booth-recoded multipliers (see [1], [2]) or MAC units are considered as having the best performance. In these multipliers, the product $y = ax$ is obtained as the sum of partial products (PPs) $2^{2r}A_r x$, $r=0,1,\ldots,n/2$-$1$, of the multiplicand $x$, and $A_r \in \{-2, -1, 0, 1, 2\}$. Main advantages of these multipliers are the ease of finding the set of potential PPs (-2x, -x, 0, x, 2x), and the relatively small number $n/2$ of PPs to be added compared to radix-2 multipliers where $n$ PPs are to be added.

The number of PPs is further reduced in radix-$T(T > 4)$, multipliers where only $n/t$ ($t = log_2T$) PPs are added (see [4–6]). In these multipliers, similarly to the case of radix-4 Booth-recoded multipliers, multiplication operation is implemented in two steps. First a list of potential PPs of the multiplicand ($x$) with all possible $t$-bit numbers are computed. Then ($n/t$, $/t = log_2T$) selected PPs from this list are shifted and added according to $t$-bit slices of the multiplier $a$.

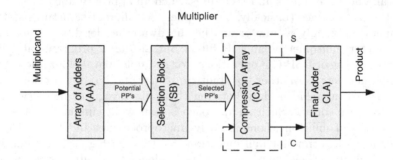

**Fig. 1.** The general structure of higher-radix multipliers.

The second step of a higher-radix multiplication method is computationally less expensive compared to the second step of Booth-recoded radix-4 multiplication. The price for this is the added complexity of the first step which includes one or more levels of shift-add operations for finding the list of potential PPs. Higher the radix, higher the "portion of complexity" moved from the second step to the first one. This is commonly considered to be the main drawback of higher-radix multipliers. However, this may turn to be an advantage in the cases where it would be possible to avoid the first step in most of multiplications by reusing the list of potential PPs. Such cases occur if, for example one of the multiplication operands is a known constant or if one multiplicand is to be multiplied with a number of multipliers. One such example is the matrix vector product where every column of the multiplier matrix is multiplied with the corresponding component of the multiplicand vector. Another example is the convolution (or Finite-Impulse-Response (FIR) filtering) where the same filter coefficient is multiplied with every sample of a long input signal. It should be noted that higher the radix, more it is beneficial to reuse the list of potential

PPs. It has no effect of reusing the list of potential partial products in radix-2 or radix-4 Booth-recoded multiplication methods since these are essentially shifted version of the input multiplicand.

Reusing the list of potential PPs leads to significant saving of the execution time of "incomplete" multiplications (without the first step). However, it still does not reduce the hardware complexity of higher-radix multipliers since a number of shifters and adder-subtractors must anyway be involved in the structure in order to support also "full" multiplications. On the other hand, it is likely, that a system involving a multiplier involves also adder-subtractors which already exist in higher-radix multipliers but are absent in radix-2 or radix-4 Booth-recoded multipliers. Thus, also this drawback may be turned to an advantage if these adders-subtractors, as well as the other blocks involved in a single multiplier structure may operate independently and, therefore may be reused for implementing other tasks.

Independent operation of component blocks of a single multiplier may, for example, be achieved by making use of reconfigurable interconnections between blocks and between blocks and I/O buses. Such an approach allows also to configure the same device (basically, a multiplier) to different structures so that it may operate not only as one or another hardware accelerator (for example a matrix-vector multiplier or an FIR filter) but also as a programmable device supporting a list of DSP-like operations (for example, parallel additions, MAC, accumulations, etc.). Another possibility is to have no interconnection between blocks but to interchange data between them via a register memory under a simple software control. Such an approach is somewhat similar to software implementation of multiplications in early microprocessors and DSPs. However, it needs much less time for multiplications as it uses a higher-radix multiplication method and special hardware blocks implementing sub-operations of this method.

Another drawback of higher-radix multipliers is related to a problem of low balancing between stages when trying to apply pipelining. However, this problem may be solved by parallelizing pipeline stages where different stages are parallelized at different levels (similar technique has been applied in [7] to achieve perfect balancing between pipeline stages of an architecture for sum-of-absolute difference computation).

In this work, we propose a higher-radix multiplication based methodology for designing processor architectures oriented to matrix-vector arithmetics. several independent groups of modifications into higher-radix multiplication method and multiplier structures are proposed making them suitable for matrix-vector arithmetics. These modifications may be applied separately or combined with each other. The proposed methodology may be used in designing different types of processor architectures ((reconfigurable) ASICs, programmable RISC/DSPs processors, *etc.*) and may have various realizations.

Main advantage of the proposed method is that the list of potential PPs may be reused whenever one multiplicand is to be multiplied with several multipliers. Another advantage is that the hardware blocks involved for high-radix multiplication may also be used independently to implement other tasks such as parallel addition/subtractions, accumulations. This allows introducing a group of modifications to high-radix multiplier structures making them reconfigurable so that single devices having two-fold functionalities of either programmable processors or reconfigurable hardware accelerators may be designed.

## 2   Higher-Radix Multipliers

Higher-radix multipliers may be classified according to the radix $T$ and according to the use or non-use of Booth recoding. However, all of these multipliers may be presented in a simple unified scheme shown on Fig. 1. Such multipliers are based on finding the product $y = ax$ of the multiplier $a$ and the multiplicand $x$ as the sum

$$y = (A_0x)2^{n/t} + (A_1x)2^{n/t-1} + \ldots + (A_{n/t-1}x)2 + A_{n/t}x \qquad (1)$$

where $A_ix, i = 1, 2, \ldots, n/t$, ($t = logT$, $T$ is the radix) are partial products (PPs) of the multiplicand $x$. The PPs are either zero or obtained by adding or subtracting $x$ with its shifts or with a constant. In Booth recoded radix-$T$ multiplication methods with $T = 8, 16$ or in non-recoded radix-$T$ multiplication methods with $T = 4, 8$, at most one addition/subtraction is needed in order to obtain the value of every potential PP since their values are selected from a subset of the set $\{-7x, \ldots, -x, 0, x \ldots, 7x, -x + C\}$ in every of these cases ($C$ is a known constant). For example, in the case of a non-recoded radix-8 multiplier, the list of potential PPs is $\{-x + C, 0, x, 2x, 3x = x + 2x, 4x, 5x = x+4x, 6x = 2(x+2x), 7x = 8x-x\}$. Therefore, all of these values may be obtained in one parallel addition and/or a shift operation. This is done at the array of adder/subtractors (AA) constituting the first pipeline stage of the multiplier (see Fig. 1).

The second pipeline stage in higher-radix multipliers is the Selection Block (SB) (see Fig. 1) which, according to bit-groups of the multiplier $a$, outputs PPs $A_ix$, $i = 0, 1, \ldots, n/t$ used in (1). In the case of, $e.g.$, non-recoded radix-8 multiplication method, PPs are formed according to non-overlapping groups each consisting of three bits of the multiplier. If, for instance $a = 011110101010$, the product $y = ax$ is obtained as $y = (3x)2^9 + (6x)2^6 + (5x)2^3 + (2x)$.

The PPs selected in the second pipeline stage are shifted and added within the last two pipeline stages. The third stage is a Compression Array (CA) that reduces all PP rows into two rows (the Sum term $S$ and the Carry term $C$). The fourth pipeline stage is an adder (Final Adder) that adds the Sum and Carry Terms. This is typically a Carry-Look-Ahead adder (CLA).

Multiply-accumulate (MAC) units may simply be derived from high-radix multiplier structures by incorporating feedbacks between the outputs and inputs of the Compression Array as shown with dashed lines on Fig. 1.

Main drawbacks of the higher-radix ($T > 4$) multipliers are related to the necessity of implementing a number of addition/subtractions for finding the list of potential PPs in the Array of Adders of the first pipeline stage. This not only makes the first pipeline stage more complicated as compared to the case of radix-4 Booth recoded multiplier but also leads to a significant unbalancing between the pipeline stages of the multiplier. In the next section we describe a methodology for designing efficient matrix-vector processor architectures based on several independent groups of modifications to higher-radix multiplication method and multiplier structures that turn the mentioned drawbacks to advantages.

# 3    The Methodology for Designing Efficient Matrix-Vector Processor Architectures

In this section, several groups of modifications to higher-radix multiplication methods are introduced in order to develop a methodology for designing efficient matrix-vector arithmetics oriented architectures. These modifications may be applied separately or combined with each other. The proposed methodology may be used in developing different types of processor architectures such as DSP-like RISC processors or ASICS, or multi-functional reconfigurable hardware accelerators/coprocessors.

## 3.1    Reuse of the List of Potential Partial Products

First modification consists of introducing so called "incomplete" multiplications differing from "full" multiplications in that the list of potential PPs for the multiplicand is assumed being pre-computed and stored in a memory so that only selection of the PPs according to bit-slices of the multiplier and summation of the selected PPs are implemented. This simple modification allows excluding the most complicated first pipeline stage from the critical path of the multiplication process whenever one multiplicand is to be multiplied by many multipliers. This is the case in, e.g. FIR filtering, and matrix-vector product. For example, in FIR filtering, potential PPs of the filter coefficients may be precomputed and stored in the memory and then reused for every location of the filter window. Thus all the multiplications (or actually MAC operations) will be reduced to "incomplete" ones where the complicated first pipeline stage is skipped and only the simple last stages are implemented. In matrix-vector product, the set of potential PPs of the components of the input vector may be obtained while multiplying the first row of the matrix to that vector. These potential PPs may then be reused while multiplying the other rows. This means, only $N$ out of $NM$ multiplications are "full" while the rest are "incomplete".

It should be noted that MAC operations implemented in a series and accumulating the results of may also be "incomplete" in the sense that the final addition may be not implemented in every accumulation step but only at the last one. Before the last accumulation step, the current Sum and Carry outputs are accumulated to the previous values via the feedback between the outputs and the inputs of the Compression Array. Thus, both the first and the last pipeline stages may be excluded from the critical path of MAC operations.

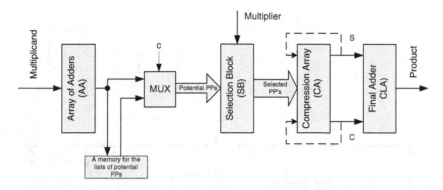

**Fig. 2.** Higher-radix multiplier structure with a memory block.

There are various ways of designing architectures that support the idea of "incomplete" multiplications. One possible solutions is illustrated on Fig. 2. Here, the reuse of the list of potential PPs is achieved by simply incorporating a memory block between the first and second pipeline stages as depicted on Fig. 2. There is a control signal $c$ according to which the memory is either open (when $c$ is set low) or closed (when $c$ is set high) for writing potential PPs from the output of the Array of Adders. The same signal $c$ controls the multiplexer having connected its first input to the output of the Array of Adders, and the second input to the memory output. Thus, the potential PPs enter to the input of the Selection Block either directly from the output of the Array of Adders (when $c$ is low) or from the memory (when $c$ is high). In the former case "full" multiplications are implemented while in the latter case "incomplete" ones are implemented.

The idea of "incomplete" multiplications may also be used in designing programmable DSP-like processors similar to the one shown on Fig. 3 (blocks and connections illustrated with dashed lines are optional in this figure). Except having a typical to such processors set of memory blocks and functional units (Registers, few smaller precision and at least one wider precision adder/subtractors), the system should now include a Compression Array and optionally a Selection Block similar to those involved in the corresponding higher-radix multiplier structure (see Fig 1). In return, the conventional multiplier may optionally be removed from the system.

There may exist connections between the Array of Adders and the Selection Block (which must exist in the system in this case) and between the Compression Array and the Wide Adder. In this case, the system actually involves a higher-radix multiplier. Therefore, "full" multiplication and MAC operations are implemented exactly according to the higher-radix multiplier scheme. That is, the multiplicand operand enters to the Array of Adders either from the internal memory or from a register. The Array of Adders computes the list of potential PPs of the multiplicand and sends it to the Selection Block. Simultaneously, the multiplier enters to the Selection Block which sends the corresponding set of

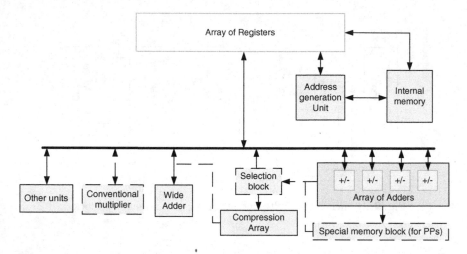

**Fig. 3.** Programmable processor architecture based on modified higher radix method.

PPs to the Compression Array. Then the obtained Sum and Carry terms enter to the Wide Adder from the Compression Array. However, also "incomplete" multiplication and MAC operations may be executed if one multiplicand is to be multiplied with many multipliers. In this case, either a special memory block (if such) or the Register Array may be used for storing the lists of potential PPs.

In another case the Selection Block, the Special Memory Unit, as well as connection between the Array of Adders and the Compression Array and between the Compression Array and the Wide Adder may be absent. In this case, the data interchange is executed via the Register Array. The Address Generation Unit will then play the role of the Selection Block. For this, it should generate the addresses of those potential PPs stored in the Register Array, that correspond to the bit slices of the multiplier operand.

Let us note that when accumulative series of MAC operations is to be implemented, then every MAC operation of the series, except the last one will employ only the Compression Array.

### 3.2 Reuse of Basic Component Blocks of Higher-Radix Multipliers

The idea of the second group of modifications is to use the basic hardware component blocks of higher-radix multipliers to execute also other than multiplication based tasks. Such modification is meaningful since the higher-radix multipliers involve, as component blocks, such basic information processing hardware as adder/subtractors and adder trees (Compression Array followed by Final CLA adder is, actually, an adder tree). Reusing the hardware components of the multipliers for additions may, in many cases, eliminate the need of including separate adders and separate multipliers into a system for matrix-vector arithmetics.

Again, this idea may have many realizations when designing matrix-vector operations oriented processor architectures. Actually one example has already been considered in the previous section. The Array of Adders, the Compression Array, and the Wide Adder of a DSP-like processor similar to the one on Fig. 3 may separately be used for addition based operations in parallel with multiplication or MAC operations or independently from them.

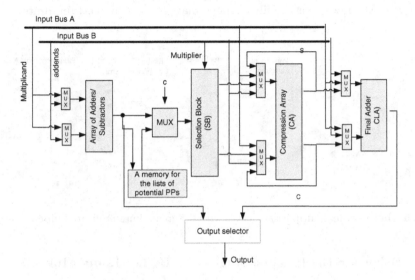

**Fig. 4.** Reconfigurability by multiplexed interconnections.

Also the basic pipelined higher-radix multiplier structure (see Figs. 1 and 2) may be modified to support addition based operations by introducing multiplexed interconnections between the main components of high-radix multipliers instead of fixed ones (see Fig. 4). "Flexible" feedbacks from the Compression Arrays to their inputs may also be introduced in such a way that they may be either active or inactive. These type of a modifications make the proposed architectures reconfigurable. Halting some of the pipeline stages and generating different control signals to the multiplexers, different configurations may be formed. For example, if only the first pipeline stage is activated then we obtain an Array of Adders/subtractors configuration. Clearly, multiplier configuration is obtained by activating all the multiplier pipeline stages and all the standard connections between them. Activating also the feedbacks of Compression Arrays, the architecture is configured to a bank of MAC units.

### 3.3 Single Device Operating as a Reconfigurable ASIC or a Programmable Processor

Next modification is based on incorporating of two nested loop counters within the control unit of a reconfigurable higher-radix multiplier structure similar to the one on Fig. 4. This allows of configuring architectures derived from a single higher-radix multiplier not only to basic DSP specific operations as in the previous section but also to several flexible hardware accelerators. For example, the same device that may be used as a programmable processor with DSP-specific operations may also be configured either to matrix-vector multiplication accelerator or to FIR filter, or to fast orthogonal transform accelerator. Moreover, the size of the matrix or the filter length may vary within certain limits.

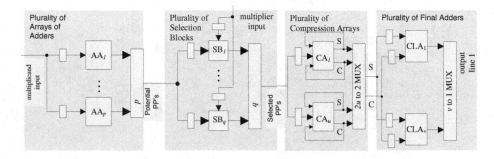

**Fig. 5.** Higher-radix multiplier structure with different times replicated pipeline stages.

### 3.4    Balancing the Pipeline Stages of a Higher-Radix Multiplier

Next, let us consider a modification that may be applied to pipelined higher radix multiplier structures in order to achieve a high-level balancing between their pipeline stages. This may be done by parallelizing every stage at different levels of parallelism. This means that replicating of every basic block of the corresponding pipeline stage of the high-radix multiplier is allowed and the number of blocks within each pipeline stage may be different from each other (see Fig. 5). The blocks within a pipeline stage are connected to the same input/output lines through demultiplexers and multiplexers and they operate in a time-interlaced manner (that is, in parallel but with a time offset of one clock cycle).

The proposed modification allows calibrating every pipeline stage to a predefined cycle time and to achieve perfect balancing between them. By replicating the basic blocks, we actually obtain a single, unified structure for a bank of devices implemented with shared blocks.

## 4    Conclusion

A high-radix multiplication based methodology for designing matrix-vector arithmetics oriented processor architectures has been proposed. Several independent modifications to higher-radix multiplication methods and multipliers structures have been suggested to be applied separately or combined with each others. Main advantage of the proposed method is that the list of potential PPs may be reused whenever one multiplicand is to be multiplied with several multipliers, a typical case in matrix-vector arithmetics. Another advantage is that the hardware blocks involved for high-radix multiplication may also be used independently to implement other tasks such as parallel addition/subtractions, accumulations. This is achieved by making higher-radix multiplier structures reconfigurable so that single device may have two-fold functionalities of either programmable processors or reconfigurable hardware accelerators. Also a methodology to balance pipeline stages of has been proposed.

# References

1. O.L. MacSorley, "High speed arithmetic in binary computers," in Proc. IRE, an. 1961.
2. A.D. Booth, "A signed binary multiplication technique," *Quarterly J. Mechan Appl. Math.*, vol. IV, part 2, 1951.
3. Wen-Chang Yeh and Chein-Wei Jen, "High-speed Booth encoded parallel multiplier design," *IEEE Trans. on Computers*, vol. 49, No 7, July 2000, pp. 692-701.
4. H. Sam and A. Gupta "A generalized multibit recoding of two's complement binary numbers and its proof with applications in multiplier implementations," *IEEE Trans. on Computers*, vol. 39, No 8, August 1990, pp. 1006-1015.
5. C.M. Conway and E.E. Swartzlander, Jr., "Product select multiplier, *Proceedings of the IEEE Twenty-Eighth Asilomar Conference on Signals, Systems and Computers*, vol. 2 pp 1388 -1392, Oct.-Nov. 1994.
6. E.M. Schwarz, R.M. Averill III, L.J. Sigal, "A radix-8 CMOS S/390 multiplier, *Proceedings of the 13th IEEE Symposium on Computer Arithmetic*, pp. 2-9, July 1997.
7. D. Guevorkian, A. Launiainen, P. Liuha, and V. Lappalainen, "Architectures for the sum of absolute differences operation," *Proceedings, of the IEEE Worshop on Signal Processing Systems (SIPS 2002)*, San Diego, California, pp. 57-62, Oct. 2002.

# Metrics for Digital Signal Processing Architectures Characterization: Remanence and Scalability

Pascal Benoit[1], Gilles Sassatelli[1], Lionel Torres[1], Didier Demigny[2], Michel Robert[1], and Gaston Cambon[1]

[1] LIRMM, UMR UM2-CNRS C5506,
161 rue Ada, 34392 Montpellier Cedex 5, France
(33)(0)4-67-41-85-69
{first_name.last_name}@lirmm.fr
[2] ETIS, UMR-CNRS 8051,
6 av. du Ponceau, 95014 Cergy Pontoise Cedex, France
(33)(0)1-30-73-66-10
{name}@ensea.fr

**Abstract.** SoCs became reality: an increasing number of products powered by this type of circuits hits the market. Reduced power consumption, increased performance are some of the usually stated benefits. Besides approaches aiming at enabling system level exploration for multiple million gates designs, like the SystemC initiative, choosing the right IP core, or the right set of parameters among those available is not straightforward. In this article we first present a generic model for digital signal processing architectures. Several metrics, later referred as Remanence and Operative Density are presented in this paper. The methodology is illustrated through a case study.

## 1 Introduction

Among the last couple of years lots of new approaches appeared [1][2]. Real innovations like coarse grain reconfigurable fabrics [2] or dynamical reconfiguration have brought numerous improvements, solving several weaknesses of traditional FPGA architectures. Besides this point, several recurrent issues remain, and the proliferation of architectures lays to an additional problem for SoC designer: choose the right IP core for a given set of specifications. Despite some works have already proposed some useful tools, like the Dehon metric [3], allowing to compare the computing density for different architectures in different silicon technologies, the need of additional metrics is now obvious. The goal of this paper is to address this characterization problem by the way of defining two metrics: remanence and scalability allow to compare more efficiently different architectures dedicated to digital signal processing.

## 2 Digital Signal Processing Architectures

Each architecture dedicated to digital signal processing exhibits benefits as well as limitations, extensively listed in [1] for Von Neumann architecture and [2][8] for re-

A. Pimentel and S. Vassiliadis (Eds.): SAMOS 2004, LNCS 3133, pp. 128–137, 2004.

configurable architectures (RA). Figure 1 depicts a general model for both processors and RAs. Depending on the architecture, each constituting element differs.

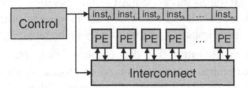

**Fig. 1.** The Generic model of DSP architectures

The constituting elements are:

- interconnect subsystem,
- array of processing elements (PE), PE structure,
- control unit,
- instruction / configuration memory.

The following architectures can be modeled:

- Processors are based on the Von Neumann paradigm [5]. Operation execution is carried out in the data path in a sequential way. Usually a single PE is present. The configuration memory is no more than a single register storing the current instruction.
- VLIW DSP: they carry out parallelism at the instruction level. A VLIW instruction consists of several RISC instructions, each one being executed in one PE.
- Fine grain RAs like FPGAs. The PE array is two-dimensional. Each PE features bit-level reconfigurable logic, often Look-Up-Table based. In most devices, no controller is present, the configuration being uploaded in the configuration memory offline.
- Coarse grain RAs Each PE often features hardwired arithmetic operators (coarse grain) instead of bit-level reconfigurable logic.

## 3   Remanence and Scalability

### 3.1   Remanence

A RA is constituted by a set of operators $N_a$ running at the clock frequency $F_e$. Each architecture is able to reconfigure $N_c$ operators each configuration cycle of frequency $F_c$. $F_c$ may be different from $F_e$, depending on the considered architecture. The *remanence* is defined by the following expression:

$$R = \frac{N_a . F_e}{N_c . F_c}$$

The remanence [6] subsequently characterizes the dynamical character of the RA by reporting the number of cycles needed to reconfigure the PE array. This criteria provides an information on the minimal amount of data to be processed between two configuration cycles.

- If the configuration phase is shadowed, a new configuration is loaded during processing. The configurations are then switched within the next clock cycle. The architecture is efficient if during this cycle most of the operators are processing data.
- If the configuration phase is not shadowed, the number of processing cycles must be greater than R for a limited overhead: usually in the range of 10 to 20 times R.

Moreover, a data parallelism of $\beta$ ($\beta$ data processed concurrently) increase according to a factor $\beta$ the minimal number of data to be processed between two configuration cycles. Therefore, the ratio between the amount of data to be computed and R figures out an important information which helps to choose between data or instruction parallelism. Besides this point, one can notice that 1/R is a metric assessing the dynamical character of an architecture. The less R, the more dynamically reconfigurable the architecture is. The system reconfiguration frequency is lower to $F_e/R$.

This metric has three main advantages:

- It reports the dynamical character of an architecture independently from its granularity: The operators can either be fine grain (CLBs) or coarse grain (multipliers, ALUs). This is enabled thanks to the use of the concept of operators instead of any lower-level consideration.
- Although some architectures provide only inter-operators path routing, this implies to stop processing while configuring. Hence, it is functionally equivalent to reconfigure the operators. It can nevertheless be more efficient to directly reconfigure the operators. For a given processing power, $N_c$ can be greater or/and require less configuration bits. This it implicitly taken into account by the remanence, thanks again to the concept of operators.
- No matter how the reconfiguration takes place. It can be done in a single pass, after the processing related to the current configuration is done, or continuously, a few operators being reconfigured each cycle while processing keeps on.

*Remanence and power consumption.* In a processor, up to 50% of the power is consumed in the control unit. Reconfiguration frequency and volume (i.e. number of bits) might consequently impact on the power consumed. Some architectures providing a 'freeze' mode (configuration frozen during a given time) can achieve interesting power savings.

The processing power $P_{proc}$ of a given architecture can be expressed as the product between the number of operators $N_a$ and the clock frequency $F_e$ ($P_{proc} \sim N_a.F_e$)The power consumed can then be expressed as:

$$P_{cons} \sim N_a.F_e.U^2$$

with U being the voltage supply. According to this formula, equivalent power saving might be achieved by either optimising $N_a$ or $F_e$. However, decreasing the clock frequency allow to decrease proportionally the voltage supply. Let assume that, the power consumed is :

$$P_{cons} \sim N_a.F_e^3$$

Then the ratio $P_{cons}/P_{proc}$ grows according to a factor $F_e^2$. For a given processing power, it is then worthwhile to increase the number of operator and reduce accordingly the clock frequency. Nevertheless, applying such an approach might increase consequently the control unit complexity and then its power consumption. This observation figures out clearly the significance of the remanence. The power consumed is proportional to the bit switching activity (each second). Hence, it is possible to define a cost in power consumption per MIPS by the way of considering both processing-related cost and configuration-switching cost.

## 3.2  Scalability

Due to the continuous technology scaling, scalability is today becoming a key issue; the problem can be stated as follows: given a customisable architecture model (in terms of number of PEs), how does the $N_a/A$ ratio grow, $N_a$ being the number of PEs and A the core area. We define the operating density Do as the ratio $N_a/A$. Hence, for an architecture fully scalable OD ($N_a$) will be constant.

Accordingly to our general model (figure 1), and assuming the core area as the sum of the constituting elements' area, architecture scalability analysis sum up to each component scalability analysis:

$$OD \sim \frac{N_a}{A_{PEs}+A_{control}+A_{config\_mem}+A_{interconnect}}$$

# 4  The Systolic Ring

The Systolic Ring architecture features a DSP-like coarse grain reconfigurable block; following an original concept (figure 2). The configuration (microinstruction code) can either come from the configuration layer (FPGA-like mode, *global mode*) or from a local sequencer (*local mode*) depicted in figure 2.

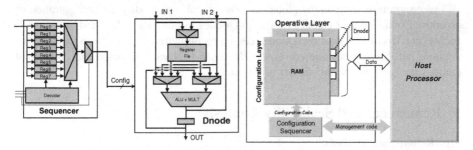

**Fig. 2.** The Dnode architecture                    **Fig. 3.** System overview

A custom instruction set RISC processor (*configuration sequencer*, figure 3) is also used in order to upload the microprograms into the local sequencers of the Dnodes set to *local mode*. It is also used to write the configuration into the configuration layer (*global mode*).

The specific structure of the operating layer is depicted on figure 4a. The Ring topology allows an efficient implementation of pipelined datapath. The switch components establish a full connectivity between two layers, refer to [4] for complete description. The Systolic Ring also provides a feedback network that proves useful for recursive operations. It allows to feedback data to previous layers by the way of using feedback pipelines implemented from *each* switch in the structure. Each other switch in the architecture has a read access on *each* other switch's pipeline. Figure 4b depicts the east switch's feedback pipeline. In addition a bus connecting all switches in the architecture and the global sequencer is available, mainly for conditional configuration: a data computed in the operating layer can be retrieved in the configuration sequencer for further analysis and thus different configuration evolution.

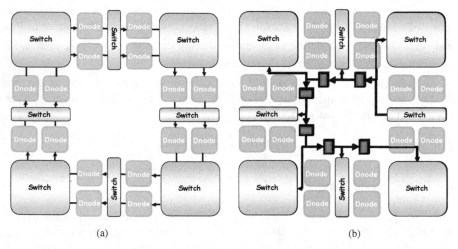

(a)                                                                      (b)

**Fig. 4.** Operating layer (a) and a switch's feedback pipeline (b)

The program running on the global sequencer is able to modify the configuration of an entire Dnode layer (2 Dnodes on the 16 Dnodes Systolic Ring depicted on figure 4) each cycle. Up to 12.5% of the Dnodes can be reconfigured each cycle in the exposed version, but this can be tailored, especially when C/N vary, C being the number of Dnodes per layer and N the number of layers.

## 5  Remanence and Scalability Analysis

### 5.1  Remanence Analysis

Considering the *global mode*, the remanence of the Systolic Ring (Figure 4) is $R_{sring\_static}$=8, 8 cycles are indeed needed to reconfigure the whole structure, $F_e$ being equal to $F_c$. As previously said, the Systolic Ring is customisable, thus the remanence can be tailored. This of course impacts the instruction size, and other parameters like memory bandwidth. This will be pointed out in the scalability section.

The *local mode* allows to change the configuration of each Dnode of the structure each cycle (assuming that all Dnodes are in local mode). However, 8 configuration cycles are needed to store a maximum length microprogram (one local sequencer register loaded per cycle, Figure 2), this microprogram being considered as a single Dnode configuration. In this case, a maximum of 64 cycles are needed, thus $R_{sring\_dynamic}=64$.

It must be pointed out that:

- A microprogram being considered as a single instruction, 8 instructions are needed to carry out a single data. Therefore, $R_{sring\_static}$ only characterizes the amount of data.
- Despite in local mode all Dnodes can modify their configuration each cycle, from a system point of view, only $R_{sring\_dynamic}$ should to be taken into account. This mode is worthwhile only when the number of cycles of the considered process is at least 10 times greater than $R_{sring\_dynamic}$. The global mode is of great interest for data parallelism while the local mode features intermediate granularity data parallelism and potential instruction parallelism.

Table 1 gives remanence values for three different architecture described below:

- Texas Instruments TMS320C62: this DSP is a powerful VLIW processor featuring 8 processing units. It reaches 1600 MIPS (max power) when running at 300MHz. The remanence $R_{C62}$ is equal to 1: it is able to reconfigure all its processing units each cycle.
- Xilinx Virtex XC2V2000 FPGA [7]: this one is partially reconfigurable, and requires 14.29 ms to be totally reconfigured at $F_c$=66 MHz. While $F_e$ is application-dependant, the ratio $F_e/F_c$ is non constant. Results depicted in table 1 are given for $F_e$=100 MHz.
- Systolic Ring: a 16 Dnodes realisation, described above in section 4.

**Table 1.** Remanence comparisons

| | TMS 320C62 | Xilinx XC2V2000 | Ring-8 | |
| --- | --- | --- | --- | --- |
| | | | Dynamic | Static |
| **Number of op.(Na)** | 8 PEs | 2688 CLBs | 8 Dnodes | |
| **Reconfigured op. / cycle** | 8 | $2.8.10^{-3}$ | 0.25 | 2 |
| **Fe/Fc** | 1 | 1 ($F_e$=66MHz) | 1 | 1 |
| **Remanence (R)** | 1 | 936540 | 64 | 8 |

As shown in table 1, the remanence of the Systolic Ring in full global mode (i.e. static) is 8, as to say, 8 cycles are required to fully reconfigure the structure. The Systolic Ring also provides a *hybrid mode*, allowing to set independently each Dnode in the structure in global or local mode. In this last case, the effective remanence is ranging from $R_{sring\_static}$ to $R_{sring\_dynamic}$. The most 'dynamically reconfigurable' architecture is however the VLIW processor. Hence, its use should be recommended for relatively irregular applications implying instruction-level parallelism. The remanence however does not give the number of PEs that one can expect to have for a given silicon area : the scalability analysis addresses this problem.

## 5.2  Scalability Analysis

As assumed in 3.2, the total area is approximated by the sum of the 4 constituting elements of our model. Two different scaling techniques are to be considered:

*Scaling technique 1: N/C tradeoff*
$N_a$ can be tailored between N (number of Dnodes per layer) and C (number of layers) according to the formula: $N_a = N.C$
   Increasing N will encourage parallelism level (either instruction or data) while increasing C will improve pipeline depth (i.e. computation parallelism).

*Scaling technique 2: MIMD approach*
It is also possible to increase $N_a$ by the way of using multiple Systolic Rings witch will lead to a MIMD (Multiple Instructions Multiple Data) like solution. This technique provides a maximal scalability, as the resulting silicon area will be proportional to the number $N_a$ of PEs.

$$\left(\frac{N_a}{A}\right)_{MIMD} = \alpha = cte$$

   In the following, only scalability issues related to technique 1 will be considered.

### *Processing elements (i.e. Dnodes)*
Given a PE of core area A, the instantiation of $N_a$ PEs occupies $\alpha A$ area units on the die, as to say this part is fully scalable, independently from the N/C ratio:

$$\left(\frac{N_a}{A}\right)_{PEs} = \alpha = cte$$

### *Control unit*
The global sequencer is a simple RISC processor featuring a specific instruction set. The 16 lower bits of the instruction format are dedicated to internal RISC management, whereas the upper ones are directly addressing a given Systolic Ring layer (configuration of N Dnodes and the corresponding switch). Figure 5 depicts the format of the instruction register used in the configuration sequencer.

**INSTRUCTION FORMAT**

| 0 | 15 16 | | | L |
|---|---|---|---|---|
| RISC instruction | Layer address | Dnodes modes | Dnodes configuration | Switch configuration |
| $A_{RISC}$ | $A_{layer\_add}$ | $A_{PRG}$ | $A_{dnodes\_conf}$ | $A_{switch\_conf}$ |

**Fig. 5.** RISC instruction format

The area $A_{part}$ corresponding to a given *part* of the instruction register will be considered proportional to the number of bits required for its coding, $M_{part}$.

- $A_{RISC}$. The size of the sequencer-related instruction is constant, thus, fully scalable.

$$A_{RISC} \sim M_{RISC} = 16$$

- $A_{layer\_address}$. $M_{layer\_address}$ bits being required for a C-layer addressing ($2^M = C$), and taking into account that C may not be a power of two:

$$A_{layer\_address} \sim M_{layer\_address} = \left| 1 + \log 2\,(C\text{-}1) \right|$$

- $A_{PRG}$. 2 bits are required to code the 4 run-modes. Hence, for N Dnodes, the required number of bits given above exhibit a maximal scalability:

$$A_{PRG} \sim M_{PRG} = 4.N$$

- $A_{dnodes\_conf}$. Again, considering that 17 configuration bits are required for each Dnode, the resulting area is:

$$A_{Dnodes\_conf} \sim M_{Dnodes\_conf} = 17.N$$

- $A_{switch\_conf}$. In order to provide a full inter-layers connectivity, let n be the number of inputs of the MUX and p the number of outputs: $C(n,p)$ addresses combinations must be supported. The availability of a bus implies to be able to write the result of any Dnode output, plus an additional bit putting the bus driver in high impedance. The resulting number of bits required is:

$$A_{switch\_conf} \sim M_{switch\_conf} = \left| 1 + Log_2(C_n^p\text{-}1) \right| + \left| Log_2(N) + 1 \right|$$

The number of inputs is determined by the expression:

$$n = 2.N + (C\text{-}1).N + 1$$

The first term is related to number of Dnodes of the upper layer, while the second is related to the feedback network: C-1 feedback network are implemented, each one constituted by the aggregation of N Dnodes outputs. The number of outputs p is equal to N (number of Dnodes per layer).

### Configuration Memory

The use of a coarse grain technology drastically decreases the size of the configuration memory. In addition, the size of the PE-only configuration memory grow linearly with the number of PEs. Only the routing-relative configuration size grows non-linearly with respects to the number of processing elements, due to the fact that the Systolic Ring provides full interlayer connectivity. The size required for the storage of a (N,C) version of the Systolic Ring is:

$$A_{config} \sim M_{config} = C.(M_{PRG} + M_{Dnodes\_conf} + M_{switch\_conf})$$

## 6   Case Study: Tailoring the Parameters

Let us suppose that the processing power needed (proportional to the number of Dnodes) corresponds to a number of Dnodes between 40 and 60. First, a C/N ratio must be selected. This ratio will be set according to the targeted applications. Let us also suppose that promoting pipeline degree seems to be more attractive for the targeted applications. Therefore, we choose a C/N ratio equal to 4. Following the area evolution as a function of C and N for one instance of the Systolic Ring, corresponding curves are plotted for several instances of the Systolic Ring. The figure 6 represents the corresponding curves. The constraint tube is then plotted for the C.N values chosen (40 and 60). In order to show the architecture dynamism, we also plot the *Remanence* curve and add it to the graph. The figure 6 shows how a Systolic Ring user can tune the architectural parameters. Indeed, in the constraint tube, many solutions are possible. Choosing for example eight Systolic Ring instances (40 Dnodes total) provide the smallest silicon area in the constraint tube. Moreover, it also will be the most dynamical solution, *i.e.* the one requiring the minimum number of cycles to configure the 40 Dnodes. However, it will be also the solution offering the worst interconnection resources (implying inter-Systolic Ring communications) and the worst processing power. At the opposite, choosing only one instance of the Systolic Ring with a total number of 60 will significantly increase the processing power (1.5 times) but also the silicon area. However, more interconnection resources will be available due to the full layer interconnectivity allowed in a single Systolic Ring instance. The increase of operators will also involve a higher *Remanence*.

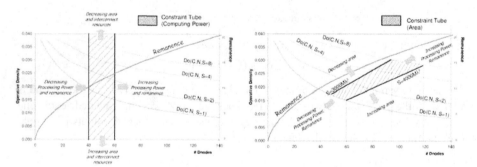

**Fig. 6.** Processing power constrained                    **Fig. 7.** Area constrained

Let us now suppose that the available silicon area is between 3000M$\lambda^2$ and 4000M$\lambda^2$ ($\lambda$ being the half width of the transistor channel). This design space defines the constraint tube. As mentioned previously, the C/N ratio must be selected. This ratio will be set according to the target applications. We choose here for example a C/N ratio equal to 4. Following the area evolution as a function of C and N for one instance of the Systolic Ring, corresponding curves are plotted for several instances of the Systolic Ring. The figure 7 depicts the related curves. The constraint tube is then plotted according to the area constraints (the two lines were extrapolated from the Systolic Ring area formalisation). The *Remanence* curve is also plotted.

The figure 7 shows how a Systolic Ring user (a platform-based designer for example) can tune his core with the architectural parameters. Indeed, in the constraint tube, many solutions are possible. For the lower bound ($3000M\lambda^2$), tradeoffs ranging from 45 to 90 Dnodes are available. This characterizes an increased operative density. This is allowed by the way of using eight instances of the Systolic Ring instead of only one. However, this multi-instantiation implies a reduced connectivity between the Dnodes of the architecture and an increased *Remanence*. For the upper bound ($4000M\lambda^2$), the processing power can also be doubled by the same means, implying the same consequences.

# 7  Conclusion

After having compared different architectures and shown the limitations of classical comparison approaches, we have presented a general methodology for the characterization of architectures dedicated to digital signal processing. This methodology is based on evaluation metrics, *Remanence* and *Operative Density*, as functions of the architecture parameters. This methodology helps the designer to choose between several architectural trade-offs, as shown for the Systolic Ring example. The architecture presented in the first section, was used as a case study for both *Remanence* and *scalability* analysis. These considerations helped to determine architecture trade-offs and also contributed to establish the limitations of the architecture considering a set of application-relative constraints (parallelism type, area, processing power). Future works take place in analysing other crucial factors in a SoC design context such as the power consumption.

# References

1. W. H. Mangione-Smith et al, "Seeking Solutions in Configurable Computing," IEEE Computer, pp. 38-43, December 1997
2. R. Hartenstein, H. Grünbacher: The Roadmap to Reconfigurable computing Proc. FPL2000, Aug.27-30, 2000; LNCS, Springer-Verlag
3. André DeHon, "Comparing Computing Machines", Configurable Computing: Technology and Applications, Proc. SPIE 3526, 2-3 November 1998.
4. G. Sassatelli, et al.: "Highly Scalable Dynamically Reconfigurable Systolic Ring-Architecture for DSP applications", IEEE Design Automation and Test in Europe (DATE'02) , pp. 553-557, mars 2002, Paris, France.
5. G. Sassatelli, "Architectures reconfigurables dynamiquement pour les systèmes sur puce", Ph.D. thesis, Université Montpellier II, France, April 2002.
6. D. Demigny, et al.: «La rémanence des architectures reconfigurables, un critère significatif des architectures», proc. of JFAAA, pp. 49-52, décembre 2002, Monastir, Tunisie.
7. Xilinx, the Programmable Logic Data Book, 2002.
8. D. Demigny, et al.. «Architecture à reconfiguration dynamique pour le traitement temps réel des images» Techniques et Science de l'Information Numéro Spécial Architectures Reconfigurables, 18(10) : 1087-1112, décembre 1999.

# Virtual Architecture Mapping: A SystemC Based Methodology for Architectural Exploration of System-on-Chip Designs

Tim Kogel[1], Malte Doerper[2], Torsten Kempf[2], Andreas Wieferink[2], Rainer Leupers[2], Gerd Ascheid[2], and Heinrich Meyr[2]

[1] CoWare Inc.
Tim.Kogel@CoWare.com
http://www.coware.com
[2] Integrated Signal Processing Systems
Aachen University of Technology, Germany
http://www.iss.rwth-aachen.de

**Abstract.** The ever increasing complexity and heterogeneity of modern System-on-Chip designs demands early consideration and exploration of architectural alternatives, which is hardly practicable on the low abstraction level of implementation models.

In this paper, a system level design methodology based on the SystemC 2.0.1 library is proposed, which enables the designer to reason about the architecture on a much higher level of abstraction. Goal of this methodology is to define a system architecture, which provides sufficient performance, flexibility and cost efficiency as required by demanding applications like broadband networking or wireless communications. The methodology also provides capabilities for co-simulating multiple levels of abstraction simultaneously. This enables reuse of the simulation environment for functional verification of synthesizable implementation models against the abstract architecture model.

During a industrial case study, this methodology is applied to the development of a 2.5 GB IP forwarding chip with Quality-of-Service (QoS) support. In this paper we share our experiences with special emphasis on the architecture exploration phase, where several architectural alternatives are evaluated with respect to their impact on the system performance.

## 1 Introduction

One of the most challenging tasks in modern System-on-Chip design projects is to map a complex application onto a heterogeneous platform architecture in adherence to the specified flexibility, performance and cost requirements. Under stringent cost constraints, the required flexibility and performance is best delivered by a heterogeneous platform employing standard as well as application specific programmable architectures and dedicated hardware blocks, which are connected by a sophisticated communication topology. As a result, the designer faces a huge design space and has to compose a system architecture from various kinds of building blocks and communication resources in order to meet the constraints of the specific application.

A. Pimentel and S. Vassiliadis (Eds.): SAMOS 2004, LNCS 3133, pp. 138–148, 2004.
© Springer-Verlag Berlin Heidelberg 2004

The traditional design flow comprises only two decoupled phases of textural specification and architecture implementation and is no longer feasible for the design of large heterogeneous systems on a single chip, because quantitative architectural considerations are difficult to estimate on paper, prior to the implementation phase. Systems are either over-engineered, thus impacting the cost, or fail to deliver the expected performance.

Due to the high level of detail inherent to implementation models, so far they can only be optimized locally and system architecture tradeoffs and optimizations are not exploited. For that reason we advocate an intermediate System Level Design phase in the design flow, where the functionality of the system is mapped to the platform architecture in an abstract manner to enable architecture optimizations across heterogeneous computational components.

The following methodical aspects have been identified to cope with requirements of System Level Design:

The foundation for our methodology is provided by the SystemC library [1], which is widely considered as the emerging EDA industry standard language for bringing together today's disjunctive worlds of system conceptualization and implementation. Hardware semantics as well as interface based design are already incorporated into the 2.0 release of SystemC and also synthesis tools become commercially available. We have supplemented SystemC with a methodology specific library to enable rapid design space exploration at the System Level.

The following section discusses the envisioned design flow followed by the technical details of methodology specific library are presented. Section 4 contains our experiences from an industry cooperation, where the framework has been deployed in the design of a NPU platform. Finally we conclude our approach and give an outlook on future research topics.

## 2   System Level Design Methodology

System Level Design is all about filling the gap between specification and implementation. In this section we first classify the abstraction levels enabled by System 2.0 and then elaborate on the proposed architecture exploration methodology.

### 2.1   Transaction-Level Modeling

SystemC 2.0 has been conceived to realize a *Transaction-Level Modeling (TLM)* style [2], where communication is abstracted from the low-level implementation details of the Register Transfer Level (RTL). The resulting improvement in terms of simulation speed and modeling efficiency enables the system architect to create an executable specification of the complete SoC architecture.

The TLM paradigm can be further subdivided by applying abstraction w.r.t data and timing accuracy. By that the manifold design problems during the definition of the system architecture can be resolved in the appropriate design step. Note that the entry level depends on the design complexity: small scale and homogenous designs start immediately at RTL whereas cycle level TLM is usually sufficient for the design of medium scale embedded systems.

140     Tim Kogel et al.

This paper addresses the conceptualization of large scale heterogenous systems, which need heterogenous computational modules and a customized communication infrastructure to meet performance and cost requirements. Thus we have conceived a *packet level TLM* modeling style for architectural exploration, i.e. the considered data granularity are sets of functionally associated data, which are combined to Abstract Data Types (ADTs).

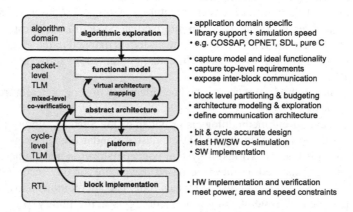

**Fig. 1.** SoC design flow

All phases in our refinement methodology depicted in figure 1 are based on SystemC and are thus interoperable. However, in this paper we particularly address the design of dedicated Hardware, so we intentionally leave out the discussion of the cycle-level TLM phase, which is mainly dedicated to the integration of Instruction Set Simulators. In the following we describe the sub-phases of our approach, i.e. functional and abstract architectural modeling as well as mixed-level co-verification.

## 2.2  Functional Model

Compared to the detailed register transfer level (RTL), simulation speed and modeling efficiency can only be improved significantly by modeling the system behavior on a much higher level of abstraction. In the functional model, the complete system behavior is partitioned only into a small number SoC building blocks instead of scattering the functionality over numerous processes as often required for a synthesizable RTL description. Abstract Data Types (ADT) replace the bit-true data representation of RTL models, such that a whole set of functionally associated data is represented as a single token, as for example an IP packet. Since the system state only changes on the arrival of a new token, we can employ pure reactive communication channels to model the data exchange between the functional blocks. This minimizes the number of the activations in the event-driven SystemC simulation kernel, which effectuates maximum simulation speed.

At the end of the functional modeling stage, the complete system behavior is captured and validated. The simulation speed as well as the modeling efficiency (measured in lines of code) is about two orders of magnitude better compared to the corresponding RTL model, which models the same functionality on a much higher level of architectural detail. The SystemC model is now prepared for the annotation of timing information, which is described in the next section.

## 2.3   Virtual Architecture Mapping

In the next design step, the functional model is mapped to the intended target architecture in order to create a performance model of the resulting system architecture. The mapping is performed virtually by annotating the timing characteristics of the target architecture to the functional model, thus the methodology enables a very fast exploration of different design alternatives. The process of timing annotation is completely orthogonal to the functionality, hence the previously validated functional system behavior is preserved.

The methodology is based on the following observation: for performance profiling purposes, the basic timing characteristics of the target architecture can be expressed by the temporal relationship of consuming, processing and producing ADT tokens.

– Pipelined architectures are able to consume and produce a token every cycle but introduce a static latency, which is determined by the number of pipeline stages.
– Data dependent modules show varying delays until the processing of the actual token is finished. In the case of a cache module for example, the processing delay of a cache read depends on whether the requested data set is in the cache or has to be fetched from the main memory.
– Resource shared modules are afflicted with an initiation interval, i.e. they are blocked for a varying amount of time during a token is processed.

As soon as the estimated timing parameters are annotated to the channels, the simulation results reflect the performance of the final system. A statistical evaluation system is associated with the channels to detect and eliminate architecture bottlenecks very early in the design flow before the time consuming implementation starts. The access statistics gathered by the bus model during a simulation run guide the selection and configuration of a specific on-chip bus.

The key mechanism of virtual architecture mapping is separating behavior inside the functional modules from timing aspects, which are captured by the communication channels. Thus we achieve a threefold orthogonalization of system level design concerns in terms of behavior, interface and timing.

## 2.4   Mixed-Level Co-verification

After the architecture is finalized, the abstract architecture model is converted into a synthesizable model. Here the same functionality has to be realized at a much lower level of detail according to the refinement steps in the SystemC synthesis guidelines. By using the SystemC synthesis [3], the implementation phase can be performed within the SystemC design environment itself. This enables a smooth transition from the refined model to the implementation model.

Since this implementation phase is highly error prone, functional verification is the most important and time consuming task in the overall design flow [4]. In our approach the effort for functional verification is drastically reduced by reusing the abstract system model as a reference for the synthesizable implementation models. For that we have generalized the well known adapter concept for communication refinement [2] to bridge the abstraction gap between packet-level and cycle-level models.

The next section describes the channel library, which has been developed to enable the exploration and co-verification methodology.

## 3    Methodology Specific Channel Library

SystemC 2.0 provides a well defined interface for its underlying event-driven simulation kernel to enable implementation of methodology specific communication channels, like e.g. data-flow fifos or HW signals. We have developed such a SystemC 2.0 compliant channel library, which provides intuitive visualization, a comprehensive set of communication and timing annotation primitives as well as support for mixed-level co-simulation.

### 3.1    MSC Visualization

Our way of modeling complex systems is illustrated by a snapshot of our graphical debugger depicted in figure 2. The simulation is visualized according to the Message Sequence Chart (MSC) principle, which is a well known tracing mechanism usually employed in SDL design environments like the TAU SDL suite [5]. For our methodology, MSC tracing provides a very intuitive visualization of a network of coarse-grain SystemC processes exchanging ADTs.

SystemC modules are represented by vertical lines, which are labeled with the module name at the top. The progress of time is vertically notated from top to bottom. Communication events are displayed by horizontal arrows between the lines of the sending and receiving processes. These arrows are labeled with signal name, the point in time and the ADT type name.

A general drawback of the MSC representation is the amount of communication events for realistic systems with tens and hundreds of SystemC modules, because the user can observe only roughly up to 15 modules and up to 40 events simultaneously. Therefore our debugger provides advanced filter mechanisms to systematically reduce the displayed data to the currently interesting communication events.

To enable dynamic filtering, the MSC debugger maintains a data-base of all communication events. This data base can be searched in multiple dimensions, e.g. time, packet type, connection name or SystemC process hierarchy. Furthermore the event filter can introspect and search for the member-fields inside the ADTs, so the MSC debugger can filter e.g. all IP-packets with a certain destination address.

MSC visualization is a built-in feature of all channels in our library, so it is enabled by just instantiating the channels without any additional code in the user modules. Further channel features like timing annotation for architectural exploration are described in the next sections.

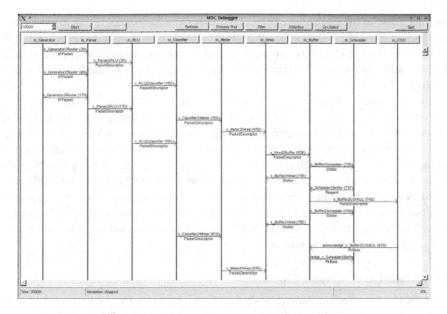

**Fig. 2.** Message Sequence Chart Visualization of the SystemC Simulation

## 3.2 Timing Annotation

Our goal is to model the architecture specific timing independently from the behavior, thus a functionally correct system model can be easily mapped to different architectures. According to the observations listed in 2.3, the channels provide methods to annotate processing delay and initiation interval. The channels are implemented hierarchically, since they incorporate internal processes to implement the mechanism for timing annotation.

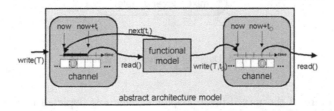

**Fig. 3.** Abstract Architecture Model

Figure 3 illustrates the creation of an abstract architecture model from the combination of the original functional model together with the channels to capture the impact on performance of the intended architecture. The right part of figure 3 shows the annotation of a processing delay $t_D$, which is passed as a second parameter of the write() method of outgoing connections. Transparently the channel takes care, that this token does not arrive at the consumer process before the specified delay $t_D$. In the same way, the left part of figure 3 shows the annotation of an initiation interval $t_I$ by calling the next() method of incoming connections. This causes the channel to suppress the arrival of tokens for the specified amount of cycles, which captures the effect of a blocking module.

Besides dedicated point to point communication, modern SoC architectures very often employ on-chip busses to improve utilization of interconnect resources. However shared busses cause a non-deterministic communication delay, which can have negative impact on the overall system performance in case of insufficient bus bandwidth. To capture this effect on the high abstraction level, we provide a generic bus model, which connects an arbitrary number of master and slave modules with a parameterizable bandwidth. A priority based bus arbitration scheme is used to resolve conflicts in case more than one master wants to perform a bus transaction at the same time. Alternatively, a Time Division Multiple Access (TDMA) based arbitration scheme allows interleaved service of simultaneous bus requests.

### 3.3   Mixed-Level Adapter Channel

The mixed-level adapter channel bridges the gap between packet-level and RT-level modules to enable block-wise functional verification, i.e. the RTL implementation is plugged into the abstract architecture model. Thus stimuli are derived from the system context and comparison of the synthesizable bit and cycle true implementation is done against the abstract architecture model. By that the significant effort for writing and verifying RT-level testbenches is avoided.

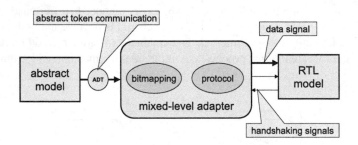

**Fig. 4.** Data- and Timing- refinement

The structure of the mixed-level adapter channels is depicted in figure 4: in the *bitmapping* engine, the adapter channel maps the ADT to the respective fields in the corresponding bit-accurate data representation. The resulting bitstream is then transfered to the protocol layer, where it is cut into slices according to the respective data width and forwarded to the RTL implementation. The *protocol* engine adds all the required control signals to reform the specified interface protocol.

A similar adapter channel implements the reverse direction to feed the output of the RTL implementation back into the packet-level environment. Here the ADT is reconstructed from the output bitstream provided by the protocol engine. Note that this concept is also capable to bridge packet-level and cycle-level TLM. Here the protocol engine calls the TLM interface methods instead of wiggling the RTL pins.

# 4  IP Forwarding Chip

In this section we present the results of an IP forwarding chip design project, where the proposed system level design methodology has been applied in cooperation with Synopsys Professional Services. We will introduce and characterize the design and illustrate the architecture mapping methodology by means of experimental results.

## 4.1  IP Forwarding with QoS Support

IP forwarding is a central part of the IP network infrastructure. This challenging application domain combines sophisticated functionality for QoS support with highest performance requirements: at OC-48 wire speed (corresponds to 2.5Gbit/s) the timing budget in the NPU for the processing of a minimum size 48Byte packet is as short as 147ns.

IP Forwarding with QoS Support according to the DiffServ proposal [6] requires a set of complex functional blocks. These are displayed in the shaded part of figure 5 together with the basic inter-block communication. The *Parser* performs checks on incoming packets and provides the following units with packet descriptors, which hold all the relevant header information of the respective IP packet. The *Route Lookup Unit* (RLU) performs forwarding of IP Packets based on the longest match table search algorithm. The forwarding decision is based upon destination IP address and the routing table. The *Classifier* classifies incoming packets into Classes of Service (CoS), so the packets are processed according to their negotiated Quality of Service parameters by the following blocks. The *Meter* measures the IP packet rate and drops packets exceeding the negotiated traffic characteristics to protect the succeeding queuer unit from unfriendly traffic streams. The *WRED* unit drops additional packets according to the weighted RED algorithm [7] to avoid throughput degradation especially for TCP traffic due to congestion. The *Queuer* stores IP packets according to their class of service until they can be forwarded to the CSIX unit. The *Scheduler* decides on the basis of the priority and the actual fill status of the packet queues in the queuer unit. Finally the *CSIX* unit segments IP packets into fixed size packets according to the standardized CSIX bus protocol to interface the switch fabric.

According to the methodology described in section 2, first a functional SystemC model is created from the functional specification document. This functional model is well suited to validate completeness and functional correctness, but does not yet impose any assumptions on the architectural realization.

## 4.2  Architecture Refinement and Exploration

Referring to the complete system view of figure 5, we first have to add an IP Packet Memory and a Memory Management Unit (MMU) to the functional model, which are necessary to store IP packets during the processing is performed by the functional units.

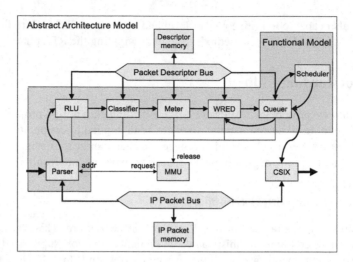

**Fig. 5.** IP Forwarding Chip

Given the specified constraints on latency and cost, the architect now has to define the general organization of the architecture. In our case, we decided to replace the expensive and inflexible point to point exchange of packet descriptors with a shared memory architecture, which is accessed through an on-chip bus.

The resulting SystemC architecture model of the IP router is running at 140k cycles per second on a 2 GHz Linux PC, thus in our case the simulation of 1 second IP traffic takes less than 12 minutes. In the following steps, the top-level structure of the router does not need to be modified. Instead, different configurations of the general system architecture depicted in figure 5 are evaluated in a very effective way by adjusting the generic model parameters and running the simulation.

An initial timing budget in terms of pipeline delay and initiation interval is annotated to each module as explained in section 2.3. The initial annotations represent an educated guess depending mostly on the experience of the designer. In our case, the timing annotations for the functional blocks are taken from a implementation on the Intel IXP2400 Network Processing Platform [8].

Based on simulations, the architect may relax some constraints, choose to tighten some others, or find out that a budget is required that is not realistic for a module. In the latter case, the architecture will be modified, e.g. resources are added or the algorithm is changed. Final budgets provide a requirement specification for later RTL implementation. The statistic evaluation of the functional blocks and the channels is used to detect bottlenecks in the system. A well-balanced system architecture provides sufficient processing power for all components.

An excerpt of the exploration results dealing with the dimensioning of the packet descriptor communication is printed in table 1. Besides the interconnect-description and -configuration we list the resource utilization and the mean delay per transaction of on the considered bus. The right column contains the overall packet latency introduced by the complete IP processing chain. Since the timing annotations of the functional units

**Table 1.** Exploration Results

| line | interconnect description | interconnect configuration | utili-zation | trn. delay in cycles | IP latency in cycles |
|------|--------------------------|----------------------------|--------------|----------------------|----------------------|
| 1 | p2p | unconstr. | 0% | 0 | 910 |
| 2 | p2p | 32bit | 8% | 22 | 1117 |
| 3 | IP_p2p | 32bit | 52% | 75 | 1117 |
| 4 | IP_bus | 64bit_prio | 78% | 149 | 1191 |
| 5 | IP_bus | 64bit_tdma | 78% | 93 | 1125 |
| 6 | pd_p2p | 32bit | 4% | 20 | 1117 |
| 7 | pd_bus | 32bit | 82% | 51 | 1582 |
| 8 | pd_bus | 64bit | 51% | 36 | 1355 |
| 9 | pd_bus | 128bit | 46% | 23 | 1142 |

are constant during the depicted experiment, the measured packet latency clearly unveils the impact of the selected communication architecture on the system level performance.

The point-to-point (p2p) communication of the functional model generates an initial traffic profile. The unconstrained p2p setup performs all communication with zero overhead, so the IP latency in line 1 reflects only the timing annotations of the functional units. The 32 bit wide p2p engine in line 2 serves as a 'lower-bound' reference configuration and not as a realistic design option. Among other unrealistic assumptions, this would implicate a packet descriptor memory with 6 read and 6 write ports , i.e. one for every connected module.

Besides an insignificant amount of local communication between the buffer and its neighboring units, the statistics generated by the p2p engine admits the classification of the on-chip traffic into two domains: (a) Parser, RLU and CSIX unit regularly access the IP memory (DRAM) to store and forward the arriving IP Packets and (b) all master blocks heavily access the packet descriptor memory.

Lines 3–5 refer to the exploration of traffic domain (a), where we examined a dedicated configuration corresponding to a multi-port IP memory and two different bus arbitration schemes connected to a single port memory. The priority based bus arbiter is obviously outperformed, because the uninterrupted transfer of long IP Packets has a negative influence on short packets. The preemptive TDMA scheduler minimizes the average delay by interleaving short and long packet transfers. The decision between configuration 3 and 5 is mainly driven by the technology dependent implementation cost of memories and wiring.

The third section in table 1 is dedicated to the exploration of a customized communication architecture for the access to the packet descriptor memory. The complete p2p mesh in line 6 is way too expensive and inefficient. Lines 7 to 9 shows the significant impact on performance of the shared bus bandwidth. Here the designer has to trade implementation cost against system performance.

## 5    Conclusion

In this paper, a system level design methodology based on the SystemC 2.0 library is presented. The outlined approach is capable to capture the complete system functionality as well as all performance relevant architecture features on the highest possible level of abstraction. The resulting modeling efficiency measured in lines of code and the simulation speed is about two orders of magnitude better compared to an RTL architecture model.

During a industry cooperation, the outlined methodology has been applied to the architecture conceptualization of an IP forwarding chip. By employing the proposed system level design methodology, a team of 3 engineers was able to demonstrate the feasibility and define a scalable and cost effective architecture within 2 months. The resulting system architecture model also serves as an executable specification and as a fast co-verification environment for the HW implementation.

Meanwhile the methodology has been extended to support HW/SW co-design [9, 10] and Network-on-Chip based communciation architectures [11].

# References

1. SystemC initiative, *http://www.systemc.org*.
2. T. Grötker, S. Liao, G. Martin, S. Swan, *System Design with SystemC.*   Kluwer Academic Publishers, 2002.
3. Cynthesizer SystemC Compiler, *Forte Design Systems, http://www.forteds.com*.
4. A. Evans, A. Silburt, G. Vrckovnik, T. Brown, M. Dufresne, G. Hall, T. Ho, and Y. Liu, "Functional Verification of Large ASICs," in *Proceedings of the Design Automation Conference (DAC)*, 1998, pp. 650–655.
5. TAU SDL suite, *Telelogic, http://www.telelogic.com*.
6. An Architecture for Differentiated Services, *http://www.ietf.org/rfc/rfc2475.txt*.
7. S. Floyd, and V. Jacobson, "Random early detection gateways for congestion avoidance," *IEEE/ACM Transactions on Networking*, vol. 1, no. 4, pp. 379–413, August 1993.
8. S. Lakshmanamurthy, K.-Y. Liu, Y. Pun, L. Huston, U. Naik, "Network Processor Performance Analysis Methodology," *Intel Technology Journal*, vol. 6, no. 3, Aug. 2002.
9. A. Hofmann, H. Meyr, R. Leupers, *Architecture Exploration for Embedded Processors with LISA.*   Kluwer Academic Publishers, 2002, iSBN 1-4020-7338-0.
10. A. Wieferink, M. Doerper, R. Leupers, Gerd Ascheid, H. Meyr, T. Kogel, "Early ISS integration into Network-on-Chip Designs," in *"Proc. Int. Workshop on Systems, Architecturs, Modeling and Simulation(SAMOS)"*, July 2004.
11. T. Kogel, M. Doerper, A. Wieferink, R. Leupers, G. Ascheid, H. Meyr, and S. Goossens, "A Modular Simulation Framework for Architectural Exploration of On-Chip Interconnection Networks," in *CODES+ISSS*, October 2003.

# Comparison of Data Dependence Analysis Tests

Miia Viitanen and Timo D. Hämäläinen

Tampere University of Technology, Institute of Digital and Computer Systems,
P.O. Box 553, FIN-33101, Tampere, Finland
timo.d.hamalainen@tut.fi

**Abstract.** Comparison of six data dependence analysis algorithms is presented. The algorithms are purposed for a parallel compiler that is being developed for a configurable multi-DSP system PARNEU. The algorithms are implemented in SUIF compiler framework and benchmarked with Perfect Club, Audio Signal Processing, and Media Bench test problems. Proprietary PARNEU programs that have been manually parallelised are also included. Performance in terms of accuracy and execution time of the data dependence algorithms has been measured and compared. The results show that the Omega test is the most accurate but also takes most execution time for benchmarks with for-loop parallelism.

## 1 Introduction

Parallel processing has traditionally been used in scientific computations in large-scale computers but now increasingly in embedded systems. This is reflected on inherently parallel, embedded processors as well as System-on-Chip implementations. However, the utilisation of parallel architectures has several difficulties, of which programming is among the worst one. This is further emphasized in configurable architectures [15].

In an ideal case, a parallel compiler takes care of the application algorithm mapping to the architecture. Such compilers have been studied intensively for parallel computers that have much resources and homogeneous architecture [2][14]. Unfortunately, those are not directly suitable for typical embedded parallel architectures [6].

Our research focuses on development of parallel compiler for a DSP based system called PARNEU [9]. It was developed for signal-processing applications, and it consists of a master and a scalable number of slave processors as well as configurable communication nodes also capable of performing simple operations. After several manual mappings of algorithms, the goal is to make the process automated.

As an essential part of this work, this paper presents results for implementation and comparison of several data dependence analysis tests. The goal is to find out the accuracy differences between the analysis algorithms with many different problems. Data dependence analysis is not only essential for automatic detection of parallelism, but also necessary for many other important compiler transformations that improve memory locality, load balancing, and reduce the overhead due to task initiation and synchronization.

A. Pimentel and S. Vassiliadis (Eds.): SAMOS 2004, LNCS 3133, pp. 149–158, 2004.

In the next two sections, we briefly introduce the PARNEU compiler and data dependence tests chosen for the comparison. After that, their implementations are discussed. The last sections present used benchmark problems and results with analysis.

## 2    Parneu Compiler

SUIF (Stanford University Intermediate Format) [8] framework has been chosen because of its ready made front-end for C and flexibility to freely modify and add new passes. An overview of the PARNEU compilation flow is depicted in Fig. 1. The sequential source code is first compiled into SUIF. Then the analysis and optimisation passes are applied. After that, the parallel code generator maps operations to the Processing Units (PU) of PARNEU. Information on the capabilities of PUs (memory, performance) and communication network is required at this phase. As a result, there are SUIF codes for each processor, which are further converted in C and compiled with the processor compiler. Communication primitives are available for the code generation. The data dependence analysis pass is performed before inserting the communication functions and parallelising the program.

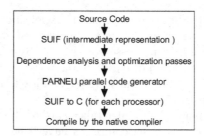

**Fig. 1.** Parallel compilation flow for PARNEU

The original SUIF paralleliser is targeted to shared- memory multiprocessors and is thus being re-written because PARNEU is a distributed memory system like many embedded systems. The standard data dependence analysis has been further improved with the implementation of other tests compared in this paper.

## 3    Dependence Tests

Data intensive signal processing and scientific algorithms often contain loops performing a set of operations on data arrays. Thus, a common way to increase performance is to exploit parallelism among iterations of a loop [13]. For this reason all of the data dependence tests chosen were limited to the analysis of this loop-parallelism. In addition, only static analysis was carried out in each test problem.

For the comparison, six dependence analysis algorithms were chosen that are **gcd test** [1], **generalised gcd test** [1], **extreme value test** [18], **Fourier-Motzkin elimination** [18], **Omega test** [12] and the standard **SUIF data dependence** approach. Detailed descriptions of the algorithms' functionality are outside the scope of this paper, but the selection criteria are considered in more detail.

One approach to form a data dependence test is to combine single test with other tests [17] to find generality, precision and complexity at the same time. Usually simple tests are used as starting point and then the more complex tests applied. For this reason both simple and complex tests were chosen.

Another criterion is to find an algorithm or combination of algorithms that is applicable to many kinds of inputs. In case of special case input algorithm, there is always the danger that the special case never occurs in the programs to be analysed. However, the standard SUIF approach to use a special case algorithm only for a suitable input is one way to use these algorithms efficiently.

The gcd test is very fast and simple. The disadvantage is that it is not accurate, because very often in practice the gcd of the coefficients turns out to be one, which of course divides any constant coefficient. The gcd test tells also nothing about the direction vector or the dependence distance. The gcd test ignores the loop bounds and simply determines whether the equation has an unconstrained integer solution. Thus, the gcd test produces a false positive, when the equation has an integer solution outside the limits but not within. This test can be applied only to single equation, which means that it can only consider a single subscript of a multidimensional array reference at a time. The gcd test has been chosen to be evaluated mainly, because it might be a good algorithm for example as the first test to the given dependence problem. If it can find independence, no other more expensive algorithm would be necessary to use in that case.

The generalised gcd test extends the gcd test to equation systems and provides only a necessary condition for dependence between two statements, i.e. answers the question if loop bounds are ignored is there an integral solution to the set of equations. The test itself is not exact; it can be used as a pre-processing step. The generalised gcd test can make other algorithms more efficient by transforming the original dependence problem into a simpler and smaller form. It eliminates the equality constraints and cuts down the number of variables per constraint.

The extreme value test considers the dependence system constraints. The method is to determine whether the dependence equation has a constrained real solution. The advantages of the extreme value test are that the test is very efficient, it can tell direction vector information and it considers the loop limits. Unfortunately, when some of the unknowns are unbounded, the method may not be able to find a lower or an upper bound for the function.

In the Fourier-Motzkin elimination, the system of linear inequalities is solved by projecting it onto a reduced number of unknowns, eliminating one unknown at a time. Fourier-Motzkin elimination as such only tells if real solutions exist or not. In addition, in the worst case, the number of inequalities may grow exponentially. Thus, the method is known to be computationally expensive [18].

The Omega test is an extension of Fourier-Motzkin elimination and thus, it has the same worst-case exponential time complexity. When performing the Omega test the loop limit values do not need to be known for the method to work. In addition, the Omega test can accurately determine distance and direction vectors.

The Omega test was chosen because evaluation between the SUIF approach and the Omega test has not been made previously. In addition, the Omega test differs in its basic principles from the approach of the variants of Banerjee's test, so it gives a new viewpoint for this evaluation. The Fourier-Motzkin elimination was evaluated, because it is a kind of "by-product" when the Omega test was implemented and in addition, it is interesting to see how many of the Omega test's independence results could be achieved only with the basic Fourier-Motzkin elimination.

The SUIF dependence analyser consists of a series of special case exact tests, each applicable to a limited domain. Thus, if the input is not of the appropriate form for an algorithm, the next test is tried. The test assortment consists of the extended gcd test, the **single variable per constraint test**, the **acyclic test**, the **simple loop residue test** and the Fourier-Motzkin elimination. The analysis also uses memorization, the technique of remembering previous test results, to capitalize on the fact that many dependence tests performed in one compilation are identical.

## 3.1  Implementation

SUIF Release 1.3.0.5 was used as the implementation environment in this work. The SUIF data dependence analysis functions are implemented in a sub-package called `dependence`. For this work, the package was taken as a template. The tests not present in the original SUIF dependence package were implemented and the new sub-package named `parneudependence`.

In the course of implementing the data dependence tests, several SUIF features were utilised. The `builder` package and the `suifmath` library of the SUIF compiler, which consists of a set of routines for the manipulation of matrices and linear inequalities, were used extensively. For example, the `linear inequality` library functions were utilised in implementation of some of the data dependence tests, like the Fourier-Motzkin elimination and the Omega test, which needed such functions.

## 4  Results

Sixteen benchmark problems were used for the evaluation of implemented data dependence analysis algorithms. The problems are listed in table below and are subsets of different kinds of benchmark suites. Perfect Club (PC) [3] problems represent scientific computations while Audio Signal Processing (ASP) [4] and MediaBench (MB) [4] DSP algorithms. The last collection is a small set of DSP-programs manually parallelised for PARNEU including DCT-based motion estimation algorithm [16], H.263 video encoder [10], matrix multiplication, Self-Organizing Map (SOM) [9] and wavelet transform [7].

Benchmarks were characterized in SUIF to find out where the data dependence analysis is applicable and what kind of analysis problems there are. Table 1 presents the characterized features and results.

**Table 1.** Characteristics of benchmark problems

| Benchmark →<br>Profile ↓ | LG (PC) | LW (PC) | NA (PC) | SR (PC) | TF (PC) | TI (PC) | Instf (ASP) | Radproc (ASP) | Rfast (ASP) | Rtpse (ASP) | mpeg2-enc (MB) | Dctmot (PARNEU) | h263enc (PARNEU) | Matrix (PARNEU) | SOM (PARNEU) | Wavelet (PARNEU) |
|---|---|---|---|---|---|---|---|---|---|---|---|---|---|---|---|---|
| Total # of for-loops | 129 | 54 | 269 | 219 | 181 | 78 | 39 | 38 | 32 | 34 | 80 | 64 | 116 | 5 | 16 | 7 |
| # of nonconstant loop cntrl. | 88 | 37 | 187 | 207 | 155 | 78 | 33 | 31 | 26 | 27 | 28 | 0 | 2 | 0 | 16 | 5 |
| # of nonconst. loop init. | 7 | 4 | 12 | 164 | 4 | 15 | 3 | 2 | 2 | 2 | 4 | 0 | 0 | 0 | 2 | 0 |
| Total # of array references | 757 | 535 | 187 | 170 | 884 | 93 | 34 | 31 | 32 | 26 | 250 | 123 | 397 | 7 | 13 | 4 |
| # of writes | 221 | 111 | 517 | 429 | 245 | 32 | 15 | 15 | 19 | 15 | 62 | 439 | 164 | 4 | 3 | 2 |
| # of reads | 536 | 424 | 135 | 127 | 639 | 61 | 19 | 16 | 13 | 11 | 188 | 796 | 233 | 3 | 10 | 2 |
| # of 1D arrays | 655 | 532 | 169 | 215 | 91 | 53 | 34 | 25 | 32 | 26 | 245 | 990 | 343 | 0 | 13 | 4 |
| # of 2D arrays | 102 | 3 | 183 | 148 | 793 | 40 | 0 | 6 | 0 | 0 | 5 | 245 | 54 | 7 | 0 | 0 |
| # of nonlinear subscripts | 2 | 7 | 115 | 0 | 0 | 0 | 0 | 0 | 0 | 0 | 47 | 0 | 0 | 0 | 1 | 0 |
| # of while-loops | 0 | 0 | 0 | 1 | 0 | 1 | 6 | 5 | 6 | 5 | 44 | 1 | 4 | 0 | 2 | 22 |

The number of *for-loops* gives an indication of how often the program could be parallelised if there was not data dependence. Only *counter-controlled* loops are considered. Non-constant loop limits in the loop condition (*initialisation* statement and *control* statement) were also included in the characterization, because they render the data dependence analysis. Some tests simply fail if this kind of situations happens.

The total number of *array references in for-loops* gives an implication how often the data dependence analysis is applicable. The number of array definitions (*writes*), the number of array uses (*reads*), the number of one-dimensional (1D) array references, the number of two-dimensional (2D) array references and the number of array references with *non-linear subscripts* are also included.

The last row in table is the number of *while*-loops, which are *logically controlled* loops. The repetition control is based on a Boolean expression rather than a counter and the data dependence analysis cannot be done in the same way as for *for*-loops.

The benefits of different data dependence analysis tests can be evaluated by comparing the number of definite dependences/independences found by the algorithm. Another factor that can be compared is the execution times of different data dependence analysis tests. This of course depends on the implementation the programmer has made and whether the program is optimised or not.

### 4.1 Measured Accuracy Results

The results of running the accuracy evaluation for the benchmark programs are seen in Table 2. The second column shows the actual number of data dependence

**Table 2.** Total number of problems and number of independence found by each test

| Benchmark | Total # of problems (100%) | GCD Test | Generalised GCD Test | Extreme Value Test | Fourier-Motzkin Elimination | Omega Test | SUIF Approach |
|---|---|---|---|---|---|---|---|
| LG (PC) | 6390 | 5455 | 5455 | 5552 | 5552 | 5552 | 5546 |
| | | 85% | 85% | 87% | 87% | 87% | 87% |
| LW (PC) | 942 | 18 | 18 | 90 | 72 | 90 | 102 |
| | | 2% | 2% | 10% | 8% | 10% | 11% |
| NA (PC) | 1801 | 6 | 6 | 6 | 6 | 6 | 6 |
| | | 0% | 0% | 0% | 0% | 0% | 0% |
| SR (PC) | 3281 | 2075 | 2075 | 2083 | 2085 | 2097 | 2077 |
| | | 63% | 63% | 63% | 64% | 64% | 63% |
| TF (PC) | 1287 | 559 | 559 | 659 | 624 | 758 | 585 |
| | | 43% | 43% | 51% | 48% | 59% | 45% |
| TI (PC) | 86 | 0 | 0 | 0 | 0 | 0 | 0 |
| | | 0% | 0% | 0% | 0% | 0% | 0% |
| Instf (ASP) | 30 | 0 | 0 | 0 | 0 | 0 | 0 |
| | | 0% | 0% | 0% | 0% | 0% | 0% |
| radproc (ASP) | 26 | 0 | 0 | 0 | 0 | 0 | 0 |
| | | 0% | 0% | 0% | 0% | 0% | 0% |
| rfast (ASP) | 2 | 0 | 0 | 0 | 0 | 0 | 0 |
| | | 0% | 0% | 0% | 0% | 0% | 0% |
| rtpse (ASP) | 21 | 0 | 0 | 1 | 0 | 1 | 0 |
| | | 0% | 0% | 5% | 0% | 5% | 0% |
| mpeg2enc (MB) | 50 | 0 | 0 | 0 | 0 | 0 | 0 |
| | | 0% | 0% | 0% | 0% | 0% | 0% |
| Dctmot (PARNEU) | 25034 | 22880 | 22880 | 22880 | 22880 | 22880 | 22880 |
| | | 91% | 91% | 91% | 91% | 91% | 91% |
| SOM (PARNEU) | 5 | 0 | 0 | 0 | 0 | 0 | 0 |
| | | 0% | 0% | 0% | 0% | 0% | 0% |
| h263enc (PARNEU) | 889 | 530 | 530 | 560 | 570 | 570 | 570 |
| | | 60% | 60% | 63% | 64% | 64% | 64% |
| wavelet (PARNEU) | 0 | 0 | 0 | 0 | 0 | 0 | 0 |
| | | 0% | 0% | 0% | 0% | 0% | 0% |
| matrix (PARNEU) | 1 | 0 | 0 | 0 | 0 | 0 | 0 |
| | | 0% | 0% | 0% | 0% | 0% | 0% |
| Accuracy % | 100% | 58.4 | 58.4 | 60.4 | 60.2 | 61.3 | 60 |

test problems that occur in a program when dependence test is called. The number of independent cases found by each test is presented in the same table in numbers as well as in terms of percentage of the total number of problems. The comparison gives an indication in how many cases the data dependence test can break the data dependence between array references and thus, improve the chances of parallelisation. In addition, the comparison gives also the number that the test has proven to be dependent or assumed to have possible dependence.

When comparing the results, it should be noted that the *Dctmot* benchmark program has considerably more data dependence problems than the other benchmarks and would dominate the total percentages. Therefore, the percentages are counted without it and listed in the last row of the table.

According to the results, the Omega test finds most of the independences. When the tests were run, the so-called "Omega test nightmare" situations were also checked. Notable is that in all the benchmark programs the Omega test had a "nightmare"-situation only three times. Thus, leaving these cases without testing and assuming them dependent does not diminish potential parallelism significantly. The Fourier-Motzkin elimination does not perform very badly either compared to other tests. Actually, the Fourier-Motzkin elimination can prove independence only 1.1% (when the *Dctmot* benchmark is excluded) less than the Omega test. However, as it can be seen the extensions to the Omega test improve the results and are thus important.

The extreme value test found independences second best, although the Fourier-Motzkin evaluation and the SUIF approach performed almost as well as it. On the other hand, because the extreme value test does not know how to distinguish the dependent cases but gives an answer of possible dependence, it does not give as good impression to the user as for example the SUIF approach. However, according to these results this test seems to be quite usable because it can even record the direction vectors.

The gcd test and the generalised gcd test performed the same as expected. The accuracy compared to others was also quite clear but still these tests should not be forgotten right away because of their simplicity. They can effectively be used as in SUIF approach ? as a preprocessing step. Quite interesting is also that the generalised gcd test proves independent only 1.6% (excluding *Dctmot*) less than the SUIF approach.

It is notable that accuracy differences between data dependence tests are not remarkably big. However, it should be kept in mind that when seeking possible parallelism from programs, pairs of references do not give the entire picture. In a loop with thousands of independent pairs, only one possible dependence can have a devastating effect on the amount of parallelism discovered. Thus, even the slightest differences between the algorithms can have positive effects to the parallelised program.

During the data dependence analysis, it was found out that the ASP and some of the PARNEU benchmark programs do not have many arrays inside the for-loops. In addition, when these were analysed with the data dependence tests, many of them were proven dependent (or *maybe* dependent) - thus, producing even the result of 0% independent.

When considered in more detail, there are a number of facts that influence the results. The problems with non-linear expressions appearing in the subscripts could be proved dependent. Variable with unknown and non-linear expressions appearing in the loop bounds also make the testing more difficult even though in some cases it could be possible to prove independence otherwise.

On the other hand, when the array references had coupled subscripts, the subscript-by-subscript tests (such as the gcd test) are inexact in a case where they cannot disprove the dependence in one of the subscripts. The percentage of found independences also seems to be unbelievably big. This is because most of them are merely constant array references. For example, array reference A[5] is always independent of A[3]. On the other hand, *renaming* can eliminate anti- and output dependences. Thus, the type of the proved dependence influences on the amount of actual parallelism available in the program.

In conclusion, the scientific applications in Perfect Club benchmarks with lots of for-loops and array references in them seemed to be the most suitable for data dependence testing and thus, for for-loop parallelisation. For these programs, the choice of a data dependence test is also significant. The most accurate for these test cases was the Omega test.

It was also found that for other than Perfect Club benchmarks the choice of the data dependence test is not so important in terms of accuracy, because all the tests performed almost the same. Many 0% results for the other benchmark programs show that the for-loop parallelisation is not the most appropriate because during the data dependence analysis many of the arrays in the for-loops were proven dependent. The 0% results also emphasize the fact that characterization of analysable programs may improve the parallelisation because suitable parallelisation schemes can be applied at once.

## 4.2   Execution Time

The tool **gprof** [5] was used to measure the execution times in a Linux Redhat 6.2 operating system. To minimize measurement errors the different data dependence analysis tests were run 100 times and an average taken for every benchmark program.

The total sum over all benchmark problem execution times is depicted in Fig. 2. The Omega test and the Fourier-Motzkin elimination take about 20% more time than other data dependence analysis tests. However, the percentage is even bigger for a single, large problem. The execution times of other tests are as expected.

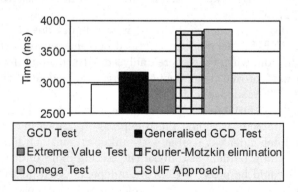

**Fig. 2.** Total sums of execution times

The gcd test as a very simple algorithm performs best. The extreme value test, although it also produces direction vector information, performs almost the same as the gcd test. The generalised gcd test performs almost the same as the SUIF approach. Thus, the SUIF data dependence approach pays only little in execution times considering that the accuracy results are quite good.

However, it should be noted that the SUIF data dependence analysis uses memorization, which means that it does not perform the data dependence test again if it is identical to a data dependence test performed earlier in that compilation. This technique could also benefit the execution times of the other tests if it was implemented on them.

## 5 Conclusions

During the work it became obvious that rather than just comparing the accuracy of the algorithm, the other properties, like the algorithm's ability to find dependence distance or direction vectors, and need for tight time constraints, has also an important effect on choosing an appropriate data dependence analysis algorithm.

The most accurate data dependence test was the Omega test. The question is if the accuracy of it pays what it looses in execution time. The long execution time of the Omega test probably makes it unsuitable for large applications or applications, which have to be compiled repeatedly. This situation is familiar with embedded system architecture exploration tools that make many iterations to e.g. give a user many possibilities to choose from. In such a loop the source code (or intermediate representation of it) is attempted to be modified, for which reason the data dependence analysis is carried out again.

For the ASP and the PARNEU programs, the choice of the data dependence test did not seem to be as significant as for Perfect Club problems according to the accuracy results. Thus, in these cases also the SUIF approach or the extreme value test can be useful. Both performed well when measuring the execution times and both have additional properties compared to the traditional gcd test and the general gcd test.

In general, the data dependence analysis solves only one problem in automatic program parallelisation and as such is not enough. In our research, we are moving on to the paralleliser, which requires also abstract representation of the physical architecture of the parallel platform. The greatest challenge is to make the compiler framework independent of the architecture, because contemporary configurable System-on-Chip designs are unique case by case. PARNEU will provide a platform to this work.

## References

1. Banerjee U, Dependence Analysis, Kluwer Academic Publishers, USA, 1997, 213 p.
2. Banerjee U, Eigenmann R, Nicolau A and Padua D A, Automatic Program Parallelization, Proceedings of the IEEE, Vol. 81, No. 2, February 1993, pp. 211-243.
3. Berry M et al., The Perfect Club Benchmarks, Effective Performance Evaluation of Supercomputer, Technical Report UIUCSRD Rep. No. 827, University of Illinois Urbana-Champaign, 1989, 48 p.
4. Embree P M, C Language Algorithms for Real-Time DSP, Prentice-Hall, 1995, 256 p.

5. Fenlason and Stallman, GNU gprof, The GNU Profiler, Available at
   http://www.gnu.org/manual/gprof-2.9.1/html_chapter/gprof_toc.html
6. Gauthier L, Yoo S, Jerraya A, Automatic Generation and Targeting of Application-
   Specific Operating Systems and Embedded Systems Software, IEEE Transactions
   on Computer-Aided Design of Integrated Circuits and Systems, Vol. 20, No. 11,
   2001, pp. 1293-1301.
7. Haapala K, Kolinummi P, Hämäläinen T, Saarinen J, Parallel DSP Implementation
   of Wavelet Transform in Image Compression, IEEE International Symposium on
   Circuits and Systems, Geneva, Switzerland, May 28-31, 2000, Vol. 5, pp. 89-92.
8. Hall M, Anderson J, Amarasinghe S, Murphy B, Liao SW, Bugnion E, Lam M,
   Maximizing Multiprocessor Performance with the SUIF Compiler, IEEE Computer, Vol. 29, No. 12, 1996, pp. 84-89.
9. Kolinummi P, Hämäläinen P, Hämäläinen T, Saarinen J, PARNEU: General-
   Purpose Partial Tree Computer, Microprocessors and Microsystems, Vol. 24, No.
   1, 2000, pp. 23-42.
10. Kolinummi P, Särkijärvi J, Hämäläinen T, Saarinen J, Scalable Implementation of
    H.263 Video Encoder on a Parallel DSP System, IEEE International Symposium
    on Circuits and Systems, Geneva, Switzerland, May 2000, Vol.1, pp. 551-554.
11. Pugh W, A Practical Algorithm for Exact Array Dependence Analysis, Commu-
    nications of the ACM, Vol. 35, No. 8, August, 1992, pp. 102-114.
12. Pugh W, The Omega Test: A Fast and Practical Integer Programming Algorithm
    for Dependence Analysis, Proceedings of the 1991 Confeqrence on Supercomputing,
    held in Albuquerque, NM USA, 1991, pp. 4-13.
13. Ramasubramanian N, Subramanian R, Pande S, Automatic compilation of loops
    to exploit operator parallelism on configurable arithmetic logic units, IEEE Trans-
    actions on Parallel and Distributed Systems, Vol. 13, No. 1, 2002, pp. 45-66.q
14. Sungdo M, Byoungro S, Hall MW, Evaluating automatic parallelization in SUIF,
    IEEE Transactions on Parallel and Distributed Systems, Vol. 11, No. 1, 2000, pp.
    36-49.
15. Thoen P, Catthoor F, Modeling, Verification and Exploration of Task-Level Con-
    currency in Real-Time Embedded Systems, Kluwer Academic Publishers, 2000,
    438 p.
16. Viitanen M, Kolinummi P, Hämäläinen T, Saarinen J, Scalable DSP Implementa-
    tion of DCT-based Motion Estimation Algorithm, Proceedings of EUSIPCO 2000,
    the X European Signal Processing Conference, Vol. 1, Tampere, Finland, Septem-
    ber. 4-8, 2000.
17. Wolfe M, Tseng C, The Power Test for Data Dependence, IEEE Transactions on
    Parallel and Distributed Systems, Vol. 3, No. 5, September 1992, pp. 591-601.
18. Wolfe M, High Performance Compiler for Parallel Computing, Addison-Wesley,
    1996, 570 p.

# MOUSE: A Shortcut from Matlab Source to SIMD DSP Assembly Code

Gordon Cichon and Gerhard Fettweis

Mobile Communcations Chair, TU-Dresden
D-01062 Dresden, Germany
cichon@ifn.et.tu-dresden.de

**Abstract.** This article presents a novel design flow called MOUSE for the effective development of digital signal processing systems in terms of development time, performance and power consumption. It uses a model in high-level language like Matlab[1] as a starting point. Utilizing techniques originating from supercomputing and dynamical compilation, these models can be translated to assembly code for specialized DSP processors of the CATS family. An implementation of terrestial digital video broadcast (DVB-T) serves as an example.

## 1 Introduction

The traditional design flow for the development of signal processing systems requires the implementation of two models of the system: First, conceptual development and prototyping is done in high-level languages like Matlab. The actual implementation then takes place in a second model, which is developed in a modeling language close to the target hardware platform.

According to [8], Matlab is the most popular language for the development of the first kind of model. It has a community of over 500,000 users.

The development of the second model is usually the major effort in the development process. It is written either in VHDL for FPGA and ASIC targets, or in low-level C and assembly language for DSP targets. Fig. 1 shows such a design flow on the left hand side.

Experience with the development of complex signal processing systems at the Vodafone Chair of Mobile Communication Systems suggests that a great amount of productivity enhancement can be achieved by cutting down the development effort of a target specific system model. For this reason, we chose to avoid reimplementing the second model from scratch, but instead to reuse the high-level model for this purpose (see Fig. 1, right hand side).

This paper presents a high-level language frontend of the MOUSE compiler system. Additionally, we provide an implementation of a transmitter and receiver for terrestial digital video broadcast (DVB-T), as a benchmark application.

---

[1] Matlab is a registered trademark of MathWorks, Inc.

A. Pimentel and S. Vassiliadis (Eds.): SAMOS 2004, LNCS 3133, pp. 159–167, 2004.

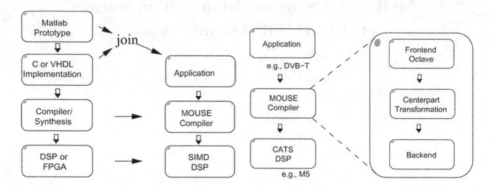

**Fig. 1.** Digital Signal Processing, Design Flow     **Fig. 2.** MOUSE development environment

## 2   Related Work

Matlab compiler [11] translates code from Matlab into generic C code. The type switching and memory management of this approach is not optimized for an environment with tight constraints on memory consumption and performance.

[3] offers a dynamic compilation technique that utilizes runtime type inference. This approach is not well-suited to embedded systems with tight memory consumption constraints, either.

[8] presents a system to compile Matlab to FPGA platforms. This kind of translation implies a data-flow driven architecture.

[9] presents a system for translating nested loop programs written in the Matlab programming language into a process network description. This kind of process network description is suitable for implementations using generic functional units constituting a systolic array.

It has been shown at the M3 processor design [15] that for many typical signal-processing applications, like wireless transmission systems, DSL, and others, an implementation using a SIMD approach can improve resource utilization and is able to reduce the demand for buffer memory between different processing elements. This is particularly the case with systems that involve data interleaving [16].

## 3   The MOUSE Design Flow

Fig. 2 shows a novel design flow for the development of a digital signal processing system based on the experience at the Vodafone chair. The Matrix Optimized Universal Signal-processing Environment (MOUSE) leverages the inherent parallelism inside vector- or matrix-based high-level development languages, such as Matlab [11], for the compilation of programs for SIMD processors.

It utilizes techniques originating from supercomputing, especially vectorizing compilation [2], [19], and the efficient translation of dynamically typed programming languages, such as Java [4].

Using this approach, high-level language models can serve directly as a source code to implementations in a SIMD architecture, like CATS DSP family [15], without the need for rewriting the algorithm in a language of lower abstraction level, such as C or VHDL.

The MOUSE compiler consists of three pieces: First, a frontend that reads the program source code and transforms it into a suitable intermediate representation. Second, the centerpart that performs dynamic type analysis, floating point to fixed point mapping, vectorization, and unique program transformations. And third, a traditional compiler backend [1, 12] that maps an intermediate representation at the level of C code to machine language.

Together, these three pieces form a tool-chain that enables rapid system development for signal processing systems. In contrast to other approaches, the proposed design flow allows the compilation of assembly code for a high-performance, low-power DSP-implementation from existing Matlab code.

A carefully written code can be translated directly without further modification. However, in larger projects, it often becomes necessary to gradually adapt the code to facilitate recognition of data types and to exploit parallelism. In contrast to dual-implementation approaches, the transition can be done within a running environment, and without breaking existing code. It can be done in a way that is integrated in the environment.

In addition to that, modifications are small and merely affect the arrangement in which statements and loops are written. However, the abstraction level and the expressiveness of the code still remain high. The necessary transformations are the ones described for Fortran in high-performance super-computing environments [2].

## 4   Octave Frontend

The frontend part of the MOUSE compiler is based on the code of the Octave interpreter. Octave accepts a substantial subset of the Matlab programming language. It is freely available under the general public license (GPL), and the Octave Frontend can be downloaded from the MOUSE homepage [5].

The MOUSE adaptation of Octave can either interpret high-level language programs, or it can act as a compiler frontend to translate programs into advanced intermediate representation (AIR), suitable for the following stages of the compiler. This intermediate representation can also be translated to the Aterm format, which is used at the Stratego project [17] at the University of Utrecht.

To achieve this functionality, a new software module has been introduced into the octave interpreter. This software module converts the internal program representation of Octave into that of AIR and writes it to a file. Conversion to Aterm is achieved by running the embedded rna2aterm converter.

RNA is a simple library that facilitates the handling of persistent tree and graph data structures. Figure 3 shows an overview of the fundamental data types available in RNA. Simple data types include booleans, strings, integers, and floating point values. Composite data types are records, arrays and lists. The composite data types can reference each other deliberately, such that graph data structures can be constructed.

The following features of Matlab are supported by the octave frontend:

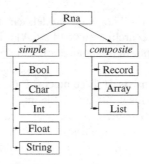

**Fig. 3.** RNA Architecture

## 4.1 Constants and Variables

- **variable**
  Variables can have an arbitrary name according to standard identifier naming rules. Types of variables are not explicitly specified in Matlab. First releases of the centerpart of the compiler will require a separate description of the types of the used variables. In future versions, automatic type inference can be accomplished either by profile based approaches [18], or by abstract interpretation [6].
- **constant**
  Constants can be integers (e.g.: 1), floating point values (e.g.: 3.14), or a vector of items enclosed in square brackets. (e.g.: [1; 2; 3]). The sophisticated parsing rules for matrices in Matlab apply.

## 4.2 Types

- **bool**
  Matlab does not allow explicit designation of values to the type boolean. However, the compiler can recognize certain expressions and variables as boolean values through the way of their creation and use. Vectorized boolean values play an important role in the parallelization of if-statements.
- **integer**
  Integer is a basic type of machine precision. In the CATS DSP design, this precision will presumably be 16 bit. Other instances of the DSP platform might work with 8 or 32 bit for this quantity. Currently, there is no support for character data types.
- **float**
  Since floating point computation is not supported by typical DSP platforms, a floating point values can be transformed globally into an integer representation using a suited transformation technique (e.g., [18] or [6]) by the compiler centerpart.
  Currently, all floating point values are represented as q.15 fixed point values by the compiler centerpart. In the process of accumulating results from vector products, 40-bit intermediate results may be generated.
- **vector**
  A vector will be distributed across the slices of the SIMD DSP processor, and the compiler will try to execute operations on vectors in a parallel way across different

slices using SIMD parallelization techniques [2]. Vectors with a constant length, and with a length of a multiple of the number of slices will experience a performance gain.

– **matrix**

A matrix is represented as a two-dimensional vector. Arranging a matrix in memory gives the compiler a degree of freedom: It can either be stored in row order or in column order. Currently, matrices are sorted in the same order as in Fortran programs.

## 4.3  Expressions

Matlab supports several different kinds of expressions:

– **primary expressions**

A primary expression is a variable name or a constant (e.g.: a, 5).

– **indexed expressions**

An indexed expression consists of an expression followed by a comma-separated list of arguments enclosed in parentheses. The individual arguments are expressions, in turn. In Matlab, an indexed expression can represent either a function call or an element access of a vector (e.g.: fun(1,5), a(5)).

– **arithmetic expressions**

Arithmetic expressions are combinations of expressions linked with arithmetic operators. Currently, the following operators are supported: + - * / & | && || ! (e.g., 1+1, a+5, a(i)+b(i)).

– **range expressions**

A range expression creates a vector filled with a sequence of values. These values start with a specific initial value, they have a constant increment, and end with a final value (e.g.: 1:n means [1; 2; ...; n], 3:3:18 means [3; 6; 9; 12; 15; 18]).

Ranges play a special role as range expressions for loops. In this case, the corresponding vector is not created explicitly. Instead, the loop induction variable is initialized with the corresponding range value for each loop body instance.

## 4.4  Statements

– **assignment statement**

An assignment statement consists of two expressions separated by an assignment operator. Currently, the following assignment operators are supported: = += -= *= /=. (e.g., a=1; a+=1 a(i)=b(i)+c)

– **if statement**

If statements are supported without restrictions.

– **while loop**

While loops are translated directly into loops on the assembly level.

– **break**
– **continue**
– **return**

The above three control flow statements facilitate expressive structured programming in the absence of goto statements.

– **for loop**
  For loops are subject to vectorization by the centerpart. The compiler tries to find loops in which there are no data dependencies between the individual instances of the loop body over the induction variable. If this case is detected, the compiler can potentially parallelize the loop using SIMD parallelization.
– **statement list**
  Statements can be chained together, separated by full stops or semi-colons.

### 4.5   Function Definition

For the development of structured programs, the definition of functions is supported by the compiler. At this time, variable length argument lists are not supported.

## 5   Benchmark Application: DVB-T

To evaluate the effectiveness of the proposed design flow, the implementation efforts of a system are compared under two different development environments: An implementation in Matlab, and an implementation in assembly language.

As benchmark application, DVB-T was chosen. It is a complex signal processing application, including Reed/Solomon, Viterbi, FFT, and interleaver algorithms. The structure of the system is shown in Figure 4.

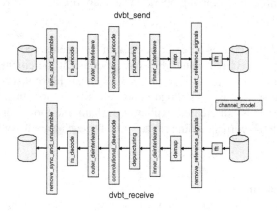

**Fig. 4.** DVB-T Overview

The DVB-T system is implemented according to the ETSI standard [7]. We considered a standard system with 2048 carriers, 16-QAM, and 2/3 puncturing. This yields a typical data rate of 14 Mbps.

The system is composed by the following modules:

– **Scrambler**
  This is a simple XOR-operation with a pseudo-random bit-sequence generated by a feedback shift register. The operation requires 2 MIPS with a stored PRBS sequence.

- **Reed/Solomon**
  This is a shortened (188,204,16) decoder. It is implemented using Berlekamp-Massey, Chien-Search, and Forney. The data rate requires 11 MIPS to perform the decoding. However, this kind of algorithm is quite control flow intensive for a DSP application, and thus serves as a good indicator for the behavior of the CATS DSPs in terms of performance, power-consumption and code density.
  Our group has also developed a Reed/Solomon decoder in assembly language, written by a student worker [13].
- **Outer Interleaver**
  A convolutional interleaver with parameters I=12, M=17.
- **Viterbi Decoder**
  This is a 64-state, soft-decision Viterbi decoder. In Matlab, we use the implementation of Kammeyer and Kuehn [10]. This is the computationally most intensive part of the system, requiring 990 MIPS for Trellis computation and 140 MIPS for traceback.
  Our group has also developed an assembly language implementation of a Viterbi-decoder which uses either 4 or 16 bit of fixed point precision [14].
- **Inner Interleaver**
  A block interleaver on OFDM symbols.
- **Mapping**
  Currently, the DVB-T system supports 16-QAM mapping.
- **OFDM-demodulation**
  This module consists of a FFT. It is computationally expensive, requiring 720 MIPS.
  The Matlab implementation uses a call to the `fft` runtime library function.

As shown above, the system requires a high data processing rate, and, for mobile applications, a low power consumption. A performance analysis of the data rate required for DVB-T shows that Viterbi needs 1130 MIPS and Reed-Solomon requires 11 MIPS for the signal processing part. Also, the whole system is supposed to run battery-powered, i.e. with a power consumption around 1 Watt.

The implemented system runs in the Matlab environment, as well as on the MOUSE Octave Frontend. It is available for download under a BSD license from the MOUSE homepage [5].

Although automatic parallelization does not work reliably in all circumstances because of Turing computability reasons, it can be concluded that with minor program modifications for fine tuning, compiled code can be made comparably fast as handwritten assembly code.

# 6  Results

As depicted in Figure 5, the Matlab implementation of Open-DVB, Version 0.3, has about 5000 lines of code in total. A significant number of these lines are comments. In addition to that, code of testbenches is more than one third of the total code. In the following comparison, comments and testbenches will not be counted. The entire DVB-T code was implemented within about three man-month.

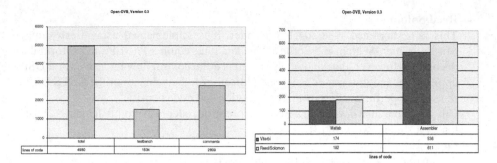

**Fig. 5.** DVB-T: total system         **Fig. 6.** DVB-T: lines of code

Two important modules, Reed-Solomon [13] and Viterbi [14], were implemented in assembly code by students. Each of these two modules took about three man-month to implement. In the following, the Matlab and assembly language implementations of these modules are compared.

Figure 6 shows the lines of code needed to implement the two algorithms in Matlab and assembly code. It can also be observed that the code lines in Matlab rarely exceed 80 columns. Due to the VLIW instruction set of the target DSP, code lines are much wider in assembly code: up to 536 columns for Viterbi and up to 611 columns for Reed/Solomon. It can be concluded that implementation in Matlab requires significantly less effort.

In addition to that, the implementation of a complex system like DVB-T on the MOUSE compiler framework serves as an indicator for its stability and correctness.

## 7 Further Work

As a next step, the implementation of the centerpart will show the viability of this approach. Modules currently under work are type inference, memory layout of data, and parallelization by vectorization. A deeper coverage of the centerpart and backend of the MOUSE compiler will be presented in a separate paper.

## Acknowledgments

The authors would like to thank K. Kammeyer and V. Kuehn for the contribution of their Viterbi decoder and D. Schoenfeld for her help with the math of Reed/Solomon. Thanks also to the CATS team and to Caroline Cichon.

This work has been sponsored in part by the German Science Foundation (Deutsche Forschungsgemeinschaft, DFG) within SFB356-A6.

## References

1. A. V. Aho, R. Sethi, and J. D. Ullman. *Compilers. Principles, Techniques, and Tools.* Addison-Wesley, Redding, MA, 1985.
2. R. Allen and K. Kennedy. *Optimizing Compilers for Modern Architectures.* Morgan Kaufmann Publishers, Burlington, MA, 2001.

3. G. Almasi and D. Padua. Majic: Compiling matlab for speed and responsiveness. In *ACM SIGPLAN PLDI*, Berlin, 2002.
4. C. Chambers. *The Design and Implementation of the Self Compiler, an Optimizing Compiler for Object-Oriented Programming Languages*. PhD thesis, Computer Science Department, Stanford University, March 1992.
5. G. Cichon. MOUSE: Matrix Optimized Universal Signal-processing Environemnt. http://www.radionetworkprocessor.com/.
6. A. Cortesi, editor. *Verification, Model Checking, and Abstract Interpretation, Third International Workshop, VMCAI 2002, Venice, Italy, January 21-22, 2002, Revised Papers*, volume 2294 of *Lecture Notes in Computer Science*. Springer, 2002.
7. ETSI. Digital video broadcasting (DVB); framing structure, channel coding and modulation for digital terrestrial television. EN 300 744 V1.4.1, 2001.
8. M. Haldar, A. Nayak, A. Choudhary, and P. Banerjee. A system for synthesizing optimized FPGA hardware from matlab™. In *Proc. of the 2001 IEEE/ACM international conference on Computer-aided design (ICCAD'01)*, pages 314–319, San Jose, CA, Nov. 2001.
9. T. Harriss, R. Walke, B. Kienhuis, and E. Deprettere. Compilation from matlab to process networks realized in FPGA. *Design Automation of Embedded Systems*, 7(4), 2002.
10. K. Kammeyer and V. Kuehn. *Matlab in der Nachrichtentechnik*. J. Schlembach-Verlag, Weil der Stadt, Deutschland, 1. auflage edition, 2001.
11. Matlab™. http://www.mathorks.com/.
12. S. Muchnik. *Advanced compiler design and Implementation*. Morgan Kaufmann Publishers, 1997.
13. Rene Beckert. Implementierung eines Reed-Solomon-Decoders fuer DVB-T auf einem hochparallelen Signalprozessor. ftp://ftp.radionetworkprocessor.com/pub/vodafone-chair/Studienarbeit-Be%ckert.pdf, 2003.
14. Rene Habendorf. Implementierung eines Viterbi-Decoders fuer DVB-T auf einem hochparallelen Signalprozessor. ftp://ftp.radionetworkprocessor.com/pub/vodafone-chair/Studienarbeit-Ha%bendorf.pdf, 2002.
15. T. Richter, W. Drescher, F. Engel, S. Kobayashi, V. Nikolajevic, M. Weiss, and G. Fettweis. A platform-based highly parallel digital signal processor. In *Proc. CICC*, pages 305–308, San Diego, USA, 2001.
16. T. Richter and G. Fettweis. Parallel interleaving on parallel DSP architectures. In *Proc. of IEEE Workshop on Signal Processing Systems (SiPS'02)*, pages 195–200, San Diego, USA, oct 2002.
17. E. Visser. Stratego: A language for program transformation based on rewriting strategies. System description of Stratego 0.5. In A. Middeldorp, editor, *Rewriting Techniques and Applications (RTA'01)*, volume 2051 of *Lecture Notes in Computer Science*, pages 357–361. Springer-Verlag, May 2001.
18. M. Willems, V. Buersgens, H. Keding, and H. Meyr. FRIDGE: Fliesskomma-Programmierung von Festkomma-DSPs. In *DSP Deutschland*, Muenchen, 1997.
19. Zima and Chapman. *Supercompilers for Parallel and Vector Computers*. Addison-Wesley, Redding, MA, 1990.

# High-Level Energy Estimation for ARM-Based SOCs

Dan Crisu[1], Sorin Dan Cotofana[1], Stamatis Vassiliadis[1], and Petri Liuha[2]

[1] Computer Engineering Laboratory, Electrical Engineering, Mathematics and Computer Science Faculty, Delft University of Technology Mekelweg 4, 2600 GA Delft, The Netherlands
{dan,sorin,stamatis}@ce.et.tudelft.nl
[2] Nokia Research Center, Visiokatu-1, SF-33720 Tampere, Finland
petri.liuha@nokia.com

**Abstract.** In recent years, power consumption has become a critical concern for many VLSI systems. Whereas several case studies demonstrate that technology-, layout-, and gate-level techniques offer power savings of a factor of two or less, architecture and system-level optimization can often result in orders of magnitude lower power consumption. Therefore, the energy-efficient design of portable, battery-powered systems demands an early assessment, i.e., at the algorithmic and architectural levels, of the power consumption of the applications they target. Addressing this issue, we developed an energy-aware architectural design exploration and analysis tool for ARM based system-on-chip designs. The tool integrates the behavior and energy models of several user-defined, custom processing units as an extension to the cycle-accurate instruction-level simulator for the ARM low-power processor family, called the ARMulator. The models we implemented take into account the particular class, e.g., datapath, memory, control, or interconnect, as well as the architectural complexity of the hardware unit involved and the signal activity triggered by the specific algorithm executed on the ARM processor. Our tool can estimate at the architectural level of detail the overall energy consumption or can report the energy breakdown among different units. Preliminary experiments indicated that the estimation accuracy is within 25% of what can be accomplished after a circuit-level simulation on the laid-out chip.

## 1 Introduction

With the advent of mobile platforms for computing and communications, system designers and integrators were confronted with a massive shortage of tools that enable early energy consumption estimation for such systems. CAD tool support for embedded system design is still limited and it addresses mainly functional verification and performance estimation.

The intricacy involved by these new electronic appliances imposed a new design paradigm to cope with the specific requirements, e.g., low cost with fast time to market, and restrictions they have. Also, energy consumption is a critical factor in system-level design of embedded portable appliances. A hardware-software co-design framework must be employed to proceed with the design from the software applications intended to run on these appliances to the final specifications of the hardware that implements the desired functionality given the above-mentioned constraints. Studies have demonstrated that circuit- and gate-level techniques have less than a $2\times$ impact on power,

A. Pimentel and S. Vassiliadis (Eds.): SAMOS 2004, LNCS 3133, pp. 168–177, 2004.

while architecture- and algorithm-level strategies offer savings of $10 - 100\times$ or more [1]. Hence, the greatest benefits are derived by trying to assess early in the design process the merits of the potential implementation. Architecture optimization corresponds to searching for the best design that optimize all objectives. Since the optimization problem involves multiple criteria (power consumption, throughput, and cost) to reach the global optimum a set of Pareto points [2] in the design space have to be found. Ideally, when designing an embedded system, a designer would like to explore a number of architectural alternatives and test functionality, energy consumption, and performance without the need to build a prototype first.

Usually, typical portable systems are built of commodity components and have a microprocessor-based architecture. Full system evaluation is often done on prototype boards resulting in long design times. Power consumption estimation can be done only late in the design process, after the prototype board was built, resulting in slow power tuning turnarounds that doesn't meet the requirement of fast time to market. On the other hand, using field programmable gate array (FPGA) hardware emulators for functional debugging, with a fast prototyping time, can neither give accurate estimates of energy consumption nor of the performance.

Among the tools preferred for early performance assessment at the algorithmic and architectural level, in the last decade, were the cycle-accurate instruction-set simulators. Unfortunately, for power consumption estimation this approach was seldom easy to follow. There were only a few academic tools for power estimation (all based on or integrated in the SimpleScalar instruction set simulator toolset framework [3], [4], [5]) and almost no commercial products.

For several target general purpose processors a number of techniques emerged in the last few years. The processor energy consumption for an instruction trace was generally estimated by instruction-level power analysis [6], [7]. This technique estimates the energy consumed by a program by summing the energy consumed by the execution of each instruction. Instruction-by-instruction energy costs, together with non-ideal effects, are precharacterized once for each target processor. A few research prototype tools that estimate the energy consumption of processor core, caches, and main memory have been proposed [8], [9]. Memory energy consumption is estimated using cost-per-access models. Processor execution traces are used to drive memory models, thereby neglecting the non-negligible impact of a non ideal memory system on program execution. The main limitation of these approaches is that the interaction between memory system (or I/O peripherals) and processor is not modeled. Cycle-accurate register-transfer level energy estimation was proposed in [4]. The tool integrates RT level processor simulator with DineroIII cache simulator and memory model. It was shown to be within 15% of HSPICE simulations.

The drawback of all the above methods to estimate the power consumption is that they are based on certain architectural templates, i.e., general purpose processors and can be hardly adapted to model system-on-chip designs.

A new approach towards high-level power estimation is presented in this paper in the context of ARMulator [10], a cycle-accurate instruction-level simulator for the ARM low-power processor family. More in particular, we developed an energy-aware architectural design exploration and analysis tool for ARM based system-on-chip de-

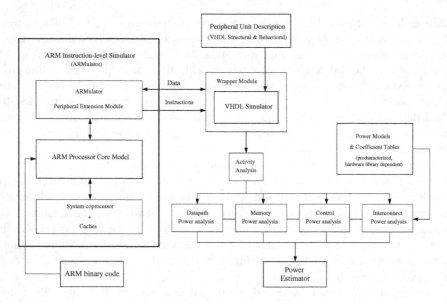

**Fig. 1.** System-on-chip simulator architecture.

signs. The tool integrates the behavior and energy models of several user-defined, custom processing units as an extension to the ARMulator. These models take into account the impact of design complexity and signal activity on datapath, memory, control, and interconnect power consumption. So far we have implemented only the tool framework and the power calculators for the datapath part. Experiments carried on employing a sample coprocessor design indicated that the accuracy of the results obtained by behavioral simulation is within 25% of that obtained using circuit simulators.

The rest of the paper is organized as follows. We present the system model and the methodology for cycle-accurate simulation of energy dissipation in Section 2. In Section 3, to validate the employed methodology we design down to the physical layout a sample coprocessor for an ARM1020T CPU core in order to run a number of realistic experiments and prove the effectiveness of the proposed high-level methodology. Finally, Section 4 presents the conclusions and describes future work in the area.

## 2 Proposed Design Exploration Framework

In this section we present our approach to estimate at the architectural level the power consumption of a coprocessor or peripheral unit coupled with an ARM CPU core on a system-on-chip.

### 2.1 System Model

Figure 1 gives an overview of the power analysis strategy that we propose.

We use this strategy for the design of peripheral units that augment or complement ARM CPU core functionality. The instruction set architecture of the ARM family of processors offers room for extensions to be added by providing the so called coprocessor instructions. Referring to the Figure 1, the inputs from the user are a description of a candidate architecture for the desired peripheral unit given in behavioral or structural VHDL and the set of data and the application program for which a power analysis is desired. The provided program is then compiled using the ARM native compiler. Usually, the code will embed, beside ARM native instructions, specific peripheral unit instructions. These specific instructions, when executed on the ARMulator (the ARM instruction set simulator), will be recognized as non-native or coprocessor instructions and they will trigger callback functions, installed using the ARMulator API (application programming interface), so specific actions (e.g., new data or commands are fed to the hardware description simulated in VHDL) can be taken. Moreover, every clock cycle, the ARMulator will sent signals to the VHDL simulator to advance the state of the simulated hardware description one more clock cycle. In this simple way the simulated hardware description will process its own data in lockstep with the ARM processor pipeline. Every clock cycle the activity on internal relevant signals is also collected and sent to the power analysis units. Rather than attempting to find a single power model for the entire chip, we take the approach of identifying four basic classes of components: datapath, memory, control, and interconnect. The total power consumption of the coprocessor or peripheral unit per program executed on the ARM processor is estimated.

The central elements of our architectural design exploration framework are:

- ARMulator, the cycle-accurate instruction set simulator for the ARM family of low-power processors;
- VHDL simulator, capable of saving the state of the simulated hardware description whenever it receives this command, also it is capable to reinitialize the hardware description with the previous saved state before it processes the new stimuli sent by the ARM CPU core simulated on the ARMulator;
- Wrapper Module, that handles the communication between ARMulator (using ARMulator API) and the VHDL simulator; it is also responsible of passing correct formatted data between ARMulator, the VHDL simulator, and the activity analysis module;
- Precharacterized Power models and Effective Capacitance Coefficient Tables Module, that contain for a library of hardware cells all the technology dependent information required by the power analysis modules to compute the power consumption; the tables are derived only once for a given library of hardware cells (more detailed explanations are given in Subsection 2.2);
- Activity Analysis Module, that feeds the Power Analysis modules (power calculators) with statistics about signal activity inside the simulated hardware description;
- Power Analysis Modules, that estimate the power consumption in the datapath, control, memory, and interconnect based on statistics received from the Activity Analysis Module and lookups in the effective capacitance coefficient tables;
- Power Estimator Module, that adds the estimates of power consumption of datapath, control, memory, and interconnect and offers the total figure of power consumption of the coprocessor or peripheral unit per program executed on the ARM processor;

The approach we have taken provide all the benefits of a co-design framework, moreover, it is also capable of power estimation:

- permits experimental partitioning schemes between features that must be provided by software and features that will be mapped in hardware;
- allows changing of the organization and order of execution of the algorithmic blocks to investigate and verify potential new architectures;
- provides methods of performance monitoring (in terms of throughput, and power consumption);
- accelerates the implementation of new algorithms and provides an environment in which to test them both individually and as part of an entire pipeline;
- allows tweaking the bit width precision and seeing potential impacts on result accuracy and performance factors.

## 2.2 Power Models

In this subsection, we will describe the methodology of modeling power consumption at the architecture level. We followed the methodology presented in [1]. The premise for the success of such methodology consists in the existence of a library of hardware cells consisting of various operators for the datapath part, gates for control logic, and bit-cells, decoders, sense amplifiers for memory cores. Depending on the estimation accuracy desired, the individual cells can be specified at gate-level if the gates employed are already characterized for power, or can be specified at the layout-level in order for the internal interconnect parasitics between individual constituent transistors to be accounted for. Once such a library exists, it can be precharacterized via gate-level, respectively circuit-level simulations, resulting in a table of effective capacitive coefficients for every element in the library. Then using only this tables and the activity statistics derived during the architectural-level simulation the power consumption can be estimated easily. This precharacterization has to be done only once and only the effective capacitive coefficients table are needed for power estimation. The precharacterization results are valid only for a specific library of hardware cells and a given IC technology.

The power estimation methodology presented in [1] analyzes separately the four main classes of chip components: datapath, memory, control, and interconnect. For the first two classes, a model called the Dual Bit Type (or DBT) model was developed which demonstrated good accuracy results, with power estimates typically within $10 - 15\%$ of results from switch-level simulations. The DBT model achieves its high accuracy by carefully modeling both physical capacitance and circuit activity. The key concept behind the technique is to model the activity of the most significant (sign) bits and least significant bits separately due to the fact they exhibit different statistical behavior as presented in Figure 2. The least significant bits are modeled as uniform white noise (UWN). The DBT model applies only to parts of the chip that manipulate data. A separate model is introduced to handle power estimation for control logic and signals. This model is called the Activity-Based Control (ABC) model. The method relies on the observation that although the implementation style of the controller (e.g., ROM, PLA, random logic, etc.) can heavily impact the power consumption, it is still possible to identify a number of fundamental parameters that influence the power consumption regardless of the implementation method. In a chip, datapath, memory, and control blocks

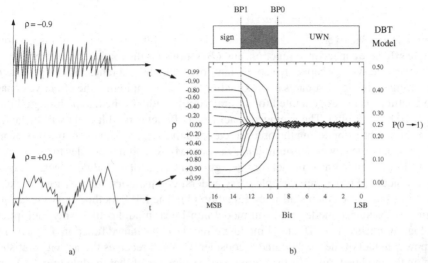

**Fig. 2.** Bit transition activity for 2 two's complement data streams modeled as Gaussian processes with different temporal correlation $\rho$: a) Activity for positively and negatively correlated waveforms. b) Bit transition activity for data streams with varying temporal correlation.

are joined together by an interconnect network. The wires comprising the network have capacitance associated with them and, therefore, driving data and control signals across this network consumes power. The precise amount of power consumed depends on the activity of the signals being transferred, as well as the physical capacitance of the wires. The DBT and ABC models provide the activity information for control and data buses, but the physical capacitance depends on the average length of the wires in each part of the design hierarchy. The average length of the wires is estimated based on the Rent's rule.

Having the library of hardware cells specified, for example, at the layout-level the library is precharacterized first with a circuit-level simulator. During the precharacterization stage of the library of hardware cells a black-box model of the capacitance switched in each module for various types of inputs is produced. If desired, these capacitance estimates can be converted to an equivalent energy, $E = CV^2$, or power, $P = CV^2f$. The black-box capacitance models can be parameterized, i.e., taking into account the size or complexity of the module. The model accurately accounts for activity as well as physical capacitance. As a result, the effect of the input statistics on module power consumption is reflected in the estimates.

For illustrative purposes, we will exemplify only briefly the modeling of the capacitance of a ripple-carry subtractor. Intuitively, the total power consumed by a module should be a function of its complexity, i.e., size. This reflects the fact that larger modules contain more circuitry and, therefore, more physical capacitance. The amount of circuitry and physical capacitance an instance of this subtractor will contain is determined by its word length, $N$. In particular, an $N$-bit subtractor can be realized by $N$ one-bit full-subtractor cells. The total module effective capacitance function should, therefore, receive an argument proportional to the word length as shown here:

$$C_T = f\,(activity\_statistics, C_{eff}N) \tag{1}$$

where $C_{eff}$ is the average capacitive coefficients per bit table, $f$ represents the total module effective capacitance function, and $C_T$ represents the total module effective capacitance. The average capacitive coefficients per bit table is obtained after a process of data fitting (using least-squares approximation method) employing the effective capacitive coefficients tables generated for several sample width of the datapath (e.g., 4 bits, 8 bits, 16 bits, 32 bits). The average capacitive coefficients per bit table will be generated for the subtractor during the precharacterization stage and stored for the time when the estimate of the power consumption is needed. Many modules besides the subtractor also follow a simple linear model for the argument of the total module effective capacitance function. For example, ripple-carry adders, comparators, buffers, multiplexers, and Boolean logic elements all obey Equation (1). The DBT method is not restricted to linear capacitance models and can model non-linear modules like array multipliers and logarithmic shifters. The total module effective capacitance function $f$ is actually the power model of the module under consideration and receives the activity statistics seen on the module terminals, the complexity parameters of that module (e.g., $N$), and a pointer to the average capacitive coefficients per bit table for that module. The reader is referred to [1] for more details. The total module effective capacitance $C_T$ represents the effective capacitance switched by that module every clock cycle during the execution of an application program on the ARM processor.

## 3   Experimental Results

To verify the power consumption prediction accuracy of the architectural space exploration tool we designed, we need to provide the following experimental setup: a precharacterized library of hardware cells, the description in VHDL of the peripheral or coprocessor to be simulated, and the binary code of the program to be simulated on the ARMulator containing calls to the coprocessor.

We precharacterized parts of a datapath library of cells (including a ripple-carry subtractor) designed in UMC $0.18\mu m$ Logic 1.8V/3.3V 1P6M GENERICII CMOS technology. We extracted from the layout the circuit of the subtractor in three variants of the datapath width: for 4 bits, 8 bits, and 16 bits. After using the method presented in Subsection 2.2 we obtained the average capacitive coefficients per bit values presented in Table 1.

We modeled in VHDL a sample coprocessor for an ARM1020T CPU core. It was designed starting from the datasheet of AMD's Am2901 four-bit bipolar microprocessor slice. The coprocessor has a datapath width of 8 bits. The coprocessor consists of a 16-word by 8-bit two-port register file, an ALU and the associated shifting, decoding and multiplexing circuitry. The 9-bit microinstruction word is organized in three groups of three bits each and selects the ALU source operands, the ALU function, and the ALU destination register. The ALU provides various status flag outputs. The ALU is capable of performing three binary arithmetic ($R + S$, $S - R$, $R - S$) and five logic functions ($R$ OR $S$, $R$ AND $S$, $\overline{R}$ AND $S$, $R$ XOR $S$, $R$ XNOR $S$).

To generate the application programs we analyzed real trace data for environmental control realized with well known microcontrollers (Intel 8051 and compatible). We ex-

**Table 1.** Average capacitive coefficients per bit for the ripple-carry subtractor.

| Transition Templates | Capacitive Coefficients (fF/bit) | | | |
|---|---|---|---|---|
| **UU/UU** | 35.12 | | | |
| **UU/SS** | 34.05 | 51.26 | 49.73 | 17.26 |
| **SS/UU** | 0.00 | 28.32 | 41.02 | 29.56 |
| **SS/SS/SS** | 0.00 | 28.33 | 41.17 | 3.15 |
| | 41.92 | 0.00 | 18.61 | 0.00 |
| | 52.13 | 25.71 | 0.00 | 0.00 |
| | 0.51 | 0.00 | 0.00 | 0.00 |
| | 0.00 | 35.42 | 0.00 | 52.12 |
| | 16.00 | 38.02 | 36.21 | 15.69 |
| | 0.00 | 55.79 | 0.00 | 0.00 |
| | 49.10 | 27.42 | 0.00 | 0.00 |
| | 0.00 | 0.00 | 69.21 | 60.01 |
| | 0.00 | 0.00 | 43.17 | 0.00 |
| | 7.65 | 32.73 | 48.82 | 10.13 |
| | 46.18 | 0.00 | 19.29 | 0.00 |
| | 0.00 | 0.00 | 0.00 | 2.41 |
| | 0.00 | 0.00 | 54.92 | 72.12 |
| | 0.00 | 0.15 | 0.00 | 46.89 |
| | 0.75 | 25.02 | 22.83 | 2.81 |

tracted the recurrent patterns of control and data in these instruction flows and generated three instruction flows A, B, and C, along with the data using biased noise generators. We used biased noise generators because in the case of our sample coprocessor there is no already developed software available. We executed these instruction flows on the ARM processor family ISA and, using the framework described in Subsection 2.1, we obtained power consumption estimates for the subtractor. They are presented in the second column of Table 2.

**Table 2.** Power consumption results for the ripple-carry subtractor.

| Instruction Trace | Power Consumption (estimated) | Power Consumption (simulated) | Relative Error (%) |
|---|---|---|---|
| A | 0.77mW | 0.91mW | -15 |
| B | 1.02mW | 0.84mW | 21 |
| C | 0.63mW | 0.61mW | 3 |

In order to find the relative error of these estimations for the ripple-carry subtractor we have to compare the results obtained employing our design exploration tool with the power consumption estimated accurately with the HSPICE circuit simulator on exactly the same excitation patterns for the ripple-carry subtractor. For this purpose we designed down to the layout-level the sample coprocessor using the library of hardware cells. The layout of the sample coprocessor is presented in Figure 3.

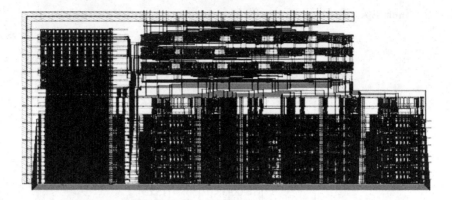

**Fig. 3.** Sample coprocessor layout. From left to right and up to down: register file, control, and datapath.

The simulation results on the extracted netlist of the ripple-carry subtractor are presented in the third column of Table 2. The clock frequency for the sample coprocessor assumed throughout these experiments is 200MHz. We have to mention here that the circuit-level simulation of the subtractor took several hours for the three instruction traces executed on the ARM processor. This clearly indicate that a circuit-level simulation of the whole coprocessor, to obtain the power consumption directly, for an instruction trace executed on the ARM processor is computationally unfeasible. The relative error between the power estimated and the power consumption obtained by circuit-accurate simulation is presented in the last column of Table 2. The power prediction accuracy is good, well within 25% of a direct circuit simulation with HSPICE.

## 4  Conclusions

A new approach towards high-level power estimation is presented in this paper in the context of ARMulator, a cycle-accurate instruction-level simulator for the ARM low-power processor family. More in particular, we developed an energy-aware architectural design exploration and analysis tool for ARM based system-on-chip designs. The tool integrates the behavior and energy models of several user-defined, custom processing units as an extension to the ARMulator. The models we implemented take into account the particular class, e.g., datapath, memory, control, or interconnect, as well as the architectural complexity of the hardware unit involved and the signal activity triggered by the specific algorithm executed on the ARM processor. Our tool can estimate at the architectural level of detail the overall energy consumption or can report the energy breakdown among different units. Preliminary experiments indicated that the estimation accuracy is within 25% of what can be accomplished after a circuit-level simulation on the laid-out chip.

Our endeavor to accurately predict power consumption within the ARM-based system-on-chip designs is an ongoing work. We have to mention that, up to date, the precharacterization of the library is done in a manual way. In the future, we intend to develop an automatic process of precharacterization. We believe that a command language with a dedicated grammar for the precharacterization process can be a possible solution. Within this approach every leaf cell in the library of hardware cells will be accompanied by a description file with specific commands for the precharacterization process. These issues will be addressed in the near future.

# References

1. Landman, P.: High-Level Power Estimation. In: International Symposium on Low Power Electronics and Design, Monterey CA (1996) 29–35
2. Micheli, G.D. In: Synthesis and Optimization of Digital Circuits. McGraw-Hill (1994)
3. Burger, D., Austin, T.M.: The SimpleScalar Tool Set, Version 2.0. Technical Report Nr. 1342, University of Wisconsin-Madison Computer Sciences Department (1997)
4. Vijaykrishnan, N., Kandemir, M., Irwin, M.J., KIM, H.S., Ye, W.: Energy-Driven Integrated Hardware-Software Optimizations Using SimplePower. ISCA 2000 (2000)
5. Brooks, D., Tiwari, V., Martonosi, M.: Wattch: A Framework for Architectural-Level Power Analysis and Optimizations. In: Proceedings of the 27th International Symposium on Computer Architecture, Vancouver, BC (2000) 83–94
6. Tiwari, V., Malik, S., Wolfe, A., Lee, M.: Instruction Level Power Analysis and Optimization of Software. Journal of VLSI Signal Processing Systems 13 (1996) 223–238
7. Tiwari, V., Malik, S., Wolfe, A.: Power analysis of embedded software: A first step toward software power minimization. IEEE Transactions on VLSI Systems 2 (1994) 437–445
8. Li, Y., Henkel, J.: A Framework for Estimating and Minimizing Energy Dissipation of Embedded HW/SW Systems. In: Proceedings of Design Automation Conference. (1998) 188–193
9. Kapoor, B.: Low Power Memory Architectures for Video Applications. In: Proceedings of 8th Great Lakes Symposium on VLSI. (1998) 2–7
10. ARM Limited: ARM Developer Suite version 1.1. (1999)

# IDF Models for Trace Transformations:
# A Case Study in Computational Refinement

Cagkan Erbas, Simon Polstra, and Andy D. Pimentel

Dept. of Computer Science, University of Amsterdam
Kruislaan 403, 1098 SJ Amsterdam, The Netherlands
{cagkan,spolstra,andy}@science.uva.nl

**Abstract.** The Sesame environment provides methods and tools for efficient design space exploration of heterogeneous embedded systems. It uses separate application and architecture models. The application model is explicitly mapped onto the architecture model and they are simulated together, using trace driven co-simulation. Since the abstraction level of the application model may not match the abstraction level of the architecture model, techniques are needed to refine the traces if necessary. In [13], we introduced integer-controlled dataflow (IDF) models to perform trace transformations for communication refinement. This paper uses these trace transformation methods to refine computational events. A simple case study, consisting of a 2D-IDCT application model mapped onto different architecture models, is used to show the capabilities of these IDF modeling techniques.

## 1 Introduction

Modern embedded systems, like those for media and signal processing, usually have a heterogeneous system architecture consisting of components in the range from fully programmable processor cores to dedicated hardware components. These systems often provide a high degree of programmability as they need to target a range of applications with varying demands. Such characteristics greatly complicate the system design, making it even more important to have good tools available for exploring different design choices at an early stage.

In the context of the Artemis project [14], we are developing the Sesame [6] modeling and simulation framework which provides modeling and simulation methods and tools for the efficient design space exploration of heterogeneous embedded multimedia systems. This framework should allow for rapid performance evaluation of different architecture designs, application to architecture mappings, and hardware/software partitionings. In addition, it should do so at multiple levels of abstraction *and* for a wide range of multimedia applications. Key to this flexibility is that separate application and architecture models are used together with an explicit mapping step to map an application model onto an architecture model. This mapping is realized by means of trace-driven co-simulation of the application and architecture models, where the execution of

A. Pimentel and S. Vassiliadis (Eds.): SAMOS 2004, LNCS 3133, pp. 178–187, 2004.

an application model generates application events that represent the application workload imposed on the architecture.

As a designer gradually refines architecture models in Sesame, the abstraction level of application models does not match the abstraction level of the refined architecture models anymore. At the same time, implementing a new refined application model for every abstraction level at the architecture layer puts too much burden on the application programmer. Due to this overhead, we do not want to hamper the re-usability of our application models and want to be able to use them with different architecture models. Therefore, new techniques are needed within the Sesame environment which will support the gradual refinement of architecture models, without causing any limitation or hindrance on the re-usability of our application models. For this purpose, in [13] we have proposed a new method to refine application traces within the simulation environment. This method combines the utilization of process and dataflow networks within a single simulation environment to perform communication refinement.

In this paper, we show how computational and communicational grain-size refinements can be performed using dataflow networks. These dataflow networks also enable us to model intra-task level parallelism at the architecture layer. To demonstrate this, we make use of a two dimensional inverse discrete cosine transform (2D-IDCT) case study. With this case study, we demonstrate how we accomplish refinement at the architecture layer without changing the application model. The rest of the paper is organized as follows: the next section gives a short introduction of the Sesame environment. Section 3 presents trace transformations and the dataflow actors within Sesame. In Section 4, we demonstrate how we accomplish computational refinement with a simple case study. Section 5 discusses the related work. Finally, Section 6 concludes the paper.

## 2   The Sesame Environment

The Sesame environment recognizes separate application and architecture models within a system simulation. An application model describes the functional behavior (i.e. computation and communication behavior) of an application. The architecture model defines architecture resources and captures their performance constraints. After explicitly mapping an application model onto an architecture model, they are co-simulated via trace-driven simulation. This allows for evaluation of the system performance of a particular application, mapping and underlying architecture. The layered structure of Sesame is shown in Figure 1.

For application modeling, Sesame uses the Kahn Process Network (KPN) model of computation [8] in which parallel processes – implemented in a high level language – communicate with each other via FIFO channels. The workload of an application is captured by instrumenting the code of each Kahn process with annotations. By executing the Kahn model, each process records its actions in order to generate its own trace of application events, which is necessary for driving an architecture model. There are three types of application events: *read* and *write* for communication events, *execute* for computation events. These

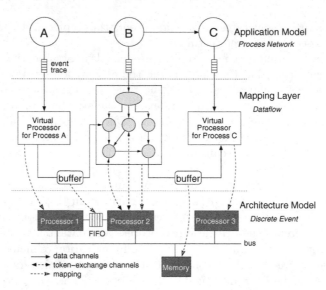

**Fig. 1.** The three layers within Sesame: the application model layer, the architecture model layer, and the mapping layer which interfaces between the former two.

events are typically coarse-grained like *read(pixel-block,channel-id)*, *write(frame-header,channel-id)*, and *execute(DCT)*.

An architecture model simulates the performance consequences of the computation and communication events generated by an application model. It solely accounts for performance constraints and does not model functional behavior, since the latter is already captured in the application model. An architecture model is constructed from generic building blocks provided by a library, which contains template performance models for processing cores, communication media (like busses) and various types of memory. Architecture models in Sesame are implemented in Pearl [6] which is a discrete-event simulation language.

To map Kahn processes from an application model onto architecture model components, Sesame provides an intermediate *mapping layer*. This layer consists of virtual processors communicating via FIFO buffers. There is a one-to-one relationship between the Kahn processes in the application model and the virtual processors in the mapping layer. A virtual processor reads in an application trace from a Kahn process via a trace event queue and dispatches the events to a processing component in the architecture model. When multiple Kahn processes are mapped onto a single architecture component, the event traces need to be scheduled. For computation events, a given policy (FCFS by default) is used. In the case of communication events, the appropriate buffer at the mapping layer is first checked whether or not a communication event is safe to occur so that no deadlock is introduced. Only when it is found to be safe (i.e., available data for read events and enough space for write events in the target buffer), communication events are dispatched to processor components in the architecture model. If a communication event cannot be dispatched, the virtual processor blocks. This means that the mapping layer accounts for synchronization latencies, while the architecture layer accounts for pure communication latencies. This is possible since both the mapping and the architecture layers are implemented in Pearl.

With the introduction of gradual refinement of architecture model components, the virtual processors are also refined with dataflow networks. The latter allows us to do simulation at multiple levels of abstraction, without modifying the application model. In Figure 1, we express this fact by refining the virtual processor for the process B with a fictive dataflow network. In the next section, we provide more insight on this refinement approach by explaining relations between the trace transformations for refinement and dataflow actors at the mapping layer.

## 3   Trace Transformations in Sesame

Refining architecture model components requires that the application events driving them should also be refined to match the architectural detail. Since we want smooth transition between different abstraction levels, we do not want to re-implement (parts of) the application models for each abstraction level. The salient way to accomplish this in Sesame is to refine the virtual processors with dataflow actors. This way, the coarse-grained application events (in the application trace) can be refined up to the desired abstraction level at the mapping layer, and subsequently be used to drive the architecture model components.

In Sesame, SDF [9] actors are utilized for trace transformations. Such a trace transformation refines application-level operations (or events) into finer-grained architecture-level operations. IDF [5] actors are subsequently used to model repetitions and branching conditions which may be present in the application code. However, as in [13], they may also be utilized within static transformations to achieve less complicated (in terms of the number of actors and channels) dataflow graphs. To give an example, the following trace transformations refine *read* ($R$) and *write* ($W$) operations such that the synchronizations are separated from real data transfers as follows [11]:

$$R \overset{\Theta_{ref}}{\Longrightarrow} cd \to ld \to sr, \tag{1}$$

$$W \overset{\Theta_{ref}}{\Longrightarrow} cr \to st \to sd \ . \tag{2}$$

Here refined architecture-level operations *check-data*, *load-data*, *signal-room*, *check-room*, *store-data*, *signal-data* are abbreviated as $cd$, $ld$, $sr$, $cr$, $st$, $sd$, respectively. The arrows between these indicate the ordering relations. The purpose of such refinements is that it, for instance, allows for moving synchronizations when a *pattern* of operations is transformed [13]. For example, in the following transformation we early check room to store data, which may be useful for a processor that cannot store data locally,

$$R \to E \to W \overset{\Theta_{ref}}{\Longrightarrow} cd \to cr \to ld \to E \to st \to sr \to sd \ . \tag{3}$$

In Figure 2, we give two dataflow graphs implementing this transformation. If the SDF actor T in Figure 2(a) is invoked initially, and if the rest of the SDF actors are also invoked in the order in which they appear on the right hand side of the equation (3), this simply constructs a *valid* schedule for the SDF graph in Figure 2(a). In all cases where the outcome of the trace transformation is a total ordering, a valid schedule is guaranteed to exist and it is constructed as explained. In general, a trace with a total ordering is called a *linear trace*. At this point we should recall that the schedules which are both *admissible* and *periodic* are valid [3]. It is easy to verify that the constructed schedule for this graph is both admissible and periodic. We see that all the actors are immediately fireable when they are invoked in the order they appear in the schedule. This makes the schedule admissible. It is also observed that when all the actors are fired, the graph returns its original state, i.e. the number of tokens on the channels remains the same, which means that the schedule is also periodic. To see this, one may alternatively write the balance equations. The same is true for the graph in Figure 2(b), in which a similar valid schedule can be easily constructed by replacing the single appearance of SDF actor T with three consecutive occurrences of the IDF switch actor.

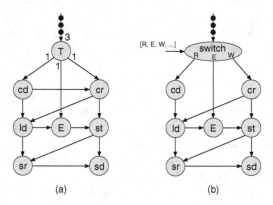

(a)                                (b)

**Fig. 2.** (a) An SDF graph for a trace transformation in Sesame (b) An IDF graph implementing the same transformation.

In Sesame, all dataflow graphs to implement linear trace transformations are constructed in this manner, so we always end up with valid schedules. We also make use of multiphase and/or multistage IDF actors, like REPEAT-BEGIN, REPEAT-END, which were first proposed in [5], to further simplify our dataflow graphs. Although IDF graphs have analyzibility problems, in Sesame we try to overcome this problem by constructing a static schedule. In most of the cases, this is possible because we may run the application model beforehand and obtain trace files representing the workload of the Kahn processes. However, one can also co-simulate the application and architecture models and schedule the IDF actors dynamically. But in this case, one cannot guarantee whether the execution is completed in finite-time or whether it is performed within bounded memory [4].

In this paper, we are interested in refining grain sizes of both computation and communication events and subsequently model parallel execution (intra-task parallelism) of these events at the architecture level. More specifically, as our Kahn application models often operate on blocks of data, we look at the following transformations,

$$R \stackrel{\Theta}{\Longrightarrow} R(l) \to \ldots \to R(l), \tag{4}$$

$$E \stackrel{\Theta}{\Longrightarrow} E(l) \to \ldots \to E(l), \tag{5}$$

$$W \stackrel{\Theta}{\Longrightarrow} W(l) \to \ldots \to W(l), \tag{6}$$

$$E(l) \stackrel{\Theta}{\Longrightarrow} e_1 \to \ldots \to e_n . \tag{7}$$

In the first three transformations, read, execute and write operations at the block level are refined to multiple (e.g., 1 block = 8 lines) corresponding operations at the line level. We represent line level operations with an 'l' in parenthesis. The last transformation further refines execute operations at line level to model multiple pipeline execute stages inside a single processor. In (7), refinement for a processor with n-stage pipeline execution is given.

## 4    Case Study

In Figure 3, the application model for a 2D-IDCT case study is given. All the Kahn processes in the application model operate at block level, i.e. they read/write and execute operations on blocks of data. The Input process writes blocks of data for the IDCT-row process which in turn reads blocks of data, executes IDCT, and writes blocks of data. The Transpose process simply performs a matrix transpose to prepare data for the IDCT-col process.

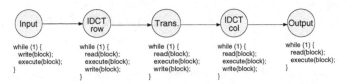

**Fig. 3.** Kahn process network for the 2D-IDCT case study.

We investigate two alternative architecture models, given in Figure 4, for this application model. Both architecture models have the same four processing elements, PE1 to PE4. The mapping of Kahn processes onto the processing elements is identical in both cases, they differ in how these communicate. In the first architecture model, they are connected via dedicated buffers while in the second architecture a shared memory is used. Each processing element is able to perform read, execute and write operations in parallel, so it can perform its task in a pipelined fashion. Input and Output processes are mapped onto PE1 and PE4, IDCT-row and IDCT-col are mapped onto PE2 and PE3, respectively. The Transpose process is not mapped onto anything, since its functionality is simply implemented as follows: the processing element on which the IDCT-row process is mapped simply writes rows of data to the memory while the processing element on which the second IDCT process is mapped reads columns of data from the memory. We should note that this type of implementation of the matrix transpose forces those processing elements, operating at line level (as we will explain later on in this section), to be synchronized at block level. This is because the second processing element cannot start processing lines until the first one is finished with the last line of data.

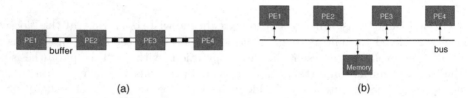

(a)                                         (b)

**Fig. 4.** Two different target architectures.

In both architectures, we modeled PE1 and PE4 to operate at block level. We first modeled PE2 and PE3, in the target architectures operating at line level, at a more abstract block level and then later refined them to operate at line level. For this reason, in the latter case, the application events from the IDCT processes need to be refined. The pattern to be refined for the IDCT processes is $R \to E \to W$. For simplicity if we assume 1 block = 2 lines then,

$$R \to E \to W \stackrel{\Theta}{\Longrightarrow} \begin{array}{l} R(l) \longrightarrow E(l) \longrightarrow W(l) \\ \qquad\qquad R(l) \longrightarrow E(l) \longrightarrow W(l) \ . \end{array} \tag{8}$$

If we define that PE2 and PE3 are processing elements with 2-stage pipeline execution units, which creates an execution pipeline inside the previously mentioned task pipeline, then from (7) with $n = 2$ we obtain,

$$R \to E \to W \stackrel{\Theta}{\Longrightarrow} \begin{array}{l} R(l) \longrightarrow e_1 \longrightarrow e_2 \longrightarrow W(l) \\ \qquad\qquad R(l) \longrightarrow e_1 \longrightarrow e_2 \longrightarrow W(l) \ . \end{array} \tag{9}$$

In Table 1, we give the simulation parameters. We have performed four simulations represented by the four columns in the table. The terms *non-refined* and *refined* indicate whether the processing elements PE2 and PE3 operate at block level or at line level. The terms *fifo* and *shared* refer to the architectures in

**Table 1.** Parameters for simulation.

|  | non-refined, shared | refined, shared | non-refined, fifo | refined, fifo |
|---|---|---|---|---|
| pipeline size | – | 3/8 | – | 3/8 |
| PE2, PE3 exec. lat. | 300 | 13/5 | 300 | 13/5 |
| PE2, PE3 data size | 64 | 8 | 64 | 8 |
| PE1, PE4 data size | 64 | 64 | 64 | 64 |
| fifo lat. | – | – | 1 … 60 | 1 … 60 |
| memory lat. | 1 … 60 | 1 … 60 | – | – |
| memory width | 8 | 8 | – | – |
| bus setup lat. | 1 | 1 | – | – |
| bus width | 8 | 8 | – | – |

Figures 4(a) and 4(b), respectively. Execution latency is measured in cycles, and data size in bytes. Memory and FIFO latencies are given in cycles/line, where 1 line is 8 bytes and 8 lines make up a block. We note that in these experiments the ratios between the parameters are more important than the actual values being used. We assume that executing a 1D-IDCT takes 300 cycles per block on a non-refined execution unit, so in a 3-stage pipelined execution unit operating on lines, the amount of work is divided by the number of stages, and by the number of lines in a block. So the execution latency of one stage in the 3-stage pipeline is 13 cycles and that of the 8-stage is 5 cycles.

In Figure 5, we give the performance graph obtained when we map the 2D-IDCT application onto the architectures in Figure 4. In all experiments, we have processed 500 blocks of input data. In the first experiment, the processing elements PE2 and PE3 operate at block level and no refinement is performed. This gives us performance results for single and double buffer implementations, i.e. where the double buffer is a 2-entry buffer so that the producer can write to it and the consumer can read from it, simultaneously. We change a single buffer to a double buffer model, simply by adding an extra initial token at the mapping layer. In the second experiment, we refined the processing elements PE2 and PE3 in the architecture model, and explored four alternative cases. For these two processing elements, we have used a 3-stage and an 8-stage execution pipeline.

For the buffers, we have again experimented with single and double buffer implementations. When we compare the single and double buffer performance of the non-refined models, we observe that it is the same until point A. After that point, as the communication latency increases, the single buffer model becomes communication bounded. The performance of the double buffer model is affected by the increased communication latency at point B, when the time to transfer a block of data becomes equal to the time it takes to perform an IDCT on a block of data. When we compare the refined models with the non-refined models, we observe that once the communication becomes a bottleneck (point A for single buffer and point B for double buffer), the advantage of having a pipelined execution unit disappears. When the models become communication bounded, the non-refined and refined models predict the same performance numbers. We note that a similar situation occurs at points C and D, when increased communication latencies negate the effect of having a longer pipeline. Finally, when we compare

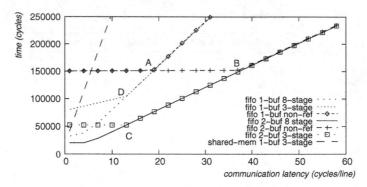

**Fig. 5.** Performance results for the FIFO architecture.

these results with the results of the shared memory architecture, we observe that in the latter, the performance is very quickly bounded by the communication, because increasing the communication latency causes contention on the shared bus. This makes the effect of pipelined execution very limited. For this reason, we only present the graph for the refined case with the 3-stage pipeline.

## 5   Related Work

Within the context of embedded systems and hardware/software codesign, as the search for models of computation continues [10], many system-level design and simulation environments [1], [14] together with system modeling languages [2], [7] have been developed. In parallel to the exploration environments that facilitate the idea of separate functionality and architecture, in Sesame we try to push this separation to even greater extents. This is achieved by an architecture-independent application model, an application-independent architecture model and a mapping step which relates these models for co-simulation. Besides, within the same simulation environment, we use multiple models of computation. It is chosen specifically in accordance with the task to be achieved. As already shown in this paper, we use process networks for application specification, dataflow networks for certain tasks at the mapping layer (e.g., trace transformations) and a discrete-event simulator to model processing components for fast simulations.

Both the Spade [12] and Archer [15] environments show a lot of similarities with the Sesame environment in the sense that they share the same philosophy by recognizing separate application and architecture models. However, each of these environments uses its own architecture simulator and follows a different mapping strategy for co-simulation.

## 6   Conclusion

In this paper, we showed how computational and communicational grain-size refinement can be performed using the IDF models which was first proposed in [13] for communication refinement. Performing a simple case study, we illustrated how easily we could model task-level parallelism and intra-task parallelism at the architecture layer. Additionally, using similar dataflow graphs, we could also model pipeline execution stages inside a single processor. While doing this, we kept the application model unaffected. Currently, we are testing our new methodology on more realistic real-life media applications. We are especially interested in investigating its efficiency in terms of modeling and simulation time when more complex applications and transformations are considered.

# References

1. F. Balarin et al. Metropolis: An integrated electronic system design environment. *IEEE Computer*, Apr. 2003.
2. L. Benini et al. SystemC cosimulation and emulation of multiprocessor SoC designs. *IEEE Computer*, Apr. 2003.
3. S. S. Bhattacharyya, P. K. Murthy, and E. A. Lee. *Software Synthesis from Dataflow Graphs*. Kluwer Academic Publishers, 1996.
4. J. T. Buck. *Scheduling Dynamic Dataflow Graphs with Bounded Memory using the Token Flow Model*. PhD thesis, Dept. of EECS, UC Berkeley, 1993.
5. J. T. Buck. Static scheduling and code generation from dynamic dataflow graphs with integer valued control streams. In *Proc. of the 28th Asilomar Conference on Signals, Systems, and Computers*, Oct. 1994.
6. J. E. Coffland and A. D. Pimentel. A software framework for efficient system-level performance evaluation of embedded systems. In *Proc. of the ACM Symposium on Applied Computing*, Mar. 2003.
7. D. Gajski et al. *The SpecC Language*. Kluwer Academic Publishers, 1997.
8. G. Kahn. The semantics of a simple language for parallel programming. In *Proc. of the IFIP Congress*, 1974.
9. E. A. Lee and D. G. Messerschmitt. Synchronous Data Flow. *Proc. of the IEEE*, Sep. 1987.
10. E. A. Lee and A. Sangiovanni-Vincentelli. A framework for comparing models of computation. *IEEE Trans. on CAD*, Dec. 1998.
11. P. Lieverse et al. A trace transformation technique for communication refinement. In *Proc. of the IEEE/ACM CODES*, Apr. 2001.
12. P. Lieverse et al. A methodology for architecture exploration of heterogeneous signal processing systems. In *Proc. of the IEEE Workshop SiPS*, Oct. 1999.
13. A. D. Pimentel and C. Erbas. An IDF-based trace transformation method for communication refinement. In *Proc. of the ACM/IEEE DAC*, June 2003.
14. A. D. Pimentel et al. Exploring embedded-systems architectures with Artemis. *IEEE Computer*, Nov. 2001.
15. V. Živković et al. Design space exploration of streaming multiprocessor architectures. In *Proc. of the IEEE Workshop SiPS*, Oct. 2002.

Systems, Architectures, Modeling,
and Simulation 2004 (SAMOS IV)

# Programming Extremely Flexible Platforms

## Keynote Speech

Kees Vissers

Xilinx Research
2100 Logic Drive
San Jose, CA 95124 USA
kees.vissers@xilinx.com

**Abstract.** Modern Platform FPGAs contain a combination of processors, embedded memory, programmable interconnect, dedicated DSP elements, and conventional lookup tables. On top of that they have multiple clock domains, very high speed Serial I/Os and a large number of pins.

This talk will focus on using all this flexibility for several applications. First I will show the programming of a JPEG2000 encoder application. This application will be shown as a program on a processor, a program on a network of processors and a high speed implementation in a dedicated architecture. The throughput of the implementations varies a factor 1000, dependent on the implementation style.

Next I will show that the inherent efficiency of direct implementations stems from avoiding a large number of instructions and from building a dedicated, optimal memory architecture. I will illustrate the structured development of MPEG4 encoders and decoders for FPGAs. I will briefly illustrate the programming environment using the Matlab and Simulink environment for FPGAs and the benefits and challenges that this environment brings.

Finally I will discuss performance analysis early in the design of various programming methods for platform FPGAs and I will illustrate ideas about programming in a component model. The talk will finish with addressing some of the industrial challenges in designing high-level mapping methods, tools and architectures for future FPGA architectures, with an emphasis on the high-performance DSP applications.

A. Pimentel and S. Vassiliadis (Eds.): SAMOS 2004, LNCS 3133, p. 191, 2004.
© Springer-Verlag Berlin Heidelberg 2004

# The Virtex II Pro™ MOLEN Processor

Georgi Kuzmanov, Georgi Gaydadjiev, and Stamatis Vassiliadis

Computer Engineering Lab, EEMCS, TU Delft, The Netherlands
{G.Kuzmanov,G.N.Gaydadjiev,S.Vassiliadis}@ET.TUDelft.NL
http://ce.et.tudelft.nl/

**Abstract.** We use the Xilinx Virtex II Pro™ technology as prototyping platform to design a MOLEN polymorphic processor, a custom computing machine based on the co-processor architectural paradigm. The PowerPC embedded in the FPGA is operating as a general purpose (core) processor and the reconfigurable fabric is used as a reconfigurable co-processor. The paper focuses on hardware synthesis results and experimental performance evaluation, proving the viability of the MOLEN concept. More precisely, the MPEG-2 application is accelerated very closely to its theoretical limits by implementing SAD, DCT and IDCT as reconfigurable co-processors. For a set of popular test video sequences the MPEG-2 encoder overall speedup is in the range between 2.64 and 3.18. The speedup of the MPEG-2 decoder varies between 1.65 and 1.94.

## 1 Introduction

The MOLEN polymorphic processor [9], a Custom Computing Machine (CCM) based on the co-processor architectural paradigm, resolves some shortcomings of many recent reconfigurable processors (e.g., opcode space explosion, modularity and compatibility problems identified for [2, 3, 6]). More specifically, the MOLEN concept suggests that for a given ISA, a single architectural extension comprising between 4 and 8 additional instructions suffices to provide an almost arbitrary number of reconfigurable functions. In addition, unlike [1, 11], the concept allows implementations with large, virtually unlimited, number of input and output parameters for the reconfigurable functions. In this paper, we present a prototype design of the MOLEN CCM utilizing a Virtex II Pro™ FPGA of Xilinx [10]. The implemented minimal PowerPC ISA augmentation comprises only four instructions and the reconfigurable hardware utilization of the prototype is extremely low with only 156 FPGA slices consumed. Experimental results indicate that this prototype realization can speedup the MPEG-2 encoder between 2.64 and 3.18 when implementing SAD, DCT and IDCT as reconfigurable functions. When implementing the IDCT operation alone, the projected speedup of the MPEG-2 decoder is between 1.65 and 1.94 for a set of popular test video sequences. The reconfigurable hardware costs of the aforementioned functions is between 8% and 53% of the utilized xc2vp20 chip, depending on the particular configuration considered.

The remainder of the paper is organized as follows. Section 2 briefly introduces the MOLEN CCM background. In Section 3, Virtex II Pro™ specific design considerations and hardware evaluation of the MOLEN prototype infrastructure are presented. Considering MPEG-2, Section 4 evaluates the prototype based on experimental results.

A. Pimentel and S. Vassiliadis (Eds.): SAMOS 2004, LNCS 3133, pp. 192–202, 2004.

Reconfigurable hardware utilization by the custom functional units and performance estimates are reported. Finally, concluding remarks are presented in Section 5.

## 2   Background on the MOLEN CCM

This section briefly describes the MOLEN $\rho\mu$-coded CCM organization, originally introduced in [9]. The two main components in the MOLEN machine organization (depicted in Figure 1) are the *Core Processor*, which is a general-purpose processor (GPP), and the *Reconfigurable Processor* (RP). The ARBITER performs a partial decoding on the instructions in order to determine where they should be issued. Instructions implemented in fixed hardware are issued to the GPP. Instructions for custom execution are redirected to the RP. Data transfers from(to) the main memory are handled by the *Data Load/Store* unit. The *Data Memory MUX/DEMUX* unit is responsible for distributing data between either the reconfigurable or the core processor. The reconfigurable processor consists of the *reconfigurable microcode ($\rho\mu$-code)* unit and the *custom computing unit* (CCU). The CCU consists of reconfigurable hardware and memory, intended to support additional and future functions that are not implemented in the core processor. Pieces of application code can be implemented on the CCU in order to speed up the overall execution of the application. A clear distinction exists between code that is executed on the RP and code that is executed on the GPP. Data must be transferred across the boundaries in order for the overall application code to be meaningful. Such data includes predefined parameters (or pointers to such parameters) or results (or pointers to such results). The parameter and result passing is performed utilizing the so-called *exchange registers* (XREGs) depicted in Figure 1.

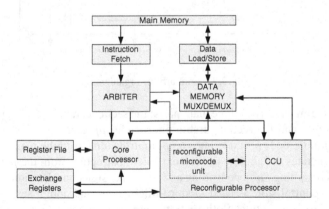

**Fig. 1.** The MOLEN machine organization

An operation, executed by the RP, is divided into two distinct phases: set and execute. The set phase is responsible for reconfiguring the CCU enabling the execution of the operation. Subsequently, in the execute phase the actual execution of the operations is performed. No specific instructions are associated with specific operations to configure and execute on the CCU as this would greatly reduce the opcode space. Instead, pointers to *reconfigurable microcode* ($\rho\mu$-code) are utilized. The $\rho\mu$-code emulates both the configuration of the CCU and the execution of implementations configured on the CCU resulting in two types of microcode: 1.) reconfiguration microcode that controls the configuration of the CCU; and 2.) execution microcode that controls the execution of the implementation configured on the CCU.

**Arbiter operation.** The arbiter directs instructions to either the core processor or the reconfigurable processor. A general view of an arbiter organization, the operation of which is entirely based on decoding the instruction flow is depicted in Figure 2. Instructions from the original GPP ISA are directed (via MUX) to the core processor. Up-on decoding of an RP instruction, "arbiter emulation instructions" are multiplexed through the core processor instruction bus to drive the GPP into a wait state. In the same time, control signals are issued (via the control block in Figure 2) to the RP (in essence the $\rho\mu$-code unit) to initiate a reconfigurable operation. The microcode location address is redirected to the $\rho\mu$-code unit and the data memory control is transferred to the RP. After an RP operation is completed, data memory control is released back to the GPP, an instruction sequence is generated to ensure that the GPP exits the wait state and the program execution continues with the instruction immediately following the executed RP instruction. More details regarding arbiter operation can be found in [5].

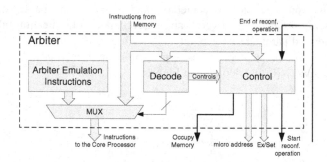

**Fig. 2.** General arbiter organization

**The $\rho\mu$-code unit** comprises three main parts: the sequencer, the reconfigurable control ($\rho$-control) store, and the reconfigurable microcode ($\rho\mu$-code) loading unit. The $\rho\mu$-code loading unit, loads $\rho\mu$-code into the $\rho$-control store from the main memory. The sequencer generates the address of the next microinstruction from the $\rho$-control store. More details regarding $\rho\mu$-code loading and related design considerations can be found in [4]. The $\rho$-control store is used to store microcodes and comprises two sections - a *set* and an *execute* section. Both sections can be identical and are further divided into a *fixed* and a *pageable* part. The fixed part stores the resident reconfiguration and execution microcode of the *set* and *execute* phases, respectively. Other microcode is stored in memory and the pageable part of the $\rho$-control store acts like a cache to provide temporal storage. For more details regarding the considered cache mechanisms and the $\rho$-control store organization, the interested reader is referred to [9].

**The MOLEN programming paradigm** is a sequential consistency paradigm targeting the MOLEN organization (for details see [7]). The complete list of the eight required

instructions, denoted as polymorphic instruction set architecture ($\pi$ISA), is as follows:
1) partial set (*p*-**set** $<address>$) performs common and frequently used configurations;
2) complete set (*c*-**set** $<address>$) *completes* the CCU's configuration to perform less
frequent functions; 3) **execute** $<address>$: controls the execution of the operations on
the CCU configured by the *set* instructions; 4) **set prefetch** $<address>$ and 5) **execute prefetch**: prefetch the needed microcodes responsible for CCU reconfigurations
and executions into a local on-chip storage (the $\rho\mu$-code unit); 6) **break**: synchronizes
the parallel execution of the RP and the GPP; 7) **movtx** $\text{XREG}_a \leftarrow \text{R}_b$ and 8) **movfx**
$\text{R}_a \leftarrow \text{XREG}_b$: move the content of general-purpose register $\text{R}_b$ to/from $\text{XREG}_a$. The
$<address>$ field in the instructions introduced above denotes the location of the re-
configurable microcode for the configuration and execution processes.

We note that it is not imperative to include all eight instructions when implementing
a MOLEN organization. In our prototype design, we have considered a **minimal** $\pi$**ISA**
which comprises four basic instructions, namely **set** (more specifically: *c*-**set**), **execute**,
**movtx** and **movfx**. By implementing the first two instructions (**set/execute**) any CCU
implementation can be loaded and executed on the reconfigurable processor. The **movtx**
and **movfx** instructions are needed to provide the input/output interface between the RP
targeted code and the remainder application code. The minimal $\pi$ISA is essentially the
smallest set of MOLEN instructions needed to provide a working scenario.

## 3   Prototype Design Considerations and Hardware Estimation

In this section, we present Virtex II Pro™ specific design considerations and evaluate the reconfigurable hardware utilized by the MOLEN prototype infrastructure, i.e.,
excluding any CCU implementations. We consider a minimal $\pi$ISA comprising the instructions **set**, **execute**, **movtx**, and **movfx**. Specific software considerations and $\pi$ISA
instruction encoding are referred. Some implementation issues are presented as well.

**The development platform.** We experimented with the Alpha Data XPL Pro™ lite
development board (ADM-XPL). As a reconfigurable hardware platform, we used a
Xilinx xc2vp20-5 device from the Virtex II Pro™ family. The MOLEN organization
has been described in VHDL and synthesized by the Xilinx XST tool of ISE 5.2, SP3.

**Software considerations.** Due to performance reasons, we do not use PowerPC special
operating modes instructions as arbiter emulation instructions (e.g., exiting power-down
modes requires an interrupt). We employed the *'branch to link register'* instruction
(**blr**) to emulate a 'wait' state and *'branch to link register and link'* (**blrl**) to move the
processor out of this state. Thus the arbiter emulation instructions (Figure 2) are reduced
to only one instruction for 'wait' and one for 'wake-up'. Implementation details and
additional performance enhancing software considerations are discussed in [5].

**Instruction encoding.** We mapped the **movtx** and **movfx** instructions to the existing
PowerPC instructions **mtdcr** and **mfdcr**. This implementation solution has been imposed by the fact that the Virtex II Pro™ PowerPC core has a dedicated interface to the
so called Device Control Registers (DCR) [10]. We implemented the XREGs as DCRs
and utilized the **mtdcr** and **mfdcr** instructions to support XREG transfers. Thus only
the **set** and **execute** instructions have to be considered for encoding. As a guideline, we
decided to closely follow the already established PowerPC instruction format. We have

chosen an opcode from the set of unused opcodes to represent both instructions. Figure 3 depicts the implemented RP instructions format, referred to as *the ρ-form*. The manner to distinguish a **set** instruction and an **execute** instruction (using the same opcode) is via instruction modifiers. This encoding allows us to utilize a 24-bits address (embedded in the instruction word) to specify the location of the microcode. Finally, we have to note that within this address field, a modifier bit R/P (resident/pageable) specifies where the microcode is located and how to interpret the address field. That is, either a location in the memory (R/P=1) or in the on-chip $ρμ$-code unit (R/P=0).

**Fig. 3.** The ρ-form: **set** (*p*-set, *c*-set) and **execute** instructions

**Memory organization.** For the memory design, we considered the on-chip memory blocks of the utilized FPGA. The available BRAM blocks in xc2vp20 allow the implementation of 128 KBytes memory for both data and instructions. The PowerPC has a Harvard architecture with separated instruction and data addressing spaces. Therefore, for better performance, we separated the main memory into two equal segments - 64 KBytes for instructions and other 64 KBytes for application data. In this case, we note that the amount of memory is limited only by the available on-chip memory. By utilizing external memories, it is possible to extend the memory volume up to the entire memory space addressable by PowerPC (i.e., 32-bit addresses). The later option, however, has not been considered in our prototype and in the experiments to follow.

**Clock domains.** Due to the polymorphic nature of the MOLEN processor and for performance efficiency, three clock domains have been implemented in our prototype:

- **PPC_clk**- clock signal to the core processor. The frequency of this signal has been set to 250 MHz, the maximum recommended for the PowerPCs in xc2vp20-5;
- **mem_clk**- clock signal to the main memory. This signal has been set to be three times lower than the PPC_clk, i.e., 83 MHz;
- **CCU_clk**- clock signal to the CCU driven by an external pin. It may be utilized by any CCU, which requires frequencies, different from the PPC_clk and mem_clk.

**Additional design parameters.** For the prototype implementation, we have considered a microcode word length of 64 bits. A 32MByte memory segment has been considered for storing microprograms into a 64-bit organized main memory. The ρ-control store has been designed to handle 8KBytes 64-bit microcode words. As primary microcode storage units for the ρ-control store, we have used the BRAM blocks of the FPGA fabric, configured as a dual port memory. Each port is unidirectional - a read-only port is used to feed the microinstruction register, while a write-only port loads microcodes from the external memory into the pageable section of the ρ-control store. The XREGs have been implemented in a single BRAM organized as $512 \times 32$-bit storage.

**Synthesis results.** Hardware costs reported by the synthesis tools are presented in Table 1. The first column displays the FPGA resources considered. Column two reports the actual values of these resources, consumed by the reconfigurable processor, without considering any CCU implementation, i.e., the $\rho\mu$-code unit and the associated infrastructure. This includes the $\rho\mu$-code loading unit, the sequencer and the $\rho$-control store. Column three presents resource utilization of the arbiter. In column four, the resources consumed by the entire MOLEN organization are displayed, including the reconfigurable processor infrastructure, the arbiter and the XREGs. Finally, columns five and six respectively present the available FPGA resources in the xc2vp20 chip and the utilized part of these resources by the MOLEN organization (in %). Synthesis results strongly suggest that the MOLEN infrastructure consumes trivial hardware resources, thus leaving virtually all FPGA resources available for CCU implementations.

**Table 1.** MOLEN Organization Synthesis Results (* without any CCU implemented)

| Device xc2vp20 Speed Grade -5 | Reconfig. Processor* | Arbiter | Total incl. XREGs | Available Resources | % |
|---|---|---|---|---|---|
| Number of Slices | 71 | 84 | 156 | 10304 | 1 |
| Number of Slice Flip Flops | 78 | 69 | 147 | 20608 | 1 |
| Number of 4 input LUTs | 171 | 150 | 322 | 20608 | 1 |
| Number of BRAMs: | 4 | N.A. | 5 | 112 | 3 |
| Maximum Frequency [MHz] | 130 | 143 | 130 | N.A. | N.A. |

# 4   Prototype Evaluation

In this section, we describe the experiments that have been carried out to evaluate the MOLEN prototype performance and report the obtained results. We target and profile the MPEG-2 application. The profiling data are used to identify and design performance critical kernels as CCU implementations. Due to memory limitations, we run only the extracted kernels on the prototype MOLEN processor and directly measure the performance gains. Using these measurements, the profiling data, and Amdahl's law, we estimate the projected overall speedup, rather than directly run the entire MPEG-2 application on MOLEN. Hardware estimations for the considered CCUs are presented.

**Software profiling results.** The first step of the experimentation involves identifying the functions that are suitable for hardware implementations. The objective is to identify the most time-consuming kernels from the application. To this purpose, we performed the measurements on a PowerPC 970 running at 1600 MHz. The considered application is the Berkeley implementation of the MPEG-2 encoder and decoder included in libmpeg2. As input data, we used a representative set of four popular video sequences, namely *carphone*, *claire*, *container* and *tennis*. Profiling results for each considered function and its descendants (obtained with the GNU profiler **gprof**) are presented in Table 2. For the MPEG2 encoder, the total execution time spent in SAD, DCT and IDCT operations (Table 2, column 6) emphasizes that these functions require around

2/3 of the total application time. Although the IDCT function in MPEG2 encoder takes only around 1% of the application time (Table 2, column 5), in the MPEG2 decoder it requires on average around 42%. Consequently, all considered functions are good candidates for hardware implementations although their individual contribution to the performance improvement may differ per sequence and application.

**Table 2.** MPEG2 profiling results for each of the considered functions and its descendants

| sequence | # frames@Resolution | MPEG2 encoder | | | | MPEG2 decoder |
|---|---|---|---|---|---|---|
| | | SAD(16x16) | DCT(8x8) | IDCT(8x8) | Total | IDCT(8 x 8) |
| carphone | 96@176x144 | 51.1 % | 12.5 % | 1.3 % | 64.9 % | 50.4 % |
| claire | 168@360x288 | 53.8 % | 11.8 % | 1.0 % | 66.6 % | 37.6 % |
| container | 300@352x288 | 56.2 % | 10.7 % | 1.0 % | 67.9 % | 40.4 % |
| tennis | 112@352x240 | 60.0 % | 9.5 % | 0.8 % | 70.3 % | 40.5 % |

**Synthesis results for the considered CCU implementations.** We implemented the functions, suggested by the profiling results, into reconfigurable hardware. Synthesis results for the xc2vp50 chip are reported in Table 3. For the SAD function, we implemented the organization proposed in [8]. The super-pipelined 16-byte version of this SAD organization (SAD16) is capable of processing one 16-pixel line (1 pixel is 1 byte) of a macroblock in 17 cycles at over 300 MHz. The 128-byte version (SAD128) processes eight macroblock lines in 23 cycles, and the 256-byte version (SAD256), processes an entire 16x16-pixel macroblock in 25. SAD256 requires more resources than available in the xc2vp20 chip, therefore we consider it for future implementation on a larger FPGA (e.g., xc2vp50). To support the DCT and IDCT kernels, we synthesized the 2-D DCT and 2D-IDCT v.2.0 cores available as IPs in the Xilinx Core Generator Tool. Considering the implemented clock domains and synthesis results (from Table 3) in our experiments, we have run the DCT and IDCT functions at mem_clk frequency (83MHz). The SAD designs were clocked by PPC_clk (250MHz).

**Table 3.** Synthesis Results per CCU implementation

| Device xc2vp20 Speed Grade -5 | SAD16 | SAD128 | SAD256 (xc2vp50) | DCT | IDCT | Available Resources |
|---|---|---|---|---|---|---|
| Number of Slices | 831 | 6807 | 13613* | 4314 | 5436 | 10304 |
| Number of Slice Flip Flops | 1448 | 11862 | 23724* | 7964 | 9876 | 20608 |
| Number of 4 input LUTs | 1390 | 11379 | 22757* | 6832 | 8624 | 20608 |
| Number of BRAMs: | N.A. | N.A. | N.A. * | 2 | 2 | 112 |
| Maximum Frequency [MHz] | 310 | 310 | 310* | 96 | 96 | N.A. |

**Experimental results.** We have embedded the considered CCU implementations within the MOLEN organization and carried out experiments in two stages:

*Stage 1.* Compile the software kernels for the original PowerPC ISA and run them on one of the PowerPC405 processors, embedded in the xc2vp20 device. The kernels have been extracted from the original application source code (the ANSI C code used for the profiling) without any further code modifications. For our experiments, we considered the same data sequences as used in the profiling phase. The PowerPC timers are initialized before a kernel is executed and are read immediately after the kernel execution has completed. Thus, the exact number of PowerPC cycles, required for the entire kernel execution can be obtained. After we derived the cycle counts for the PowerPC ISA software runs, we initiated the next stage of the experiment.

*Stage 2.* The kernel software code is substituted with a new piece of code to support πISA. The corresponding kernel CCU configuration is present in the reconfigurable processor. Identically to the preceding experimentation stage, we obtain the exact number of PowerPC cycles required to complete the entire kernel operation on MOLEN.

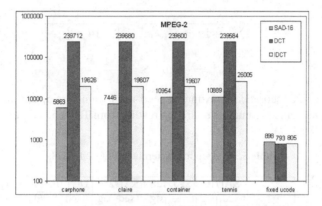

**Fig. 4.** Cycle numbers for kernels execution in original PowerPC ISA and fixed $\mu$-code in πISA

Figure 4 depicts the measured cycles obtained in the two experimentation phases. The first four chart groups present cycle counts for the original PowerPC ISA. The last chart group presents the cycle numbers, consumed by MOLEN while processing the same data. In this figure, only fixed microcode implementations are depicted. In addition, we have considered both fixed and pageable microcode implementations for SAD16 and SAD128. Table 4 reports cycle numbers for executing these SAD implementations over a single macroblock. After obtaining the execution cycle numbers for each kernel both on PowerPC and MOLEN, the kernel speedup is calculated for all data sequences with respect to each CCU implementation. Table 5 presents the calculated kernel speedups.

**Table 4.** Cycle numbers per macroblock for different SAD implementations

|                     | SAD16 | SAD128 | SAD256 |
|---------------------|-------|--------|--------|
| fixed microcode     | 898   | 311    | 264    |
| peageable microcode | 914   | 331    | 284    |

**Projected application speedup.** To calculate the projected speedup of the entire application, we employed the well known Amdahl's law, utilizing the following notations. Let us assume $T$ to be the execution time of the original program (say measured in cycles) and $T_{SEi}$ - time to execute kernel $i$ in software, which we would like to speed-up in reconfigurable hardware. Assume $T_{\rho i}$ is the execution time (in $\pi$ISA) for the reconfigurable implementation of kernel $i$. Assuming $a_i = \frac{T_{SEi}}{T}$ and $s_i = \frac{T_{SEi}}{T_{\rho i}}$, the speed-up of the program with respect to the reconfigurable implementation of kernel $i$ is:

$$S_i = \frac{T}{T - T_{SEi} + T_{\rho i}} = \frac{1}{1 - \left(a_i - \frac{a_i}{s_i}\right)} \tag{1}$$

Identically, assuming $a = \sum_i a_i$, all the kernels potential candidates for reconfigurable implementation would speed-up the program with:

$$S = \frac{T}{T - \sum_i T_{SEi} + \sum_i T_{\rho i}} = \frac{1}{1 - \left(a - \sum_i \frac{a_i}{s_i}\right)}, \tag{2}$$

$$S_{max} = \lim_{\forall s_i \to \infty} S = \frac{1}{1 - a} \tag{3}$$

Where $S_{max}$ is the theoretical maximum speed-up. Parameters $a_i$ are the profiling results from Table 2 and parameters $s_i$ are the results from Table 5.

**Table 5.** Speedup for Different MPEG-2 Kernels

|  | SAD16 | | SAD128 | | SAD256 | | DCT | IDCT |
|---|---|---|---|---|---|---|---|---|
|  | fixed | pag. | fixed | pag. | fixed | pag. | fixed | fixed |
| carphone | 6.5 | 6.4 | 18.9 | 17.7 | 22.2 | 20.6 | 302.3 | 24.4 |
| claire | 8.3 | 8.1 | 23.9 | 22.5 | 28.2 | 26.2 | 302.2 | 24.4 |
| container | 12.2 | 12.0 | 35.2 | 33.1 | 41.5 | 38.6 | 302.1 | 24.4 |
| tennis | 12.1 | 11.9 | 35.0 | 32.9 | 41.2 | 38.3 | 302.1 | 32.3 |

The projected speedup figures for the entire MPEG-2 encoder and MPEG-2 decoder applications are reported in Table 6. It can be observed that SAD128 and SAD256 CCU implementations clearly outperform SAD16 due to their parallel processing organization. That is, depending on the CCU implementation, the entire application speedup

**Table 6.** Speedup per kernel for the Entire MPEG2

|  | encoder | | | | | | | | decoder |
|---|---|---|---|---|---|---|---|---|---|
|  | SAD16 | | SAD128 | | SAD256 | | DCT | IDCT | IDCT |
|  | fixed | pag. | fixed | pag. | fixed | pag. | fixed | fixed | fixed |
| carphone | 1.76 | 1.76 | 1.94 | 1.93 | 1.95 | 1.95 | 1.14 | 1.01 | 1.94 |
| claire | 1.90 | 1.89 | 2.06 | 2.06 | 2.08 | 2.07 | 1.13 | 1.01 | 1.56 |
| container | 2.07 | 2.06 | 2.20 | 2.20 | 2.21 | 2.21 | 1.12 | 1.01 | 1.63 |
| tennis | 2.22 | 2.22 | 2.40 | 2.39 | 2.41 | 2.41 | 1.10 | 1.01 | 1.65 |

can be severely affected. The projected overall speed up figures for the entire MPEG-2 encoder and MPEG-2 decoder applications are reported in Table 7. For the MPEG-2 encoder, the simultaneous configuration of the SAD128, DCT, and IDCT operations employing fixed microcode implementations has been considered. For the MPEG-2 decoder, only the IDCT has been implemented. Columns, indicated by label "theory" contain the theoretically achievable maximum speedup calculated with respect to Equation (3). Columns labelled by "impl." have been calculated employing Equation (2) and contain data for the projected speedups with respect to the considered MOLEN implementation. Results in Table 7 strongly suggest that the actual speedup of the MPEG-2 encoder and decoder obtained during our practical experimentation very closely approach the theoretically estimated maximum possible speedups.

**Table 7.** Overall MPEG2 Speedup

|  | MPEG2 encoder* | | MPEG2 decoder | |
|---|---|---|---|---|
|  | theory | impl. | theory | impl. |
| carphone | 2.85 | 2.64 | 2.02 | 1.94 |
| claire | 2.99 | 2.80 | 1.60 | 1.56 |
| container | 3.12 | 2.96 | 1.68 | 1.63 |
| tennis | 3.37 | 3.18 | 1.68 | 1.65 |

\* fixed $\mu$-code SAD128 + DCT + IDCT

# 5    Conclusions

In this paper, we presented a prototype design of the MOLEN polymorphic processor, a custom computing machine based on the co-processor architectural paradigm. The prototype was implemented on a Xilinx Virtex II Pro™ FPGA. One of the PowerPC cores embedded in the Virtex II Pro™ FPGA was used as a general purpose processor and the reconfigurable fabric operated as a reconfigurable co-processor. The paper presented hardware synthesis results for the MOLEN infrastructure and for three custom computing units implemented as reconfigurable processors, namely SAD, DCT and IDCT. The reconfigurable hardware costs of the aforementioned functions were between 8% and 53% of the utilized xc2vp20 chip, depending on the particular configuration considered. The performance of the design was evaluated by experiments. More precisely, the MPEG-2 application was accelerated very closely to its theoretical limits by implementing SAD, DCT and IDCT as reconfigurable co-processors. The MPEG-2 encoder overall speedup was in the range between 2.64 and 3.18 while the speedup of the MPEG-2 decoder varies between 1.65 and 1.94. These results proved the viability of the MOLEN concept and showed its potentials for accelerating complex real-life applications at trivial hardware costs.

# References

1. F. Campi, M. Toma, A. Lodi, A. Cappelli, R. Canegallo, and R. Guerrieri. A VLIW Processor with Reconfigurable Instruction Set for Embedded Applications. In *ISSCC Digest of Technical Papers*, pp. 250–251, Feb 2003.
2. M. Gokhale and J. Stone. Napa C: Compiling for a Hybrid RISC/FPGA Architecture. In *Proc. IEEE Symp. on FCCM*, pp. 126–135, 1998.
3. S. Hauck, T. Fry, M. Hosler, and J. Kao. The Chimaera Reconfigurable Functional Unit. In *Proc. IEEE Symp. on FCCM*, pp. 87–96, 1997.
4. G. Kuzmanov, G. N. Gaydadjiev, and S. Vassiliadis. Loading rm-code: Design considerations. In *Proc. Third Intl. Workshop on Systems, Architectures, Modeling, and Simulation (SAMOS'03)*, pp 8–11, 2003.
5. G. Kuzmanov and S. Vassiliadis. Arbitrating Instructions in an $\rho\mu$-coded CCM. In *Proc. 13th Intl. Conf. FPL'03*, Springer-Verlag LNCS, vol. 2778, pp. 81–90, 2003.
6. A. L. Rosa, L. Lavagno, and C. Passerone. Hardware/Software Design Space Exploration for a Reconfigurable Processor. In *Proc. DATE 2003*, pp. 570–575, 2003.
7. S. Vassiliadis, G. N. Gaydadjiev, K. Bertels, and E. M. Panainte. The molen programming paradigm. In *Proc. Third Intl. Workshop on Systems, Architectures, Modeling, and Simulation (SAMOS'03)*, pp. 1–7, 2003.
8. S. Vassiliadis, E. Hakkennes, S. Wong, and G. Pechanek. The Sum-of-Absolute-Difference Motion Estimation Accelerator. In *Proc. 24th Euromicro Conf.*, pp. 559–566, 1998.
9. S. Vassiliadis, S. Wong, and S. Cotofana. The MOLEN $\rho\mu$-Coded Processor. In *11th Intl. Conf. FPL'01*, Springer-Verlag LNCS, vol. 2147, pp. 275–285, 2001.
10. Xilinx Corporation. *Virtex-II Pro Platform FPGA Handbook*, v.1.0, 2002.
11. A. Ye, N. Shenoy, and P. Banerjee. A C Compiler for a Processor with a Reconfigurable Functional Unit. In *ACM/SIGDA Symp. on FPGAs*, pp. 95–100, 2000.

# Reconfigurable Hardware
# for a Scalable Wavelet Video Decoder
# and Its Performance Requirements

Dirk Stroobandt[1], Hendrik Eeckhaut[1], Harald Devos[1], Mark Christiaens[1],
Fabio Verdicchio[2], and Peter Schelkens[2]

[1] Ghent University, ELIS Dept., Sint-Pietersnieuwstraat 41, 9000 Gent, Belgium
{dstr,heeckhau,hdevos,mchristi}@elis.UGent.be
[2] Vrije Universiteit Brussel, ETRO Dept., Pleinlaan 2, 1050 Brussel, Belgium
{fverdicc,pschelke}@etro.vub.ac.be
http://www.elis.UGent.be/resume/

**Abstract.** Multimedia applications emerge on portable devices everywhere. These applications typically have a number of stringent requirements: (i) a high amount of computational power together with real-time
performance and (ii) the flexibility to modify the application or the characteristics of the application at will. The performance requirements often
drive the design towards a hardware implementation while the flexibility
requirement is better served by a software implementation. In this paper
we try to reconcile these two requirements by using an FPGA to implement the performance critical parts of a scalable wavelet video decoder.
Through analytical means we first explore the performance and resource
requirements. We find that modern FPGAs offer enough computational
power to obtain real-time performance of the decoder, but that reaching
the necessary memory bandwidth will be a challenge during this design.

## 1 Introduction

When designing a new multimedia system one would usually prefer to implement
most of the functionality in software running on a general purpose processor. This
improves the ease and flexibility of the design process and avoids the high cost of
designing an ASIC. Still, often the performance requirements of the multimedia
system are such that specific hardware is necessary. Then again, ASICs do not
offer flexibility of the functionality after implementation. For example, an ASIC
designed for doing JPEG compression utilizing Huffman encoding will become
useless when application changes require arithmetic encoding. This generally
results in an overdimensioning of the ASIC so that it can accommodate all the
required operations of the multimedia system even if these operations may only
be needed infrequently. In software such overdimensioning has little consequence
but in hardware it increases the complexity of the design and the production cost.

With the emergence of high-performance FPGAs (field programmable gate
arrays) [1], we have access to both the required performance and enough flexibility. In the RESUME project (Reconfigurable Embedded Systems for Use in

A. Pimentel and S. Vassiliadis (Eds.): SAMOS 2004, LNCS 3133, pp. 203–212, 2004.

scalable Multimedia Environments [2]) we explore the usefulness of FPGAs for the design of multimedia systems. We are building (among others) a *scalable* wavelet based video decoder [3,4]. By "scalable" we mean that it allows one to easily change the quality of service (QoS), i.e., the frame rate, resolution, color depth, ... of the decoded video without having to change the video stream used by the decoder (except for skipping unnecessary blocks of data without decoding) or having to decode the whole video stream if only part of it is required.

Such a scalable video decoder has advantages for both the server (providing video streams) and the clients. The server only needs to produce one video stream for all clients and the client can easily change the decoding parameters to optimize the use of the display, the required processing power, the required memory, etc. A scalable video decoder is a perfect fit for the use of FPGAs since it can be reconfigured each time the QoS requirements change while still performing in real-time.

Our current goal in the project is to design the scalable video decoder such that we can semi-automatically generate a range of different FPGA configurations by simply changing the QoS requirements that need to be met. These implementations will form a near Pareto-optimal set of configurations that each have optimal performance for a certain set of requirements and cost function.

In the remainder of this paper we present an overview of the decoder in Section 2 and point out its scalability features in Section 3. Section 4 presents the results of profiling the software version of the decoder. Section 5 contains some preliminary performance estimates and a description of the first implementation. Finally, in Section 6, we detail the future evolution of our project.

## 2    System Overview

The encoded video in our system consists of a reference frame per group of 16 pictures (GOP), a set of motion vectors describing the movement of image parts in the other GOP frames and error frames. These are all encoded by a wavelet transform and the resulting bit stream is further reduced by an entropy encoder. The wavelet video decoder that we need to decode these images is described by the high-level overview shown in Figure 1. The "parser" P receives a bit stream representing the compressed video, analyzes its structure and extracts only the relevant parts for the further decoding process. The "wavelet entropy decoder"

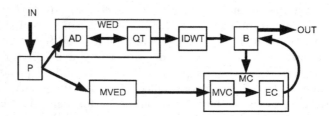

**Fig. 1.** High-level overview of the video decoder.

(WED) decodes entropy encoded parts of the bit stream into wavelet transformed frames. It consists of two strongly interconnected parts: the "arithmetic decoder" (AD) and the "quadtree decoder" (QT) [5, 6]. This close cooperation improves the compression ratio that is achieved but hinders the independent implementation of these components. The "inverse wavelet transform" (IDWT) takes a wavelet transformed frame and computes an inverse wavelet transform producing either a reference image (the first image of a GOP) or an error frame. "Motion vector entropy decoding" (MVED) performs the entropy decoding of the motion vectors and "Motion compensation" (MC) does the actual reconstruction of the final video frames. It is composed of the "motion vector compensation" (MVC) and the "error correction" (EC). The MVC takes two reference frames and a set of motion vectors. It constructs a first estimate of the resulting video frame by combining translated blocks of the reference frames. The corresponding error frame is added in EC in order to 'fine-tune' the first estimate and to produce the final image. Finally, the "reorder buffer" (B) puts the decoded frames in the correct order resulting in the final video stream.

## 3   Exploiting the Scalability

We can distinguish the scalability of the decoder QoS from the scalability of the hardware cost. The former may include the frame rate, the resolution of the frames, the accuracy (cfr. PSNR - Peak Signal to Noise Ratio), the availability of colors, ... The latter contains parameters such as required chip area, power consumption, network bandwidth, ... It is clear that all these parameters are not independent of each other. Here, we discuss the influence of the parameters that describe the QoS scaling on the calculation cost.

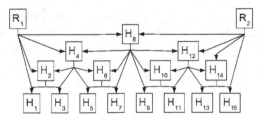

**Fig. 2.** The temporal decomposition of one GOP. The arrows illustrate which frames are used to reconstruct (via motion compensation) other frames at lower decomposition levels. $R_1$ and $R_2$ are reference frames, the $H_i$ are reconstructed (intermediate) frames.

**Frame rate:** Different frame rates are possible through a dyadic temporal decomposition [7] of the video stream. This is illustrated in Figure 2. The decoder can choose to which (temporal) level the stream is decoded. Each extra level doubles the frame rate. Because the frames are grouped in GOPs of 16 frames and the full video streams are played at 30 frames per second, the possibilities are 30, 15, 7.5, 3.75 and 1.875 frames per second.

**Resolution:** In the encoder a 2-D discrete wavelet transform (DWT) in K levels is performed on the error and reference frames. The $0^{th}$ level has the total frame as input and generates four subbands LL, HL, LH and HH. In the next levels the same action is performed on the LL-subband of the previous level. This is a low resolution version of the original frame. The inverse discrete wavelet transform (IDWT) in the decoder performs the inverse transformation and can stop at an arbitrary level, thus influencing the resolution of the video. The wavelet entropy decoding (WED) of the unused high frequency subbands can also be omitted.

**Image quality:** The quadtree entropy decoder decodes a bit stream containing the quantized wavelet encoded frames, bit plane per bit plane, starting with the most significant plane. Resources can be economized when some less significant bit planes are omitted. This results in a lower quality (measured by, e.g., the PSNR) of the decoded frames.

# 4   A Rough Profile of the Decoder

In this section, we try to obtain a rough estimate of where the computationally expensive parts of the decoding system are located. Therefore, we profiled the decoding algorithm based on a preliminary C/C++ implementation (on a standard PC[1]). Note that we are dealing here with prototype code, written for ease of modification, not for optimal speed. Therefore the results in this section are only intended as a rough, first estimate of the computational costs of the different blocks of the decoder.

## 4.1   PSNR

Execution time alone is not enough to evaluate our scalable codec. We also need a measure for the quality of decoded sequences: the PSNR of the decoded frames vs. the original frames. It is defined as follows: if $Y_{i,j}$, $U_{i,j}$ and $V_{i,j}$ and $Y'_{i,j}$, $U'_{i,j}$ and $V'_{i,j}$ are the luminance and the two chrominance channels of a YUV 4:2:0 image and its reconstructed version, both with resolution $r \times s$, then the PSNR is defined as

$$10 \log_{10} \frac{255^2 \frac{3}{2} rs}{\sum (Y - Y')^2 + \sum (U - U')^2 + \sum (V - V')^2} \qquad (1)$$

The PSNR provides a measure for the quality of one decoded frame; for the quality of the entire video stream we use the mean PSNR. However, since we are dealing with temporal scalability we also need a quality measure when the original and decoded sequence have a different frame rate. There are two options to be able to compare all frames: either reduce the frame rate of the original sequence by removing frames (called 'Reduced Frame Rate (RFR) PSNR') or inflate the rate of the decoded sequence by duplicating frames before the PSNR

---

[1] Pentium IV 2.0 GHz, 512MiB RAM

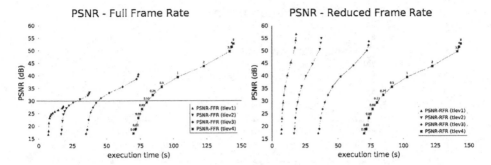

**Fig. 3.** The RFR and FFR PSNR for the Foreman sequence. The bit rates (bpp) are only labeled for the curve of sequences decoded at maximum frame rate (time level 4); the values for the other curves are the same. It obviously takes more time to decode more frames and the higher the bit rate the better the quality. For FFR PSNR, the effect of a lower frame rate (less time levels) is clearly visible.

is calculated (*'Full Frame Rate (FFR) PSNR'*). While RFR PSNR does not assign a quality loss to low frame rates (because it discards high frame rates), FFR PSNR considers a lower frame rate as lower quality. Both approaches are used in the following experiments.

We decoded a variety of different (encoded) sequences for a number of different bit rates while measuring the execution time and the resulting PSNR. In this paper, the bit rate is defined as the number of (decoded) bits per pixel. Note that this is different from the number of bits per second. Two streams with the same bit rate but a different frame rate for example will not have the same number of bits per second because the total number of pixels is different. The considered sequences are reference sequences widely used for video coding research. The results for all sequences were very similar and in this paper we present results for the "Foreman" sequence, consisting of 288 CIF frames ($352 \times 288$ pixels $+ 2 \times 176 \times 144$ pixels for the color channels) which (@30Hz) equals 9.6s of video.

The results for the Foreman sequence are illustrated in Figure 3, for reduced and full frame rate. The PSNR is of course the same for both approaches when all frames are decoded (time level 4). When the quality is measured with the full frame rate PSNR the effect of a lower frame rate is clearly visible. For reduced frame rate PSNR on the contrary, we observe no significant impact on the PSNR.

In Figure 4 we plotted the execution time of the three major time consuming blocks of the algorithm versus the bit rate. Only the Wavelet Entropy Decoding (WED) depends on the bit rate. For higher bit rates this is the most time consuming block of the decoding algorithm. Motion Compensation (MC) is independent of the bit rate but varies for different sequences (depending on the actual values of the motion vectors). The share of the Inverse Discrete Wavelet Transform (IDWT) is rather limited and independent of both bit rate and sequence; each frame needs exactly the same number of computations.

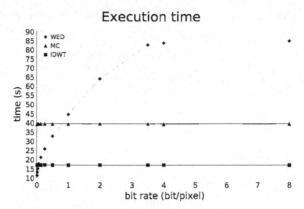

**Fig. 4.** The execution time for Wavelet Entropy Decoding (WED), Inverse Discrete Wavelet Transform (IDWT) and Motion Compensation (MC) (Foreman sequence).

## 4.2   Experiment

In Figure 3 and Figure 4 we can see that we are far from a real-time (software) implementation. Therefore we experimented with different configurations of the decoding algorithm, skipping either interpolation or error frame correction or reducing the bit rate. The results of these experiments can be found in [8] and resulted in a few configurations that could be decoded in real-time (but with reduced quality of course). To decode images at full frame rate and impeccable quality, we need a hardware implementation.

## 5   Estimations and Implementation

To be able to choose a hardware platform, the requirements of the application need to be known. This includes the amount of necessary memory, the bandwidth to the memory and some measures for the computing power. As their exact quantities are only known after implementation, estimations have to be made.

The requirements depend on and scale with the QoS of the video. Only estimations for the maximal QoS (30 frames/s, QCIF or CIF-format) are listed here because these will result in the requirements for the hardware. Estimations for other QoS are interesting to illustrate the trade-offs between different quality and hardware cost parameters. One of the goals of the project is the validation of these estimation techniques and the development of new estimation techniques.

The decoding algorithm was provided as Matlab/C++ code that was written for ease of developing and not for minimal execution time. The following estimations are based on the underlying algorithms, so that redundant calculations and operations in the code are not taken into account.

Some of the blocks in the system have a very deterministic behavior (e.g., the inverse wavelet transform). They repeatedly perform the same actions on constant amounts of data. Others are extremely data dependent (e.g., quadtree);

the data arrives at varying rates (compressed) and needs varying amounts of operations. For these blocks only the worst case requirements are calculated.

## 5.1 Data Types

In the C code, the most frequently used data types are floating point and integer. For a hardware implementation, fixed point numbers and integers with limited range should be used. Therefore a study of the relation between performance and range or accuracy of the variables was made, showing that each fixed point number can be stored in 2 bytes or less (floating point = 4 bytes). Larger word lengths are only needed for intermediate results and calculations on the FPGA.

## 5.2 Memory Requirements

Arrays and variables in the software source are allocated for a longer time than really needed. To calculate the real memory requirements one should limit the lifetime of each array and variable to the minimum so that memory can be reused. Also the size of the data types differs from the software implementation as described in the previous paragraph.

If we assume that all components of the decoder will need to be working in parallel (e.g., in a pipelined fashion) the total memory requirement is the sum of the requirements of the different components. Table 1 gives an overview.

**Table 1.** Memory requirements (in Byte) of the decoder.

|                      | QCIF    | CIF       |
|----------------------|---------|-----------|
| Reorder buffer       | 228,096 | 912,384   |
| Motion compensation  | 44,541  | 172,845   |
| IDWT                 | 76,032  | 304,128   |
| Quadtree decoder     | 120,384 | 481,636   |
| Arithmetic decoder   | 86,888  | 342,144   |
| Total                | 555,941 | 2,213,037 |

## 5.3 Computational Requirements

Can a modern FPGA (e.g., Xilinx Virtex-II or Altera Stratix) cope with the amount of computations that are needed for decoding the video stream in real-time? Let us look at the different components of the decoder.

- Previous implementations [9] of arithmetic decoders have shown that this component fits in a very small part (a few %) of a modern FPGA.
- The quadtree decoder has a rather low computational cost but will be I/O bound since it has a large number of accesses to a large data structure with bad locality.

– The inverse wavelet transform has a good temporal and spatial locality so we believe it will be computation bound. For a wavelet transform of degree 4 using the Bior 5.5 filter (the largest filter) we need $2.5 \times 10^6$ multiplications and $4.5 \times 10^6$ additions per CIF-frame or $754 \times 10^6$ multiplications/s and $135 \times 10^6$ additions/s.
– The motion compensation (without interpolation) performs $6.08 \times 10^6$ additions/s and $3.04 \times 10^6$ shifts/s. As shifts can be hard-wired they can be ignored.
– In the worst case, the interpolator performs $231 \times 10^6$ multiplications/s and $220 \times 10^6$ additions/s.

A Virtex-II 2000 speed grade 5 has 56 18 bit×18 bit multipliers that can run at 105 MHz. This results in $5.88 \times 10^9$ multiplications/s which is more than sufficient. Additions are substantially less expensive and should not be a problem either.

**Table 2.** Bandwidth (MiB/s) between components.

|  | QCIF | | CIF | |
|---|---|---|---|---|
|  | In | Out | In | Out |
| Reorder buffer | 1.09 | 11.35 | 4.35 | 45.41 |
| Motion compensation | 11.84 | 1.09 | 47.36 | 4.35 |
| IDWT | 2.18 | 1.22 | 8.7 | 4.89 |
| Quadtree decoder | < 2.18 | 2.18 | < 8.7 | 8.7 |
| Arithmetic decoder | < 2.18 | < 2.18 | < 8.7 | < 8.7 |
| Total | 19.46 | 21.29 | 77.81 | 68.79 |

### 5.4 Bandwidth Requirements

An overview of the bandwidth required between components is shown in Table 2 (the interpolator is integrated in the motion compensation). This table does not show the bandwidth between a component and its (local) memory, required for the internal operation of that component.

Here the quadtree decoder might prove to be a problem. It requires a fairly large work memory that is accessed very frequently in irregular patterns. This type of behavior excludes the possibility of efficient caching. Further experimentation has to show if a real-time implementation of the quadtree decoder is feasible. We expect that the typical behavior of this component is much better than our worst case (426 MiB/s internal bandwidth) assumptions.

The IDWT may also prove difficult due to the fact that it needs to traverse the frame multiple times. In a naïve implementation (not block-based) 46.22 MiB/s is necessary.

### 5.5 Conclusion Regarding the Estimates

The major conclusions are that the necessary internal bandwidth is the most restrictive bottleneck, that the targeted wavelet entropy decoder has a high compression performance but its sequential nature and memory access pattern hampers an elegant hardware implementation and that memory requirements are quite modest. Luckily, earlier work has shown that embedded entropy decoders can be implemented efficiently [10]. Modern FPGAs should offer enough calculation power to implement the video codec.

### 5.6 Current Status of the Implementation

Starting from the rough Matlab/C++-implementation we used for profiling, we molded the algorithm into a more hardware-friendly form. We transformed all floating point operations to fixed point (without a loss in quality) and optimized the memory use both in footprint and in bandwidth. We completely rewrote the motion compensation code which resulted in a faster than real-time compensation of CIF frames on a Pentium IV 2 GHz. From the wavelet code, irrelevant calculations were removed and symmetry properties are now exploited. Even after extensively optimizing the wavelet entropy coding algorithm it still remained too complex to achieve a fast implementation in hardware. We are currently in the process of developing a new WED algorithm which can be implemented more efficiently and more easily in hardware while still supporting quality scalability.

The optimized C-code of the IDWT was refined to SystemC, RTL-level. This code can be automatically translated to VHDL and synthesized. The IDWT was included in a modular design on a Stratix FPGA. This modular design allows for easy addition or removal of modules that share common resources like access to the memory or the PCI-bus. This allows us to choose independently between a software and a hardware version for each module. All blocks of the decoder will follow the same design trajectory as explored for the IDWT.

## 6  Future Work

As stated in the introduction it will be possible to configure the FPGA design of the scalable video. For each block a set of different parameterizable or scaled versions will be constructed. This will effectively yield hundreds of different implementations of the video decoder that each are nearly "optimal". Optimality is clearly defined by a cost function that takes into account such factors as low power consumption, small FPGA requirements, low memory requirements, . . . given that a certain QoS must be achieved. A future goal of our project is to devise techniques to evaluate the performance/cost of a configuration of the FPGA without actually having to instantiate that design. These may be based on SLIP (System Level Interconnect Prediction) techniques [11].

Another avenue of research we will investigate is how to simultaneously run multiple multimedia applications on the same FPGA or on multiple FPGAs. Finally, we want to further explore the ideal architecture supporting all this scalability and a further elaboration of the new WED needs further examination.

# 7    Conclusions

There is an ever increasing demand for scalable multimedia applications. Software may not be able to cope with the high performance requirements but reconfigurable hardware combines flexibility with high performance.

This paper considers a scalable wavelet video decoder. It shows that modern FPGAs should offer enough computational power but the necessary bandwidth, the sequential nature and the memory access pattern of the wavelet entropy decoder may hamper the implementation.

This preparatory work is a crucial step in the exploration of the usefulness of FPGAs in multimedia systems. With the proposed evaluation of the performance/cost of FPGA implementations and the study of the reconfiguration possibilities, we will be able to fully grab the performance requirements for reconfigurable hardware to be used for scalable video decoder applications.

## Acknowledgments

This research is supported by I.W.T. grant 020174, F.W.O. grant G.0021.03 and by GOA project 12.51B.02 of Ghent University. Harald Devos and Peter Schelkens are supported by the fund for scientific research Flanders (F.W.O.).

## References

1. DeHon, A.: The density advantage of configurable computing. IEEE Computer **33** (2000) 41–49
2. The RESUME project: Reconfigurable Embedded Systems for Use in Scalable Multimedia Environments. (http://www.elis.UGent.be/resume)
3. Taubman, D., Zakhor, A.: Multirate 3-D subband coding of video. IEEE Trans. Image Proc. **3** (1994) 572–588
4. Woods, J.W., Lilienfield, G.: A resolution and frame-rate scalable subband/wavelet video coder. IEEE Trans. Circ. and Syst. Video Techn. **11** (2001) 1035–1044
5. Munteanu, A.: Wavelet Image Coding and Multiscale Edge Detection - Algorithms and Applications. Ph.D. thesis, Vrije Universiteit Brussel (2003)
6. Munteanu, A., Cornelis, J., Van der Auwera, G., Cristea, P.: Wavelet image compression - the quadtree coding approach. IEEE Trans. Inf. Techn. in Biomedicine **3** (1999) 176–185
7. Turaga, D., van der Schaar, M.: Unconstrained motion compensated temporal filtering. In: ISO/IEC JTC1/SC29/WG11, m8388, MPEG 60th meeting. (2002)
8. Devos, H., Eeckhaut, H., Christiaens, M., Verdicchio, F., Stroobandt, D., Schelkens, P.: Performance requirements for reconfigurable hardware for a scalable wavelet video decoder. In: CD-rom Proc. ProRISC Workshop on Circuits, Systems and Signal Processing, STW, Utrecht (2003)
9. Xie, Y., Wolf, W., Lekatsas, H.: A code decompression architecture for VLIW processors. In: 34th Ann. Intl. Symp. Microarchitecture. (2001) 66–75
10. Schelkens, P.: Multidimensional Wavelet Coding - Algorithms and Implementations. Ph.D. thesis, Dept. ETRO, Vrije Universiteit Brussel, Brussel (2001)
11. Stroobandt, D.: A Priori Wire Length Estimates for Digital Design. Kluwer Academic Publishers, Boston / Dordrecht / London (2001)

# Design Space Exploration for Configurable Architectures and the Role of Modeling, High-Level Program Analysis and Learning Techniques

Pedro C. Diniz

University of Southern California / Information Sciences Institute
4676 Admiralty Way, Suite 1001
Marina del Rey,California 90292, USA
pedro@isi.edu

**Abstract.** Reconfigurable computing architectures promise to substantially increase the performance of computations through the customization of data-path and storage structures best suited to the specific needs of each computation. The need to synthesize, either fully or partially, the structure of the target architecture while simultaneously attempting to optimize the mapping of the computation to that architecture creates a vast design space exploration (DSE) challenge. In this paper we describe current approaches to this DSE problem using program analysis, estimation, modeling and empirical optimization techniques. We also describe a unified approach for this DSE challenge in which these techniques can be complemented with history- and learning-based approaches.

## 1 Introduction

Reconfigurable computing systems offer the promise of substantial performance improvements over traditional computing architectures as they allow for the development of custom data-path and storage structures suited to the particular needs of each computation. For example, a numerically-intensive computation could take advantage of a large number of arithmetic units to operate in parallel over different data items whereas a memory-intensive computation, could use localized storage structures (*e.g.,* tapped-delay lines or RAM blocks) to hold frequently used data values.

This promise of reconfigurable computing comes at the expense of a substantial increase in complexity of the mapping of computations described in traditional imperative programming languages such as C, MatLab or Java. Besides the complexity of uncovering the concurrency in the computations, either statically or using run-time compilation techniques, any approach that aims at fully exploiting the potential of reconfigurable computing must synthesize (partially or fully) the target architecture the computations are to be mapped onto.

To address the very challenging problem of a combined architecture exploration and computation mapping, researchers have developed sophisticated

A. Pimentel and S. Vassiliadis (Eds.): SAMOS 2004, LNCS 3133, pp. 213–223, 2004.

design-space-exploration (DSE) prototype systems. Typically, these systems revolve around the idea of iteratively improving a combined hardware/software design by applying a set of program mapping steps and transformations and observing the resulting overall performance. This iterative process terminates when a feasible design is obtained and/or no significant process is likely to occur in subsequent iterations of the design's refinement.

This iterative DSE process is, in many cases, lengthy and error prone. For example, when targeting Field-Programmable-Gate-Array (FPGA) configurable systems, just the Place-and-Route (P&R) step of a design mapping can take hours. If a design is not feasible, *i.e.*, it does not fit in the allocated time or hardware resources, designers have to rethink their approach and choose among one of many design alternative paths. To address this issue, researchers have extensively used modeling and estimation techniques as a way to accelerate the design exploration. Instead of waiting for a design to be fully synthesized/compiled, estimation and modeling allows compiler/synthesis tools to make decisions about which partitions and sequences of transformations are likely to yield best results without having to explicitly apply them. The obvious drawback is the potential discrepancy between the models, the estimates, and the reality.

In this paper we introduce a new approach that helps mitigate some of the accuracy and duration aspects of current DSE that rely exclusively on estimation and/or modeling techniques. In the approach described here, a compiler would use the experience from previous mappings to guide, and accelerate the application of program transformations to new mappings in a *history-based* approach. Because the variety and diversity of each input code is extremely large, we suggest the utilization of program analysis for the definition and quantification of *structural* similarities between codes. This similarity matching approach would allow the compiler to select a good basis for the set of program transformations to apply. Given an initial selection of program transformations and mapping decisions, should help the compiler in quickly determining a feasible mapping upon which it can improve with other techniques. This can even be coupled with *learning-based* techniques. Over time, and given the wealth of knowledge about previously successful and unsuccessful mapping decisions, a compiler could derive knowledge, for instance in the form of a *rule-based* approach, to derive knowledge about which transformations work best with which codes' features.

This paper is organized as follows. Section 2 describes current approaches to DSE using a combination of analysis, estimation, modeling and empirical optimization techniques. Section 3 outlines a unified approach combining existing techniques with history- and learning-based approaches. Section 4 presents preliminary results that suggest the applicability of some aspects of the proposed approach and in section 5 we conclude.

## 2   Current Design-Space-Exploration Efforts

We now outline the basic DSE flow and describe current research efforts in the area of mapping computations expressed in high-level imperative programming languages to fine-grained configurable architectures, most notably architectures that rely on FPGAs as their basic computing devices. Reconfigurable architec-

tures with coarser-grained computing elements, (*e.g.* the RaPiD [1], the XPP
Array [2] or even the hybrid Garp processor [3]), typically mitigate the issue
of area capacity and clock rate definition to a combination of a functional unit
allocation, binding and scheduling. We also discuss architecture exploration efforts for the embedded systems arena, where estimation, modeling and empirical
optimization techniques have been explored.

Figure 1 depicts a generic DSE flow. In this flow an input program, typically
described in a high-level imperative programming language, is translated to an
output program specification, for instance using VHDL or Verilog along with
some specification, either full or partial, of the target architecture the transformed output program is to be executed on. Along this process the input program is subject to a series of program partitioning and mapping refinements.
At each stage of this refinement process, the system evaluates the performance
of the current solution in terms of well defined *goodness* metrics. Using the results of these metrics, the system either settles for a solution or uses the results
of the performance metrics using a set of predefined transformation strategies
to select one, among many, possible program transformation. Once the refinement is achieved the system generates an output program specification, using
the appropriate target architecture tools.

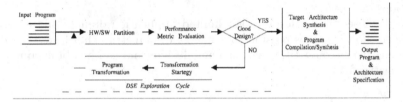

**Fig. 1.** Generic Design Space Exploration Flow.

## 2.1   Estimation and Modeling for FPGAs

The problem of estimation of area and execution time for FPGAs deals with
several issues. First, the execution of a design can exploit pipelining execution
techniques not necessarily apparent in a sequentially specified program. Second,
mapping steps such as P&R use algorithmically complex solutions that include
Simulated Annealing combined with a variety of heuristics. Lastly, the mapping
relies on technology-specific transformations besides low-level resource sharing
that are difficult to model.

To address these difficulties, researchers have developed approaches to derive
very fast and accurate FPGA area and speed metrics for small image processing
kernels relying on empirically derived linear and quadratic regression models [4,
5]. The basic approach is to build the program's data flow graph and aggregate
the area and timing information for the critical path in the graph from a library
of previously characterized modules. Typically, these approaches do not exploit
important high-level transformations that current tools perform such pipelining
or resource sharing.

In terms of execution time, researchers have develop simple, but effective execution models that exploit the program data and control dependences and use software pipelining techniques. In [6] the authors derive a core data-path from a the body of a loop nest and then use software pipelining techniques combined with area and speed estimates for the basic operators to derive accurate execution time metrics.

## 2.2    Metrics for Guiding Transformations

Estimation of area and speed is only part of the solution in DSE. When a design is infeasible or impractical, a strategy for applying transformations that will generate alternative candidate designs is needed.

Derrien and Rajoupadyhe [7] describe an array partitioning strategy that takes into account the memory hierarchy and I/O bandwidth. They use an analytical performance model (relying on pipelining execution techniques) to derive an optimal *loop-tiling* for a loop nest. So *et. al.* [8] use the notion of *balance* between memory operations and computation along with an *efficiency* metric that recognizes diminishing returns to evaluate the relative merit of designs. Their compiler uses estimates for area and number of control-steps, extracted from commercially available synthesis tools, to select a good *loop-unrolling* factor for the loops in a nest.

Both these efforts, despite their limited application domain and evaluation contexts, show that it is possible to define guiding metrics that lead to hardware designs that are competitive with manual designs and can be obtained in a very small faction of time.

## 2.3    Architecture Exploration for Embedded Systems

Other research projects have used estimation and modeling techniques to address the problem of architectural design exploration. The core of these efforts has focused on the embedded systems arena using either architecture-specific tools, commercial synthesis tools or their own prototype compilation and synthesis tools.

The PICO project [9] uses estimates from the scheduling of loop iterations, to determine which loop transformation(s) lead to shorter scheduling time and therefore minimal completion time, on a array of customizable VLIW processors. The MILAN project [10] provides a DSE environment for a System-on-Chip (SoC) architecture. MILAN evaluates several possible partitions of the computation among the various system components (processor, memory, special purposed accelerators) using simulation techniques to derive area, time and power estimates. Halambi *et. al.* [11] describe a tool-kit generator system to allow designers to evaluate the impact of SoC architectural characteristics on the execution of the applications. The system generates a compiler and a simulator to profile the application's execution. Designers use the output of the execution to understand what the performance is and why and make suitable modifications to the target SoC architecture.

## 3    A Unified Approach

The approach suggested in this paper uses a combination of estimation, modeling of the impact of program transformations and architectural elements along with history- and learning-based approaches. The approach uses estimates and modeling to bypass the long cycles induced by pure empirical (test-based trials) approaches. It uses program analysis to determine the applicability of specific program-level transformations as well as architecture-level transformations. To support the flexibility of a systems in which both architecture and input program can be simultaneously transformed, we proposed a flexible *rule-based* approach. While the system can be boot-strapped with a set of predefined rules for the application of both program and architecture transformations, as time evolves with the application of the system to many designs, we envision a smart compilation and synthesis systems that would be able to derive new rules from application characteristics in order to improve future system mappings. Figure 2 outlines this vision that we describe in more detail below.

At the center of this flow is a representation of the *program* as a collection of units that comprise the input program. Each unit can be transformed using a different sequence of transformations and have *affinities* with different *architectural elements*. These architectural elements can also be *synthesized* from the ground up, possibly using the description of the program units as this way the program-element affinity is maximized. Alternatively, one can combine using a set of architectural transformations coarser-grain architectural elements out of finer-grain elements.

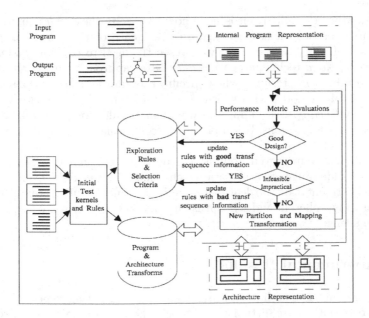

**Fig. 2.** Unified Design Flow Approach.

Ultimately finding a good architecture amounts to striking a balance between the efficiency of the mapping of the individual program units to the set of architecture elements and the efficiency (both in area and execution rate) of the elements themselves. In this search, the compiler/synthesis tool will rely on performance metrics either defined by an external source (typically the programmer via some language mechanism such as a real-time constructs) or by defining a set of default goodness metrics such as wall-clock time, area constrains, power, etc.

To guide the application of both architectural and program transformations the tool will rely on two sets of *rules*. Rules that specify which program and architecture transformations are valid with respect to other transformations and also with respect to each architecture elements, and rules that specify how performance metrics should be achieved, *i.e.. strategy rules*. Using this *rule-based* approach, a system would alternate between using transformation rules and strategy rules until a good design is reached. At each step of the design refinement process, the system could even accumulate knowledge about which transformations sequences results in perceived (or real) performance improvements and which do not. For extreme flexibility such knowledge should also be captured in the form of new rules to be used in the same or in future mappings.

Finally, the proposed design flow could also use transformation rules from a set of predefined sample kernels extensively transformed and mapped to a wide range of architectural elements. By finding similarities between the structure of these predefined sample kernels and the structure of the input program, the tool could boot-strap the exploration process by choosing a transformation sequences associated with the predefined sample kernels as a starting point for the exploration.

Besides the very important issue of how to specify these *rules*, another more important issue lies on how to ensure convergence of the search in a practical amount of time. To this effect we foresee the need to combine *history-based* and *learning-based* techniques. An *history-based* approach can be as simple as a look-up table to determine when specific program transformations were applied profitably to codes with which *structural* features and target architecture elements. A *learning-based* approach would *infer* rules for profitable, and nonprofitable transformations, based on the current design while ensuring internal rule consistency.

As with other unproven approaches the overall design flow outline above combines a wide range of optimization techniques, from flexible (even reversible) program representations to learning techniques. Successfully integrating these techniques in a coherent and self-consistent system might prove to be the biggest design challenge.

## 4    Experimental Results

We now present some preliminary results aimed at validating some of the ideas of the approach outlined in section 3. The goal of these experiments is to observe the similarities in relative behavior between versions of different code kernels when subject to the same program transformations. We first observe the similarities between kernels that have the same input/output and data access structure but different computational granularities. We then observe the difference between those and the behavior for a kernel with a very distinct structure.

## 4.1   Methodology and Sample Kernel Codes

We carry out this experiment using three kernel codes with strong similarities: a Finite-Impulse-Response (FIR), a pattern-matching computation (PAT) and a masking-accumulation computation (MSK). These codes use a memory access behavior that is identical in structure as depicted in figure 3. We further compare two versions of MSK with different lengths for one of its input data set. Finally, we use a matrix-matrix multiply computation (MAT) for $16 \times 16$ sized matrices to observe the differences in performance behavior between kernels with different computational structures.

```
for m = 0 to M
  sum = 0;
  for n = 0 to N
    sum += coeff[n]*input[m+n];
  end for
  out[m] = sum;
end for
```

**Fig. 3.** Computational and Memory Structure for FIR, PAT and MSK.

For each kernel we have developed a C reference specification and manually translated the C code to behavioral VHDL in order to synthesize them onto a Xilinx Virtex™ XCV 1K BG560 FPGA. We converted each behavioral specification to structural VHDL using Mentor Graphics' Monet™ high-level synthesis tool. We then used Synplify Pro 6.2 and the Xilinx ISE 4.1i tool set for logic synthesis and Place-and-Route (P&R). After P&R we extracted the real area and clock rate for each design and used the number of clock cycles derived from simulation of the structural design with the memory latency information of our target FPGA board (read latency of 6 clock cycles and write latency of 1 clock cycle) to calculate wall-clock execution time.

For each kernel we applied a specific program transformation: *scalar replacement*. Using *scalar replacement* a compiler, or in it absence the designer, can *cache* in a register the data fetched in one iteration of a loop to be reused at a latter iteration. This caching allows the design to avoid fetching or storing data from or to an external memory resulting in substantial savings. We manually applied this *scalar replacement* transformation (described in detail in [12]) to exploit reuse at different loop levels of the nests in each code. For the kernels FIR, PAT and MSK there are no data reuse opportunities for their innermost loops as illustrated in the example code in figure 3. For the outer loop, however, reuse can be exploited by capturing both the coeff array values in N registers which are loop invariant with respect to the outer loop, and N-1 values of the input array variable to be used in subsequent iterations of the outer loop. In this experiment we define distinct code versions corresponding to data reuse being exploited at different loop levels. For the purpose of this experiment we have also used RAM blocks present in our target FPGA for one of the code version as a substitute for discrete registers. Versions that uses RAM blocks will trade-off space for internal bandwidth as the registers arranged in RAM blocks are much more compact in terms or area than discrete registers. For performance comparisons, we used as base line the code version v1 that exploits no reuse at any level of the loop nest. In this base version, and except for scalar variables, all array accesses are executed via memory operations.

## 4.2   Results

Figure 4 depicts the results for the hardware implementations exploiting data reuse at different loop levels. In these plots, version v1 denotes the *base* code in which no reuse is exploited at any level; versions v2 and v3 denote the versions where reuse is exploited exclusively using registers at loop levels 1, 2 respectively. In these particular kernels v1 and v2 lead to the same design as there is no possible data reuse to be exploited in the innermost loop. Finally, version v4 exploits reuse at the top loop level of the nest but uses internal RAM blocks rather than registers.

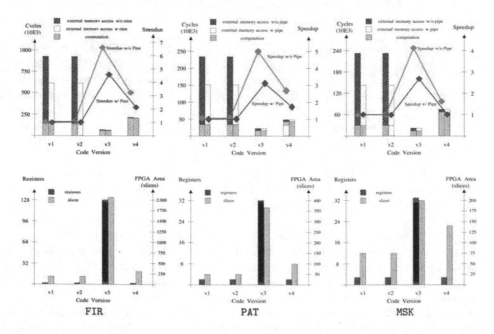

**Fig. 4.** Experimental Results for FIR, PAT and MSK.

For each kernel we present two plots. The first plot depicts the number of clock cycles of the actual computation as well as of the corresponding memory operations with and without pipelined memory access execution modes. In the same plot we present the speedup with respect to the original version (v1) using the same memory access mode. The speedup calculation uses the actual clock rate obtained from the hardware implementation of each design after P&R. In the second plot we present the number of registers used to exploit reuse and the FPGA area in terms of slices[1].

As can be seen from the plots in figure 4, exploiting data reuse at all levels of the loops dramatically reduces the number of memory accesses across all three kernels and consequently the performance of the implementations. The performance behavior for the three kernels is almost identical with the expected difference in scaling. The largest performance gains are attained for version v3 that exploits data reuse at the outermost loop at a steep price of the largest area and registers implementation cost. Versions v4 show some improvement over the bases version at a very low area cost when compared against the best performing versions v3.

In summary, these results underscore the similarities of performance behavior for kernels with almost identical computational structures. This is hardly surprising given that these three kernels have the same loop nest structure and data access patterns. Consequently, specific program transformations will exploit identical opportunities.

Figure 5 depicts the results for two variants of the MSK kernel, the MSK_16 and the MSK_32 respectively. These variants differ in the number of iterations of the inner loop which translates into different number of registers required to fully exploit the data reuse. As expected having a larger number of loop iterations leads to an increase in the of memory operations. The benefit of a larger number of registers is therefore larger leading to higher speedup values. In terms of area and registers there is a simple scaling effect. This relative behavior is expected as the two MSK codes have the same structure and the designs are nowhere near the FPGA capacity limits to exhibit unpredictable performance anomalies due to a clock degradation caused by poor P&R results.

The comparison against the MAT kernel is more striking. Despite performing a comparable number of *read* and *write* operations and having similar computational grainularities (specially FIR and MAT) these kernels have very different structure. For MAT there is a sustained performance improvement as more registers are being used due to the reduction of the number of memory operations. This behavior is more evident in MAT since this kernel has a richer loop nesting structure and consequently a richer set of data reuse opportunities at various loop levels. For the code version that uses the RAM blocks (in this case v5) there is even an improvement in the design clock rate that leads to an even greater performance improvement over the versions that use exclusively registers for exploiting data reuse.

---

[1] In the area metric we have excluded the slides due to the RAM blocks in any of the designs since they are fixed for every design whether the design uses them or not.

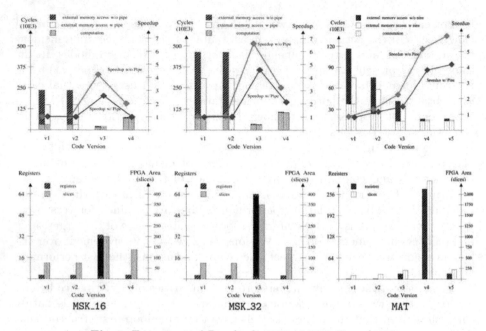

**Fig. 5.** Experimental Results for MSK_16, MSK_32 and MAT.

## 4.3   Discussion

In this experiment we focused on a rather sophisticated transformation, *scalar replacement*, rather than commonly used loop transformations such as *loop unrolling*. The results presented here support two main ideas. First, without considering target architecture capacity limitations, computations with very similar structures do exhibit similar opportunities for the application of the transformations. As such, versions that result from the application of program transformations with the same parameters yield very similar relative behavior *i.e.*, similar trends in performance and resource usage. Second, the same computation with different parameter values, in our case the loop bounds, will lead to *scaled* performance metrics as long that the resource constraints of the target architectures are not violated. Finally, and most importantly, codes with different opportunities for the application of the transformation will very likely lead to very different relative performance behaviors.

Clearly, these observations cannot possibly be extrapolated for arbitrary values of the parameters of both the transformations or the the input codes. We suspect that these observations are valid for a range of transformation's parameters and sequence of transformations that do not stress the capabilities of the mapping tools and/or for which the resulting designs do not stress the capacity limits of the target devices.

# 5   Conclusion

In this paper we have surveyed current approaches to the very challenging problem of design-space-exploration (DSE) for reconfigurable computing architectures with an emphasis on FPGA-based architectures. We have described the role of program analysis in selecting possible program transformation and of estimation in accelerating the evaluation of the impact of those transformations. We have described a unified approach for DSE that combines, program analysis, estimation, modeling and learning techniques. Successfully integrating these techniques in a coherent and self-consistent system might prove to be the biggest challenge. While we are far from being able to evaluate the feasibility and effectiveness of such a comprehensive system, the preliminary experimental results presented here validate specific aspects of the proposed approach.

# References

1. Cronquist, D., *et. al.*: Specifying and Compiling Applications for RaPiD. In: In Proc. IEEE Symp. on FPGAs for Custom Computing Machines (FCCM'98). (1998) 116–125
2. XPP Technologies, Inc.: The XPP White Paper. Release 2.1.1 edn. (2002)
3. Hauser, J., Wawrzynek, J.: Garp: A MIPS Processor with a Reconfigurable Coprocessor. In: Proc. of the IEEE Symp. on FPGAs for Custom Computing Machines. (1997)
4. Kulkarni, D., Najjar, W., Rinker, R., Kurdah, F.: Fast Area Estimation to Support Compiler Optimizations in FPGA-based Reconfigurable Systems. In: IEEE Symp. on Field-Programmable Custom Computing Machines (FCCM). (2002)
5. Nayak, Haldar, M., Choudhary, A., Banerjee, P.: Accurate Area and Delay Estimators for FPGAs. In: Proc. of the 2002 Design Automation and Test in Europe Conference and Exhibition (DATE02), IEEE Computer Society Press (2002)
6. Liao, J., Wong, W.F., Mitra, T.: A Model for the Hardware Realization of Loops. In: Proc. of the 2003 Intl. Symp. on Field Programmable Logic (FPL'03). (2003) 334–344
7. Derrien, S., Rajoupadyhe, S.: Loop Tiling for Reconfigurable Accelerators. In: Proc. of the Int. Symp. on Field-Programmable Logic (FPL01). (2001)
8. So, B., Hall, M., Diniz, P.: A Compiler Approach to Fast Hardware Design Space Exploration for FPGA Systems. In: Proc. of the 2002 ACM Conference on Programming Language Design and Implementation (PLDI'02), ACM Press (2002)
9. Kathail, V., Aditya, S., Schreiber, R., Rau, B., Cronquist, D., Sivaraman, M.: PICO: Automatically designing custom computers. In: IEEE Computer. (2002)
10. Bakshi, A., Prasanna, V., Ledeczi, A.: MILAN: A Model Based Integrated Simulation Framework for Design of Embedded Systems. In: Proc. of the 2001 ACM Workshop on Languages, Compilers, and Tools for Embedded Systems (LCTES'01). (2001)
11. Halambi, A., *et. al.*: EXPRESSION: A Language for Architecture Exploration through Compiler/Simulator Retargetability. In: Proc. of the Conf, on Design Automation and Test Europe (DATE99). (1999)
12. So, B., Hall, M.: Increasing the Applicability of Scalar Replacement. In: Proc. of the 2004 ACM Symp. on Compiler Construction (CC'04), ACM Press (2004)

# Modeling Loop Unrolling: Approaches and Open Issues*

João M.P. Cardoso[1] and Pedro C. Diniz[2]

[1] University of Algarve, Faculty of Sciences and Technology
Campus de Gambelas, 8000-117 Faro, Portugal, INESC-ID, Lisbon, Portugal
jmpc@acm.org
[2] University of Southern California / Information Sciences Institute
4676 Admiralty Way, Suite 1001, Marina del Rey, Calif. 90292, USA
pedro@isi.edu

**Abstract.** Loop unrolling plays an important role in compilation for Reconfigurable Processing Units (RPUs) as it exposes operator parallelism and enables other transformations (*e.g.,* scalar replacement). Deciding when and where to apply loop unrolling, either fully or partially, leads to large design space exploration problems. In order to cope with these vast spaces, researchers have explored the application of design estimation techniques. Using estimation, tools can conduct early evaluation of the impact and interplay of transformations in both the required resources and expected performance. In this paper we present some of the current approaches and issues related to estimation of the loop unrolling impact when targeting RPUs.

## 1 Introduction

Reconfigurable systems offer the promise of significant performance improvements over traditional computing architectures as they allow for the development of custom data-path structures suitable to each computation particular needs. For example, a data-intensive computation might take advantage of a large number of multiply-accumulate units whereas an image-processing, memory-intensive computation can use a customized tapped-delay line storage structure to hold windows of pixel values.

Unfortunately, programming such systems requires programmers to assume the role of hardware designers and master hardware-oriented programming languages, making reconfigurable computing technology inaccessible to a wider audience. The typical approach to map computations to RPUs requires programmers to engage in a lengthy and error-prone design cycle. Programmers will apply a sequence of transformations attempting to expose more concurrency in their computations, and then use existing tools to generate a working hardware design specification.

The variety of transformations programmers can apply to their computations when mapping them to RPUs leads to an immense search exploration problem. The use of *pragmas* to control the application of program transformations (*e.g.,* [1]) leads to inflexible mapping strategies that need to be updated when the target hardware changes.

---

* This work is partially supported by the Portuguese Foundation for Science and Technology (FCT) – FEDER and POSI programs – under the CHIADO project. João Cardoso gratefully acknowledges the donation by PACT XPP Technologies, Inc, of the XPP development suite (XDS) software.

A. Pimentel and S. Vassiliadis (Eds.): SAMOS 2004, LNCS 3133, pp. 224–233, 2004.

In addition, it limits the definition of optimization strategies to the syntax and capabilities of the *pragma* interface. Empirical approaches (*e.g.*, [2]) might not be viable when compiling to RPUs. The transform-and-test is very time-consuming as it typically includes low-level synthesis and Place-and-Route (P&R) steps. In addition, and unlike in traditional processor architectures, the designs resulting from the application of a set of program transformations might be infeasible if they do not fit in the available RPU resources or require a clock rate that is unsupported.

To mitigate the practical issues in dealing with such vast design spaces, researchers have successfully used estimation techniques, in addition to well defined criteria [3], to aggressively search large spaces while yielding designs that are very close to designs that programmers would be able to derive. Other authors have also used estimations coupled with program analysis and modeling to show that it is possible to predict the impact of various loop transformations when mapping computations to hardware designs for Field-Programmable-Gate-Arrays (FPGAs) [4].

In this paper we focus on area and performance estimation approaches for the application for a very important program transformation – *loop unrolling*. Unrolling of a loop mainly consists of replications of its body corresponding to consecutive iterations. This transformation is always legal, as it always respects the program control and data dependences, and exposes to the body of the unrolled loop a potentially large number of parallel operations. Unrolling enables the exploitation of Instruction-Level-Paralellism (ILP) subject to the data and control dependences. Even when the number of the exposed operators exceeds the number of available functional units, it is possible through the use of virtualization and resource sharing techniques to exploit the available computational parallelism. In addition, loop unrolling, in particular when unrolled fully, can enable the reuse of data across the newly exposed inner loop leading to a substantial reduction of the number of memory access if the reused data is kept in registers.

Despite its extensive use in high-end and embedded computing arenas, loop unrolling in the context of reconfigurable computing architectures exhibits new trade-offs and implementation issues. In this paper we address issues concerning the estimation of the impact of loop unrolling in reconfigurable computing architectures, surveying recent approaches, and presenting what we believe are still open research issues. We also present results that illustrate the benefits of estimation loop unrolling for a specific reconfigurable architecture, the XPP [5], and for two specific kernels.

This paper is organized as follows. In section 2 we outline a generic compilation flow for reconfigurable architectures and sketch the role of estimation in section 3. In section 4 we survey current methods for predicting the impact of loop unrolling. In section 5 we briefly present a new method for estimation of loop unrolling and present some experimental results of the application of this method. In section 6 we describe a set of open issues and conclude in section 7.

## 2   Compilation for Reconfigurable Computing Platforms

Researchers have developed numerous approaches to facilitate the task of mapping computations expressed in high-level abstractions to reconfigurable architectures [6].

In Figure 1 we illustrate a generic compilation and synthesis flow for reconfigurable architectures. The front-end exposes fine-grain as well as coarse-grain parallelism, through the application of architecture-driven optimizations (*e.g.*, floating- to fixed-point transformations, bit-width narrowing, etc.) and architecture-neutral transformations (*e.g.*, loop transformations). More advanced transformations include data partitioning of the array variables across multiple memories and/or the replication of read-only variables, in order to increase overall data bandwidth availability.

As contemporary reconfigurable computing platforms include microprocessors, typically assuming the role of host processors, the front-end must also partition the computation between the microprocessor and the RPUs. This partitioning might be guided by performance's maximization, energy savings, design costs, etc. The computation assigned to the processors is compiled using their native compiler and includes a library to interact with the RPU via a set of predefined memory-mapped registers [7] or via communication library internals structures [8].

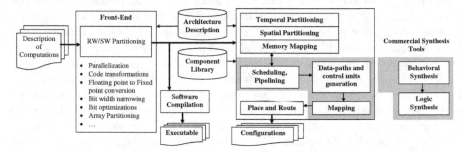

**Fig. 1.** Typical compilation flow for reconfigurable computing platforms

After the high-level Hardware/Software partitioning carried out by the front-end, the flow engages in a series of architecture-aware transformations. For example, the system can perform temporal and spatial partitioning. Temporal partitioning refers to the splitting of the input program in sections that will be executed by time-sharing the RPUs, whereas, spatial partitioning refers to the splitting of the input program in sections that will be executed on multiple RPUs. Overall resource allocation (*e.g,*. mapping of variables to memories, striping of array across memories), binding and scheduled is performed at this stage. As the last phases, and once a scheduled is defined, the flow may use architecture-dependent synthesis tools to generate the executable code for the various RPUs. For example, systems that use FPGAs can use existing commercial synthesis tools (*e.g.*, Monet™ and Synopsys BC™). Others have developed their own tools geared towards specific features of their target reconfigurable architectures (*e.g.*, [9]).

Loop constructs play an important role in the specification of a large class of array-based computations, ranging from matrix operations to digital image processing operators. A number of loop transformations (*e.g.,* unrolling, tiling, distribution (fission), jamming (fusion), interchanging and reversal) [10] transform the original code to improve specific aspects of the execution (*e.g.,* memory footprint, energy) or simply enable other more profitable transformations.

Loop unrolling is a commonly used transformation as it decreases the loop over-head while increasing the opportunities for ILP. Unrolling a loop by a factor of $N$ is accomplished by replicating the statements of the body corresponding to $N$ consecutive iterations and propagating the iteration index to the corresponding statements. Unrolling is also used to expose more array references and therefore facilitate data reuse in the unrolled loops. Occasionally, due to I/O constraints and lack of further potential for optimizations, unrolling is either infeasible or simply non-profitable.

As an example, consider the smooth image processing kernel presented in Figure 2a. In this example we have a 2-dimensional FIR filtering kernel, over an array variable representing an input image, using a 3-by-3 window. Figure 2b depicts a simple 1-dimensional FIR filtering kernel used in our experiments in section 5.

Figure 3 presents results obtained by compiling, with the XPP-VC compiler [11], the example to the XPP platform [5], exploring loop unrolling. The results show both the achieved speedups and the ratio of required resources with loop unrolling versus the original implementation. Mapping the original source code without code transformations might not expose sufficient operation level parallelism to justify its execution in an RPU. The exploration of loop unrolling of the four available loops may lead to distinct and often substantial performance improvements.

```
...
const int K[9] = {...};
...
for(r=0;r<DIM;r++) {  // L1
 for(c=0;c<DIM;c++) {  // L2
  sum = 0;
  for(rw=0;rw<3;rw++) {    // L3
   for(cw=0;cw<3;cw++) {    // L4
    sum+=IN[r*DIM+c+rw*DIM+cw]
       *K[rw*3+cw];
   }
  }
  sum = sum >> 4;
  OUT[r*Dim + c] = sum;
  }
}...
(a)
```

```
#define M 128 // #samples
#define N 18  // #taps
...
const int h[N] = {...};
...
for(j=0;j<M;j++) {  // L1
 sum = 0;
 for(i=0;i<N;i++) {  // L2
  sum += x[i+j]*h[i];
 }
 y[j] = sum >> 15;
}
...
(b)
```

**Fig. 2.** Examples: (a) smooth image processing filter (2D-FIR); (b) 1D-FIR

As revealed by this simple example, there are many choices of unrolling amounts for the various loops in a computation. A problem facing programmers is on how to find a good, or even optimal, loop unrolling factor that will lead to the best performance for a certain set of resource constraints.

## 3   Role of Estimation

Estimation (*e.g.*, of size or latency) plays an important role in helping a compiler to quickly evaluate a wide range of transformations with respect to their impact on the quality of the resulting design. A compiler/synthesis tool can use estimates to quickly navigate a large design space, in effect performing a design-space-exploration (DSE), which would otherwise be impractical for the average designer.

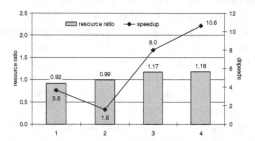

**Fig. 3.** Effects of loop unrolling when mapping a 2D-FIR example on the XPP reconfigurable array. Each array variable is mapped to a distinct memory

The work in the DEFACTO project illustrates the benefit of using area and clock rate estimates from Behavioral Synthesis. The DEFACTO compiler uses two metrics of goodness for the designs, balance and efficiency in guiding the application of loop unrolling for FPGA designs. The compiler attempts to unroll as much as possible until it reaches a balanced design or begins suffering from diminishing returns [3] in the resulting design This limited experience shows that even using estimates, as opposed to the real implementation metrics, allows a compiler to make correct decisions about which loop unrolling factors to apply [4].

Linear regression techniques have been used in the MATCH compiler [12] to model the number of resources and the delay of library operators (*e.g.,* arithmetic units with varying bit-widths) for FPGA designs. To account for the additional resources after P&R, a multiplier factor is used. With respect to mapping Matlab descriptions, the authors have reported predictions within 16% of the total resources used and within13% of the attained clock frequency.

When targeting coarse-grained RPUs, one can perform estimation of high-level constructs directly to the RPU resources avoiding some intermediate mapping steps. In the case of bit-widths surpassing the granularity of the RPU, a decomposition intermediate step is required. Irrespective of the target architecture granularity, a pressing issue with reconfigurable architectures is the difficulty in predicting the extra resources after the P&R phase as, for robustness, most of existing commercial tools use simulated annealing techniques. Nevertheless, other authors have shown that it is possible to combine empirical modeling and behavioral synthesis estimation to predict the size of complete FPGA-based designs [13].

## 4   Predicting the Impact of Loop Unrolling

We now briefly describe recent approaches in predicting the impact of loop unrolling for mapping computation to reconfigurable and embedded platforms. In general, existing efforts have focused on well-behaved loops *i.e.,* loops without irregular control flow, and statically known iteration space, for which there is wealth of static program analysis information. In [14] the authors describe an algorithm to find the optimal loop unrolling factors for nested loops when targeting VLIW processors. The method, which can be adapted to reconfigurable architectures, considers a saturation factor due to instruction cache limit bearing similarities to the resource constraints on RPUs. In [15] the authors describe an approach to predict the impact of various loop optimizations on cache performance in the context of embedded processors. For each loop transformation the authors present an analytical model that captures loop header and array references characteristics.

Liao *et. al.* [16] present an approach to estimate the impact of the loop unrolling factor and software pipelining on innermost loops. The approach requires some runs (i.e., loop unrolling is performed for some cases) to tune the parameters used by analytical models (for number of resources and performance). Specifically, P&R is realized for a number of design instances and then a linear approximation method is used. The model is not powerful enough to fully estimate the optimum unrolling factor and the use of software pipelining, given the resource constraints, without the use of instruction scheduling and/or the results of a number of solutions in the huge design space exploration. Although the results are very promising, there is no strong evidence that the model works for other type of loops and the needed runs make difficult to use it in an exploration environment. However, since in some benchmarks only the innermost loops are migrated to the reconfigurable logic of the computing system, the approach can truly assist design decisions.

Finally, So *et. al.* [3] describe a fully automated system where the compiler uses behavioral synthesis estimates along with *balance* and *efficiency* metrics to guide the application of loop unrolling to both inner and outermost loops in a nest.

Although some proposed techniques may be applied, such as enhanced DSE approaches without revealing all the design space, it is obvious that research on techniques to find optimal unrolling factors without explicitly carry out unrolling and without traversing the entire compilation flow are required. With respect to compilation for RPUs, techniques exploring the unrolling factor without generating the hardware for each implementation and/or without mapping each design will truly help design decisions.

## 5  New Approach

We now describe a new model to predict the impact of full loop unrolling on the execution time and on the number of required resources, without explicitly performing it. Note that with respect to execution time only relative accuracy is needed. The estimation of the number of resources needed may only also need relative accuracy if accurate numbers about the implementation of the original code can be obtained.

In this approach each loop is labeled with the following parameters: number of iterations (*Iter*); number of cycles of the critical path length of the loop body not taking into account to inner loops latency (*CPL*); maximum number of successive memory accesses to each memory contributing to the *CPL* (*maxSucMem*); remain number of memory accesses in the *CPL* (*restMem*); number of cycles of the *CPL* only devoted to computing (*Comp*); number of resources for the loop body and for loop control; number of resources specially used to index each array variable (which are removed if the array is eliminated); and an identifier of the loop status (*i.e.*, unrolled or not).

The estimation of the *CPL* and the number of cycles devoted to memory accesses for each loop body is achieved by doing a static list scheduling, assuming a previous binding of array variables to the memories of the system. To estimate the execution cost of loop i, we consider equations (1), (2), and (3) when the loop is pipelined, the loop is fully unrolled, or the loop is neither fully unrolled nor pipelined, respectively. We assume that only innermost loops are pipelined.

$$ExecCostLoop_i = LoopCtr_{overhead} + R_{overhead} + CPL_i + (Iter_i - 1) \times Pipe_i \qquad (1)$$

$$ExecCostLoop_i = R_{overhead} + CPL_i + (Iter_i - 1) \times Pipe_i \qquad (2)$$

$$ExecCostLoop_i = LoopCtr_{overhead} + (R_{overhead} + CPL_i) \times Iter_i \qquad (3)$$

In the equations above $LoopCtr_{overhead}$ and $R_{overhead}$ represent execution cost overheads of each loop control structure and for having a number of references to the same memory, respectively; $Pipe_i$ represents the length of each pipelining stage or *maxSucMem*, when the former exceeds the pipeline stage. Note that $R_{overhead}$, $Pipe_i$, and $CPL_i$ can have different values for the same loop, since full unrolling may increase or decrease the number of references to the same memory.

Each array reference in the original code is represented by a *Reference Vector* (RV) of N elements, where N is the maximum number of nested loops plus one. For the example in Figure 2a we obtain the RVs depicted in Figure 4a. The first element from left represents the root code and is referred by level 0. The other elements represent nested levels from the outermost to the innermost loop. The rightmost number element corresponds to an array reference in the body of the loop related to that vector element (*e.g.*, the rightmost 1 in reference IN is related to the reference in loop L4). The symbol ⊥ represents the absence of references in the corresponding loop.

When a loop is unrolled, the number of references is updated by multiplying the number of iterations of the loop being unrolled by the number of references of each RV's element, starting on the element positioned at that loop to the leftmost element (outermost level). This accounts for the fact that an RV with references in a certain loop body may have, after loop unrolling, a different number of references to the array variable (see Figure 4 for some examples).

Yet another parameter represents the case when some references can be removed from the code as due to unrolling if they become loop invariant. For instance, references to array K can be removed if loops L3 and L4 are both fully unrolled. This information is represented in the model with information defining when the reference is removed (*e.g.*, remove RV#3 when the element 3 equals 9, means that when the number of references in position loop 3 of RV#3 is 9, the references represented by this reference vector can be removed). Information about when data reuse can be exploited, by *e.g.*, adding rotating registers, is specified in a similar way. Each RV is also labelled with the number of resources used by common sub-expressions when the loop is unrolled, the number of resources related to the array access and the contribution of each reference to the *maxSucMem* and *restMem* parameters.

| RV#1(load, memID, IN):<br><1; 1; 1; 1; 1> | IN:<br><3; 3; 3; 3; 3> | IN:<br><14; 1; 1; 1; 1> | IN:<br><42; 3; 3; 3; 1> |
|---|---|---|---|
| RV#2(load, memID, K):<br><1; 1; 1; 1; 1> | K:<br><3; 3; 3; 3; 3> | K:<br><14; 1; 1; 1; 1> | K:<br><42; 3; 3; 3; 1> |
| RV#3(store, memID, OUT):<br><1; 1; 1; ⊥; ⊥> | OUT:<br><1; 1; 1; ⊥; ⊥> | OUT:<br><14; 1; 1; ⊥; ⊥> | OUT:<br><14; 1; 1; ⊥; ⊥> |
| (a) | (b) | (c) | (d) |

**Fig. 4.** Reference Vectors: (a) for the original code of Figure 2a; (b) loop L4 (3 iterations) is unrolled; (c) loop L1 (14 iterations) is unrolled and then (d) loop L2 is also unrolled

The estimation of the number of resources is based on the computational structures present at the source level. When a loop is unrolled, usually a simple multiplication of the resources for the loop body by the number of iterations is sufficient to determine the total number of resources. The number of resources for the memory accesses takes into account the structures of MUX/DEMUX-type operations needed.

We used the reference vectors approach described above to explore full loop unrolling when targeting the XPP, a coarse-grained, data-driven, reconfigurable array [5]. In these experiments we use the two examples shown in Figure 2 and automatically obtain the results for all possible fully unrolling cases of the loops in each code. The results in Figure 5 illustrate the resource and execution cost ratios (real and estimated) between the mapping of the original code and when unrolling of certain loops is performed. For the 2D-FIR (Figure 5a) the ratios are for the following unrolled loops: (a) L4; (b) L3; (c) L3 and L4. For the 1D-FIR (Figure 5b) the ratios are related to the innermost loop unrolled for four numbers of taps.

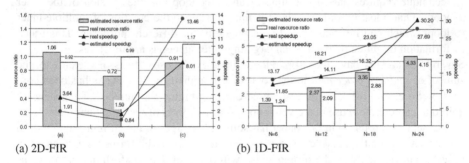

(a) 2D-FIR            (b) 1D-FIR

**Fig. 5.** Comparison between estimations and real results

Despite tracking very well the observed implementation for the various cases, we notice some, non-negligible mismatch on the relative accuracy between the predicted and observed execution time. Since the overall latency predictor considers optimally pipelined loops, mismatches are subject to occur when, due to resource constraints, full pipeline balancing is not achieved. In order to predict such difficult effect further study and experimentation is required. Notice also that the reference vectors furnish a suitable model to traverse the complex design space offered by loop unrolling.

## 6  Open Issues

The estimation of loop transformations are of great importance since the exploration spaces can be too large and therefore very time consuming. With respect to *loop unrolling* the following issues require further research:

- Loop unrolling can be applied to achieve better performance but its use can lead to designs requiring more resources than the available. Thus, the exploitation of loop unrolling also needs to take into account the use of temporal partitioning, assisted with *loop distribution* and *loop dissevering* [17].
- Loop unrolling usually conduces to other optimizations but such effects are not easy to quantify without performing it. For instance, it might further lead to substitution of more subsequent memory accesses by shift- or rotate-registers (also named as register promotion). This eliminates redundant memory accesses across loop iterations by reusing data fetched in earlier accesses and cached in registers.
- Due to the additional resources needed for loop pipelining, predictors should be able to quantify the trade-off between resources and achieved performance.
- Other loop transformations are even more difficult to predict but they might be required to achieve acceptable performance gains. For instance, loop strip-mining can be applied to inner loops to create two loops nested, which may permit the parallelization of instances of the new inner loop when each instance computes on data sets located on different memories, or on the same memory with more than one port. Loop merging (fusion) can increase the efficiency of loop pipelining.
- Another aspect is that loop unrolling has been focused mostly on innermost loops. Despite its importance, the impact of *unroll-and-jam* is difficult to predict since the technique requires partial unrolling of an outer loop and then fusion of the inner loops. Outermost unrolling without jamming leads to the creation of multiple inner loops which can be transformed independently for different purposes. This transformation might be relevant when targeting heterogeneous architectures.

Several researchers have recently addressed some of these efforts. For example, the subject of *scalar replacement* in the context of compilation for FPGAs has been covered by So et al. [18]. They have focused on determining the number of registers required to capture the reuse in a given loop nest at all levels of the loop hierarchy.

The scheme proposed in this paper has some advantages to the current used models. It does not require the presence of perfected nested loops and it furnishes a mechanism to automatically traverse the design space without explicitly performing loop unrolling. However, further experiments must be done to continuing the model validation and evaluation and to include partial loop unrolling prediction.

## 7  Conclusion

This paper discusses some of the emerging modeling techniques to predict the impact of loop unrolling when mapping loops to reconfigurable computing architectures in terms of number of resources and performance. The techniques vary widely for fine- and coarse-grain reconfigurable architectures and several success cases have been reported in the literature for limited contexts warranting further research.

# References

1. W. Böhm, et al., "Mapping a Single Assignment Programming Language to Reconfigurable Systems," in *The Journal of Supercomputing*, Kluwer Academic Publishers, vol. 21, no. 2, Feb. 2002, pp. 117-130.

2. S. Triantafyllis, et al., "Compiler Optimization-Space Exploration," in *Proc. of Int'l Symposium on Code Generation and Optimization (CGO'03)*, San Francisco, CA, USA, 2003.

3. B. So, M. Hall, and P. Diniz, "A Compiler Approach to Fast Hardware Design Space Exploration for FPGA Systems," In *Proc. of ACM Conference on Programming Language Design and Implementation (PLDI'02)*, Berlin, Germany, June 17-19, 2002.

4. B. So, P. Diniz, and M. Hall, "Using Estimates from Behavioral Synthesis Tools in Compiler-Directed Design Space Exploration", In *Proc. of Design Automation Conference (DAC'03)*, June 2003.

5. PACT XPP Technologies, Inc., "The XPP White Paper," Release 2.1.1, March 2002.

6. J. Cardoso, P. Diniz, and M. Weinhardt, "Compilation for Reconfigurable Computing Platforms: Comments on Techniques and Current Status," *INESC-ID Technical Report*, RT/009/2003,, Oct. 2003.

7. M. Gokhale, J. M. Stone, and E. Gomersall, "Co-synthesis to a hybrid RISC/FPGA architecture," In *Journal of VLSI Signal Processing Systems for Signal, Image and Video Technology*, Vol. 24, No. 2, March 2000, pp. 165-180.

8. Annapolis Micro Systems Inc., "WildStar Reconfigurable Computing Engines. User's Manual R3.3," 1999.

9. S. Goldstein, et al., "PipeRench: A Reconfigurable Architecture and Compiler," In *IEEE Computer*, Vol.33, No. 4, April 2000, pp. 70-77.

10. M. Wolfe, *High Performance Compilers for Parallel Computing*, Addison-Wesley, 1996.

11. J. Cardoso, and M. Weinhardt, "XPP-VC: A C Compiler with Temporal Partitioning for the PACT-XPP Architecture," in *Proc. of Int'l Conference on Field Programmable Logic and Applications (FPL'02)*, LNCS 2438, Springer-Verlag, Sept. 2002, pp. 864-874.

12. A. Nayak, et al., "Accurate Area and Delay Estimators for FPGAs," in *Proc. Design Automation and Test in Europe (DATE'02)*, March 2002, Paris, France, pp. 862-869.

13. J. Park, P. Diniz, and S. Raghunathan, "Performance and Area Modeling of Complete FPGA Designs in the Presence of Loop Transformations," In *Proc. of Int'l Conference on Field programmable Logic (FPL'03)*, LNCS, Springer-Verlag, Berlin, August 2003.

14. A. Koseki, H. Komatsu, and Y. Fukazawa, "A Method for Estimating Optimal Unrolling Times for Nested Loops," in *Proc. of Int'l Symposium on Parallel Architectures, Algorithms and Networks (ISPAN'97)*, Taipei, Taiwan, 1997, IEEE CS Press, pp. 376-382.

15. M. Zhao, B. R. Childers, and M. L. Soffa, "Predicting the impact of optimizations for embedded systems," in *ACM SIGPLAN Symposium on Languages, Compilers, and Tools for Embedded Systems (LCTES'03)*, San Diego, CA, USA, June 2003.

16. J. Liao, W.F. Wong, and M. Tulika, "A Model for Hardware Realization of Kernel Loops," in *Proc. of 13th Int'l Conference on Field Programmable Logic and Application (FPL'03)*, LNCS 2778, Springer-Verlag, Sept. 2003, pp. 334-344.

17. J. Cardoso, "Loop Dissevering: A Technique for Temporally Partitioning Loops in Dynamically Reconfigurable Computing Platforms," in *Proc. of Reconfigurable Architectures Workshop (RAW'03)*, Nice, France, April 2003.

18. B. So, and M. Hall, "Increasing the Applicability of Scalar Replacement", In *Proc. of Int'l Conference on Compiler Construction (CC'04)*, ACM Press, 2004.

# Self-loop Pipelining and Reconfigurable Dataflow Arrays

João M.P. Cardoso[1,2]

[1] Faculty of Sciences and Technology, University of Algarve
Campus de Gambelas, 8000 – 117 Faro, Portugal
[2] INESC-ID, Lisbon, Portugal
jmpc@acm.org

**Abstract.** This paper presents some interesting concepts of static dataflow machines that can be used by reconfigurable computing architectures. We introduce some data-driven reconfigurable arrays and summarize techniques to map imperative software programs to those architectures, some of them being focus of current research work. In particular, we briefly present a novel technique for pipelining loops. Experiments with the technique confirm important improvements over the use of conventional loop pipelining. Hence, the technique proves to be an efficient approach to map loops to coarse-grained reconfigurable architectures employing a static dataflow computational model.

## 1 Introduction

Dataflow machines [1] have been promising to overcome the poor-support of parallelism of von Neumann architectures since the early 70's [2]. However, their envisaged use has been transcended by efforts on augmenting the parallel processing capabilities of traditional processors (*e.g.*, VLIW). There is now a strong believe that it will be very difficult to take full advantage of the Moore's Law using traditional processor architectures. Since dataflow computing is a natural paradigm to process data streams, it is a very promising solution for stream-based computations, which indeed are becoming increasingly important. Some researchers have already focused on synthesizing programs to ASICs behaving in a static dataflow fashion [3]. One of the reasons is the avoidance of centralized control units, which is an ideated goal since the evidence that interconnection delays are becoming preponderating.

Processor arrays, namely wavefront [4] and data-driven arrays [5], have been introduced in the 80's. They devised a scalable and effective fashion to directly support the dataflow computational model and have been revived by some reconfigurable architectures (*e.g.*, KressArray [6]). The dataflow computing model has been used in signal processing and other applications. Recently, research efforts on dataflow computing have been conducted (see, for instance, [7]), especially its usage in reconfigurable computing due to the fact that it naturally supports computing in space. Asynchronous dataflow FPGAs (Field Programmable Gate Arrays) [8] and coarse-grained architectures with dataflow semantics (*e.g.*, WaveScalar [9]) are focus of recent research efforts with encouraging results.

A. Pimentel and S. Vassiliadis (Eds.): SAMOS 2004, LNCS 3133, pp. 234–243, 2004.

Coarse-grained reconfigurable architectures (see *e.g.*, [10] for information on several architectures) are promising computing platforms. Some of them mix concepts of data-driven arrays with the reconfiguration properties of the programmable logic devices (*e.g.*, FPGAs). Two such examples are the KressArray [6] and the XPP [11]. Although using coarse-grained architectures significant speedups have been achieved, the capability to compile from a high-level imperative programming language, and to still achieving noticeable speedup impact, has not been fully proved, apart from results on mapping specific algorithms. One of the reasons is the reduced focus on researching reconfigurable architectures to unburden the compilation phases and to map more effectively some typical computational structures.

This paper examines some of the most relevant characteristics of the reconfigurable architectures, operating under the dataflow computational model, introduces some compilation techniques to target static dataflow reconfigurable architectures, illustrates some architecture operations to assist compilation, and shows a new loop pipelining technique, named *self loop pipelining* (SLP). Moreover, this paper also aims to address the following questions:

- With respect to other reconfigurable architectures, are data-driven architectures a better target for software compilation?
- What is the impact when using *self loop pipelining*?

This paper is organized as follows. Next section introduces some of the coarse-grained, data-driven, reconfigurable architectures. Section 3 briefly explains some architecture features to support computational structures, and section 4 summarizes compilation techniques for those architectures. Section 5 explains the SLP technique, and focuses on the impact of the technique on a number of benchmarks. Finally, concluding remarks and ongoing and future work issues are sketched in section 6.

# 2  Data-Driven Array Architectures

Data-driven architectures usually use a handshaking protocol to control the data flow, in such a way that the execution of each functional unit (FU) starts when data is present in the required inputs and next result can start to be computed or output (due to previous consumption or absence of output tokens).

Specific hardware implementations can be constructed using FUs or regions of FUs behaving according to the static dataflow model (*e.g.*, [3]). As has been aforementioned, another approach is the use of data-driven reconfigurable arrays (*e.g.*, [11]), either working asynchronous, synchronously, or both. Note, however, that the static dataflow computing model [1] is the simplest to implement in VLSI. There is no strong evidence the complexity required by the dynamic dataflow model [1] is worth to be implemented (it permits to directly map recursive functions, *e.g.*, [12]).

A data-driven array mainly consists of a matrix of N×M PEs and interconnection resources (as an example, see in Figure 1 a simple scheme of the XPP architecture [11]). Dataflow operations, which are implemented by PEs, include usual arithmetic and logic operations, and especial operations to deal with conditional branches.

Conditional branches require BRANCH (SWITCH, DISTRIBUTOR, or DEMUX) and MERGE (JOIN, SELECT, or MUX) operations [1]. BRANCH is used to route data items to one of the two outputs based on a control event (usually named control token). Standard MERGE operations do not have an enabling rule and just output the first data item present in one of the two inputs. There are, however, different implementations of MERGE. One MERGE uses a control signal to select between the two input data tokens and discards the data token (*i.e.*, the token is consumed but not copied to the output) not selected. According to the enabling rule, there are also different MERGE implementations. One only triggers the execution when the control token and the two data tokens are ready, the other one triggers the execution as soon as the control token and the selected data token are ready (this type of evaluation is called lenient in [3]).

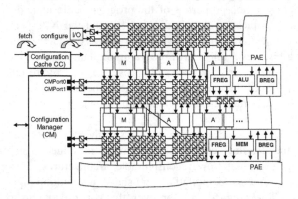

**Fig. 1.** Simple diagram of the PACT XPP architecture (notice that the picture does not show many architecture's details). PAEs are elements of the architecture that can include an ALU or a memory. The PAEs with memories are located in the left and rightmost columns of the array. Each PAE also includes two more elements: FREG and BREG. These elements can perform special operations and can be used as pipeline stages

Other special operators are specifically used to discard tokens, e.g., the T- and F-Gates used in some dataflow machines, which copy input data to output when the control token has value "true" or when has value "false", respectively [2].

Enhanced dataflow architectures integrate the semantics of imperative programming languages to manipulate array variables (e.g., load/store operations). Two strategies are used for load/store ordering: ordering conducted according to statically labeling of program references (*e.g.*, WaveScalar [9]); ordering explicitly accomplished by control tokens (*e.g.*, XPP [11]). When memories are located in special PEs, array structures are used to access them, and MERGE operations without discard are needed to multiplex data tokens (*e.g.*, XPP). Other architectures use a data sequencer to stream data to the array (*e.g.*, KressArray).

The interconnections are responsible to flow data and control tokens. Their bit-width is a property dependent on the granularity of the PE. Architectures with explicit lines for control events also include 1-bit width interconnections (*e.g.*, XPP). Others use the data buses to flow either data or control tokens. Note that each interconnection implicitly has lines to implement the handshake mechanism.

Each configuration defines the operations in the PEs and the interconnections among them. Additional units are needed to control array reconfiguration. For efficient support of the configuration flow, architectures may include on-chip configuration manager (CM) and configuration cache (CC), as is the case of the XPP. Such amenities enable efficient and effective implementations of large programs by using temporal partitioning, especially when the number of resources to map a given algorithm exceeds the array resources [13][14].

Table 1 illustrates some of the characteristics of four data-driven arrays: Function Processor [12], KressArray [6], WASMII [16], XPP [11], and WaveScalar [9]. The first three were introduced in the early 90's. They have been pioneer work, as far as reconfigurable computing is concerned. The XPP is a commercial architecture introduced in the late 90's. The WaveScalar is one of the most recent research efforts attempting to build a decentralized dataflow machine and was introduced in the beginning of the 2000's.

Among several distinguishing features, we choose the schemes used to support load/store operations, to map loops, some differences in the operations and interconnect structures of the array and on the static or dynamic dataflow model of computation, as the main representative ones. Some of the arrays use special horizontal and vertical buses (*e.g.*, XPP), others explicitly use PEs for routing and provide interconnections between PEs in a mesh (*e.g.*, KressArray) or in a hexagonal topology (*e.g.*, Function Processor). Although some advantages and disadvantages of using different properties may be enumerated, a study of the impact of those properties, on, *e.g.*, performance, is still required. Notice, however, that with respect to reconfiguration support several differences could be sketched.

**Table 1.** Data-driven array architectures. (1) on inputs of each cell (configured as FIFOs or LIFOs); (2) Input/output queues, to store data for different waves; (3) A data-sequencer streams data to array; (4) Explicit connections to on- and off-chip memories; (5) Load/store operations can be performed in any PE

| Architecture | Dataflow Model | Programming Language | Special buffers in FUs? | Memory semantics |
|---|---|---|---|---|
| Function Processor [12] | Dynamic | Functional programming language | Yes[(1)] | No |
| KressArray [6] | Static | ALE-X (C-based) | No | No[(3)] |
| WASMII [16] | Static | Dataflow language (DFC) | No | No |
| XPP [11] | Static | C or NML (native language) | No | Yes[(4)] |
| WaveScalar [9] | Dynamic | C | Yes[(2)] | Yes[(5)] |

## 3 Support to Computational Structures

Besides work on using dataflow languages to program data-driven arrays [1], some efforts have been conducted to use imperative programming languages (*e.g.*, [17]). However, lack of specific machine operations to effectively support high-level languages has been one of the major difficulties to attain more efficient compilation results. Although apparently tailored for computations alike the ones described in high-level languages, coarse-grained reconfigurable architectures require further research both on compiler techniques and on operators support. For instance, special functionalities can be directly supported by primitive operations. One of such features permits to implement a counter with a single PE of the architecture (as is the case in the XPP). The counter is one of the operators that truly assists the mapping of high-level languages, specifically well-behaved FOR loops.

Another example is the support of load/store operators in any PE of the architecture (*e.g.*, WaveScalar), without needing to route, for instance, PEs to a port (*e.g.*, with selection capability) of the specific memory cell. One or more buses can be provided to exclusively access memories. Special labeling of the array references in the code [9] and arbitration in order to preserve load/store ordering can be used.

Another issue arises when, in a certain configuration, array resources need to be shared. This needs special control, to route distinct sources by the correct order to the input of the cell being shared, and to route each data item being output from the shared cell to the correct destination. This kind of structures can be implemented by SWITCH and MERGE operators and using control structures to generate the correct event sequences to accomplish the correct paths. The shared resources can be I/O ports for streaming data, which need to be steered to the correct PE (see Figure 2a). For this type of computations, two new operations can be ideated: SE-PAR and PAR-SE. They perform continuously serial to parallel and parallel to serial operations on the input data, respectively. SE-PAR has one input (A) and two outputs (X and Y). The operator repeatedly alternates data on the input to either X and Y (see Figure 2b). PAR-SE has two inputs (A and B) and one output (X). It repeatedly outputs to X the inputs in A and B, in an alternating fashion. Both operators can really assist compilation, fully decentralizes the needed control, without requiring additional resources.

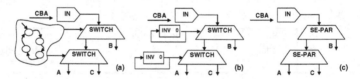

**Fig. 2.** Routing sequentially each item in a data stream to a distinct destination. Use of SWITCH operators and control structures to create a different path for each item: (a) a centralized; (b) decentralized; (c) naturally decentralized by using SE-PAR operators

MERGE operators with lenient behavior have been already used in [3]. They are important for conditional constructs, because they permit to continue computing as soon as data produced on the selected branch arrive (no need to wait for the data produced by the other branches).

In this type of architectures pipelining is, as in other computational models, very important. Register stages are added to full balance different paths in order to achieve maximum throughput. When PEs with input/output FIFOs are used, pipeline balancing may in some cases be naturally achieved without adding extra pipeline stages (and thus sophisticated pipeline balancing algorithms are not required). However, a study about the impact of FIFOs' size on the achieved performance for a set of representative benchmarks needs to be carried out. FIFO queues are also important structures for some implementations, especially when a delay of some stages is needed. This can be accomplished using a number of simple FIFOs in sequence, but that may require several PEs. Therefore, their direct support should be considered.

The presented schemes can be directly supported by data-driven arrays to assist the mapping of computational structures described in high-level languages. Moreover, they enclose the necessity to experimentally evaluate some design decisions in order to design a new data-driven array.

As a final remark, when compiling to reconfigurable hardware (see, for instance, [15]), a specific architecture to implement the input algorithm is synthesized. The architecture is usually composed of a data-path and a centralized control unit. Operations performed by the data-path are statically schedule and its execution is then controlled by the FSM (Finite State Machine) generated from the scheduling. Being a centralized control mechanism, it leads to difficulties to achieve the maximum performance, since the complexity to fully pipeline large examples and to tune the timing constraints to be used by place and route tools. Data-driven arrays do not need a centralized control unit, the operations are not statically schedule, and it is the data flow that dynamically imposes the execution of a particular operation (notice, however, that it is possible to statically define an order among operations using control tokens). Both data and control tokens flow concurrently through the array structures, and the implementation therefore naturally exposes fine-grain parallelism and multiple flows of control.

# 4  Compiling to Dataflow Array Architectures

Mapping computational structures to dataflow architectures is almost direct when straight-line code is input and each operation in the code can be directly implemented by a PE of the target architecture. The handshaking mechanism permits to abstract the mapping from the timing details associated when the computational structures are implemented using a data-path and a centralized control unit (timing-driven model).

When mapping conditional constructs (such as *if-then-else* statements) MERGE and SWITCH operations can be used. These two operations can also be used to implement loops. SWITCH operations are used to select the data flow through the loop structures (during iterations) or to path it to the structures beyond the loop (after loop completion).

To map imperative programming languages to a dataflow machine, the input computational structures can be transformed to the Program Dependence Web (PDW) [18], a representation that extends the Static Single Assignment (SSA) form [19] and the Program Dependence Graph (PDG) [20]. The PDW contains all the needed information for control-, data-, and demand-driven interpretation, and thus it can be used to generate the DFG akin to the required dataflow structure.

Selection points are explicitly represented in the SSA-form by $\Phi$-functions. Those points can be directly implemented with MERGE operations with discard. The PDW uses the Gated Single Assignment (GSA) to generate the control conditions. Instead of using only the SSA $\Phi$-functions, the PDW uses three types of functions ($\mu$, $\gamma$, and $\eta$).

μ-functions are used to represent selection points between loop carried values and loop initializations (MERGE operation). γ-functions are used to control forward data flow (MERGE operation). Finally, η-functions are used to control passage of values out of loop bodies (*i.e.*, they are used to forward final data values after loop completion). η-functions can be translated to SWITCH nodes. Operations to forward a copy or to discard the input data item may also be used (*e.g.*, T- and F-gate). Note that as opposite to non dataflow modes, where operations using a certain assignment are scheduled to time steps where data are already available, here we have to ensure that only data that must be used arrive to destination.

To enable the firing of some operations, control tokens are used, either directly (*i.e.*, as a form of predicate execution controlled by guards) or as control mechanisms to cease the data flow. Architectures with PEs with firing rules enabled by special control inputs can almost directly implement predicated execution (*e.g.*, XPP). When these type of firing rules are not directly supported, special operators can be added to enable/disable the data flow to destinations. Nevertheless, when speculative execution is used enable/disable firing is not needed as long as the data generated in paths not taken are discarded.

In the end, some transformations on the DFG may be necessary to be ready for placement and routing on the data-driven array. Pipeline balancing is usually performed during the place and route phase (*e.g.*, XPP).

Note however that for efficient compilation several optimizations are still required (see, for instance, [3]), such are the cases of software pipelining and elimination of redundant memory accesses (*e.g.*, inter-iteration register promotion [21]). A novel dataflow specific optimization, called *loop decoupling*, has been introduced in [3]. It slices a loop into multiple independent loops that may run ahead from each other. To ensure that no data-dependences are violated they use a token generator operator. It dynamically controls the dependence distance between decoupled loop iterations.

## 5   Self-loop Pipelining (SLP)

One of the most efficient design optimizations is pipelining. Pipelining is a form of overlapping different steps of computations. The use of pipelining leads usually to significant performance improvements. With respect to loops, *software pipelining* is a fundamental technique to improve throughput.

As far as dataflow computing is concerned, efficient loop execution has been achieved through *dataflow software pipelining* [22]. The approach uses balancing techniques to exploit maximum throughput. Balancing is achieved by the use of a certain number of register stages or FIFOs in each arc of the dataflow model.

Consider the example in Figure 3a. Figure 3b shows a pipelined implementation. The CNT module represents a counter which starts at a given number, increments by a certain quantity until a certain limit is not exceeded. Using a data-driven model with handshaking, the counter only furnishes a new value if the previous one has already been consumed.

To enable optimal software pipelining, full balancing of paths is required (see Figure 3b), *i.e.*, the counter indexing consecutive elements of the arrays A, B and C, requires that the two paths arriving to the destination memory where array C is located are balanced. The two paths are related to the operations computing the data items to be stored in the array C, and to the address generation structure. For balancing, elements behaving as simple registers have been inserted.

Now we briefly introduce *self loop pipelining* (SLP), a novel technique for pipelining loops. Figure 3c shows the main concept. The original centralized counter, responsible for the control iterations of the FOR loop, is duplicated and now two decentralized counters are responsible for the loop control behavior. The counters are decoupled and synchronize indirectly due to the data flow. As is depicted, there are now two independent paths furnishing the index value (i) to access array elements. Note that another correct SLP implementation would use three counters (one for each memory).

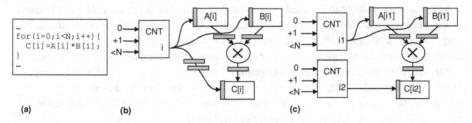

(a)                    (b)                                        (c)

**Fig. 3.** Loop pipelining on data-driven machines: (a) simple example - each array is mapped to a distinct memory; (b) traditional loop pipelining; (c) the proposed *self loop pipelining* technique. Rectangles in gray represent pipeline stages

With SLP, loops are naturally executed in a pipelining fashion. The technique is based on duplicating the cyclic hardware structures responsible to loop control (in the example is implemented using a counter, but usually can be implemented using a hardware cyclic structure), in order they are autonomously executed, with synchronization being naturally achieved by the data flow. It can be applied to all kind of loops (DO-WHILE, WHILE, and FOR), and also to nested loop structures. Using SLP, innermost loops with conditional constructs can also be pipelined without conservative loop pipelining implementations (which are usually based on the maximum critical path length of the loop body). The technique requires fewer resources for balancing (*i.e.*, fewer registers or smaller FIFOs) and less sophisticated balancing efforts than previous software pipelining techniques.

We have semi-automatically mapped some benchmarks to the XPP [11] using SLP. The architecture performs each PE operation and communicates data between elements (*i.e.*, PEs or interconnection registers) in a single clock cycle.

The results are now compared with loop pipelining implementations automatically achieved with the XPP-VC compiler [17]. When applying SLP to various DSP kernels (*max, auto correlation, weighted vector sum, block move, gourad, and median*) [23], performance improvements are achieved. With SLP we obtain from 1.2% to 68.4% fewer execution cycles, and even fewer needed PEs for most examples.

The improvements achieved with SLP have origins in the more relaxed *pipeline balancing* requirements and in the unneeded matching of branches on conditional constructs to achieve the maximum throughput.

Our ongoing work focuses on more experiments and on extending our compiler [15] to target static dataflow machines, including the use of the SLP technique.

## 6  Conclusions

This paper discusses some interesting reconfigurable array architectures computing in a dataflow fashion. Promising research efforts to compile imperative software languages to those kinds of architectures are also introduced. One of the techniques is a novel form of loop pipelining, named *self loop pipelining*.

*Self loop pipelining* can be used to pipeline loops in data-driven architectures based on the ready-acknowledge principle of operation. It involves replication of the hardware structures responsible for the control of loop iterations. The proposed technique has been applied for mapping a number of benchmarks to the XPP. Results, achieving performance improvements and fewer required resources, strongly confirm its importance. Ongoing and future work aims compilation techniques to automatically apply the technique. Future work should also embrace experiments with static dataflow models with input/output FIFOs in the functional units.

## Acknowledgments

This work is in part supported by the Portuguese Foundation for Science and Technology (FCT) - FEDER and POSI programs - under the CHIADO project. The author gratefully acknowledges the donation by PACT XPP Technologies, Inc, of the XPP development suite (XDS) software.

## References

1. H. Veen, "Dataflow machine architecture," in *ACM Computing Surveys*, Vol. 18, Issue 4, Dec. 1986, pp. 365-396.
2. J. B. Dennis, D.P. Misunas, "A computer architecture for highly parallel signal processing," in *Proc. ACM National Conference*, ACM, New York, Nov. 1974, pp. 402-409.
3. M. Budiu, *Spatial Computation*, Ph.D. Thesis, CMU CS Technical Report CMU-CS-03-217, Dec. 2003.
4. S. Y. Kung, et al., "Wavefront Array Processors - Concept to Implementation," in *IEEE Computer*, vol. 20, no. 7, July 1987, pp. 18-33.
5. I. Koren, et al., "A Data-Driven VLSI Array for Arbitrary Algorithms," in *IEEE Computer*, October 1988, pp. 30-43.

6. R. Hartenstein, R. Kress, and H. Reinig, "A Dynamically Reconfigurable Wavefront Array Architecture," in *Int'l Conference on Application Specific Array Processors (ASAP'94)*, Aug. 22-24, 1994, pp. 404-414.

7. W. A. Najjar, E. A. Lee, and G. R. Gao, "Advances in the dataflow computational model," in *Parallel Computing*, vol. 25, 1999, Elsevier Science B.V., pp. 1907-1929.

8. J. Teifel, and R. Manohar, "Highly Pipelined Asynchronous FPGAs," in *ACM Int'l Symposium on Field-Programmable Gate Arrays (FPGA'04)*, Monterey, CA, USA, Feb. 2004.

9. S. Swanson, et al., "WaveScalar," In *36th Annual Int'l Symposium on Microarchitecture (MICRO-36)*, Dec., 2003.

10. R. Hartenstein, "A Decade of Reconfigurable Computing: a Visionary Retrospective," In *Int'l Conf. on Design, Automation and Test in Europe (DATE'01)*, Munich, Germany, March 12-15, 2001, pp. 642-649.

11. PACT XPP Technologies, Inc., "The XPP White Paper," Release 2.1.1, March 2002, http://www.pactxpp.com.

12. J. Vasell, J. Vasell. "The Function Processor: A Data-Driven Processor Array for Irregular Computations," in *Future Generation in Computer Systems*, 8(4), 1992, pp. 321-335.

13. João M. P. Cardoso, "Loop Dissevering: A Technique for Temporally Partitioning Loops in Dynamically Reconfigurable Computing Platforms," in *10th Reconfigurable Architectures Workshop (RAW'03), Nice, France, April 2003*, IEEE Computer Society Press.

14. João M. P. Cardoso, and Markus Weinhardt, "From C Programs to the Configure-Execute Model," in *Proc. of the Design, Automation and Test in Europe Conference (DATE'03)*, Munich, Germany, March 3-7, 2003, IEEE Computer Society Press, pp. 576-581.

15. João M. P. Cardoso, and Horácio C. Neto, "Compilation for FPGA-Based Reconfigurable Hardware," in *IEEE Design & Test of Computers Magazine*, March/April, 2003, vol. 20, no. 2, pp. 65-75.

16. X. Ling, et.al., "WASMII: An MPLD with Data-Driven Control on a Virtual Hardware," in *Journal of Supercomputing.*, Vol.9, No.3, 1995, pp.253-276.

17. João M. P. Cardoso, and Markus Weinhardt, "XPP-VC: A C Compiler with Temporal Partitioning for the PACT-XPP Architecture," in $12^{th}$ *Int'l Conference on Field Programmable Logic and Applications (FPL'02)*, LNCS 2438, Springer-Verlag, 2002, pp. 864-874.

18. K. J. Ottenstein, R. A. Ballance, and A. B. Maccabe, "The program dependence web: a representation supporting control-, data-, and demand-driven interpretation of imperative languages," In *ACM Conference on Programming Language Design and Implementation (PLDI'90)*, 1990, pp. 257-271.

19. R. Cytron, et al., "Efficiently Computing static single assignment form and the control dependence graph," In *ACM Transactions on Programming Languages and Systems*, vol. 13, no. 4, October 1991, pp. 451-490.

20. J. Ferrante, K. J. Ottenstein, and J. D. Warren, "The program dependence graph and its use in optimization," in *ACM Transactions on Programming Languages and Systems*, vol. 9, no. 3, July 1987, pp. 319-349.

21. S. Carr, D. Callahan, and K. Kennedy, "Improving register allocation for subscripted variables," In *Proc. of ACM Conference on Programming Language Design and Implementation (PLDI'90)*, June 1990, ACM Press.

22. G. R. Gao, *A Code Mapping Scheme for dataflow Software Pipelining*, Kluwer Academic Publishers, 1991.

23. Texas Instruments, Inc., "TMS320C6000™ Highest Performance DSP Platform," 1995-2003, http://www.ti.com/sc/docs/products/dsp/c6000/benchmarks/62x.htm#search

# Architecture Exploration
# for 3G Telephony Applications Using
# a Hardware–Software Prototyping Platform[*]

François Charot, Madeleine Nyamsi, Patrice Quinton, and Charles Wagner

Irisa, Campus de Beaulieu, 35042 Rennes Cedex, France
{charot,mnyamsi,quinton,wagner}@irisa.fr

**Abstract.** Third generation mobile telephony applications require very efficient architectures, often implemented as a System on a Chip (SoC). Designing such architectures from the specification of the application requires fast prototyping techniques based on models of computation as well as efficient prototyping platforms. We consider here the implementation of a WCDMA uplink emitter and receiver on a LYRTECH hardware–software platform including a DSP and a FPGA. We explain how the application can be explored using MATLAB, SIMULINK, a DSP model, and the MMAlpha environment for high-level synthesis. The first results and conclusions of this exploration are presented and discussed.

## 1 Introduction

Third generation mobile telephony applications require very efficient architectures, most often implemented as a System on a Chip (SoC). Their complexity and the numerous design steps necessary to go from their high-level specification to their final implementation call for new methods to explore architectures for such applications.

We present a case study of architecture exploration for the physical layer of a 3G mobile telephony application based on Wide-band Code Division Multiple Access (WCDMA) [4, 11]. Architecture proposals for WCDMA are numerous and strongly depend on the algorithmic variants considered and on the targeted hardware. In [2], Dahmane et al. study the VLSI implementation of WCDMA receivers; Rajagopal et al. [10] consider Digital Signal Processor (DSP) implementation of multi-user channel estimation and detection algorithms for base station receivers. In [7], the same authors compare the implementation of a rake receiver on a DSP, a Field Programmable Gate Array (FPGA), and a new reconfigurable architecture called DART.

Our exploration uses the SignalMaster Hardware–Software prototyping platform designed by Lyrtech[1]. This platform allows one to map some parts of a data-flow design on a DSP and/or on a FPGA. The application is designed using

---

[*] This work is supported by the IST project 2000–30 026, Ozone
[1] See http://www.lyrtech.com/

A. Pimentel and S. Vassiliadis (Eds.): SAMOS 2004, LNCS 3133, pp. 244–253, 2004.

blocks of a SIMULINK library. Various tools allow one to generate C code from the blocks, and, provided equivalent VHDL descriptions are in the libraries, the same blocks can be mapped on a XILINX Virtex-II FPGA. The platform is delivered with a software environment that provides interface adapters in order to automatically connect blocks that are mapped on different components.

The design of an architecture for such a complex application faces several challenges. First, the structure of the application, as described by its initial specification, is very different from that of the final implementation. Thus, application restructuring is compulsory: this is a very time-consuming and error-prone task.

Second, each component of the design has to be targeted to a chosen technology for optimal performance: software on a general purpose processor, software on an DSP, special-purpose hardware, or static data on integrated memories. The generation of the targeted components may require a lot of effort, especially if optimized implementations are sought.

Third, predicting and/or estimating the performances of each block on various target technologies is needed in order to drive the choice of the architecture. Again, this task is far from easy, since a good estimation requires a lot of effort as well as specialized tools.

Finally, assembling and interconnecting components in the architecture is also a very difficult task, as interfaces are well-known to require as much effort to be designed than the components themselves.

The remaining of this paper is organized as follows. In section 2, we describe the WCDMA application that served as a support for our exploration. Section 3 presents the LYRTECH prototyping platform as well as a brief description of the MmAlpha software tool that was the basis for generating automatically VHDL blocks. In section 4, we detail the approach that we followed in order to explore architectures for this application. In section 5, we present the results obtained by following this methodology. Section 6 concludes this paper.

## 2   The WCDMA Model

WCDMA is a 3G asynchronous mobile communication system defined by the European norm. Signal is organized as 10 ms frames; a frame contains 15 slots, each one of which containing 2560 chips. The chip frequency is $3, 84$ Mcps. The WCDMA signal is modulated at 2 GHz in a frequency band of 5 Mhz. The receiver is a multi-user, multi-rate rake receiver using pilot bits. This model allows informations from several users to be transmitted, and it takes into account interferences due to the multiple paths followed by the signal while traveling from the emitter to the receiver. In this paper, we consider the WCDMA uplink, where the receiver is a *base station* collecting signals sent by several *mobile users*.

### 2.1   Structure of the Emitter

Fig. 1 shows the typical components of an emitter.

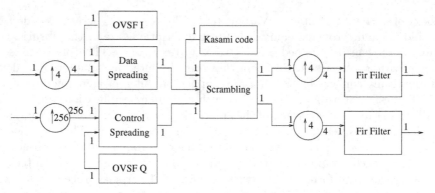

**Fig. 1.** Structure of a WCDMA emitter.

**Signal spreading:** multiplication of the input signal (both data and code) by orthogonal variable length codes (OVSF). In this step, data signal as well as control signal are oversampled and multiplied by a code that allows the receiver to separate the various users.

**Scrambling:** the (complex) signal which results from spreading is multiplied by a complex code (here, a Kasami code).

**Filtering:** the last step consists in applying $\alpha = 0.22$ roll-off factor Nyquist filter to the oversampled scrambled signal.

## 2.2   Structure of the Receiver

The receiver (in the base station) is much more complex, as it has to compensate for the transformations undergone by the signal in the transmission channel, and to cope with the multiple users and multiple paths interferences. We consider a

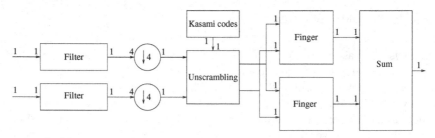

**Fig. 2.** Two *finger* rake receiver.

rake receiver [4] as shown in Fig. 2. Before entering a finger, the signal is filtered by the same Nyquist filter as seen in the emitter, then it is undersampled by 4, and finally, it is unscrambled thanks to a complex multiplication by the complex conjugates of the Kasami's code. Each finger comprises the following elements (see Fig. 3):

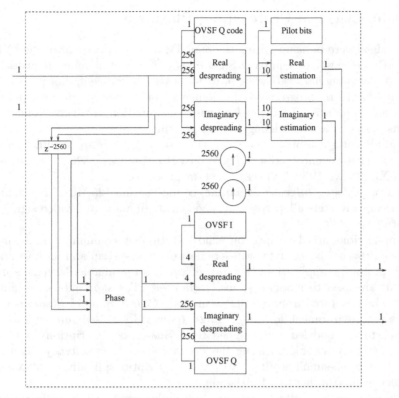

**Fig. 3.** Structure of a finger.

**Channel parameters estimation:** the channel parameters (amplitude and phase) are estimated by means of *pilot bits* which are sent repeatedly as part of the control signal. The imaginary part of the signal is correlated with the OVSFQ code, then summed up. This gives a complex estimation of the phase and amplitude distortion of the channel. Its effect is mapped to the one slot delayed input signal in order to compensate for the effect of the channel.

**Despreading:** the phase compensated output signal is despreaded using the (complete) OVSF codes.

## 2.3 Characteristics of the WCDMA Application

A WCDMA emitter and receiver system is a complex application for several reasons. First, it contains some very high performance tasks (such as filtering) that require a dedicated VLSI implementation. Second, the various parts of the system have different clock rates, and this makes the control quite complex. It should also be noted that the above rake receiver is one of the simplest structure that one can consider.

# 3    The LYRTECH Prototyping Platform

Our designs were built up xusing the SignalMaster environment of the LYRtech Signal Processing (LSP) company. SignalMaster is an autonomous, network accessible, prototyping hardware system. Its software environment allows a SIMULINK specification to be progressively implemented on a DSP and a FPGA processor. Functional simulation, hardware/software co-simulation, real-time simulation, as well as optimization and debugging are possible.

SignalMaster comprises two PCI bus connected hardware modules: a signal processing heterogeneous system based on a 167 Mhz TMS C320C6701 Texas DSP, and a XILINX XC2V3000 VIRTEX II FPGA processor.

A VIM (*Velocity Interface Mezanine*) connector and 125 Mhz, 12 bits, analog-numerical converters allow real-time acquisition of audio and video signal to be performed.

Applications are developed on a host station. A communication controller handles Ethernet based data transfers between the system and its host station.

To prototype applications, several softwares are available. MATLAB and SIMULINK are used to model systems; *Real-Time Workshop* allows optimized C code to be generated from SIMULINK models; *Code Composer Studio* is the development environment for the TMS320 DSP; *System Generator* allows FPGA systems to be modeled and mapped from SIMULINK descriptions; VHDL synthesis for FPGA is achieved using the *Leonardo Spectrum* software; MODELSIM allows one to co-simulate VHDL–SIMULINK descriptions; finally, XILINX ISE 5.1 is a placement/routing tool for the FPGA.

LSP provides two software modules (DSPlink and FPGAlink) to help generate software and/or hardware interfaces for either DSP or FPGA systems. Various bus, serial, and register based communication interfaces between the DSP and the FPGA are also available.

## 3.1    The MmAlpha Environment

During our investigation, we also used the MMAlpha environment to specify some blocks using the ALPHA applicative language, and to transform these specifications into parallel architectures. Based on research on automatic systolic synthesis [9], Alpha [5] is a functional language which was designed to express both recurrence equation specifications and hardware descriptions of regular iterative arrays. MMAlpha has been used to design applications pertaining to signal processing, multimedia, and bio-informatics [8].

MMAlpha targets both Asics and FPGAs. The final output of the compilation process is a VHDL program that can be synthesized with vendor tools.

An Alpha program – called a *system* – is a set of equations, each one of which is an indexed expression whose indexes span an integral polyhedron, that is to say, a set of integer coordinate points delimited by linear inequalities.

In MMAlpha, the synthesis process consists of applying a set of transformations – e.g. uniformization, scheduling, mapping – until the generation of a VHDL description becomes possible.

# 4    Exploration Methodology

In this section, we cover some of the steps that were needed in order to explore various implementations of the application.

## 4.1    Reference Behavioral Specification

Our first step was to obtain a behavioral, executable specification of the application. A MATLAB version, where each function reads and writes files, was developed. This version formed a functional reference model that was used to check the correctness of any other further developed version.

## 4.2    Data-Flow Specification

From the reference version, we designed a synchronous data flow (SDF) [6], paper specification. In this model, the application is decomposed into elementary blocks called *nodes*. Nodes correspond to *atomic* functions, each one of which being implemented using hardware or software, depending on performance sought.

In the SDF model, communication between nodes are modeled by *tokens*. A node consumes and produces a fixed amount of data tokens. A SDF graph allows the communication pattern of the application to be modeled: an arc between two nodes shows a communication, positive integers at the origin (resp. at the extremity) of an arc denote the amount of token produced (resp. consumed) by the producer (resp. consumer). In Fig. 1 and 3, the number of tokens of each arc are represented.

The SDF model allows one to check that a given system can be executed and finds out a schedule whenever it is possible. A well-known tool to help model SDF systems is PTOLEMY (although it was not used here).

## 4.3    Data-Flow Executable Version

A SIMULINK version was then built up from the SDF version of the second step. SDF nodes were directly mapped to SIMULINK library blocks whenever such blocks were available, or mapped to complex SIMULINK blocks using the hierarchical editor. Tests files for further implementations were generated.

Notice that the SIMULINK model has a slightly different semantics from that of SDF: instead of modeling communications, SIMULINK identifies *clocks* that drive the execution of the system.

## 4.4    Versions for Co-simulation and Performance Estimation

The SIMULINK version produced several results, depending on the way each block was implemented.

 – Software DSP implementations of some blocks. This is simplified in the LYRTECH environment by the *Real-Time Workshop* tool that generates automatically ANSI-C programs for any SIMULINK model. Such a program can then by run on the platform TMS processor.
 – Hardware implementation on the FPGA, and co-simulation with the host processor.

The *System Generator* tool of Xilinx automatically produces a hardware description configuration from a SIMULINK version. However, the effort needed is higher than to generate C code.

### 4.5 Mixed Hardware–Software Co-simulation Versions

By selecting the parts that one wants to map on the DSP and those to be executed on the FPGA, various mixed hardware–software versions may be generated and evaluated.

Note that one important step in the design of hardware for signal processing applications is not considered in this paper, namely, the choice of an appropriate fixed-point representation. The interested reader will find in [7] relevant information regarding this topic.

## 5 Experimental Results

In this section, we present preliminary results obtained on the WCDMA application. These results concern mainly the emitter, although the specifications of the complete application were modeled at the functional and data-flow level as well as in ALPHA.

### 5.1 Estimating the Number of Operations of the Emitter

The number of operations of the emitter can be easily obtained from its SDF model. A 10 ms frame contains fifteen, 2560 chips slots. The number of operations needed for each sample of a N taps filter is N multiplications, and $N-1$ additions. Six multiplications and two additions are needed for scrambling and spreading. As the frequency of the filter is 4 times that of the initial signal, and there are two filters, the number of operations (additions and multiplications) needed for a frame is therefore $15 \times 2560 \times 16N$ operations. For a 33 taps filter, this amounts to about 2 Gops.

In terms of multiplication accumulations (MAC), the total number of operations corresponds to 1 Giga MAC per second.

### 5.2 Various Implementations

As explained in the methodology, various implementations were designed. We consider successively implementations of the FIR filter, then implementations of the full emitter on the DSP and on the FPGA.

**Fir.** The symmetric, 33 taps, 13 bits coefficients FIR filter was implemented on the VIRTEX II chip from various specifications:

1. A parallel version with distributed arithmetic provided by Xilinx [1] (XILINX FIR).
2. A parallel ALPHA version, using the $18 \times 18$ multipliers of the VIRTEX II FPGA (ALPHA mults).

3. The same parallel ALPHA version, where multipliers were implemented as gates (ALPHA gates).
4. A parallel, combinational FIR, designed by assembling multipliers and adders of the XILINX library (MAC FIR).
5. The same parallel, combinational FIR, where the serial adder was replaced by a tree pipelined adder (Tree FIR).

Table 1 shows the results of these implementations. For each design, this table provides the clock estimation (after placement and routing), the latency of the design, the number of look-up table (LUT) used, the number of multipliers used, and finally, the equivalent gate count.

**Table 1.** Comparison of various fir implementations.

|             | XILINX FIR | ALPHA mults | ALPHA gates | Mac FIR | Tree FIR |
|-------------|-----------:|------------:|------------:|--------:|---------:|
| Clk (ns)    | 6          | 12          | 12          | 68      | 8        |
| #LUT        | 1,221      | 1,482       | 3,462       | 1,401   | 1076     |
| Latency     | 11         | 33          | 33          | 1       | 7        |
| # Gates     | 51,436     | 256,012     | 142,020     | 183,441 | 184,500  |
| # Mult      | -          | 32          | -           | 32      | 33       |
| # Ram blocks| -          | 1           | 1           | -       | -        |

The XILINX parallel, distributed arithmetic, version of the FIR is clearly the most efficient both in term of speed and surface.

The ALPHA versions do not take into account the fact that the filter is symmetric, which would simplify the design. The comparison of the ALPHA gates version with the XILINX version shows a factor of 2 in speed and a factor 3 in surface in favor of the latter one.

The tree of adder version is a little bit more complex in term of surface, but faster than the ALPHA version.

**Co-simulation of emitter on DSP.** The SIMULINK description of the FIR (using the XILINX distributed arithmetic FIR) was translated in C and co-simulated on the DSP. In this execution, data are read and written on the host station, and the DSP is synchronized with the host station.

For each fir sample, 990 DSP cycles were needed. At 167 MHz, one cycle lasts 6 ns, and 990 cycles correspond therefore to 5.93 $\mu$s per FIR frame, i.e. a chip requires $4 \times 5.93 = 23.7\,\mu$s. As a chip lasts 260 ns, this is 91 times real-time.

As a bottom line, the number of operations that the DSP is capable is $334 \times 10^6$ MAC per second, i.e., 6 times real-time. This shows that the SIMULINK C code is about 15 times less efficient than the best possible code.

**Full FPGA version.** Two versions were synthesized and evaluated. The first one uses multiplier blocks. The estimated clock after placement and routing was 12.5 ns. 6 multipliers and 5 RAM blocks were used, giving a total of 432,132 equivalent gates. The second version implemented multipliers directly on the chip. The clock was 11 ns, and the number of gates was 398,600.

A clock of 11 ns corresponds to 44 ns for a 260 ns chip, i.e., about 6 times faster than real-time. Therefore, an implementation of the filter using only 6 cells would be sufficient here.

### 5.3   Discussion

The use of such a platform really helps exploring architectures for a signal processing application. Indeed, a single framework allows different implementations to be quickly developed and tested, while checking that the results keep consistent with the reference implementation.

Two features of the platform were especially useful. First, communications between the host station, the DSP and the FPGA are easily developed by means of communication adapters: as interfaces are known to be the trickiest part of a design, one saves a lot of design time. Second, tools to compile SIMULINK functions to DSP help getting quickly a coarse DSP version. Although the result may be far from an optimized version, one gets figures that could help targeting the type of architecture that would be needed to implement the application.

The above results also show that FPGA implementations may reach very high performances, here more than 100 times faster than the DSP implementation. However, this comes with the price of developing new representations of the application, as all SIMULINK blocks are not available in the hardware library. The use of high-level synthesis tools such as MMAlpha is therefore very interesting, as it allows hardware to be quickly developed and evaluated.

## 6   Conclusion

We have presented the use of a prototyping platform to explore architectures for the WCDMA 3G telephony standard. We have shown a methodology to use this platform by building a reference MATLAB version, then a data-flow version, implement this data-flow version using SIMULINK, then map and evaluate parts of the design on either DSP or FPGA. Our experiment on the emitter part of the WCDMA application gave some figure of performances of the DSP and of the FPGA implementations.

This experiment shows the great potential of such a platform to quickly experiment various architectures. In particular, it makes it quite easy to map and interconnect components on different technologies, and to simulate their behavior within the complete application.

In [3], another approach to architecture exploration consists in a SystemC software co-simulation of the application together with its environment. We believe this approach to be complementary to ours: it is more accurate, but certainly slower. It is therefore best suited to simulate an architecture, after it has been selected among various other possibilities, possibly using our approach. Moreover, getting SystemC equivalent implementations of the SIMULINK blocks would accelerate the design of the system.

# Acknowledgments

The authors would like to thank Pascal Scalart, Daniel Ménard and Olivier Sentieys for their help in understanding the WCDMA application, and in particular, for providing an initial MATLAB reference version of the WCDMA.

# References

1. Distributed Arithmetic FIR Filter, V7.0. Product Specification, Xilinx, Inc., Mar. 2002.
2. A. O. Dahmane and D. Massicotte. Wideband CDMA Receivers for 3G Wireless Communications: Algorithm and Implementation Study. In *IASTED Wireless and Optical Communiaction*, July 17-19 2002.
3. A. Fraboulet, T. Risset, and A. Scherrer. Fast and Accurate Hardware–Software Prototyping with SOCLIB & MMALPHA. In *Samos IV*, Samos, Greece, July 2004.
4. H. Holma and A. Toskala. *WCDMA for UMTS: Radio Access For Third Generation Mobile Communication*. John Wiley & Son, second edition, 2002.
5. Le Verge, C. Mauras, and P. Quinton. The ALPHA Language and its Use for the Design of Systolic Arrays. *Journal of VLSI Signal Processing*, 3:173–182, 1991.
6. E. Lee and D. Messerchmitt. Synchronous Data Flow. *Proceedings of the IEEE*, 75(9), Sept. 1987.
7. D. Menard, M. Guitton, S. Pillement, and O. Sentieys. Design and Implementation of WCDMA Platforms: Challenges and Trade-offs. In *International Signal Processing Conference (ISPC'03)*, Dallas, US, Apr. 2003.
8. A. Mozipo, D. Massicotte, P. Quinton, and T. Risset. A Parallel Architecture for Adaptative Channel Equalization Based On Kalman Filter Using MMAlpha. *1999 IEEE Canadian Conference on Electrical & Computer Engineering*, pages 554–559, May 1999.
9. P. Quinton and Y. Robert. *Systolic Algorithms and Architectures*. Prentice Hall and Masson, 1989.
10. S. Rajagopal, S. Bhashyam, J. Cavallaro, and B. Aazhang. Efficient VLSI Architectures for Multiuser Channel Estimation in Wireless Base-Station Receivers. *Journal of VLSI Signal Processing*, 31(2):143–156, June 2002.
11. S. Verdu. *Multiuser Detection*. Cambridge University Press, 1998.

# Embedded Context Aware Hardware Component Generation for Dataflow System Exploration

John McAllister[1], Roger Woods[1], and Richard Walke[2]

[1] Institute for Electronic, Communication and Information Technology (ECIT),
Queens University Belfast, Belfast, BT9 5AH, UK
{jp.mcallister,r.woods}@ee.qub.ac.uk
[2] Real Time Embedded Systems (RTES), QinetiQ Ltd., St. Andrew's Road, Great Malvern,
Worcestershire WR14 3PS, UK
walke@signal.qinetiq.com

**Abstract.** Techniques for the rapid deployment and architectural exploration of complex digital signal processing algorithms on embedded processor platforms are gaining popularity. These become significantly more complicated when dedicated hardware components need to be integrated. The models on which such design methodologies and tools are based highlight the system level inflexibility with both pre-designed intellectual property cores and most customized component creation techniques. This paper presents a technique for overcoming these deficiencies using a dataflow model of computation, by allowing flexible circuit architectures to be created that can be optimized as desired, providing increased throughput with no extra resource usage in some situations.

## 1  Introduction

Modern high-end Digital Signal Processing (DSP) systems can be implemented on embedded multi-processor platforms, using packet switched (PS) inter-processor communication technology. Model of computation (MOC), in particular dataflow (DF) [1], based techniques are well known for their rapid prototyping abilities [2,3]. DF is attractive as it provides capabilities for deadlock detection, determinacy and static schedulability across multiple processors in certain instances [4]. However, as important, is the system level architecture exploration capabilities of these models and associated tools [3] which alter the algorithm environment to trade-off throughput, resource usage and memory requirements in the embedded implementation.

The major benefit of these techniques have so far mostly been in the software solution domain, as their inherent programmability allows easy actor manipulation as required by the system level exploration techniques. Dedicated hardware solutions restrict this ability since the behaviour of the actor is fixed at design time and is costly to change. The use of programmable hardware components in the form of Field Programmable Gate Array (FPGA) would suggest an easing of this restriction, but at present there is no design methodology to support this. This is the focus of this paper.

Custom hardware synthesis from multi-rate dataflow graph (MRDFG) specification is primarily realized by one of two techniques: a one-to-one translation from multi-rate DFG to hardware component network, as characterized by solutions includ-

A. Pimentel and S. Vassiliadis (Eds.): SAMOS 2004, LNCS 3133, pp. 254–263, 2004.

ing actors and high levels of interconnecting FIFO queue buffers [5, 6]; alternatively conversion to a single-rate *signal flow graph* (SFG) allows use of existing architectural synthesis techniques [7] ideally suited to FPGA realization [8]. The system level flexibility of this latter approach is limited as conversion from a MRDFG to a SFG complicates the design process and more importantly means that the result is a point solution in the DFG level design space. Despite this, the dataflow MOC origins of this technique and the highly efficient results make its use an attractive proposition, allowing the user to trade off highly efficient solutions with the ability to effectively traverse the *system* design space using DFG manipulations. Significant enhancements to the approach are given here.

This paper is organized as follows. Section 2 outlines typical DFG manipulations used in system level architecture exploration, and highlights how SFG architectural synthesis techniques are insufficient. Section 3 describes an advanced synthesis technique to overcome these deficiencies which is demonstrated in section 4.

# 2 Dataflow System Architecture Exploration

## 2.1 DFG Rapid Prototyping Fundamentals

A DFG describes *actors* connected by *arcs* carrying *streams* of *tokens* which may be scalar, vector or matrix. In the process of actor *firing*, tokens are *consumed* from input arcs and *produced* on output arcs. Iterations of the dataflow system schedule [4], involve actor *execution*, which consists of a series of actor firings. The schedule dictates the number of tokens which must pass between producer and consumer actor in an iteration. The *threshold* $(T)$ of an actor dictates the number of tokens produced/consumed in actor firing, and hence dictates the number of firings in an execution. The times an actor fires in a single iteration is known as the *natural granularity* $(G_n)$ which may be altered by a *granularity multiplier* $(G_m)$, to give the actual granularity $(G_a)$. When partitioned across multiple processing resources, inter-processor communication send and receive $(S/R)$ actors are implicitly inserted into the system, and the resulting graph statically scheduled as much as possible to minimise run time scheduling overhead. Fig. 1(a) shows a simple DFG where input matrices are transformed by two matrix operators $A_m$ and $B_m$. Actor token thresholds are indicated by the values inside circular actor ports. A partitioned implementation is shown in Fig 1(b) where actors are partitioned onto separate processors, and communicate using a packet PS scheme.

## 2.2 DFG Token Manipulation

In the DFG of Fig. 1(a), $T$ and $G_n$ for all actors is 1. When each DFG component is implemented, tokens transferred from one actor to another manifest themselves as memory storage locations where the size of the tokens will dictate memory needs. If computations on high order tokens (e.g. matrices) can be expressed as parallel computations on lower order tokens (e.g. vectors) the additional parallelism can be exploited to partition across a greater number of processors, increasing throughput at the cost of extra resources. It is obvious, therefore, that manipulation of actor token type is one transformation which can be used to trade off throughput, processing resource and memory requirements. If the matrices in Fig 1(a) have 10 rows, the computations on each may then be partitioned into 10 parallel vector operation streams (Fig. 2).

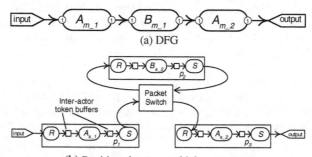

(a) DFG

(b) Partitioned across multiple processors

**Fig. 1.** Matrix Token System

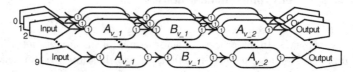

**Fig. 2.** Family of Vector DFGs

$A_m$ and $B_m$ can be converted to $n$ parallel vector actors which are represented as a PGM family [9] of actors. Each family member may be partitioned to separate processors to maximize parallelism, thereby increasing throughput and reducing memory per processor. For very large matrices (e.g. 1000 rows), maximum row parallelism is impractical for exploitation and a compromise family size/memory size value must be found. This manipulation is a type of algorithmic engineering commonly used in such dataflow programming environments, for trading off throughput, processing resource, and memory requirements. To allow this exploration, actors and their implementations must be *token polymorphic*.

## 2.3   DFG Threshold/Granularity Manipulation

It is rare in an embedded DF system implementation that the system will operate at $G_n$ as, quite often, the physical manifestation of send ($S$) and receive ($R$) operations have a fixed defined threshold, i.e. they do not operate until a certain number of tokens are supplied. Low threshold/granularity system operation can also result in expensive run-time overhead associated with system scheduling and inter-processor communication in real-time systems. This physical limitation constrains the DFG in a way that is not apparent at the algorithmic level. The ability to operate at varying $G_a$ levels is fundamental to the high level embedded system exploration capabilities of DF programming environments. Actors which have fixed thresholds *must* have flexible granularity constraints to allow use, exploration and reuse in DF design environments. DFG actor implementations must be *granularity polymorphic*. It will now be shown how SFG semantics and architectural synthesis methods are overly restrictive for such an approach.

## 2.4 SFG Deficiencies for DFG Synthesis

SFGs are single-rate DFGs (SRDFGs) [4], where every SFG actor executes precisely once in a DFG schedule iteration. This is a significant drawback for components generated from SFGs as these represent "point" solutions in the DF system spectrum, as outlined in previous sections. Converting a relevant portion of MRDFG to a SFG according to multi-rate activity and threshold [7] makes two important assumptions of the system. The SFG assumes single rate synchronicity between input data streams and actor firing, which has a fixed threshold of 1. A SFG also assumes input token atomicity, i.e. every element of an input token is assumed available simultaneously and consumed accordingly, which is certainly not the case in PS systems. These are major drawbacks if the component is to undergo system level manipulation, or is to be reused in another DF system. Consider the DFG of Fig. 3(a) with the equivalent SFG shown in Fig 3(b).

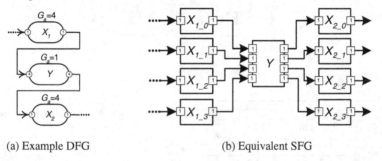

(a) Example DFG                    (b) Equivalent SFG

**Fig. 3.** DFG/SFG Comparison

In the Fig 3(a), $T$ of Y is 4, and the 4 tokens are consumed simultaneously. For $T = 8$, the number of inputs to Y would double in the SFG. This is because SFG architectural synthesis produces *fixed T* solutions. Since $T$ is fixed, so is $G_a$ for a specific DFG. Hence SFG architectural synthesis produces fixed $T$ and $G_a$ solutions for DFG systems. If the DFG of Fig 3(a) was a family member which operates on scalar tokens, DFG level token manipulation to implement a single vector processor would require SFG re-generation and synthesis because SFG synthesis produces *fixed token* designs. These two restrictions constrain the number of DFG configurations that an SFG generated component can process. In traditional SFG synthesis, an isolated portion of DFG portion produces a point solution which is now unacceptable. A new approach is needed which trades off SFG architectural synthesis efficiency with DFG level flexibility. The greater the implementation efficiency for a range of DFG configurations, the flexible it is at the DFG level. The greater the flexibility, the less efficient a point solution will be.

# 3   System Implementation Ethos

## 3.1   Processing Node Structure

In this approach, portions of DFG are separated into one or more 'pools', for conversion to SFG and architectural synthesis, producing an implementation node known as a Signal Flow Object (SFOs) (Fig. 4) for each pool. Computation, communication and control are all isolated in the SFO. The processing part is considered as a 'white box' component [11] exposing input and output data interfaces, and supplied with information on configurable aspects for timing purposes. This style of node architecture is not new [6,12] but it is important to note that the local SFO control allows system level architecture optimisation to be realized by altering the behaviour of the controller only. The controller supplies state information to the processor, switching the component state in the case of multi-stream operation.

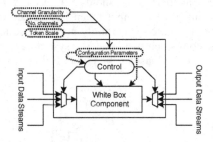

**Fig. 4.** SFO Structure

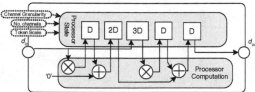

**Fig. 5.** 2 Stage Pipelined FIR White Box Component

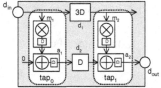

**Fig. 6.** 2 Stage FIR Processor

## 3.2   White Box Function Unit Structure

The structure of a white box component is visualised as in Fig. 5 for a two stage pipelined FIR filter. The component is regarded as a purely computational portion, provided with a particular set of tokens, known as the computation state $c$, defined by the delays on the inputs to the computation portion. This is computed and returned to the state arbitration unit. The component should be scalable to allow maximum flexibility in terms of number of data streams, stream token type, and stream $G_a$. The major obstacle to achieving this is proper arbitration of data state space, $s$, of the component, as defined by the delays in the circuit. In the view of this methodology, the role of SFG architectural synthesis is to generate the structure of the computation portion, and a scalable state portion. The scaling and implementation of the state is determined by the stream/token/$G_a$ activity of the component.

### 3.3  Base Processor Synthesis

SFG architectural synthesis produces a *base* processor, which defines the minimum level of DFG behaviour in terms of $T$, $G_a$, number of input streams, and input token dimension that the processor can support. The processor cannot be used for any values less than these, but by configuration can implement supersets. For example, a two stage FIR filter processor architecture with a base configuration of scalar token, unity threshold, unity $G_a$, single stream operation undergoes architectural synthesis to produce the processor structure of Fig 6. This is augmented by parameterisable size data storage on all subcomponent outputs, the size of which and the nature of how the delays are implemented are the key to parameterisable system level manipulation.

### 3.4  Token Type Manipulation

A SFG input vector (Fig. 7(a)) is streamed one scalar element at a time when PS communication is used (Fig. 7(b)). Thus no input/output multiplexing/demultiplexing, as would normally be required in the SFG generated component, is required as the assumption of simultaneous availability of token elements need not hold. The *single cycle token type* (SCTT) of the data is a scalar, whilst the *packet token type* (PTT) is a vector. Thus in transforming from a scalar to a vector processor, the type of data consumed and processed in any clock cycle by the processor is identical, rendering SFG manipulation and re-synthesis unnecessary. The state of the scalable processor $S=\{s\}$ in the base processor (i.e. scalar) configuration. A vector input can be considered to be multiple input ($n$) base token streams. $S$ is now a superset of the $n$ sets of $s$, one for each algorithmically independent input stream, as shown in (1).

$$S = \{s_1, s_2, ..., s_n\}\tag{1}$$

Similarly, the computation state C of the multistream processor, which for one input stream is $C=\{c_{1\_1},c_{1\_2},c_{1\_3},...\}$, cycles in turn through the computation state due to the n processor states, as shown in (2).

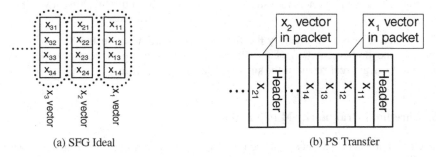

(a) SFG Ideal                                              (b) PS Transfer

**Fig. 7.** Actor Vector Token Transfer

$$C = \{c_{1\_1}, c_{2\_1}, ..., c_{n\_1}, c_{1\_2}, c_{2\_2}, ..., c_{n\_2}, ...\} \tag{2}$$

This is achieved by an *n*-slowing operation on the SFG. Since the processor architecture derived from SFG architectural synthesis is merely a retimed form of the original SFG [7], *n* slowing the processor architecture achieves the desired effect, where *n* is the number of SCTT in the PTT. It is worth noting that for processors with a pipeline period greater than 1, this slowing can be achieved without any extra resource usage for tokens with algorithmically independent elements, but gives an *n* factor throughput increase. The parameterisation of token scale effects the structure of the base processor in the following well defined way:

*i.* Edges are *n-slowed* [7] by the factor given by (3),

$$factor = n \left\lceil \frac{max(u_c)}{\alpha_o} \right\rceil \tag{3}$$

where $max(u_c)$ is the maximum subcomponent utilisation (expressed as a fraction between zero and 1), and $\alpha_o$ the base token processor pipeline period

*ii.* Subcomponent output delays are scaled to length $(n-1)L$, where $L$ is the number of pipeline stages in the subcomponent.

Step (*i*) ensures all subcomponents are 100% utilised, whilst (*ii*) ensures all the subcomponent delays are scaled appropriately for scheduling duplication. The token scalable FIR filter processor structure for an *n* scalar PTT is shown in Fig 8.

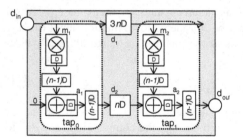

Fig. 8. 2 Stage FIR Vector Processor

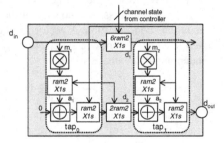

Fig. 9. 2 Stage FIR Multi-Stream Variable Granularity Component

The value of *n* is controlled by the 'token scale' parameter on the SFO of Fig. 4. Note that the implementation of the state scaling by the use of configurable length delay chains is a direct result of the single cycle switching from $c_{n\_x}$ to $c_{n+1\_x}$.

## 3.5  Threshold/Granularity Manipulation

It is clear that a wider ability is needed to map the DFG components to a single hardware-shared processor with an arbitrary number of input streams of arbitrary $G_a$.

This scaling has a similar effect on $S$ as for the token transform, in (1), but, in this case, the effect on $C$, the computation state, is rather different as shown by (4).

$$C = \{c_{1\_1}, ..., c_{1\_G}, c_{2\_1}, ..., c_{2\_G}, ...c_{n\_1}, ..., c_{n\_G}, c_{1\_G+1}, ..., c_{1\_2G}, ...\} \qquad (4)$$

For high granularity, multiple stream operation, $s_i$ is iterated $G_a$ times, before switching to the next $s$. This repeats $n$ times, where $n$ is the number of input streams multiplexed onto the processor. The stream switching is controlled by the SFO control unit, and it only remains for the core to implement the proper state capacity for the operations. The entire computational resource of the component is dedicated to a single input stream for $T*G_a$ cycles. This type of load-compute-store behaviour requires last data state retention for each stream for multiple cycles (until the next iteration for that stream). The fabric of modern FPGA is ideally suited to implementing this type of behaviour via the use of distributed RAM blocks [10] which have synchronous write/asynchronous read operations, thereby maintaining the same timing profile as a simple delay. They are also hardware inexpensive, meaning that this type of high granularity stream hardware sharing can be intuitively and relatively inexpensively implemented without SFG redesign giving the 2 stage FIR component in Fig. 9.

# 4  Design Example

This section applies the technique to an 8 stage Normalised Lattice Filter (NLF) component [7], as shown in Fig. 10(a). The NLF stage SFG is shown in Fig. 10(c). SFG architectural synthesis is used to generate a base scalar token, unity threshold, unity granularity, single stream base processor. The base processor token NLF (BS-NLF) is generated by a hierarchical SFG architectural synthesis solution [8], and is shown in Fig. 10(b), with the stage processor structure shown in Fig. 10(d). To demonstrate the flexibility of this approach, the processor will be configured for operation on 4, 8 and 68 element vector tokens (4BS-NLF, 8BS-NLF and 68BS-NLF respectively), and for operation on 16 streams of 4 element vectors with $G_a=16$ (16S4BS-NLF). These examples were chosen to demonstrate the optimisation capability of the transforms described here, highlight the flexibility of the generated structures and are all performed without re-performing MRDFG to SFG translation and SFG architectural synthesis.

Implementation is on a Xilinx XC2V6000-6 device. All circuits described in this table utilise 39 embedded Virtex2 *mult18x18s* components. BS-NLF (Fig.10(b)) has a pipeline period of 4 clock cycles. Since the adder and multiplier subcomponents are all pipelined by a single stage, the circuit is only 25% efficient given that all the subcomponents can compute new input cycles every clock cycle. However, adapting this configuration for a 4 element vector, unity threshold, unity granularity, single stream operation (4BS-NLF) allows an increase in computational performance of the processor by a factor 4 with no additional hardware, as shown in row 2 of Table 1.

Increasing vector length to 68 elements shows constant additional hardware usage with throughput increased by a factor of 4.6 over BS-NLF. The hardware resource overhead at this point is rendered insignificant in terms of absolute extra FPGA resource used by the vast programmable logic resource of modern FPGA, and is a small price to pay for the flexibility. It can, however, be minimised by performing the initial

SFG architectural synthesis in the knowledge that system level manipulation is to occur. Although this technique is not described here, results for the 8 and 68BS-NLF components synthesised using it (8BS-NLF2/68BS-NLF2) show considerable resource overhead reductions.

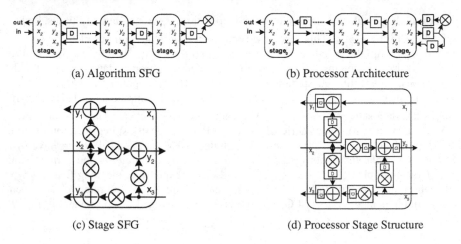

(a) Algorithm SFG

(b) Processor Architecture

(c) Stage SFG

(d) Processor Stage Structure

**Fig. 10.** 8 Stage NLF Algorithm and Processor Structure

**Table 1.** Synthesis Results For DF Configurations of SFG Generated NLF Component

| | Slices | 4 Input LUTS | | | FDE | Throughput |
|---|---|---|---|---|---|---|
| | | Logic | SRL16E | RAM16S | | (MSamples/s) |
| BS-NLF | 332 | 184 | - | - | 605 | 38.14 |
| 4BS-NLF | 332 | 184 | - | - | 605 | 152.56 |
| 8BS-NLF | 620 | 186 | 583 | - | 1136 | 176.56 |
| 68BS-NLF | 620 | 186 | 583 | - | 1,136 | 176.56 |
| 16S4BS-NLF | 618 | 186 | 7 | 816 | 152 | 132.40 |
| 8BS-NLF2 | 481 | 186 | 207 | - | 874 | 167.17 |
| 68BS-NLF2 | 583 | 186 | 407 | - | 1078 | 168.03 |

## 5   Conclusions

A new approach to flexible hardware component synthesis for use and reuse in DF systems has been presented. The system level deficiencies of SFG architectural synthesis solutions have been highlighted. Despite this, the highly efficient processor structures generated by these approaches provide a good foundation for a wider design methodology. SFG architectural synthesis techniques generate a base processor configuration with minimum level of token size, threshold and input streams. By manipulating supersets of this processor schedule, a high degree of DF system flexibility is possible in terms of input token type, number of input streams and granularity. This technique can achieve high levels of increase in throughput for no resource expense for processors with high order pipeline periods. By recognising that this type of manipulation will be applied to the component at the SFG architectural synthesis stage the resource overhead associated with high levels of integration can be reduced. Since the size of a DFG pool which is translated to a single processing node is undefined (provided it is part of a static schedule) then it is possible, by adjusting the size of the pool, to trade off the implementation efficiency with high level architecture design space.

## Acknowledgments

The contribution of Jasmine Lam and Darren Reilly to this work is acknowledged. This work is part of a collaborative project between Queens University Belfast, QinetiQ Ltd. and BAE Systems ATC and is supported by the Department of Education and Learning (DEL) Northern Ireland and the UK Ministry of Defence Corporate Research Programme.

## References

1. Lee, E.A., Parks, T.M.: Dataflow Process Networks. Proc. IEEE, vol. 83 (1995), 773-801.
2. Lauwereins, R., Engels, M., Adé, M., Peperstraete, J.A.: Grape-II: A Rapid Prototyping Environment for DSP Applications, Computer, vol. 28 (1995), 35-43
3. Madahar, B.K., et al: How Rapid is Rapid Prototyping? Analysis of ESPADON Programme Results. EURASIP JASP, vol. 6 (2003), 580-593.
4. Lee, E.A., Messerschmitt, D.G.: Synchronous Data Flow. Proc. IEEE, vol. 75 (1987), 1235-1245.
5. Williamson, M., Synthesis of Parallel Hardware Implementations from Synchronous Dataflow Graph Specifications. University of California, Berkeley (1998).
6. Stefanov, T., Zissulescu, C., Turjan, A., Kienhuis, B., Deprettere, E.: System Design Using Kahn Process Networks: The Compaan/Laura Appoach. In Proc. Design Automation and Test in Europe (DATE) (2004)
7. Parhi, K.K.: VLSI Digital Signal Processing Systems Design and Implementation. Wiley, 1999
8. Yi, Y.:DSP Architectural Synthesis Tools for FPGAs. Queens University Belfast (2003).
9. Kaplan, D.J., Stevens, R.S., Processing Graph Method 2.1 Semantics. (2002)
10. Xilinx Inc., Virtex-II Platform FPGA Handbook. (2001).
11. Bingmann, O., Rosenstiel, W.: Resource Sharing in Hierarchical Synthesis. Proc. Int'l Conf. on Computer Aided Design (ICCAD) (1997).
12. Zepter, P., Grötker, T., Meyr, H.: Digital receiver design using VHDL generation from data flow graphs. Proc. 32$^{nd}$ Design Automation Conference (DAC) (1995), 228-233

# On the (Re-)Use of IP-Components in Re-configurable Platforms

Jérôme Lemaitre[1], Sylvain Alliot[1], and Ed Deprettere[2]

[1] ASTRON, Oude Hoogeveensedijk 4, Dwingeloo 7990, Netherlands
[2] LIACS, Leiden university, Netherlands

**Abstract.** When mapping high-throughput signal processing applications onto heterogeneous platforms, parts of these applications will most likely be mapped into re-configurable components. The current trend of automating such mappings assumes that one can transform application specification to implementation specification without delving deep into details. This implies that one has to rely on the (re-)use of IP components, even when it remains unknown what the final exact specification of the implementation components will be. When it comes to 1) (re-)using of IP components, 2) porting of designs from one platform (component) to another, and 3) relying on IP components in high-level (task-level) application to (re-configurable) platform (component) mapping, the design requirements and constraints are not well defined. To find out what they should be, we have conducted two case studies around the (re-)use of IP components; one focusing on the porting issue, and one dealing with the automated task-level mapping. The goal of these case studies was to identify and resolve the problems that come with the so-called completion logic or glue logic that hinders fast and accurate IP embedding in a high-level implementation specification and description.

## 1 Introduction

Platform-based design [5] has emerged from the need to reduce design costs. A platform consists of a number of processing units on the one hand, and a communication, synchronization, and storage infrastructure on the other hand. The processing units are typically taken from a library of re-usable components. In many cases, both the application and the (platform) architecture are heterogeneous: different parts of the application are specified differently (using imperative languages, finite state machine and/or dataflow models, discrete event languages, etc) depending on the nature of the architecture components they have to be mapped into: programmable, configurable, dedicated, etc. [4]. To avoid too much abstract talking, we now assume that we deal with a high-throughput signal processing application (such as phased array signal processing) and that our application has been partitioned. We also assume that one of the partitions - say a Filter Bank (FB) is to be mapped onto a re-configurable processing unit, say a FPGA. At this stage of the design, the challenge is to provide methods and tools to map the FB onto the FPGA in such a way that:

A. Pimentel and S. Vassiliadis (Eds.): SAMOS 2004, LNCS 3133, pp. 264–273, 2004.

- We can rely on IP modules to specify our FPGA implementation.
- We do not have to refine our FB specification to the level of the IP module details.
- The integration of the IP modules in the implementation specification that matches the FB application specification is accurate and fast.
- Neither the FB's refinement nor the FPGA's detailed internals are frozen.
- The final implementation is optimal.

To find out whether these objectives are feasible and, if not, what is missing so far, we have conducted two case studies to identify the problems, if any, and to extract from our findings a list of requirements and constraints that may serve as a guide to the development or improvement of new or existing mapping strategies. The first case study deals with a handcrafted mapping of a polyphase filter bank application onto a FPGA component with emphasis on the IP integration completion logic and the portability of IP-based implementations across different FPGA fabrics. The second case study addresses the automated mapping of an application into a FPGA at a level of abstraction above IP module details. From these case studies we draw some general conclusions on IP integration for portability. The remaining of the paper is organized as follows. In section 2, we specify our first case study, and present our findings. In section 3, we present our second case study and the lessons we learned from it. Then, we propose our requirements and constraints for fast and accurate mapping methods.

## 2   Case Study I: Completion Logic and Portability

In this section we first present the problem statement. Next we briefly introduce the polyphase filter bank application. We, then, look into the specification of this application, given that it is to be mapped into a FPGA component. Finally, we move on to the implementation in two different FPGA fabrics, the completion logic problem, and the portability issue.

### 2.1   Problem Statement

IPs are available for implementing functions on a re-configurable platform without delving into the details of the mapping. It reduces the development time [2] to reach a satisfactory design. Integrating IPs has an impact on the design portability, as they are not platform independent. By this IP integration we avoid the refinement of our FB specification to the level of the IP module details. However,

- Application requirements can change as well as the architecture of the FPGA platform.
- IP modules implement behaviour that is not perfectly matching the specification.
- IP interfaces are not standardized.

Thus, the completion logic for the IP integration needs to evolve. We want to evaluate here the constraints and efforts needed to make an IP based design portable. The result needs to satisfy a number of objectives that are summarized in Table 1. Some of these can be conflicting (e.g. optimisation and development time) but need to be considered. The balance of these objectives for a particular design is a global optimality that is in terms of the metrics given in Table 1.

**Table 1.** Global optimality.

| Maximize | Minimize |
|---|---|
| Throughput | Resource usage |
| Reliability | Development time |
| Scalability | Dependence |
| Re-usability | Maintenance |

## 2.2 Application: Polyphase Filterbank

As an example of a high throughput signal-processing algorithm we implemented a polyphase filterbank (FB). Roughly speaking, a polyphase filterbank consists of a number of FIR filters whose inputs are derived from a decimated stream of signal samples and whose output are DFT transformed with an FFT as shown in Fig. 1. See standard text books [1] for details.

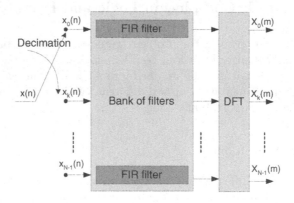

**Fig. 1.** Functional diagram of the FB.

## 2.3 Application Specifications for FPGA Implementation

The hardware implementation must be parallel and distributed in order to reach high throughputs. Therefore, choices must be made concerning the level of distribution and parallelism. These choices determine the partitioning of the application on the hardware. In the FB application, the functions (decimation, filters and FFT) are separated in blocks as is shown in Fig. 1. Inside the shaded filter block, filters are mapped on a set of N MACs (Multiplier Accumulator) and memories. The FFT is a higher grain function that can be integrated as an IP module in the implementation. We propose to map the FB on two FPGA platforms from different manufacturers (Stratix from Altera [7] and Virtex-II Pro from Xilinx [8]) to evaluate the portability of a design. These two platforms offer distributed local memory and embedded multipliers that can be seen as low grain IPs.

### 2.4 Implementation: Glue Logic and Portability Issues

Each FFT IP used for the FB implementation has a specific interface and their utilisation varies. One is accessing vectors stored in a buffer whereas the other one receives samples as tokens. The data formats as well as the function transformations are not equivalent. The control of the interface, then, must be dedicated in order to match this specificity. The low grain IPs (embedded multipliers, DSP or specific memory blocks) are controlled also by means of completion logic to accommodate the IP specificities.

The completion logic corresponds to local controllers in the sense that only the main control signals (start/stop/reset) of the IP and the I/O data flow manipulations (read/write addresses) are considered. This type of controller is also synchronized at system-level to operate only on flows of data. Its internal synchronization does not interact with the upper level synchronization (Globally Asynchronous, Locally Synchronous (GALS)). Therefore the upper layer control can be easily ported and the only control that needs to be changed is the local one, which is block (or IP) specific. The FB application is implemented on a Stratix EP1S20 and a Virtex-II Pro XC2VP20. The results are given in Table 2 in terms of cells (logic elements: LE), embedded multipliers (EM), memory (Mem) and speed. Given the same throughput requirements, the implementations satisfy the same objectives in terms of size, memory usage etc. as defined in Table 1.

**Table 2.** Polyphase filterbank benchmark on Stratix and Virtex-II Pro.

| Target | IP cores | LE(k) | EM | Mem(kbits) | Speed(MS/s) |
|--------|----------|-------|-----|-----------|-------------|
| Stratix | 4, pipe, float | 10.5 | 32x9 bits | 200 | 80 |
| Virtex-II Pro | 1, fix | 7.5 | 12x18 bits | 200 | 80 |

There are variations observed in the implementation size concerning the logic elements (cells). For one implementation, IPs are pipelined and each IP is controlled independently. In the other case, only one IP is controlled and this reduces the resource usage. Both the high grain IP interfacing and the IP specification forced us to re-write the completion logic for these functions while porting from one design to the other. Nonetheless, the application partitioning remained the same. For the functions implemented with low grain IPs only minor changes in the completion logic were needed for synchronization purposes. This was possible because the interface controllers and IP functions were parameterised in the original design. Some of the FB sub-systems application refinement could also be unfolded and skewed to adapt to the different platforms constraints. In order to synchronize and check the integrated design, about half of the time was spent on simulations. The rest of the time was mainly spent on writing completion logic.

# 3   Case Study II: Automated Task Level Mapping

In the previous section we have considered a hand-crafted FPGA implementation of a high-throughput signal processing application. We paid particular attention to problems related to completion logic and portability when it comes to the integration of IP components and the effect of these on implementation cost in terms of effort, time, and loss of optimality. In the last decade, several research groups in academia and industry have been proposing and prototyping methods and tools for the (semi-) automated mapping of applications into platforms, or at least parts of applications into parts (components) of platforms. See e.g., [6], [10], [11]. Given the list of challenges in the introduction, we have been particularly interested in ascertaining whether these approaches can lead to designs and implementations that can compete with our handcrafted references. Compete in the sense of global optimality, e.g. the trading of the resource usage against the development time.

## 3.1   Automated Mapping of an Application into a FPGA

In the approaches given above, the implementation is facilitated with high levels of specification for example in Matlab, Simulink or C. One approach followed by the CAD industry [10] [11] is a graphical specification. We experimented with the implementation of the FB with a Simulink entry: DSP Builder (Altera [7]) and System Generator for DSP (Xilinx [8]). We draw here some conclusions.

Positive aspects:

- They allow combination of portable, platform independent VHDL together with IPs.
- They facilitate the integration of manufacturer IPs by providing a fast and easy to use simulation, verification and debugging environment.

Limitations:

- The implementation specification relies on specific libraries that are manufacturer dependent.
- The specification can not be parameterized.

In particular, it implies that the application requirements cannot be modified without rewriting the completion logic. This is also the case when porting onto another platform. It can be concluded that these tools cannot be used to specify a complex system with multiple functions. However, they have been used successfully to fast-prototype elements of the system with a reliable test environment.

Another approach to avoid the manual refinement of the application without graphical entries was tested. We used the Compaan tool [17] to extract the parallelism of a cross-correlation application specified in a subset of Matlab. The specification is automatically transformed in a process network specification. With the Laura tool [18], this network is mapped onto the FPGA platform. Laura can generate the skeleton of the partitioned application, with a controller for each partition. It leaves space for the designers to integrate the actual functions the way they want (e.g. IPs). Each function and its dedicated controller are surrounded by FIFOs to physically separate the partitions.

Positive:

- Compaan helps the refinement of a high level specification and can shorten the time to analyze the partitioning.
- Laura can generate the skeleton of the network to encapsulate IPs.

Limitations:

- The completion logic generated automatically uses about 35 % more resources for this case study than the hand crafted design.
- IPs need to be integrated after each generation of the VHDL skeleton.
- The IPs optimum performances are not reached. In this case study the loss in the maximum operating frequency was about 40 %.

In particular, it implies that if the requirements or the FPGA platform are changed, the intermediate completion logic and interfaces can be generated again for the system but the IPs need to be re-inserted with their glue logic and the integrated design re-verified. In addition, in the system implemented, the IP performances are not optimally exploited. A modification of the VHDL for performance optimization is possible but involves modifications on the others blocks of the design that are complex. If the generated code is modified, the advantage of a fast code generation is lost and moreover the design cannot be ported as this operation would be necessary for every instance of the system specification. The optimizations are for instance the use of particular resources (e.g. local memories on a platform) in the mapping phase or the customization of the buffer sizes or the channel time multiplexing. Of course the development time can be traded against the optimum resource usage on the component and it can be considered as an optimal solution for implementing small scale but complex applications.

## 3.2   Discussion

We discuss here the results obtained with the automated approaches and according to our objectives of optimization. In particular, for the cases we studied, there are multiple point to point connections in between processes and the distribution of tokens on the network becomes complex. The task of distributing

the data is not automated when using a graphical entry tool for the specification. Therefore only a few cases can be developed fast in practice (i.e. power
of 2 in the module multiplicity). On one hand, this is a limitation in terms of
scalability and reusability. Scalability because allocating multiple instances of a
single IP (like a FIR filter in the FB design) would imply to interface all the
IPs to the rest of the design by hand. Reusability because the schematics need
to be reentered. On the other hand, this kind of design is easy to verify with
the test environment that is provided together with Simulink. It improves the
reliability of the design process. Last but not least, designing with such tools is
a way to obtain relatively high throughput and low resource usage for simple
designs (close to handcrafted designs). However, the end result is a prototype
that is dependent on a FPGA fabric.

The Compaan-Laura tool chain automatically controls the distribution of
tokens on the networks. As already mentioned, it mainly results in an increase in
the resource usage and a suboptimum throughput. However, this approach helps
to scale designs in an efficient way by modifying only the high-level specifications.
Indeed, it was possible to scale the correlator IP to build a cross correlator simply
by modifying the specifications of the Matlab code (entry of Compaan). This
scalability provided by this tool is then a way to reach the reuse of IP, but the
completion logic problem is not completely solved with this approach. Verifying
the distribution of the tokens on the implementation and at inter-task level is
not an easy task as patterns are not regular. Even if the Compaan-Laura tool
chain is currently platform dependent, it could support different targets in the
future.

The comparisons between handcrafted designs and the two semi-automated
approaches evaluated in this paper are summarized in Table 3 with respect to
the criteria given in Table 1.

**Table 3.** Design approaches and observations with respect to global optimality criteria
for the case studies. (1) satisfactory; (2) can be improved; (3) limitation.

|  | Handcrafted | Simulink entry | Compaan-Laura |
|---|---|---|---|
| Throughput | 1 | 2 | 3 |
| Resource usage | 1 | 1 | 3 |
| Reliability (verification) | 3 | 2 | 2 |
| Scalability | 2 | 3 | 1 |
| re-usability | 2 | 3 | 2 |
| Development time | 3 | 1 | 2 |
| Dependence | 2 | 3 | 2 |

To strengthen these observations and reproduce them in the future, procedures need to be elaborated that are more precise. Indeed, a-priori knowledge
on the flows and the applications is a bias in this comparison and particularly
for the development time.

### 3.3 Requirements and Constraints for Fast and Accurate Mapping Methods

We identified in the case studies the difficulties in re-using a design. This is a time consuming task particularly if the systems are complex and if different platforms are considered. This problem is similar to designing a multi-platform multi-requirement IP. A higher level of abstraction can be reached for the specification only if the interfaces in between the blocks can be easily glued. The fast and accurate mapping methods are devised for generating a skeleton code automatically around IPs. However the completion logic around the IP cannot be re-used. This is due to the non-standard control and interfacing of IPs. For an automated mapping to be feasible, the IP interfaces should be described and characterized. OCP-IP [9] provides a uniform and common interface for IPs. OCP- IP guides a designer in generating an IP interface that could be wrapped into the generated code of a more complex system. This could reduce the efforts particularly when a systematic code generation approach is followed. Another constraint comes from the mapping onto the platform's embedded components that are not only treated as independent IPs. A coarse description of the platform targeted needs to be provided for the mapping to be accurate according to designer's requirements for optimization. The designer's intervention is still required to force a mapping decision (equivalent to a compilation directive) to explore alternatives.

Multiple implementation options must be tried and their validity checked. It is a time consuming task that must be assisted. A fast test environment should be provided. The behavioral models of the IP functions must be available in the high-level specification language. From there, it should allow for the generation of the test vectors at every level of abstraction and in between every functional block. In this way iterative refinement methods can be supported and larger designs can be handled. The FB implementation is also an IP that should be re-used on different platforms as part of a larger system. In this system, the FB is re-configured by and synchronized with an external control interface. This control arbitrates other subsystems on the chip and communicates with external controllers. This top down control hierarchy is illustrated in the system hierarchy shown in Fig. 2 where the IPs must be glued and configured to allow for cross platform interactions. Moreover the FB is interfaced with other subsystems and to low grain IPs such as I/O lines (e.g. LVDS, Rocket I/O). We need to specify these interfaces uniformly such that designs can be ported and efficiently reused.

## 4   Related Work

Organizations such as Virtual Socket Interface Alliance [13] or the Object Management Group [14] are currently specifying open interfaces standards for components to be integrated into sockets. Others such as the System Design Industrial Council-Telecom (SYDIC-Telecom) [15] analyse also the design flows in relation with specification languages and formalism analysis to address the issues of design re-use starting from a system level conceptual level. Voros [3] contributed

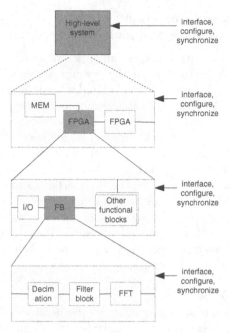

**Fig. 2.** Hierarchy of the designs.

to this research by identifying the common basis in all these approaches in particular the parameterization issue [12] in various aspects of granularity and the encapsulation of IPs in an object oriented system design [16]. Objects provide for a structural representation of the information through all abstraction levels.

## 5   Conclusion

Two case studies have been conducted around the reuse of IPs in re-configurable components. They allowed for identification of the problems that come with completion logic for accurate IP embedding. We first implemented a high throughput signal processing application across different FPGA fabrics. The specified implementation matched our requirements. However, difficulties were encountered for adapting to different IP controls and interfaces. Then we used tools to automate the mapping at higher levels of abstraction. This approach helped to shorten the overall implementation specification time but we encountered many disparities between the tools we manipulated, especially concerning IP interfacing and (re-)use of completion logic. Finally, we proposed directions for improving the high-level design tools with respect to these issues. First, they should support the specification of an IP wrapper that can be interfaced in a systematic way. Second, these tools should automate the mapping procedure from a unique high-level specification of the system. This includes both a high level specification of the application and of the architecture. The tools could allow then for fast iterations in this design space.

# References

1. R. Crochiere and L. Rabiner. Fundamental of Multirate Signal Processing. Prentice-Hall, 1983
2. M. Keating and P. Bricaud. Reuse Methodology Manual, 3rd edition. Kluwer Academic Publishers, 2002
3. N. S. Voros. System Design Reuse, Chapter 7, pp 79- 99. Kluwer Academic Publishers, 2003
4. S. Alliot. Architecture Exploration for Large Scale Array Signal Processing Systems. PhD thesis, December 2003, Leiden University, The Netherlands
5. A. Sangiovanni-Vincentelli. Defining platform- based design. EEDesign of EE-Times, February 2002
6. T. Harris et al. Compilation from Matlab to Process Networks Realized in FPGA. Kluwer Academic Publishers, Apr. 2002
7. http://www.altera.com
8. http://www.xilinx.com
9. Open Core Protocol International Partnership http://www.ocpip.org/about/ocp
10. http://www.mentor.com/fpga
11. http://www.synopsys.com
12. T. Givaris, F. Vahid, J. Henkel. System-Level Exploration for Pareto-optimal Configurations in Parameterized SoC, Proc. IEEE/ACM ICCCAD, Nov. 2001
13. VSI, Virtual Socket Interface Alliance, http://www.vsi.org
14. OMG, Object Management Group, http://www.omg.org
15. CSYDIC-Telecom, System Design Industrial Council of European Telecom Industries, http://sydic.vitamib.com
16. F. Doucet and R. Gupta. Microelectronic SoC Modeling using Objects and their Relationships. 1st Online Symposium for Electrical Engineers, may 2003
17. B. Kienhuis, E. Rypkema, and E. Deprettere. Compaan: Deriving Process Networks form Matlab for Embedded Signal Processing Architectures. In Proc. Of the 8th International workshop on the Hardware/Software Codesign (CODES), May 2000
18. C. Zissulescu, T. Stefanov, B. Kienhuis, and E. Deprettere. LAURA:Leiden Architecture Research and Exploration Tool. In Proc. 13th Int. Conference on Field Programmable Logic and Applications (FPL'03), Sept. 2003

# Customising Hardware Designs
# for Elliptic Curve Cryptography

Nicolas Telle, Wayne Luk, and Ray C.C. Cheung

Department of Computing, Imperial College,
180 Queen's Gate, London, England

**Abstract.** This paper presents a method for producing hardware designs for Elliptic Curve Cryptography (ECC) systems over the finite field $GF(2^m)$, using the optimal normal basis for the representation of numbers. A design generator has been developed which can automatically produce a customised ECC hardware design that meets user-defined requirements. This method enables designers to rapidly explore and implement a design with the best trade-offs in speed, size and level of security. To facilitate performance characterisation, we have developed formulæ for estimating the number of cycles for our generic ECC architecture. The resulting hardware implementations are among the fastest reported, and can often run several orders of magnitude faster than software implementations.

## 1 Introduction

Elliptic curve cryptography (ECC) is a public key cryptography system which is superior to the well-known RSA cryptography: for the same key size, it gives a higher security level than RSA. This paper presents a method for producing hardware designs for ECC systems over $GF(2^m)$, using the Optimal Normal Basis (ONB) for the representation of numbers.

The unique feature of our approach is a design generator which can automatically produce a customised ECC hardware design that satisfies specific user-defined requirements. This method enables designers to rapidly explore and implement a design with the best trade-offs in speed, size and level of security.

When optimised for speed, our design generator produces ECC designs with extensive parallelisation and pipelining. These designs do not involve instructions, to avoid overhead associated with instruction fetch and decode. Our architecture is generic: for instance, a user-defined parameter controls the amount of parallelism in evaluating field multiplication. Once this and other parameters are decided, various design-specific constants, wiring patterns and data widths are generated automatically.

To facilitate performance characterisation, we have developed formulæ for estimating the number of cycles for our generic ECC architecture. These formulæ are expressed in terms of various customisation parameters, such as the key size, the amount of parallelism in function evaluation, and the number of cycles for basic operations like point addition and point multiplication.

As an example, for a key size of 270 bits, a point multiplication, which is the slowest operation in the ECC method, can be computed in 0.36 ms with our hardware design

A. Pimentel and S. Vassiliadis (Eds.): SAMOS 2004, LNCS 3133, pp. 274–283, 2004.

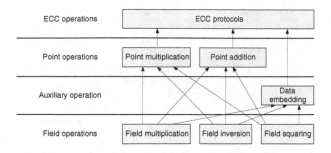

**Fig. 1.** Interactions between different operations.

implemented in an XC2V6000 FPGA at 66 MHz. In contrast, an optimised software implementation requires 196.71 ms on a dual-Xeon computer at 2.6 GHz; so our FPGA design is more than 540 times faster, while its clock speed is almost 40 times slower than the Xeon processors.

Previous work includes: reconfigurable finite-field multiplier [6], ASIC designs for field operations over specific $GF(2^m)$ fields [10], an ECC processor on a smart card device [13], and recent FPGA implementations for ECC designs [1, 2, 5, 7, 8, 11]. We shall first present our ECC architecture, followed by implementation details and results, and finally a comparison of various designs.

## 2   ECC: Architecture

This section describes the operations supported by our ECC architecture. These operations include field multiplication, field inversion, point multiplication and so on, and their interaction is summarised in Figure 1. In the following, $m$ is the key size for our ECC architecture, which is a characteristic of the field.

**Field multiplication.** We first develop an architecture for field multiplication. The multiplication of two elements of $GF(2^m)$ defined using a normal basis, $c = a \times b$, is defined by the coefficients $c_k$ ($k \in [0, m-1]$) where

$$c_k = \sum_{j=0}^{m-1} \sum_{i=0}^{m-1} a_{i+k} b_{j+k} \lambda_{ij}$$

The $\lambda_{ij}$'s are the elements of the *multiplication matrix* $\Lambda$, which are either 0 or 1. Every sum of inner product in the above equation can be written in the form:

$$\sum_{i=0}^{m-1} a_{i+k} b_{j+k} \lambda_{ij} = b_r(a_p + a_q)$$

for some $r, p, q \in [0, m-1]$, except for $j = 0$ where (for some $r, p \in [0, m-1]$):

$$\sum_{i=0}^{m-1} a_{i+k} b_{j+k} \lambda_{ij} = b_r(a_p)$$

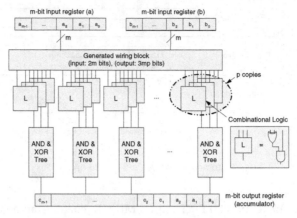

**Fig. 2.** Parametic field multiplier design.

Our architecture is based on having $p$ copies of a serial $m$-bit multiplier running in parallel. Figure 2 shows the datapath of our field multiplier. The wiring block is automatically generated for different $m$ values and is described in Section 4.

**Field inversion.** The algorithm used for field inversion is based on *Fermat's theorem* which states that in a normal basis:

$$a^{-1} = a^{2^m - 2} = \left(a^{(2^{m-1}-1)}\right)^2$$

Using this formula to compute an inverse, it would require $m$ multiplications. The following reduces the complexity of the inversion, as it is easy to calculate $x^{2^{(m-1)/2}+1}$ where $x$ is shifted $(m-1)/2$ times and then multiplied by $x$.

$m - 1$ is even: $a^{(2^{m-1}-1)} = a^{(2^{(m-1)/2}+1)\cdot(2^{(m-1)/2}-1)} = \left(a^{2^{(m-1)/2}-1}\right)^{2^{(m-1)/2+1}}$

$m - 1$ is odd:
$$a^{(2^{m-1}-1)} = a^{(2(2^{(m-2)/2}-1)(2^{(m-2)/2}+1)+1)} = \left((a^{2^{(m-2)/2}-1})^{2^{(m-2)/2}+1}\right)^2 \cdot a$$

The algorithm is described below:

Input: $a \in GF(2^m)$ to be inverted
Output: $x = a^{-1}$

  - $x \leftarrow a$ ; $s \leftarrow log_2(m) - 1$
  - while $s \geq 0$
      • $r \leftarrow$ right shift $m$ by $s$ bits
      • $y \leftarrow$ left shift $x$ by $\lfloor r/2 \rfloor$
      • $y \leftarrow$ multiply $x$ by $y$
      • if $x$ is odd
              $y \leftarrow$ left shift $y$ by 1 bit
              $y \leftarrow$ multiply $x$ by $y$
      • $x \leftarrow y$
      • $s \leftarrow s - 1$
  - $x \leftarrow$ left shift $x$ by 1 bit
  - return $x$

If we consider the time to perform a multiplication is much longer than the time to perform a shift operation, the number of cycles for this algorithm can be approximated by the following equation where $T_{mult}$ represents the number of cycles to perform a field multiplication:

$$(\log_2(m-1) + \text{number\_of\_bits\_set\_in}(m-1) - 1) \times T_{mult}$$

**Field squaring and field addition.** Field squaring is simply a left rotation in hardware and field addition is an XOR operation. Therefore these two functions take up little space in hardware.

**Point multiplication.** This part presents the point operations based on the following elliptic curve:

$$y^2 + xy = x^3 + a_2x^2 + a_6$$

Let $P$, $P_1$ and $P_2$ be three points of an elliptic curve $E$ and assume that the property $P_2 - P_1 = P$ holds. Let the (affine) $x$-coordinate of $P_i$ ($i \in \{1, 2\}$) be $X_i/Z_i$ where $X_i$ and $Z_i$ are the first and third projective coordinate of $P$.

It can be shown that the $y$-coordinate of any of the three points are not required in computing the $x$-coordinate ($X/Z$) of $P_1 + P_2$ or of $2P_i$. Hence, in the main loop of the algorithm, we can get rid of these $y$-coordinates and use the above formula to compute the $x$-coordinate of $2P_i$ and $P_1 + P_2$ at each step. When the main computation is over, we can get the $y$-coordinate of the result point by using the following formula which is proved in [9]:

$$y_1 = (x_1 + x) \cdot ((x_1 + x) \cdot ((x_2 + x) + x^2 + y)/x) + y$$

The improved Montgomery algorithm for point multiplication becomes:

---

Input: $k \in GF(2^m)$ ($k = (k_{l-1}, \cdots, k_1, k_0)$), $P(x, y)$ a point of a certain curve $E$ defined by $a_2$ and $a_6$
Output: $Q = k \cdot P$

- $X_1 \leftarrow X; Z_1 \leftarrow 1; X_2 \leftarrow x^4 + a_6; Z_2 \leftarrow x^2$
- for $i$ from $l - 1$ downto 0 do
    if $k_i = 1$ then
        $(Z_1, X_1) \leftarrow Madd(X_1, Z_1, X_2, Z_2)$;
        $(Z_2, X_2) \leftarrow Mdouble(X_2, Z_2)$
    else
        $(Z_2, X_2) \leftarrow Madd(X_2, Z_2, X_1, Z_1)$;
        $(Z_1, X_1) \leftarrow Mdouble(X_1, Z_1)$
- return $Q = Mxy(X_1, Z_1, X_2, Z_2)$

where:

- $Madd(X_1, Z_1, X_2, Z_2)$ returns $(Z_3, X_3)$ where
  $Z_3 = (X_1 \cdot Z_2 + X_2 \cdot Z_1)^2$ and $X_3 = x \cdot Z_3 + (X_1 \cdot Z_2) \cdot (X_2 \cdot Z_1)$,
- $Mdouble(X_1, Z_1)$ returns $(Z_3, X_3)$ where
  $Z_3 = Z_i^2 \cdot X_i^2$ and $X_3 = X_i^4 + a_6 \cdot Z_i^4$,
- $Mxy(X_1, Z_1, X_2, Z_2)$ returns $Q(x_1, y_1)$ where
  $x_1 = X_1/Z_1$ and $y_1 = (x_1 + x) \cdot ((x_1 + x) \cdot (x_2 + x) + x^2 + y)/x + y$.

---

This algorithm requires $6l + 10$ multiplications and only one inversion, where $l$ is the number of bits needed to represent $k$ in base 2. The value of $l$ is usually close to the value of $m$. The algorithm used for point multiplication is mainly sequential, since each step of the loop needs the results of the previous step to start.

Since the two functions $Madd$ and $Mdouble$ can be computed independently in parallel, the number of cycles for point multiplication can be reduced by 33.3%. The reason is that the $Madd$ function requires 4 field multiplications, and the $Mdouble$ function requires 2 field multiplications; both functions take the time of 6 field multiplications to execute sequentially, while a parallel design takes the time of 4 field multiplications. This improvement is significant, since each step in the loop is executed around $m$ times, where $m$ is typically between 100 and 500. This flexible field multiplication function can be made large or small, fast or slow depending on the performance required. Since other functions involve extensive use of the field multiplier, an optimised design is crucial and has a large impact on the final ECC system.

**Point addition and point subtraction.** Although point addition is not as common as point multiplication, some security protocols require both. The algorithm used to compute this operation is simple. Adding $P(x_1, y_1)$ and $Q(x_2, y_2)$ $(P \neq Q)$ gives $R(x_3, y_3)$ where:

$$\theta = (y_2 - y_1)/(x_2 - x_1)$$
$$x_3 = \theta^2 + \theta + x_1 + x_2 + a_2$$
$$y_3 = \theta(x_1 + x_3) - y_1$$

The details of the algorithm are not included here. Our system will also support point subtraction. To compute subtraction, we develop an algorithm that can invert a point. The negation of a point $P(x, y)$ is $-P(x, x + y)$. The addition algorithm requires 1 field inversion and 2 field multiplications. The point inversion algorithm takes negligible time, as it only requires an XOR operation.

**Data embedding.** Data embedding embeds data onto a point of an elliptic curve. Not all elements of $GF(2^m)$ are $x$-coordinate of a point of a given elliptic curve, and the ECC technique only allows the encryption of a point. It is therefore necessary to embed data into a point in order to encrypt them.

It has been shown that, given a specific elliptic curve, if 5 *don't care* bits are appended to $m - 5$ bits of data, there always exists at least one value of the don't care bits for $x$ to stay on the curve. The skeleton of the embedding algorithm is the following:

---

Input: $d$ data written in base 2 (the data must be of length $m - 5$ bits)
Output: $M(x, y)$ point in which the data to be encrypted are stored

- $x \leftarrow append(d, 00000_2)$
- while not $on\_curve(x)$
    increment $x$
- $compute\_y(x)$
- return $M(x, y)$

---

where $on\_curve(x)$ checks if $x \in GF(2^m)$ is the $x$-coordinate of a point of the curve that we are working on. $compute\_y(x)$ returns the $y$-coordinate of one of the two points whose $x$-coordinate is $x$. The equation of the curve is

$$y^2 + xy = x^3 + a_2 x^2 + a_6 \Rightarrow y^2 + xy + f(x) = 0$$

where $f(x) = -(x^3 + a_2 x^2 + a_6)$. Let $y = zx$, the equation becomes (if $x \neq 0$):

$$(xz)^2 + x^2 z + f(x) = 0 \Rightarrow z^2 + z + c = 0$$

where $c = f(x) \cdot x^{-2}$. The function $on\_curve(x)$ is described below:

---

Input: $x \in GF(2^m)$ bits
Output: true if $x$ is the $x$-coordinate of a point, false otherwise

- $c \leftarrow (x^3 + a_2 x^2 + a_6) \cdot x^{-2}$
- $trace \leftarrow$ XOR of all bits in $c$
- if $trace = 1$ then
        return false
- else
        return true

---

We compute $-f(x) \cdot x^{-2}$ instead of $f(x) \cdot x^{-2}$ since $\forall u \in GF(2^m)$, $-u$ is defined by $u + (-u) = 0$, that is $u$ XOR $(-u) = 0$ and $-u = u$. To compute the $y$-coordinate given the $x$-coordinate, We can rewrite the equation we are working on as ($i \in [0, m-1]$):

$$z = z^{1/2} + c^{1/2} \Rightarrow z_i = z_{i-1} + c_{i-1}$$

Moreover, if $z$ is a solution of our equation, then the other solution is $z + 1$. It is easy to prove this by assuming $z^2 + z + c = 0$ and by calculating

$$\begin{aligned}(z+1)^2 + (z+1) + c &= z^2 + 2z + 1 + z + 1 + c \\ &= z^2 + z + c + 2(z+1) \\ &= z^2 + z + c = 0\end{aligned}$$

In this proof, an addition is just an XOR operation in $GF(2^m)$, then $\forall u \in GF(2^m)$, $2u = 0$. Since $z + 1$ is actually $\bar{z}$ in a normal basis, in one of the two solutions the least significant bit will be 0 and the other one will be 1. As a result, the least significant bit of the solution that we are looking for is equal to 0. We then further compute all the other bits one by one. To compute the $y$ value, we simply multiply $z$ by $x$.

The algorithm that performs the operation $compute\_y(x)$ is described below:

---

Input: $x \in GF(2^m)$ (and $c$ calculated in function $on\_curve(x)$)
Output: $M(x, y)$ a point of the curve we are working on

- $z_0 \leftarrow 0$
- for $i$ from 1 to $m - 1$
        $z_i \leftarrow z_{i-1} + c_{i-1}$
- $y \leftarrow x \cdot z$
- return $y$

---

**Table 1.** Number of clock cycles required for each function to execute.

| Operation | Number of cycles |
|---|---|
| Field operations | |
| Addition | 1 |
| Squaring | 1 |
| Multiplication | $4 + 2\lfloor m/p \rfloor$    or    $2 + (2m/p)$ if $m$ is divisible by $p$ |
| Inversion | $2 + (\lceil log_2(m) \rceil - 2)(3 + T_{mult}) + s(m-1)(3 + T_{mult}) + ns(m-1)$ |
| Point operations | |
| Addition | $12 + 2T_{mult} + T_{inv}$ |
| Subtraction | $1 + T_{point\_add}$ |
| Multiplication | $28 + 10T_{mult} + T_{inv} + (m - \lceil log_2(k) \rceil) + (\lceil log_2(k) \rceil - 1)(14 + 6T_{mult})$ |
| Data embedding | $6 + 3T_{mult} + nb\_attempts(8 + T_{inv} + T_{mult})$ |

## 3   ECC: FPGA Implementation

This section presents the implemention of our design to produce a customizable encryption/decryption system. We have implemented our designs in Handel-C [3]. The key components in our design are: field operations (multiplication, inversion, squaring, addition), point operations (multiplication, addition), and data embedding.

Functions are implemented as shared logic. They will only be mapped once on the hardware. We then generate the routing logic and the control logic to send the appropriate data to these functions and fetch the result when necessary. The system performance has been optimised by exploring the maximum possible parallelism between operations and high-level descriptions. We also notice that because these functions called each other many times and have to send large values (usually two or three $m$ bits values) to each other every time, the design's speed is limited by parameter passing. To tackle this problem, all function calls have been pipelined.

The estimation of the number of clock cycles required by each function is presented in Table 1. Notations for this table include: $T_{mult}$, $T_{inv}$ and $T_{point\_add}$ represent the number of cycles of field multiplication, field inversion and point addition functions respectively, and $s(x)$ and $ns(x)$ represent the number of set bits and of clear bits in the binary representation of $x$. The $nb\_attempts$ in the data embedding formula represents the number of times the data need to be incremented to find the $x$-coordinate of a point.

## 4   Automatic Generation and Customisation

This section presents a code generator which can automatically generate an implementation with optimised speed, size and level of security. The major customisable elements of a cryptosystem are: the key size $m$, the degree of parallelism $p$, and the protocols of the system.

**Code generator.** We develop a program that takes a valid ONB $m$-value (type I or type II optimal normal basis) and the degree of parallelism in the field multiplication function, and produces synthesizeable Handel-C code. The code generator first computes the $\Lambda$ table for the given $m$ using the algorithm presented in [14]. This algorithm generates an $m \times 2$ matrix (Lambda) where the $j^{th}$ row contains two values of $i$ for which:

if $GF(2^m)$ has an ONB of type I: $2^i + 2^j$ equals 1 or 0 in mod $(m + 1)$,
if $GF(2^m)$ has an ONB of type II: $2^i \pm 2^j$ equals $\pm 1$ in mod $(2m + 1)$.

When $j = 0$, there is only one value of $j$ that satisfies the equations. From the $\Lambda$ table, we generate the wiring pattern required by our field multiplication design. This wiring rearranges the $m$-bit inputs a and b into $3p$ $m$-bit variables:

```
inputa1[0],···,inputa1[p-1],
inputa2[0],···,inputa2[p-1],
inputb[0],···,inputb[p-1],
```
where:
```
inputb[i]_k (the k^th bit) is b_(2k-i),
inputa1[i]_k is a_(Lambda[k,0]+k-i),
inputa2[i]_k is a_(Lambda[k,1]+k-i).
```

The code generator computes all the constants that are used by various functions. In particular, it computes $s = \lfloor m/p \rfloor$ and $r = m \bmod p$ used in field multiplication. It also calculates the size of these variables and some other values such as the constant 1 in $GF(2^m)$ which is an $m$-bit variable with all its bits set.

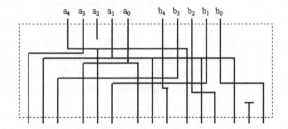

**Fig. 3.** Example of a wiring block when m = 5 and p = 1.

**Protocol generator.** The protocol generator enables users to choose appropriate encryption protocols for their applications. For example, a system can easily implement an encryption/decryption protocol using a particular elliptic curve. Users can store their private keys in the FPGA.

## 5 Results and Evaluation

In this section, we compare the performance of various software and hardware implementations for point multiplication, which is the bottleneck of ECC systems. We have implemented the software design [14] on a dual-processor Intel Xeon 2.66GHz with 4 GB of RAM. We also compare our design with the fastest existing FPGA ECC cryptosystem over $GF(2^m)$. The comparison for serial and parallel designs on different $m$ and $p$ values, where $p$ refers to the degree of parallelisation, is presented in Table 2. Our hardware design has been implemented on an RC2000 board containing an XC2V6000

FPGA chip. It can cope with values of $m$ up to 453 for $p = 1$ or $m = 418$ for $p = 8$. The "Speedup" column shows the performance gain of our design over other methods. This gain is due to our architecture which does not involve instruction fetch and decode.

**Table 2.** Comparison between our design and the reference designs [8, 14]. The symbol (*) denotes extrapolated results based on published data for different $m$ values.

| $p$ | Our design time(ms) | Software [14] time(ms) | speedup | Hardware (serial) [8] time(ms) | speedup | Our design time (ms) | Hardware (parallel) [8] time(ms) | speedup |
|---|---|---|---|---|---|---|---|---|
| | | | $m = 162$ | | | | $m = 113$ | |
| 2 | 2.51 | 45.67 | 18.20 | 9.39* | 3.74 | 1.23 | 2.6 | 2.11 |
| 8 | 0.69 | 45.67 | 66.18 | 9.39* | 13.61 | 0.36 | 1.06 | 2.94 |
| 16 | 0.39 | 45.67 | 117.10 | 9.39* | 24.08 | 0.21 | 0.81 | 3.86 |
| 32 | 0.24 | 45.67 | 190.29 | 9.39* | 39.13 | 0.13 | 0.79 | 6.08 |
| 56 | 0.15 | 45.67 | 304.47 | 9.39* | 62.60 | - | - | - |
| | | | $m = 270$ | | | | $m = 473$ | |
| 2 | 6.84 | 196.71 | 28.76 | 27.99* | 4.09 | 20.68 | 69.2 | 3.35 |
| 8 | 1.79 | 196.71 | 109.89 | 27.99* | 15.64 | 5.38 | 19.1 | 3.55 |
| 16 | 0.95 | 196.71 | 207.06 | 27.99* | 29.46 | 2.78 | 12.7 | 4.57 |
| 32 | 0.55 | 196.71 | 357.65 | 27.99* | 50.89 | - | - | - |
| 56 | 0.36 | 196.71 | 546.41 | 27.99* | 77.75 | - | - | - |

We also compare our design with other existing hardware cryptosystems. Table 3 shows the performance improvement by using our design (with the maximum implementable value for $p$) for the $m$-values that have been published. We adopt maximum parallelism since a large speed improvement can be obtained by a small area increase.

**Table 3.** Comparison between our design and other existing hardware designs. PB stands for polynomial basis and ONB stands for optimal normal basis.

| Name | Year | Platform | Basis | $m$ | Timing | Slices | Our timing (largest $p$) | speedup |
|---|---|---|---|---|---|---|---|---|
| Rosner [15] | 1998 | XC4062 | PB | 168 | 4.47 ms | 956 | 0.12 ms | 37.25 |
| Orlando [12] | 2000 | XCV400E | PB | 167 | 0.21 ms | 1512 | 0.12 ms | 1.75 |
| Ernst [4] | 2001 | XC4085XLA | ONB | 155 | 1.3 ms | 2346 | 0.12 ms | 10.83 |
| Leong (serial) [8] | 2002 | XCV1000 | ONB | 173 | 11.1 ms | 2148 | 0.12 ms | 92.5 |
| Leong (parallel) [8] | 2002 | XCV1000 | ONB | 113 | 0.75 ms | 8753 | 0.09 ms | 8.3 |
| Gura [5] | 2002 | XCV2000E | PB | 163 | 0.14 ms | 15768 | 0.12 ms | 1.16 |
| Kerins [7] | 2002 | XCV2000 | PB | 176 | 6.9 ms | - | 0.12 ms | 57.5 |
| Bednara (LFSR) [1] | 2002 | XCV1000 | PB | 191 | 3.72 ms | - | 0.15 ms | 24.8 |
| Bednara (parallel) [1] | 2002 | XCV1000 | PB | 191 | 0.50 ms | - | 0.15 ms | 3.33 |
| Nguyen [11] | 2003 | XC2V6000 | PB | 233 | 3.35 ms | - | 0.20 ms | 18.75 |

We find $m$ and $p$ vary linearly with the area. Given $p = 2$, for $m = 113$ the design requires 9001 FPGA slices whereas for $m = 270$, it requires 20555 slices. So increasing the key by 2.4 times (or increasing the security level radix by $\sqrt{2^{270} - 2^{162}}$), the design needs 2.3 times as many slices.

# 6    Summary

A customisable pipelined and parallelized Elliptic Curve Cryptography design for various field operations has been proposed. This design supports various parameters, such as the key size and the degree of parallelism to enable tradeoff between level of security, design size and speed. A code generator and protocol generator have been developed to facilitate fast implementation. Performance analysis shows that our design, the fastest amongst existing hardware implementations, at 66MHz can compute a point multiplication up to 540 times faster than a software ECC application on a dual-Xeon 2.66GHz computer. Our on-going and future work includes functional extensions, speed improvement, resource minimization, and exploring use of reconfiguration.

**Acknowledgments.** The support of Celoxica, Xilinx, the Croucher Foundation and UK EPSRC (Grant number GR/R 31409, GR/R 55931, GR/N 66599) is gratefully acknowledged.

# References

1. M. Bednara, M. Daldrup, J. Gathen, J. Shokrollahi and J. Teich, Reconfigurable Implementation of Elliptic Curve Crypto Algorithms. Reconfigurable Architectures Workshop, 2002.
2. M. Bednara et. al., Tradeoff Analysis of FPGA Based Elliptic Curve Cryptography. Proc. IEEE International Symposium on Circuits and Systems, vol V, pp. 797–800, 2002.
3. Celoxica, *Handel-C Language Reference Manual for DK2.0*, Document RM-1003-4.0, 2003.
4. M. Ernst et. al., Rapid Prototyping for Hardware Accelerated Elliptic Curve Public-Key Cryptosystems, Proc. Workshop on Rapid System Prototyping, pp. 24-29, 2001.
5. N. Gura et. al., An End-to-End Systems Approach to Elliptic Curve Cryptography, Cryptographic Hardware and Embedded Systems, LNCS 2523, pp. 349-365, Springer, 2002.
6. M. Jung, F. Madlener, E. Ernst and S.A. Huss, A Reconfigurable Coprocessor for Finite Field Multiplication in $GF(2^m)$, IEEE Workshop on Heterogeneous reconfigurable SoC, 2002.
7. T. Kerins et. al., Fully Parameterizable Elliptic Curve Cryptography Processor over GF($2^m$), Field-Programmable Logic and Applications, LNCS 2438, pp. 750-759, Springer, 2002.
8. P.H.W. Leong and K.H. Leung, A Microcoded Elliptic Curve Processor using FPGA Technology, IEEE Transactions on VLSI Systems, Vol. 10, No. 5, pp. 550-559, 2002
9. J. López and R. Dahab, Fast Multiplication on Elliptic Curves over $GF(2^m)$ without precomputation, Cryptographic Hardware and Embedded Systems, LNCS 1717, pp. 316-327, Springer, 1999.
10. E.D. Mastrovito, VLSI Architectures for Computation in Galois Fields, PhD Thesis, Linköping University, 1991.
11. N. Nguyen, K. Gaj, D. Caliga and T. El-Ghazawi, Implementation of Elliptic Curve Cryptosystems on a Reconfigurable Computer, Int. Conf. on Field Prog. Tech., pp. 60-67, 2003.
12. G. Orlando and C. Paar, A High Performance Reconfigurable Elliptic Curve for $GF(2^m)$, Cryptographic Hardware and Embedded Systems, LNCS 1965, pp. 41-56, Springer, 2000.
13. H. Pietiläinen, Elliptic Curve Cryptography on Smart Cards, MSc Thesis, Helsinki University of technology, 2000.
14. M. Rosing, Implementing Elliptic Curve Cryptography, Manning Ed, 1999.
15. M. Rosner, Elliptic Curve Cryptosystems on Reconfigurable hardware, MSc Thesis, Worcester Polytechnic Institute, 1998.
16. A. Woodbury, Efficient Algorithms for Elliptic Curve Cryptosystems on Embedded Systems, MSc Thesis, Worcester Polytechnic Institute, 2001.

# Dynamic Hardware Reconfigurations: Performance Impact for MPEG2

Elena Moscu Panainte, Koen Bertels, and Stamatis Vassiliadis

Computer Engineering Lab
Delft University of Technology, The Netherlands
{E.Panainte,K.Bertels,S.Vassiliadis}@et.tudelft.nl

**Abstract.** In this paper, we study the impact dynamic reconfiguration has on the performance of current reconfigurable technology. As a testbed, we use the Xilinx Virtex II Pro, the Molen experimental platform and the MPEG2 encoder as the application. We show for the MPEG2 encoder that a substantial overall performance improvement, up to 34 %, can be achieved when SAD, DCT and IDCT functions are executed on the reconfigurable hardware when the compiler anticipates and separates configuration from execution. This study also considers the impact inappropriate scheduling can have on the overall performance. We show that slowdowns of up to a factor 1000 are observed when the configuration latency is not hidden by the compiler. Our experiments show that appropriate scheduling allows to exploit up to 97% of the maximal theoretical speedup.

## 1 Introduction

The development of architectural improvements is a complex process as it deals with a large number of highly interconnected factors. An improvement in one component does not necessarily result in an improved system performance. This complexity increases considerably as heterogeneous architectures are included. The combination of a general purpose processor (GPP) and a Field Programmable Gate Array (FPGA) is becoming increasingly popular (e.g. [1], [2], [3]) as it allows developers to better partition and manage their projects (e.g. [4], [5] and [6]). Reconfigurable computing is a new style of computer architecture which, thanks to the availability of high density programmable logic chips, allows the designer to combine the advantages of both hardware (speed) and software (flexibility). A general paradigm that eliminates the shortcomings of other approaches in reconfigurable computing is described in [7] and in [8] and is referred to as the Molen Programming Paradigm. An important drawback of RC paradigm is the huge reconfiguration latency of the actual FPGA platforms. Based on the work described in [9] where a compiler for the Molen approach was presented, this paper addresses some open issues which primarily involve the hardware reconfiguration impact on performance. As will be explained in the remainder of this paper, the potential speedup of the kernel hardware executions can be completely wasted by inappropriate repetitive hardware reconfigurations.

A. Pimentel and S. Vassiliadis (Eds.): SAMOS 2004, LNCS 3133, pp. 284–292, 2004.

In this paper, we investigate the impact on the overall performance for the MPEG 2 benchmark of hardware reconfiguration in two cases: a) the straightforward approach when each hardware execution is preceded by the coresponding hardware configuration and b) when the hardware configuration can be anticipated and efficiently scheduled referring to the hardware execution. In this paper, we only Analise MPEG 2 encoder benchmark. Whenever in the remainder of the paper, we mention MPEG 2, we refer only to MPEG 2 encoding phase.

The main contributions of the paper can be summarized as follows:

- Based on profiling results, we determine that the maximal performance improvement of the Molen approach versus the pure software approach for the MPEG 2 benchmark that can be achieved by hardware execution of the kernel operations SAD, DCT and IDCT is about 65 %. We consider a set of real hardware implementations of these kernels and determine that the kernels hardware execution is up to 31x faster than the pure software execution.
- We estimate that, in the straightforward approach when each hardware execution is preceded by the coresponding hardware configuration, the huge reconfiguration latency of the hardware reconfiguration can slowdown the MPEG 2 benchmark by 3 order of magnitudes.
- A scheduling that anticipates the hardware configuration can eliminate the previous described drawback and provide a performance improvement up to 97 % from the maximal performance improvement of MPEG 2 benchmark.

The paper is organized as follows: in the next section, we present the Molen programming paradigm and describe a particular implementation, called the Molen processor. Section 3 describes the necessary compiler extensions for the Molen programming paradigm. Consequently, we present a profiling experiment and analyze the impact on performance of the hardware reconfiguration for the MPEG 2 benchmark. Finally, we conclude by discussing future research directions.

## 2    The Molen Programming Paradigm

The Molen programming paradigm [8] is a sequential consistency paradigm for programming CCMs possibly including a general purpose computational engine(s). The paradigm allows for parallel and concurrent hardware execution and is intended (currently) for single program execution. It requires only a one time architectural extension of few instructions to provide a large user reconfigurable operation space. The added instructions include **SET** $< address >$ implying that at a particular location the hardware configuration logic is defined and **EXECUTE** $< address >$ that serves to control the executions of the operations on the reconfigurable hardware. In addition, two MOVE instructions for passing values to and from the GPP register file and the reconfigurable hardware are required.

For the moment, we only consider code fragments in the form of functions having a number of parameters. These parameters are passed to special reconfigurable hardware registers denoted as Exchange Registers (XRs). In order to maintain the correct program semantics, the code is annotated and Custom Computing Machine (CCM) description files provide the compiler with implementation specific information such as the addresses where the SET and EXECUTE code are to be stored, the number of exchange registers, etc. It should be noted that this programming paradigm allows modularity, meaning that if the interfaces to the compiler are respected and if the instruction set extension (as described above) is supported, then custom computing hardware provided by multiple vendors can be incorporated by the compiler for the execution of the same application. The modular approach also implies that the application can be ported to multiple platforms with mere recompilation.

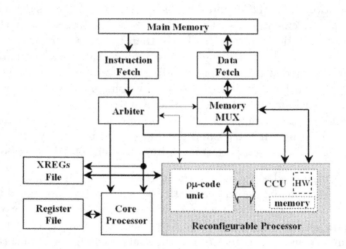

**Fig. 1.** The Molen machine organization

Finally, it is noted that every user is provided with at least $2^{(n-op)}$ directly addressable functions, where n represents the instruction length and 'op' the opcode length. The number of addressable functions can be easily augmented to an arbitrary number by reserving additional opcodes for indirect opcode accessing.

**The Molen Reconfigurable Processor:** The Molen $\rho\mu$-coded processor has been designed having in mind the programming paradigm previously presented. The Molen machine organization is depicted in Figure 1. The arbiter performs a partial decoding of the instructions fetched from the main memory and issues them to the corresponding execution unit. The parameters for the FPGA reside in the Exchange Registers. In the Molen approach, an extended microcode - named reconfigurable microcode - is used for the emulation of both SET and EXECUTE instructions. The microcode is generated when the hardware implementation for a specific operation is designed and it cannot be further modified.

# 3  Compiler Extensions
# for the Molen Programming Paradigm

The compiler system relies on the Stanford SUIF2[10] (Stanford University Inter-mediate Format) Compiler Infrastructure for the front-end, while the back-end is built over the framework offered by the Harvard Machine SUIF[11]. The last component has been designed with retargetability in mind. It provides a set of back-ends for GPPs, powerful optimizations, transformations and analysis passes. These are essential features for a compiler targeting a CCM. We have currently implemented the following extensions for the x86 processor:

- A special pass in the SUIF front-end identifies the code that is mapped on the reconfigurable hardware. Using special pragma annotation, all the calls of those functions are marked for further modification.
- The Instruction Set has been extended with SET/ EXECUTE instructions at both MIR (Medium Intermediate Representation) level and LIR (Low Intermediate Representation) level.
- Exchange Registers (XRs) are added to the Register File Set. These regis-ters are used for passing operation parameters to the reconfigurable hard-ware and returning the computed values after the operation execution. In order to avoid dependencies between the RU and GPP, the XRs receive their data directly from the GPP registers. The XR allocation phase, introduced in Machine SUIF at LIR level, precedes the GPP register allocation. The conventions introduced for the XRs are implemented in this pass.
- Code generation for the reconfigurable hardware is performed when trans-lating SUIF to Machine SUIF IR, and affects the function calls marked in the front-end.

An example of the code generated by the extended compiler for a function call when the considered function is executed on the reconfigurable fabric is presented in Figure 2. The standard function call is replaced by the appropriate instructions for sending parameters (two for the considered example) to the reconfigurable hardware in XRs, hardware configuration phase, hardware execution and finally returning the computed result to the GPP registers. The presented code is at Medium-level Intermediate Representation (MIR), before register allocation and code finalization passes.

```
mov   $vr2.s32 ← param1
movtx $vr1.s32(XR) ← $vr2.s32 # send param1 in XR
mov   $vr4.s32 ← param2
movtx $vr3.s32(XR) ← $vr4.s32 # send param2 in XR
set   address_op1_SET        # hardware configuration
exec  address_op2_EXEC       # hardware execution
movfx $vr6.s32 ← $vr5.s32(XR) # return result
mov   res ← $vr6.s32
```

**Fig. 2.** MIR Code generated by the Molen compiler

Certain information about the target architecture such as microcode address of SET and EXECUTE instructions, the number of XRs, the fixed XR associated with each operation, etc. are extracted by the compiler from a description file.

## 4    A MultiMedia Based Evaluation

In order to evaluate the impact on performance of the hardware configuration we consider the MPEG2 encoder multimedia benchmarks and the test sequences presented in Table 1. Building on previous work [9][7], we look at the following time consuming functions that are implemented in reconfigurable hardware: SAD (sum of absolute-difference), 2D DCT (2 dimensional discrete cosine transform) and IDCT (inverse DCT). As explained before, we consider a Molen machine organization with an x86 as the Core Processor. More specifically, the compiler generates code for the x86 architecture while the measurements are performed on an AMD Athlon XP 1900+ at 1600 MHz.

**Table 1.** MPEG test sequences

| Name | # frames | Resolution |
|------|----------|------------|
| carphone | 96 | 176x144 |
| claire | 168 | 360x288 |
| container | 300 | 352x288 |
| football | 125 | 352x240 |
| foreman | 300 | 352x288 |
| garden | 115 | 352x240 |
| mobile | 140 | 352x240 |
| tennis | 112 | 352x240 |

**MPEG 2 Profiling Results for Pure Software Execution.** We first compute the number of cycles each function consumes for the input sequences given in Table 1, when executed on the target GPP without reconfigurable hardware acceleration. These profiling results for the MPEG2 encoder benchmarks are presented in Table 2. The cumulated time spent by SAD, DCT and IDCT functions (Table 2, column 3,5 and 7) in the pure software approach represents about 65 % of the total MPEG2 execution time. In consequence, the hardware acceleration of these functions (as proposed in the Molen approach) can produce a significant speedup of the MPEG2 encoder up to 3x. The results from Table 2, column 3 suggest that the SAD function is the best candidate for hardware implementation as it can provide up to around 40 % performance improvement. Whereas for the encoding phase, IDCT cannot yield substantial performance improvement, in decoding, this function is heavily used and can produce a significant performance increase.

**MPEG2 Performance Estimation for Molen CCM Execution.** As the presented Molen CCM is not currently implemented, we determine the perfor-

**Table 2.** Profiling results for MPEG2 encoder

| Video | SAD (16x16) | | DCT (8x8) | | IDCT (8x8) | |
|---|---|---|---|---|---|---|
| sequence | # Cycles | % Time | # Cycles | % Time | # Cycles | % Time |
| carphone | 997 | 31.69 | 37796 | 28.19 | 2612 | 1.95 |
| claire | 1092 | 36.46 | 37796 | 26.44 | 2177 | 1.53 |
| container | 1008 | 34.44 | 37590 | 27.04 | 2208 | 1.59 |
| football | 1484 | 42.74 | 37537 | 22.93 | 2827 | 1.73 |
| foreman | 1298 | 39.93 | 37572 | 24.35 | 2193 | 1.42 |
| garden | 1311 | 40.21 | 37594 | 24.70 | 2463 | 1.62 |
| mobile | 1092 | 35.95 | 37536 | 26.30 | 2519 | 1.77 |
| tennis | 1344 | 41.23 | 37531 | 24.39 | 2221 | 1.44 |
| Average | 1203 | 37.83 | 37593 | 25.54 | 2402 | 1.63 |

mance of the Molen CCM based on the measured profiling results for the GPP included in the MOLEN CCM as follows:

$$n_{Molen} \simeq n_{X86} - n_f + n_{call} \cdot cost \qquad (1)$$

$$cost = x_{SET} + y_{EXEC} \qquad (2)$$

where

- $n_{Molen}$: the total number of GPP cycles spent in the considered application by the Molen processor;
- $n_{X86}$: the total number of GPP cycles when the considered;
- function $f$ is implemented on the FPGA application is executed exclusively on the GPP;
- $n_f$: the total number of GPP cycles spent in function $f$ when the considered application is performed only on the GPP;
- $n_{call}$: the number of calls to function $f$ in the considered application;
- $cost$: the number of cycles for one execution of function $f$ on FPGA;
- $x_{SET}$: the number of GPP cycles required for one configuration of the FPGA for function $f$;
- $y_{EXEC}$: the number of GPP cycles required for one execution on the FPGA of function $f$; for the considered hardware implementation, the execution time is not dependent on the input data.

In our experiments, we have measured the values for $n_{X86}$, $n_f$ and $n_{call}$ included in Formula 1. To this purpose, we used the *Halt* library[12] available in Machine SUIF. This library is an instrumentation package that allows the compiler to change the code of the program being compiled in order to collect information about the program own behavior (at run-time). In order to minimize the impact of external factors on the measurements, we run the applications in single mode and with the highest priority in Linux.

**Hardware Execution and Reconfiguration.** Before discussing the hardware acceleration, we present the target FPGA platform included in our experiments. We used the Xilinx Virtex II Pro, XC2VP20 chip and the 2D DCT and 2D IDCT cores available as IPs in the Xilinx Core Generator Tool as well as the SAD implementation presented in [7]. After synthesis, the area required by each function is given in Table 3, column 3. We measured the hardware execution time of each function in terms of the target Athlon processor cycles, given in Table 3, column 3. Based on the characteristics of the XC2VP20 chip, for which a complete configuration of 9280 slices takes about 20 ms, we estimate the reconfiguration time for the considered functions as presented in Table 3, column 2.

**Table 3.** Hardware configuration and execution parameters

| Op | Area | EXEC | HW Speedup | SET | | SET_MAX | | SET/SET_MAX |
|---|---|---|---|---|---|---|---|---|
| | [slices] | [cycles] | | [ms] | [cycles] | Mean | st.dev | |
| SAD | 831 | 133 | 9 x | 2 | 3200000 | 1070 | 167 | 2991 |
| DCT | 4314 | 1184 | 31 x | 10 | 16000000 | 36409 | 80 | 439 |
| IDCT | 5436 | 1200 | 2 x | 12 | 19200000 | 1202 | 225 | 15973 |

We basically performed two experiments to assess not only the impact of hardware acceleration but also the impact of an appropriate scheduling of the reconfiguration phase.

**A Simple Hardware Reconfiguration Scheduling.** On the basis of the hardware execution times from Table 3 and the average software execution time given in Table 2 column 2,4,6, we determine that the hardware acceleration of the considered kernels (Table 3, column 4) is up to 31x. However, a direct scheduling where the corresponding SET and EXECUTE instructions for hardware configuration and hardware execution are consecutively executed for each operation can completely waste the hardware speedup. In this consecutive scheduling, the hardware reconfiguration is each time performed before the hardware execution. Due to the huge reconfiguration latency and repetitive hardware configuration imposed by this scheduling, the use of reconfigurable hardware can slowdown the MPEG2 benchmark (computed as $n_{Molen}/n_{X86}$ using Formula 1) by 2-3 orders of magnitude (Table 4, row 2) compared to complete execution on the GPP alone.

Based on the profiling result (Table 2), reconfigurable hardware execution times (Table 3) and Formula 1, we determine the upper boundary for a SET instruction latency that ensures that the Molen CCM is not slower than the pure software approach ($n_{Molen} \simeq n_{X86}$). We refer to this boundary as SET_MAX and is described by:

$$SET\_MAX \simeq \frac{n_f}{n_{call}} - y_{EXEC} \qquad (3)$$

The mean SET_MAX values and standard deviations are presented in Table 3, (columns 7-8). We notice that the complete hardware configuration of the currently available FPGA platforms (SET) accounts for 3-4 orders of magnitude (see Table 3, column 9) more reconfiguration time than SET_MAX and produces for the MPEG 2 benchmark a performance decreasing of 2-3 order of magnitude

(Table 3, last column). In consequence, without an appropriate scheduling of the SET instructions, the overall performance is decreased due to the huge reconfiguration latency in spite of the faster hardware execution time. Such an appropriate scheduling is discussed in the rest of this section.

**Out of Loop Hardware Reconfiguration.** The above presented limitation can be eliminated by simply scheduling the hardware configuration phase as early as possible. This transformation can be particularly beneficial when there is only one operation executed in hardware included in a loop-body. This situation is encountered in MPEG2 encoder for all three considered functions. In the rest of this section, we estimate the effect of this transformation on the performance of the Molen processor. In this respect, we use the ceteris paribus approach meaning that we look at the influence of each function individually to estimate the performance improvement while considering that none of the other functions are implemented in reconfigurable hardware. As we previously explained, performing the hardware configuration before each hardware execution can decrease the performance for the Molen processor versus the GPP alone. Nevertheless, removing the unnecessary repetitive SET instructions (when the hardware is already configured) results in a significant performance improvement (computed as $\frac{n_f - n_{call} * y_{EXEC} - x_{SET}}{n_{X86}}$). The performance efficiency (presented in Table 4, row 4) emphasizes that the individual improvement of each function is very close to the maximum possible improvement.

**Table 4.** MPEG 2 encoder performance results with and without anticipated hardware configuration

| Video sequence | SAD | DCT | IDCT |
|---|---|---|---|
| Simple Scheduling Slowdown | 1012 x | 108 x | 131 x |
| Out-of-loop Scheduling Performance Impr | 33.61 % | 24.68 % | 0.75 % |
| Theor. Maximal Performance Impr | 37.83 % | 25.54 % | 1.63 % |
| Performance Efficiency | 89 % | 97 % | 46 % |

We emphasize that the execution of both SAD and DCT simultaneously on the reconfigurable hardware will not provide a cumulative performance improvement due to the required switching of configurations in order to preserve the overall application behavior. The compiler optimizations are expected to play a key role in handling these more complicated cases.

## 5  Conclusions

In this paper, we used the compiler technology developed to support the Molen programming paradigm to study the conditions under which substantial performance improvements can be obtained with hardware acceleration using CCM's. Based on profiling results, we showed that potential speedups can be completely outweighed by inappropriate scheduling of the reconfiguration instruction. When theoretically a performance improvement of up to 40 % is achievable, the slow-down caused by improper scheduling can be as large as a factor 1000 (e.g. for SAD). We also showed that given a suitable scheduling up to 97 % of the maximal performance improvement can be obtained.

Future research will focus on compiler optimizations to allow for concurrent execution. We also intend to extend the compiler to take into account complex knowledge about the target reconfigurable platform and thus to achieve an efficient schedule of the different operations performed on the reconfigurable fabric.

# References

1. Campi, F., Toma, M., Lodi, A., Cappelli, A., Canegallo, R., Guerrieri, R.: A VLIW Processor with Reconfigurable Instruction Set for Embedded Applications. In: In ISSCC Digest of Technical Papers. (2003) 250–251
2. Sima, M., Vassiliadis, S., S.Cotofana, van Eijndhoven, J., Vissers, K.: Field-Programmable Custom Computing Machines - A Taxonomy. In: 12th International Conference on Field Programmable Logic and Applications (FPL). Volume 2438., Montpellicr, France, Springer-Verlag Lecture Notes in Computer Science (LNCS) (2002) 79–88
3. Becker, J.: Configurable Systems-on-Chip : Commercial and Academic Approaches. In: Proc. of 9th IEEE Int. Conf. on Electronic Circuits and Systems - ICECS 2002, Dubrovnik, Croatia (2002) 809–812
4. Gokhale, M.B., Stone, J.M.: Napa C: Compiling for a Hybrid RISC/FPGA Architecture. In: Proceedings of FCCM'98, Napa Valley, CA (1998) 126–137
5. Rosa, A.L., Lavagno, L., Passerone, C.: Hardware/Software Design Space Exploration for a Reconfigurable Processor. In: Proc. of DATE 2003, Munich, Germany (2003) 570–575
6. Ye, Z.A., Shenoy, N., Banerjee, P.: A C Compiler for a Processor with a Reconfigurable Functional Unit. In: ACM/SIGDA Symposium on FPGAs, Monterey, California, USA (2000) 95–100
7. Vassiliadis, S., Wong, S., Cotofana, S.: The MOLEN $\rho\mu$-Coded Processor. In: 11th International Conference on Field Programmable Logic and Applications (FPL). Volume 2147., Belfast, UK, Springer-Verlag Lecture Notes in Computer Science (LNCS) (2001) 275–285
8. Vassiliadis, S., Gaydadjiev, G., Bertels, K., Moscu Panainte, E.: The Molen Programming Paradigm. In: Proceedings of the Third International Workshop on Systems, Architectures, Modeling, and Simulation, Samos, Greece (2003) 1–7
9. Moscu Panainte, E., Bertels, K., Vassiliadis, S.: Compiling for the Molen Programming Paradigm. In: 13th International Conference on Field Programmable Logic and Applications (FPL). Volume 2778., Lisbon, Portugal, Springer-Verlag Lecture Notes in Computer Science (LNCS) (2003) 900–910
10. (http://suif.stanford.edu/suif/suif2)
11. (http://www.eecs.hardvard.edu/hube/research/machsuif.html)
12. M.Mercaldi, Smith, M.D., Holloway, G.: The Halt Library. In: The Machine-SUIF Documentation Set, Hardvard University (2002)

# Compiler and System Techniques
# for SoC Distributed Reconfigurable Accelerators[*]

Joël Cambonie[1], Sylvain Guérin[2], Ronan Keryell[2], Loïc Lagadec[3],
Bernard Pottier[3], Olivier Sentieys[4], Bernt Weber[2], and Samar Yazdani[3]

[1] STMicroelectronics/MPU
[2] ENST-Bretagne/LIT
[3] Université de Bretagne Occidentale/A&S
[4] Université de Rennes 1/IRISA

**Abstract.** To answer new challenges, systems on chip need to gain flexibility and FPGAs need to gain structure. We propose a general framework for SoC architectures and software tools in which different kind of processing units are programmed at high level. We show a reconfigurable unit suitable for this framework and we draw the outline of a super-compiler able to address such an architecture.

## 1 Introduction

Adding some on-chip flexibility is very attractive to extend the lifetime of a sub-micron ASIC product and to capitalize on the engineering cost but one faces the trouble of an heterogeneous system having different units programmed with different languages. These units can be powerful processors, micro-programmable architectures, reconfigurable data-paths, or fine-grain embedded FPGAs. The global view includes an operating system that runs on a control processor, leading the execution of distributed processes. Each process has its program broken into tasks that can run on different units, based on performance requirement and resource availability. The system has a global view of task status coming from the units, communications and synchronizations being achieved on packet or transaction bases. The main objective is to draw the full figure of a software oriented reconfigurable system, including real hardware, low level tools for reconfigurable units, and compiler techniques to be developed.

The case of reconfigurable units is perhaps the most difficult challenge, because their usual hardware description tools are not usable in a software flow. Section 2 presents a mixed grain reconfigurable unit associating memories, operators and fine grain resources primarily chosen for a wireless modem. The general flow shown in figure 1 can use a decomposition in scalar processing and stream processing. Cooperation between the two sides can be loose or tight. The strategy of mapping on reconfigurable units uses a first layer where the concurrency is represented by cooperating processes. Code for these processes is produced in the form of a graph of operations compatible with target architectures. Then these graphs are mapped to the available hardware. Higher level tools can make

---

[*] Thanks due to research programs from STSI, RNTL and CNRS/STIC POMARD

A. Pimentel and S. Vassiliadis (Eds.): SAMOS 2004, LNCS 3133, pp. 293–302, 2004.

their decisions based on feedbacks coming from the low
level tools. In section 4 we
present a tool structure for
mapping on units mixing
logic (FPGA) and arithmetic
levels (data path units). Section 5 shows the different
level of concurrency in the
system organization. Sec-
tion 6 discuss code generation for this scheme from
high-level language down to
the basic software using
high-performance computing
techniques.

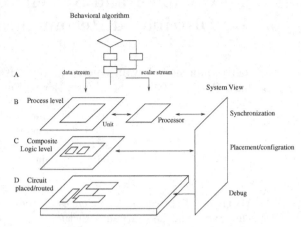

**Fig. 1.** Simplified flow for multi-target compilation
$(A \to B)$, synthesis $(B \to C)$ and system activities

## 2    A Reference Architecture

Reconfigurable architectures have received significant attention in recent years,
and some directions have emerged that combine desirable features such as low
power and flexibility [11, 6] for portable signal processing applications. One idea
is that, from an energy perspective, coarse grain arithmetic functions with programmable interconnects outperform instruction based processors where the
storing in cache and decoding of the wide instructions account for a significant
energy overhead. On the contrary, FPGA is less efficient on context switching,
and so the area efficiency is bad, since more functions must be mapped at the
bit level on the matrix, in order to meet real time constraints. From an other
standpoint, future generation of ASIC has to face the challenge of increasing
computing power at low cost, which obviously is incompatible with a fine grain
flexibility. This is why a promising direction for *soft* ASIC design is heterogeneous architectures, combining application specific IPs selected by profiling the
set of targeted applications, together with some quantity of configurable fabric,
flexibly interconnected, with task synchronization being performed by a micro
controller.

The previous SOC architecture of a programmable baseband processor for an
OFDM modem combined dedicated IP, fine grain FPGA, micro controller and a
crossbar bus interconnect on a single die [14]. To increase the area efficiency
and computing power of the FPGA, a mixed grain configurable fabric has been
developed, encapsulated into a system wrapper that permits multi-threaded communication with the system bus. The configurable fabric has been described at
the RT-level, validated by simulation of configurations generated from various
functions used in the 802.11a OFDM modem. It has been synthesized in $130nm$
ST Microelectronics' technology, and is integrated on a test chip. Die size is 14
$mm^2$ for the composite coarse plus fine grain fabric.

This section focuses on the configurable fabric architecture description, its internal structure and how it interacts with the rest of the system.

## 2.1   Configurable Fabric

This device is composed of four different types of resources organized as separate interconnected networks, called coarse networks in the following. These are: fine grain LUT, ALU, RAM, and address generator (AG) networks.

- The fine grain network provides bit-level computing resources. It is a standard embedded FPGA with 350 available bi-directional ports and 32×32 LUT.
- The ALU network is composed of 16 rows of two tiles. Each tile has two 8-bit registered ALUand one 16-bit registered multiplier, with local and global interconnect resources for data and register control.
- Each row has four dual-port static RAM of 256×8-bit capacity appearing as shared memory onto the processor address space. RAMs are connected to the global data interconnect.
- Each row has also address generators connected to the RAM by a local bus.

Basic resources are statically configured to perform elementary operations. For each resource, data are selected from or connected to the interconnect by multiplexors. The segmented bus is configurable through a set of switches to perform local interconnections. ALU, RAM and AG coarse networks constitute the set of coarse grain resources, while the FPGA is the network of fine grain resources. Coarse networks are made of vertically stacked rows with horizontal connections on their left and right sides, so that by simple abutment of the three networks, the horizontal global signals can propagate. The horizontal bus width is 117 bits for one row. The three abutted coarse networks are now called composite coarse network.

The composite coarse has 16×117 bi-directional data and control wires available for connection with the fine grain. In order to have a regular connection density through the rows between fine grain and coarse composite network, configurable multiplexors are added to select horizontal busses from coarse composite network to be connected to the 350 available fine grain ports (see figure 2(a)). The close coupling of the fine grain with the coarse grain allows efficient mapping of mixed control and data processing. All bit level state machines and data processing being efficiently mapped on the fine grain, while word level arithmetic is mapped on the coarse composite. The vertical global lines that propagate through each network are selectively connected to the data ports of the fabric.

## 2.2   System Wrapper

The configurable fabric is embedded into a SOC. It supports on-the-fly reconfiguration, and multi-threaded applications. This encapsulation with a system-wrapper permits communication with the system, as shown in figure 2(b). The main I/O port is connected to the system crossbar bus, steering incoming data

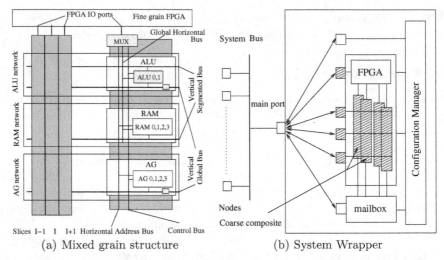

(a) Mixed grain structure          (b) System Wrapper

**Fig. 2.** Two architecture views

from bus towards one of the six internal input ports: four bi-directional data ports are connected to the fabric, 1 to the configuration port (write only), and the last to the mailbox port. The main output port takes data from the five internal output ports among which four are the data ports and a mailbox port. Priority is assigned on a fixed order basis.

Data exchange between fabric and system are performed in two different modes: (1) receiving and sending data to the other peripherals of the system is achieved through the data ports connected to the crossbar bus, (2) data exchange with the processor are executed through the multi-bank dual ported shared memory embedded into the fabric. The mailbox ensures synchronization of the tasks running on the fabric with the rest of the system. It decodes messages coming through the bus from other peripherals and produces control signals for the fabric, and on occurrence of conditions in the processing from the fabric, it generates message to be sent on the bus to the other peripherals. For instance, configuration commands are sent through the mailbox to the configuration manager, which returns acknowledgment on completion. This is also a way of interrupting the software to change context on events occurring in the data-path.

## 3   Application of an 802.11a Receiver

The 802.11a is an OFDM based WLAN standard, where payload data are preceded by a preamble for receiver synchronization. Some functions are advantageously performed by dedicated coprocessors (FFT, Viterbi, Demapping) connected to the main bus, while the other functions can be mapped on the configurable fabric (preamble detection, carrier offset frequency estimate, channel estimate, channel equalizer, deinterleaver and descrambler). The section describes how the different phases of the receiver algorithm are mapped on the fabric, and the kind of interactions occurring between fabric and other processors.

In a first phase, where the receiver is waking up, a preamble detection algorithm is mapped on the fabric. This function jointly performs detection and CFO estimate in real time. A call to a Cordic rotation (rotor) in the process is implemented on a dedicated coprocessor. Once a detection criterion is met, a message is sent via the mailbox to the processor that reads data produced by the fabric from the shared memory.

Those data will be used to generate data dependent configuration for the next phase. Processor will then order reconfiguration of the data-path for the following step: channel estimate using long preambles. Again when this step is done, a partial reconfiguration is performed to support the payload data processing, of which channel equalizer, de-interleaving and descrambling are mapped on the mixed grain fabric. Figure 3 shows the different processes composing the receiver,

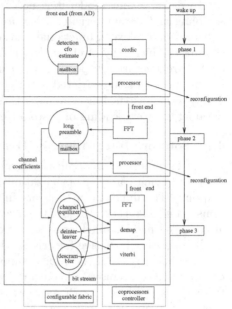

**Fig. 3.** 802.11 baseband receiver with the 3 main phases triggered by microcontroller (short and long preamble detection, then payload)

and how the fabric interacts with other coprocessors and controller via shared memory, mailbox and system bus along the phases.

Practical mapping of the OFDM preamble detection and CFO estimation is shown in figure 3 in the form of pipeline of medium grain processes communicating by shared memories. A simple implementation is achieved by connecting memories to operative parts. The control of this pipeline needs a control process that feed status information to the global control of the system. The stages are loops implementing correlation computations.

## 4   Physical Synthesis for Reconfigurable Units

Physical synthesis is the translation of a software description of the application into resource allocation for a given target architecture, its internal state and constraints. In MADEO, it necessitates two inputs. The first one is the application description appearing as a hierarchical graph of operations including symbolic operations, primitives, logic based operations or memories. As MADEO tools are generic, they need to be characterized by an architecture definition to do their work: placing, routing, resource allocation, interactive or programmed editing and configuration generation. The second input is the target architecture described with grammar oriented tools conforming to an abstract model.

To define a unit model it is necessary to write or generate a program assembling and parameterizing a hierarchy of hardware elements such as wires, registers, multiplexers, functional unit, etc. Wires can be single lines, structured channels or hierarchy of channels. Tools support parameterized channel size to enable architecture prospection under place and route control. Functional units can be specified as a restricted set of permitted symbolic operations (e.g. ALUs) or any $n$-inputs logic function (e.g. LUTs). The model can be extended by custom parameters or embedding of custom elements.

### 4.1   Software Integration for Heterogeneous Units

Physical synthesis of an application graph is based on interleaved two-steps operations implying compiler optimizations from Madeo front-end [10] and physical mapping. The upper layer tools are in charge of mapping to architecture functions, based on its knowledge of the target unit, and on type information provided at compile time. Detailed types are set of values used to produce optimized logic as the interval alternative for arithmetic operators.

The first stage of this compiler supports classical optimizations such as dead code and NOPs removal. Then, in the flow for addressing fine grain FPGAs, the logic is produced as PLAs representing the hierarchical graph of lookup-tables. Last, we use logic synthesis to perform technology adaptation. Coarse grain graph elements are hardware primitives such as addition/multiplication that will be allocated on the data-path.

Madeo flow integrates floor-planning, place and route, and physical characteristics computation. The default floor-planning policy is based on the TCG algorithm from Lin and Chang, the placement algorithm relying on a simulated annealing algorithm; the global routing uses a PATH-FINDER-like algorithm on top of a maze router, performing the point-to-point routing.

### 4.2   Interactions with Higher Levels

Inside Madeo, the physical and logical layers interact in a cyclic way. The physical layer tools enable *architecture exploration* by enumerating the available resources in order to let the compiler parameterize its behavior. The compiler creates hierarchical graphs of components, called *composite parts*, in conformity with the unit resources: logic tables, registers, operators and memories. The physical layer handles composite parts ensuring the migration from the high level to physical mapping. Then it outputs *physical characteristics* back to the high level compiler. As an illustration of these interactions, place and route tools return hierarchical modules that are pieces of configuration with relative position[8]. These modules are analyzed regarding several performances criteria such as temporal or geometrical characteristics, and resource use. Other criteria such as power consumption estimation can also be added. These informations are sent back to higher level compilers or editing tools, so that optimization trade-offs could be found.

Regarding the modules produced by Madeo, several policies can be considered. One policy is to keep these modules if they can be reused in the context of the application, as for producing pipeline stages or regular design components. Another policy is to archive these modules in a database for further reuse. Madeo has now provisions to keep modules as hardware dependent libraries associated to high level object-oriented behaviors, or simple software definitions.

To conclude with physical synthesis, the proposed tools are generic, but the architectural model specializes them transparently. The effort to produce an architecture model is relatively small. The approach strongly reduces the development time, and improves the software quality as any improvement is widespread to all architectures. As for the fabric, the same tools operate over the entire architecture. As an example, as every function unit "publishes" the functions it can implement, every node of the graph of operations the compiler produce, can be assigned a set of primitive function candidates. Once the placement is done, routing computes routes from pins to pins, without regards to the net's width or the kind of routing channels, thus fine grain and medium grains can be managed in the same framework.

## 5    System Aspects

Heterogeneous systems on chip require an assembly of complex software and CAD tools since it is necessary to address different hardware supports with transparency. The objectives to remember are to reach the best possible compromise between: (1) costs and delays for application developments, (2) energy consumption, silicon resource and computing efficiency.

The first objective implies to use efficient development methodologies, supporting very high level specifications and modular design (objects). The second objective is obtained by using a gradation of targets going from processors to reconfigurable units, and IP modules.

A view of a computer at work is an operating system controlling hardware resources and application processes. Processes can be divided into small tasks implementing concurrent or sequential computations. The system model has three components: (1) hardware resource description, (2) application processes, (3) algorithms for scheduling and allocating resources.

An advantage of the SoC approach of architecture toward unstructured FPGAs is the level of organization provided by the network, I/Os and the control processor. Reconfigurable resources are allocated as unit chunks, communication are simple transactions from unit to unit, or message passing. In this case the knowledge of the SoC organization is enough to allow the OS to act. A more difficult issue is the case where reconfigurable units are shared between tasks. This situation is highly desirable to make an efficient use of the hardware when data arrives at unscheduled time or at irregular rates. Overloading means that processes can migrate from the active state to an inactive state swapped to the local configuration memory, or to the external memory. To enable the system to operate, it is mandatory to structure processes into set of tasks that will be mapped on the different units.

The flow model where data are fed to an accelerator is simple and convenient for multimedia or signal processing algorithms. In this case, computations are organized as pipelines of medium grain task graphs. Tasks implement one step in an algorithm, act independently from peers. They embed their own control and processing parts. The application pipeline is managed by a control task receiving status informations from the stages, and enabling the communications between them. The control process communicates at its turn with a node management process that holds the status of the different applications, active or inactive, communicates with the OS, and manages partial reconfiguration and swaps.

This structural organization can be described in a CSP-fashion, with the remark that the computation graph is not statically mapped to the computer, but dynamically processed by the OS and the skeleton thread running on the control processor. Code for tasks are generated as physical circuit descriptions for reconfigurable units, programs for compute intensive processors or microcode for microprogrammable units. In the case of configured circuits, the physical description is a bitmap block associated to a geometry, and correspondence between high level variables and registers. At runtime, the bitmap will be merged with other task bitmaps and loaded to configuration memory. The bitmap contains the registers initial values or context values during a swap-out operation.

## 6    Towards General Purpose Compiling

During the past few years, the main concentration in the domain of embedded systems has been on high performance in a cost effective manner i.e. flexibility and power efficiency but the switch from general-purpose to multimedia workloads allows alternative architectures. Since Reconfigurable architectures such as SCORE [5] and RaPiD [4] rely heavily on compilation processes, consistent software paradigms [15] for programming custom computing machines are becoming the need of the day.

Vector ISA has some advantages over scalar ISA to exploit the computation pipeline [7, 9] and out-of-order, speculative techniques or aggressive simultaneous multithreading [13] can be used to boost the efficiency but may have adverse effects to real-time processing. Since the computation throughput often increases the processor-memory gap, the separation of memory access and computation streams in decoupled architectures [12] is interesting since it allows out-of-order execution between the two streams.

Since many parallelism levels that were used in the high-end computers are now found in SoC, the same compilation techniques can be used to compile high level programs to control software and hardware descriptions.

If we look at compiling for distributed memory computers for example, a program is split in different parts running on various processors with their own memory. Since a processor cannot directly access data in the memory of another processor the compiler analyze the code to insert communications primitives where such accesses are needed. In the same way, to generate a program for an heterogeneous computer we need to add communication or interface code between the controller, the various hardware operators, the memories, the bus. This is why we have used super-computing compilation techniques to our control code and hardware specification problem: global memory emulation by compilation [3] to generate memory access code or DMA initialization and HPF style compilation [2] to distribute the computation on the computational entities of the SoC.

To achieve such a code generation from classical higher-level numerical languages such as Fortran or C to a closer architectural description in SmallTalk for the MADEO tool of the project we have used the PIPS compiler framework [1] that is developed since 1988 as a modular compiler for high performance computing. This project began as an automatic vectorizer for vector machines but evolved later toward automatic parallelization, code optimizing, code transformation, HPF compilation and reverse engineering.

Many analyses and code transformations developed in PIPS first for high performance computing are reused here in a more hardware context. Automatic parallelization transformations using precise analysis of the code based on a linear algebra framework are used to split the code in several parts. A coarse grain parallelization is used to find different coarse grain processes that will keep the different processors and co-processors of the SoC busy with some support of the operating system run-time. A fine grain parallelization inherited from vectorization for SIMD machines is used to exploit the massive parallelism available in the configurable co-processors.

To cope with inter-procedural programs, memory accesses are modeled with polyhedral regions to express the array memory usage between different parts of the program and generate the communication operators with minimal temporary memory buffers. The programmer can specify with some pragma which parts of the code will be executed on a reconfigurable engine and the region analysis will determine the input and output data to handle between the control code or memory and the hardware accelerators.

The remaining program that has not been transformed into a hardware form becomes a control program running on the SoC processors with calls to the reconfigurable operators and data-paths. Since the reconfigurable operator programs can be pretty-printed in both MADEO format or high level C or Fortran form, the later one allows an easy functional simulation of the global program by just running it on a regular computer as with other systems such as SystemC or SpecC.

**Conclusion.** This project perspectives are highlighted by giving an interpretation of the heterogeneous reconfigurable SoC architecture related to known concepts in computer architecture.

Taking benefits from the reconfiguration we propose to enable a variety of programming methods for the units, including fine tuned application support for multimedia or signal processing, general purpose support with pipelined accelerators, domain specific application supports (such as cellular automata), virtual machine implementations. The program level use of these supports is envisioned as a co-operation of two threads, one for control and memory operations, executed on the CPU, the others executed on reconfigurable units.

Several of our objectives have yet been reached: portability of synthesis on reconfigurable units is no more a concern, and the architecture developed at STMicroelectronics open the way for attractive distributed reconfigurable processing. Several threads of work are currently followed for code generation, that includes architecture synthesis for signal processing, and general purpose pipelined processing under compiler control.

# References

1. C. Ancourt, F. Coelho, B. Creusillet, and R. Keryell. How to add a new phase in pips: the case of dead code elimination. In *6th Workshop on Compilers for Parallel Computers (CPC'96)*, December 1996.
2. C. Ancourt, F. Coelho, F. Irigoin, and R. Keryell. A linear algebra framework for static hpf code distribution. *Scientific Programming*, 6(1):3–27, Spring 1997. Special Issue — High Performance Fortran Comes of Age.
3. C. Ancourt and François Irigoin. Automatic code distribution. In *3rd Workshop on Compilers for Parallel Computers (CPC'92)*.
4. D. C. Cronquist C. Ebeling and P. Franklin. RaPiD - reconfigurable pipelined datapath. In *FPL96*, number 1142 in LNCS, September 96.
5. E. Caspi, M. Chu, R. Huang, J. Yeh, J. Wawrzynek, and A. DeHon. Stream computations organized for reconfigurable execution. *FPL'2000, LNCS 1896*, 2000.
6. R. David, S. Pillement, and O.Sentieys. *Low Power Electronics Design*, chapter Energy-Efficient Reconfigurable Processsors. CRC Press, edited by C. Piguet, 2003.
7. R. Espasa, M. Valero, and J.E. Smith. Vector architectures: Past, present and future. *International Conference on Supercomputing*, 1998.
8. E. Fabiani, C. Gouyen, and B. Pottier. Intermediate level components for reconfigurable platforms. In *SAMOS'03*. Springer, LNCS, 2003.
9. C. Kozyrakis and D. Patterson. Vector vs. supersclar and VLIW architectures for embedded multimedia benchmarks. *35th Intl. Symp. on Microarchitecture*, 2002.
10. L. Lagadec, B. Pottier, and O. VillellasGuillen. An LUT-based high level synthesis framework for reconfigurable architectures. In *SAMOS'02*. M. Dekker, 2002.
11. J. Rabaey. Reconfigurable computing a solution to low power programmable DSP. *Proceedings ICASSP*, 1997.
12. J. E. Smith. Decoupled access/execute computer architectures. *In ACM Transactions on Computer Systems*, November 1984.
13. D. Tullsen, S. Eggers, and H. Levy. Simultaneous Multithreading: Maximizing on-chip parallelism. *ISCA95*, 1995.
14. L. Vanzago, B. Bhattacharya, J. Cambonie, and L. Lavagno. Design space exploration for a wireless protocol on a reconfigurable platform. *DATE'02*, 2002.
15. S. Vassiliadis, G. Gaydadjiev, K. Bertels, and E. Panainte. The Molen programming paradigm. In *SAMOS'03*. Springer LNCS, 2003.

# Design Space Exploration with Automatic Selection of SW and HW for Embedded Applications

Júlio C.B. Mattos[1], Antônio C.S. Beck[1], Luigi Carro[1,2], and Flávio R. Wagner[1]

[1] Federal University of Rio Grande do Sul, Computer Science Institute
Av. Bento Gonçalves, 9500, Campus do Vale, Porto Alegre, Brasil
{julius,caco,carro,flavio}@inf.ufrgs.br
[2] Federal University of Rio Grande do Sul, Electrical Engineering
Av. Oswaldo Aranha 103, Porto Alegre, Brasil

**Abstract.** This paper presents a methodology for automatic selection of software and hardware IP components for embedded applications. Design space exploration is achieved by the correct selection of a SW-IP block to be executed in a platform containing different implementations of the same ISA. These different versions of the same ISA dissipate a different amount of power and require a different number of cycles to execute the same program. This way, by making the software execute on a different processor to achieve the required power or energy of an application, one can fine tune the platform for the desired market.

## 1 Introduction

Embedded systems are everywhere, in consumer electronics, entertainment, communication systems and so on. Embedded applications demand varying combinations of requirements like performance, power, cost, among others. Since different platforms and IP cores are available, precise technical metrics regarding these factors are essential for a correct comparison among alternative architectural solutions, when running a particular application.

To the above physically related metrics, one should add another dimension, which is software development cost. In platform-based design, design derivatives are mainly configured by software, and software development is where most of the design time is spent. But the quality of the software development also directly impacts the mentioned physical metrics.

Presently, there is wide variety of Intellectual Property (IP) blocks such processors cores with a several architecture stiles, like RISC, DSP, VLIW. Also, there is an increasing number of software IPs that can be used in a complex embedded systems design. Thus, with wide range of SW and HW IP solutions, the designer has several possibilities and need methodologies and tools to make an efficient design exploration.

Presently, the software designer writes the application code and relies on a compiler to optimize it [1][2][3]. However, it is widely known that design decisions taken at higher abstraction levels can lead to substantially superior improvements. Software engineers involved with software configuration of embedded platforms, however, do not have enough experience to measure the impact of their algorithmic decisions on

A. Pimentel and S. Vassiliadis (Eds.): SAMOS 2004, LNCS 3133, pp. 303–312, 2004.

issues such as performance and power. Moreover, different applications have different resource requirements during their execution. Some applications may have a large amount of instruction-level parallelism (ILP), which can be exploited by a processor that can issue many instructions per cycle. Other applications have little amount of ILP, which can be executed by a single processor.

The software design exploration is done mainly by software optimizations. There are several works using software optimizations like [1][2][4]. The hardware design exploration is done by selecting the right/best architecture for one application, like [5][6][7].

This paper proposes a pragmatic approach, consisting in the use of a software library, a set of different processor cores (but with the same instruction set), and a design space exploration tool to allow an automatic software and hardware IP selection. The software IP library contains alternative algorithmic implementations for routines commonly found in embedded applications, whose implementations are previously characterized regarding performance, power, and memory requirements for each processor core.

During the execution of an application, each different implementation of the ISA can be turned on or off so that the platform can achieve the desired execution time within limits for power dissipation, or energy consumption. Thus we can have different levels of optimization, one on the software level, and another on the hardware level, selecting the best core providing different performance levels and consuming different levels of power.

By exploring design alternatives at the algorithmic level and the architectural level, that offer a much wider range of power and performance, the designer is able to automatically find, through the exploration tool, corner cases. As a very important side effect, the choice of an algorithm and an architecture that exactly fits the requirements of the application, without unnecessarily wasting resources.

This paper is organized as follows. Section 2 discusses related work in the field of embedded software optimization and hardware exploration. Section 3 presents our approach to design space exploration, introducing the software IP library and the platform (HW IP cores). Section 4 presents the design exploration tool and experimental results, and Section 5 draws conclusions and introduces future work.

## 2   Related Work

In software design exploration there are several work mainly based in software optimizations. Power-aware software optimization has gained attention in recent years. It has been shown [8] that each instruction of a processor has a different power cost. Instruction power costs may vary in a very wide range and are also strongly affected by addressing modes. By taking these costs in consideration, a 40% power improvement obtained by code optimizations is reported [8]. Reordering of instructions in the source code has been also proposed [9], considering that power consumption depends on the switching activity and thus also on the particular sequence of instructions, and improvements of up to 30% are reported. In [10], an energy profiler is used to identify critical arithmetic functions and replace them by using polynomial approximations and floating-point to fixed-point conversions.

In [4], a library of alternative hardware and software parameterized implementations for Simulink blocks that present different performance, power, and area figures is characterized. Although some code optimizations may improve both performance and power, many other improve one factor while resulting in worse figures for the other one. Recent efforts are oriented towards automatic exploration tools that identify several points in the design space that correspond to different trade-offs between performance and power. In [5], Pareto-optimal configurations are found for a parameterized architecture running a given application. Among the solutions, the performance range varies by a factor of 10, while the power range varies by a factor of 7.5. In [6], the best performance/power figures are selected among various application-to-architecture mappings.

These solutions exploiting the architecture to obtain the best option for a particular application In [7], a methodology to automates the design of applications-specific computer systems is proposed. This approach uses a application written in C as input and generates a VLIW processor and a optional nonprogrammable accelerator (one or more units) to execute compute-intensive loops.

Kumar [11] presents an interesting idea using a heterogeneous multi-core architecture with the same ISA to reduce power dissipation. During an application executing, system software evaluates the resource requirements of the application and chooses the most appropriate core. In [12], a methodology for architecture exploration of heterogeneous signal processing systems is proposed. This exploration starts from executable specifications modeled as Kan Process Networks and the result is the architecture capable of executing the applications within system constraints. [13] also presents a technique for exploration of architectural alternatives mapping an application on to the best architecture solution.

## 3  The Proposed Approach

In the proposed design space exploration approach, illustrated in Figure 1, the design starts with an application specification at a high level of abstraction, and the application code is automatically generated by a tool. This tool allows design space exploration based on software IP library and a set of cores different implementations of the same ISA. Note that, in this approach, the designer does not need to know the target platform, because this information is used only for the library characterization. Differently from traditional design flow, where the designer must know the target platform, and all optimizations are trusted to the compiler.

The software IP library contains different algorithmic versions of the same function, like sine, table search, square root, IMDCT (Inverse Modified Discrete Cosine Transform), thus supporting design space exploration. Considering a certain core (HW IP) and for each algorithmic implementation of the library functions, it measures the performance, the memory usage, and energy and power dissipation. This way, the characterization of the software library is performed according to physical related aspects that can be changed at an algorithmic abstraction level.

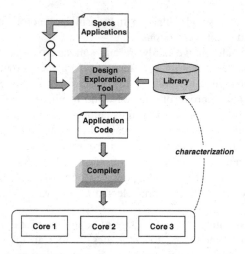

**Fig. 1.** The design space exploration approach

On hardware level, this approach uses different implementations of the same Instruction Set Architecture providing range solutions on performance, power and son on. This architecture is capable of supporting native Java instructions, since Java is a widespread language in the arena of embedded systems.

Thus, this methodology allows the automatic selection of software and hardware IPs to better match the application requirements. Moreover, if the application constraints might change, for example with tighter energy demands or smaller memory footprint, a different set of SW and/or HW IPs might be selected.

Using this methodology the space design exploration has several options to provide a final solution using different combination of SW IPs and HW IPs. Using only a single core and different algorithmic versions of the same function the designer has a good set of alternatives. However, when multiple cores are used the range of solutions is hugely increased.

### 3.1  Software Exploration

As it has been already mentioned, the library contains different algorithmic versions of the same function, thus supporting design space exploration. Each algorithmic implementation of the library functions is measure in terms of performance (in cycles), the memory usage (for data and instruction memories), and energy and power dissipation.

Since embedded systems are found in many different application domains, this investigation has been started using classical functions: Sine – Two ways to compute the sine of an angle are provided. One is a simple table search, and the other one uses the CORDIC (Coordinate Rotation Digital Computer) algorithm [14]; IMDCT – The Inverse Modified Discrete Cosine Transform is a critical step in decompression algorithms like those found in MP3 players. Together with windowing, it takes roughly 70% of the processing time [15]. Others functions are implemented like Table Search, Square Root and Sort.

## 3.2  Hardware Exploration

For hardware exploration we use a platform composed by different core implementations of the same ISA. The platform is based on different implementations of a Java microcontroller, called FemtoJava [16]. The FemtoJava Microcontroller implements an execution engine for Java in hardware through a stack machine compatible with Java Virtual Machine (JVM) specification. A CAD environment that automatically synthesizes an Application Specific Instruction-Set Processor (ASIP) version of the Java microcontroller for a target application [16] is available, using only a subset of instructions critical to the specific application.

This paper presents three different versions of the FemtoJava processor: multicycle, pipeline and a VLIW one. The multicycle version supports stack operations through stack emulation on their register files. This approach reduces the memory access bottleneck of the stack machine, improving performance.

The second architecture is the pipelined version [17], which has five stages: instruction fetch, instruction decoding, operand fetch, execution, and write back. The first stage, instruction fetch, is composed by an instruction queue of 9 registers. The first instruction in the queue is sent to the instruction decoder stage. The decoder has four functions: the generation of the control word for that instruction, to handle data dependencies, to analyze the forwarding possibilities and to inform to the instruction queue the size of the current instruction, in order to put the next instruction of the stream in the first place of the queue.

Stack and the local variable pool of the methods are available in the register bank. Once the operands are fetched, they are sent to the fourth stage, where the operation is executed. There is no branch prediction, in order to save area. All branches are supposed to be not taken. If the branch is taken, a penalty of three cycles is paid.

The write back stage saves, if necessary, the result of the execution stage back to the register bank, again, using the SP or VARS as base. There is a unified register bank for the stack and local variable pool, because this facilitates the call and return of methods where each method is located by a frame pointer in the stack. Thanks to the forwarding technique in the stack architecture, the write back stage is not always executed, and hence there a re meaningful energy savings when compared to a regular 5 state pipeline of a RISC CPU.

The VLIW processor is an extension of the pipelined one. Basically, it has its functional units and the instruction decoders replicated. The additional decoders do not support the instructions for call and return of methods, since they are always in the main flow. The local variable storage is placed just in the first register file, when the instructions of other flows need the value of a local variable, they must fetch from there. Each instruction flow has its own operand stack, which has less registers than the main operand stack, since the operand stacks for the secondary flows do not grow as much as the main flow grows.

The VLIW packet has a variable size, avoiding unnecessary memory accesses. A header in the first instruction of the word informs to the instruction fetch controller how many instructions the current packet has. The search for ILP in the Java program is done at the bytecode level. The algorithm works as follows: all the instructions that depend on the result of the previous one are grouped in an operand block. The entire Java program is divided in these groups and they can be parallelized respecting the functional unit constraints. For example, if there is just one multiplier, two instructions that use this functional unit can not be operated in parallel.

### 3.3 Results on Hardware and Software Exploration

To illustrate the results of library characterization using different algorithmic versions of the same function and different cores (multicycle, pipeline and a VLIW version with 2 words), there are two routines selected: the sine and the Inverse Modified Discrete Cosine Transform. The results in terms of performance, power and energy are obtained using the CACO-PS simulator [18].

Table 1 and 2 illustrates the characterization of the alternative implementations of the sine function. Table 1 shows the software results that do not depend on hardware and table 2 shows the results that depend on hardware. There are some entries that are pretty obvious. Since Cordic is a more complex algorithm, program memory size is larger than with Table Look-up (table 1), as well as the number of cycles required for computation for all the cores (table 2). It is interesting to notice, however, that when the resolution increases, the amount of data memory increases exponentially for the Table Look-up algorithm, but only sublinearly for the Cordic algorithm. The increase in memory reflects not only in the required amount of memory, but also in the power dissipation of a larger memory.

**Table 1.** Sine Characterization (software dependent)

| Characteristic | | Cordic | Table |
|---|---|---|---|
| *Program size* (bytes) | | 206 | 88 |
| *Data mem* | 1° | 184 | 220 |
| (bytes) | 0.5° | 184 | 400 |
| | 0.1° | 184 | 1840 |

The table 2 presents the results in terms of performance, power and energy, using a frequency equal 50 MHz and Vdd equal 3.3v. It is obvious that the pipeline and VLIW architectures provide the better results in terms of cycles, the best results in terms of performance is the combination of sine calculation as simple table search and VLIW architecture, but the worst results in terms of power. The best combination in terms of power but worst in terms of energy is the sine using Cordic and Multicycle core.

**Table 2.** Sine Characterization (hardware dependent)

| Characteristic | Cordic | | | Table | | |
|---|---|---|---|---|---|---|
| | *Multi* | *Pipeline* | *VLIW2* | *Multi* | *Pipeline* | *VLIW2* |
| *Performance* (cycles) | 2447 | 755 | 599 | 136 | 65 | 55 |
| *Power* (mW) | 11.8092 | 16.1626 | 22.9019 | 13.4431 | 17.8235 | 20.1606 |
| *Energy* (ηJ) | 577.9421 | 244.0559 | 274.4414 | 36.5652 | 23.1705 | 22.1779 |

Tables 3 and 4 show the main results of the characterization of the four different implementations of the IMDCT function. The IMDCT3 implementation has the better results in terms of performance in all architectures, but the size of program memory significantly increases. The opposite happens with the IMDCT implementation, which has far better results in terms of program memory, but consumes more cycles. In terms of power (using a frequency equal 50 MHz and Vdd equal 3.3v) the best combination are the IMDCT1 and IMDCT2 with multicycle core, but this combination does not have good results in terms of energy. Table 4 shows that the best results in terms of performance are the results that execute in VLIW core, since the IMDCT routine has lot of parallelism.

**Table 3.** IMDCT Characterization (software dependable)

| Characteristic | IMDCT | IMDCT1 | IMDCT2 | IMDCT3 |
|---|---|---|---|---|
| *Program size* (bytes) | 344 | 2,137 | 4,260 | 15,294 |
| *Data mem* (bytes) | 3546 | 3546 | 3546 | 3546 |

**Table 4.** IMDCT Characterization (hardware dependable)

| Characteristic | IMDCT | | | IMDCT1 | | |
|---|---|---|---|---|---|---|
| | *Multi* | *Pipeline* | *VLIW2* | *Multi* | *Pipeline* | *VLIW2* |
| *Performance* (cycles) | 140300 | 40306 | 33051 | 97354 | 31500 | 19325 |
| *Power* (mW) | 8.8533 | 20.0533 | 24.9227 | 8.6595 | 17.8944 | 25.3609 |
| *Energy* (µJ) | 24.8424 | 16.1654 | 16.4744 | 16.8607 | 11.2735 | 9.8021 |

**Table 4.** IMDCT Characterization (hardware dependable) (cont.)

| Characteristic | IMDCT2 | | | IMDCT3 | | |
|---|---|---|---|---|---|---|
| | *Multi* | *Pipeline* | *VLIW2* | *Multi* | *Pipeline* | *VLIW2* |
| *Performance* (cycles) | 92882 | 30369 | 17329 | 51345 | 18858 | 9306 |
| *Power* (mW) | 8.6483 | 17.7355 | 27.2193 | 9.1435 | 17.3849 | 34.5890 |
| *Energy* (µJ) | 16.0654 | 10.7722 | 9.4334 | 9.3894 | 6.5569 | 6.4380 |

# 4  Design Space Exploration Tool

In the examples presented above, the design space concerning performance, power, energy, and memory footprint was large. However, the availability of different alternatives of the same routine is just a first step in the design space exploration of the application software. One must notice that embedded applications are seldom implemented with a single routine. There is another level of optimization, which concerns finding the best mix of routines among all possible combinations that may exist in an embedded application.

Currently, we are adapting a design exploration tool that maps the routines of an embedded program to an implementation using instances of the software IP library, so as to fulfil given system requirements. The user program is modeled as a graph, where the nodes represent the routines, while the arcs determine the program sequence. The weight of the arcs represents the number of times a certain routine is instantiated.

To generate the application graph representing the dynamic behavior of the application, an instrumentation tool was developed. This instrumentation tool allows the dynamic analysis of Java Class files, generating a list of invoked methods with its corresponding number of calls, which can be mapped to the application graph.

In the exploration tool, before the search begins, the user may determine weights for power, delay and memory optimization. It is also possible to set maximum values for each of these variables. The tool automatically explores the design space and finds the optimal or near optimal mapping for that configuration.

The cost function of the search is based on a trade-off between power, timing, and area. Each library option is characterized by these three factors. The exploration tool normalizes these parameters by the maximum power, timing and area found in the library. The user can then select weights for the three variables. This way, the search can be directed according to the application requirements. If area cost, for example, must be prioritized because of small memory space, the user may increase the area weight. Although one characteristic might be prioritized, the others are still considered in the search mechanisms. There are two search mechanisms. The first one is an exhaustive search. For small programs, this search runs in acceptable times. For larger problems, since we are dealing with an optimization problem of multiple variables, we implemented a genetic algorithm.

Usually, an embedded system can have different running applications. Currently, the design exploration tool is not able to manipulate more than one application on different architectures. To eliminate this restriction each application is modelated as a graph and the design exploration tool is executed several times (one time for each application/processor core), thus the tool selects the correct combination of routines for each processor. Finally, the results are a set of applications, where each application has its own set of routines and which processor core they will be executed that minimizes either power or energy, while maintaining the desired system performance.

The methodology can be better understood through an example. Let us take, for instance, one embedded application that must execute the IMDCT (present in MP3 players, for example) and Crane algorithm (control algorithm that controls a crane). These applications must run in parallel and the power has the highest priority. All the processor cores are running at 50MHz. The crane algorithm must execute less than 5 mili seconds and the IMDCT function must have less than 7 Kbytes of memory space and the application must respond in at most 0.5 mili seconds.

Table 5 presents the results of one instance of the Crane and one instance of IMDCT the implementation. This table shows that the best option to execute the crane algorithm is the multicycle core, this core provides the best result in terms of power and satisfies the execution time. The IMDCT function has a cosine function that has smaller impact in terms of overall performance. Table 5 shows the IMDCT results that follows: muticycle implementation shows the best combination in terms of performance (IMDCT3 core with a table look-up cosine calculation); pipeline implementation shows the best combination in terms of performance (IMDCT3 core with a table lookup cosine calculation) and finally the VLIW implementation shows the best combination in terms of performance and power (IMDCT1 core with a table look-up cosine calculation).

The IMDCT results present that the only combination that fulfils the above restrictions is the VLIW implementation. Because, the best multicycle implementation do not satisfy the requirements in terms of performance and the pipeline satisfies the performance but do not satisfy the memory space. However, the VLIW core must be select to satisfy the execution time requirements and memory space. Thus, an embedded systems application shows the use the correct/best option in terms of SW routines and processor cores to satisfy the system requirements.

**Table 5.** Crane and IMDCT Results for different processors cores

| Characteristic | Crane | | | IMDCT | | |
|---|---|---|---|---|---|---|
| | *Multi* | *Pipeline* | *VLIW2* | *Multi* | *Pipeline* | *VLIW2* |
| ***Performance*** (cycles) | 179022 | 78287 | 68008 | 56241 | 21198 | 21305 |
| ***Power*** (mW) | 13.6235 | 15.9823 | 16.6761 | 9.5177 | 17.4333 | 24.8776 |
| ***Energy*** (µJ) | 48.7781 | 25.0241 | 22.6821 | 10.7057 | 7.3910 | 10.6005 |

## 5 Conclusions

This paper proposed a new methodology for design space exploration using automatic selection of software and hardware IP components for embedded applications. It is based on a software IP library and a set of cores with the same ISA, the library is previously characterized each core and uses a tool for automatic design space exploration and SW and HW IP selection.

Experimental results have confirmed the hypothesis that there is a large space to be explored based on algorithmic decisions taken at higher levels of abstraction, much before compiler intervention. Selecting the right algorithm/right architecture might give orders of magnitude of gain in terms of physical characteristics like memory usage, performance, and power dissipation. As a future work, we plan to modify the design space exploration tool making possible that routines of the same application can be mapped onto different processors cores.

## References

1. Dutt, N., Nicolau, A., Tomiyama, H., Halambi, A.: New Directions in Compiler Technology for Embedded Systems. In: Asia-Pacific Design Automation Conference, Jan. 2001. Proceedings, IEEE Computer Society Press (2001).
2. Dalal, V., Ravikumar, C.P.: Software Power Optimizations in an Embedded System. In: VLSI Design Conference, Jan. 2001. Proceedings, IEEE Computer Science Press (2001).
3. Kandemir, M., Vijaykrishnan, V., Irwin, M.J., Ye, W.: Influence of Compiler Optimizations on System Power. In: IEEE Transactions on VLSI Systems, vol. 9, n. 6 (2001).

4. Reyneri, L.M., Cucinotta, F., Serra, A., Lavagno, L.: A Hardware/Software Co-design Flow and IP Library Based on Simulink. In: Design Automation Conference 2001, Las Vegas, June 2001. Proceedings, ACM (2001).

5. Givargis, T., Vahid, F., Henkel, J.: System-Level Exploration for Pareto-optimal Configurations in Parameterized Systems-on-a-chip. In: International Conference on Computer-Aided Design, San Jose, Nov., (2001).

6. Nandi, A., Marculescu, R.: System-Level Power/Performance Analysis for Embedded Systems Design. In: Design Automation Conference, June 2001. Proceedings, ACM (2001).

7. Kathail, V., Aditya, S., Schreiber, R., Rau, B.R., Cronquist, D.C., Sivaraman, M.: PICO: Automatically Designing Custon Computers. In IEEE Computer, September (2001).

8. Tiwari, V., Malik, S., Wolfe, A.: Power Analysis of Embedded Software: a First Step Towards Software Power Minimization. In: IEEE Transactions on Very Large Scale Integration (VLSI) Systems, vol. 2, n. 4, Dec., (1994).

9. Choi, K., Chatterjee, A.: Efficient Instruction-Level Optimization Methodology for Low-Power Embedded Systems. In: International Symposium on System Synthesis, Montréal, Oct. 2001. Proceedings, ACM (2001).

10. Peymandoust, A., Simunic, T., De Micheli, G.: Complex Library Mapping for Embedded Software Using Symbolic Algebra". In: Design Automation Conference, New Orleans, June 2002. Proceedings, ACM (2002).

11. Kumar, R., Farkas, K.I., Jouppi, N.P., Ranganathan, P., Tullsen, D.M.: Single-ISA Heterogeneous Multi-Core Architectures: The Potential for Processor Power Reduction. In: International Symposium on Microarchitecture, (2003).

12. Lieverse, P., van der Wolf, P., Deprettere, E., Vissers, K.: A Methodology for Architecture Exploration of Heterogeneous Signal Processing Systems. In: Joranl of VLSI Signal Processing, vol. 29 (2001) 197-206.

13. Mariatos, E.P., Birbas, A.N., Birbas, M.K.: A Mapping Algorithm for Computer-Assisted Exploration in the Design of Embedded Systems. In: ACM Transactions on Design Automation of Electronic Systems, vol. 6, n.1, Jan. 2001, ACM (2001).

14. Omondi, A. Computer Arithmetic Systems: Algorithms, Architecture and Implementation. Prentice Hall (1994).

15. K.Salomonsen, S.Søgaard, E.P.Larsen. Design and Implementation of an MPEG/Audio Layer III Bitstream Processor, Master Thesis, Aalborg University (1997).

16. Ito, S., Carro, L., Jacobi, R.: Making Java Work for Microcontroller Applications. In: IEEE Design & Test of Computers. vol. 18, n. 5, Sept-Oct (2001).

17. Beck, A. C., Carro, L.: Low Power Java Processor for Embedded Applications. In: IFIP 12th International Conference on Very Large Scale Integration, Germany, December (2003).

18. Beck, A. C., Wagner, F.R., Carro, L.: CACO-PS: A General Purpose Cycle-Accurate Configurable Power Simulator. In: 16th Symposium on Integrated Circuits and Systems Design. São Paulo, Brazil, Sept. 2003. Proceedings, IEEE Computer Society Press (2003).

# On Enhancing SIMD-Controlled DSPs
# for Performing Recursive Filtering

Michael Hosemann and Gerhard Fettweis*

Vodafone Chair Mobile Communications Systems
Dresden University of Technology
01062 Dresden, Germany
{hosemann,fettweis}@ifn.et.tu-dresden.de

**Abstract.** Many digital signal processors (DSPs) and also microprocessors are employing the single-instruction multiple-data (SIMD) paradigm for controling their data paths. While this can provide high computational power and efficiency, not all applications can profit from this feature. One important application of DSPs are recursive filters. Due to their data-dependencies they can not exploit the capabilities of SIMD-controlled DSPs. This paper introduces enhancements of the SIMD control paradigm to accommodate recursive filters. Three methods for calculating recursive filters on SIMD-controlled DSPs and their requirement's for control and data transfer are presented. Their performance and hardware requirements are evaluated to determine the most efficient solution in terms of the AT-product.

## 1 Introduction

Digital Signal Processors (DSPs) are more and more widely used in signal processing applications since they can provide the flexibility which is needed in a world of evolving standards, changing requirements and costly bug fixes in dedicated application specific integrated circuits (ASICs). To minimize the size and performance penalty paid for the flexibility and achieve a high computational power, many state-of-the-art DSPs employ the single-instruction multiple-data (SIMD) paradigm for control. SIMD schemes are also finding their way into the multimedia extensions of microprocessors, e.g., MMX$^{TM}$ or SSE$^{TM}$.

One important application of DSPs are recursive filters. They are employed mainly in audio processing, e.g. [1], but also other applications [2]. Due to their data-dependencies they can not exploit the capabilities of SIMD-controlled DSPs as non-recursive (FIR) filters can. There are multiple ways of speeding-up the computation of recursive filters: Previously, we analyzed the data-dependencies [3] and also introduced algebraic transformations to allow for computing recursive filters in SIMD-structures at the cost of computational overhead [4]. Other approaches in literature employ pipelining instead of parallization for speedup [5] or require multiple-instruction schemes for parallel calculations [6, 7].

* This work was sponsored in part by Deutsche Forschungsgemeinschaft (DFG) within SFB358-A6

A. Pimentel and S. Vassiliadis (Eds.): SAMOS 2004, LNCS 3133, pp. 313–322, 2004.
© Springer-Verlag Berlin Heidelberg 2004

This paper introduces another approach, enhancing the SIMD control scheme itself to accommodate recursive filters without introducing much hardware overhead. Several techniques for enhancing SIMD control will be presented and their hardware overhead and performance will be analyzed to find the most efficient solution.

## 2    Parallel Calculation of Recursive Filters

### 2.1    Data Dependencies

The data dependencies limiting the available data parallelism can be seen in equation 1.

$$y_k = \sum_{m=1}^{M-1} a_m \cdot y_{k-m} + \sum_{n-0}^{N-1} b_n \cdot x_{k-n} \tag{1}$$

For the calculation of each output value $y_k$ the previous output values $y_{k-1}$ through $y_{k-M-1}$ must be available. Hence, it is impossible to complete the calculation of multiple output values at the same time, as can be done for FIR-filters [8]. Instead, if multiple output values shall be computed in parallel, their calculation can only be completed one output value at a time. This leads to the parallel calculation methods elaborated upon in the following section which were derived in [3]. We will review the data transfer and control requirements of these methods in the following sections.

### 2.2    Method 1: Calculation of One Output Value per Data Path

A data flow graph of an exemplary filter with $N = 4$ and $M = 5$, mapped upon a processor with 3 or more data paths is shown in figure 1. Each output value is calculated on one particular data path. From the data flow graph the following observations can be made for the data transfer and control requirements:

- Coefficients are always loaded into data path number 0 (left) and then transfered to the other data paths by a Zurich-Zip.
- Data are loaded into data path number zero as well as higher-number data paths. This will require a parameter for the load instruction. The data are then broadcasted to multiple, but sometimes not all, data paths. Again, this will require special parameters for the broadcast instruction.
- The calculated output values are written back to memory and also broadcasted to the data paths to the right of the calculating data path. The broadcast is already covered by the previous point, the store operation will require a special parameter for the source data path.
- During the prologue, data paths have to be activated one by one, during the epilogue they have to be deactivated again.
- For fixed-point processors, e.g. one with 16 bit, no contents of accumulators, which e.g. are 40 bit wide, have to be transfered between data paths.

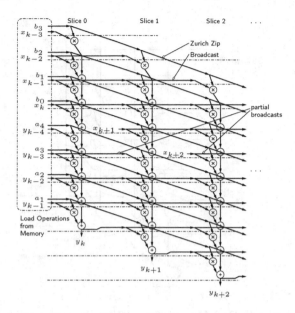

**Fig. 1.** Data Flow for calculating a IIR filter with $N = 4$ and $M = 5$

If more output samples than available data paths have to be calculated, multiple sets of calculation must be performed. The epilogues and prologues of consecutive sets can be overlapped. However, this will require higher control efforts. For overlapping sets the time to calculate $Y$ outputs of a filter with $N + M - 1$ taps on a processor with $P$ data paths and $T_T$ cycles per tap can be determined as:

$$T_{Y,P} = \max(N+M-1, P) \cdot T_T \cdot \left\lceil \frac{Y}{P} \right\rceil + (N+M-1) \cdot T_T + T_T \cdot \mathrm{rem}\,(Y,P) + 2. \quad (2)$$

For non-overlapping sets, further denoted as method 1a, this execution time increases to:

$$T_{Y,P} = \big((N+M-1) \cdot T_T + (P-1) \cdot T_T + 2\big) \cdot \left\lceil \frac{Y}{P} \right\rceil$$
$$+ (N+M-1) \cdot T_T + \mathrm{rem}\,(Y,P) \cdot T_T + 2. \quad (3)$$

## 2.3    Method 2: Calculation of one Filter Tap per Slice

The data flow graph of the second method to calculate multiple output values in parallel is shown in figure 2. Here, each filter tap is calculated on one data path. This requires transferring the accumulated intermediate results between data paths. Since in fixed-point processors the accumulated values have a higher bit-width than the samples or coefficients, this can lead to higher bandwidth requirements for the data transfers. But still, basically the same kinds of data transfer operations as before are required.

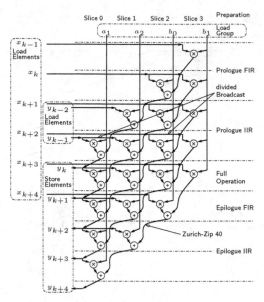

**Fig. 2.** Data Flow for Calculating One Tap per Slice

For calculating filters where the number of taps is larger than the number of data paths, multiple sets of calculations for one output have to be performed. Intermediate instead of final results have to be stored and later be reloaded for further accumulation. Also, if the number of taps is not divisible by the number of data paths, some data paths will have to run idle during the last set of calculations. Again, consecutive sets of operations can be overlapped at the cost of more parallel load and store operations. For overlapped calculations, the calculation time can be determined as:

$$T_Y = (P - 1) \cdot T_T + \max(Y, P) \cdot T_T \cdot \left\lceil \frac{N + M - 1}{P} \right\rceil + 2. \qquad (4)$$

For non-overlapping sets, further denoted as method 2a, this execution time increases to:

$$T(Y) = ((P - 1 + Y) \cdot T_T + 2) \cdot \left\lceil \frac{N + M - 1}{P} \right\rceil + Y \cdot T_T + 2 + \mathrm{rem}(Y, P) \cdot T_T. \quad (5)$$

## 2.4   Method 3: Parallel Calculation of One Output Value Using Tree-Addition

For comparison, we also include a third method, where just one output value is calculated at a time. First, the taps are calculated in parallel and second summed up in a tree pattern. This method requires special data transfers for the tree addition. They deviate from the SIMD paradigm but are otherwise fairly simple to implement since they can reuse the connections which are required for the Zurich-Zips mentioned above. Method 3 achieves the following calculation times:

$$T_{Y,P} = Y \cdot \left( \left\lceil \frac{N+M+1}{P} \right\rceil \cdot T_T + 2 \cdot \min\left( \lceil \mathrm{ld}(P) \rceil, \lceil \mathrm{ld}(N+M+1) \rceil \right) \right) + 2 \quad (6)$$

## 3   Required Control Structures

After presenting three different methods for calculating recursive filters is parallel, we will now analyze the control structures which are required for implementing these methods. The control structures for one set of calculations following both variant 1 and 2 can be seen as in figure 3 a). During the prologue, one data path begins the calculation of one filter tap and the other data paths are switched on one after another for the calculation of the next filter taps. At the same time, data are transfered only to the active data paths.

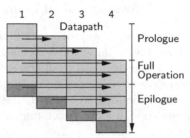

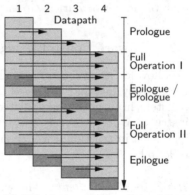

**a)** Calculation of One Set of Outputs

**b)** Calculation of Two Sets of Outputs

During full operation, all data paths are active and data are transfered between all of them.

During the epilogue, data paths have to be switched off one after another after calculating all their filter taps. Also, data are only transfered between the active data paths. For method 1, after calculating the last filter taps, denoted by the darker grey boxes, the outputs have to be written back to memory and transfered to other data path. This requires different instructions than the calculation of the other, preceding, taps.

**Fig. 3.** Control Structures

This lets us conclude that we have to solve two problems: First, we need to activate and deactivate data paths. Second, we need to provide addresses to the data transfers to control their source and destination.

If we like to overlap two sets of calculations, the required control structures become a bit more complex, as can be seen in figure 3 b). A true prologue is only performed for the first, epilogue only for the last set of calculations. Overlapping epilogue and prologue of two sets of calculations yields a new phase of operation where no data paths have to be (de-)activated but different operations have to be performed in certain data paths and data transfers have to be split. These split data transfers will require more addresses.

How to answer these control needs will be laid out in the following section.

# 4    Enhanced SIMD-Control

After analyzing the control requirements in the previous section, we will now propose control techniques which can fulfill these requirements. For each technique a qualitative assessment of the hardware requirements is presented, exact number will follow in the next section.

## 4.1    Software Control Using Immediates

A very simple way of controlling data path's activities and data transfers is by supplying immediates for each instruction. One immediate bit would be set for each active data path (its activity bit) and source and destination for data transfers are also specified as numerical values.

Since immediates must be set in every cycle, it is not possible to write program code in loops which may also increase the required program memory size.

*Hardware Requirements.* This technique requires $P$ bits for data path activation, one time ld$P$ bits for each load or store instruction and two times ld$P$ bits for each broadcast or Zurich-Zip instruction.

## 4.2    Software Control Using Registers

To allow for using loops in program code we designed a second scheme, where the activity bits and addresses are supplied by control registers. These control registers, in turn, are manipulated by small ALUs which have to be controlled by instructions in each cycle. Since these instruction can remain the same, e.g. an increment instruction, throughout some time, these instructions can be included in loop bodies.

*Hardware Requirements.* The width of the instruction word will remain about the same as in the previous method, since the registers must be specified in the data transfer instructions. Additionally, the register manipulation units must be controlled. However, the overall program memory requirements will be lower, since less lines of code will be required. Also, chip area for the registers and ALUs is required but quite small.

## 4.3    Hardware Control Using State-Machines

The previous techniques used registers manipulated by software controlled ALUs. Since this software control is fairly regular, we will replace it with hardware state-machines in this technique. The idea is illustrated in figure 4. The left part shows the program code, the middle part the corresponding state of the activity and address registers and the right part the active data paths and data transfers.

The INIT instructions initialize the registers of the state machine and set the operation mode, e.g. INIT Adr2 1 ++ sets address register 2 to 1 and also sets

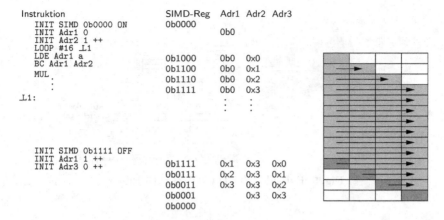

| Instruktion | SIMD-Reg | Adr1 | Adr2 | Adr3 |
|---|---|---|---|---|
| INIT SIMD 0b0000 ON | 0b0000 | | | |
| INIT Adr1 0 | | 0b0 | | |
| INIT Adr2 1 ++ | | | | |
| LOOP #16 _L1 | | | | |
| LDE Adr1 a | 0b1000 | 0b0 | 0x0 | |
| BC Adr1 Adr2 | 0b1100 | 0b0 | 0x1 | |
| MUL . | 0b1110 | 0b0 | 0x2 | |
| : | 0b1111 | 0b0 | 0x3 | |
| _L1: | : | : | | |
| | | | | |
| | | | | |
| INIT SIMD 0b1111 OFF | | | | |
| INIT Adr1 1 ++ | | | | |
| INIT Adr3 0 ++ | 0b1111 | 0x1 | 0x3 | 0x0 |
| | 0b0111 | 0x2 | 0x3 | 0x1 |
| | 0b0011 | 0x3 | 0x3 | 0x2 |
| | 0b0001 | | 0x3 | 0x3 |
| | 0b0000 | | | |

**Fig. 4.** Extended SIMD Control with State-Machines

the increment mode with saturation. The increment is carried out at each loop iteration. Because of the state-machine, this technique influences program behavior similar to a CISC processor. This technique might not be easily supported by a compiler.

*Hardware Requirements.* The hardware requirements for this technique consist of the registers and ALUs for manipulating them and is very small. The instructions for setting up the state machine can use already existing instruction slots, e.g. for program control, and hence do not increase the size of the instruction word.

### 4.4  Skewed SIMD Control

When looking at the required control structure one can note, that it is basically a skewed SIMD structure. This means, the instruction executed on one data path is the same instruction as the one that was executed on the neighboring data path one loop iteration before. We are exploiting this observation to create a control technique that does not rely on activating and deactivating data path but skewed SIMD instructions. The technique is illustrated in figure 5.

The left side does depict the control structure to be realized. The right side shows a block diagram of the control hardware. Additionally to the usual program memory, instruction decoder, and distribution of control signals, a buffer, second instruction decoder and a SIMD control unit are added. The buffer holds a copy of the program code of the first phase. One decoder decodes the instructions of the first phase, the second decoder decodes instructions of the second phase. The decoded control signals of both decoders are distributed to all data paths. However, the SIMD control unit selects the one or other set of control signals for each data path. The SIMD control unit again contains a state-machine which is set up at the beginning of the calculation of a recursive filter. For each loop iteration it advances its state so that data paths are switched from the

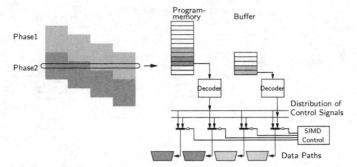

**Fig. 5.** Extended SIMD Control with Buffer

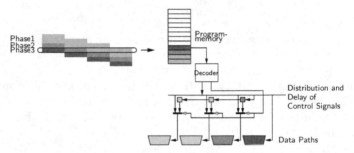

**Fig. 6.** Extended SIMD Control with Pipeline

first to the second phase. If the loop body contains just a single instruction, the control technique can be simplified to a pipeline-like structure, depicted in figure 6. Here, the decoded signals are delayed between the data paths just like in a pipeline.

*Hardware Requirements.* The hardware requirements are determined by the program buffer, second decoder and the SIMD control unit. Depending on the ISA and buffer size, the buffer and decoder will form the largest part. For the pipeline technique, the hardware requirements are determined by the number and size of the pipeline registers.

### 4.5 Comparison of Hardware Requirements

After proposing the various control techniques, we will compare their hardware requirements in order to find the most efficient solution. The hardware requirements were estimated for the UMC 0.13 $\mu$m silicon technology, where one gate-equivalent occupies $5.13\mu m^2$ and one bit of single port memory, used for program memory, occupies about $3\mu m^2$. We also assume that the processor features a VLIW-like ISA with instruction word sizes of about 170 bit and very simple decoders. These assumptions stem from our currently developed DSP for which we performed the work described in this paper.

The hardware requirements for the proposed control methods are presented in figure 7a). It can be seen, that the software control method with immediates requires the largest chip area due to its program memory consumption. The methods for skewed SIMD control require quite large chip area, too. However, these values are for our particular ISA and might be much smaller for ISAs with smaller instruction words. The smallest method is the hardware control with state-machine.

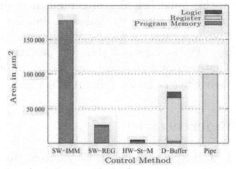

**a)** Area Requirements

However, area consumption is not the only criteria for an efficient solution. Performance also has to be taken into account. For this paper we calculated the execution time $T$ for each of the presented calculation schemes for 200 output values of a filter with 20 taps. This should be a reasonable assumption for applications where data is processed in frames. The cycle time of the processor is not affected by the control method since it is determined by the data paths. Hence, we can calculate the efficiency $E = \frac{1}{A \cdot T}$ where $A$ represents the consumed die area.

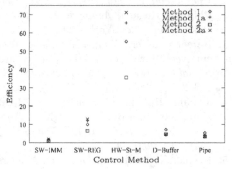

**b)** Efficiency for Control Hardware Only

The efficiency, normalized on the method with the lowest efficiency for just the control hardware is presented in figure 7b). Due to its small area consumption, hardware control with state-machines yields by far the best efficiency. However, the area consumption must be viewed for the whole DSP, where also area for memories and data paths must be accounted for. This has been done in figure 7c) where we included the area for 1Mbit of data memory. It can be

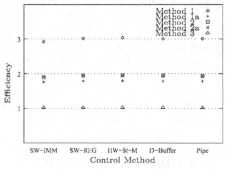

**c)** Efficiency for Complete DSP

**Fig. 7.** Comparison of Hardware Requirements and Efficiency for the Proposed Control Techniques

seen that the different hardware requirements of the control schemes play less of a role compared to the calculation schemes. Hence, issues like compiler- and programmer-friendlyness should also be taken into account when choosing a method for enhancing SIMD-controls.

# 5  Conclusions

In this paper we first presented three methods for speeding-up the calculation of recursive filters by exploiting data level parallelism. We analyzed the required control structures for the methods and presented several techniques for enhancing SIMD-controlled DSPs to perform parallel calculation of recursive filters. The hardware requirements for the proposed techniques were determined and their efficiency was compared by means of the AT-product.

# References

1. J. Huopaniemi and M. Karjalainen, "Review of digital filter design and implementation methods for 3-d sound," in *Proceedings of the 102nd Convention of the Audio Engineering Society, Preprint 4461*, 1997.
2. Philip A. Regalia, *Adaptive IIR Filtering in Signal Processing and Control*, Marcel Dekker, Inc., New York, 1995.
3. Rainer Schaffer, Michael Hosemann, Renate Merker, and Gerhard P. Fettweis, "Recursive Filtering on SIMD-Architectures," in *Proceedings of IEEE Workshop on Signal Processing Systems 2003 (SIPS'03)*, Seoul, Korea, 27.-29. Aug. 2003, pp. 263–268.
4. J. Pablo Robelly, Gordon Cichon, Hendrik Seidel, and Gerhard P. Fettweis, "Implementation of Recursive Digital Filters into Vector SIMD DSP Architectures," in *Proceedings of International Conference on Acoustics, Speech and Signal Processing, ICASSP 2004*, 2004.
5. Keshab K. Parhi and David G. Messerschmitt, "Pipeline Interleaving and Parallelism in Recursive Digital Filters – Part I: Pipelining Using Scattered Look-Ahead and Decomposition ," *IEEE Transactions on Acoustics, Speech, and Signal Processing*, vol. 37, no. 7, pp. 1099–1117, July 1989.
6. Haigeng Wang, Nikil D. Dutt, and Alexandru Nicolau, "Exploring Scalable Schedules for IIR Filters With Resource Constraints ," *IEEE Transactions on Circuits and Systems – II: Analog and Digital Signal Processing*, vol. 46, no. 11, pp. 1367–1379, Nov. 1999.
7. Michael A. Soderstrand and Antonio E. de la Serna, "Minimum Denominator-Multiplier Pipelined Recursive Digital Filters," *IEEE Transactions on Circuits and Systems – II: Analog and Digital Signal Processing*, vol. 42, no. 10, pp. 666–672, Oct. 1995.
8. J.-P. Beraud, "Digital Signal Processor Architecture with plural Multiply/Accumulate Devices," Tech. Rep., IBM, Armonk, N.Y., 1992.

# Memory Bandwidth Requirements
# of Tile-Based Rendering

Iosif Antochi[1], Ben Juurlink[1], Stamatis Vassiliadis[1], and Petri Liuha[2]

[1] Computer Engineering Laboratory,
Electrical Engineering, Mathematics and Computer Science Faculty,
Delft University of Technology,
Mekelweg 4, 2628 CD Delft, The Netherlands
{tkg,benj,stamatis}@ce.et.tudelft.nl
[2] NOKIA Research Center, Visiokatu-1, SF-33720 Tampere, Finland
petri.liuha@nokia.com

**Abstract.** Because mobile phones are omnipresent and equipped with displays, they are attractive platforms for rendering 3D images. However, because they are powered by batteries, a graphics accelerator for mobile phones should dissipate as little energy as possible. Since external memory accesses consume a significant amount of power, techniques that reduce the amount of external data traffic also reduce the power consumption. A technique that looks promising is tile-based rendering. This technique decomposes a scene into tiles and renders the tiles one by one. This allows the color components and z values of one tile to be stored in small, on-chip buffers, so that only the pixels visible in the final scene need to be stored in the external frame buffer. However, in a tile-based renderer each triangle may need to be sent to the graphics accelerator more than once, since it might overlap more than one tile. In this paper we measure the total amount of external data traffic produced by conventional and tile-based renderers using several representative OpenGL benchmark scenes. The results show that employing a tile size of $32 \times 32$ pixels generally yields the best trade-off between the amount of on-chip memory and the amount of external data traffic. In addition, the results show that overall, a tile-based architecture reduces the total amount of external data traffic by a factor of 1.96 compared to a traditional architecture.

## 1 Introduction

A huge market is foreseen for wireless, interactive 3D graphics applications, in particular games[1]. The resources required to run such applications are usually considerable, while the resources offered by low-power devices are rather limited. Specifically, since such devices are powered by batteries they should consume as little energy as possible. Furthermore, the amount of chip area of such systems is severely limited.

External memory accesses are a major source of power consumption [2, 3]. They often dissipate more energy than the datapaths and the control units. A promising technique to reduce the amount of external data traffic and, hence, the power-consumption is tile-based rendering. This technique decomposes a scene into tiles and renders the tiles one by one. The advantage of this is that the color components and z values of one tile can be stored in small, on-chip buffers, so that only the pixels visible in the final

A. Pimentel and S. Vassiliadis (Eds.): SAMOS 2004, LNCS 3133, pp. 323–332, 2004.

scene need to be stored in the external frame buffer. In other words, tile-based rendering reduces the problem of overdraw. On the other hand, however, a tile-based renderer may require that each triangle to be sent to the graphics accelerator more than once, since a triangle might overlap more than one tile. Moreover, given that the amount of chip area is limited, very little area can be devoted to local memory. So, we are faced with two opposite goals: reduce the amount of external memory traffic as much as possible while, at the same time, using as little internal memory as possible.

In this paper we examine the memory bandwidth requirements for tile-based 3D graphics accelerators. First, we examine how the amount of external data traffic varies with the tile size. The results show that a tile size of $32 \times 32$ pixels yields the best trade-off between the data traffic volume and the amount of area dedicated to on-chip buffers. By increasing the tile size beyond $32 \times 32$ pixels, the amount of external data traffic is only marginally reduced. Also, decreasing the tile size under $32 \times 32$ pixels, increases the external data traffic substantially. Second, we measure how much external data traffic is saved by a tile-based renderer compared to a traditional renderer. The results show that the tile-based architecture reduces the total amount of external data traffic by a factor of 1.96 compared to the traditional architecture.

This paper is organized as follows. After discussing related work in Section 2, we describe the conventional and tile-based rendering models in Section 3. In Section 4, the results of our experiments are presented. First, we determine the influence of the tile size on the amount of external data traffic. Second, we measure how much external data traffic is saved by employing a tile-based architecture instead of a conventional architecture. Conclusions and future work are given in Section 5.

## 2  Related Work

Tile-based architectures were initially proposed for high-performance, parallel renderers [4–6]. Since tiles cover non-overlapping parts of a scene, the triangles that intersect with these tiles can be rendered in parallel. In such architectures it is important to balance the load on the parallel renderers [7, 8]. These studies, however, present statistics relevant for high-end parallel graphics, while we consider a low-power architecture in which the tiles are rendered sequentially one-by-one and the available memory bandwidth is rather limited when compared with parallel tile-based rendering.

Low-power tile-based architectures [9, 10] were proposed, but no measurements of the total required bandwidth were presented. For instance, in [9] it is shown only that the tile-based approach reduces the traffic between the renderer and the external memory for various scene sizes. However, there is no indication of how the overall data traffic is affected by the tile size. The work presented in [10] focuses on compatibility problems for tile-based renderers and shows how they can be avoided.

Other papers discussing tile rendering (e.g., [11]) are mainly concerned by the *overlap* (the number of tiles that a primitive covers) of triangles with respect to tile size. Only the traffic between the CPU or main memory to the accelerator was considered. We consider the total data traffic, i.e., not only the traffic from the CPU or main memory to the accelerator but also the traffic between the accelerator and the frame buffer.

The amount of external data traffic can also be reduced by decreasing the amount of transfered texture data. Three techniques to reduce the texturing traffic are texture

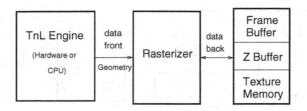

**Fig. 1.** Organization of a traditional renderer.

caching, texture compression, and texturing mechanism. Texture caching is one of the most efficient techniques to reduce the data traffic generated by a renderer. In [12] it is shown that even a 256-byte, direct-mapped cache can significantly reduce the amount of texture traffic. By using texture compression [13, 14] texture traffic can be even further reduced since less data is transferred from the texture memory to the renderer. Recently Möller and Ström proposed a new texturing mechanism called Pooma [15]. Pooma fetches fewer texels from the texture memory than traditional methods at the expense of slightly lower image quality.

## 3 Rendering Methods

In this section we describe the basic organization of a traditional and a tile-based renderer and briefly discuss the factors that contribute to the amount of external data traffic.

The organization of a conventional rasterizer is depicted in Fig. 1. The *Transform and Lighting (TnL) Engine* processes the geometry data at the vertex level. It performs primitives coordinate changes and lighting computations. Modern PC-class graphics accelerators perform (part of) the transform and light stages, but since our target platform is a low-power, low-cost accelerator for mobile phones, we assume they are performed by the host CPU. After the vertices have been processed, they are sent to the rasterizer as primitives such as points, lines, and triangles. After that, the rasterizer scan-converts each triangle into fragments (pixels which may or may not be visible in the final image). It also performs texturing if it is enabled. Finally, for each fragment it is determined if the fragment is obscured by another fragment using, for instance, a z (depth) buffer algorithm. One access to the z buffer is needed to retrieve the old z value and, if the current fragment is closer to the viewpoint than all previous fragments at the same position, the z value of the current fragment is written to the z buffer. Furthermore, if the z test succeeded, the current fragment is written to the frame buffer.

In a tile-based renderer, each scene is decomposed into regions called *tiles* which can be rendered independently. This allows to store the z values and color components of the fragments corresponding to one tile in small, on-chip buffers, whose size (in pixels) is equal to the tile size. This implies that only pixels visible in the final scene need to be written to the external frame buffer. However, tile-based rendering requires that the triangles are first sorted into bins that correspond to the tiles. Furthermore, since a triangle might overlap more than one tile, it may have to be sent to the rasterizer several times.

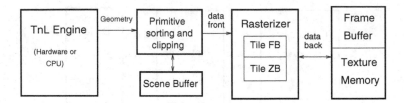

**Fig. 2.** Organization of a tile-based renderer.

The organization of a basic tile-based renderer is depicted in Fig. 2. First, the primitives are sorted according to the tile partitioning and stored in a so-called scene buffer. This may be performed by the CPU or the rasterizer. In this paper it is assumed that it is performed by the CPU. Furthermore, in our measurements we do not include the data traffic required to sort the primitives because it can be accomplished in many different ways. After the primitives have been sorted, the tiles are rendered one by one. First, the primitives that overlap the current tile are sent to the rasterizer. Thereafter, the data associated with the current tile is fetched from the external frame buffer to the local tile frame buffer. This is necessary for blending if the application does not clear the frame buffer when it starts to render a new frame. Furthermore, the tile z buffer is cleared. If the application clears the frame buffer when it starts to render a new frame, the external z buffer is no longer needed. If not, the old z values have to be fetched from the external z buffer. After all primitives that overlap the current tile have been rendered, the content of the tile frame buffer is written to the external frame buffer.

We now briefly describe the amount of external data traffic generated by each method. As depicted in Fig. 1 and Fig. 2, the data traffic between the graphics chip and other components of the system such as the CPU, main memory, and the frame buffer can be divided into two categories:

1. The data sent from the host CPU (or main memory) to the accelerator. It consists of geometrical data needed to describe the primitives, texture data, and changes to the state of the rasterizer such as enable/disable depth test, change texture wrapping mode, etc. We refer to this component as *data_front*.
2. The data transferred between the accelerator and dedicated graphics memory or memories. Since the frame buffer, z buffer, and texture memory are too large to be placed on-chip, they must be allocated off-chip. This component will be referred to as *data_back*.

The *data_front* term is usually dominated by the amount of geometrical data needed to describe the primitives. The amount of texture data is, in the long run, negligible. We remark that with texture data we mean here the traffic needed to copy the texture images to the dedicated texture memory. This is necessary because the application may reuse the texture space after it has passed a pointer to this space to the rasterizer. It does not include the traffic needed to perform texturing. This component is included in the *data_back* term.

In a traditional renderer, the amount of geometrical data is proportional to the number of primitives. In a tile-based renderer, however, each primitive might have to be sent to the rasterizer several times. In particular, if a primitive overlaps $n$ tiles, it needs to be transmitted to the rasterizer $n$ times. Thus, in a tile-based renderer, the *data_front* component is affected significantly by the amount of *overlap*, which is the average number of tiles covered by each primitive.

Therefore, a tile-based renderer actually increases the *data_front* component compared to a conventional renderer. The *data_back* term, however, is significantly reduced by a tile-based renderer. Because the color components and the z values of the fragments belonging to a particular tile can be kept in small, on-chip buffers, only pixels visible in the final image have to be written to the external frame buffer. Furthermore, provided the application clears the z buffer when it starts to render a new frame, the traffic between the rasterizer and the external z buffer is eliminated completely. In a traditional renderer, on the other hand, many fragments might be written to the external frame buffer which are not visible in the final image because they are obscured by other pixels. Thus, in a conventional renderer, the *data_back* component is affected significantly by the amount of *overdraw*, which can be defined as the number of fragments written to an external buffer divided by the image size.

Concluding, while a tile-based renderer produces more external traffic for geometrical data than a traditional renderer (depending on the amount of overlap), it generates less traffic between the rasterizer and the off-chip frame and z buffers (depending on the amount of overdraw).

## 4   Experimental Results

In this section the experimental results are presented. First, in Section 4.1, the benchmarks, tools, and some simulation parameters are described. Thereafter, in Section 4.2 we study how the amount of external data traffic varies with the tile size. Finally, in Section 4.3, we compare the total amount of off-chip memory traffic produced by a tile-based renderer to the amount of traffic generated by a conventional renderer.

### 4.1   Experimental Setup

In order to compare the traditional and tile-based architectures we used 6 of the 7 components of the benchmarking suite proposed in [16]: Q3H, Tux, Aw, ANL, GRA, and DIN. The Q3H profile corresponds to a demo of the Quake III 3D FPS game. Tux is a 3D racing game available on Linux platforms. The Aw (Awadvs-04) profile is part of the Viewperf 6.1.2 package. The ANL, GRA, and DIN are 3D VRML models for which "fly-by" scenes were created and traced.

The statistics were gathered using several tools. First, we used our OpenGL tracer to generate the benchmarks traces which were fed to the Mesa library. The Mesa library performed primitive back-face culling and generated lists of remaining primitives that were sent to our accelerator simulator. For the tile-based architecture we used tile sizes of $\{16, 32, 64\} \times \{16, 32, 64\}$ pixels, and the window size was $640 \times 480$ pixels for all benchmark suite components.

Because texturing exhibits high data locality and because small, direct-mapped caches do not require a large amount of area nor consume a significant amount of

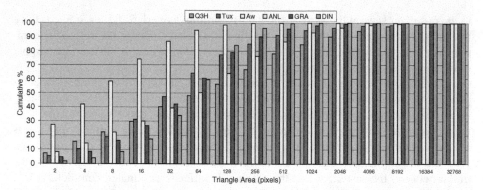

**Fig. 3.** Triangles histogram. This figure shows the cumulative percentage of triangles having an area lower than a defined size.

power [12, 17], we have employed a tiny (256-byte) direct-mapped, on-chip texture cache. We have used our own trace-driven cache simulator to measure the miss ratio of the texture cache.

In order to simulate the 9 possible tile sizes configurations for all workloads on our rasterizer simulator in an acceptable time interval (several weeks), we have rendered approximatively 60 frames from each workload evenly distributed across the workload. For the skipped frames, however, we have not skipped the state change information so that the appropriate state information was committed to the renderer before each frame was rendered.

### 4.2    Tile Size vs. External Data Traffic

In this section we determine how the amount of external data traffic varies with the tile size. Since the tile size determines the size of the local frame and z buffer, and because the amount of chip area is severely limited, we want to employ the smallest tile size possible while, at the same time, reducing the amount of off-chip data traffic as much as possible.

As a first indication of an appropriate tile size, Fig. 3 depicts the cumulative percentage of triangles up to a certain size. It can be seen that by far the most (93%) triangles are smaller than 1024 pixels. Very few triangles (7%) are larger than 1024 pixels. This indicates that more than 93% triangles might fit in a tile size of 1024 (e.g., $32 \times 32$) pixels. However, even if most triangles are smaller than say, $32 \times 32$ they still can overlap multiple tiles if the tile size is $32 \times 32$. Therefore, a better indication of an appropriate tile size is the number of triangles sent to the rasterizer.

Table 1 depicts the number of triangles transferred to the rasterizer for various tile sizes. As explained in Section 3, this data usually dominates the *data_front* component of the total external data. The last row shows the number of triangles transferred if the tile size is equal to the window size. The overlap factor for a specific tile size can, therefore, be obtained by dividing the number of triangles transferred for that tile size by the number given in the last row.

Obviously, if the tile size increases, the number of triangles transferred to the raster-izer decreases, since there is less overlap. However, as remarked before, it is important to use as little internal memory as possible and, therefore, a trade-off needs to be made. It can be seen that using a tile size of less than $32 \times 32$ can increase the number of triangles transferred significantly. For example, if we employ a tile size of $16 \times 16$ in-stead of $32 \times 32$, the amount of geometrical data sent to the rasterizer increases by a factor of 2.02 for the Q3H benchmark and by a factor of 1.97 for the Tux benchmark. On average, using the geometric mean, a tile size of $16 \times 16$ increases the number of triangles sent by a factor of 1.62 compared to $32 \times 32$ tiles. On the other hand, employ-ing tiles larger than $32 \times 32$ reduces the amount of geometrical data only marginally. For example, the geometric mean of the reduction resulting from employing $64 \times 64$ tiles instead of $32 \times 32$ tiles is 1.35. This indicates that a tile size of $32 \times 32$ is the best trade-off between the number of triangles sent to the rasterizer and the size of the internal buffers.

**Table 1.** Number of triangles transferred as a function of the tile size for each benchmark.

| Tile size | Q3H | Tux | AW | ANL | GRA | DIN |
|---|---|---|---|---|---|---|
| | Benchmarks | | | | | |
| $16 \times 16$ | 21,300 | 8,204 | 15,627 | 18,731 | 9,416 | 9,416 |
| $16 \times 32$ | 15,600 | 6,101 | 14,464 | 13,850 | 8,215 | 7,905 |
| $16 \times 64$ | 13,009 | 5,143 | 13,911 | 11,555 | 7,624 | 7,142 |
| $32 \times 16$ | 14,662 | 5,539 | 14,187 | 14,823 | 7,183 | 7,954 |
| $32 \times 32$ | 10,526 | 4,148 | 13,090 | 10,689 | 6,217 | 6,591 |
| $32 \times 64$ | 8,671 | 3,576 | 12,567 | 8,745 | 5,742 | 5,904 |
| $64 \times 16$ | 11,360 | 4,225 | 13,480 | 12,910 | 6,071 | 7,216 |
| $64 \times 32$ | 8,006 | 3,245 | 12,416 | 9,150 | 5,223 | 5,928 |
| $64 \times 64$ | 6,518 | 2,813 | 11,908 | 7,308 | 4,807 | 5,278 |
| $640 \times 480$ | 3,404 | 1,822 | 10,768 | 4,321 | 3,603 | 4,083 |

### 4.3   Tile-Based vs. Conventional Rendering

In this section we measure the total amount of external data traffic produced by a tile-based renderer for a tile size of $32 \times 32$ and compare this to the amount of off-chip memory traffic generated by a conventional renderer.

Figure 4(a) presents the amount of data traffic sent from the CPU to the rasterizer (the *data_front* component of the total traffic) for the tile-based as well as the conven-tional renderer. It also breaks down the *data_front* term into state change data and geo-metrical data. As expected, the tile-based architecture generates more *data_front* traffic than the traditional architecture. On average, using the geometric mean, the tile-based architecture increases the amount of *data_front* traffic by a factor of 2.66 compared to the conventional renderer. The figure also shows that the amount of *data_front* traffic is dominated by the geometrical data and that the increase is due for a large part to the increase in the amount of geometrical data transferred.

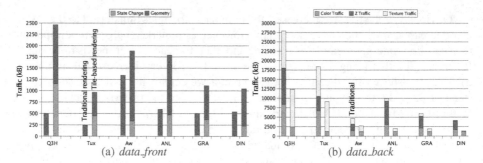

**Fig. 4.** The front and back data traffic components.

Figure 4(b) depicts the amount of data transferred between the rasterizer and the off-chip color and z buffers and texture memory (the *data_back* term). Furthermore, the *data_back* component has been split into data transferred from/to the color buffer, z-buffer, and texture memory. Due to the fact that our rasterizer simulator is much slower when rendering larger tile sizes due to the fact that some of the used data types, when scaled, can no longer be mapped directly to native data types, and the texture miss ratio changed only marginally for tiles with sizes from $16 \times 16$ up to $64 \times 64$, we have approximated the texture traffic for a traditional renderer with the texture traffic generated by a $64 \times 64$ tile-based rasterizer. On average, the tile-based architecture reduces the *data_back* traffic by a factor of 2.71 compared to the traditional renderer (geometric mean). Furthermore, for the conventional architecture the *data_back* traffic is dominated by the traffic between the rasterizer and the frame/z buffers, whereas in a tile-based renderer this traffic is eliminated almost completely. For a tile-based renderer, the texture traffic is the largest component of the *data_back* traffic.

Finally, Figure 5 depicts the total amount of external data traffic produced by the conventional and the tile-based renderer. The total traffic has been divided into *data_front* and *data_back* traffic. It can be seen that since the amount of *data_back* traffic is much larger than the amount of *data_front* traffic, the tile-based architecture reduces the total amount of external traffic significantly. The geometric mean of the traffic reductions over all benchmarks is a factor of 1.96. However, the advantage of tile-based rendering is workload dependent and the results show that tile-based rendering is more suitable than traditional rendering for workloads with low overlap and high overdraw, while for workloads with high overlap and low overdraw, the traditional rendering should be used. Since the workloads from our benchmark suite do not exhibit high overdraw, the results obtained for the tile-based renderer are not significantly better than traditional rendering.

## 5   Conclusions and Future Work

In this paper we have presented a comparison of the total amount of external data traffic required by traditional and tile-based renderers. For tile-based renderers, based on the total data traffic variation with respect to the on-chip memory (tile size), a tile size

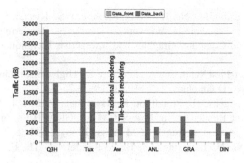

**Fig. 5.** Total external data transferred (kbytes) per frame for a tile-based and a traditional architecture.

of $32 \times 32$ pixels was found to yield the best trade-off between the amount of on-chip memory and the amount of external data traffic. We have also shown that tile-based rendering reduces the total amount of external traffic due to the considerable data traffic reduction between the accelerator and the off-chip memory while maintaining an acceptable increase in data traffic between the CPU and the renderer. Considering that external memory accesses consume a significant amount of power, this indicates that tile-based rendering might be a suitable technique for low-power embedded 3D graphics implementations. We mention, however, that the reduction in bandwidth of tile-based rendering when compared to traditional rendering depends significantly on the workload used. For workloads with a high overlap factor and low overdraw, the traditional rendering can still outperform the tile-based rendering, while for workloads with a low overlap factor and high overdraw, the tile-based rendering is more suitable than traditional rendering.

As future work, we intend to investigate the implications of using multitexturing for tile-based architectures. Furthermore, since the amount of texture traffic is significant for a tile-based renderer, we intend to investigate texture compression techniques. Finally, we are currently investigating the memory bandwidth required for sorting the geometrical primitives into bins corresponding to the tiles.

# References

1. ARM Ltd.: ARM 3D Graphics Solutions. Available at http://www.arm.com (2002)
2. Catthoor, F., Franssen, F., Wuytack, S., Nachtergaele, L., Man, H.D.: Global Communication and Memory Optimizing Transformations for Low-Power Signal Processing Systems. In: Proc. VLSI Signal Processing Workshop. (1994)
3. Fromm, R., Perissakis, S., Cardwell, N., Kozyrakis, C., McGaughy, B., Patterson, D., Anderson, T., Yelick, K.: The Energy Efficiency of IRAM Architectures. In: Proc. $24^{th}$ Annual Int. Symp. on Computer Architecture, ACM Press (1997) 327–337
4. Fuchs, H., Poulton, J., Eyles, J., Greer, T., Goldfeather, J., Ellsworth, D., Molnar, S., G. Turk, B.T., Israel, L.: Pixel-Planes 5: A Heterogeneous Multiprocessor Graphics System Using Processor-Enhanced Memories. Computer Graphics, Vol. 23, No. 3 (July 1989) 79–88
5. Molnar, S., Cox, M., Ellsworth, D., Fuchs, H.: A Sorting Classification of Parallel Rendering. IEEE Comput. Graph. Appl. **14** (1994) 23–32 IEEE Computer Society Press.

6. Humphreys, G., Houston, M., Ng, R., Frank, R., Ahern, S., Kirchner, P.D., Klosowski, J.T.: Chromium: A Stream Processing Framework for Interactive Rendering on Clusters. In: Proc. $29^{th}$ Annual Conf. on Computer Graphics and Interactive Techniques (SIGGRAPH 2002). (2002) 693–702

7. Mueller, C.: The Sort-First Rendering Architecture for High-Performance Graphics. In: Proc. Symp. on Interactive 3D Graphics, ACM Press (1995) 75–84

8. Chen, M., Stoll, G., Igehy, H., Proudfoot, K., Hanrahan, P.: Simple Models of the Impact of Overlap in Bucket Rendering. In: Proc. ACM SIGGRAPH/Eurographics Workshop on Graphics Hardware, Lisbon, Portugal, ACM Press (1998) 105–112

9. PowerVR: 3D Graphical Processing (Tile Based Rendering - The Future of 3D), White Paper. http://www.beyond3d.com/reviews/videologic/vivid/PowerVR_WhitePaper.pdf (2000)

10. Hsieh, E., Pentkovski, V., Piazza, T.: ZR: A 3D API Transparent Technology for Chunk Rendering. In: Proc. $34^{th}$ ACM/IEEE Int. Symp. on Microarchitecture MICRO-34. (2001)

11. Cox, M., Bhandari, N.: Architectural Implications of Hardware-Accelerated Bucket Rendering on the PC. In: Proc. 1997 SIGGRAPH/Eurographics Workshop on Graphics Hardware, ACM Press (1997) 25–34

12. Antochi, I., Juurlink, B., Cilio, A., Liuha, P.: Trading Efficiency for Energy in a Texture Cache Architecture. In: Proc. $4^{th}$ Int. Conf. on Massively Parallel Computing Systems (MPCS'02). (2002)

13. Beers, A.C., Agrawala, M., Chaddha, N.: Rendering from Compressed Textures. In: Proc. $23^{rd}$ Annual Conf. on Computer Graphics and Interactive Techniques, ACM Press (1996) 373–378

14. Fenney, S.: Texture Compression Using Low-Frequency Signal Modulation. In: Proc. ACM SIGGRAPH/Eurographics Conf. on Graphics Hardware, Eurographics Association (2003) 84–91

15. Akenine-Möller, T., Ström, J.: Graphics for the Masses: A Hardware Rasterization Architecture for Mobile Phones. ACM Trans. Graph. **22** (2003) 801–808

16. Antochi, I., Juurlink, B., Vassiliadis, S., Liuha, P.: GraalBench: A 3D Graphics Benchmark Suite for Mobile Phones. In: Proc. ACM SIGPLAN/SIGBED Conf. on Languages, Compilers, and Tools for Embedded Systems (LCTES'04). (2004) (to appear)

17. Hakura, Z.S., Gupta, A.: The Design and Analysis of a Cache Architecture for Texture Mapping. In: Proc. $24^{th}$ Annual Int. Symp. on Computer Architecture. (1997)

# Using CoDeL to Rapidly Prototype Network Processsor Extensions

Nainesh Agarwal and Nikitas J. Dimopoulos

Department of Electrical and Computer Engineering
University of Victoria
Victoria, B.C., Canada
{nagarwal,nikitas}@ece.uvic.ca

**Abstract.** The focus of this work is on techniques that promise to reduce the message delivery latency in message passing environments, incuding clusters of workstations or SMPs. We are introducing *Network
Processing* extensions, and present a preliminary implementation using
CoDeL to rapidly design and prototype these extensions.

## 1 Introduction

Network Processors provide environments that facilitate the processing of communication traffic. These may address message latency or be specifically focused
in the rapid and ongoing changes of protocols [1].

The focus of this work is on techniques that promise to reduce the message
delivery latency in message passing environments, incuding clusters of workstations or SMPs. We have developed predictive techniques which adaptively
predict the target of subsequent communications from sequences of past communication requests. These techniques have proven very effective with hit rates
in excess of 90% for scientific and engineering workloads [3, 4].

The information provided by these predictors can be used to manage the
communication environment so that the delivery of the intended message is facilitated and its latency is minimized. The main contributors to latency are
the copying operations needed to transfer and bind a received message to the
consuming process/thread. To reduce this copying overhead, we introduce architectural extensions comprising of specialized *network cache* and instructions
to manage the operations of this *cache* [3]. The predictive techniques discussed
previously will be used in the cache replacement policies.

In this work we report our using the hardware description language CoDeL
[2], which we have developed, to rapidly prototype network processor extensions.

CoDeL (Controller Description Language), targets the specification and design at the behavioral level. CoDeL is a procedural language in which the order
of the statements implicitly represents the sequence of activities. It extracts
the data and control flow from the program automatically, assigns the necessary
hardware blocks and exploits inherent parallelism. It is similar to the C programming language and is therefore easy to learn. The CoDeL compiler is written in

A. Pimentel and S. Vassiliadis (Eds.): SAMOS 2004, LNCS 3133, pp. 333–342, 2004.

C and it compiles a source CoDeL program to produce synthesizable VHDL code. The control path is extracted automatically and sequences operations and the storing of results. Optimizations include automatic parallelization of non-dependent assignment statements. The generated VHDL code can be targeted to any technology including PLD, FPGA or ASIC.

This paper is organized as follows. Section 2 presents a description of the architectural extensions introduced to support efficient processing of sending and receiving of messages in a tightly coupled parallel processing environment, section 3 discusses the use of CoDeL in specifying and rapidly prototyping these extensions, and we finally conclude with section 4.

## 2   Network Processor

High performance computing is increasingly concerned with efficient communication across the interconnect. System Area Networks (SAN), such as Myrinet [7], provide high bandwidth and low latency while several user-level messaging techniques have removed the operating system kernel and protocol stack from the critical path of communications [11, 14]. A significant portion of the software communication overhead is attributed to message copying. As shown in Fig. 1, these are: from the send buffer to the system buffer (1), from the system buffer to the network interface (NI) (2), and from the network interface to a system buffer (3), and finally to the receive buffer (4). At the send side, user-level messaging layers use programmed I/O or DMA to avoid system buffer copying.

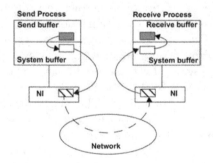

**Fig. 1.** The network interface controller

When a message arrives at the receiving side it is buffered if the receive call has not been posted yet. Several techniques have been developed that try to alleviate the latency introduced by this buffering. These include VMMC, VMMC-2 [10], Fast sockets [13], MPI-LAPI [5] or re-mapping, and copy-on-write techniques [8]. Prediction techniques have been proposed in the past to predict the future accesses in distributed shared memory (DSM) [9] and to predict message destinations in message-passing systems [4, 12].

## 2.1   Integrating Message Predictors with the Network Interface

In this section, we discuss how a message predictor [4] can be used and integrated into the network interface to help achieve zero-copy communication [3]. Since we predict the sequence of message reception calls, we can move the next-to-be-used message near the place that will be consumed. This is most efficiently done if the message is moved to the cache of the processor that will consume it. Predictors then would be incorporated in the replacement policies of caches and pages that hold received messages. Predictors would reside beside the network interface and monitor the message reception patterns predicting the expected message to be consumed next. The network interface uses these predictions to place early arriving messages into the cache. However, these early arriving messages will not be bound to the consuming process/thread until the appropriate receive message is issued.

Ideally, if the data destined to be consumed by a consuming process/thread, has been cached, the process/thread will encounter minimum delay in consuming this data. If the data is to be delivered by the network, as we discussed earlier in this work, the late binding required by a two sided protocol, introduces a significant overhead. Our aim is to introduce architectural extensions that will facilitate the placement of the message data in a cache, bound and ready to be consumed by the consuming thread/process. We accomplish this through the introduction of a special network cache and extensions to the ISA. We consider that a message includes, in addition to the payload, a message ID which may be part or the total MPI message envelope. The message ID is used to identify the message and bind it to its target address. We consider two memory spaces: *Network memory space*: This is where network buffers are allocated and where received messages live waiting to be bound to the process address space. *Process memory space*: This is the process memory address space where process objects, including bound messages, live. To facilitate late binding, we introduce a separate network cache that can distinguish the two memory spaces.

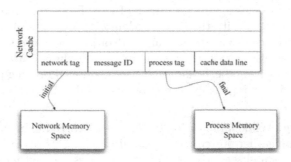

**Fig. 2.** The *process* and *network* memory spaces and their relation through the network cache

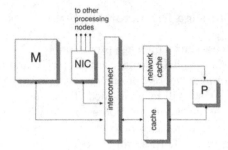

**Fig. 3.** The overall architecture of a network-extended node

**Operation.** We assume messages of length identical to that of a cache line. We assume a separate network cache the structure of which and its associativity will be further elaborated in section 3. The network cache includes three separate tags. The *network tag* is associated with the Network Memory Space, while the *process tag* is associated with the Process Memory Space. A separate *message ID tag* holds the message ID. All three tags can be searched associatively.

On its arrival, a message is cached in the network cache. The *network tag* is set to the address of the buffer in network memory space that is allocated to the message and the *message ID tag* is set accordingly. The message lives at the network cache and it migrates to the Network Memory Space according to a cache replacement policy, which utilizes the prediction heuristics discussed in [4], to replace the message that is least likely to be consumed next. The *message ID* and the *network tag* of a replaced message are held by a link translation buffer so that the message can be located and reloaded into the cache quickly.

**Late Binding.** A *receive call* targeting a message on the network cache will invalidate the message ID and network tags and will set the process tag to point to the address of the object destined to receive the message in Process Memory Space. The buffer in Network Memory space is now released and it can be garbage collected. Similarly the link translation buffer entry is invalidated concluding the late binding of the message to its target object. From this point onward, the cache line is associated with the Process Memory Space. On cache replacement, the message is written back to its targeted object in Process Memory Space and eventually to the data cache. Both the data cache and the network cache are searched for cached objects, and the aforementioned binding process ensures that the object is not replicated in the *network* and *data* caches.

**Early Binding.** While late binding binds an early arriving message to a subsequent receive, an earlier posted receive could prepare and reserve a cache line in the network cache and set the corresponding *process_tag* and *message ID_tag* in anticipation of a subsequent message. When the message indeed arrives in the future, it is placed directly into the reserved cache line and becomes available to the process immediately. This *early binding* functionality is only introduced here, and has not been implemented yet.

**Other Considerations.** As outlined in [3], the network cache mechanism can be suitably extended to accommodate larger messages by dividing these messages into blocks and suitably annotating them. Also, very large messages can be handled in a very similar manner by introducing special *network TLBs* which incorporate the *message ID* and both a *process* and *network* virtual addresses.

**ISA Extensions.** In a general architecture, one may implement a network processor by including a few specialized, network-specific instructions that facilitate the implementation of the late binding operations described earlier.

- *network_load*
- *network_store*
- *remap*

The *network_load* and *network_store* instructions are identical to the standard load and store instructions with the exception that they cause the networked cache to be searched according to the network tag. No other cache is searched. Regular load and store instructions target both the normal data cache and the network cache and the network cache is searched according to the *process tag*.

The remap *message_id, new_process_tag* instruction remaps the cache line identified by the *message_id* to the *new process tag*. The *message_id* and *new_process_tag* are in registers. The *new_process_tag* corresponds to the virtual address of the object which is to receive the message. The exact operation of the *remap*instruction is discussed in [3]. The *message_ID* is used as a key to search the network cache for the presence of the identified message. Upon a cache hit, the physical address corresponding to the *new_process_tag* is written into the cache. Upon a cache miss, the link translation buffer is queried based on the *message_ID* to yield the *network_tag* and bring the corresponding cache line into the cache. This may be done as part of the remap instruction, or it may be emulated in software depending on its complexity and the achieved miss rate for the remap operations. The network tag is reset and one of the processor status bits is set/reset to indicate the success or failure of the instruction.

## 3   Implementation

Using CoDeL we have implemented a network cache and its controller towards achieving a zero-copy messaging environment. The implemention is composed of four modules: the *network cache controller*, the *network register file*, the *process register file*, and the *message LTB*. as presented in figure 4.

The implementation reflects the fact that the network cache is associatively searched on any of the three tags (i.e. *network, process* or *message ID*). As it is depicted in figure 4, we have implemented a conventional 4-way set-associative cache that stores the cache line and the *network tag*. The *message ID* indexes the *message LTB* whose entries contain valid *network addresses*. The present implementation assumes a 16 bit *message ID* and a 64K entry LTB. In the

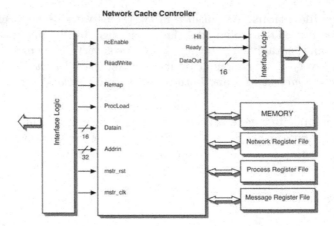

**Fig. 4.** Network Cache Architecture

future, we intend to implement a q-way set associative cache as the *message_ID* section to allow for longer *message ID*s and to minimize the required storage.

The *process* tags are kept in the *message* and *process* sections respectively, while the payload in these sections consist of pointers that point to the cache line in the *network* section that keeps the actual data. This means that whenever the *remap* or *load* instruction is executed an indirection needs to take place where a pointer in the *message* or *process* section is obtained first. The pointer is then used to access the correct cache block in the *network* section. It is this manipulation of pointers that allows the avoidance of any data copying.

For our 256 entry cache we have chosen a 4-way set associative architecture. The 32 bit network and process adresses are broken down as shown in figure 5. Each cache line is 32bytes long. The *network, process* and *message* sections are implemented as register files, and the *network cache controller* simply facilitates the accessing and manipulation of the information stored in those registers to implement the cache functionality described in Section 2.

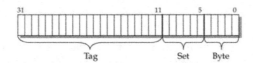

**Fig. 5.** Network and Process Address Structure

## 3.1   Network Controller

The *network cache controller* section is implemented using CoDeL. It interacts with the register files in the three other sections to implement a 4-way set associative cache that is accessed through any of the *network, message ID* or *process* tags. The register files include a four port output ensuring that information from all four members in a set can be retrieved concurrently. The cache is write-back, and implements a *write-allocate* on a cache miss on a write[1].

**Message ID.** A message ID being part of the message needs to be placed in the appropriate entry in the *network cache* structure. As we discussed earlier, we use the *message ID* tag to identify the appropriate message to be bound to a process through the *remap* instruction. In this implementation, we assume that the *message ID* occupies the first two bytes of a message. Thus a *network store* targeting the first word of the message will store the *message ID* in the first two bytes of the cache line, and to the corresponding entry of the *message* LTB, it will store the *network buffer address* assigned to the message. We also insist that the network buffers used to store the messages have boundaries which are multiples of the message size (32 bytes). In future implementations we plan to relax these restrictions by implementing a true caching environment for the *message* LTB facilitated by special modes of the *network store* and *network load* instructions which will allow us to manipulate the entries of the *message* LTB explicitly. Figure 6 shows the planned structure.

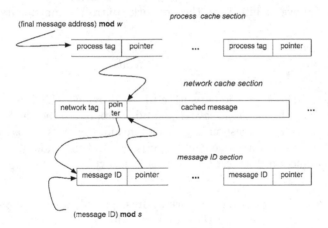

**Fig. 6.** The planned structure of the *message ID* and *process* sections

**Process Cache Section.** The Process Cache Section is organized as a 4-way set associative cache. It consist of two entries, one that stores the process tag

---

[1] A modified write-allocate on a cache miss on a write could be considered if one considers that messages are atomic and are not modifiable. Under this assumption, a message is stored into the network buffer only once, and stays there until it is bound to its destination process. Thus, the cache line could be populated with the elements of the message as they are brought in from the NIC, declared dirty, and written back to the network buffer only on replacement. The implementation of this scheme however, depends on the message being atomic, and thus on the ability to lock a cache line while the message is being brought in. This can be implemented by having explicit cache line lock/unlock capabilities.

and the other that stores a pointer to the cache line that stores the message itself in the network section. Since the network address and the process address are not correlated, and in order to avoid unnecessary cache replacements, the set associativity of this section should in reality be greater than that of the network section. This, we plan to implement in a future revision of the structure. The process tag consists of the base of the data structure to which the message is bound. Thus, the index to an item within the cache line, is calculated as the difference between the *process tag* and the real address of the item. The *remap* instruction sets the *process tag* and the pointer pointing to the particular cache line that is bound through the *remap* instruction. The cache line remains in the network section until it is deemed replaceable. On replace, any cache lines already in the regular data cache which include addresses covered by the bound message block in the network cache, are written back and declared invalid before the message block is itself written into the process space starting at the address specified in the *process tag*[2].

We expect that most of the accesses to the bound message in the process space will happen immediately following the *mpi_receive* (i.e. immediately following the execution of a *remap*) and as such it is advantageous to keep the bound message in place in the network cache, ensuring no cache misses.

Using the above architecture, the network controller implements 4 required instructions.

- *network_load*
- *network_store*
- *remap*
- *load*

**network_load.** Based on the network address provided, the four *network tags* are retrieved from the *network register file* and compared to the address provided. If a match occures, the corresponding cache line and the message ID are provided as output. On a cache miss, the cache line is brought in randomly replacing an existing cache line which is written back only if dirty.

**network_store.** Based on the network address provided, the four *network tags* are retrieved and compared to the provided address. On a match, the data is written in the designated cache line and at the designated index, and the cache line is marked as dirty. On a miss, the standard write-allocate with random replacement is followed. As per the discussion earlier, the *network_store* instruction is also used to store the *message ID tag*.

**remap.** The *remap* instruction utilizes the *message ID* and the *new process virtual address*. It is assumed that a *new process address* is generated based on

---

[2] We are currently exploring the possibility of cache-to-cache copying from the network cache directly to the regular data cache, to ensure fast write-back. This can be done expeditiously if blocks covering the addresses of the bound message are already in the data cache. If this is not the case, then these blocks must be brought into the data cache, and only then the network cache-to-data cache transfer can take place.

the *new process virtual address* from a look-aside buffer. The *message ID* is used to retrieve the *network address* from the *message* LTB. *new process address* is used to target a corresponding set in the process section. A randomly chosen entry is replaced with the *new process address* and the pointer to the cache line holding the message identified by the previously obtained *network address*. The *message ID tag* and *network tag* are invalidated to indicate the successful conclusion of the *remap*.

**load.** The *load* instruction targets both the network cache and the regular data cache. The process cache section provides the pointer to the referenced cache line which is used to retrieve the referenced datum. If both the network cache and the regular data cache respond, the datum from the network cache supercedes the one from the regular data cache. This convention is adopted since the network cache will respond only if a valid message has been bound.

## 3.2  Complexity

The register file modules were implemented in VHDL. Each of these required about 60 lines of VHDL code. The network controller module, written in CoDeL, required about 697 lines of code, and generated close to 4011 lines of VHDL code.

Under simulation we see that the *network_load* instruction requires 15 clock cycles, the *network_store* takes 29 cycles, the *remap* takes 29 cycles, while the *load* requires 21 cycles.

## 4  Conclusions and Discussion

In this work we presented a preliminary design of a *Network Processor* extension. Our primary purpose was to ensure a self consistent design, and prove the capabilities of our CoDeL design environment. We have concluded both goals successfully, and through this process, we have establish several points both to our design and to the CoDeL environment that need attention. We have enumerated some of the issues in the main text and we plan to incorporate these in future revisions of the design. Additionally, we plan to investigate ways that the described extensions can be incorporated to an existing processor core.

Finally, a few comments on CoDeL. We found that although CoDeL provides a wonderful protyping environment there are certain deficiencies. First CoDeL lacks the ability to specify register arrays. If it allowed creation of arrays, the register files could be implemented within CoDeL with great ease.

Second, although the CoDeL compiler attempts to discover data dependencies and parallelizes the architecture based on these dependencies, it is not able to do this effectively. It would be extremely useful if the language allowed user defined sequential and parallel constructs. This could yield better parallelism.

## Acknowledgment

This work was supported by grants from NSERC and the University of Victoria.

# References

1. Farshad Khunjush, M. Watheq El-Kharashi, Kin F. Li, and Nikitas J. Dimopoulos "Network Processor Design: Issues and Challenges" *Proceedings, 2003 IEEE Pacific Rim Conference on Communications, Computers and Signal Processing* pp. 164-168, Victoria, Aug. 2003
2. R. Sivakumar, V. Dimakopoulos, and N. Dimopoulos 'CoDeL: A Rapid Prototyping Environment for the Specification and Automatic Synthesis of Controllers for Multiprocessor Interconnection Networks, *Proceedings, SAMOS III 3d International Workshop on Systems, Architectures, Modeling and Simulation* pp. 58-63, Samos, July 2003
3. Ahmad Afsahi and Nikitas J. Dimopoulos, "Architectural Extensions to Support Efficient Communication Using Message Prediction, *Proceedings, 16th Annual International Symposium on High Performance Computing Systems and Applications, HPCS2002,* pp. 20-27, June 2002
4. Ahmad Afsahi and Nikitas J. Dimopoulos, "Efficient Communication Using Message Prediction for Cluster of Multiprocessors, *Fourth Workshop on Communication, Architecture, and Applications for Network-based Parallel Computing, CANPC'00,* Lecture Notes in Computer Science, No. 1797, pp. 162-178, January, 2000.
5. D. H. Bailey, T. Harsis, W. Saphir, R. V. der Wijngaart, A. Woo and M. Yarrow, The NAS Parallel Benchmarks 2.0: Report NAS-95-020, NASA Ames, Dec. 1995.
6. A. Basu, M. Welsh, T. V. Eicken, Incorporating Memory Management into User-Level Network Interfaces, Hot Interconnects V, August 1997.
7. M. Blumrich, K. Li, R. Alpert, C. Dubnicki, E. Felten, and J. Sandberg, A Virtual Memory Mapped Network Interface for the SHRIMP Multicomputer, Proceedings, 21st Annual International Symposium on Computer Architecture, 1994, pp. 142-153.
8. N. J. Boden, D. Cohen, R. E. Felderman, A. E. Kulawik, C. L. Seitz, J. N. Seizovic and W-K. Su, Myrinet: A Gigabit-per-Second Local Area Network, IEEE Micro, Feb. 1995.
9. H. Chu, Zero-copy TCP in Solaris, Proceedings of the USENIX Annual Technical Conference, 1996, pp. 253-263.
10. J. J. Dongarra and T. Dunigan, Message-Passing Performance of Various Computers, Concurrency: Practice and Experience, Volume 9, Issue 10, 1997, pp. 915-926.
11. C. Dubnicki, A. Bilas, Y. Chen, S. Damianakis and K. Li, VMMC-2: Efficient Support for Reliable, Connection-Oriented Communication, Proceedings of the Hot Interconnect97, 1997.
12. J. Kim and D. J. Lilja, Characterization of Communication Patterns in Message-Passing Parallel Scientific Application Programs, Proceedings of the Workshop on Communication, Architecture, and Applications for Network-based Parallel Computing, HPCA-4, February 1998, pp. 202-216.
13. S. S. Mukherjee and M. D. Hill, Using Prediction to Accelerate Coherence Protocols, Proceedings of the 25th Annual International Symposium on Computer Architecture, 1998.
14. S. H. Rodrigues, T. E. Anderson and D. E. Culler, High-Performance Local Area Communication with Fast Sockets, USENIX 1997, Jan. 1997. R. Sheifert, Gigabit Ethernet, Addison-Wesley, 1998.

# Synchronous Transfer Architecture (STA)

Gordon Cichon, Pablo Robelly, Hendrik Seidel, Emil Matúš,
Marcus Bronzel, and Gerhard Fettweis

Mobile Communcations Chair, TU-Dresden
D-01062 Dresden, Germany
cichon@ifn.et.tu-dresden.de

**Abstract.** This paper presents a novel micro-architecture for high-performance and low-power DSPs. The underlying Synchronous Transfer Architecture (STA) fills the gap between SIMD-DSPs and coarse-grain reconfigurable hardware. STA processors are modeled using a common machine description suitable for both compiler and core generator. The core generator is able to generate models in Lisa, System-C, and VHDL. A special emphasis is placed on the good synthesis of the generated VHDL model.

## 1 Introduction

This paper presents a novel architecture for digital signal processing that allows effective compiler support. In this architecture, many different algorithms share the available computational resources. In addition, the resulting hardware is suitable for high-performance, low-power applications, as they occur in battery-powered devices. Furthermore, the hardware implementation is streamlined: As much as possible of the hardware models is generated by our tool-chain. Both the compiler and the core generator use the same machine description in order to create an integrated design flow.

## 2 Related Work

[5, 6] performed evaluations about instruction set effectiveness and utilization. The observation that compilers could hardly utilize the full flexibility offered by the increasingly complex instruction sets, and that code size and performance do not directly correspond, led to the development of RISC architectures [8]. RISC architectures simplify instruction processing, and thus allow much higher clock rates at the cost of a large instruction footprint. Instruction level parallelism adds substantial overhead to instruction processing, e.g. for larger caches, register renaming, branch prediction, dynamic instruction scheduling, register files with many ports, etc. (see [5]).

Digital signal processors (DSP) have to meet real-time constraints in the worst case scenario. Saving die area and power is more important than compiler-friendliness. Therefore, classical DSPs avoid the overhead of dynamic instruction scheduling by supplying CISC instructions for specific high-throughput tasks. These instructions don't consume a lot of memory while exploiting the full degree of parallelism available. A typical example is a MAC (multiply-accumulate) instruction that performs a multiplication, an addition, two address calculations with circular buffering and bit-reverse addressing, and two loads at once, coded with 16 bits of instruction memory.

A. Pimentel and S. Vassiliadis (Eds.): SAMOS 2004, LNCS 3133, pp. 343–352, 2004.

Many features of general purpose processors have been adopted in the area of DSPs: Texas Instruments [11] based their high-performance DSP platform on a VLIW architecture. Intel [9] presented a superscalar implementation of the ARM RISC core with SIMD extensions. These processors show high performance and can react flexibly to dynamic situations like cache misses and branch misprediction.

With an increasing degree of instruction level parallelism, wiring dominates computational capacity. [4] presents the Transport Triggered Architecture (TTA) to alleviate this problem: It reduces the amount of interconnection resources and number of register file ports while enabling efficient code generation by compilers.

Still, these extensions are not sufficient to satisfy the demand of even more performance-hungry DSP applications. With the rise of FPGAs, high-performance signal processing applications shift towards reconfigurable computing. In order to maintain flexibility, application specific processors (like [12]) propose to identify application specific tasks for implementation in custom functional units.

For further analysis, we refer to the definition of the efficiency metrics Remanence and Scalability in [2]. According to this metric, a VLIW processor can be regarded as a very quickly reconfigurable (low remanence) piece of coarse-grain reconfigurable hardware. We will use this notion to define a fusion of processor and reconfigurable hardware.

## 3   The Architectural Template of STA

The hardware resources in a processor or reconfigurable hardware architecture can be classified according to their usage: A processor contains a portion dedicated to instruction processing (e.g. instruction memory, instruction decoder, branch prediction) and a portion dedicated to data processing (e.g. data path, ALU, FPU). Reconfigurable hardware dedicates resources to reconfiguration (e.g. storage of configuration, programmable switching matrix) and resources for computation (e.g. adders, multipliers).

Particularly for battery powered applications, it is desirable to spend as little resources as possible to programmability or reconfigurability. A possible way to achieve this goal is SIMD architecture, in which several data processing resources share a single instruction processing resource.

To reinforce the reduction of resources dedicated to reconfigurability, it is desirable to simplify the instruction processing portion as much as possible without affecting the performance of the data processing portion. The predictable execution nature of digital signal processing applications do not require the flexibility of a superscalar architecture. A VLIW or a TTA [4] architecture would be a good choice. This paper proposes a simplification of the TTA architecture.

While VLIW architectures require expensive crossbar switches for the construction of bypasses between the functional units, TTA architectures require local queues for collecting operands and a controller that determines when exactly an operation is to be started. In the predictable execution environment of DSPs, we propose to trigger the execution of instructions explicitly by supplying control signals from the instruction word. We call this architecture Synchronous Transfer Architecture (STA).

Figure 1 shows the architectural template of STA: the design is split up into an arbitrary number of functional units, each with arbitrary input and output ports. To facilitate

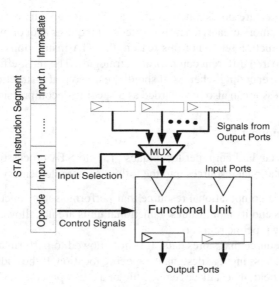

**Fig. 1.** STA Control Path

synthesis and timing analysis, it is required that all output ports are buffered. Each input port is connected to an arbitrary number of output ports. Alternatively, they may originate from immediate fields in the instruction word as well. For each computational resource, a segment of the STA instruction word contains the control signals (opcode) for the functional unit and the multiplexer controls to control the sources of all input ports and associated immediate fields.

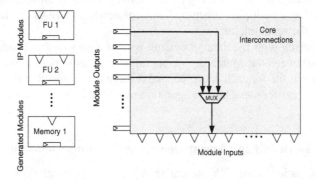

**Fig. 2.** STA Data Path

Figure 2 shows all input multiplexers together forming a switching matrix between the output and input ports. In total, the system constitutes a synchronous data flow network. The switching matrix may implement arbitrary connections depending on the application, performance, and power-saving requirements. Such an interconnection network can also be constructed in a hierarchical fashion.

The STA architecture poses a new challenge: Storing uncompressed STA instruction segments in memory creates a new bottleneck: It requires a lot of memory and huge bandwidth for instruction fetch. For this reason, the STA instructions need to be compressed. [13] compared different compression strategies. The most efficient ones seem to be 2D run-length encoding schemes. It should be noted that instruction processing of a superscalar processor can also be regarded as a specific decompression technique.

### 3.1 Compiler Support

In order to apply standard compiler techniques [1, 7] to STA processors, it is required to separate computational resources into the following complementary types:

- **behavior**, i.e. a computational resource that performs some function based on its control signals and its input values. Functional units are not allowed to contain any state excepting pipeline registers.
- **state**, i.e. a resource that stores data. It is not allowed to perform any computation and uses an address input to designate a specific location. If the address comes from an immediate field, it acts like a register file of a RISC processor. Otherwise, it acts like a memory.

Assuming that it is possible to route data between any resources, the Tomasulo algorithm for dynamic scheduling in superscalar processors described in [5] is applicable. With STA processors however, Tomasulo's algorithm can be performed statically by the compiler. The STA interconnection matrix acts like the bypass connections found in classical processors.

It should be noted that the data processing part of any processor can be reinterpreted as an STA processor by assuming an STA-conforming module partition: Each register, register file, or memory turns into an STA-state and each combinatorial circuitry turns into an STA-behavior. E.g., a multiplier containing an accumulator (MAC) can be modeled as a multiplier functional unit connected to a register file containing a single register, the accumulator.

The comparison with the data processing part of a superscalar processor yields a sufficient criterion for the routability of operands, as mentioned above: If there is a designated register file for each data type, and if there is a connection from each port of that type to that register file. This configuration resembles a VLIW processor without a bypass.

### 3.2 Synthesis-Friendly Implementation of the STA Interconnection Matrix

At the implementation of the STA interconnection matrix, particular care has to be taken of the realization of multiplexers. It turned out to be most advantageous to place these multiplexers directly at the core toplevel without wrapping them into a module.

Depending on the library, synthesis can split the multiplexers into NAND gates, as depicted in Figure 3. During the later design phases, the first NAND gate can be placed near the output of the source resource, while placing the second NAND gate near the input port of the target resource. This placement has the advantage of making the the resulting circuitry particularly fast and power-saving.

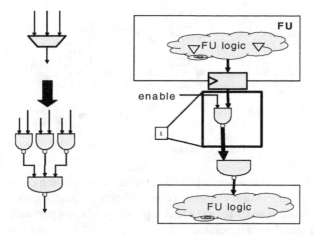

**Fig. 3.** Implementation of STA Interconnection Matrix

The first NAND gate can be dimensioned as the driver for the following long wire to the target. It also acts as a power gate for the switched signal. Thus, toggling or recharging of the long wire is prevented in cases when the data are not used at the target.

# 4    The Integrated Design Flow

Our group created an integrated design flow for the efficient development of STA processors. A formal machine description is used by both compiler and core generator. An UML-diagram overview over the format is shown in Figure 4.

The design flow of our core generator is depicted in Figure 5. It can be freely used for evaluation purposes at our web site [3]. The web site also provides more detailed documentation and the sample processor model *minimal*.

## 4.1    ISA Layout

The core generator first computes an optimized instruction set layout for the given architecture. For this purpose, the binary encodings for instructions and multiplexer controls

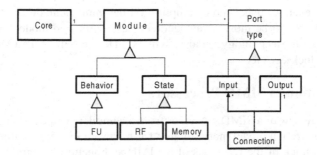

**Fig. 4.** Machine Description: UML Diagram

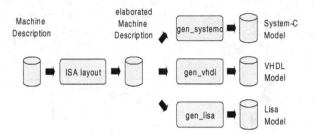

**Fig. 5.** Core Generator: Design Flow

are determined. The binary encodings also determine the bit width of the corresponding fields in the instruction word. Correlated control fields are placed close to each other in the instruction word in order to improve compression efficiency. Finally, a report about the instruction encoding is generated.

### 4.2 Simulation Models

For simulation and software debugging purposes, a machine model for the Lisa system [14] is generated. The core generator handles the features necessary to support STA and SIMD constructs in Lisa effectively. The generated model contains generated behaviors for all instructions, as well as all code related to the switching matrix. The core generator also generates an assembly preprocessor to support a human-readable entry of parallel programs. Lisa, in turn, generates assembler, linker, and a machine simulator with a debugger.

Alternatively, the core generator can generate a System-C model of the processor.

### 4.3 Synthesis Models

The core generator also generates a synthesis friendly VHDL model. The generated parts consist of a VHDL package with constant definitions, a core toplevel with interconnection wires and multiplexers, different types of decompressing instruction decoders, register files with debug capability, memories using technology dependent hardmacros with debug capability, and stubs for the implementation of functional units. In addition to that, the core generator generates synthesis scripts for ASIC- and FPGA-libraries. A proprietary debug interface for in-circuit debugging is inserted automatically.

The core generator makes no assumption on the implementation of the functional units. It turned out to be most advantageous to use optimized models obtained from third parties, e.g. the technology foundry, Synopsys DesignWare, Altera Megafunctions, Xilinx DSP-Blocksets, etc.

## 5   Application to SIMD Processors

The conceptual view of a SIMD processor from a compiler perspective is different than the perspective from a model more suitable for hardware implementation: A compiler needs to keep track of the resources of a SIMD-architecture that are controlled by a common instruction. Conceptually, such a SIMD-unit performs a vector-computation

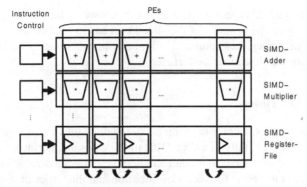

**Fig. 6.** SIMD Processors

subject to instruction scheduling. These units are shown as horizontal rectangles in Figure 6, e.g. a SIMD-adder, a SIMD-multiplier, and a SIMD register file. Please note that the term slice refers only to the conceptual representation in Figure 6 and does not imply any restriction on its geometric implementation.

Nevertheless, an efficient hardware implementation can only be derived if modules are prouped into slices or tiles shown as verticals rectangles. Thus, the modules are internally tightly wired, while there is little communication between them. A slice can once be physically placed and routed with a minimal degree of unnecessary freedom, and then be replicated to produce the desired parallelism.

## 5.1  Slice Recognition

The first step to automatically generate the processor core is to recognize the units that· can actually be split into slices. Units that do not perform vector-processing are not subject to the transformation process described in the later steps.

The sliceability of a functional unit can be determined from the machine description by taking into account three indications:

- If the unit inputs or outputs vector data at its ports
- If the behavior of a unit performs vector processing
- Explicit specification by the processor designer

Special care has to be taken of sliceable units that contain scalar ports: Integer types can trivially be reinterpreted as a vectors of single bits. With this technique, the result flags of SIMD-units can be processed by integer scalar units. Another trivial mapping is to generate a broadcast operation for scalar input ports. In other cases, a user-defined mapping has to be specified by the processor designer.

## 5.2  SIMD-Unit Fission

The second step is to break up the sliceable SIMD-units. This operation is performed by replacing each sliceable unit with a corresponding sliced one. The sliced unit has the same number of input and output ports, while the type of each port is replaced by its corresponding scalarized type. E.g., if the port type used to be *vector of my_type*, it is replaced by *my_type*. The behavior of the sliced unit has to be specified accordingly.

If a unit requires inter-slice communication, additional communication signals have to be inserted into the sliced unit's interface.

## 5.3   Slice-Module Fusion

The third step of the procedure is to group all sliced units into a new module that represents the physical layout entity of a slice. This module has an interface containing input and output ports for all signals that connect sliced and unsliced units with each other. Additionally it contains ports for slice identification and inter-slice communication.

Within each slice, a synthesis-friendly multiplexer matrix is generated as described above for all locally interconnected signals (see Fig. 7, the multiplexer inside the slice).

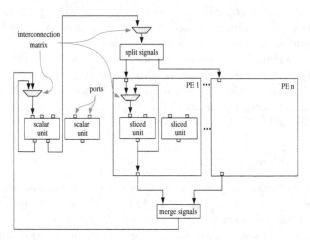

**Fig. 7.** Interconnection Network with Sliced and Unsliced Functional Units

## 5.4   Processor Integration

The fourth and final step builds a processor model containing the replicated slice module, the non-sliceable functional units, and a synthesis friendly interconnection network (see Fig. 7).

Special care needs to be taken of signals that cross the slice boundary:

– **connection from outside to inside**
   For connections to input ports at SIMD-units, only inputs that originate from unsliced units are handled by a second multiplexer outside the slice. As depicted on the upper side of Figure 1, the resulting vector signal is split into its components and connected to the scalarized inputs of the corresponding slices. Inside the slice, the signal is connected to the second multiplexer generated by the fusion step.

– **connection from inside to outside**
For output signals originating from output ports inside slices which needs to be connected to input ports of unsliced units, all individual scalarized signals originating from inside the slices have to be merged to vector signals (see lower side of Fig. 7).

## 6    Discussion and Further Work

We presented a novel micro-architecture tailored to high-performance, low-power DSPs. For this new architecture, we are able to generate hardware implementations in an efficient integrated design flow. We used the SIMD paradigm to decrease the amount of resources required to provide programmability.

The performance of an STA processor is determined by the parallelism of its computational resources. It allows to build high-performance processors from libraries of primitive functions. This allows for better resource sharing than other approaches that require to identify specific application specific operations.

In traditional design flows, either two different models of the processor have to be developed and maintained, or a compiler-type model has to be used for synthesis. In contrast to that, our core generator automatically converts a compiler-type machine model into a synthesis-type machine model.

The novel architecture has been tested on a wide variety of systems: A DVB-T receiver, a 802.11/UMTS combo chip, and an OFDM transceiver system. Synthesis and power simulation results show that the proposed architecture is actually suitable for high-performance and low-power DSPs. The results show that programmable solutions are competitive with hardwired solutions. A complete implementation example is presented in [10].

## Acknowledgments

Thanks to the CATS team and to my sister Caroline Cichon.

This work has been sponsored in part by the German Science Foundation (Deutsche Forschungsgemeinschaft, DFG) within SFB356-A6.

## References

1. A. V. Aho, R. Sethi, and J. D. Ullman. *Compilers. Principles, Techniques, and Tools.* Addison-Wesley, Redding, MA, 1985.
2. P. Benoit, Sassatelli, Torres, Demigny, Robert, and Cambon. Metrics for digital signal processing architectures characterization: Remancence and scalability. In *Proc. of Third International Workshop on Systems, Architectures, Modeling, and Simulation (SAMOS'03)*, pages 102–107, Samos, Greece, July 2003.
3. G. Cichon. MOUSE online core generator.
   http://www.radionetworkprocessor.com/gencore.php.
4. H. Corporaal. *Microprocessor Architecture from VLIW to TTA.* John Wiley & Sons, 1997.

5. J. Hennessy and D. Patterson. *Computer Architecture, a Quantitative Approach.* Morgan Kaufmann Publishers, Inc., San Francisco, CA, 1996.
6. A. Lunde. Empirical evaluation of some features of instruction set processor architectures. *Commun. ACM*, 20(3):143–153, 1977.
7. S. Muchnik. *Advanced compiler design and Implementation.* Morgan Kaufmann Publishers, 1997.
8. D. A. Patterson. Reduced instruction set computers. *Commun. ACM*, 28(1):8–21, 1985.
9. S. Santhanam. StrongArm 110: A 160MHz 32b 0.5W CMOS ARM processor. In *Proceedings for HotChips VIII*, August 1996.
10. H. Seidel, E. Matúš, G. Cichon, P. Robelly, M. Bronzel, and G. Fettweis. An automatically generated core-based implementation of an OFDM communication system. In *Proc. of Fourth International Workshop on Systems, Architectures, Modeling, and Simulation (SAMOS'04)*, Samos, Greece, July 2004.
11. L. Truong. The VelociTI™ architecture of the TMS320C6xxx. In *HotChips IX Symposium*, August 1997.
12. A. Wang, E. Killian, D. Maydan, and C. Rowen. Hardware/software instruction set configurability for system-on-chip processors. In *Proc. DAC 2001*, 2001.
13. M. Weiß and G. P. Fettweis. Dynamic codewidth reduction for VLIW instruction set architectures in digital signal processors. In *3rd. Int. Workshop in Signal and Image Processing (IWSIP '96)*, pages 517–520, Jan. 1996.
14. V. Zivojnovic. LISA - machine description language and generic machine model for HW/SW co-design. In *IEEE Workshop on VLSI Signal Processing*, 1996.

# Generated DSP Cores for Implementation of an OFDM Communication System

Hendrik Seidel, Emil Matúš, Gordon Cichon, Pablo Robelly,
Marcus Bronzel, and Gerhard Fettweis

Mobile Communcations Chair, TU-Dresden
D-01062 Dresden, Germany
seidel@ifn.et.tu-dresden.de

**Abstract.** Application tailored signal processors fill the gap between ASICs and general purpose DSPs. Single Instruction Multiple Data (SIMD) Signal Processors offer high computational power with low control overhead. This paper describes the development of a multi-processor OFDM-System x using automatically generated SIMD-DSP Cores. The focus of this case of study was the test of our integrated design flow which is based on our core generation tool. We show how with our design methodology we reduce the design cycle in comparsion with other HW/SW Co-design tools and traditional design flows.

## 1 Introduction

Signal processing applications for high end communication devices require two different types of application specific signal processors: The first type is a highly optimized DSP core with a complex instruction-set to handle the demanding application specific computational requirements. The second type is a more generic small processor core which can be used with different application specific cores or as a stand-alone-core for low data rate applications. Powerful tools are needed to minimize the time needed for designing and validating these DSPs. Therefore, the required software toolchain should be generated together with a processor core which enables efficient reuse of previously created hardware units. This can be achieved using a dedicated hardware library together with a capable architecture template which facilitates short and frequent design cycles.

The STA (Synchronous Transfer Architecture) [2] is such a template. A compiler-friendly machine description describes DSP cores. Then, the machine description is used by GenCore [1] to create hardware and simulation models of application tailored DSP cores. Compared to the more general processor design tools like CoWare/LisaTek [7], PEAS-III [5] and EXPRESSION-ADL [4] which are more targeting RISC and CISC architectures, GenCore is focusing on SIMD vector DSP architectures. In our case of study we have developed an OFDM broadcasting system using an STA-I/O Processor and an STA SIMD DSP on receiver and transmitter side.

A. Pimentel and S. Vassiliadis (Eds.): SAMOS 2004, LNCS 3133, pp. 353–362, 2004.

## 2   Case Study: OFDM

OFDM is used in numerous digital communication systems: DVB, ISDB and DAB for digital broadcasting, IEEE802.15.3a and IEEE802.11a for wireless networking and ADSL modems for wireline communication. These systems are transmitting IP, video and audio streams with data rates up to multiple Mbit/s. High performance ASICs [3] and multi-DSP solutions are used for embedding these standards into set- top-boxes, PCMCIA-cards or mobile terminals.

In our first design we have developed an initial platform to compute the basic algorithms of these standards. The primary goal was to demonstrate the feasibility of our generated platform concept in order to achieve short design cycles. In a first case study we have developed a simple OFDM based communication system with transmitter and receiver. Both comprise two different STA based DSP cores which have been integrated on a single FPGA: The generic STA-I/O Processor and STA-OFDM SIMD DSP. For a rapid prototyping of the system, the design is implemented on two Stratix25 FPGA development boards (shown in figure 1) with ADCs and DACs for baseband signal processing. The input and output of the OFDM system consists of an uncoded data stream which is transferred via a USB 2.0 interface to a host PC for post processing.

**Fig. 1.** Development Board Setup

### 2.1   Functional Blocks

For the OFDM System, we implemented functional blocks similar to those being used in DVB-T/H broadcasting systems. Each functional block at the transmitter has a corresponding block at the receiver as shown in figure 2. At the transmitter the Input Data from a Host-PC is mapped to QPSK-symbols. After insertion of BPSK pilot carriers (Barker Sequence) the IFFT (with decimation in frequency) is calculated. The resulting time domain signal is finally converted into an analogue signal using a dual DAC with 500kHz sampling frequency. At the receiver the incoming symbols are oversampled at 2MHz with a dual ADC. Depending on the cross-correlation results after the FFT, the phase of the incoming stream is shifted by the synchronisation unit. Every forth symbol is stored

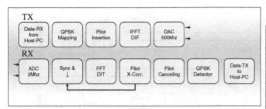

**Fig. 2.** OFDM Transmitter and Receiver (Block Diagram)

**Table 1.** OFDM parameters

| | |
|---|---|
| Total number of carriers | 64 |
| Data carriers (QPSK) | 48 |
| Pilot carriers (BPSK) | 7 |
| Barker-Code | |
| Bits per OFDM symbol | 96 |
| Sample rate | > 500kHz |

into the memory. After calculation of the FFT, the BPSK pilot signals are cross-correlated with the barker sequence and the complex result is stored for later use in the synchronisation unit. Following the detection process, the received data is sent to a Host-PC. [6] The OFDM parameters are shown in table 1. For the first implementation the sample rate was set to 500kHz, but 3-4 times higher sample rates are possible as shown in paragraph 4.

## 3  SoC Development

After analyzing the system requirements and the underlying algorithms a first draft of the SoC concept was designed. In order to guarantee a short time frame for design and testing, we decided to reduce custom hardware design to a minimum and generate as much as possible automatically from our core generation tools. Instead of having a communication bus between the processors and the peripheries, we deviced a small automatically generated STA-processor as DMA controller, IO processor and task scheduler. This OFDM-IO processor manages all data transfers. The SIMD OFDM-DSP signal processor was added to the OFDM-IO as a Co- Processor. The OFDM-DSP computes all signal processing algorithms described in paragraph 2.1. It provides an interface to its scalar memory. A program halt is indicated by a control flag. The sequencer of the OFDM-DSP is controlled by the OFDM-IO processor. With machine descriptions of both processors, two instances of the STA- architectural template were generated using GenCore. Many VHDL[1]-components available from previous designs could be reused for this OFDM SoC. Only a few new components had to be added to the design. To ensure that the design fits on the 25k cells of the FPGA, a rough cell-count estimation was performed. The whole design was synthesized and routed without doing any previous functional tests of the system to get an estimate of the expected cell area for the final design. Software and hardware development were started with the first release of our SoC. Figure 3 provides an overview of our SoC design flow.

### 3.1  Processor Design

*STA with GenCore:* The core generation tool GenCore creates instances of the synchronous transfer architecture template. In STA, a functional unit is defined

---

[1] Very High Speed Integrated Circuit Hardware Description Language

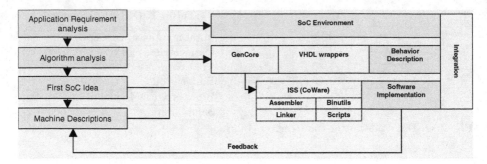

**Fig. 3.** Integrated Design Flow with GenCore

as module with output registers and input multiplexers. The input multiplexers of each functional unit are connected to one or more output registers of other functional units. Depending on the application, power, area and performance constraints, this multiplexer network is more or less complex. Functional Units perform computation. Register files and memories store states.

To describe a STA-based processor, a special machine description format is used. The format is called RNA and is based on annotated graphs [8]. The machine description is subdivided into 6 major sections:

- Types
- Toplevel
- Register Files
- Memories
- Functional Units
- Operations

A LISA[9] model and a VHDL framework[2] are generated based on the STA-architecture template and machine description. The VHDL framework consists of memories[3], register files, an instruction decoder, a multiplexer network and functional unit VHDL-wrappers. The VHDL-wrappers have to be filled with a behaviour description of the functional unit. With every new operation the multiplexer network and decoder are adjusted automatically. Implementation errors are minimized by having just a single VHDL-file to be changed by hand if new instructions are added.

*Design Space Exploration:* STA-processor design is done on three abstraction levels:

1. Instruction Set Simulation with the CoWare LISA ISS Debugger for software development and cycle count optimization.
2. VHDL-Model Simulation using Synopsys/Scirocco for hardware debugging. (For silicon implementations in this layer performance, area and power estimations are done)

---

[2] The VHDL framework is generated by GenCore, not by CoWare Tools
[3] Only ALTERA memories are supported

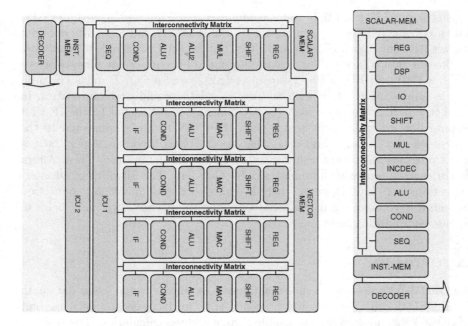

**Fig. 4.** OFDM-DSP Block Set          **Fig. 5.** OFDM-IO Block Set

3. FPGA prototyping to test the processor with other hardware devices and to run tests like bit error rate calculations.

The ISS is used as reference for the other abstraction levels. Therefore, the first step in the hardware debugging process is the comparison of VHDL-model and FPGA-prototype with the ISS.

In Table 2 the different simulation and emulation methods are listed. Adequate debugging methods could be chosen from this set.

**Table 2.** Comparsion of the test and development platforms of STA-processors

|  | ISS | VHDL-Simulation | FPGA-prototype |
|---|---|---|---|
| Simulation time | Medium | Very High | Very Low |
| Debugging Information | High | High | Very Low |
| Coverage | Software | Software/Hardware | Software/Hardware |
| Cost | Low | Low | Low - Medium |

## 3.2   OFDM-DSP

The OFDM-DSP is a fixed point SIMD parallel signal processor (A block diagram is shown in Figure 4) with a high degree of instruction level parallelism. The vector part of the DSP consists of 4 parallel data paths. Each data path consists of an ALU, a multiply and accumulate (MAC) unit, a barrel-shifter (BS) unit, a register (REG) file, a conditional unit (COND) and a conditional data transfer (IF)-unit. With IF units and COND units, the DSP is able to parallelize conditional data transfers. The Scalar data path of the processor consists of two ALUs, a MUL, a REG, a BS, a sequencer (SEQ) and a COND unit. The data path is principally involved with address calculations and program control. In the vector part of the processor, the COND unit is connected to the IF-Unit for data flow control. In the scalar part, the COND unit is connected to the sequencer for conditional branches. The processor has three single port memories: a program Memory, a scalar memory and a vector memory. These Altera Memories were generated automatically by GenCore. The bitwidth of all interconnections is 16 bits. However, there is a single exception: a 32 bit connection between the Accumulator of the MAC Unit and the barrel shifter unit, helps to increase computation accuracy.

### 3.3   OFDM-IO

The OFDM-IO processor, as shown in figure 5, is similar to the scalar data path of the OFDM-DSP. Instead of the second ALU, an increase and decrease unit (INCDEC) was implemented to enable simple address calculation. The Instruction Level parallelism of STA-processors enables efficient data transfers between Functional Units and Memories. The OFDM-DSP and the I/O ports are connected to the OFDM-IO within functional unit -wrappers. Hence, both units have input multiplexers and output registers like standard functional units e.g. an ALU or an MAC. Specialized instructions to write or read the ADC/DAC and to access the USB 2.0 Interface exist. Data exchange with the OFDM-DSP is done via direct memory access.

### 3.4   Environment

The OFDM-IO processor is embedded into the operational environment (figure 6). The environment of the processor consist of the:

– input and output baseband signal channels,
– input and output data (RX/TX) channels,
– debug interface,
– debug input and output signal channels,
– clock generator.

PC, as master, controls the OFDM transceiver over the general purpose USB 2.0 interface. USB slave controller is located in the transceiver. The data RX/TX channels and debugging port are implemented in the USB slave controller. Optionally also input/output baseband signal channels could be used to emulate ADC and DAC interfaces. Debug interface enables address, data in/out and control signal generation. All memory resources of both IO and DSP processors are accessible at any time over debug interface. Thus, the processor memory

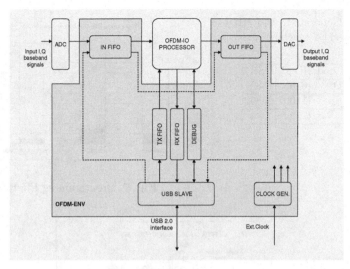

**Fig. 6.** SoC Environment

down/up load from/to PC is possible. In the receiver mode the input I,Q base-band signals are digitized by ADCs and stored to the input FIFO buffers. The OFDM-IO processor reads the signal samples to be processed from input FIFO buffer and serves them to the DSP processor. The demodulated data is send to RX data channel and received by host over USB interface. In the transmit-ter mode, the data to be transmitted is send by host to TX data channel over USB interface. IO processor reads the data from TX FIFO buffer and passes them to OFDM-DSP. Output baseband signal generated by OFDM- IO proces-sor is stored to ouput FIFO buffers. Output FIFOs are directly connected to DA converters to produce analogue baseband signal.

## 4   Results

The presented design was implemented within 5 weeks by two engineers. The processor design and its implementation were finished after three weeks. The main hardware implementation effort was spent on the environmental devices like the USB 2.0 Interface and converters. Software development was started in the second week of the development process after the LISA description was generated from the first version of our STA- machine description.

*Hardware Description:* In Table 3 the complexity of STA-MD code is compared to the generated LISA and VHDL Code. Also in consideration of the fact that a handwritten LISA or VHDL model is smaller than our generated models, a STA-machine description is less complex than LISA and VHDL description.

To represent the implementation effort for each of the processors we have calculated the lines of code of the VHDL-models. The comparison is shown in figure 7. We distinguish between generated code, handwritten code and code

**Table 3.** Generated ADL/HDL-Code from STA-machine description

| Lines of code | IO-P | DSP |
|---|---|---|
| STA-MD | 619 | 1389 |
| LISA | 11007 | 27892 |
| VHDL | 2592 | 4784 |

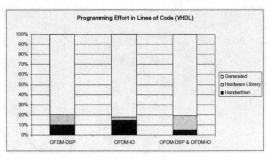

**Fig. 7.** Programming Effort

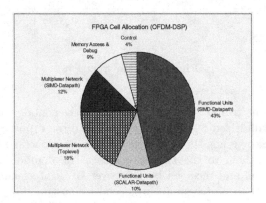

**Fig. 8.** FPGA Cell Allocation

taken from a hardware library. We assume that we have to build the hardware library from scratch. If we look at both processors, the code taken form a hardware library increases. A next implementation based on this design will have even more code taken from a hardware library. This high reusability is based on the fact that the STA-architecture is extremely structured.

*Hardware Implementation:* Synthesis and Place and Route were done with the Altera Quartus II Software without any manual optimization or detailed timing constraints. The OFDM-IO consumes 5179 cells, the OFDM-DSP 16686 cells and the environmental devices 575 cells. Overall 85% of the 25k FPGA cells were used. A detailed partitioning of the cells for the OFDM-DSP is shown in Figure 8. Most of the Cells were spend on functional units and the multiplexer network. The control overhead of the DSP is only 4%. The current size of the multiplexer network compared to the functional units is alarming. For a redesign we have to decrease the number of available connections. For STA-based designs a simple profiling tool is able to detect not frequent or never used multiplexer states. A complexity decimation of 50%-75% could be reached with little effort.

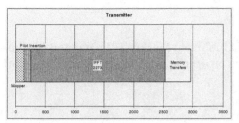

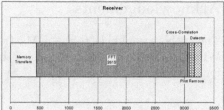

**Fig. 9.** Clock Cycles Transmitter          **Fig. 10.** Clock Cycles Receiver

*Software Implementation:* In figure 9 and 10 the Clock Cycles for each algorithm are presented. Mapping, Detecting, Pilot Insertion and Removal take only a little percentage of the overall computational effort. The main parts are IFFT/FFT and Memory Transfers. The memory transfers can be integrated into the FFT and IFFT calculations, hence FFT and IFFT remain as major part of the whole computation. The IFFT (DIF) was implemented after the FFT (DIT). Thus, the developer was more familiar with the architecture as he programmed the FFT a second time. As the theoretical limit for the FFT with a 4 Slice SIMD parallel DSP with one MAC-Unit in each slice and a single port data memory is about 192 clock cycles, the current implementation has high optimization potential. About 500 clock cycles for FFT and 1000 clock cycles to compute a complete OFDM-frame is feasible. Therefore, the system is able to transmit or receive with a core clock rate of 40MHz at 2.5Mhz sampling frequency. This results in a maximal transmission rate of 3.84Mbit/s.

To use this system for real applications, the synchronization has to be more sophiticated and forward error correction and equalizsation techniques have to be implemented. A RF-frontend has to be added, as well.

## 5   Conclusion

Our integrated design flow which is based on our core generation tool is suitable for fast VLSI prototyping. Common implementation failures as well as effort could be reduced by generating most of the source code automatically. Special features for automatic SIMD-processor generation allow for enlarging the design with little effort. The OFDM Transmitter and Receiver have been developed within five weeks by two engineers. Test and Verfikation is simplified by the structured STA-approach and the high hardware resusability.

With further software optimization, uncoded OFDM Transmission with a data rate up to 3.84Mbit/s is possible. A weak spot of the current architecture implemenation is the large multiplexer network. This problem has to eliminated by removing not used interconnections in future.

In consideration of the fact that we spent most of the development time on embedding the environmental devices, design tools have to be developed to face this problem.

## Acknowledgements

The authors would like to thank Martin Goblirsch, Markus Ullmann und Markus Winter for valuable contributions to this project and Winnie-Kathrin Ahlendorf for realizing XP.

## References

1. Gordon Cichon, Pablo Robelly, and Hendrik Seidel. *STA Core Generator Manual.* TU-Dresden, 2003. www.radionetworkprocessor.com.
2. Gordon Cichon, Pablo Robelly, Hendrik Seidel, Marcus Bronzel, and Gerhard Fettweis. Synchronous transfer architecture (sta). In *Proc. of Fourth International Workshop on Systems, Architectures, Modeling and Simulation (SAMOS'04),* Samos, July 2004.
3. Babak Daneshrad, Jr. Leonard J. Cimini, and Manny Carloni. Clusterd-ofdm transmitter implementation. In *Proc. IEEE PIMRC'96,* pages 1064–1068, Tapipei, Taiwan, Oct 1996.
4. A. Halambi and P. Grun. Expression: A language for architecture exploration through compiler/simulator retargetability, 1999.
5. Akira Kitajima, Makiko Itoh, Jun Sato, Akichika Shiomi, Yoshinori Takeuchi, and Masaharu Imai. Effectiveness of the asip design system peas-iii in design of pipelined processors. In *Proceedings of the 2001 conference on Asia South Pacific design automation,* pages 649–654. ACM Press, 2001.
6. John G. Proakis and Dimitris G. Manolakis. *Digital Signal Processing.* Prentice Hall, third edition, 1996.
7. CoWare LISATek prodcut family. Automated embedded processor design and software development tool generation.
8. *RNA.* http://www.rna.cichon.com.
9. Vojin Zivojnovic, Stefan Pees, and Heinrich Meyr. Lisa - machine description language and generic machine model for hw/sw co-design, 1996.

# A Novel Data-Path for Accelerating DSP Kernels[*]

Michalis D. Galanis[1], G. Theodoridis[2], Spyros Tragoudas[3],
Dimitrios Soudris[4], and Costas E. Goutis[1]

[1] University of Patras, Patras, Greece
{mgalanis,goutis}@vlsi.ee.upatras.gr
[2] Aristotle University, Thessalonica, Greece
theodor@physics.auth.gr
[3] Southern Illinois University, Carbondale, USA
spyros@engr.siu.edu
[4] Democriteus University, Xanthi, Greece
dsoudris@ee.duth.gr

**Abstract.** A high-performance data-path to implement DSP kernels is proposed in this paper. The data-path is based on a flexible, universal, and regular component to optimally exploiting both inter- and intra-component chaining of operations. The introduced component is a combinational circuit with steering logic that allows in easily realizing any desirable complex hardware unit, called template; so that the data-path's performance benefits by the intra-component chaining of operations. Due to the component's flexible and universal structure, the Data Flow Graph is realized by a small number of such components. The small numbers of the used components coupled with a configurable interconnection network allow adopting direct inter-component connections and optimally exploiting any inter-component chaining possibility over to the existing template-based methods. Also, due to universal and flexible structure of the component, scheduling and binding are accomplished by simple, yet efficient, algorithms achieving minimum latency at the expense of an area penalty and a small overhead at the control circuit and clock period. Results on DSP benchmarks show an average latency reduction of 20%, when the proposed data-path is compared with a high-performance data-path.

## 1 Introduction

Digital Signal Processing (DSP) and multimedia applications usually spend most of their time executing a small number of code segments with well-defined characteristics, called kernels. To accelerate the execution of such kernels, various high-performance data-paths have been proposed [1-4]. Research activities in High-Level Synthesis (HLS) [1, 3, 5, 6, 8] and Application Specific Instruction Processors (ASIPs) [2], [7, 9] have proven that the use of complex resources instead of primitive ones improves the performance of the data-path. In these works, at the behavioral level, complex operations (or complex instructions) are used instead of groups of primitive ones, while at the architectural level the complex operations are implemented by optimal custom-designed hardware units, called *templates* or *clusters*. A template may be a specialized hardware unit or a group of chained units. Special hardware is used for common-appeared operations (e.g. multiply-add). Chaining is the

---

[*] This work was partially supported by the project IST-34793-AMDREL funded by the E.C. Also, it was partially funded by the Alexander S. Onassis Public Benefit foundation

A. Pimentel and S. Vassiliadis (Eds.): SAMOS 2004, LNCS 3133, pp. 363–372, 2004.
© Springer-Verlag Berlin Heidelberg 2004

removal of the intermediate registers between the primitive units improving the total delay of the units combined. The templates either can be obtained by an existing library [1, 3], or can be extracted by the kernel's Data Flow Graph (DFG) [2, 4], [8-9].

Corazao et al. [1] shown that templates of two levels with at most two operations per level can be used together with primitive resources to derive a high-performance data-path. Given a library of templates, a method for implementing a portion of the DFG, which corresponds to the critical path, was proposed. Primitive resources implement the rest of the DFG. The reported results show high performance gains with an affordable area increase. Although intra-template chaining of (usually) two operations is exploited, chaining among operations assigned in distinct templates is not utilized. Thus, the templates and primitive resources exchange data through the register bank, which results in a latency increase. Also, as the library consists of many different templates, complex algorithms are needed to cover the DFG.

Kastner et al. [2] addressed the definition of complex instructions (templates) for an application domain. The templates implemented in ASIC technology are embedded in a hybrid reconfigurable system consisting of the templates and FPGA units. They observe that the number of operations per template is small and conclude that simple pairs of operations are the most appropriate templates for DSP applications. However, as FPGA units implement the uncovered DFG operations, the system's performance is reduced and the power consumption is increased. Cathedral [3] HLS system generates a high-performance data-path that consists of special components called Application Specific Units (ASUs). ASUs are clusters of operations comprised of chained units that match selected parts of the application's Signal Flow Graph. The chained units of an ASU, which are called Abstract Building Blocks (ABBs), are available from a given library. SFG matching is achieved via manual clustering of operations into more complex ones. However, direct connections among ABBs are not permitted resulting in non-optimal exploitation of chaining.

Rao and Kurdahi [4] examined the regularity extraction in a digital system and presented a methodology for clustering operations based on the structural regularity. They showed that identifying clusters in a circuit can simplify an important CAD problem -system-level clustering - resulting in simplifications in several design tasks. Cadambi and Goldstein [8] proposed a constructive bottom up approach to generate single-output templates. In both methods the generated templates are restricted to the area and number of their inputs and outputs, while a complete graph covering is not achieved.

Cong et al. [9] addressed the problem of generating application-specific instructions for configurable processors aiming at improving delay. The instruction generation considers only Multiple-Input Single Output (MISO) format, which cannot take into advantage of register files with more than one write port. The pattern library is selected to maximize the potential speedup, subject to a total area constraint. Nevertheless, this does not exclude the generation of a large number of different patterns, which complicates the step of application mapping. The mapping stage is formulated as a minimum-area technology mapping problem and it is solved by a binate covering problem, which is an NP-hard problem with high complexity.

This paper proposes a high-performance data-path to realize DSP kernels. The aim is to overcome the limitations of the existing template-based methods regarding the exploitation of chaining and to fully utilize both intra- and inter-template chaining. This is achieved by introducing a uniform and flexible component (template) called

Flexible Computational Component (FCC). The FCC is a combinational circuit consisting of a 2x2 array of nodes, where each node contains one ALU and one multiplier. Each FCC is able to easily realize complex operations. Due to the universality and flexibility of the FCC the DFG is fully covered and realized by a small number of FCCs; thus direct inter-FCC connections exist to fully exploit chaining between nodes of different FCCs in contrast to existing template-based methods [1,2,9]. Furthermore, the stages of synthesis are accommodated by unsophisticated, yet effective, algorithms for scheduling and binding with the FCCs. A set of experimental results shows that the proposed data-path achieves higher performance than primitive resource- and existing template-based data-paths. The performance gain stems from the features of the FCC data-path and the respective synthesis methodology.

The rest of the paper is organized as follows. Section 2 presents the detailed architecture and the main features of the FCC. The synthesis methodology for executing applications in the proposed data-path is given in section 3, while section 4 presents the experimental results. Finally, section 5 concludes the paper.

## 2  FCC-Based Data-Path

### 2.1  Architecture Description

The proposed data-path architecture consists of: (a) the FCCs, (b) a centralized register bank, and (c) a reconfigurable interconnection network, which enables the inter-FCC connections.

The FCC's internal architecture is shown in Fig. 1. It consists of four nodes whose interconnection is shown in Fig. 1a, four inputs (*in1, in2, in3 in4*) connected to the centralized register bank, four additional inputs (*A, B, C, D*) connected to the register bank or to another FCC, two outputs (*out1, out2*) also connected to the register bank and/or to another FCC, and two outputs (*out3, out4*) whose values are stored in the register bank. Multiplexers are used to select the inputs for the second-level nodes. Concerning the FCC's structure chaining of two operations is achieved. This is in compliance with the conclusions of [1, 2, 9] regarding the number of nodes in their proposed templates. An FCC with chaining larger than two levels could have been considered, but it has been shown in [1] that templates with depth larger than two comes with high area and time penalties and more control overhead, as well. Also, it has been proved in [2, 9] that templates with two operations in sequence contribute the most in the performance gains.

Each FCC node consists of two computational units that are a multiplier and an ALU as shown in Fig. 1b. Both these units are implemented in combinational logic to exploit the benefits of the chaining of operations inside the FCC. The flexible interconnection among the nodes is chosen to allow the control-unit to easily realize any desired hardware template by properly configuring the existing steering logic (i.e. the multiplexers and the tri-state buffers). The ALU performs shifting, arithmetic (add/subtract), and logical operations. Each time either the multiplier or the ALU is activated according to the control signals, Sel1 and Sel2, as shown in Fig. 1b. Each operation is 16-bit, because such a word-length is adequate for the majority of the DSP applications.

The direct connections among the FCCs in the data-path are implemented through a configurable full crossbar interconnection network. This interconnection scheme introduces a routing overhead, which is small - not degrading the performance - when the number of the FCCs is a small constant, e.g. equal to 4. When a large number of FCCs is required to support a high concurrency of operations, the simple crossbar network cannot be used efficiently. In this case we can use an interconnection structure similar to those used in supercomputing domain. Such an interconnection network is the fat-tree [10]. For the FCC data-path, a modification of this network structure like the one presented in [11] can be used. Particularly, connecting FCCs into clusters, we can create an efficient interconnection network. Firstly, $k$ FCCs are clustered and connected via a switch device, which provides the full connectivity among the $k$ FCCs. Then, $k$ clusters are recursively connected together to form as a supercluster and so on. It was showed that a value of $k=4$ results in large performance gains [11]. Any two FCCs can be connected with fewer than $2\log_k N-1$ switch devices, where $N$ is the total number of FCCs in the data-path. Thus, the interconnect delay increases logarithmically with the number of FCCs in the data-path and not in a quadratic manner as in a crossbar network, where $O(N^2)$ switches are required. Although, a fat-tree like scheme can be also employed by the existing methods, the interconnect delay of the introduced data-path is smaller as it consists of a smaller number of regular and uniform hardware resources (FCCs) compared to the data-path derived by the existing template-based methods. In other words fewer switches are required for implementing the interconnection for the FCC data-path, since their number is smaller than the template instances.

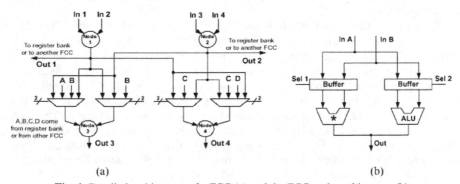

(a)                                                                (b)

**Fig. 1.** Detailed architecture of a FCC (a) and the FCC node architecture (b)

## 2.2  Data-Path Characteristics

It is adopted that there is trade-off between area and performance when templates are used to implement a data-path. In general, the template-based data-path has larger area but better performance compared with a data-path implemented by primitive resources. The area of our data-path is the sum of the area of the FCCs and the area of the external to the FCCs steering, wiring and control logic. However, as we target to accelerate DSP kernels, the data-path is a resource-dominated circuit [5], which means that its area is dominated by the computational resources (i.e. the FCCs). To minimize the area overhead due to FCCs, we perform post synthesis optimization by a procedure called *FCC instantiation*. In particular, when a unit (ALU or multiplier) in an FCC node and/or a whole FCC node is not used at any control steps (c-steps) of the scheduled DFG, then it is not included in the final data-path.

When the FCC data-path is compared with a data-path implemented by primitive resources or templates, extra control signals are required to configure the proposed data-path. However, the control-unit can be designed in such a way that does not introduce extra levels of combinational logic; thus the critical path is not affected. This can be achieved by grouping control signals to define a subset of the control state in a c-step. This feature is supported by the majority of the advanced CAD synthesis tools [12], where the control-unit can be automatically synthesized under a given delay constraint. For example, the extra control signals that are required to set-up the connections and enable the proper operations inside the FCC, can be grouped to form a subset. In this way, the delay of this control-unit is not increased compared to a data-path consisting of templates and/or primitive resources. Regarding the power consumption, each time an operation is assigned to a FCC node, only one unit either the multiplier or the ALU is activated by properly controlling the corresponding buffers. When a FCC node is not utilized at a c-step, neither the multiplier nor the ALU are activated, thus reducing the power consumption.

Compared with a data-path realized by templates [1, 2, 9], the FCC's critical path increases due to the delays of (a) two tri-state buffers, and (b) a 4-to-1 multiplexer. To have an indication of this delay increase, an experiment has been performed. Two multipliers in a sequence are considered as template. We described the FCC and the two multipliers in sequence in structural VHDL. The multiplication unit is a 16-bit Booth-Wallace. We synthesized both designs in an ASIC CMOS process at $0.13\mu m$ and an increase in delay of 4.2% has been measured. Thus, the performance improvements of our data-path over the template-based one are not negated (see Table 1), since the measured % delay increase (and thus the % increase in clock cycle period) is significantly smaller than the expected reduction of the latency cycles.

Also, exploiting the generality and flexibility of the FCC, the DFG can be implemented by a small number of FFCs allowing to use direct inter-FCC connection and thus to exploit chaining of operations assigned to different FCCs (inter-template chaining). To clarify this, a motivational example is shown in Fig. 2, where both the templates and the DFG's nodes perform two-operand computations. Observing the DFG, it is evident that there is a similarity regarding the computational structures appeared in the three steps (c-steps). However, the available templates have a fixed structure without appropriate steering logic that should allow the control unit to configure them and exploit the aforementioned similarity in the DFG. Thus, to achieve minimum latency, the DFG is implemented by 8 template instances (Fig. 2b). Regarding the exploitation of the inter-template chaining let as assume that direct connections among the templates of Fig. 2b are not allowed. Then, the templates communicate each other through the register bank and two clock cycles are required to perform the computations at each c-step. For instance at the first step of Fig. 2b. If direct inter-template connections are not allowed the result of operation $x$ is produced and stored in the register bank at the first cycle and it is consumed by operation $y$ at the second clock cycle. Thus, the absence of direct inter-template connection results in non-optimal chaining exploitation and latency increase.

On the other hand considering the structure of the FCC component the DFG is realized by only two FCC instances allowing to adopt direct inter-FCC connections and thus to exploit inter-component chaining of operations.

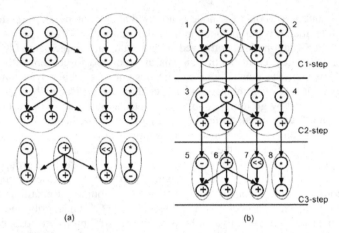

**Fig. 2.** Available templates (a), DFG covering by templates (b)

# 3   Synthesis Methodology

The introduced data-path offers a lot of advantages to develop unsophisticated, yet efficient, synthesis algorithms. As the data-path consists of one type of resources, (i.e the FCC) resource allocation can be accomplished by a simple algorithm. The universal and flexible structure of the FCC further simplifies binding allowing in achieving a full DFG covering using only FCCs. Also, the flexibility of the whole data-path provided by the FCC and the interconnection network gives extra freedom to realize the DFG by a small number of FCCs, while inter- and intra-FCC chaining is fully exploited. To implement an application onto the FCC data-path, a synthesis methodology has been developed. The methodology consists of (a) scheduling of DFG operations, and (b) binding with the FCCs. The input is an unscheduled DFG. For scheduling and binding Control Data Flow Graphs (CDFGs) the methodology is iterated through the DFGs comprising the CDFG of an application [5].

We consider that the data-path is realized by a fixed number of FCCs. Hence, scheduling is a resource-constrained problem with the goal of latency minimization. We accomplish scheduling by developing a scheduler based on list scheduling, which is widely used in HLS and compilers. The priority function of the scheduler is derived by properly labeling the DFG's nodes. The nodes are labeled with weights of their longest path to the sink node of the DFG [5], and they are ranked in decreasing order. The most urgent operations are scheduled first. In our data-path the list scheduler handles one resource type, thus it is simpler than a list scheduler, which handles various types of resources. This happens since the input DFG consists of ALU and/or multiplication type of operations and each FCC node contains ALU(s) and a multiplier; thus each DFG node is considered of one resource type (i.e. the FCC).

The pseudo-code of the binding algorithm is illustrated in Fig. 3. The input is the scheduled DFG, where each c-step has $T_{prim}$ clock period, and this type of c-step is called from here after $c\text{-}step_{prim}$. For example, $T_{prim}$ can be set to the multiplier's delay, so each DFG node can occupy one $c\text{-}step_{prim}$, since all DFG nodes have, in this case, unit execution delay. The binding algorithm maps the DFG nodes to the FCC nodes in a row-wise manner. We define a term called *FCC_index* that it is related to the new period $T_{FCC}$ of the c-steps (i.e. the clock period), after the binding is performed. It represents the current level of FCC operations that bind the DFG nodes. The *FCC_index* takes the values of 0 and 1, as the FCC consists of two levels of operations. Also, the clock period $T_{FCC}$ is set so as each operation is executed in one cycle. The algorithm covers the operations in *c-step*$_{prim}$ (s) for *FCC_index* equal to 0 or until there are no DFG nodes left uncovered in a *c-step*$_{prim}$. Then it proceeds with *FCC_index* equal to 1, if there are DFG nodes left to be covered. This procedure is repeated for every FCC in the data-path. The binding starts from the FCC assigned to the number 1, and it is continued, if it is necessary, for the next FCCs in the data-path. A FCC is not utilized, when they are no DFG nodes to be covered. Also, an FCC is partially utilized when there is no sufficient number of DFG nodes left and the mapping to FCC procedure (*map_to_FCC*) has already been started for this FCC. If there are *p* FCCs in the data-path the maximum number of operations per *c-step*$_{prim}$ is equal to 2*p*, as each FCC level consists of two nodes.

```
do {
  for the number of FCCs
  for (FCC_index=0; FCC_index<2; FCC_index++)
   while (col_idx < 2 && col_idx < number of DFG nodes not covered)
      map_to_FCC (dfg_node, FCC_index, col_idx)
   end while;
  end for;
 end for;
} while (the DFG is covered)
FCC_instantiation();              /* Instantiating the FCCs */
Determine_register_bank_size();   /* Defining the register bank size */
```

**Fig. 3.** The proposed binding algorithm

## 4   Experimental Results

A prototype tool has been developed in C++ to demonstrate the efficiency of the proposed data-path in well-known DSP benchmarks. The first set of benchmarks contains data flow structures described in VHDL, which have been used extensively in the HLS domain. The second set is described in C and consists of: (a) a set of DSP kernels from the Mediabench suite [13], and (b) an in-house JPEG encoder and an IEEE 802.11a OFDM transmitter. The DFGs were obtained from the behavioral VHDL descriptions using the CDFG tool of [14], while for extracting the DFGs from the C codes, the SUIF2 compiler [15] was used. Regarding the DFGs shown in the first column of Tables, the *ellip* to *wdf7* are extracted from the HLS benchmarks, the *jpeg* to *ofdm* from the in-house benchmarks, and the *gsm_enc* till the end from the Mediabench suite.

We synthesized the control-units of small DFGs (*fir11*, *volterra* and *ellip*) for a data-path consisting of two FCCs and we have measured their delay. The specification of the control-units has been performed manually (that's why small DFGs were used), since by this time we do not support a method for automatically defining control-units from the scheduled and bounded DFG. The DFGs that have been considered are the: *fir11*, *volterra* and *ellip*. For the synthesis of the derived control-units, a 0.13μm CMOS process has been used. The average delay of the control-units is a small fraction (bellow 10%) of the delay imposed by the FCC. This indicates that the delay of the control-unit does not affect the critical-path of the proposed data-path. Analogous results in the control-unit's delay are expected for DFGs consisting of large number (e.g *gsm_enc*) of nodes.

For the selected set of benchmarks, another *experiment* was performed which showed that a data-path with two FCCs achieves an average latency cycles decrease of 58.1%, when compared with a data-path composed of primitive resources. The clock cycle of the primitive resource data-path is set to the ALU delay. So, for this data-path, a multiplication operation takes two cycles to complete. As already mentioned, for the FCC data-path, the clock period is set for having unit execution delay. It can be easily proved that the performance of the proposed data-path is higher when $T_{FCC} < 2.4 \cdot T_{prim}$, where $T_{FCC}$ and $T_{prim}$ is the clock period for the FCC and the primitive resource based data-path, respectively. The previous relation has been satisfied after comparing the FCC delay with a 16-bit ALU delay, where both resources implemented in structural VHDL and synthesized at 0.13μm ASIC process using the Leonardo Spectrum™ tool. The results showed that $T_{FCC} = 2.14 \cdot T_{prim}$. If the physical layout of the FCC is manually optimized, then the $T_{FCC}$ should become smaller. Similar constrains, have been also satisfied for other template-based methods as in [1, 2, 9], where properly designed templates outperformed the combination of primitive resources.

A *third experiment* was performed to compare the performance and the area utilization of the introduced data-path with another high-performance data-path, which is composed of complex hardware units (i.e. templates). The template library consists of the following templates: *multiply-multiply*, *multiply-alu*, *alu-alu*, and *alu-multiply*. These templates are chosen because they are proposed by the majority of the existing methods [1, 2, 9] to be used to derive high-performance data-paths for DSP kernels. The FCC data-path consists of three FCCs, so six operations can be executed concurrently. The assumptions of this experiment are: (a) template partial matching is enabled, and (b) the clock period for all the synthesized template-based data-path is set to the delay of the *multiply-multiply* template (i.e. unit execution delay for all the templates). The template partial matching enables the full DFG covering, without needing extra primitive resources to be present in the data-path. As shown in subsection 2.2, the delay of a FCC is marginally larger than a *multiply-multiply* template. Since, our design decision is to set the clock period $T_{FCC}$ for having unit execution in a FCC data-path, it is a fair assumption to consider that the clock period is the same in both data-paths. Hence, assumption (b) is made so as the performance comparison in Table 1 is straightforward.

To derive the latency for the template data-path, covering with templates is performed in the unscheduled DFG and then scheduling is performed by a proper developed list scheduler. The binding with the templates is performed so as the available primitive computational resources (multipliers and/or ALUs) in each c-step is equal with the ones available from the FCC-based data-path.

**Table 1.** Latency cycles and area results when FCC approach is compared with a template-based data-path when 6 operations are executed concurrently

| DFG | Latency cycles | | Latency decrease (%) | Area increase (%) | |
|---|---|---|---|---|---|
| | Template-based | FCC-based | | Multiplier | ALU |
| ellip | 9 | 6 | 33.3 | 0.0 | 12.5 |
| fir11 | 7 | 6 | 14.3 | 66.7 | -40.0 |
| nc | 9 | 7 | 22.2 | -14.3 | 0.0 |
| volterra | 8 | 6 | 25.0 | 9.1 | 0.0 |
| wavelet | 9 | 7 | 22.2 | 33.3 | -41.7 |
| wdf7 | 9 | 7 | 22.2 | 20.0 | 20.0 |
| jpeg | 66 | 54 | 18.2 | 33.3 | -29.4 |
| ofdm | 28 | 23 | 17.9 | 50.0 | -14.3 |
| gsm_enc | 80 | 69 | 13.8 | 100.0 | -33.3 |
| gsm_dec | 92 | 73 | 20.7 | 140.0 | 20.0 |
| mpeg2 | 8 | 6 | 25.0 | 125.0 | 50.0 |
| Rasta | 15 | 13 | 13.3 | 140.0 | -7.7 |
| **Average** | | | **20.7** | **58.6** | **-5.3** |

Table 1 shows the results in latency and area when *three* FCCs are used to realize the DFGs of the benchmarks applications. As illustrated in Table 1, the FCC data-path achieves better performance than the data-path consisting of templates, since fewer cycles are required to implement the benchmarks. The area overhead of the FCC-based data-path is measured in terms of the number of multipliers and ALUs. A negative number in area increase indicates a decrease. For the case of *two* FCCs, an average reduction in latency of 20.4% has been reported. The average increase, in this case, for the multipliers' area is 53.8% and a decrease in the ALUs' area of 10.4%. The increase in the multiplier's area is due to the fact that in the considered DFGs the majority of operations were of ALU type, and in this case the relative usage of the FCC node as an ALU was greater than the usage as a multiplier.

**Table 2.** Template instances used in template-based data-path when 4 operations are executed concurrently

| DFG | Template instances | | | | |
|---|---|---|---|---|---|
| | mul-mul | mul-alu | alu-mul | alu-alu | Total |
| ellip | 0 | 2 | 2 | 2 | 6 |
| fir11 | 2 | 2 | 0 | 2 | 6 |
| nc | 3 | 1 | 3 | 1 | 8 |
| volterra | 2 | 2 | 0 | 2 | 6 |
| wavelet | 2 | 2 | 0 | 3 | 7 |
| wdf7 | 0 | 4 | 2 | 0 | 6 |
| jpeg | 0 | 4 | 2 | 4 | 10 |
| ofdm | 1 | 3 | 2 | 4 | 10 |
| gsm_enc | 0 | 4 | 0 | 4 | 8 |
| gsm_dec | 0 | 3 | 0 | 4 | 7 |
| mpeg2 | 0 | 3 | 0 | 3 | 6 |
| rasta | 0 | 3 | 1 | 3 | 7 |

Table 2 shows the number of the template instances of the template-based data paths when 4 operations are executed concurrently in each c-step. It is clear that due the absence of the flexible templates the generated data-paths are realized by a large number of templates instances preventing the adoption of direct inter-template connections and thus the inter-template chaining exploitation. In particular, when four operations are executed concurrently at each c-step, the FCC-based data-paths are realized by only two FCCs while the template-based data-paths are implemented by a lot of template instances.

## 5 Conclusions

A high-performance data-path to accelerate computational-intensive DSP kernels has been presented. Chaining is optimally exploited resulting in a latency reduction. Compared, with a high-performance data-path produced by existing template-based method, an average latency reduction of approximately 20% is achieved, while synthesis is accomplished by simple, yet efficient synthesis.

## References

1. M. R Corazao et al., "Performance Optimization Using Template Mapping for Datapath-Intensive High-Level Synthesis", in IEEE Trans. on CAD, vol.15, no. 2, pp. 877-888, August 1996.
2. R. Kastner et al., "Instruction Generation for Hybrid Reconfigurable Systems", in ACM TODAES, vol 7., no.4, pp. 605-627, October, 2002.
3. W. Geurts, F. Catthoor, S. Vernalde, and H. DeMan, "Accelerator Data-Path Synthesis for High-Throughput Signal Processing Applications", Boston, MA: Kluwer, 1996.
4. D. Rao and F. Kurdahi, "On Clustering for Maximal Regularity Extraction", in IEEE Trans. on CAD, vol.12, no. 8, pp. 1198-1208, August, 1993.
5. Giovanni De Micheli, "Synthesis and Optimization of Digital Circuits", McGraw-Hill, International Editions, 1994.
6. D. Gajski et al. "High-Level Synthesis: Introduction to Chip and System design", Boston, MA. Kluwer, 1997.
7. M. Jain et al. "ASIP Design Methodologies: Survey and Issues", in Proc of Int. Conf. on VLSI Design, pp. 76-81, 2001.
8. S. Cadambi and S. C. Goldstein, "CPR: a configuration profiling tool", in Symp. on Field-Programmable Custom Computing Machines (FCCM), 1999.
9. J. Cong et al., "Application-Specific Instruction Generation for Configurable Processor Architectures", in Proc. of Int. Symp. on FPGA 2004, 2004.
10. C.E. Leiserson, "Fat-Trees: Universal Networks for Hardware Efficient Supercomputing", in IEEE Trans. on Computers, vol 43., no. 10, pp. 892-901, Oct. 1985.
11. Y. Lai, "Hierarchical Interconnection Structures for Field Programmable Gate Arrays", in IEEE Trans. on VLSI, vol 5., no. 2, pp. 186-196, June 1997.
12. Cadence BuildGates™, www.cadence.com.
13. C. Lee et al., "MediaBench: a tool for evaluating and synthesizing multimedia and communications systems", in Int. Symposium on Microarchitecture, 1997.
14. CDFG toolset, http://poppy.snu.ac.kr/CDFG/cdfg.html.
15. M. W. Hall et al., "Maximizing multiprocessor performance with the SUIF compiler", Computer, vol. 29, pp. 84-89, 1996. (URL: http://suif.standford.edu)

# Scalable FFT Processors
# and Pipelined Butterfly Units

Jarmo Takala and Konsta Punkka

Tampere University of Technology, P.O.Box 553, FIN-33101 Tampere, Finland
{jarmo.takala,konsta.punkka}@tut.fi

**Abstract.** This paper considers partial-column radix-2 FFT processors. The efficiency of processors based on bit-parallel multipliers, distributed arithmetic, and CORDIC is analyzed with the aid of logic synthesis.

## 1 Introduction

Discrete Fourier transform (DFT) is one of the most important tools in the field of digital signal processing. Due to its computational complexity, several fast Fourier transform (FFT) algorithms have been developed over the years. The most popular FFT algorithms are the Cooley-Tukey algorithms originally proposed in [1]. It has been shown that the decimation-in-time (DIT) algorithms provide better signal-to-noise-ratio than decimation-in-frequency algorithms when finite word length is used [2]. In addition, in-place algorithms are often used due the principal simplicity of the operand storage; the memory locations holding the operands for a computational recursion are replaced by the results of recursion.

Based on the previous, the most popular Cooley-Tukey FFT is the radix-2 DIT FFT with bit-reversed input and in-order output. A $2^k$-point FFT can be presented with tensor product formulation as [3]

$$F_{2^k}^{\mathrm{DIT}} = \left[ \prod_{i=0}^{k-1} \left(I_{2^i} \otimes F_2 \otimes I_{2^{k-i-1}}\right) \left(I_{2^i} \otimes T_{2^{k-i}}\right) \right] P_{2^k}^r$$

$$T_J = \left(I_{J/2} \oplus D_{J/2}\right)$$

$$D_{J/2} = \mathrm{diag}\left(W_J^k\right),\ 0 \leq k < J/2$$

$$F_2 = \begin{pmatrix} 1 & 1 \\ 1 & -1 \end{pmatrix} \tag{1}$$

where $\oplus$ and $\otimes$ denote Kronecker sum and product, respectively, $I_k$ is the identity matrix of order $k$, and $F_2$ is the 2-point DFT matrix. $P_N^r$ is a bit-reversed permutation matrix of order $N$ reordering a vector $X = (x_0, x_1, \ldots, x_{N-1})^T$ to a vector $Y = (x_{rev(0)}, x_{rev(0)}, \ldots, x_{rev(N-1)})^T$, where the bit-reverse function, $rev(\cdot)$, reverses the order of the bits in the binary representation of the element indices. The complex coefficients $W_J^k$ are called twiddle factors and defined as

$$W_J^k = \exp\left(-\frac{\jmath\, 2\pi k}{J}\right) \tag{2}$$

A. Pimentel and S. Vassiliadis (Eds.): SAMOS 2004, LNCS 3133, pp. 373–382, 2004.

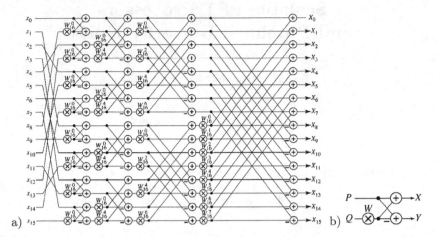

**Fig. 1.** Radix-2 decimation-in-time bit-reversed input, in-order output FFT: signal flow graphs of (a) 16-point FFT and (b) DIT butterfly operation.

where $\jmath$ is the imaginary unit. The signal flow graphs of 8-point and 16-point radix-2 DIT FFT with bit-reversed input and in-order output are illustrated in Fig. 1(a) and (b). The arithmetic kernel of DIT FFT is the butterfly operation defined as

$$X = P + WQ$$
$$Y = P - WQ \tag{3}$$

and its signal flow graph is shown in Fig. 1(c).

There are several ways to exploit the inherent parallelism in the DIT FFT algorithms. In general, the parallel FFT parallel can be divided into the following principal classes [4]: fully parallel, pipelined (alternatively cascaded), column, and partial-column. In first three classes, the number of butterfly units computing the butterfly operation are dependent on the transform length, which implies that the performance of the computational structure cannot be tailored according to the requirements of the given application. In partial-column approach, the number of butterfly units can be varied, this it allows trading implementation cost, i.e., area, against time, i.e., computation speed. The partial-column approach can also be combined to pipeline class, which results in parallel pipelines as proposed, e.g., in [4, 5].

There are also other implementation alternatives than the higher level organization, which have a great impact on the performance and efficiency of the realization. Implementations based on bit-parallel multipliers (e.g., in [6]), coordinate rotations (CORDIC) (e.g., in [7]), and distributed arithmetic (DA) (e.g., in [8, 9]) have been reported. In addition, the memory requirements and the twiddle factor storage, in particular, has become important.

This paper considers design of application-specific radix-2 FFT processors where the parallelism can be tailored according to the requirements of the given

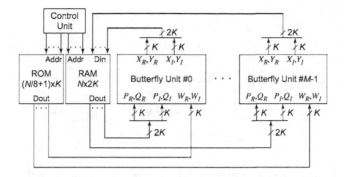

**Fig. 2.** Block diagram of partial-column FFT processor.

application. We also compare three different approaches to compute the radix-2 butterfly operation.

## 2    Partial-Column Radix-2 FFTs

In an $N$-point radix-2 FFT, there are $N/2$ butterfly operations in each butterfly column as seen in Fig. 1. Since the butterfly operations within a single column are data-independent, they can be computed in parallel. The principal idea in partial-column FFT is to compute $M$ butterfly operations at a time such that $1 < M < N/2$. This allows the number of butterfly computation units to be selected according to the requirements of the given application. In this sense, partial-column processing is scalable where as in pipeline and column FFTs the number of butterfly units is dependent on the FFT size. The organization of the proposed partial-column FFT processor is described in the following sections.

### 2.1    Organization

In general, the partial-column processing is performed in such a way that the operands required by a single butterfly unit, i.e., two operands for radix-2 butterfly, are transferred simultaneously from the memory. In our approach, the butterfly units are pipelined in a sense that a single operand ($2K$-bit word if real and imaginary part take $K$ bits each) is transferred to the butterfly unit at a time, thus each butterfly unit has a dedicated bus to and from memory as illustrated in Fig. 2. Such an arrangement increases the computation time but this can be compensated by increasing the number of butterfly units. The structure of butterfly units reminds the structure used in pipeline FFTs where the advantage is that some of the arithmetic units can be reused during the operation. This is due to the fact that there are more clock cycles available for the computation.

Our approach is to minimize the RAM storage, thus the computation is performed in-place, i.e., results of radix-2 butterfly are store into the same memory locations where the operands were obtained. Therefore, $N$ complex-valued

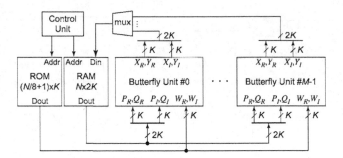

**Fig. 3.** Block diagram of partial-column FFT processor when throughput of butterfly units is $1/(2M)$.

memory locations are needed for an $N$-point FFT. The organization requires that there are $2M$-ports in the RAM memory when $M$ butterfly units with throughput of one are used, i.e., each unit consumes one operand and produces one result at each cycle.

This can be arranged with multi-port memories but more area-efficient approach is to use interleaved memories with a conflict-free access scheme. Such a scheme for FFT computation is described, e.g., in [10]. This arrangement will require that for an $N$-point FFT, there are $2M$ single-port memories with $N/(2M)$ words and the memories are interconnected with a permutation network.

If the throughput of the butterfly units is less than one, the number of memory ports is reduced. An interesting case is the throughput of butterfly unit is $1/(2M)$, i.e., the total number of data transfers, reads and writes, matches the memory bandwidth of a single port memory. In this case, the organization of the processor is slightly different as depicted in Fig. 3. If lower throughput units are used, it is still possible to increase the parallelism by adding butterfly unit groups in such a way that the total data transfer rate is one at each group and one port in the memory is allocated to each group.

### 2.2   Butterfly Unit

An essential portion of the cost and characteristics of butterfly unit is defined by the realization of complex multiplication. In this paper, we have considered three different methods based on bit-parallel multipliers, CORDIC, and DA. All these result in different structures for computing the butterfly operations and these are discussed in the following sections.

**Bit-Parallel Multiplier.** The definition of complex multiplication implies that four multipliers and two adders are needed to perform the operation:

$$WQ = (W_R + jW_I)(Q_R + jQ_I) = W_RQ_R - W_IQ_I + j(W_RQ_I + W_IQ_R) \quad (4)$$

The previous equation implies that the critical path is through a multiplier and adder. The number of multipliers can be reduced by rewriting (4) into a different

**Table 1.** Characteristics of complex multiplication with 16-bit precision on an $0.11\mu$ ASIC technology.

| | Four multipliers Eqn. (4) | | Three multipliers Eqn. (5) | |
|---|---|---|---|---|
| Clock Constraint [MHz] | 100 | 200 | 100 | 200 |
| Delay [ns] | 9.7 | 4.8 | 9.8 | 5.4 |
| Area [kgates] | 4 610 | 5 820 | 4 200 | 5 540 |
| Power Consumption [mW] | 2.3 | 5.9 | 2.3 | 6.2 |

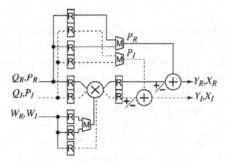

**Fig. 4.** Block diagram of radix-2 butterfly computation based on bit-parallel multipliers. All the signals are real-valued and dashed lines indicate imaginary data.

form and there are several ways to perform such a reduction as described in [11]. In this paper, we have considered the following version:

$$WQ = W_I (Q_R - Q_I) + Q_R (W_R - W_I)$$
$$+ \jmath [W_I (Q_R - Q_I) + Q_I (W_R + W_I)] \tag{5}$$

This equation implies that only three multipliers but five adders are needed for complex multiplication. This suggests that more efficient implementation can be obtained. However, the drawback is longer critical path, i.e., path through a multiplier and two adders, which requires the logic synthesis tool to use faster components to fulfill the timing requirements compared to the previous case. This is illustrated in Table 1, which shows that there is no dramatic area or power consumption difference between the implementations. However, the delay is considerably shorter in four multiplier case, thus we have used this realization in our experiments.

The table also shows that a noteworthy saving in power consumption can be obtained if two clock cycles can be allocated for the complex multiplication. This, in turn, is possible in our case when operands enter through a common bus, thus two clock cycles are available for the pipelined butterfly computation. This, however, requires that the operand $Q$ in (3) enters the butterfly unit before the operand $P$.

**CORDIC.** Since a complex number can be interpreted as a vector in imaginary plane and, in FFT, the twiddle factors are roots of unity, i.e., norm of a twiddle factor vector is one, the multiplication by twiddle factors can be realized by rotating the vector. The CORDIC algorithm is a well-known iterative method to perform such a rotation. The basic equations to be iterated are [9]

$$x_{Rk+1} = x_{Rk} + \text{sign}(z_k)x_{Ik}2^{-k} \tag{6}$$

$$x_{Ik+1} = x_{Ik} + \text{sign}(z_k)x_{Rk}2^{-k} \tag{7}$$

$$z_{k+1} = z_k - \text{sign}(z_k)\tan^{-1}(2^{-k}) \tag{8}$$

where $k$ denotes the iteration, $x_{Rk}$ and $x_{Ik}$ are the coordinates of the vector at iteration $k$, and $x_k$ is the angle at iteration $k$. Multiplication $QW_N^n$ is started with initial conditions $z_0 = -\frac{2\pi n}{N}$, i.e., rotation angle of twiddle factor $W_N^n$, $x_{R0} = Q_R$, and $x_{I0} = Q_I$. The computation requires values of $\tan^{-1}$ in (8) to be stored into a ROM but the storage requirements are small; typically for a $K$-bit precision, approximately $K$ iterations are needed implying need to store $K$ values of $\tan^{-1}$.

The drawback of the algorithm is that the magnitude of vector increases at each iteration. This scaling needs to be compensated but fortunately the scaling is constant. Therefore, in our experiments, we have used a multiplier with constant multiplicand to compensate the magnitude.

Since the CORDIC algorithm is iterative, the butterfly unit based on CORDIC may obtain new operands after $K$ cycles when $K$-bits are used for real and imaginary part implying throughput of $1/K$. A block diagram of a butterfly unit used in the analysis in this paper is depicted in Fig. 5(a).

In order to increase the throughput, the iterations of CORDIC algorithm can be separated into independent stages implying a pipelined realization. For a $K$-bit precision, $K$ pipeline stages are need which results in an increase in area due to the pipeline registers. However, the throughput of such a pipelined unit is 1. The block diagram of a butterfly unit based on the pipelined CORDIC is illustrated in Fig. 5(b). This reminds the butterfly units used in pipelined FFT processors. It should be noted that, in this approach, all the operands are fed through the complex multiplication, thus every second rotation angle needs to be zero, i.e., operand $P$ in (3) is not rotated.

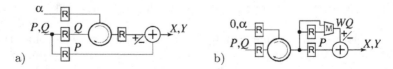

**Fig. 5.** Block diagram of radix-2 butterfly computation based on CORDIC: (a) iterative and (b) pipelined iterative version. All the signals are complex-valued except rotation angle, $\alpha$.

**Table 2.** All the possible values of $q_R(a_R, a_I)$ and $q_I(a_R, a_I)$ in (11) and (12).

| $a_R$ $a_I$ | $q_R(a_R, a_I)$ | $q_I(a_R, a_I)$ |
|---|---|---|
| 0  0 | $-(W_R - W_I)$ | $-(W_R + W_I)$ |
| 0  1 | $-(W_R + W_I)$ | $+(W_R - W_I)$ |
| 1  0 | $+(W_R + W_I)$ | $-(W_R - W_I)$ |
| 1  1 | $+(W_R - W_I)$ | $+(W_R + W_I)$ |

**Distributed Arithmetic.** The complex multiplication can be performed with the aid of distributed arithmetic as described in [12]. The principle can be described as follows. Let $x$ be a $K$-bit number in two's complement representation consisting of bits $(a_{(K-1)}, \ldots, x_{(1)}, x_{(0)})$, where $x_{(0)}$ is the least significant bit. Then $x$ can be expressed as

$$
\begin{aligned}
x &= \frac{1}{2}x - \frac{1}{2}(-x) \\
&= \frac{1}{2}\left[ -\left(x_{(K-1)} - \overline{x_{(K-1)}}\right) + \sum_{k=0}^{K-2} \left(2^{k+1-K}\left(x_{(k)} - \overline{x_{(k)}}\right)\right) - 2^{1-K} \right] \quad (9)
\end{aligned}
$$

where $\overline{x_k}$ is complement of bit $x_k$. This equation can be used in (4), which results in the following:

$$
\begin{aligned}
2WQ = {}&-q_R(Q_{R(K-1)}, Q_{I(K-1)}) + \sum_{k=0}^{K-2}\left(q_R(Q_{R(k)}, Q_{I(k)})2^{k+1-K}\right) \\
&+q_R(0,0)2^{1-K} + {}_{\jmath}\left[-q_I(Q_{R(K-1)}, Q_{I(K-1)})\right. \\
&\left.+ \sum_{k=0}^{K-2}\left(q_I(Q_{R(k)}, Q_{I(k)})2^{k+1-K}\right) + q_I(0,0)2^{1-K}\right] \quad (10)
\end{aligned}
$$

where functions $q_R(\cdot, \cdot)$ and $q_I(\cdot, \cdot)$ are defined as

$$
q_R(a_R, a_I) = (a_R - \overline{a_R})W_R - (a_I - \overline{a_I})W_I \quad (11)
$$
$$
q_I(a_R, a_I) = (a_R - \overline{a_R})W_I + (a_I - \overline{a_I})W_R \quad (12)
$$

All the possible values of $q_R(\cdot, \cdot)$ and $q_I(\cdot, \cdot)$ are listed in Table 2, which shows that for each twiddle factor $W$ it is enough to store two real values, $-(W_R - W_I)$ and $-(W_R + W_I)$. Then complex multiplication can be performed in bit-serial fashion by accumulating these store values based on the bits in the real and imaginary part.

In this paper, we have used the butterfly structure from [12]. However, the original structure has bit-serial inputs and outputs, which implies need for 1-bit memories. Since such memories were not available in the technology libraries and we are targeting to word-wide memories, we included parallel-to-serial converters into the input and used bit-parallel complex adder-subtracter to perform

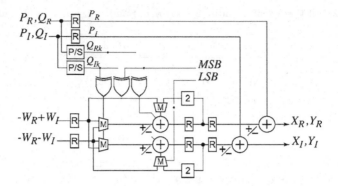

**Fig. 6.** Block diagram of radix-2 butterfly computation when complex multiplication is realized with distributed arithmetic. P/S: Parallel-to-serial converter.

the add/subtract in butterfly. The block diagram of resulting butterfly unit is illustrated in Fig. 6.

### 2.3   Operand and Twiddle Factor Storage

The in-place property of the FFT algorithm in (1) allows the input operands and intermediate and final results, to share the same memory locations. This, however, requires that the input sequence is stored into the RAM memory in bit-reversed order, which is easy to arrange by reversing the address bits when the input vector is stored into the RAM. The in-place operand access during the actual computations can be realized with the aid of address rotation [13].

The actual RAM address for operand access is obtained from a linear address by rotating a field in the least significant end of the linear address one bit to the right. The width of the field to be rotated depends on the butterfly column. In the first column, field is zero bits and, in the second column, it is one bit. In general, the memory address at butterfly column $S$ is obtained by rotating $S$ least significant bits in the linear address to the right. The address generation procedure at each butterfly column in a 64-point FFT is illustrated in Fig. 7(a). Operand address generator realizing the previous procedure can be implemented with the aid of two cascaded rows of multiplexers as illustrated in Fig. 7(b). The

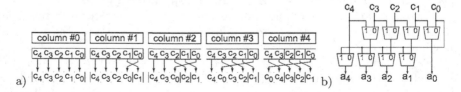

**Fig. 7.** Operand access for a 64-point FFT: (a) principle and (b) implementation. $c_4 \ldots c_0$: linear address bits. $a_4 \ldots a_0$: RAM address bits.

upper row of multiplexers is used to select the length of the bit field to be rotated. The lower row of multiplexers connects the least significant bit to the correct output.

In an $N$-point radix-2 FFT, there are $N/2$ different complex-valued twiddle factors. However, these factors can be computed from $N/8 + 1$ complex-valued numbers with the aid of an add/subtract unit [14]. On the other hand, there are $N/4+1$ different real-valued magnitudes present in the real and imaginary parts, thus the twiddle factors can be formed easily by fetching the magnitudes from a table and taking complement when needed. However, this arrangement requires that two memory accesses to the ROM table are needed. This is possible with the proposed pipelined butterfly units since the operand access takes two cycles.

The previous method can be applied directly to butterfly units based on bit-parallel multipliers. The DA based butterfly units require sum and difference of the real and imaginary parts, thus an additional add/subtract unit is needed. Butterfly units based on CORDIC need no ROM tables since the angles can be generated easily from counters synchronizing the overall operation.

## 3    Comparison

We have described the previous butterfly units in VHDL language using 16-bit precision for arithmetic units. the descriptions have been synthesized onto a $0.11\mu$ ASIC technology with Synopsys logic synthesis tools. We have also analyzed the power consumption of the implementations by obtaining the switching activity with simulations and the information is fed to Synopsys tools to obtain realistic estimate on power consumption. Since the iterative units, i.e., iterative CORDIC and DA, have throughput of 1/16, we have increased the number of units to reach the throughput of 1 in all units. The results are listed in Table 3.

Since the FFT processor contains the same 32-bit $N$-word RAM memory and the cost of control unit, according to our experiments, is negligible in terms of area and power consumption, the only difference is the ROM memory for the twiddle factor storage. Butterfly units based on bit-parallel multipliers and DA need an 16-bit $N/4 + 1$ word ROM while this is not needed in CORDIC based butterfly units. Based on the memory synthesis results, the CORDIC based FFT will use less area when $N > 2^{14}$. However, from the power consumption point of view, CORDIC will be more efficient when $N > 2^{21}$.

## 4    Conclusion

In this paper, we have proposed general organization for partial-column FFT processors and described three methods to construct pipelined radix-2 butterfly units. We have discussed in-place operand access in radix-2 FFT and twiddle factor storage. The proposed butterfly units have been synthesized onto a $0.11\mu$ ASIC technology and the results show that butterfly units based on four bit-parallel multipliers and two adders are efficient in terms of area and power

**Table 3.** Characteristics of butterfly units with 16-bit word width. Clock constraint during the logic synthesis was 200 MHz.

|                        | Bit-Parallel Multiplier | Pipelined CORDIC | Iterative CORDIC | DA     |
| ---------------------- | ----------------------- | ---------------- | ---------------- | ------ |
| Number of units        | 1                       | 1                | 8                | 8      |
| Max. clock period [ns] | 4.8                     | 4.9              | 4.8              | 4.8    |
| Area [kgates]          | 5 820                   | 14 900           | 40 640           | 14 400 |
| Power Consumption [mW] | 5.9                     | 19.7             | 64.8             | 16.8   |

when modest FFT sizes are needed. When extremely long FFTs are needed, the pipelined CORDIC should be considered.

# References

1. Cooley, J., Tukey, J.: An algorithm for the machine calculation of the complex Fourier series. Math. Comput. **19** (1965) 297–301
2. Tran-Thong, Liu, B.: Fixed-point fast Fourier transform error analysis. IEEE Trans. Acoust., Speech, Signal Processing **24** (1976) 563–573
3. Granata, J., Conner, M., Tolimieri, R.: Recursive fast algorithms and the role of the tensor product. IEEE Trans. Signal Processing **40** (1992) 2921–2930
4. Gorman, S.F., Wills, J.M.: Partial column FFT pipelines. IEEE Trans. Circuits Syst. II **42** (1995) 414–423
5. Wold, E.H., Despain, A.M.: Pipeline and parallel-pipeline FFT processors for VLSI implementations. IEEE Trans. Comput. **33** (1984) 414–426
6. Wosnitza, M., Cavadini, M., Thaler, M., Tröster, G.: A high precision 1024-point FFT processor for 2D convolution. In: Dig. Tech. Papers IEEE Solid-State Circuits Conf., San Francisco, CA (1998) 118–119
7. Despain, A.M.: Fourier transform computers using CORDIC iterations. IEEE Trans. Comput. **23** (1974) 993–1001
8. Berkeman, A., Öwall, V., Torkelson, M.: A low logic depth complex multiplier using distributed arithmetic. IEEE J. Solid-State Circuits **35** (2000) 656–659
9. Wanhammar, L.: DSP Integrated Circuits. Academic Press, San Diego, CA (1999)
10. Takala, J., Järvinen, T.: Stride permutation access in interleaved memory systems. In Bhattacharyya, S.S., Deprettere, E.F., Teich, J., eds.: Domain-Specific Processors: Systems, Architectures, Modeling, and Simulation. Marcel Dekker, New York, NY (2004) 63–84
11. Wenzler, A., Lüder, E.: New structures for complex multipliers and their noise analysis. In: Proc. IEEE ISCAS. Volume 2., Seattle, WA (1995) 1432–1435
12. White, S.A.: A simple FFT butterfly arithmetic unit. IEEE Trans. Circuits Syst. **28** (1981) 352–355
13. Chu, E., George, A.: Inside the FFT Black Box: Serial and Parallel Fast Fourier-Transform Algorithms. CRC Press, Boca Raton, FL (2000)
14. Hasan, M., Arslan, T.: FFT coefficient memory reduction technique for OFDM applications. In: Proc. IEEE ICASSP. Volume 1., Orlando, FL (2002) 1085–1088

# Scalable Instruction-Level Parallelism

Chris Jesshope

Department of Computer Science, University of Amsterdam,
Kruislaan 403, 1098 SJ, Amsterdam, The Netherlands
bossman@mac.com

**Abstract.** This paper presents a model for instruction-level distributed computing that allows the implementation of scalable chip multiprocessors. Based on explicit microthreading it serves as a replacement for out-of-order instruction issue; it defines the model and explores implementations issues. The model results in a fully distributed implementation in which data is distributed to one register file per processor, which is scalable as the number of ports in each register file is constant. The only component with less than ideal scaling properties is the the switching network between processors.

## 1   Some Issues in Current Microprocessor Design

Over the last twelve years Moore predicts a packing density increase of 256 in silicon die with a corresponding speed increase of 16. Whereas we see speed increases better than predicted, the same is not true of system-level concurrency. The history of the PPC processor (see http://www.rootvg.net/RSmodels.htm) shows that clock speed has increased at twice the predicted rate, i.e. from 33Mhz to 1Ghz but that increases in system-level concurrency do not track packing density. The PPC microprocessor has evolved from a 32-bit single-issue to a 64-bit, five-way issue design. It is difficult to obtain high IPC in out-of-order issue microprocessors and so a factor of two in effective issue width and a factor of two in bit-level concurrency is we get from this 256 increase in packing density. It seems that our linear minds can not differentiate between $e^t$ and $e^{3t}$ as they both seem discontinuous to us.

The faster than predicted clock speed is due to a finer pipeline division. The smaller than predicted concurrency is simply because we do not understand concurrency well enough, especially at the instruction level. There are also many factors contributing to the problem; for example the need for binary code compatibility. Looking at modern microprocessors, more and more area is being used for on-chip memory to mitigate against the high latencies of off-chip access, typically 25-33% of the chip area[1]. Also instruction issue logic is becoming more and more complex and typically takes as much silicon area as the on-chip memory. Instruction issue complexity is due to a poor scaling of the out-of-order approach, which grows with at least the square of the issue width[2]. Finally the register file is not scalable[3]. Register file capacity is related to issue width and the cell size to the square of the issue width. This means that as issue width

A. Pimentel and S. Vassiliadis (Eds.): SAMOS 2004, LNCS 3133, pp. 383–392, 2004.

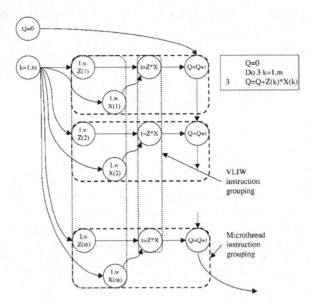

**Fig. 1.** Dependency graph for FORTRAN DO loop.

is increases, there is a cubic scaling of register file area, which will very quickly dominate chip area, speed and power considerations.

All three issues can be improved significantly. If a microprocessor can tolerate high latency, then it is possible to replace large on-chip caches with more processors. It will also be shown that instruction issue and register file area can be designed to be scalable. The solution requires explicit concurrency controls and distributed synchronisation to be added to an ISA and these in turn require a move away from binary-code compatibility. Backward compatibility can be retained at some cost in efficiency but recompilation or binary translation of legacy code is required to obtain speedup.

## 2   The Concurrency Model and Its Restrictions

### 2.1   Introduction to the Model

The model proposed in this paper is one based on the concept of micro-threading. It uses multiple threads within a single context and provides a schedule-independent description of concurrency. VLIW or the more abstract EPIC also define explicit concurrency but over a fixed schedule of instructions, giving problems with non-deterministic timing, as any delay in one operation delays the entire schedule.

Figure 1 shows a dependency graph for a simple FORTRAN loop illustrating how instructions are grouped in VLIW, where each group is issued simultaneously and must complete before the next is issued. EPIC differs from VLIW in that it could encode the schedules shown, whereas VLIW would sequentialise these packets into issue-width units.

Micro-threading groups instructions in sequences, where each group is called a *micro-thread* and the collection of groups, is called a *family of microthreads*, in this case over all iterations in the FORTRAN loop. Instructions in different threads can be executed concurrently in any schedule subject to data dependencies; they can be interleaved arbitrarily in a single pipeline to give latency tolerance or can be executed on multiple pipelines in a chip multiprocessor. Instructions issue in a single thread is sequential with the overall schedule determined by data availability. Micro-threads are short sequences of instructions created dynamically with their own register window, which execute and terminate on the processor they are allocated to.

## 2.2   Background

The microthreaded model was first proposed in 1996 [4] and has been refined and evaluated over time[5]. A number of other papers have also considered similar models, the earliest being nano-threads in [6], a limited form of microthreading using only two contexts to tolerate memory latency. There is now a relatively large body of similar work describing the usage of threads for pre-fetching and tolerating memory latency, e.g. [7] and [8].

## 2.3   Concurrency Controls

Micro-threading can be based on any ISA and can be designed to maintain full backward compatibility, allowing existing binary code to run without speedup. Alternatively, binary-to-binary translation can be used to obtain backward compatibility with a more efficient implementation and potential speedup. For backward compatibility, just five instructions are required to implement the concurrency controls. These are:

- an instruction to create a family of threads Cre
- an instruction to effect a context switch Swch
- an instruction to terminate a thread (and invoke a new context) Kill
- a instruction that waits for all other threads to terminate Bsync
- an instruction to terminate all other threads Brk

Using these instructions, the FORTRAN code in figure 1 can be translated into the microthreaded code shown below, where the main thread creates a family of m threads to execute the loop, defined by the *create control block* at the label do3. It should be noted that this family carries a dependency defined by the scaler variable Q, from the main thread in $S0 via the $S0/$D0 pair in each thread, through to the last iteration, where the value of Q is written to memory. The dependency distance from the create control block determines how these pairs of registers are bound over the family of threads.

```
            .data            # create control block
do3:        .word 1          # start index
            .word m          # last index
            .word 1          # skip between indices
            .word 1          # distance between dependencies
            .word 2          # number of $L registers per thread
            .word 1          # number of $S registers per thread
            .word body       # pointer to the code
            .word last       # optional code for last thread (used)
main:       mv $S0 $G0       # initialise Q to zero for first thread
            cre do3          # create family of threads for loop
            bsync            # wait for thraeds to complete
            finish           # done!
body:       lw $L1 Z($L0)    # for all but last index value do
            lw $L2 X($L0)    # load two values - $L0 contains index
            mul $L1 $L1 $L2  # multiply
            swch             # context switch as loads may miss cache
            add $S0 $D0 $L1  # add result to value from previous thread
            kill             # terminate thread
last:       lw $L1 Z($L0)    # last is as above except...
            lw $L2 X($L0)
            mul $L1 $L1 $L2
            swch
            add $S0 $D0 $L1
            swch
            sw $S0 Q($G0)    # ...it stores the result to Q
            kill
```

Note that the index value is wiitten to the first local regsiter for a thread when it is created ($L0). A number of local and shared registers (also defined in the control block) are allocated dynamically when the thread is created so long as there are sufficient registers on the target processor. Instruction interleaving in a pipeline is defined by explicit context switching between the threads allocatd to it and is required after an instruction that has a data dependency on any of its operands. In this code there are two examples, using the result of the lw instruction, which is dependent on a cache hit and reading the $D0 register, which is dependent on a previous thread writing the corresponding $S0 register. Explicit context switching at the instruction fetch stage avoids flushing the pipeline at the register read stage if either operand is found to be empty. When a register read fails and the pipeline is executing instructions from another thread, the micro-context of the instruction is stored in the *empty* register to suspend that thread. When data is written to the register, that context is reactivated. This action implements synchronisation as a blocking read between threads or between a thread and the memory system.

Because the model is defined on a single context, transfer of control between functions results in a single thread of control and threads other than that executing the call or return are killed. The synchronisation model works only at the instruction level and there is no synchronisation on memory. Concurrent writes to memory must be controlled by synchronisation at the register level. In the example, the loop-to-loop dependency is carried in registers and only written to Q in the last thread. If every thread wrote Q, the order of execution of the threads might result in the wrong value being stored in memory. Finally, a dependency distance of zero defines a family of independent threads, which have no dependency relation between them nor to the thread that created them. A non-zero dependency distance defines a chain of dependencies that follows iteration order with thread i being dependent on thread i-d, where i is the ith thread created and d is the dependency distance defined in the create control block.

## 2.4   Register Partitioning

The register namespace in the microthreaded model is partitioned logically according to the type of communication being performed. An implementation would map each partition onto an appropriate register file and associated access mechanisms. The microthreaded model identifies four classes of variables, which are:

- *invariants*, which give rise to broadcast communication. Such variables are global and can be read and written by any thread. They are represented by a specifier $Gi in the assembly language;
- *dependencies*, which give rise to pair-wise communication between two threads. They are written by one thread and read by another. They are called Shared in the producer thread and represented by a specifier $Si and are called Dependent in the consumer thread and represented by a specifier $Di. It should be noted that $Si(producer)=$Di(consumer);
- all other variables are called Local and used for communicating data within a single thread or between the memory system and that thread . These are represented by $Li.

Each class of variable is allocated as a logical register window as mechanisms for access to each will differ. The state of a thread includes information to locate the various register windows in the register file(s).

## 3   Implementing the Model

A recent article [9] reviewed billion transistor architectures, seven years on from a special issue on the same topic. It highlights two areas where current approaches have failed to provide solutions to the trends in chip architecture. The first and perhaps the most important is the shrinking percentage of the chip that is reachable within a single clock cycle, this has become more critical with the superclocked processor cores that are now being designed. It mandates a partitioning that allows multiple, independent clocking zones that communicate asynchronously. The other factor is that of power dissipation and any implementation of a chip multiprocessor must address both of these issues.

Figure 2 shows a distributed implementation of the microthreaded model. In this architecture, the GCQ iterates the *create control block* to individual processors, where registers are allocated and state is created for the threads. Thread state is stored in the LCQ and this and the register files are fully distributed. A single bus provides access to the GCQ for creating threads. Although only one processor may access this bus in any cycle, analysis of code in [10] shows that thread creation is a low-frequency event. The GCQ iterates the m iterations, to n processors so that each processor has at most $\lceil \frac{m}{n} \rceil_c$ threads allocated to it. The iteration proceeds so long as all processors have LCQ slots and registers available, otherwise iteration waits until resources are released. Registers are allocated by the RAU using parameters passed to it by the GCQ ,and those registers are initialised to empty. The first of the $L registers is also written with the thread's index value. Threads are scheduled from the LCQ to the local pipeline only when the required code is in the I-cache, so no I-cache miss stalls will occur on a context switch.

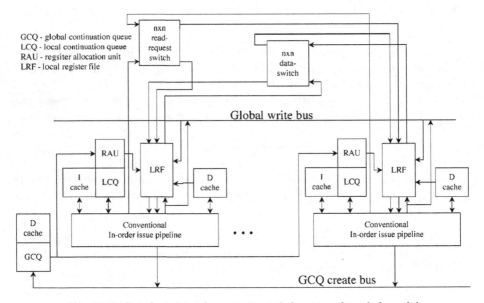

**Fig. 2.** A distributed implementation of the microthreaded model.

Each register in each LRF implements an i-structure having two operations, i-store, which sets the register to the full state and writes data to it and i-read, which, if the register is full, reads the data stored otherwise saves a reference to the thread reading it. The i-read instruction must therefore reactivate any suspended thread it finds waiting there. These operations requires a two-bit overhead on each register to encode the full, empty and waiting states, and a state machine controller for each port of the register file.

The model defines three different types of communication specified over the four classes of register window, where each must have an access mechanism that can be mapped onto this distributed implementation. It is trivially easy to distribute the local register window, as accesses to it are from only one thread but there is still a requirement for synchronisation. It is possible for both ALU and memory system to deliver data in an unscheduled manner, e.g in an iterative operation or a cache miss. Distributing the global window is not so simple, as it is shared between all threads. As any thread may wite to this window an implementation must include arbitration to resolve this. The implementation shown, replicates the global window in all processors and provides a single *global write bus* with arbitration between processors for writes to this window. Reads then become local and require no special implementation. Writes occur locally as normal but get reflected in the other processors asynchronously.

The final question to be asked is whether the shared and dependent windows can also be distributed to local register files and the answer to this will depend the number of concurrent reads to these registers. If this number grows with the number of processors, there is nothing to be gained from distributing these windows. The $S and $D windows allow only pair-wise communication, the $S window is in the namespace of a single producer thread and the $D window is in the namespace of one or more consumer threads. A $D window is mapped onto the $S window by the dependency relationship between the threads. Many-to-one mappings between $D and $S windows are possible but the multiple threads that define these $D windows cannot concurrently read the same location in their respective $D windows, as this would violate the i-structure limitation, of holding only a single continuation. This restriction must be enforced by the compiler. What it means is that the number of concurrent reads to the $S/$D window is bounded above by the range of the register specifier and this provides a model constraint that allows distributed implementation. Note that the $D and $S windows may be allocated to different processors so thread state must also contain the processor id of the producer to its $D window.

Reads and writes to the $S window are no different to the $L window, as they are local to that thread, but reads to the $D window must trap to a special access mechanism to the producer's $S window. It is importrant to decouple the local pipeline from this potentially remote register read and this requires the thread reading the $D register to context switch and be suspended locally, which in turn requires that the $D window, conceptually just a mapping onto the producer's $S window, be physically allocated to the consumer thread. Each register location in the $S/$D window thus becomes a shared pair, connected asynchronously by the switching network. A read to $D suspends the thread locally but only if the location is empty. This initiates a read to the potentially remote $S register, where the request may itself suspend waiting for data. Any network or synchronisation delay is tolerated by executing other microthreads, given sufficient local concurrency. Note that after data has been delivered, any subsequent read to the same location becomes local, so multiple reads to a shared variable incur only one remote access.

## 3.1   Allocating Registers

The abstract model partitions the registers at the ISA level in order to differentiate different access mechanisms, namely local, broadcast and pair-wise communication. An implementation requires this partitioning to identify the special access requirements. There are two cases that require special treatment. The first is a write to the global window, which must trigger an arbitration for the global write bus. Note that a local buffer can avoid any processor stalls due to peaks in traffic. The second is a read from the $D window, which, on finding an empty register, must trigger a read to the corresponding $S window wherever it is located. If it is local, it will cause an access to the producer thread's $S window locally, if it is remote it will do this via the switching network on a remote processor. Note that the base address for the producer thread must be available to the consumer thread in all such binary communications, regardless of the location of the producer thread.

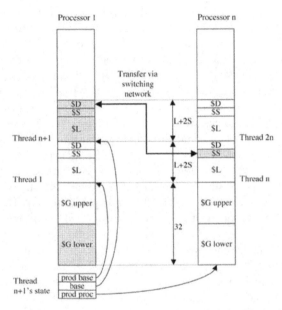

**Fig. 3.** Register allocation showing the state of thread n+1. Note that thread n+1 is dependent on thread n and all registers accessible to thread n+1 are illustrated by shading.

Using a conventional RISC ISA as a basis for the implementation gives a five-bit register specifier. A balanced implementation, based on the analysis in [10], would divide this address space equally between global and local variables for any created thread, which means that they would access to 16 locations in the $G window and 16 locations shared between the $L, $S and $D windows. Assuming that a thread requires L locals and S shared variables (these are specified in the create control block), then a single window is allocated for every thread with L+2S locations, where L+2S ≤ 16. Each thread requires S registers for its own $S window and another S for the $D window that is linked to its producer's $S window. To maintain backward compatibility for legacy code, the main thread would have to have access to all 32 addressable locations and, as the main thread in micro-threaded code has no dynamically allocated registers, its $G window could also have 32 locations. Only the first 16 of these registers, would be available to threads that were dynamically created.

In thread code, the compiler would translate addresses to $G to the lower half of the register specifier range and to $L, $S and $D to the upper half. In the main thread, the compiler would also translate the $S window to a location in the upper global window. The hardware would trap writes to $G using the ms bit of the specifier and a single base address associated with each thread would allow access to $L, $S and $D windows. For reads to empty locations greater than L+S, the hardware would trap to a mechanism to read the producer's $S window. The thread's state also needs the base address of its producer window and the processor the producer thread is running on. This is illustrated in figure 3. Note that when a read to $D is accessed from the producer's $S window it is read from an address S locations lower in that window. The three components of thread state must be passed through the pipeline to the register read stage. These are the base address for the thread (this is also required at the writeback stage), the base address for its producer thread and the processor on which the producer thread is mapped.

# 4    Conclusions

This paper has introduced a model of explicit concurrency, that is dynamic and which can be used as a target for the compilation of existing sequential languages. The code produced exploits instruction-level concurrency across all kinds of loop structures. In order to schedule code using these explicit concurrency controls the model also requires distributed synchronisation on registers, implemented as an i-structure, which is restricted to binary communications, i.e. communication between one producer and one consumer thread. This model supports a general model of sequential computation at the high-level language with concurrency produced automatically by the compiler. Such a model was very successful on the vector supercomputers of the past. Unlike the vectorisation in these predecessors, this model will still generate concurrent code even if the sequential source exhibits dependencies between the iterations of a loop. Excess concurrency on each processor is available to allow data-driving scheduling with efficient mechanisms for context switching and synchronisation.

It is also shown in this paper that such a model may be implemented on a distributed collection of in-order pipelines, with dynamic allocation of registers to threads. Unlike an out-of-order issue processor, where the synchronisation namespace is much smaller than the physical register pool, in this model the synchronisation namespace is potentially larger than the physical register pool. This means that concurrency is no longer limited by hardware implementation constraints but is limited only by the concurrency exposed in the loop structures in the source code.

The distributed implementation proposed is totally asynchronous, allowing for the implementation of all global communication by asynchronous means. Three global bus/network structures are required. The first is a switching network to perform the binary synchronisation, the second is a broadcast bus for broadcasting global variables and the last is a bus for creating a global description of the families of threads that implement the loop concurrency. Global communication is known to be a big issue in current and future systems and papers on asynchronous interconnect are already appearing in the literature[11]. This model and outline implementation therefore provides a way forward from the current problems faced in out-of-order, speculative instruction processing. The only potential problem with this model is that existing sequential code will not provide speedup unless some form of binary-code translation is provided that performs a parallelisation on legacy binary code. Finally power need only be dissipated on those processors executing threads, with control being determined by the instruction scheduling mechanism and no power is lost due to speculation errors, which must surely be a problem in current processor designs.

# References

1. R P Peterson et. al. (2002) Design of an 8-wide superscalar RISC microprocessor with simultaneous multithreading, *ISSC Digest and Visuals Supplement*.
2. J Burns and J Gaudiot (2001) Area and system clock effects on SMT/CMP processors, *Intl. Conf. on Parallel Architectures (PACT 01)*, pp211-221, IEEE.
3. I Par, M Powell and T Vijaykumar (2002) Reducing register ports for higher speed and lower energy, *Proc. 35th annual ACM/IEEE international symposium on Microarchitecture*, pp 171 - 182 , ACM ISBN ISSN:1072-4451 , 0-7695-1859-1
4. A Bolychevsky, C R Jesshope and V B Muchnick, (1996) Dynamic scheduling in RISC architectures, *IEE Trans. Computers and Digital Techniques* ,**143**, pp309-317.
5. C R Jesshope (2003) Multithreaded microprocessors evolution or revolution, *Proc. ACSAC 2003: Advances in Computer Systems Architecture*, Omondo and Sedukhin (Eds.), pp 21-45, Springer, LNCS 2823 (Berlin, Germany), ISSN0302-9743, Aizu, Japan, 22-26 Sept 2003.
6. L Gwennap, (1997) DanSoft develops VLIW design. *Microproc. Report*, **11**, 2 (Feb. 17), 1822.
7. Y Solihin, J Lee and J Torrellas, (2003) Correlation Prefetching with a User-Level Memory Thread, *IEEE Trans. on Parallel and Distributed Systems*, **vol. 14**, no. 6.
8. C Zilles and G Sohi (2001) Execution-based prediction using speculative slices, *Proc. Intl. Symposium on Computer Architecture*.
9. D Burger and J R Goodman (2004) Billion-transistor architectures: there and back again, *IEEE Computer*, **37**, 3, pp22-28.
10. C R Jesshope (2004) Microthreading, a model for distributed instruction-level concurrency, submitted to *Parallel Processing Letters* (on-line at: http://www2.dcs.hull.ac.uk/people/csscrj/papers.html).
11. A Lines(2004) Asynchronous interconnect for synchronous SoC design, *IEEE Micro*, **24**, 1, pp32-41.

# A Low-Power Multithreaded Processor
# for Baseband Communication Systems

Michael Schulte[2], John Glossner[1,3], Suman Mamidi[2],
Mayan Moudgill[1], and Stamatis Vassiliadis[3]

[1] Sandbridge Technologies, 1 North Lexington Ave., White Plains, NY, 10512, USA
jglossner@sandbridgetech.com
http://www.sandbridgetech.com

[2] University of Wisconsin, Dept. of ECE, 1415 Engineering Drive, Madison, WI, 53706, USA
{schulte,mamidi}@engr.wisc.edu
http://mesa.ece.wisc.edu

[3] Delft University of Technology, Electrical Engineering,
Mathematics and Computer Science Department, Delft, The Netherlands
s.vassiliadis@its.tudelft.nl
http://ce.et.tudelft.nl

**Abstract.** Embedded digital signal processors for baseband communication systems have stringent design constraints including high computational bandwidth, low power consumption, and low interrupt latency. Furthermore, these processors should be compiler-friendly, so that code for them can quickly be developed in a high-level language. This paper presents the design of a high-performance, low-power digital signal processor for baseband communication systems. The processor uses token triggered threading, SIMD vector processing, and powerful compound instructions to provide real-time baseband processing capabilities with very low power consumption. Using a super-computer class vectorizing compiler, the processor achieves real-time performance on a 2Mbps WCDMA transmission system.

## 1 Introduction

General purpose processors have utilized various microarchitectural techniques such as deep pipelines, multiple instruction issue, out-of-order instruction issue, and speculative execution to achieve very high performance. Recently, simultaneous multithreading (SMT) processors, where multiple hardware thread units simultaneously issue multiple instructions per cycle, have been deployed [1]. These techniques have produced performance increases at high complexity and power dissipation costs.

In the embedded DSP community, power dissipation and real-time processing constraints have typically precluded general purpose microarchitectural techniques. Rather than minimize average execution time, embedded DSP processors often require the worst case execution time to be minimized in order to satisfy real-time constraints. Consequently, VLIW or statically scheduled microarchitectures with architecturally visible pipelines are typically employed. Unfortunately, exposing pipelines may pose

A. Pimentel and S. Vassiliadis (Eds.): SAMOS 2004, LNCS 3133, pp. 393–402, 2004.

interrupt latency restrictions, particularly if all memory loads must complete prior to servicing an interrupt. Furthermore, on-chip memory access in DSP systems has traditionally operated at the processor clock frequency. Although this eases the programming burden and allows single cycle on-chip memory accesses, it often restricts the maximum processor clock frequency.

In this paper, we describe a compound instruction set architecture and an ultra low power multithreaded microarchitecture, in which multithreading is utilized to reduce power consumption and simplifying programming. We also describe a non-blocking fully interlocked pipeline implementation with reduced hardware complexity that allows the on-chip memory to operate significantly slower than the processor cycle time without inducing pipeline stalls.

## 2  Sandblaster Processor Design

Sandbridge Technologies has designed a multithreaded processor capable of executing DSP, embedded control, and Java code in a single compound instruction set optimized for handset radio applications [2-4]. The Sandbridge Sandblaster design overcomes the deficiencies of previous approaches by providing substantial parallelism and throughput for high-performance DSP applications, while maintaining fast interrupt response, high-level language programmability, and low power dissipation.

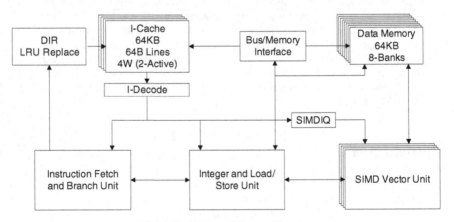

**Fig. 1.** Sandblaster Microarchitecture

Fig. 1 shows a block diagram of the Sandblaster microarchitecture. The processor is partitioned into three units; an instruction fetch and branch unit, an integer and load/store unit, and a SIMD vector unit. The design utilizes a unique combination of techniques including hardware support for multiple threads, SIMD vector processing, and instruction set support for Java code. Program memory is conserved through the use of powerful compounded instructions that may issue multiple operations per cycle. The resulting combination provides for efficient execution of DSP, control, and Java code.

## 2.1  Processor Pipeline

Processor pipelines for one particular implementation of the Sandblaster DSP are shown in Fig. 2. The pipelines are different for various operations. The Load/Store (Ld/St) pipeline is shown to have nine stages. The first stage fetches and decodes the instruction. This is followed by a read from the general-purpose register file. The next stage generates the address to perform the Load or Store. Five cycles are used to access data memory. Finally, the result is written back to the register file. Once an instruction from a particular thread enters the pipeline, it runs to completion. It is also guaranteed to write back its result before the next instruction from the same thread tries to read the result.

| | | | | | | | | | |
|---|---|---|---|---|---|---|---|---|---|
| Ld/St | Inst Dec | RF Read | Agen | XFer | Int Ext | Mem 0 | Mem 1 | Mem 2 | WB |
| ALU | Inst Dec | Wait | RF Read | Exec 1 | Exec 2 | XFer | WB | | |
| I_Mul | Inst Dec | Wait | RF Read | Exec 1 | Exec 2 | Exec 3 | XFer | WB | |
| V_Mul | Inst Dec | VRF Read | Mpy1 | Mpy2 | Add1 | Add2 | XFer | VRF WB | |

**Fig. 2.** Processor Pipelines

Similarly, there are multiple (variable) stages for the other execution pipelines. The integer and load/store unit has two execute stages for arithmetic and logic (ALU) instructions and three execute stages for integer multiplication (I_MUL) instructions. The Wait stage for the ALU and I_MUL instructions causes these instructions to read from the general-purpose register file one cycle later than Ld/St instructions. This helps reduce the number of register file read ports. The vector multiplication (V_MUL) has four execute stages - two for multiplication and two for addition. An additional transfer (Xfer) stage is allocated between the computation of a result and writing the result back to the register file to account for delays due to long wires in deep submicron design.

An important point is that the write back stages of the instructions are staggered. This allows a single write port to be implemented, but provides the same functionality as multiple write ports. The processor does not stall provided threads issue as even/odd pairs. This allows the register files to be banked, giving the power dissipation of a single write port, but able to completely sustain the code sequence given in Fig. 3. With the complexity of a single write port per register file, the processor can sustain more than 3.9 taps per cycle on typical DSP filters. This includes the overhead of entering and exiting the loop.

## 2.2  Compound Instructions

The Sandblaster architecture is a compound instruction set architecture. Historically, DSPs have used compound instruction set architectures to conserve instruction space encoding bits. In contrast, VLIW architectures are often completely orthogonal, but only encode a single operation per instruction field, such that a single VLIW is composed of multiple instruction fields. This has the disadvantage of requiring many instruction bits to be fetched per cycle, as well as significant register file write ports. For example, Texas Instrument's TMS320C62x VelociTi processor fetches up to eight 32-bit instructions each cycle [5]. It has two general-purpose register files and each register file has 16 read ports and 10 write ports [5]. Both these features contribute heavily to power dissipation.

In the Sandblaster architecture, specific fields within a 64-bit compound instruction may issue multiple compound operations, including SIMD vector operations. Each field controls a different execution unit, and restrictions may apply if a particular operation is chosen. Most classical DSP instruction set architectures are compound. In contrast, a VLIW instruction set architecture may allow a completely orthogonal specification and then fill in any unused issue slots either in hardware or through no operation instructions (NOPs).

Fig. 3 illustrates the compound nature of our architecture. It shows a single compound instruction with three compound operations. This instruction implements the inner loop of a vector sum-of-squares computation. The first compound operation, lvu, loads the vector register vr0 with four 16-bit elements and updates the address pointer r3 to the next element. The vmulreds operation reads four fixed-point (fractional) 16-bit elements from vr0, multiplies each element by itself, saturates each product, adds all four saturated products plus an accumulator register, ac0, with saturation after each addition, and stores the result back in ac0. Further details on the vmulreds instruction are provided in Section 4. The loop operation decrements the loop count register lc0, compares it to zero, and branches to address L0 if the result is not zero.

```
L0:  lvu %vr0, %r3, 8
||   vmulreds %ac0,%vr0,%vr0,%ac0
||   loop %lc0,L0
```

**Fig. 3.** A Single Compound Instruction for a Sum of Squares Loop

All the code shown in Figure 3 is encoded in a single 64-bit compound instruction. Each compound operation, including each vector operation, is specified with at most 21 bits. Like most DSP architectures, arbitrary operations are not specifiable within the same instruction. The 64-bit instruction shown in Fig. 3 may require 256 bits or more to encode on a VLIW machine. Furthermore, since the pipeline in a VLIW machine typically produces architecturally visible side effects (i.e. it is not transparent), it may take a deeply software pipelined loop to obtain single-cycle throughput, thereby exploding the instruction storage requirements. To further distinguish our approach from VLIW and exposed pipeline architectures, each instruction is completely interlocked and architecturally defined to complete with no visible pipeline effects. This is critical for fast interrupt processing.

# 3 Low Power Multithreading

Multithreading is a well-known technique for hardware and software acceleration. The Denelcor HEP was designed circa 1979 [6]. In this design, multiple instructions could be simultaneously active from multiple threads. It was required that each thread complete the current instruction prior to issuing a subsequent instruction. When only one thread issues an instruction each cycle and threads progress in sequence, this is termed barrel multithreading or interleaved multithreading [7].

More recent embodiments of multithreaded processors make use of simultaneous multithreading (SMT) [1, 7]. In this approach, multiple thread units may issue multiple instructions each cycle. When combined with superscalar techniques such as out-of-order processing, the additional hardware required for SMT is not significant. Although SMT may reduce power dissipation in superscalar processors, superscalar and SMT techniques both consume significant power [8]. They also make it difficult to determine the worst case execution time, since instructions are scheduled dynamically, rather than at compile time.

## 3.1 Decoupled Logic and Memory

As technology improves, processors are capable of executing at very fast cycle times. Current state-of-the-art performance for 0.13um technologies can produce processors faster than 3GHz. Unfortunately, current high-performance processors consume significant power. If power-performance curves are considered for both memory and logic within a technology, there is a region that provides approximately linear increase in power for linear increase in performance. Above a specific threshold, there is an exponential increase in power for a linear increase in performance. Even more significant, memory and logic do not have the same threshold.

For 0.13um technology, the logic power-performance curve may be in the linear range until approximately 600MHz. Unfortunately, memory power-performance curves are at best linear to about 300MHz. This presents a dilemma as to whether to optimize for performance or power. Fortunately, the Sandblaster implementation of multithreading allows the processor cycle time to be decoupled from the on-chip memory (e.g., cache) access time. This allows both logic and memory to operate in the linear region, thereby significantly reducing power dissipation. The decoupled execution does not induce pipeline stalls due to the multithreaded pipeline design.

## 3.2 Token Triggered Threading

Fig. 1 shows the microarchitecture of the Sandblaster processor. In a multithreaded processor, threads of execution operate simultaneously. An important point is that multiple copies (e.g. banks and/or modules) of memory are available for each thread to access. The Sandblaster architecture supports multiple concurrent program execution by the use of hardware thread units (contexts). The microarchitecture supports up to eight concurrent hardware threads. The microarchitecture also supports multiple operations being issued from each thread.

The Sandblaster processor uses a form of interleaved multithreading called Token Triggered Threading ($T^3$). As shown in Fig. 4, with $T^3$ each thread is allowed to simultaneously execute an instruction, but only one thread may issue an instruction on a cycle boundary. This constraint is also imposed on round robin threading. What distinguishes $T^3$ threading is that each clock cycle a token indicates the subsequent thread that is to issue an instruction. Tokens may be sequential (e.g. round-robin), even/odd, or based on other communication patterns. Compared to SMT, $T^3$ has much less hardware complexity and power dissipation, since the method for selecting threads is simplified, only a single compound instruction issues each clock cycle, and dependency checking and bypass hardware is not needed, as explained in the next section. Baseband processing applications have sufficient thread level parallelism to support several concurrent hardware threads. For example, our implementation of WCMDA has 32 threads that can operate concurrently.

**Fig. 4.** Token Triggered Threading

# 4 Vector Processing Unit

Fig. 5 shows a high-level block diagram of the SIMD vector processing unit (VPU), which consists of four vector processing elements (VPEs), a shuffle unit, a reduction unit, and a multithreaded 2-bank accumulator register file. The four VPEs perform arithmetic and logic operations in SIMD fashion on 16-bit, 32-bit, and 40-bit fixed-point data types. High-speed 64-bit data busses allow each PE to load or store 16 bits of data each cycle in SIMD fashion. Support for SIMD execution significantly reduces code size, as well as power consumption from fetching and decoding instructions, since multiple sets of data elements are processed with a single instruction [9].

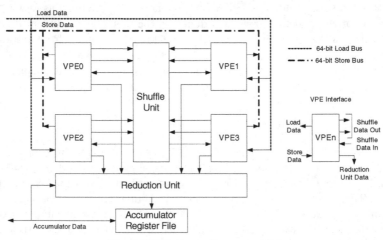

**Fig. 5.** SIMD Vector Processing Unit

The shuffle unit transfers data between the VPEs, and is useful when implementing various DSP algorithms, such as FFTs and DCTs, which require data to be processed and then rearranged [10]. The shuffle unit reduces the number of data memory accesses needed to perform these algorithms by allowing data to be rearranged within the VPU, instead of having to store data out to memory and then retrieve it in a different order. The reduction unit takes results from the VPEs, adds them to or subtracts them from an accumulator register file operand, and then stores the result of the reduction back in the accumulator register file. The reduction unit and accumulator register file accelerate the computation of dot products and similar vector operations.

Each VPE contains a 2-bank multithreaded vector register file (VRF), a multiply-accumulate (MAC) unit, a shifter, a compare-select unit, a logic unit, and an adder. To reduce dynamic power dissipation, clock gating is employed such that when performing an operation in a particular unit, the inputs to other units do not change. All of the VPE functional units support operations on 16-bit, 32-bit, and 40-bit operands, except for the MAC unit, which only multiplies 16-bit operands and can then add a 32-bit or 40-bit accumulator. Multiplication of numbers larger than 16 bits is not necessary for most DSP algorithms in our application domain, and support for it would lead to an unacceptable increase in area, cycle time, and power consumption. When required, 32-bit multiplications are implemented with multiple 16-bit multiplications. The MAC unit, shifter, and adder all support both saturating and wrap-around arithmetic operations. DSP algorithms in our application domain typically use saturating arithmetic with 32-bit accumulators and wrap-around arithmetic with 40-bit accumulators.

Most SIMD vector instructions go through eight pipeline stages. For example, a vector MAC instruction goes through the following stages: Instruction Decode, VRF Read, Mpy1, Mpy2, Add1, Add2, Transfer, and Write Back. The Transfer stage is needed due to the long wiring delay between the bottom of the VPU and the VRF. Since there are eight cycles between when consecutive instructions issue from the same thread, results from one instruction in a thread are guaranteed to have written their results back to the VRF by the time the next instruction in the same thread is ready to read them. Thus, the long pipeline latency of the VPEs is effectively hidden, and no data dependency checking or bypass hardware is needed. This is illustrated in Fig. 6, where two consecutive vector multiply instructions issue from the same thread. Even if there is a data dependency between the two instructions, there is no need to stall the second instruction, since the first instruction has completed the Write Back stage before the second instruction enters the VRF Read stage.

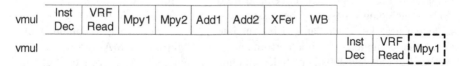

**Fig. 6.** Two Consecutive Vector Multiply Instructions that Issue from the Same Thread

The VRF in each VPE has eight 40-bit register file entries per thread. Since both a vector MAC operation (with three vector source operands and one vector destination operand) and a vector load or store operation (with one vector destination or source operand) can appear in the same compound instruction, a VRF designed using a standard implementation requires four read ports and two write ports.

To reduce the number of ports, the VRF uses a novel technique, which divides it into two register banks; one for even threads and one for odd threads. Register accesses by certain source and destination operands are delayed, such that in a given cycle each register file bank has at most two operands being read and one operand being written. For example, when a MAC operation and a store operation appear in the same compound instruction, the two multiplier operands are read from the VRF immediately following the instruction decode stage, but the accumulator and store operands are read one cycle later (i.e., during the Mpy1 stage). Thus, the accumulator and store operands are read from one bank of the register file, while the next instruction, which issues from a different thread, reads at most two operands from the other bank.

The reduction unit and accumulator register file are used with the VPEs to perform dot products and similar vector operations, which are required in many DSP applications. In particular, Global System for Mobile communication (GSM) standards, which are fundamental components of second and third generation cell phone technology, frequently perform dot products with saturation after each multiplication and each addition. To be compliant with GSM standards, the results produced by GSM algorithms much be identical (bit-exact) to the results obtained when the algorithms are executed serially with saturation after each operation. Since saturating arithmetic operations are not associative, most DSP processors execute saturating dot products in GSM algorithms sequentially, which degrades performance.

The Sandblaster processor executes roughly ($k/4$) vmulreds instructions to perform a $k$-element saturating dot product. This computation is similar to the sum of squares computation shown in Fig. 3, except the vmulreds instruction changes to

```
vmulreds %ac0,%vr0,%vr1,%ac0
```

and data is also loaded into vr1. For each vmulreds instruction, four pairs of vector elements are multiplied in parallel by the MAC units in the four VPEs. The reduction unit then adds the results from the VPEs, along with an operand from the accumulator register file, with saturation after each addition. The result from reduction unit is then written back to the accumulator register file to be used in the next instruction.

## 5   SDR Implementation Results

Sandbridge Technologies has developed a complete Software Defined Radio (SDR) product, including a baseband processor and C code for the UMTS WCDMA FDD-mode physical layer standard. Using an internally developed super computer class vectorizing compiler, real-time performance on a 2Mbps WCDMA transmission system has been achieved. This includes all chip, symbol, and bit-rate processing. Fig. 7 shows the performance requirements for 802.11b, GPRS, and WCDMA as a function of SB3000 utilization for different transmission rates. The SB3000 contains four Sandblaster cores and provides processing capacity for full 2Mbps WCDMA FDD-mode including chip, symbol, and bit-rate processing.

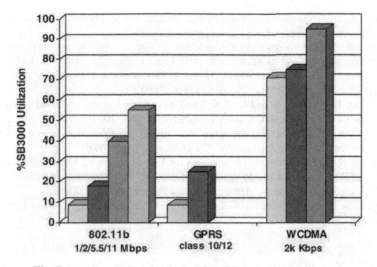

**Fig. 7.** Processor Utilization in Baseband Communication Systems

## 6  Conclusion

This paper has presented the design of a high-performance, low-power processor for baseband communication systems. The design uses a unique combination of token triggered threading, SIMD vector processing, and powerful compound instructions to provide very low power consumption and real-time baseband processing capabilities. Having validated our low power design approach with working 0.18um silicon and having implemented complete baseband processing on our core, we can provide a terminal class SDR baseband processor with power dissipation appropriate for commercial terminals.

## References

1. D. M. Tullsen, S. J. Eggers, H. M. Levy: Simultaneous Multithreading: Maximizing on-chip Parallelism. 22nd Annual International Symposium on Computer Architecture (June, 1995) 392-403
2. J. Glossner, D. Iancu, J. Lu, E. Hokenek, and M. Moudgill: A Software Defined Communications Baseband Design. IEEE Communications Magazine, Vol. 41, No. 1 (January, 2003) 120-128
3. J. Glossner, T. Raja, E. Hokenek, and M. Moudgill: A Multithreaded Processor Architecture for SDR. The Proceedings of the Korean Institute of Communication Sciences, Vol. 19, No. 11 (November, 2002) 70-84
4. J. Glossner, M. Schulte, and S. Vassiliadis: A Java-Enabled DSP. In E. Deprettere, J. Teich, and S. Vassiliadis (eds.): Embedded Processor Design Challenges, Systems, Architectures, Modeling, and Simulation (SAMOS). Lecture Notes in Computer Science, Vol. 2268. Springer-Verlag, Berlin (2002) 307-325

5. N. Seshan: High VelociTI Processing: Texas Instruments VLIW DSP Architecture. IEEE Signal Processing Magazine, vol.15, no 2 (March 1998) 86-101

6. B. J. Smith: The Architecture of HEP. In J. S. Kowalik (ed.) Parallel MIMD Computation: HEP Supercomputer and Its Applications. MIT Press, Cambridge, MA, (1985) 41–55.

7. T. Ungerer, B. Robič, and J. Šilc: A Survey of Processors with Explicit Multithreading. ACM Computing Surveys, vol. 35, no. 1 (March 2003) 29-63

8. J. S. Seng, D. M. Tullsen, and G. Z.N. Cai: Power-Sensitive Multithreaded Architecture. International Conference on Computer Design, (September, 2000) 199-208

9. J. Sebot and N. Drach: SIMD Extensions: Reducing Power Consumption on a Superscalar Processor for Multimedia Applications. Cool Chips IV (April 2001)

10. R. B. Lee: Subword Permutation Instructions for Two-Dimensional Multimedia Processing in MicroSIMD Architectures. Proceedings of the IEEE 11th International Conference on Application-Specific Systems, Architectures and Processor (July 2000) 3-14

11. B. Parhami, Computer Arithmetic: Algorithms and Hardware Designs. Oxford University Press, New York (2000)

# Initial Evaluation of Multimedia Extensions on VLIW Architectures

Esther Salamí and Mateo Valero*

Computer Architecture Department, UPC, Barcelona
{esalami,mateo}@ac.upc.es

**Abstract.** Media processing has motivated strong changes in the focus and design of processors. The inclusion of $\mu$SIMD multimedia extensions such as MMX is a cost effective option to improve the performance of those regions of the program with large amounts of DLP. This paper provides an initial evaluation of $\mu$SIMD and vector-SIMD enhanced VLIW architectures. We show that these two architectures execute respectively an average of 40% and 57% fewer operations than the reference VLIW architecture. However, when most of the available DLP parallelism has been exploited via multimedia extensions or wide-issue static scheduling, the remaining of the program exhibits only modest amounts of ILP (1.40 operations per cycle for a 8-issue width architecture). We claim that, in general, vector-SIMD extensions achieve the highest speed-ups while still reducing the fetch pressure, although for wide-issue $\mu$SIMD architectures reach a similar performance at a lower cost.

## 1   Introduction

Improvements in semiconductor technology have a direct repercussion in microprocessor performance. Further speedups come from exploiting some kind of available parallelism. *Instruction Level Parallelism* (ILP) is a set of processor and compiler design techniques that speed up execution by causing individual machine operations to execute in parallel [1]. On the other hand, the *Data Level Parallelism* (DLP) paradigm, tries to specify with a single machine operation a large number of operations to be performed on independent data.

*Superscalar* processors are the most traditional ILP implementation for the general purpose domain. However, it is widely assumed that current superscalar processors cannot be scaled by simply fetching, decoding and issuing more instructions per cycle [2]. Branches, the instruction cache bandwidth, the instruction window size, the register file and the memory wall are relevant problems to solve.

*Very Long Instruction Word* (VLIW) processors are another form of ILP implementation. The first generation of VLIW processors were successful in the

---

* This work has been supported by the Ministry of Science and Technology of Spain and the European Union (FEDER funds) under contract TIC2001-0995-C02-01 and by the European HiPEAC network of Excellence. We also acknowledge the Supercomputing Center of Catalonia (CESCA) for supplying the computing resources.

A. Pimentel and S. Vassiliadis (Eds.): SAMOS 2004, LNCS 3133, pp. 403–412, 2004.

scientific domain, and it has also been the architecture of choice for most media embedded processors. However, some relevant facts, such as code compatibility and non-deterministic latencies, have contributed to the belief that VLIW processors are not appropriate for the general-purpose domain. At present, a revival of the VLIW execution paradigm is observed. HP and Intel have recently introduced a new style of architecture known as *Explicitly Parallel Instruction Computing* (EPIC) [3] and a specific architecture implementation: the *Itanium Processor Family* (IPF). EPIC retains compatibility across different implementations without the complexity of superscalar control logic.

Media processing has motivated strong changes in the focus and design of processors. In the general purpose domain, these changes have been very straightforward with the inclusion of $\mu$SIMD multimedia extensions such as SSE [4] or Altivec [5]. Current multimedia extensions provide good performance at a low cost, but they fail to scale adequately. This problem is addressed in [6] and they propose to enhance superscalar processors with MOM, a matrix ISA extension that is basically an hybrid between conventional vector and MMX-like ISAs. This vector-SIMD extension also arises as a competitive option in the embedded media domain [7].

A very promising alternative is the inclusion of SIMD (either $\mu$SIMD or vector-SIMD) extensions in a VLIW processor, since it would be able to exploit DLP parallelism by means of the SIMD operations and ILP by using wide-issue static scheduling. However, a real media program is composed of heterogeneous regions of code with highly variable levels of parallelism: some of them with large amounts of DLP and the other ones with only modest amounts of ILP. When those regions with high DLP achieve high performance via wide scheduling or multimedia extensions, the performance of the serial regions of code becomes the main performance bottleneck. At this point, a full reorganizing of the program code is required to expose more parallelism to the processor. Multimedia vector-SIMD extensions provide the processor the ability to exploit the DLP typical of multimedia kernels while keeping the low fetch bandwidth required in the serial regions of codes.

The focus of this paper is to provide an initial evaluation of VLIW architectures with $\mu$SIMD and vector-SIMD multimedia extensions. Sections 2 and 3 describes the modeled architectures and the simulation framework. Section 4 presents quantitative data such as the number and type of operations, the performance speed-ups, the memory behavior and the scalability of the vector and non-vector regions. Finally, section 5 concludes the paper.

## 2    Modeled Architectures

We have evaluated 2, 4 and 8 issue width VLIW architectures and the $\mu$SIMD and vector-SIMD multimedia extended versions described below. Table 1 summarizes the general parameters of the nine architectures under study. In order to support the hight computational demand of multimedia applications, our configurations are quite aggressive in the number of arithmetic functional units.

**Table 1.** VLIW processor configuration ($m$ = multiplication, $d$ = division)

| Resource | Latency | VLIW 2 / 4 / 8 -issue | +MMX 2 / 4 / 8 -issue | +VMMX 2 / 4 / 8 -issue |
|---|---|---|---|---|
| integer unit | $1, 5\,(m), 17\,(d)$ | 2 / 4 / 8 | 2 / 4 / 8 | 2 / 4 / 8 |
| vector unit | $1, 5\,(m)$ | – | 2 / 4 / 8 | 1x4 / 2x4 / 4x4 |
| branch unit | 2 | 1 | 1 | 1 |
| L1 ports | 3 | 1 / 2 / 4 | 1 / 2 / 4 | 1 / 1 / 2 |
| L2 ports | 12 | – | – | 1x2 / 1x4 / 1x8 |

## 2.1   Reference VLIW Architecture

The reference processor is a 2-issue load/store VLIW core. The engine is able to
fetch one instruction word per cycle. Each instruction word can hold up to two
different operations, being one of them a memory and/or a branch operation
at the most. All integer operations are 1 single cycle, except for multiplication
and division that have a latency of 5 and 17 cycles respectively and branches
take 2 cycles. It includes 80 general purpose registers, 96 1-bit predicate registers
(used to store branch condition and predicates) and 20 branch target registers
(to store the target address of branches).

Table 2 summarizes the main parameters of the L1 and L2 data caches. The
first level data cache is a 32 KB, 4-way set associative cache with one port for the
reference 2-issue width architecture. We consider pseudo-multi-ported caches for
the configurations with greater number of ports. Latencies are 3 cycles for the
first level cache, 12 cycles for the second level and 500 cycles to main memory.
We have not simulated the instruction cache since our benchmarks have small
instruction working set. The compiler schedules all memory operations assuming
they hit in the first level cache and the processor is stalled at run-time in case
of a cache miss or bank conflict.

## 2.2   $\mu$SIMD Extensions

We have enhanced the basic model with a $\mu$SIMD register file together with
additional vector units able to operate on up to eight 8-bit items in parallel.
We have used the emulation libraries described in [8] to hand-write the applications with a $\mu$SIMD ISA extension fairly similar to Intel's SSE integer opcodes.
This $\mu$SIMD extension provides 67 opcodes and 64-bit $\mu$SIMD registers. In the
remaining of the paper, this architecture is named VLIW+MMX.

## 2.3   Vector-SIMD Extensions

In [8] we proposed a matrix ISA that is basically an hybrid between conventional
vector ISAs and $\mu$SIMD MMX-like ISAs. Figure 1 shows a comparison between
a $\mu$SIMD (*MMX* in the figure) and a vector-SIMD operation (labeled *VMMX*).
It provides matrix registers with 16 64-bit words each and 192-bit packed accumulators (similar to those proposed in the MDMX multimedia extension [9]).

**Table 2.** Cache hierarchy configuration (*WT* = write-though, *WB* = write-back, *NWA* = no-write-allocate, *WB depth/retire* = write buffer entries/retire-at-X policy)

|                     | L1       | L2          |
|---------------------|----------|-------------|
| size                | 32 K     | 128 K       |
| number of ports     | 1 / 2 / 4 | 1          |
| port width (bytes)  | 8        | 16 / 32 / 64 |
| number of banks     | 8        | 2           |
| sets per bank       | 32       | 256         |
| associativity       | 4        | 2           |
| line size (bytes)   | 32       | 128         |
| write policy        | WT       | WB          |
| allocate policy     | NWA      | NWA         |
| latency             | 3        | 12          |
| MSHR entries        | 8        | 8           |
| WB depth / retire   | 8 / 4    | 8 / 4       |

Both the register file and the vector-SIMD functional unit are clusterized in 4 independent vector lanes where the different vector elements are interleaved. Therefore, up to four $\mu$SIMD-operations from the same matrix operation can be performed per cycle. We refer to this architecture as VLIW+VMMX.

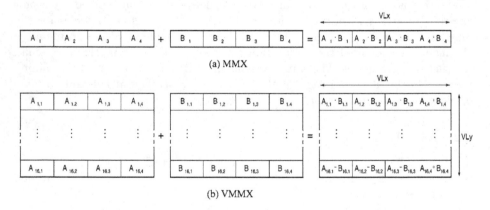

**Fig. 1.** Comparison between a MMX operation and a VMMX operation

In the same way as conventional vector instructions, +VMMX memory patterns have the potential to allow a smart exploitation of the spatial locality. For our study we use the *vector cache* proposed in [10]. The vector cache is a two-bank interleaved cache targeted at accessing stride-one vector requests by loading two whole cache lines (one per bank) instead of individually loading the vector elements. Then, an interchange switch, a shifter, and a mask logic correctly align the data. Scalar accesses are made to the L1 conventional data cache, while vector accesses bypass the L1 to access directly the L2 vector cache. If the L2 port is $B\times$ 64-bit wide, these accesses are performed at a maximum rate of $B$ elements when the stride is one, and at 1 element per cycle for any other stride. A coherency protocol based on an exclusive-bit policy plus inclusion is used to guarantee coherency.

Note that this architecture is not balanced against the same way VLIW or +MMX architectures because we consider it as an alternative to wider issue machines. For example, the 4-way +VMMX arithmetic capability is comparable to that of the 8-way +MMX configuration, but not to the 4-way +MMX. However, we wish to highlight the simpler one port L1 data cache design.

## 3   Methodology

For our experiments we have used *Trimaran*. Trimaran [11] is a compiler infrastructure for supporting state of the art research in compiling for ILP architectures. The system is currently oriented towards EPIC architectures. It is comprised by Impact, a compiler front-end for C, which performs machine independent optimizations, Elcor, a compiler back-end which performs machine-dependent optimizations, instruction scheduling and register allocation, and a cycle-level simulator of the parameterized architecture. To expose sufficient ILP it makes use of advanced techniques such as Superblock or Hyperblock formation. The architecture space is characterized by HPL-PD [12], a parameterized processor architecture.

The Impact front-end included in the public release of Trimaran has been replaced by an internal version of Impact able to perform interprocedural pointer analysis. So, our scalar versions of code include the memory disambiguation inherent in the vector versions. We have used emulation libraries to hand-write the applications with the before described +MMX and +VMMX extensions. The HPL-PD machine description has been enhanced with the new operations, register files and functional units. The compiler has been modified to detect the emulation functions calls and replace them by the related low level operations. The simulator has also been extended to include the new ISAs and a detailed memory hierarchy.

## 4   Quantitative Analysis

For our study we have selected three multimedia applications: the JPEG, MPEG2 and GSM encoders, representative enough of image, audio and video workloads. For each of the benchmarks we have evaluated the impact of the multimedia extensions in the overall number of operations and execution time.

### 4.1   Operation Breakdown

Figure 2 shows the dynamic operation count for the benchmarks under study. Note that by the term operation we refer to each of the machine level operations inside one instruction word. Results are normalized by the dynamic operation count of the plain VLIW architecture. The graph on the left shows the operations classified into five categories: control, scalar memory, scalar arithmetic, vector memory and vector arithmetic. In the graph on the right, we have distinguished the contribution of each region inside the full application. Regions from $R1$ to $R3$ are the fractions of code that has been vectorized in the +MMX and +VMMX versions (for example, in MPEG2, $R1$ accounts for the distance computation and $R2$ and $R3$ for the forward and inverse two dimensional DCT). Region $R0$ always refers to the remaining scalar portion of code.

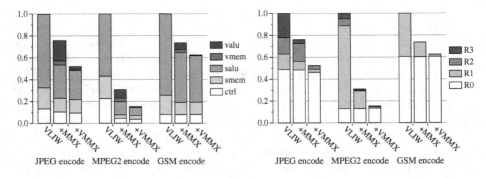

**Fig. 2.** Normalized dynamic operation count by type and by regions

From the results we clearly observe that the vectorized versions of code require to execute much less operations than the scalar versions. As seen in the figure, the +MMX architecture executes about 40% fewer operations than the plain VLIW, and the +VMMX an average of 57% fewer operations. The obvious reason is that +MMX/+VMMX architectures can pack several micro-operations into a single operation. Moreover, there is an additional reduction on the number of operations involved in the loop-related control. Another important contribution is the semantic richness of each ISA to perform operations such as the sum of absolute differences or saturation arithmetic.

The overall operation reduction is strongly dependent on the average vector length (the average number of micro-operations per +MMX/+VMMX operation) and the vectorization percentage of the program. Table 3 shows the average vector length for the benchmarks under study. Note that the potential maximum vector length is 8 for the +MMX architecture and 16x8 for the +VMMX. Most multimedia kernels are characterized by nested loops with very small loop counts, which usually results on low or moderate vector lengths in conventional vector architectures. However, the +VMMX ISA leverages quite fair vector lengths, due to its capability to vectorize two inner nested loops.

As far as the vectorization percentage is concerned, we were very surprised to find that it was less than 50% for two of the benchmarks, although it is not the case for the MPEG2, where the distance computation plus the DCT transforms

**Table 3.** Average vector length

|              | +MMX | +VMMX |
|--------------|------|-------|
| JPEG encode  | 3.64 | 13.04 |
| MPEG2 encode | 6.54 | 48.00 |
| GSM encode   | 2.41 | 25.60 |

account for 87% of the overall dynamic operation count. From the second graph in fig. 2, it can be seen that the +VMMX ISA achieves to reduce the number of operations of the vector regions to a minimum (less than 10% of the total dynamic operation count).

## 4.2   Performance

Figure 3 shows the performance results with and without realistic cache simulation. The speed-up is related to the reference 2-way VLIW architecture with perfect memory. By perfect memory we consider that all accesses hit in cache, but with the corresponding latency. That is, all scalar accesses are served after 3 cycles of latency and all vector accesses in the +VMMX configurations go to the L2 and take 12 cycles plus the additional cycles to serve all vector data elements.

As it was to be expected, both +MMX and +VMMX architectures outperform the plain VLIW architecture. This is mainly due to the smaller number of operations to execute and to the higher parallelism of these operations (to execute more that one micro-operation each). More interesting is the fact that, in average, the performance of a $X$-way +VMMX architecture is comparable to that of a $2X$-way +MMX or a $4X$-way VLIW one. This is due to the fact that +VMMX greatly reduces the fetch pressure by packing an order of magnitude more micro-operations per operation than +MMX, making it an ideal candidate for embedded systems, where high issue rates are not an option.

We can also see that the gap between the different architectures decrease with the way of the machine. For example, while the 2-way +VMMX exhibits a factor of 1.21X of performance improvement (in average) over the 2-way +MMX, the 8-way +VMMX only outperforms the 8-way +MMX in a 1.03X. That means that a wide enough +MMX architecture is able to exploit as ILP the parallelism that the +VMMX architecture exploits as DLP.

Additionally, we observe that the +VMMX architectures exhibit the highest performance degradations when considering a realistic memory system. This fact may seem counterintuitive, since vector architectures are well known for their capability to tolerate memory latency. Two reasons explain this behavior. First, the +VMMX vector lengths are not long enough to take benefit of this characteristic. Second, VLIW architectures are very sensitive to non-deterministic latencies. During the scheduling, the compiler assumes that all vector accesses have a stride of one, and the processor stalls at run-time if this assertion is not true. For example, in the case of having a 4 x 64-bit wide port to L2, a vector load with vector length 16 would be scheduled as taking 16 ($= 12 + 16/4$) cycles.

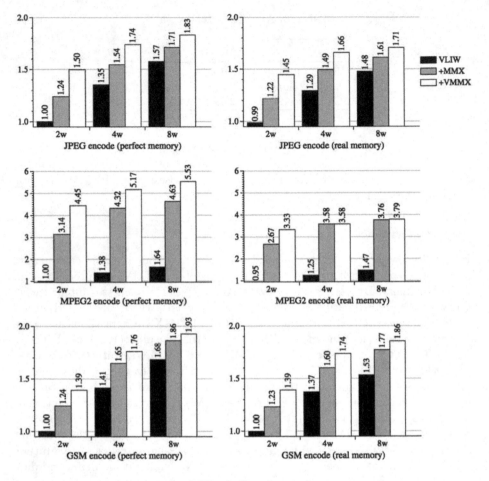

**Fig. 3.** Speed-up

However, if it actually had a stride different from one, it would take at least 28 (= 12 + 16) cycles to execute, and the processor would be stalled at run-time for at least 12 cycles. That is exactly what happens in the MPEG2 benchmark, in which the main function (distance computation) has a stride different from one, and this results in a hight performance degradation (up to 45%). Apart from this, all benchmarks exhibit high hit ratios and very low performance degradation when considering realistic memory.

### 4.3   Scalability

Table 4 shows the average number of operations per cycle and the average speed-up for the scalar and vector regions of code separately. It confirms our belief that the non-vector regions of code do not benefit from scaling the way of the machine above 4 issue width. Fetching 1.4 operations per cycle does not pay off the hardware complexity of a 8-way architecture. Even though the +VMMX ISA achieves very hight speed-ups in the vector regions (up to 19X in GSM), the scalar region of code fails to scale and becomes the limiting factor for performance improvement.

**Table 4.** Scalability of scalar and vector regions of code (*OPC* = operations per cycle, $\mu OPC$ = micro-operations per cycle, $S$ = speed-up)

|            | Scalar regions | | Vector regions | | | Full program | | |
|            | OPC | S | OPC | $\mu$OPC | S | OPC | $\mu$OPC | S |
|------------|------|------|------|-------|-------|------|------|------|
| 2w VLIW    | 1.14 | 1.00 | 1.80 | 1.80  | 1.00  | 1.46 | 1.46 | 1.00 |
| 2w +MMX    | 1.14 | 1.00 | 1.72 | 5.34  | 3.13  | 1.32 | 2.54 | 1.75 |
| 2w +VMMX   | 1.13 | 0.99 | 0.91 | 9.18  | 9.27  | 1.06 | 2.11 | 2.12 |
| 4w VLIW    | 1.34 | 1.14 | 3.06 | 3.06  | 1.68  | 1.96 | 1.96 | 1.33 |
| 4w +MMX    | 1.33 | 1.14 | 3.18 | 9.87  | 5.75  | 1.71 | 3.32 | 2.29 |
| 4w +VMMX   | 1.33 | 1.14 | 1.12 | 11.04 | 10.60 | 1.26 | 2.43 | 2.39 |
| 8w VLIW    | 1.40 | 1.18 | 4.40 | 4.40  | 2.40  | 2.26 | 2.26 | 1.52 |
| 8w +MMX    | 1.39 | 1.18 | 4.86 | 14.24 | 8.12  | 1.86 | 3.56 | 2.45 |
| 8w +VMMX   | 1.39 | 1.19 | 1.38 | 13.39 | 12.81 | 1.34 | 2.56 | 2.52 |

For the +MMX and +VMMX versions we also show the average number of micro-operations executed per cycle. The +VMMX ISA obtains the highest speed-ups while still keeping low fetch bandwidth requirements. However, for wide enough issues, the +MMX ISA exhibits more flexibility to benefit from wide static scheduling and reaches significant micro-operations per cycle rates.

# 5   Conclusions

This paper has provided an initial evaluation of $\mu$SIMD and vector-SIMD enhanced VLIW architectures for three full applications of audio, video and image processing. For wide issue architectures, the $\mu$SIMD extensions arise as the most cost-effective option, providing good performance at a reasonable cost. However, we have demonstrated that there is a significant part of the program which does not take benefit of increasing expensive resources such as the fetch bandwidth and the number of memory ports. Vector-SIMD extensions provide the best performance and reduce the fetch pressure and the L1 ports requirements. Adding two +VMMX units to a 4-issue width VLIW architecture leads to speed-ups ranging from 1.26X to 2.86X while fetching only between 0.82 and 1.76 operations per cycle. A wide port to the L2 provides the bandwidth required by the vector regions of code and allows to have a single port to L1. On the other hand, we have also shown that +VMMX architectures do not perform well in front of non stride-one memory references and exhibit the highest performance degradations when considering a realistic memory system.

# References

1. Schlansker, M., Rau, B.R., Mahlke, S., Kathail, V.: Achieving high levels of instruction-level parallelism with reduced hardware complexity. Technical Report HPL-96-120, Hewlett–Packard Laboratories (1994)
2. Johnson, M.: Superscalar Microprocessor Design. Prentice-Hall, Englewood Cliffs, New Jersey (1991)
3. Schlansker, M.S., Raw, B.: Epic: Explicitly parallel instruction computing. In: IEEE Computer. (2000) 37–45
4. Intel: Pentium iii processor: Developer's manual. Technical report, INTEL (1999)
5. Nguyen, H., John, L.K.: Exploiting SIMD parallelism in DSP and multimedia algorithms using the altivec technology. In: International Conference on Supercomputing. (1999) 11–20
6. Corbal, J.: N-Dimensional Vector Instruction Set Architectures for Multimedia Applications. PhD thesis, UPC, Departament d'Arquitectura de Computadors (2002)
7. Salamí, E., Corbal, J., Espasa, R., Valero, M.: An evaluation of different dlp alternatives for the embedded media domain. In: 1st Workshop on Media Processors and DSPs. (1999)
8. Corbal, J., Espasa, R., Valero, M.: Exploiting a new level of dlp in multimedia applications. In: 32nd international symposium on Microarchitecture. (1999) 72–79
9. SIG: Mips extension for digital media with 3d. Technical report, MIPS Technologies, Inc (1997)
10. Quintana, F., Corbal, J., Espasa, R., Valero, M.: Adding a vector unit on a superscalar processor. In: International Conference on Supercomputing. (1999) 1–10
11. Lab., H.P., Group, R.I., Group, I.: Trimaran user manual (1998) http://www.trimaran.org/docs.html.
12. Kathail, V., Schlansker, M., Rau, B.R.: Hpl-pd architecture specification: Version 1.1. Technical Report HPL-93-80(R.1), Hewlett–Packard Laboratories (2000)

# HIBI v.2 Communication Network for System-on-Chip

Erno Salminen, Vesa Lahtinen, Tero Kangas, Jouni Riihimäki,
Kimmo Kuusilinna, and Timo D. Hämäläinen

Tampere University of Technology, Institute of Digital and Computer Systems,
P.O. Box 553, FIN-33101, Tampere, Finland
erno.salminen@tut.fi

**Abstract.** This paper presents a communication network targeted for
complex system-on-chip (SoC) and network-on-chip (NoC) designs. The
Heterogeneous IP Block Interconnection v.2 (HIBI) aims at maximum
efficiency and energy saving per transmitted bit combined with guaranteed quality-of-service (QoS) in transfers. Other features include support
for arbitrary topologies with several clock domains, flexible scalablility
in signalling and run-time reconfiguration of network parameters. HIBI
has been implemented in VHDL and SystemC and synthesized in 0.18
CMOS technology with area comparable to other NoC wrappers. HIBI
data transfers are shown to approach the maximum theoretical performance for protocol efficiency.

## 1 Introduction

Network-on-chip (NoC) can be regarded as the third wave of system-on-chip
(SoC) designs after intellectual property (IP) block-based [1][2] and platform-
based [4] methodologies. The third wave focuses on how to reuse not only IP
blocks but also on-chip communication networks. Communication networks, as a
research topic, have well established in multi-processor and multi-computer systems [5][6][7]. Many topologies that were originally intended for super computers
are now proposed as backbones for SoCs and NoCs. However, their original form
may lead to unexpected problems in SoC environment. A regular and symmetric topology, such as a mesh, fits well for dataflow type of processing with static
scheduling and allocation of tasks. This is different from contemporary SoCs,
such as [8][9], that include several clock domains that are not necessarily synchronized and some of the blocks are from time to time shut down for power saving.
The overall computation is heterogeneous and still quality-of-service (QoS) in
terms of guaranteed latency and/or throughput must be met for data transfers.
We begin with a review of network design issues and related work. Motivation,
key design constraints, and advanced features of HIBI v.2 and its implementation are described in Sections 3 and 4. Low-level implementation details, such
as bus signal encoding schemes, are beyond the scope of this paper. Finally, in
Section 5, synthesis results and performance analysis are given with the help of
a case study. Section 6 concludes the paper.

A. Pimentel and S. Vassiliadis (Eds.): SAMOS 2004, LNCS 3133, pp. 413–422, 2004.

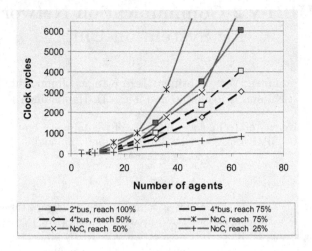

**Fig. 1.** Clock cycles for total exchange

## 2  Related Work

Most on-chip networks have utilized a bus network due to its simple implementation, but signal propagation delays in deep sub-micron technologies restrict the size of a practical single bus. AMBA [10] is a widely used, centrally arbited on-chip bus that supports two-level hierarchical structures. Silicon Backplane [11] bus uses distributed, two-level arbitration and pipelined transfers. For other on-chip buses a survey can be found in [12] which indicated that fixed constraints dominate the properties of contemporary buses. For example, number of agents and the available bus widths are limited, leading to constrained scalability. We believe that it is better to keep such properties parameterizable to cover a wider range of applications and let application and implementation technology define the limits instead of the protocol. Lately, a lot of research has gone into adopting packet-switched NoCs [13][14]. Proteo network is a topology-free packet-switched NoC concept [14]. The current implementation suffers from large buffering overhead. Moraes *et al.* propose a mesh-based packet-switched NoC utilizing worm-hole routing [15]. Their best-effort routing algorithm has a notable latency of ten cycles per switch. A router introduced by Rijpkema *et al.* offers guaranteed service with time division multiplexing [16]. SPIN network uses a packet-switched fat-tree network [17]. Valtonen *et al.* consider a homogeneous cellular NoC with special attention on testability and error tolerance [18]. Three major problems are readily apparent with contemporary NoCs: large area due to buffering inside communication network, lack of guaranteed service, and lack of common test cases for performance comparisons.

Zeferino *et al.* have analyzed the switching point when mesh-based NoC becomes preferable over simple bus having no hierarchy [19]. Using the same equations, Fig. 1 shows clock cycles for total exchange for mesh-based NoC, hierarchical two-bus and four-bus networks with different degrees of locality. Locality is expressed as proportion of reachable agents. Figure 1 shows that even a two-bus network will offer comparable performance to a mesh-based NoC when at least half of the agents must be reached. If locality or the number of agents is higher, a system having more bus segments could be chosen. This suggests that the switching point will shift to a higher number of agents than presented in [19] because it does not consider hierarchical buses. The signal lines get shorter as the number of segments increases, but they are still likely to be longer than in a mesh topology. In hierarchical networks, the mapping of processes onto computation resources is a critical step to keep most of the communication within a small area and still ensure load balancing. A fixed topology does not allow application-specific optimization of communication topology. Optimization may be targeted toward performance by adding more communication links when needed or toward area by removing links to avoid an overkill topology. Therefore, the topology should be scalable and modified easily to support various applications efficiently. The choice of the most suitable topology depends on the requirements of the targeted application.

# 3   HIBI v.2 Overview

The design objectives behind HIBI v.2 were to design a topology-independent, scalable, and still high-performance network. Special attention was paid to configurability, efficiency of the protocol in terms of energy and performance per transmitted bit, and quality of service. It is based on previously presented Heterogeneous IP Block Interconnection v.1 (HIBI v.1) [20][21]. HIBI is used to construct modular, hierarchical structures with distributed arbitration and multiple clock domains.

## 3.1   Buffering and Signaling

The model of computation used in HIBI design approach assumes bounded first-in-first-out (FIFO) buffers between processes. A simple FIFO interface can be adapted to more complex interfaces such as the OCP (Open Core Protocol)[22]. To avoid excess buffering, the received data should be read from the FIFO as soon as possible, for example by using a direct memory access (DMA) controller. Therefore, the buffer space in HIBI wrapper is not defined by the *amount* of transferred data, but the *latency* of reading data from the wrapper. The scheme resembles worm-hole routing, but the links are not reserved for the whole duration of the transfer. The functional unit may use a different clock than the wrapper.

## 3.2   Quality-of-Service

Arbitration is distributed to wrappers, meaning that they can decide the correct time to access the bus by themselves and no central arbiter is required. A two-level arbitration scheme, a combination of time division multiple access

(TDMA) and competition, is used in HIBI. In TDMA, time is divided into repeating time frames. Inside frames, agents are provided time slots when they are guaranteed an access to the communication channel. Competition is based either on round-robin or priority. The second level mechanism is used to arbitrate the unassigned or unused time slots. Priority arbitration as a second level method attempts to guarantee a small latency for high priority agents whereas round-robin provides a fair arbitration scheme. TDMA arbitration is beneficial for energy saving because transfer times are known in advance and, therefore, timing shutdown and predictive power-up operations is simple. The application can actively set the power save modes through configuration memory. The HIBI implementation pays special attention to minimizing the arbitration latency by removing empty cycles from the arbitration process by pipelining.

### 3.3   Run-Time Reconfiguration

HIBI allows the run-time configuration of all arbitration parameters to minimize latency by network tuning. Also the cycle counters can be reset to an arbitrary clock cycle value within the time frame to keep time slots in the correct place with respect to data availability. The resynchronization may be triggered by a specific monitor unit, which monitors how effectively time slots are used and starts the reconfiguration if needed [23]. Furthermore in HIBI v.2, the second-level arbitration method may be changed at run-time between priority and round-robin or both of them can be disabled. When the second-level arbitration is disabled, only basic TDMA is used and a HIBI wrapper reserves the bus always for the whole allocated time-slot.

In HIBI v.2, three methods are used to decrease configuration latency. First, by making use of the bus nature, each common parameter can be broadcast to all wrappers. Second, enabling the reading of configuration values simplifies the procedure as the whole configuration does not have to be stored in the configuring device. The configuring agent can read the old parameter values to help determine the new. Third, additional storage capacity for multiple parameter pages has been added to enable rapid change of all parameters. When a configuration page changes, all the parameters in network are updated immediately using one bus operation. It is possible to store a specific configuration for every application (phase) in its own configuration page to enable fast configuration switching.

### 3.4   Circuit and Packet-Switching

Bus throughput can be scaled up by using hierarchical bus structures as shown in Section 2. Figure 2 depicts a system with a hierarchical HIBI network. The key is to locate the agents that communicate frequently in the same segment to provide small latency. Clustering makes the optimization easier since segments can operate with various data widths and clock frequencies. The implementation area and power consumption are lowered by making the segments as slow

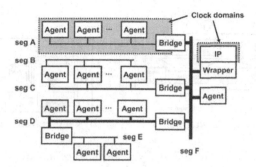

**Fig. 2.** Example of a hierarchical bus network

and narrow as possible but still meeting the application requirements. Transfers inside a bus segment are circuit-switched but HIBI v.2 bridges utilize the packet-switched principle so that bus segments are not circuit-switched together. Instead, the data is stored inside the bridge until it gets an access to the other segment. If the bridge cannot buffer all the data, the transfer is interrupted until the bridge has written some of the data to the next bus segment. Once the data is stored inside the bridge, the source segment is free for other transfers. It is possible that a bridge buffers parts from multiple transfers.

### 3.5   Data Transfer Operations

In HIBI v.2, all operations can be targeted either to a single agent or to a group of agents with multicast. All data arrive in-order. In HIBI v.2, data may be sent with different priorities. High priority data, such as control messages, bypass the normal data transfers resulting in smaller latency. This does not change the timing of bus reservations, but it selects what is transferred first. HIBI v.2 has multiplexed address and data lines whereas HIBI v.1 uses separate address and data lines. HIBI v.2 implementations can be made smaller than HIBI v.1 because signal lines are removed and less storage capacity is needed for the addresses. On the other hand, the saved area can be used for wider data transfers to increase the available bandwidth. HIBI protocol does not require any specific control signals, but message-passing is utilized when needed. HIBI v.1 assumes strictly non-blocking transfers and omitted handshake signals to minimize transfer latency. One handshake signal was added to HIBI v.2. As a result, blocking models of computation can be used in system design and the depth of FIFOs is considerably smaller.

## 4   HIBI v.2 Implementation

HIBI v.2 was implemented with synthesizable VHDL and SystemC. In addition, the SystemC simulation model has an embedded performance monitor which is used to analyze and tune the architecture to better fit the application.

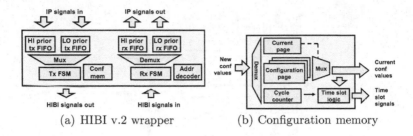

    (a) HIBI v.2 wrapper       (b) Configuration memory

**Fig. 3.** Structure of HIBI v.2 wrapper and configuration memory

## 4.1   Signaling

The bus signals are *Reset, Clock, Data, Address Valid, Command, Lock,* and
*Target Full.* The number of data bits can be freely chosen. The signal Address
Valid indicates when an address is transferred on the data lines. Three bits are
needed for Command to present eight different network operations. Handshaking
is done with the Target Full signal. All signals are shared and no point-to-point
signalling is required. On IP side, there are separate FIFO/OCP interfaces for
every data priority. Furthermore, the power control signals can be routed out of
the wrapper if the IP block can utilize them. An OR network was selected for
bus signal resolution.

## 4.2   Wrapper Structure

HIBI v.2 wrapper is depicted in Fig. 3(a). The modular wrapper structure may
be tuned to better meet the application requirements by using different versions
of the internal units or even leaving out properties that are not needed in a
particular application. The main parts are buffers for transferring and receiving
data and the corresponding controllers. The transfer controller takes care of distributed arbitration. Configuration memory stores all arbitration and addressing
parameters. Message bypassing is implemented by adding an extra FIFO along
with the data FIFO. A multiplexer is placed between the transmit FIFOs and
the transfer controller so that the controller sees only a single FIFO that it can
access. The separate multiplexer allows this method to be expanded to support
priorities in excess of two without changing the control.

    The structure of the configuration memory is illustrated in Fig. 3(b). It in-
cludes multiple configuration pages for storing the parameter values, a register
storing the number of currently active page, and a clock cycle counter. Current
configuration values and time slot signals are fed to the transfer controller. The
receive controller takes care of writing new values to the configuration memory.
Configuration values can be written to non-active pages before they are used to
minimize the risk of conflict when the configuration procedure is yet to be completed. Naturally, having multiple pages results in larger implementation area. A
way to reduce area is to restrict the configuration options by hardwiring values.

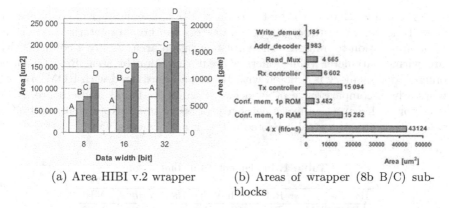

(a) Area HIBI v.2 wrapper

(b) Areas of wrapper (8b B/C) sub-blocks

**Fig. 4.** Area of HIBI v.2 wrapper and its sub-blocks

Still, it is possible to leave some parameters to be configured at run-time. For example, allowing clock counter synchronization and the use of multiple hardwired configuration pages might be a good compromise for many applications.

### 4.3 Structure of HIBI Bridge

A bridge is constructed by connecting two wrappers together. If the connected bus segments use different clock frequencies, handshaking logic is needed between the two wrappers. One option is to mix channels of different widths in a hierarchical system in which the bridges are responsible for the data width adaptation. Segments having only simple peripheral devices could use a slow and narrow bus while the main processing parts have higher capacity buses.

## 5  HIBI v.2 Performance

### 5.1  Synthesis Results

The HIBI v.2 wrapper was synthesized using a 0.18 micron technology. The results do not include the wiring or place-and-route information. Areas for four different wrapper configurations with three different data widths are shown in Fig. 4. FIFO definition *3,3,0,0* means that data buffer sizes are 3 words and message FIFOs are absent. Both A and B cases use a hardwired configuration. Version C and D allow new configuration values to be written at run-time. Furthermore, version D has two configuration pages. The maximum frequency is in the range of 200 to 300 MHz depending on the sizes of FIFO buffers and configuration memory used.

Currently the configuration memories and FIFO buffers are implemented with flip-flops to support soft IP core methodology, which results in rather large area. This is illustrated in Fig. 4 for an eight-bit wrapper (B and C). In this case, the FIFO buffers occupy half of the wrapper area. Still, the area of FIFO

buffers is smaller than in the first version of HIBI. The number of configuration
pages, time slots, and the width of parameters can be parameterized according
to the application to minimize the implementation area. Figure 4 confirms that
hard-wiring parameter values offers a great reduction in area. Register-based
configuration memory is denoted with RAM and hardwired with ROM. Table 1
shows a brief comparison to other network wrappers found in literature. ARM
processor is shown as an example of a processing node. Note that the buffers
mainly determine the area of Proteo network not the data width.

**Table 1.** Implementation comparison

| IP | Ref | Tech | Width | Gates | $mm^2$ | MHz |
|---|---|---|---|---|---|---|
| ARM7TDMI | [24] | 0.18 | 32b | - | 0.62 | 80-115 |
| HIBI v.2 (A) | | 0.18 | 32b | 7k | 0.08 | 200-300 |
| HIBI v.2 (C) | | 0.18 | 32b | 15k | 0.18 | 200-300 |
| NoC Cell | [15] | - | 32b | 10k | - | - |
| NoC Cell | [16] | 0.12 | 32b | - | 0.26 | 166/500 |
| NoC Cell | [18] | 0.35 | 16b | 15k | - | 110-267 |
| Proteo | [14] | 0.18 | 8b | 16k | 0.20 | - |
| SPIN | [17] | 0.13 | 32b | - | 0.24 | 200 |

## 5.2   Performance Evaluation

Fair comparison of networks is difficult since there are no widely accepted benchmarks or reported implementations simply do not offer enough information. The
performance of HIBI v.2 protocol was tested with a test case similar to the
one described by Saastamoinen *et al.* [14] (pp. 193-213) that provides at least
a starting point. The application reads 10x10 byte pictures from source memory, processes the data, and writes 10x10 byte result pictures to target memory.
Our test case model assumes minimum latency of 10 cycles for processing and
five cycles for memory reads. The architecture includes eight processing units,
single-ported source and target memories, and either single- or dual-bus 8-bit
HIBI v.1 or v.2. Round-robin was used as the arbitration method. Single- and
dual-bus networks are similar to *seg A* and *seg B+C* in Fig. 2, respectively.

Doubling the bus width or adding another bus naturally improves the performance but the improvement is less than two-fold because requests and ac-
knowledgements cannot utilize the increased bandwidth or the task pipelining is
inefficient. Our simple application model does not perform any handshaking between processing units and therefore they all start requesting source data at the
same time. Memory sends slices of the picture to all requesting processors and
the processing cannot start until the whole picture has been received. Therefore,
the processing is delayed. Consequently, one of the buses is idle for a long time
and execution time does not improve much from the single bus topology. Figure
5(a) shows the measured run time for processing one picture in each processor.

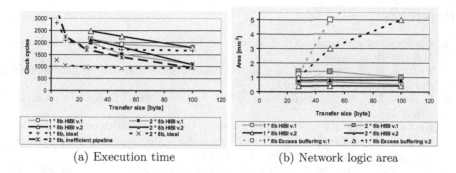

(a) Execution time                    (b) Network logic area

**Fig. 5.** Results of the case study

Both dual-bus HIBI networks have 15-35% smaller execution times for subsequent pictures when the time for filling the pipeline has only a minor effect. Figure 5(b) illustrates the estimated area for different networks.

The area of HIBI v.2 is smaller than HIBI v.1 with all transfer sizes. As noted earlier, the latency of functional unit determines the required buffer space instead of the packet size. In contrast, storing all packets inside the network logic, like store-and-forward method, would result in area consumption to be linearly dependent on packet size. Estimated area for buffering the whole packet is shown with a dashed line in Figure 5(b), which clearly indicates why this is not a preferable method. Comparison with results of Saastamoinen *et al.* [14] (about 2500 cycles, 4.4 $mm^2$ with 28B/tx) shows that even a single HIBI bus provides better performance than a Proteo ring network with considerably smaller area cost. Adding a second bus to HIBI network improves performance nearly 40% and the area is still smaller than in Proteo.

## 6   Conclusions

In this paper, with our HIBI scheme, we have shown that a number of useful operations, such as architecture orthogonalization, QoS, and heterogeneous structures, can be implemented based on a non-traditional bus network. Especially, the proposed arbitration and configuration mechanisms offer great potential for both execution time and energy optimization. HIBI can be regarded as a NoC because it scales upwards, theoretically to arbitrary topologies, but particularly to hierarchical and fat bus structures. The data transfer capacity can, therefore, be chosen relatively freely while maintaining well known and easily programmable architectures. Furthermore, the presented synthesis results show that HIBI implementations have performance indicators and implementation areas that are acceptable for contemporary SoCs.

# References

1. Chang, H. *et al.*: Surviving SoC Revolution. Kluwer Academic Publishers, Norwell, MA (1999)
2. Keating, M., Bricaud, P.: Reuse Methodology Manual 2nd edn. Kluwer Academic Publishers, Norwell, MA (1999)
3. Rowson, J.A., Sangiovanni-Vincentelli A.: Interface-Based Design. In proc. DAC (1997) 178-183
4. Keutzer, K., *et al.*: System-Level Design: Orthogonalization of Concerns and Platform-Based Design. IEEE Trans. Computer-Aided Design of Integrated Circuits and Systems, vol. 19, issue 12 (2000) 1523-1543
5. Scherson, I.D., Youssef A.S.: Interconnection Networks for High-Performance Parallel Computers. IEEE Computer Society Press, Los Alamitos, CA (1994)
6. Varma, A., Raghavendra, C.S. (eds.): Interconnection Networks for Multiprocessors and Multicomputers Theory and Practice. IEEE Computer Society Press, Los Alamitos, CA (1994)
7. Zalewski, J. (ed.): Advanced Multiprocessor Bus Architectures. IEEE Computer Society Press, Los Alamitos, CA (1995)
8. Park, J.H., *et al.*: MPEG-4 video codec on an ARM and AMBA. In proc. Workshop and Exhibition on MPEG-4 (2001) 95-98
9. Dutta, S., *et al.*: Viper: A Multiprocessor SoC for Advanced Set-Top Box and Digital TV Systems. IEEE Design and Test of Computers, vol. 18, issue 5 (2001) 21-31
10. ARM Limited: AMBA Specification Rev 2.0. (1999)
11. Sonics Inc.: Sonics uNetworks Technical Overview Revision A21-1. (2000)
12. Salminen, E., *et al.*: Overview of Bus-based System-On-Chip Interconnections. In proc. ISCAS (2002) II-372 - II-375.
13. Benini, L., de Micheli, G.: Networks on chips: A New SoC Paradigm. Computer, vol. 35, issue 1 (2002) 70-78
14. Jantsch, A., Tenhunen, H. (eds.): Networks on Chip. Kluwer Academic Publishers, Dordrecht, The Netherlands (2003)
15. Moraes, F., *et al.*: A Low Area Overhead Packet-Switched Network on Chip: Architecture and Prototyping. In proc. IFIP VLSI-SOC (2003) 174-179
16. Rijpkema, E., *et al.*: Trade Offs in the Design of a Router with Both Guaranteed and Best-Effort Services for Network on Chip (Extended version). IEEE Proc. Computers and Digital Techniques, vol 150, issue 5 (2003) 294-302
17. Andriahatenenaina, A., Greiner, A.: Micro-network for SoC: Implementation of 32-port SPIN Network. In proc. DATE (2003) 11128-11129
18. Valtonen, T., *et al.*: An Autonomous Error-tolerant Cell for Scalable Network-on-Chip Architectures. In proc. Norchip (2001) 198-203
19. Zeferino, C.A., et. al.: A Study on Communication Issues for System-on-Chip. In proc. SBCCI (2002) 121-126
20. Kuusilinna, K., *et al.*: Low-Latency Interconnection for IP-Block Based Multimedia Chips. In proc. PDCN (1998) 411-416
21. Lahtinen. V., *et al.*: Interconnection scheme for continuous-media systems-on-chip. Microprocessors and Microsystems vol. 26, issue 3 (2002) 123-138
22. OCP-IP Alliance: Open Core Protocol Specification, Release 1.0, Portland, OR (2001)
23. Kangas, T., *et al.*: System-on-Chip Communication Optimization with Bus Monitoring. In proc. DDECS (2002) 304-309
24. ARM Limited: ARM7 Thumb Family Flyer. (2003)

# DIF: An Interchange Format
# for Dataflow-Based Design Tools

Chia-Jui Hsu, Fuat Keceli, Ming-Yung Ko,
Shahrooz Shahparnia, and Shuvra S. Bhattacharyya

Department of Electrical and Computer Engineering,
and Institute for Advanced Computer Studies
University of Maryland, College Park, 20742, USA

**Abstract.** The dataflow interchange format (DIF) is a textual language that is
geared towards capturing the semantics of graphical design tools for DSP system design. A key objective of DIF is to facilitate technology transfer across
dataflow- based DSP design tools by providing a common, extensible semantics
for representing coarse-grain dataflow graphs, and recognizing useful sub-
classes of dataflow models. DIF captures essential modeling information that is
required in dataflow-based analysis and optimization techniques, such as algorithms for consistency analysis, scheduling, memory management, and block
processing, while optionally hiding proprietary details such as the actual code
that implements the dataflow blocks. Accompanying DIF is a software package
of intermediate representations and algorithms that operate on application models that are captured through DIF. This paper describes the structure of the DIF
language together with several implementation and usage examples.

## 1 Introduction

Modeling of DSP applications based on coarse-grain dataflow graphs is widespread in
the DSP design community, and a large and growing set of DSP design tools support
such dataflow semantics [2]. Since a variety of dataflow modeling styles and accompanying semantic constructs have been developed for DSP design tools (e.g., see [1,
4, 5, 8, 11, 14, 15]), a critical problem in the process of technology transfer to, from,
and across such tools is a common, vendor-independent language, and associated
suite of intermediate representations and algorithms for DSP-oriented dataflow modeling. This paper describes a preliminary version of a *dataflow interchange format*
(*DIF*) for addressing this problem.

As motivated above, DIF is not centered around any particular form of dataflow,
and is designed instead to express different kinds of dataflow semantics. Our present
version of DIF includes built-in support for synchronous dataflow (SDF) semantics
[14], which have emerged as an important common denominator across many DSP
design tools and support powerful algorithms for analysis and software synthesis [3].
DIF also includes support for the closely related cyclo-static dataflow (CSDF) model
[4], and has specialized support for various restricted versions of SDF, in particular,
homogeneous and single-rate dataflow, which are often used in multiprocessor scheduling and hardware synthesis. Additionally, support for Boolean dataflow (BDF) [5]
and parameterized dataflow [1], and for general constructs involving dynamic, vari-

A. Pimentel and S. Vassiliadis (Eds.): SAMOS 2004, LNCS 3133, pp. 423–432, 2004.
© Springer-Verlag Berlin Heidelberg 2004

able-parameter dataflow quantities (production rates, consumption rates, and delays) is provided in DIF. DIF also captures hierarchy, and arbitrary non-dataflow attributes that can be associated with dataflow graph nodes (also called *actors* or *blocks*), edges, and graphs.

## 2  The Language

DIF is designed to be exported and imported automatically by tools. However, unlike other interchange formats, DIF is also designed to be read and written by designers who wish to understand the dataflow structure of applications or the dataflow semantics of a particular design tool, or who wish to specify an application model for one or more design tools using the features of DIF. *Indeed, DIF provides the programmer a unique, integrated set of semantic features that are relevant to dataflow modeling.* As a result, DIF is not based on XML, which is more for pure data exchange applications, and is not well-suited for being read or written by humans. Due to the emphasis on readability, DIF supports *C*/Java-style comments, allows specifications to be modularized across multiple files (through integration with the standard *C* preprocessor), and is based on a block-structured syntax.

A dataflow graph definition in DIF consists in general of six blocks of code: *topology*, *interface*, *refinement*, user-defined and built-in *attributes,* and *parameters*. These code blocks are contained in a main block defining the dataflow graph. Note that each block is optional without violating language basics. Using the *basedon* keyword, a graph can inherit the same topology as another graph while overriding arbitrary attributes and parameters. Figure 1 illustrates the general form of a graph definition block. The optional *keyword* on the first line denotes the type (form of dataflow). Further details on the different graph types available are described in Section 3.

### 2.1  Defining the Topology of a Dataflow Graph

The topology definition of a graph consists of node and edge definition blocks. These define the sets of nodes and edges, and associate a unique identifier with each node and each edge. Since dataflow graphs are directed graphs, edges are specified by their source and sink node identifiers. A node definition may also include a port association (described further in Section 2.2) for interfacing to other graphs. The lower left side of Figure 2 shows an example of a topology definition block.

### 2.2  Hierarchical Graphs

Given the importance of hierarchical design in graphical design tools, a necessary feature of the DIF language is the general ability to associate a node of a graph with a "nested" subgraph. Such hierarchical nodes are called *supernodes* in DIF terminology. In addition to providing for hierarchy, this supernode feature allows for reuse of graph specifications: a topological pattern that appears multiple times in a graph can be defined as a separate graph and every occurrence in the original graph (parent graph) or in multiple graphs can be replaced with a single node.

A graph can be declared as a nested subgraph in the *refinement* block of a parent graph. For a graph to be declared as a subgraph, it should have an *interface* block, which includes a list of directed ports. A port will then be associated either with a node (in the *topology* block) or with one of the ports of a super node (in the *refinement* block).

Further details and examples of the hierarchy mechanism in DIF can be found in [10].

```
[keyword] graph graphID [basedon graphID] {
    params {
        param prm1, prm2, ...;
        domain (prm1, {1, 2, ...});
        domain (prm2, [1, 5]);
        ...
    }
    interface {
        input portID portID ...;
        output portID portID ...;
    }
    topology {
        nodes { nodeID [:portID ] nodeID [:portID ] ...}
        edges {
            edgeID sourceINodeID sinkNodeID;
            edgeID sourceINodeID sinkNodeID;
            ...
        }
    }
    refinement {
        subgraphID nodeID
            subPortID:edgeID subPortID:PortID ...;
        subgraphID nodeID
            subPortID:portID subPortID:edgeID ...;
        ...
    }
    attribute attributeName {
        edgeID value ;
        nodeID value ;
        ...
    }
    ...
    [built-in attribute] {...}
    ...
}
```

**Fig. 1.** A sketch of a dataflow graph definition in DIF. Items in boldface are DIF keywords. Italicized words are to be defined by the user. Parts in braces are optional.

## 2.3 User-Defined and Built-In Attributes

DIF supports assigning attributes to nodes, edges, and graphs. There are two types of attributes: *user-defined* and *built-in. User-defined attributes* are attributes with arbitrary names that can take on any value assigned by the user. *Built-in attributes* are predefined attributes, which have associated keywords in the DIF language, and are usually handled in a special way by the compiler. An example of a built-in attribute is the *delay* parameter of graph edges.

## 2.4 Parameters

Parameterization of attribute values is possible in DIF with the *params* block. The capability of defining a possible set of values (*domain*) for an attribute instead of a specific value provides useful support for dynamic and reconfigurable dataflow graphs. The domain of a parameter can be an enumerated set of values, an interval, or a composition of both forms.

## 2.5  The *basedon* Feature

Using the *basedon* keyword, a graph that has the same topology as another graph, but with different attribute or parameter values can be defined concisely with just a reference to the other graph. The user can change selected parameter and attribute values by overriding them in *attribute* and *params* blocks of the new graph.

## 3  Dataflow Support

This *DIF package* is a Java-based software package for DIF that is being developed, along with the DIF language, at the University of Maryland. Associated with each of the supported dataflow graph types is an intermediate representation within the DIF package that provides an extensible set of data structures and algorithms for analyzing, manipulating, and optimizing DIF representations. Also, conversion algorithms between compatible graph types (such as CSDF to SDF or SDF to single-rate conversion) are provided. Presently, the collection of dataflow graph algorithms is based primarily on well-known algorithms (e.g., algorithms for iteration period computation [9], consistency validation [14], and loop scheduling [3]), and the contribution of DIF in this regard is to provide a common repository and front-end through which different DSP tools can have efficient access to these algorithms. We are actively extending this repository with additional dataflow modeling features and additional algorithms, including more experimental algorithms for data partitioning and hardware synthesis. Below is a summary of the dataflow models that are currently supported in DIF.

### 3.1  DIF Graphs

*DIF graphs* are the default and most general class of dataflow graphs supported by DIF. DIF graphs can be specified explicitly using the *dif* keyword. In DIF graphs, no restriction is made on the rate at which data is produced and consumed on dataflow edges, and other types of specialized assumptions, such as statically-known delay attributes, are avoided as well. In the underlying intermediate representation, an arbitrary Java object can be attached to each node/edge incidence to represent the associated dataflow properties. In the inheritance hierarchy of the DIF intermediate representations, DIF graphs are the base class of all other forms of dataflow. In this sense, all dataflow graphs modeled in DIF are instances of DIF graph. Furthermore, if a tool cannot export to any of the more specialized versions of dataflow supported by DIF, it should export to DIF graphs.

### 3.2  CSDF Graphs

In restricted versions of the DIF graph model that are recognized in DIF, the number of data values (tokens) produced and consumed by each node may be known statically and edge delays may be fixed integers. For example, *CSDF* graphs, based on the cyclo-static dataflow model [4], are specified by annotating DIF graph definitions with the *csdf* keyword. In CSDF graphs, production and consumption rates can vary between node executions, as long as the variation forms a certain type of periodic pattern. Consequently, values of these rates are integer vectors. These vectors are associated with CSDF graph edges using the *production* and *consumption keywords*. For example, the code fragment

```
production {e1 [1 1 2 4]; e2 [2 2 3];}
```

associates the periodic production patterns

$$(1, 1, 2, 4, 1, 1, 2, 4, \ldots) \quad \text{and} \quad (2, 2, 3, 2, 2, 3, \ldots)$$

and with edges $e1$, and $e2$, respectively.

## 3.3 SDF Graphs

Similar to CSDF graphs, token production and consumption rates of synchronous dataflow (SDF) graphs [14] are known at compile time, but they are fixed rather than periodic integer values. SDF graphs are specified using the *sdf* keyword, and the arguments of *production* and *consumption* specifiers in SDF graphs are required to be integers, as in:

```
production {e1 4; e2 3;}
consumption {e1 5; e2 2;}
delay {e1 1; e2 2;}
```

The last statement, which is permissible in other DIF graph types as well, associates integer-valued delays to the specified edges.

## 3.4 Single Rate and HSDF Graphs

*Single rate* graphs are a special case of SDF graphs where the production and consumption values on each edge are identical. In single rate graphs, nodes execute ("fire") at the same average rate [3]. In the slightly more restricted case of *homogeneous* SDF (HSDF) graphs, production and consumption values are equal to one for all edges. Instead of *production* and *consumption* attributes, DIF uses the *transfer* keyword for edges in single rate graphs. DIF does not associate an attribute for token transfer volume in HSDF since it is not variable.

## 3.5 Parameterized Dataflow Graphs

Parameterized dataflow [1] graphs can be represented in DIF using the parameterization and hierarchy facilities of DIF. Specifically, separate subgraphs can be defined for the *init*, *subinit*, and *body* subsystems of a parameterized dataflow model, and variable parameters with associated parameter value domains can be defined and linked to outputs of the init or subinit graphs through user-defined attributes.

## 3.6 Other Dataflow Graphs

Boolean-controlled dataflow (BDF) [6] is a form of dynamic dataflow for supporting data-dependent DSP computations. A dynamic actor produces or consumes a number of tokens depending on the incoming data values during each firing. In BDF, the number of tokens produced or consumed by a dynamic actor is restricted to be a two-valued function of the value of a control token. For example, the *Switch* actor in BDF consumes an input token and a control token. If the control token is true, the input token is sent to an outgoing edge labeled *True*, otherwise it is sent to an outgoing edge labeled *False*. BDF graphs are specified using the *bdf* keyword and a syntax is provided for specifying control inputs to BDF actors and their relationships to other incident edges.

Interval-Rate Locally-static Dataflow (ILDF) [18] is proposed to analyze dataflow graphs whose component data rates are not known precisely at compile time. In ILDF graphs, the production and consumption rates remain constant throughout execution (locally-static), but only the minimum and maximum values (interval-rate) of these constants are given. DIF is capable of representing ILDF graphs by parameterizing the production and consumption rates of ILDF edges and specifying the intervals of those parameters.

In addition to the aforementioned dataflow models, a variety of other dataflow models are being explored for inclusion in DIF.

## 4   DIF Language Implementation

The DIF package includes a parser that converts a DIF specification into a suitable, graph-theoretic intermediate representation based on the particular form of dataflow used in the DIF specification. This parser is implemented using a Java-based compilercompiler called *SableCC* [7]. The flexible structure of the compiler enables easy extensibility for different graph types.

Using *DIF writer* classes, it is also possible to generate DIF files from intermediate representations (graph objects) in the DIF package. The default writer is the DIF graph writer, which generates a DIF graph specification, and custom writers can be constructed by extending the DIF graph writer base class to handle semantic additions/ restrictions by converting them to appropriate built-in attributes, structural conventions, etc.

The DIF package builds on some of the packages of Ptolemy II [13]. In particular, the attribute features of DIF are built on the rich classes for managing attributes in Ptolemy II, and the intermediate representations of DIF build on the *graph* package of Ptolemy II, which provides data structures and algorithms for working with generic graphs.

## 5   Examples

This section illustrates some further examples of the utility of the DIF package.

### 5.1   Ptolemy

We have developed a back-end for Ptolemy II that generates DIF graphs from dataflow- based Ptolemy II models. An example of Ptolemy-to-DIF conversion through this back-end is shown in Figure 2. A front-end that converts DIF specifications into Ptolemy II models is under development.

## 5.2   MCCI Autocoding Toolset

Another usage example of DIF is in the Autocoding Toolset of Management, Communications, and Control Inc. (MCCI) [16]. This tool is designed for mapping large, complex signal processing applications onto high-performance multiprocessor platforms.

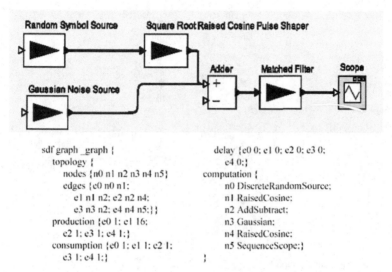

Fig. 2. Ptolemy II model of a PAM communication system that is exported to DIF. This example represents the functionality of each node as a *computation* attribute, which is derived from the Ptolemy II library definition.

Through a DIF-generating back-end developed at MCCI, the Autocoding Toolset supports generation of DIF specifications after partitioning the application.

Figure 3 shows a synthetic aperture radar (SAR) application developed in the Autocoding Toolset. The functional requirements of SAR processing consist of four logical processes: data input and conditioning, range processing, azimuth processing and data output. The Autocoding Toolset partitions the application into five parts dividing the azimuth processing into two parts. Figure 3(a) shows the top level functional definition graph and Figure 3(b) shows the *range* subgraph with its DIF definition. *Range* processing of data includes conversion to complex floating point numbers, padding the end of each data row with zeros, multiplying by a weighting function, computing the FFT, and multiplying the data by the radar cross-section compensation.

## 5.3   Visualization and Benchmark Generation

The DIF package contains facilities to generate DIF specifications of randomly-generated, synthetic benchmarks. This can be useful for more extensive testing of tools and algorithms beyond the set of available application models. The benchmark generator is based on an implementation of Sih's dataflow graph generation algorithm

[17], which constructs application-like graphs by mimicking patterns found in practical dataflow models.

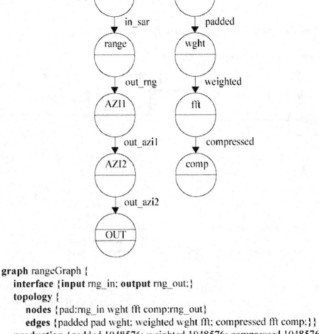

(c)
```
graph rangeGraph {
    interface {input rng_in; output rng_out;}
    topology {
        nodes {pad:rng_in wght fft comp:rng_out}
        edges {padded pad wght; weighted wght fft; compressed fft comp;}}
    production {padded 1048576; weighted 1048576; compressed 1048576;}
    consumption {padded 1048576; weighted 1048576; compressed 1048576;}
    delay {padded 0; weighted 0; compressed 0;}
}
```

(d)
```
graph SAR {
    ...
    refinement {
        rangeGraph range rng_in:in_sar rng_out:out_rng;
    }
    ...
}
```

**Fig. 3.** (a) The top-level partitioned application graph of a SAR application in the MCCI Autocoding Toolset. (b) Range processing. (c) Range processing in DIF. (d) Range processing instantiation in SAR. Note that although 3(c) is a single rate graph, the Autocoding Toolset presently exports this in the more general form of a DIF graph. This example is adapted due to space constraints.

DIF specifications and intermediate representations can also be converted automatically into the input format of *dot* [12], a well-known graph-visualization tool.

# 6  Summary

This paper has presented the dataflow interchange format (DIF), a textual language for writing coarse-grain, dataflow-based models of DSP applications, and for communicating such models between DSP design tools. The objectives of DIF are to accommodate a variety of dataflow-related modeling constructs, and to facilitate experimentation with and technology transfer involving such constructs. We are actively extending the DIF language, including the set of supported dataflow modeling semantics, and the associated repository of intermediate representations and algorithms.

# Acknowledgements

This research is sponsored in part by DARPA (contract #F30602-01-C-0171, through the USC Information Sciences Institute), and the Semiconductor Research Corporation (contract #2001-HJ-905).

# References

1. B. Bhattacharya and S. S. Bhattacharyya. Parameterized dataflow modeling for DSP systems. *IEEE Transactions on Signal Processing*, 49(10):2408-2421, October 2001.
2. S. S. Bhattacharyya, R. Leupers, and P. Marwedel. Software synthesis and code generation for DSP. *IEEE Transactions on Circuits and Systems — II: Analog and Digital Signal Processing*, 47(9):849-875, September 2000.
3. S. S. Bhattacharyya, P. K. Murthy, and E. A. Lee. Synthesis of embedded software from synchronous dataflow specifications. *Journal of VLSI Signal Processing Systems for Signal, Image, and Video Technology*, 21(2):151-166, June 1999.
4. G. Bilsen, M. Engels, R. Lauwereins, and J. A. Peperstraete. Cyclo-static data flow. In *Proc. ICASSP*, pages 3255-3258, May 1995.
5. J. T. Buck and E. A. Lee. Scheduling dynamic dataflow graphs using the token flow model. In *Proc. ICASSP*, April 1993.
6. J. T. Buck. *Scheduling Dynamic Dataflow Graphs with Bounded Memory Using the Token Flow Model*. Tech. Report UCB/ERL 93/69, Ph.D. Thesis, Dept. of EECS, University of California, Berkeley, 1993.
7. E. Gagnon. *SableCC, an object-oriented compiler framework*. Master's thesis, School of Computer Science, McGill University, Montreal, Canada, March 1998.
8. G. R. Gao, R. Govindarajan, and P. Panangaden. Well-behaved programs for DSP computation. In *Proc. ICASSP*, March 1992.
9. K. Ito and K. K. Parhi. Determining the iteration bounds of single-rate and multi-rate dataflow graphs. In *Proc. IEEE Asia-Pacific Conference on Circuits and Systems*, December 1994.
10. F. Keceli, M. Ko, S. Shahparnia, and S. S. Bhattacharyya. First version of a dataflow interchange format. Technical report, Institute for Advanced Computer Studies, University of Maryland at College Park, November 2002.
11. B. Kienhuis and E. F. Deprettere. Modeling stream-based applications using the SBF model of computation. In *Proceedings of the IEEE Workshop on Signal Processing Systems*, pages 385-394, September 2001.
12. E. Koutsofios and S. C. North. *dot* user's manual. Technical report, AT&T Bell Laboratories, November 1996.

13. E. A. Lee. Overview of the Ptolemy project. Technical Report UCB/ERL M01/11, Department of EECS, UC Berkeley, March 2001.
14. E. A. Lee and D. G. Messerschmitt. Synchronous dataflow. *Proceedings of the IEEE*, 75(9):1235-1245, September 1987.
15. M. Pankert, O. Mauss, S. Ritz, and H. Meyr. Dynamic data flow and control flow in high level DSP code synthesis. In *Proc. ICASSP*, 1994.
16. C. B. Robbins. *Autocoding Toolset software tools for automatic generation of parallel application software*. Technical report, Management, Communications & Control, Inc., 2002.
17. G. C. Sih. *Multiprocessor Scheduling to account for Interprocessor Communication*. Ph.D. thesis, Department of EECS, UC Berkeley, April 1991.
18. J. Teich and S. S. Bhattacharyya. Analysis of dataflow programs with interval-limited datarates. In *Proceedings of the International Workshop Systems, Architectures, Modeling, and Simulation*, Samos, Greece, July 2004. To appear.

# Scalable and Modular Scheduling

Paul Feautrier

LIP, Ecole Normale Superieure de Lyon
69364 Lyon Cedex 07, France
Paul.Feautrier@ens-lyon.fr

**Abstract.** Scheduling a program (i.e. constructing a timetable for the
execution of its operations) is one of the most powerful methods for automatic parallelization. A schedule gives a blueprint for constructing a
synchronous program, suitable for an ASIC or a VLIW processor. However, constructing a schedule entails solving a large linear program. Even
if one accepts the (experimental) fact that the Simplex is almost always
polynomial, the scheduling time is of the order of a large power of the
program size and of the maximum nesting level of its loops. Hence the
method is not scalable. The present paper presents two methods for improving this situation. Firstly, a big program can be divided into smaller
units (processes) which can be scheduled separately. This is *modular
scheduling*. Second, one can use projection methods for solving linear
programming problems incrementally. This is especially efficient if the
dependence graph is sparse.

## 1 Introduction

One of the challenges in the design of embedded system is to devise methods
for the automatic or semi-automatic construction of application-specific devices
from a behavioral specification.

I only consider here the case of compute intensive systems, which are mostly
found in signal processing applications (audio and video processing, radar software, telephony, etc.). Here the computing time cannot be neglected, the amount
of data is huge, and the need for safety is not stringent. At present, applications
(or parts thereof) in this field are first modeled in very high level languages
(mostly, Matlab), then mapped by hand on a variety of architectures, and then
implemented in a mixture of medium level code (C), assembly code and hardware specification languages like VHDL. The design process is lengthy, complex,
error-prone, and does not lend itself to the exploration of the solution space.

The aim of this paper is to sketch another approach, in which the application
is specified as a system of communicating processes, each process being written
in a medium-level language like C. I will explain how such a specification can be
converted to a synchronous program, suitable for instance for a VLIW processor
or as a first step in the design of an ASIC. One begins by constructing a schedule,
which gives the instant at which each operation in the program is executed. The
problem of regenerating a program from a schedule has been first studied by

A. Pimentel and S. Vassiliadis (Eds.): SAMOS 2004, LNCS 3133, pp. 433–442, 2004.

Irigoin [1] and considered by many other scholars. Very efficient solutions (with associated software) [2, 3] are available today.

The aim of this paper is to propose two methods for applying scheduling to large applications. The first method consists in modifying the basic scheduling algorithm to achieve better scalability. In the second method, I investigate under which conditions a program can be divided into modules which can be scheduled independently. This second method has the added advantage that it may be the key to reuse of hardware or software components in parallel applications.

In the next sections I define which type of modules are suitable for parallel programming and review the basic scheduling algorithm. In section 4, I explain how to improve the scheduling time of one process provided that the dependence graph is sparse. Section 5 explains how to do modular scheduling. In the conclusion, I present some open problems and discuss future work.

## 2   Communicating Regular Processes

Communicating Regular Processes are a variant of Kahn Process Networks [4] and of Communicating Sequential Processes [5]. The main difference is that regularity conditions are imposed on processes in order to allow temporal analysis of the full system.

### 2.1   Definitions

**Processes.** A process is a sequential program which can communicate with other processes through channels (see below). With the exception of channels, all variables are local to one process and are not visible from other processes. The code of a process can be written in any convenient algorithmic language. I use C here, but other choices are possible: Pascal, Fortran and others.

The code of a process is *regular*, or has static control [6]. Statements are assignments and bounded loop statements. All variables are considered part of some array, scalars being zero-dimensional arrays. Loops are of the arithmetics progression variety, and the loop upper and lower bounds are affine forms in numerical or symbolic constants and surrounding loop counters. The only method of address calculation is subscripting into arrays of arbitrary dimension. The subscripts must be affine forms in constants and surrounding loop counters.

The iteration vector of a statement is a list of its surrounding loop counters, from outside inward. The iteration vector of $S$ must belong to the iteration domain of $S$, $D_S$, which is constructed from the bounds of the surrounding loops. Under the assumption that the program is regular, iterations domains are convex polyhedra (or, more precisely, sets of integral points inside polyhedra).

An iteration of $S$ or *operation* is written $\langle S, x \rangle, x \in D_S$. The set of operations of a process $P$ is the disjoint union:

$$E_P = \bigcup_{S \in P} \{\langle S, x \rangle \mid x \in D_S\},$$

and the set of operations of a process system is $E = \cup_P E_P$. In more abstract contexts, I may simply write $u \in E$ for a generic operation. $<_{\text{seq}}$ is the sequential order of execution.

**Channels.** A channel is an array of arbitrary dimension which is used as a communication medium from a process to another process. Channels are unidirectional. One process is declared as the writer to a channel. Considered as an array, each cell of the channel must be written no more than once by its writer. Writing to a channel is non-blocking.

On the other hand, a channel may have any number of readers, and there are no constraints on the pattern of reading. Reading is not destructive: a value remains in a channel at least as long as some process may have some use for it. If a process reads a cell which has not yet been defined, it blocks until a definition happens.

One can prove that these restrictions on processes and channels are enough to guarantee that the channel contents are the same for all executions of a CRP system, and are independent of relative processor speeds or scheduling decisions. The detailed proof will be given elsewhere.

## 2.2   An Example

The following trivial example specify a system in which a producer generates an infinite stream of values which are sent to a consumer which compute a sliding mean. I hope that the extensions to C are clear for the reader.

```
channel float A[];

process producer(){
   int i;
   for(i=0;;i++)
W:   A[i] = f(i);
}
```

```
process consumer(){
   float s;
   int i;
Z: s = 0.0;
   for(i=0;;i++)
R:    s = 0.5*(s + A[i]);
}
```

## 2.3   Dependences

Data dependences were defined, as early as 1966, for the purpose of parallelization [7]. For each operation $u$, let $R(u)$ be the set of memory cells that are read by $u$ and $W(u)$ be the set of cells which are modified by $u$. Two operations $u$ and $v$ from the same process ($u <_{\text{seq}} v$) are in dependence if at least one of the three sets $W(u) \cap W(v)$ (output dependence), $W(u) \cap R(v)$ (flow dependence) and $R(u) \cap W(v)$ (anti-dependence) is not empty. The dependence relation is written $u\,\delta\,v$.

Assume now that the cell which causes the dependence is a channel cell. Before defining a dependence, one has to decide how to order the two dependent operations. This is not self-evident in the case of channels, since the dependent operations do not belong to the same process. In accordance with the intended semantics, I assume that the dependence is always from the write operation to a read, or that the write always occurs before any read to the same cell.

# 3   Scheduling

## 3.1   Target Architectures

In contrast to the above programming model, most of today electronic systems are synchronous: there is one global clock, and all changes of state occur in relation to the clock. Example of synchronous systems are VLIW processors and ASIC/FPGA special purpose circuits. A generic VLIW processor will be the main target architecture in what follows.

## 3.2   Schedules

A schedule is a function which assign a starting time to all operations in a program. In other words, a schedule is a function from $E$ to the set of time values, $T$, and is a way of specifying an execution order. $T$ may be any ordered set. The order associated to $\theta$ is:

$$u <_\theta v = \theta(u) < \theta(v).$$

The favorites for $T$ are $\mathbb{N}$ and $\mathbb{N}^d$, lexicographically ordered. This second case gives rise to the so-called multidimensional schedules.

The execution order which is defined by a schedule must be legal, i.e. it must extend the dependence relation:

$$\forall u, v \in E : u\,\delta\,v \Rightarrow \theta(u) < \theta(v). \tag{1}$$

To solve this functional inequality, one has to postulate a shape for $\theta$. The usual choice is that $\theta(\langle S, x\rangle)$ is an affine form in the iteration vector, $x$:

$$\theta(\langle S, x\rangle) = h_S.x + k_S, \tag{2}$$

where $h_S$ is the timing vector of $S$ and $k_S$ is a scalar offset. For regular programs, this choice has the advantage that everything in (1) becomes affine, and that powerful results from the theory of linear inequalities, like Farkas lemma [8], can be used to characterize the solutions. The reader is refered to [6, 9] for details. A short review of the method will be given below.

## 3.3   Solving the Scheduling Constraints

The first step of the solution consists in splitting formula (1) according to the source and sink of the dependence. For a given pair of statements, $S$ and $T$, the constraint now reads:

$$\forall x \in D_S, y \in D_T : \langle S, x\rangle\,\delta\,\langle T, y\rangle \Rightarrow \theta(\langle S, x\rangle) < \theta(\langle T, y\rangle). \tag{3}$$

Then, one has to eliminate the quantifiers on $x$ and $y$. This can be done either by the vertex method [10], or by making use of Farkas lemma. Whatever the method, (3) can be shown to be equivalent to a system of affine constraints[1]:

---

[1] Here and in what follows, I assume that constant terms have been included in the matrices by the well known homogeneous coordinate trick.

$$M_{ST}(h_S, k_S)^T + N_{ST}(h_T, k_T)^T \geq 0. \tag{4}$$

$M_{ST}$ and $N_{ST}$ are constant matrices which can be computed from the program text. The direct application of Farkas lemma introduces new unknowns, the Farkas multipliers, which can be eliminated along the lines of [6].

Lastly, one can solve (4) using any convenient linear programming algorithm.

In some cases, the scheduling constraints are not feasible, because not all programs can be executed in linear time on many processors. One can resort in this case to multidimensional schedules, whose parallel latency is polynomial. The construction of multidimensional schedules is explained in [9]. I will ignore this point in this preliminary paper.

## 4    Scalability

The number of unknown in a scheduling problem is of the order of the number of statements times the mean depth of loop nests. The number of dependences is in general quadratic in the program size, and the number of constraints per dependences is again proportional to the mean nesting depth. Lastly, the Simplex algorithm, while exponential in the worst case, has a high probability of being cubic in the number of unknowns or constraints, when these two numbers are of the same order of magnitude. Hence, the direct solution of the scheduling constraints by linear programming does not scale well.

### 4.1    Stepwise Scheduling

To go further, one has to observe that the constraint matrix is sparse, or, rather, block sparse: see (4). If one compress each block $M_{ST}$ or $N_{ST}$ to a single cell, one gets the incidence matrix of the dependence graph.

If the scheduling problem is solved by a variant of the simplex algorithm, one cannot make use of this sparsity to speed up the resolution: the simplex has *fillup*. The solution is to use projection algorithms. The projection of a set $D$ in $\mathbb{R}^{n+1}$ along its first dimension is:

$$\text{Proj}(D, y) = \{x \mid \exists y : y.x \in D\}. \tag{5}$$

It is well known that if $D$ is a polyhedron, so is $\text{Proj}(D, y)$. For polyhedra, there are several projection algorithms:

- The simplest one is the Fourier-Motzkin algorithm. Its complexity is super exponential. Part of this complexity is due to the fact that the resulting system of constraints contains many redundant inequalities.
- One can also use parametric linear programming as in PIP [11]. The complexity is less, but the result still has many redundancies.
- Lastly, if one knows the Minkowski representation of $D$, it is easy to find the Minkowski representation of its projection. From that, one can reconstruct an irredundant constraint system with the Chernikova algorithm.

The last solution is probably the best one, especially since there exists an efficient implementation [12]. However, for the preliminary experiments that are reported here, I have used the Fourier-Motzkin algorithm coupled to a naive redundancy elimination method.

Whatever the projection algorithm, once the final feasibility test has succeeded, one can reconstruct values for the eliminated variables by back-propagation. This suggest the use of the following algorithm:

- For each statement $S$:
  - Collect all the rows of the constraint matrix where $h_S$ has a non-zero coefficient.
  - Eliminate $h_S$.
  - Remember the bounds for $h_S$.
- If the resulting system is trivially unfeasible (like $-1 \geq 0$) stop. No schedule exists.
- For each statement $S$ in reverse order:
  - The bounds for $h_S$ are constants. Select a value within the bounds for $h_S$ (e.g. the lower bound).
  - Substitute these values in all other bounds.

Experience with a limited set of programs shows that while this technique does not reduce much the number of constraints, the number of unknown at each elimination step decreases sharply, which is a big improvement since the Fourier-Motzkin algorithm is super exponential in the number of unknowns.

The order in which statements are eliminated is obviously important for the scalability of the algorithm. One may devise many heuristics for selecting the next victim: select for instance the statement with lowest degree in the dependence graph. Systematic evaluation of this and others heuristics is left for future work.

## 5   Modularity

In language and compiler design, the standard definition of a module is "a part of a program which can be *partially* compiled without reference to other parts". Traditionally, the result of partial compilation is called an *object*. When all modules have been compiled, another processor, the *linker*, is needed to finish the construction of the program. Modularity has many advantages. Modules promote reuse and increases the readability of programs. Also, in case of a modification, one recompile only the affected module(s). As we have seen earlier, the natural unit of compilation for a parallel program is the *process*.

### 5.1   Channel Schedules

Going back to the scheduling constraints (1), one can see that processes are not independent, as there will be relations between the schedules of the writer and the readers of each channel. This does not allow modular scheduling. The solution is to provide some "insulation" between processes.

Observe that each cell in a channel $A$ is written only once at a definite time by statements from only one process. Therefore, one can postulate the existence of a channel schedule $\theta(\langle A, x \rangle)$ such that the value $A[x]$ is guaranteed to be available at time $\theta(\langle A, x \rangle)$ (and later). For simplicity, I will assume that $\theta$ is affine. There is a loss of generality here, but I believe it is not important for most programs and can be easily corrected in other cases.

With this definition, a channel dependence can be split in two parts:

- On the write side, a cell is not available before it has been written. Let $S : A[\omega_A(x)] := \cdots$ be a statement that writes into $A$:

$$\theta(\langle A, \omega(x) \rangle) \geq \theta(\langle S, x \rangle) + 1 \qquad (6)$$

- On the other side, a cell cannot be read before it is available. Let $R : \cdots :=$ $\cdots A[\rho_A(x)] \cdots$ be a statement that read $A$:

$$\theta(R, x) \geq \theta(\langle A, \rho_A(x) \rangle). \qquad (7)$$

The 1 in formula (6) is intended to represent a propagation delay through the channel. I have arbitrarily inserted this delay on the write side, but many other configurations can be used without changing the overall method.

## 5.2   The Modular Algorithm

Let $h_P$ be the concatenation of the timing vectors for all statements in process $P$, and let $h_A$ be the timing vector for array $A$. After application of the Farkas algorithm to (6) or (7) and elimination of the Farkas multipliers, the shape of the constraint matrix is as follows.

For each process $P$ there is a system $U_P h_P \geq 0$ which represents the constraints generated by the inner dependences in $P$. The matrix $U_P$ is block sparse, and each of its blocks is one of the $M_S$ or $N_S$ blocks in formula (4). For each process $P$ and each channel $A$ which is connected to $P$ there is a system $V_{AP} h_P + W_{AP} h_A \geq 0$ which represents the constraints generated by the communication dependences of the system. These observations suggest the following modular scheduling algorithm.

1. Construct the constraint matrix for each process and its adjacent channels.
2. For each process $P$ eliminate $h_P$ from the constraints:

$$U_P h_P \geq 0, \ V_{PA} h_P + W_{PA} h_A \geq 0, \ \text{for all } A \text{ connected to } P \qquad (8)$$

This first pass of compilation is modular, in so far as this can be done one process at a time, without reference to other processes. The result is a system of constraints on channel schedules.

3. When all such *communication constraints* have been computed (or collected from a repository), they can be solved as a whole, giving a solution for the channel schedules. Again, the communication constraints matrix is block-isomorphic to the communication graph of the whole system, and has a high probability of being sparse. This is the only place where the system has to be considered *in toto*.

4. The solution for the channel schedules can then be substituted in the bounds for the coefficients of the schedules, and these coefficients can be recovered by back-substitution.
5. It remains to gather all schedules and submit them to a code generator. With present day tools [3], there is no hope of staying modular there, unless one deals with highly specialized architectures. However, tools like CLooG are quite efficient and can handle very large programs.

Consider the example of Sect. 2.2. The first step is to compile the two processes. Let:

$$\theta(\langle W, i \rangle) = \alpha i, \ \theta(\langle Z \rangle) = \beta, \ \theta(\langle R, i \rangle) = \gamma i + \delta, \ \theta(\langle A, x \rangle) = \epsilon x + \phi.$$

The producer has no data dependence, hence the only constraint is a communication constraint:

$$i \geq 0 \Rightarrow \epsilon i + \phi \geq \alpha i + 1.$$

Application of the Farkas algorithm gives $\phi \geq 1$ and $\epsilon \geq \alpha$ after elimination of the multipliers. After elimination of $\alpha$, the only remaining constraint is $\phi \geq 1$.

In the consumer there is a flow dependence from $Z$ to $R$, which gives $\delta \geq \beta+1$, and a flow dependence from $R$ to itself, which gives $\gamma \geq 1$. Lastly, there is a communication dependence from $A$ to $R$ which entails $\phi \leq \delta$ and $\epsilon \leq \gamma$. The next step is the elimination of $\beta, \gamma$ and $\delta$ from the system of constraints:

$$\delta - \beta - 1 \geq 0, \ \gamma \geq 1, \ \phi - \delta \geq 0, \ \gamma - \epsilon.$$

The resulting system is empty. The only communication constraint is $\phi \geq 1$ whose smallest solution is $\phi = 1$. From there, one may reconstruct the schedules:

$$\theta(\langle W, i \rangle) = 0, \ \theta(\langle Z \rangle) = 0, \ \theta(\langle R, i \rangle) = i + 1, \ \theta(\langle A, x \rangle) = 1.$$

This solution is not satisfactory, since one has to deposit an infinite number of values in $A$ in one clock cycle. An easy way out is to slow down the producer by introducing a dependence:

```
C:   t = f(i);
W:   A[i] = t;
```

The schedules become:

$$\theta(\langle C, i \rangle) = 2i, \ \theta(\langle Z \rangle) = 0, \ \theta(\langle W, i \rangle) = 2i + 1, \ \theta(\langle A, x \rangle) = 2i + 2, \ \theta(\langle R, i \rangle) = 2i + 2.$$

Notice that it was not necessary to recompile the consumer. These schedules correspond to a VLIW program whose kernel is:

| clock cycle | C | W | R |
|:-----------:|:-:|:-:|:-:|
| even | * | | * |
| odd | | * | |

# 6    Related Work

While the literature on automatic parallelization is enormous, and the literature on scheduling is only slightly smaller, the problems of modular parallelization and of modular scheduling have not been extensively considered by the academic community, let alone industry.

In [13], the unit of modularity is the procedure, whose effect is summarized by computing *regions*. The drawback of this method is that one can find parallelism between procedure calls, and also inside procedures, but not parallelism that requires a transformation involving both a procedure and its calling context.

Nearer to the subject of this paper, Risset and Quinton [14] have defined structured scheduling for *systems* in the ALPHA specification language [15]. Systems can be scheduled independently. The schedules of several systems are then composed to give the global schedule. This is possible only if somewhat stringent restrictions are imposed on systems.

The use of processes in parallel programming dates back to the commencement of the subject. Kahn Process Networks [4] have been a source of inspiration for the present paper. The main difference is that in KPN, there are no constraints on the definition of each process – which may not be a program in the usual sense – hence their *a priori* analysis and compilation is almost impossible. This results in the present situation, where KPN are only used for simulation or even direct execution. In contrast, CRP systems can be checked statically or compiled into synchronous programs.

# 7    Conclusion and Future Work

This paper is very preliminary and many problems have to be solved if this proposal is to become a practical solution for the design of embedded systems. Let me quote some of them.

In the above description, there is nothing to bound the size of a channel. One needs a way of constructing schedules under the additional constraint that each channel uses no more than a given amount of memory. Let us note that the inverse problem (finding the amount of memory needed to support a given schedule) has been the subject of much research and that good solutions are known [16, 17].

For complexity reasons, as soon as resources are in a fixed finite amount, the restriction to affine schedules is no longer tenable. One has to use *many-dimensional schedules*. While there are methods for constructing such schedules [9], building their modular extension is by no means obvious.

Many problems in, e.g., image processing, are outside the regular (or polytope) model. One may sometime obviate this difficulty by overestimating dependences, or by encapsulating the irregular program parts, or by asking for help from the programmer. There is much work to be done in this direction.

# References

1. Ancourt, C., Irigoin, F.: Scanning polyhedra with DO loops. In: Proc. third SIG-PLAN Symp. on Principles and Practice of Parallel Programming, ACM Press (1991) 39–50
2. Quilleré, F., Rajopadhye, S., Wilde, D.: Generation of Efficient Nested Loops from Polyhedra. International Journal of Parallel Programming **28** (2000) 469–498
3. Bastoul, C.: Efficient code generation for automatic parallelization and optimization. In: ISPDC'03 IEEE International Symposium on Parallel and Distributed Computing. (2003) to appear, http://www.prism.uvsq.fr/users/cedb/.
4. Kahn, G.: The semantics of a simple language for parallel programming. In Holland, N., ed.: IFIP'94. (1974) 471–475
5. Hoare, C.A.R.: Communicating sequential processes. Communications of the ACM **21** (1978)
6. Feautrier, P.: Some efficient solutions to the affine scheduling problem, I, one dimensional time. Int. J. of Parallel Programming **21** (1992) 313–348
7. Bernstein, A.J.: Analysis of programs for parallel processing. IEEE Trans. on El. Computers **EC-15** (1966)
8. Schrijver, A.: Theory of linear and integer programming. Wiley, NewYork (1986)
9. Feautrier, P.: Some efficient solutions to the affine scheduling problem, II, multi-dimensional time. Int. J. of Parallel Programming **21** (1992) 389–420
10. Quinton, P.: The systematic design of systolic arrays. In Fogelman, F., Robert, Y., Tschuente, M., eds.: Automata networks in Computer Science, Manchester University Press (1987) 229–260
11. Feautrier, P.: Semantical analysis and mathematical programming; application to parallelization and vectorization. In Cosnard, M., Robert, Y., Quinton, P., Raynal, M., eds.: Workshop on Parallel and Distributed Algorithms, Bonas, North Holland (1989) 309–320
12. Wilde, D.: A library for doing polyhedral operations. Technical Report 785, Irisa, Rennes, France (1993)
13. Triolet, R., Irigoin, F., Feautrier, P.: Automatic parallelization of FORTRAN programs in the presence of procedure calls. In Robinet, B., Wilhelm, R., eds.: ESOP 1986, LNCS 213, Springer-Verlag (1986)
14. Quinton, P., Risset, T.: Structured scheduling of recurrence equations: Theory and practice. In: Proc. of the System Architecture MOdelling and Simulation Workshop. Lecture Notes in Computer Science, 2268, Samos, Greece, Springer Verlag (2001)
15. Leverge, H., Mauras, C., Quinton, P.: The ALPHA language and its use for the design of systolic arrays. Journal of VLSI Signal Processing **3** (1991) 173–182
16. Lefebvre, V., Feautrier, P.: Optimizing storage size for static control programs in automatic parallelizers. In Lengauer, C., Griebl, M., Gorlatch, S., eds.: Europar'97. Volume 1300 of LNCS., Springer (1997) 356–363
17. Darte, A., Schreiber, R., Villard, G.: Lattice-based memory allocation. In: 6th ACM International Conference on Compilers, Architectures and Synthesis for Embedded Systems (CASES 2003). (2003)

# Early ISS Integration into Network-on-Chip Designs

Andreas Wieferink[1], Malte Doerper[1], Tim Kogel[2],
Rainer Leupers[1], Gerd Ascheid[1], and Heinrich Meyr[1]

[1] Institute for Integrated Signal Processing Systems,
Aachen University of Technology, Germany
wieferink@iss.rwth-aachen.de
http://www.iss.rwth-aachen.de
[2] CoWare, Inc.
tim.kogel@coware.com
http://www.coware.com

**Abstract.** Future signal processing SoC designs will contain an increasing number of heterogeneous programmable units combined with a complex communication architecture to meet flexibility, performance and cost constraints. Designing such a heterogeneous MP-SoC architecture bears enormous potential for optimization, but requires a system-level design environment and methodology to evaluate architectural alternatives effectively.

Recently, efficient tool frameworks have been proposed to support the design space exploration for large scale embedded systems. The technique presented in this paper allows integrating retargeteable Instruction Set Simulators (ISS) into such an exploration framework very early in the design flow.

In a dual-processor JPEG decoding case study, we illustrate the effectiveness of this approach.

## 1   Introduction

The ever increasing System-on-Chip (SoC) complexity along with the ever shrinking time-to-market constraints pose enormous challenges to conceptualize, implement, verify and program today's SoCs. The traditional flow to directly implement the hardware on Register-Transfer-Level (RTL) after having a textual architecture specification available does not work for these complex embedded systems any more.

Thus, several flows have been suggested which close the gap between the un-timed architecture specification and the RTL implementation by inserting suitable design steps in between. These are based on architectural models having an abstraction level higher than RTL. Their modeling effort as well as simulation performance is multiple orders of magnitude superior. This allows real design space exploration since iteration cycles are very efficient, compared to the expensive redesign costs and turnaround cycles on RT-Level.

For both domains, the system modules themselves as well as the communication between these modules, efficient abstract modeling techniques have been introduced. In table Fig. 1, these abstraction levels are classified.

For the inter-module communication, all levels higher than RTL are covered by the new Transaction-Level-Modeling (TLM) paradigm [1]. They have in common that the

A. Pimentel and S. Vassiliadis (Eds.): SAMOS 2004, LNCS 3133, pp. 443–452, 2004.

| communication accuracy | data accuracy | timing accuracy | software accuracy |
|---|---|---|---|
| TLM | packets | un-timed | functional specification |
| | | timed | performance model |
| | bytes/ words | transaction | instr. accurate ISS |
| | | transfer | cycle accurate ISS |
| RTL | bit-vectors | cycle | HDL processor model |

**Fig. 1.** Modeling Abstraction Levels

pin wiggling on the interfaces is not modeled in detail any more, but is replaced by condensed Interface Method Calls (IMC). A distinction within this large TLM abstraction level can be done with respect to the accuracy of data and timing. *Bytes/words accurate* TLM can achieve a significant performance gain against RTL without sacrificing cycle accuracy when modeling at *transfer* timing level. *Packet level* TLM, in contrast, obtains further large gains in simulation efficiency especially by modeling a whole burst of data transfers as one single communication event.

Also the system modules can be modeled on a variety of abstraction levels. Due to rising flexibility constraints, silicon area is more and more filled by programmable SoC modules, especially by the relatively power efficient Application Specific Instruction set Processors (ASIPs). Also software running on a processor can be modeled more efficiently above RTL. This can either be done applying an Instruction Set Simulator (ISS), which actually can simulate execution of the final application software, or it can be modeled with an abstract module which just uses annotated execution delay estimations or does not contain timing at all.

It can be observed that the communication accuracy on the *timed packet* TLM abstraction level is very good [2]. But the *performance model* for the abstract processor modules normally applied on this level cannot deliver reliable information. CPU load, impact of the RTOS, SW response time and the on-chip communication traffic shape as caused by the instruction caches can hardly be analyzed without an ISS.

Thus, we present the integration of fast instruction accurate ISSs already into a *packet level* system simulation framework to combine its advantages of high simulation speed and efficient design exploration capabilities with the accuracy of an ISS.

The following section presents related work in system level design. In section 3, the system exploration framework this work is based on is summarized. Section 4 then more detailed motivates the need for the early ISS integration. The advantages of the ISS availability for meaningful design space exploration is then presented in section 5. Next, a dual-processor case study is presented in section 6. Finally, section 7 concludes this work.

## 2   Related Work

Heavy research on all abstraction levels between functional specification and RTL is currently done to cope with the ever increasing SoC complexity problem. The research on the packet level TLM abstraction level is addressing efficient and fast design space exploration for huge SoCs. Various system level design frameworks are proposed addressing design space exploration for partitioning and mapping [3, 4] as well as conceptualization and performance analysis [5]. This work is based on [5] because of its high flexibility and modularity. Basically, any of these system level design frameworks could be extended with retargeteable ISSs.

Traditionally, mixed HW/SW systems are not integrated and co-simulated before the RTL abstraction level is reached [6]. But the low simulation speed and the time consuming modeling on this detailed level prohibits architectural exploration and embedded software development.

Thus it is desirable to have accurate software models already on higher abstraction levels. Recently, efforts have been done to integrate Instruction Set Simulators already on bytes/words accurate TLM level [7–9]. In this paper, fast instruction accurate processor simulators have even been coupled into a packet level simulation framework to very early take advantage of the high ISS accuracy.

By integrating ISSs automatically generated by the retargeteable LISA processor design platform [10], this approach is very generic. It allows the system designer either to integrate processors purchased or reused as IP, alternatively he also could conceptualize an own optimally tailored ASIP for the respective task. In principle, another retargeteable processor exploration framework like ISDL [11], EXPRESSION [12], nML [13], MIMOLA [14] could also have been chosen. We selected the LISA [10] platform because of its powerful simulators as well as due to its support for C compiler generation [15] and for full RTL generation.

## 3   NoC Exploration Framework

An important design challenge in the exploration process is to find an optimal mapping of processing elements to a complex communication architecture. This disciplined exploration of different communication architectures has recently been subsumed under the Network-on-Chip (NoC) design paradigm.

The NoC exploration framework applied here [5] is implemented on top of the SystemC library [16]. The application's functionality is captured by system modules, which communicate to each other by exchanging data packets (Fig. 2). Master modules like processor cores actively initiate transactions, while slave modules, e.g. memories, can only react passively. All communication between these functional modules is encapsulated by the NoC channel module. The actual communication topology can be easily configured by selecting the respective network engine and parameterizing it accordingly (e.g., for AMBA AHB or STBus). These network engines determine the latency and throughput during simulation according to the selected network type (point-to-point, bus, crossbar, etc).

## 4   Early ISS Integration

In the system level NoC exploration framework, data exchange is modeled on the high abstraction level of packet transfers. This temporal and data abstraction is one of the key techniques to enable the high system level simulation performance. As shown in

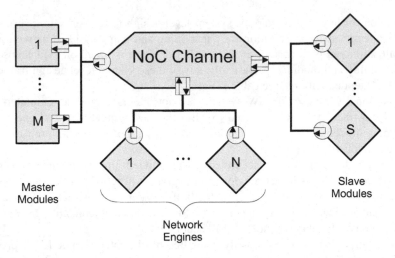

**Fig. 2.** NoC Channel Overview

several case studies [17, 5], it is beneficial to model a burst transfer as one single event, neglecting ever-recurring low-level implementation details. This is straight forward for the data communication as occurring in networking applications. Here, one data burst contains functionally associated data, e.g. the Route Lookup (RLU) information for an IP packet. In case of applications with higher data locality than networking, data caches can drastically reduce access latencies, and they introduce a packet oriented but totally different traffic characteristic on the NoC infrastructure. Thus, modeling the impact of the data caches already leads to a significant accuracy enhancement. For this, the abstract modules have to be equipped with data cache models; they do not need to be replaced completely yet for this issue.

But in the final SoC design, processor cores mostly execute the master module functionality to meet flexibility constraints. Especially in case of complex, MMU and cache equipped processors like the MIPS32 core, the program code also needs to be transferred over the NoC if (and only if) a program cache miss occurs. The cache behavior highly affects the performance of the processor, and it can have high influence on the network traffic and thus on the performance of the remaining modules. Even more, the impact of the processor architecture itself, e.g. if it is a VLIW processor or an optimally tailored ASIP, and the impact of the RTOS on the software execution time can hardly be estimated on the very high abstraction level. These issues make it nearly impossible to annotate accurate timing budgets to the master modules.

Thus, we propose very early ISS integration into the system level NoC platform. After the system architect has excluded lots of architectural alternatives, he needs a more detailed model for further design decisions. For example, is it sufficient to integrate a Common-Of-The-Shelf (COTS) processor or is it necessary to optimally tailor an own ASIP. When replacing the abstract functional module with a processor simulator, one can exploit the accurate NoC framework capabilities efficiently especially for cached data transfers. A data packet then has the granularity of a cache line.

Recent developments in Design Automation more and more ease the task of migrating from an abstract master module model to software running on an ISS. When using a processor design environment like LISA [10], an initial customized instruction accurate processor model is available within a few man weeks. Applying the LISATek Processor Designer tools [18], a processor simulator, an assembler, a linker, and with some amount of additional manual specification even a C compiler can be generated automatically for the specified architecture [15]. This allows compiling (or recoding) the application code for the target architecture already now, which enables profiling and verifying the final software very early.

Alternatively, already existing LISA processor models could be integrated easily into the NoC framework to explore on this high abstraction level if the efficiency and computational power of these purchased or own IP blocks is suitable for the respective task.

So far, integrating LISA processors into their system context was earliest possible when a *bytes/words accurate* TLM model of the bus is available [9]. The technique presented in this paper allows coupling ISS directly into the abstract NoC simulation framework. All profiling, statistics and debugging capabilities provided by the NoC exploration framework is used for analyzing the cache traffic characteristics and optimizing the overall system architecture.

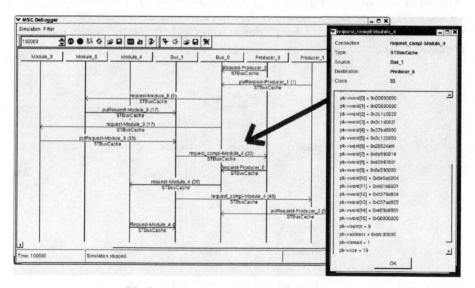

**Fig. 3.** NoC as observed by the MSC debugger

## 5  NoC Design Space Exploration

Having integrated the LISA processor models into the NoC simulation framework, its design exploration capabilities can again be used to also deeply analyze the processor related issues in system context. This section illustrates the debugging and profiling capabilities of the NoC simulation framework.

## 5.1  Debugging

In Fig. 3, a dual processor STBus system is observed in a Message Sequence Chart
(MSC) diagram. Every system module is displayed as a vertical line, and every packet
transfer appears as an horizontal arrow with the time stamp annotated in brackets. In
the simulation shown here, the program caches of both processors (Producer_0 and
Producer_1), of course, have a cache miss at system startup. The memory requests are
put over a shared symmetric STBus model (Bus_0 for requests and Bus_1 for responses)
to the respective memory modules (Module_x). The contents of every packet can be
displayed by clicking onto the corresponding communication arrow. In Fig. 3, the first
cache line returned to Producer_0 is shown.

Powerful filtering mechanisms in the MSC debugger together with the LISATek
multiprocessor debugger front-end [19] assist the system architect in detecting bugs
and deadlocks as soon as possible.

## 5.2  Profiling

As soon as the debugging has succeeded and the timed MP-SoC model is working
correctly, the system designer now can move forward and profile the communication
behavior of the current platform. In Figure 4, an automatically generated traffic graph
for the same dual processor system is shown. Accumulated over the full duration of
the system simulation, the number of packet transfers between the system modules is
displayed as weighted arrows.

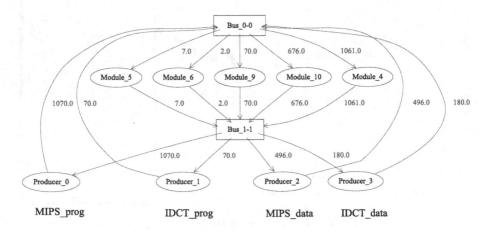

**Fig. 4.** Traffic graph generated by the NoC environment

There are several other visualizations available, for example buffer fill state his-
tograms, to further assist the designer in detecting bottlenecks. Together with the processor profiling capabilities of the LISATek tools, the user gets valuable hints to improve
the overall system performance early in the design flow.

# 6  Dual-Processor JPEG Case Study

The outlined early ISS integration has been applied on a dual-processor system optimized for decoding JPEG images. This section first describes the target application, as
well as the development of the final SoC topology. Then, the simulation accuracy of the
NoC framework is compared to the cycle accurate TLM reference.

## 6.1  JPEG Decryption System

The considered application is a JPEG-2000 decompression algorithm decoding a
150x100 sized bitmap. Both the C original source code of the algorithm and the sample bitmap are freely available from the JPEG group's web page [20]. We modified
the code to run it jointly on two processor cores: First, a specially designed IDCTcore
coprocessor for calculating the inverse discrete cosines transformation (idct), which is
the algorithmic core of JPEG decryption. Second, a MIPS32 processor core performs
the remaining, i.e., the control and file I/O tasks. Both processors share a common data
memory, and each of them accesses a personal program memory.

The bus topologies and cache topologies that have been explored are depicted in
Fig. 5 and Fig. 6, respectively.

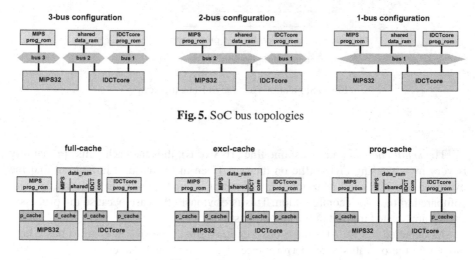

**Fig. 5.** SoC bus topologies

**Fig. 6.** SoC cache topologies

## 6.2  Simulation Accuracy

In Fig. 7, for different cache configurations the number of cycles consumed to decode
the given bitmap is shown. In the *full-cache* system configuration, cache consistency
is ensured easily by flushing and invalidating the data cache after a processor's task
is performed. The *excl-cache* configuration avoids this problem by only caching memory regions exclusive to one processor. The synchronization of the two processors is
interrupt-based.

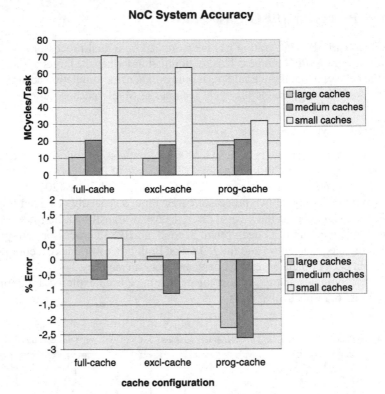

**Fig. 7.** Simulation Accuracy (1-bus topology)

The *small caches* contain just one line (16 words), thus the cache miss probability is very high, causing high traffic on the bus. Even in this case, it turned out that the overhead of a 2-bus and 3-bus topology does not obtain a significant performance gain compared to the 1-bus configuration. This is obviously the case because the processor caches are located in front of the system bus(es).

As depicted in Fig. 7 for the 1-bus topology, the cache size in contrast has a high impact on the overall system performance. The difference between *small caches* and *large caches* is up to a factor of 7, the program cache size impact alone still leads to a factor of two. These factors would even be higher for slower memories behind the AMBA bus. The program cache size is an example for a property which is very difficult to annotate to an abstract processor module.

We compared the cycle counts against a reference system with the same ISSs, but connected to CoWare TLM AMBA AHB bus models [21]. In any of the system configurations, the estimation error introduced by the packet level NoC bus models is lower than 3 %. This is due to the fact that the currently deployed generic bus model of the NoC simulation framework does not yet take all AMBA AHB pipeline effects into account.

# 7   Conclusion

Integrating LISA processors into abstract NoC exploration frameworks combines the high accuracy of ISSs for the processor modules with the flexibility and simulation speed of the NoC simulation framework for the communication modeling. A seamless design flow is obtained by smoothly stepping forward from full abstract simulation to the cycle true TLM world, initially reusing the NoC communication models.

# References

1. T. Grötker, S. Liao, G. Martin, S. Swan. *System Design with SystemC*. Kluwer Academic Publishers, 2002.
2. Ariyamparambath, M. and Bussagila, D. and Reinkemeier, B. et al. A Highly Efficient Modeling Style for Heterogeneous Bus Architectures. In *International Symposium on System-on-Chip*, Tampere (Finland), Nov 2003.
3. Vladimir D. Zivkovic, Ed Deprettere, Erwin de Kock, Pieter v. d. Wolf. Fast and Accurate Multiprocessor Architecture Exploration with Symbolic Programs. In *Proc. Int. Conf. on Design, Automation and Test in Europe(DATE)"*, 2003.
4. D. Gajski, J. Zhu, R. Dömer, A.Gerstlauer, S. Zhao. SpecC: Specification Language and Methodology. In *Kluwer Academic Publishers*, 2000.
5. T. Kogel, M. Doerper, A. Wieferink et al. A Modular Simulation Framework for Architectural Exploration of On-Chip Interconnection Networks. In *The First IEEE/ACM/IFIP International Conference on HW/SW Codesign and System Synthesis*, Newport Beach (California USA), Oct 2003.
6. J. Notbauer, T. Albrecht, G. Niedrist,S. Rohringer. Verification and management of a multimillion-gate embedded core design. In *DAC*, 1999.
7. P. Paulin P. Magarshack. System-on-chip beyond the nanometer wall. In *DAC*, 2003.
8. W. Cesario, A. Baghdadi, L. Gauthier et al. Component-Based Design Approach for Multicore SoCs. In *DAC*, 2002.
9. A. Wieferink, T. Kogel, G. Braun et al. A System Level Processor/Communication Co-Exploration Methodology for Multi-Processor System-on-Chip Platforms. In *Proceedings of the Conference on Design, Automation & Test in Europe (DATE)*, Paris, France, Feb 2004.
10. A. Hoffmann, T. Kogel, A. Nohl et al. A Novel Methodology for the Design of Application Specific Instruction-Set Processor Using a Machine Description Language. In *IEEE Transactions on Computer-Aided Design of Integrated Cicuits and Systems (TCAD) vol. 20 no. 11*, pages 1338–1354. IEEE, Nov 2001.
11. G. Hadjiyiannis, S. Devadas. Techniques for Accurate Performance Evaluation in Architecture Exploration. *IEEE Transactions on Very Large Scale Integration (VLSI) Systems*, 2003.
12. P. Mishra, P. Grun, N. Dutt, and A. Nicolau. Processor-memory co-exploration driven by an architectural description language. In *Intl. Conf. on VLSI Design*, 2001.
13. A. Fauth and J. Van Praet and M. Freericks. Describing Instruction Set Processors Using nML. In *Proceedings of the European Design & Test Conference*, Mar. 1995.
14. R. Leupers. HDL-based Modeling of Embedded Processor Behavior for Retargetable Compilation. In *Proc. Int. Symp. on System Synthesis*, Sep. 1998.
15. M. Hohenauer, H. Scharwaechter, K. Karuri et al. A Methodology and Tool Suite for C Compiler Generation from ADL Processor Models. In *Proceedings of the Conference on Design, Automation & Test in Europe (DATE)*, Paris, France, Feb 2004.
16. SystemC initiative. *http://www.systemc.org*.

17. T. Kogel, A. Wieferink, R. Leupers et al. Virtual Architecture Mapping: A SystemC based Methodology for Architectural Exploration of System-on-Chip Designs. In *Int.Workshop on Systems, Architecturs, Modeling and Simulation (SAMOS)*, Samos (Greece), July 2003.
18. LISATek Product Line. *CoWare, http://www.coware.com.*
19. Wieferink, A. and Kogel, T. and Nohl, A. et al. A Generic Toolset for SoC Multiprocessor Debugging and Synchronisation. In *IEEE International Conference on Application-Specific Systems, Architectures and Processors (ASAP)*, The Hague (Netherlands), June 2003.
20. Official JPEG homepage. *http://www.jpeg.org.*
21. ConvergenSC. *CoWare, http://www.coware.com.*

# Cycle Accurate Simulation Model Generation for SoC Prototyping

Antoine Fraboulet[1], Tanguy Risset[2], and Antoine Scherrer[2]
(Lip, ENS-Lyon, Citi, Insa-Lyon, Inria, UCBL, CNRS, EPML Soclib*)

[1] Citi, Insa-Lyon, 21 av. Jean Capelle, 69621 Villeurbanne Cedex
antoine.fraboulet@insa-lyon.fr
[2] LIP, ENS Lyon, 46 allée d'Italie, 69364 Lyon Cedex 07
{tanguy.risset,antoine.scherrer}@ens-lyon.fr

**Abstract.** We present new results concerning the integration of high level designed IPs into a complete System on Chip. We first introduce a new computation model that can be used for cycle accurate simulation of register transfer level synthesized hardware. Then we provide simulation of a SoC integrating a data-flow IP synthesized with MMAlpha and the SocLib cycle accurate simulation environment. This integration also validates an efficient generic interface mechanism for data-flow IPs.

## 1 Introduction

With the advent of multi-processors system on chip (MPSOC), fast cycle accurate hardware simulation is a major issue in the design process. Because most hardware design projects now include a significant software part, the simulation time increases a lot when it becomes precise enough to model highly unpredictable mechanisms such as cache misses or bus/network contentions. In addition the ideal design scheme where one could easily re-use IPs designed elsewhere, as it is naturally done in software development, is far from today's habits mainly because of the lack of standardization of communication protocols between IPs.

The SocLib[1] initiative proposes some advances in the resolution of these problems. First it proposes to write simulation models of IPs using SystemC with precise rules at various level of refinement: *Transaction Level Modeling* (TLM) for software-like prototyping and *Cycle Accurate, Bit Accurate Modeling* (CABA) for a cycle accurate simulation of the IP. Then, it proposes to use VCI (Virtual Component Interface [1]) communication low level protocol to interface easily various IP. Finally it suggests a certain programming style that enables the possibility of writing very efficient simulation engines (closer to step by step simulation than to event driven simulation [2]).

---

* The authors would like to thank members of the Asim group in LIP6 Lab. for many fruitful discussion as well as for the production of many simulation models and tools used in this paper.
[1] http://soclib.lip6.fr/

A. Pimentel and S. Vassiliadis (Eds.): SAMOS 2004, LNCS 3133, pp. 453–462, 2004.

During the design of a MPSOC, some IPs are re-used (processors, memories, DMA, etc.) but some (usually few of them) must be designed specifically for the application targeted. The design of these new IPs and the integration in the global system must be fast to prototype rapidly the whole application. For many years now, people have been working on *high level synthesis* to reduce the time, effort and potential errors due to manual design of hardware. These research have lead to prototypes and industrial tools that perform this *semi-automatic* design of hardware from high level (functional or behavioral) specifications. One can check the following academic tools: MMAlpha [3], Gaut [4], Paro [5], Compaan [6], Hugh [7] and the industrial initiatives: Pico [8] (Synfora, spin off from HP), CriticalBlue [9] and probably many more to come. Most of these tools address specific target circuits to reduce the search space during refinement, many of them target data-flow computations (sometimes referred to as *stream processing*) widely used in signal processing applications. This is the case for MMAlpha that is used in this work to generate highly parallel hardware accelerators for signal processing filters. It is important to notice that the *de facto* failure of general high level synthesis tools such as *behavioral compiler* from Synopsys highlighted the fact that high level synthesis was intrinsically difficult to achieve and that the long research effort provided to produce the tools mentioned above was justified.

However, most of these tools are now faced to the problem of integrating their IPs in MPSOC simulation and synthesis environments. The two most important problems encountered as soon as integration is envisaged are:

1. The choice of a communication protocol that provides data to the IP. This choice is driven by many factor: the simplicity of the protocol, the size and power of the hardware necessary for it and its impact on the performance of the global system.
2. The generation of a simulation model for the hardware synthesized which is compatible with the simulation platform used.

This paper explains which solutions were chosen for the MMAlpha tool and it also extracts some underlying generic solutions that can be re-used for other tools. More precisely, we propose a new target computation model for the translation from classical structural RTL representation of hardware to finite state machine representation. We also present an efficient algorithm for performing the translation. This algorithm has been used for CABA simulation model generation from MMAlpha. The generated simulation model have been integrated into a simple SoC composed of a MIPS R3000 processor, a standard RAM, a generic interconnect and a hardware accelerator generated with MMAlpha. This platform runs a simple signal processing program filtering audio files. Apart from the validation of the above mentioned computation model, this experiment was used to validate the SocLib approach and the use of a generic interface scheme for connecting external IPs generated by high level design tools in such a framework.

In section 2 we introduce the new computation model that we would like to promote for high level design tools. In Section 3 we present the SoC simulation performed using SocLib and MMAlpha. we have improve the interface mechanism between that hardware and software that was presented in [10] so that it can be reused for any data-flow IP in the SoC platform, simulation results concerning the whole SoC platform are presented there too.

## 2  FSM Representation for RTL Simulation Models

Now that high level synthesis tools are gaining importance, the question is raised of how to generate efficient simulations models from internal representation of the tools which usually corresponds to *classical* RTL representation. In this generation process, a crucial issue is the efficiency of the CABA simulation. The community now widely agree that finite state machine (FSM) is a good computation model for simulation because it can be easily understood by designers and it can be efficiently simulated. Following initial ideas of Jennings [11], many works have focussed on the problem of improving MPSOC simulation performances by reducing the inefficiency introduced by event driven simulation. In particular, the results of [2] state that if the FSM is represented in the form of Moore-Mealy machine, the simulation kernel can produce much more efficient simulations.

A moore-mealy machine is an automaton with an internal state and three functions: the `transition` function, the `moore` function and the `mealy` function. The standard definition of these functions is the following: the `transition` function uses the inputs and the current internal state to update the internal state. The `moore` function uses the internal state to provide outputs and the `mealy` function uses the inputs and the internal state to produce output (see the left of figure 2). In hardware component modeling, the internal state is composed of the internal registers of the component and the state is computed at each clock cycle.

This section present a new computation model that improves SystemC code quality and performances when it is used for RTL hardware modeling. A more precise description of this new model can be find in the research report [12].

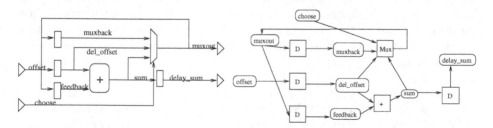

**Fig. 1.** Original Jennings' RTL example and its representation as a RTL graph

### 2.1  A New FSM Model for Hardware Modeling

In [11], Jennings introduced the *directed cyclic bipartite graph*, referred here as the RTL GRAPH, for abstracting RTL descriptions. We use the original Jennings' example in figure 1 to illustrate it (in the following we denote by the *module* the whole hardware component to be abstracted).

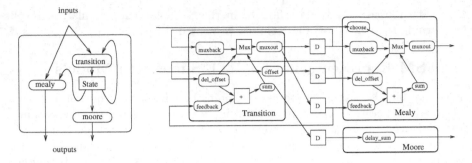

**Fig. 2.** The standard Moore-Mealy machine used for writing CABA simulation models of IPs (on the left) and its application for the hardware of figure 1

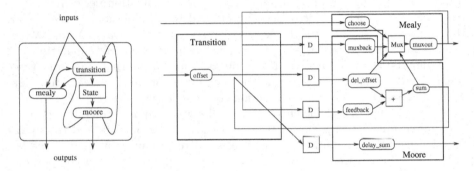

**Fig. 3.** The new machine used for writing CABA simulation models of IPs (on the left) and its application for the hardware of figure 1

Applied on the RTL graph of figure 1, a straightforward algorithm for generating a Moore-Mealy machine will lead to the graph represented on the left of figure 2. The computations that are used in more than one function (here `transition` and `mealy`) are duplicated. Code duplication can be error prone (if the code is modified during the debugging process for instance) and it also implies an increased complexity during simulation because computation will be done twice.

We propose to distribute the computations performed by the hardware in the three FSM functions without duplicating any one. For this we use a slightly modified definition of the three functions: the `moore` function inputs are unchanged, the `mealy` function will take as input some inputs of the module and some outputs of the `moore` function. Both functions `moore` and `mealy` will produced outputs that will be used by the transition function (while in the original definition, the `transition` function used only module inputs and register outputs). This is illustrated on the left of figure 3.

With this target model in mind, a possible FSM for the module of figure 1 would be the one of figure 3 where no code duplication occurs. The construction of this FSM can simply consist of a rewriting of the RTL graph. Indeed, each hardware operator will be present in one and only one of the three functions: transition, moore or mealy. A clever traversal of the RTL graph will label each hardware operator of the graph with the type of function it belongs to (transition, moore or mealy). The nets will be classified too, but they may be duplicated if they are connected to operators of different type (we want the operands and results of an operator to be of the same type, this will ease the translation to a programming language).

The algorithm is *efficient* in the sense that its complexity is linear, assuming that one can have access in a constant time to registers. Indeed, each node of the graph is traversed only once (except for the duplications at the end of the algorithm but we can safely assume that the number of registers is small compared to the total number of nodes of the graph). It is *clever* in the sense that it does not duplicate any computation, hence the resulting simulation model of the hardware will be faster. The complexity of the graph on the right of figure 2 and figure 3 illustrates it.

A more detailed description of the algorithm can be found in [12].

## 2.2   RTL Simulation Experiments with SystemC

In a SystemC implementation of this new FSM machine, we must ensure that the three methods corresponding to mealy, moore and transition functions are evaluated in a valid order. In [12], we explain precisely how it can be ensure in the SystemC framework.

For our experiments we have derived a specific hardware module: a non-pipelined version of the DLMS filter presented in [13, 3]. The RTL version of the architecture has been derived with MMAlpha from the same specification as the one used in [3]. The designer chose not to pipeline the architecture and hence obtained moore and mealy computations in each cell. Moreover, each mealy computations are connected from cell to cell, hence a complex dynamic scheduling occurs at simulation run time. This architecture is composed of N cell with N-2 identical cells.

We generated SystemC code compliant with the model introduced above for this architecture with N=30 and N=60 cells. This gave rise to three type of cell: the first cell of the array, the last cell of the array and the middle cell repeated N-2 times. Each of these SystemC cell where implemented with this new FSM machine convention. Then we took the middle cell and modify it by hand so that it can stick to the classical Moore-Mealy machine. This consisted in duplicating some of the code to use only cell inputs or register outputs in each method. It is worth noting that this represented an increase of 60% of the computations lines and 120% in the number of variables declared in the methods.

These simulation where done with systemC-2.0.1 on linux operating system (processor pentium 4M, 1.4 GHz with 512 Mo ram). C++ Compilation was done with GCC 3.3 without any optimization options. We also did the simulation with the SystemCass simulation kernel [2]. The results are presented in table 1.

These results show an improvement, between 30% and 50%, in the simulation performances obtained by SystemC simulation with the new model compared to

**Table 1.** Simulation performances, in seconds, for a simulation of 100 000 clock cycles

|              | SystemC | | SystemCass | |
|--------------|-----------|-------------|-----------|-------------|
|              | new model | Moore-Mealy | new model | Moore-Mealy |
| Cell         | 0.58      | 0.76        | 0.13      | 0.2         |
| module N=30  | 8.82      | 15.07       | 3.09      | 5.1         |
| module N=60  | 17.56     | 30.63       | 6.14      | 10.34       |

equivalent hardware described as a classical Moore-Mealy machine. Simulation with SystemCass show that our improvement can be added to the simulation acceleration provided by static scheduling techniques. Note that simulation performance of SystemC and SystemCass should not be compared here because SystemCass currently does not implement real bit-true mechanism for handling the sc_int type (int type is used). The simulation time decrease is not huge, but we point out that this is not only the main advantage of our new coding style, it has other advantages: (i) it suppresses code duplication which is error prone, and (ii) it generates simulation models that are closer to final RTL implementation. This property could be used, for instance to derive automatically VHDL RTL models from the corresponding SystemC cycle accurate simulation models.

## 3    SoC Platform Simulation

Choosing the good simulation platform is a crucial issue in MPSOC design because it implies a non-negligible investment for using the environment and developing the simulation models. Commercial tools may offer powerful environment but the lifetime of a tool will frequently be much shorter than the lifetime of an IP. We believe that the open source nature of SystemC[2] is adapted to this kind of constraint. We have used SocLib for setting up the SoC simulation environment and the MMAlpha tool for high level synthesis of dedicated hardware.

The main component of SocLib is currently a set of open source SystemC CABA simulation models for common IPs (MIPS processor, RAM, NoC, busses, DMA,...). The SocLib simulation models use the VCI (Virtual Component Interface [1]) communication low level protocol to interface with other IPs.

In this framework, a MPSOC platform consists of a set of hardware IPs together with some software code running on the programmable IPs (here the MIPS processor), which imply the use of a compiler. We used GCC targeted to MIPS core. As we used a generic network on chip interconnect (and not a standard bus), it is mandatory to provide a simple operating system that ensure correct behavior of the whole system (memory coherency, exception handling, etc.). Hence to be usable, SocLib must be associated to such an operating system compatible with the compiler used. We are currently using Mutek [14] which provides a very light implementation of the Posix threads API.

---

[2]  http://www.systemc.org/

MMAlpha [3] is a toolbox for designing regular parallel architectures (systolic like) from recurrence equation specifications expressed in the Alpha language. It is one of the only existing tools that really automate the refinement of a software specification downto RTL description within the same language: Alpha. MMAlpha's methodology for refinement successively introduces time (global synchronous clock), space (Mapping to 1 or 2-D array of processors), control generation and finally RTL level generation.

We have developed a translator from AlpHard (hardware description language, subset of Alpha) to SystemC, based on the principles explained in section 2. The translator also provides testbench that allow hierarchical debugging and which uses a stimuli file format which is common to the C code generator and the VHDL code generator of MMAlpha.

## 3.1   The SoC Platform

We have chosen a classical linux audio signal processing application called *Gramofile*. Gramofile processes audio files (.wav format) and proposes various simple filters like LP's tick removal. We have extracted a simple filter (referred as `filter.c`), and translated it in Alpha by hand. The translation was validated by replacing the original `filter.c` file by the C code generated from the `filter.alpha` by MMAlpha. Through all the refinement stages of MMAlpha, this C translation can be used to test the validity of the current description.

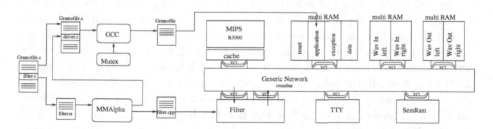

**Fig. 4.** The SoC simulated and the global design methodology. Blank square box represent C++ simulation models of IPs

The target platform chosen and the software design method are represented on figure 4. A single MIPS R3000 processor with its associated data and instruction cache is used. Standard memories are used for storing the program and data, a special memory is used for semaphores. A dedicated component is used for displaying output (referred as TTY). The hardware accelerator performing a filter is generated with MMAlpha. All these components are connected via VCI ports to a simple network. The software running on the MIPS, in addition to bootstrapping information, is composed of the gramofile program cross-compiled with GCC to a MIPS target. In this gramofile program, a specific function (referred as `filter.c`) has been translated in Alpha (MMAlpha input language) in

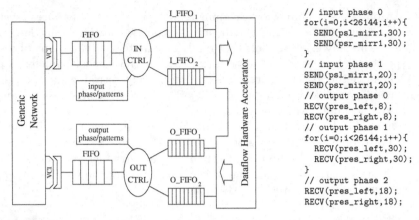

```
// input phase 0
for(i=0;i<26144;i++){
    SEND(psl_mirr1,30);
    SEND(psr_mirr1,30);
}
// input phase 1
SEND(psl_mirr1,20);
SEND(psr_mirr1,20);
// output phase 0
RECV(pres_left,8);
RECV(pres_right,8);
// output phase 1
for(i=0;i<26144;i++){
    RECV(pres_left,30);
    RECV(pres_right,30);
}
// output phase 2
RECV(pres_left,18);
RECV(pres_right,18);
```

**Fig. 5.** Hardware and Software interfaces for MMAlpha data-flow IP. Controllers must be configured according the software communication pattern used in the software driver on the right hand side. Both the hardware and software can be parameterized to allow a maximum throughput using burst communications and/or stream interleaving

order to generate the hardware accelerator IP. During this high level synthesis process, MMAlpha generates a `driver.c` which replaces the `filter.c` function in gramofile and ensures that data are correctly exchanged between the memory and hardware accelerator.

In this paper we do not describe precisely the design of the accelerator with MMAlpha (see [3] for details), the RTL representation obtained in Alphard for a simple mean filter is composed of F=8 cell containing two additions and some register each, plus a shift for the final division. This accelerator is associated with an interface (mentioned hereafter as the Alpha *controller*) which connects on the bus and carefully dispatches the data coming from/to the memory on the right input/output ports, this is represented on figure 5. The controller is based on the principles explained in [10] extended to handle burst mode (see [12] for details). Note also that this hardware accelerator comes with a *driver* represented on the right of figure 5, i.e. a piece of software code that will replace the original `filter.c` function in the C code. This driver is also generated by MMAlpha together with a set of parameters that tunes the controller accordingly.

### 3.2   System and Simulation Performances

The SoC simulation results are presented in the table 2. In this implementation we used a simple memory transfer mechanism driven by the processor. This dual read/write generates a significant overhead due to memory access and system interconnect latency taken into account for each word transfered by the processor to the accelerator or back to memories. This overhead can be overcome by using a DMA engine to speedup memory copies using burst transfers between the memories and the hardware accelerator.

**Table 2.** Performances obtained from the complete SoC simulation

| | |
|---|---|
| complete simulation time | 29.21 s |
| complete simulation cycles | 600000 cycles |
| simulation speed | 20540.9 cycles/seconds |
| hardware pipeline throughput | 20450 cycles |

It is interesting to compare these results with approach of Quinton et al. [15] where a very similar application is prototyped by using emulation on a real platform (Lyrtech SignalMaster, with a DSP and a FPGA) rather than simulation. Their implementation uses an API provided by Lyrtech for hardware-software interface (roughly the equivalent of our interface controller and driver), unfortunately we have no precise estimation of the performance of the interface. In [15] the simulation time of the complete application per filter sample is approximately $6\mu s$ while our simulation reaches $29.21/20450 \simeq 1.4ms$ per filter sample (250 times slower for a simpler application). Hence, the prototyping approach is much better as soon as simulation time is targeted. However, if cycle accurate simulation is sought, our interface mechanism is much closer to what will be on the final chip than the one used in [15] and the behavior of our simulation is exactly what will occur on the real system.

## 4   Conclusion

In this paper we have presented an efficient computation model for performing cycle accurate hardware simulation of RTL description of hardware. This representation is particularly useful for high level synthesis tools that provides *generated* simulation models rather than manually written simulation models. We have validated the simulation time improvements provided by this new computation model but we believe that the quality of the code generated is a more important advantage of our model.

We have also presented a complete SoC simulation integrating IPs coming from different places: manually written IPs developed for standard SoC platform and a hardware accelerator IP generated with MMAlpha and associated with a generic hardware interface and software driver, both generated by MMAlpha. This integration is a case for the use of the SocLib environment and it also highlighted the good efficiency of our generic hardware/software mechanism.

## References

1. Alliance, V.: Virtual component interface standard (ocb specification 2, version 1.0) (2000)
2. Pétrot, F., Hommais, D., Greiner, A.: A simulation environment for core based embedded systems. In: Annual Simulation Symposium, Atlanta, GA, U.S.A (1997) 86–91

3. Guillou, A.C., Quinton, P., Risset, T., Wagner, C., Massicotte, D.: High level design of digital filters in mobile communications. Technical Report 1405, Irisa (2001)
4. Sentieys, O., Diguet, J., Philippe, J.: Gaut: a high level synthesis tool dedicated to real time signal processing application. In: EURO-DAC. (2000) University booth stand.
5. Bednara, M., Teich, J.: Interface synthesis for fpga based vlsi processor arrays. In: Proc. of the International Conference on Engineering of Reconfigurable Systems and Algorithms (ERSA 02), Las Vegas, Nevada, U.S.A. (2002)
6. Kienhuis, B., Rijpkema, E., Deprettere, E.: Compaan: Deriving process networks from matlab for embedded signal processing architectures. In: 8th International Workshop on Hardware/Software Codesign (CODES'2000). (2000)
7. Augé, I., Donnet, F., Gomez, P., Hommais, D., Pétrot, F.: Disydent: a pragmatic approach to the design of embedded systems. In: Design, Automation and Test in Europe Conference and Exhibition (DATE'03 Designers' Forum), Paris, France (2002)
8. R. Schreiber et al.: High-Level Synthesis of Non Programmable Hardware Accelerators. In: IEEE International Conference on Application-specific Systems, Architectures and Processors (ASAP 2000), Boston (2000)
9. Hounsell, B., Taylor, R.: Co-processor synthesis a new methodology for embedded software acceleration. In: Design, Automation and Test in Europe Conference and Exhibition (DATE'03 Designers' Forum), Paris, France (2004)
10. Derrien, S., Guillou, A.C., Quinton, P., Risset, T., Wagner, C.: Automatic synthesis of efficient interfaces for compiled regular. In: Internationnal Samos Workshop on Systems, Architectures, Modeling and Simulation (Samos), Samos, Grece (2002)
11. Jennings, G.: A case against event-driven simulation for digital system design. In: Proceedings of the 24th annual symposium on Simulation, IEEE Computer Society Press (1991) 170–176
12. Fraboulet, A., Risset, T., Scherrer, A.: Cycle accurate simulation model generation for soc prototyping. Technical Report 2004-18, LIP (2004)
13. Naresh, R.S., Keshab, K.P.: Pipelined Adaptative DFE Architecture Using Relaxed Look-Ahead. IEEE Transactions on Signal Processing **43** (1995) 1368–1385
14. Pétrot, F., Gomez, P.: Lightweight implementation of the posix threads api for an on-chip mips multiprocessor with vci interconnect. In: Design, Automation and Test in Europe Conference and Exhibition (DATE'03 Designers' Forum), Munich, Germany (2003)
15. Charot, F., Nyamsi, M., Quinton, P., Wagner, C.: Architecture Exploration for 3G Telephony Applications Using a Hardware–Software Prototyping Platform. In: Proc. of Samos IV, Samos, Greece (2004)

# Modeling Instruction Semantics in ADL Processor Descriptions for C Compiler Retargeting

Jianjiang Ceng[1], Weihua Sheng[1], Manuel Hohenauer[1], Rainer Leupers[1],
Gerd Ascheid[1], Heinrich Meyr[1], and Gunnar Braun[2]

[1] Aachen University of Technology (RWTH)
Integrated Signal Processing Systems
Aachen, Germany
[2] CoWare, Inc.
Aachen Germany

**Abstract.** Today's Application Specific Instruction-set Processor (ASIP) design methodology often employs centralized Architecture Description Language (ADL) processor models, from which software tools, such as C compiler, assembler, linker, and instruction-set simulator, can be automatically generated. Among these tools, the C compiler is becoming more and more important. However, the generation of C compilers requires high-level architecture information rather than low-level details needed by simulator generation. This makes it particularly difficult to include different aspects of the target architecture into one single model, and meanwhile keeping consistency.

This paper presents a modeling style, which is able to capture high- and low-level architectural information at the same time and drives both the C compiler and the simulator generation without sacrificing the modeling flexibility. The proposed approach has been successfully applied to model a number of contemporary, real-world processor architectures.

## 1 Introduction

Today, application specific instruction-set processors (ASIPs) are used in a number of System-on-Chip (SoC) designs, because of their balance between computational efficiency and flexibility. Due to the diversity of the application domains that ASIPs are specialized in, one of the most important steps in designing ASIPs is architecture exploration, i.e. iteratively refining the architecture for the target application through exploiting different design space parameters such as instruction-set, pipeline structure, etc. This iterative approach demands that each time when the architecture is tuned, the software tools such as compiler, assembler, linker and simulator should be updated and be available as soon as possible so that the tuning result can be examined to find out the potential improvement for the next iteration. For this reason, architecture description languages (ADLs) are developed to aid the design of ASIPs. From an ADL model, software tools such as C compiler, assembler, linker, and instruction-set

A. Pimentel and S. Vassiliadis (Eds.): SAMOS 2004, LNCS 3133, pp. 463–473, 2004.

simulator, can be automatically generated, which significantly improves design efficiency.

However, the generation of C compilers has different requirements on instruction modeling than other tools, e.g. simulators, which makes it difficult to include different aspects of the architecture into a single model. Instruction-set simulators need the knowledge in detail about how the architecture executes an instruction, e.g. internal data manipulations, side effects calculation, cycle-accurate pipeline activities, etc. In contrast, C compilers view these instructions from a much higher, semantics-oriented abstraction level. They need to know the purpose of instructions rather than their execution in the architecture.

In this paper, we describe an extension of LISA 2.0 [13], a widespread industrial ADL, towards the modeling of instruction semantics for C compiler retargeting. The design of this extension aims at enabling the description of high-level instruction behavior with a minimum design effort. With this extension, embedded processor designers can generate a C compiler conveniently from a LISA processor model. Moreover, our approach helps not only the C compiler generation. In [6], we described the technique of simulator generation based on the work described in this paper and the related model consistency issues. Combined with the C compiler generation capability, our approach fulfills the demands for consistent tool generation from a single ADL model, and does not sacrifice flexibility. As the tool generation exceeds the scope of this paper, here we will focus on the new language constructs.

The rest of this paper is organized as follows: section 2 shortly discusses the approaches of related works. An overview of the LISA ASIP design methodology is given in section 3. Section 4 reviews several important principles in the LISA language. Section 5 describes in detail the design criteria and the extension of the language, which is the core of this paper. Section 6 presents the modeling results of several real-world processors. Finally, section 7 concludes the whole paper.

## 2   Related Work

Within the last decade, a variety of ADLs has been developed to support ASIP design. However, not all of them support the generation of compilers. One important architecture-specific component in the compiler is the code selector. It performs the task to translate the intermediate representation (IR) of the applications into assembly instructions. To generate a code-selector for a processor architecture, the knowledge of instruction *semantics*, i.e. what instructions do, is needed. Because most of the ADLs known today were originally designed to automate the generation of a specific embedded processor design tool, e.g. simulator, and later extended to other tools, different modeling styles were developed to support the generation of code-selectors. Based on the nature of the information provided, these ADLs can be classified into three categories: structural, behavioral and mixed.

The MIMOLA [5] language belongs to the structural ADL category. Its modeling style is similar to that of the VHDL hardware description language. The instruction set information is extracted from the register-transfer level (RTL) module netlist for use in code selector generation [16]. The software programming model of MIMOLA is an extension of PASCAL.

ISDL [9] is classified as behavioral ADL. It provides the means for hierarchical specification of instruction sets. During the code selector generation, the correlation between the target processor operations and the compiler basic operations comes from the behavior description of each instruction [11]. Because ISDL cannot model the structural details for pipelining, cycle accurate simulator generation is not possible.

nML [8] and EXPRESSION [10] are two mixed ADLs. nML was designed from its beginning to provide a formalism for instruction set modeling. The instruction set of the processor is described in a hierarchical style. The roots of the hierarchy are instructions, and the intermediate elements are partial instructions. Both instructions and partial instructions have *action* sections, which describe the behavior of instructions. Although nML is claimed as a behavioral/structural ADL, it lacks the capability of describing detailed micro-architecture structure, which limits the capability of simulator generation. The code-selection from EX-PRESSION processor models relies on a so-called "Generic Machine" [1], which has a RISC instruction set architecture similar to that of the MIPS. *Operation-mapping* sections in EXPRESSION processor models are exclusively used to define the mapping between target processor instructions and one or more generic machine instructions on assembly level. The EXPRESS compiler first translates the input application to generic instructions, which are then replaced by target instructions.

The LISA 2.0 language [12] belongs to mixed behavioral/structural ADLs. The language allows the description of the micro-architecture behavior with arbitrary C/C++ code, which achieves high flexibility of modeling and very fast simulation speed for a broad range of contemporary RISC, VLIW, NPU, DSP, and ASIP architectures. In [14], we have described our overall LISA 2.0 based C compiler generation framework. Using ACE's CoSy system [2] as a backbone, it enables semi-automatic retargeting of C compilers from LISA processor models. A restriction of this earlier version is the need for manual interaction to specify the code-selector description in the compiler backend. The extension described in the following sections makes this manual interaction largely superfluous, and thus, permits to generate the code selector from a LISA model.

# 3   System Overview

The work described in this paper is based on the *LISATek Processor Designer*, an embedded processor design platform available from CoWare, Inc [7]. The core of the platform is the LISA 2.0 ADL. It supports the automatic generation of efficient ASIP development tools such as instruction-set simulator, debugger/profiler, assembler, and linker. Furthermore, the platform also provides the capability of generating VHDL, SystemC and Verilog hardware description language models for hardware synthesis. A retargetable C compiler, which is driven

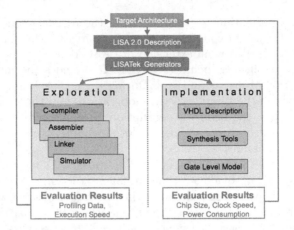

**Fig. 1.** LISA 2.0 Based ASIP Design Flow

by the same ADL model used for the generation of other tools, has been recently seamlessly integrated into the platform, too. Because the problem of model inconsistency and the need to use various special-purpose description languages are avoided by using one single ADL model, this ADL-driven ASIP design approach can achieve very high design efficiency.

## 4   Lisa Language

A LISA model basically consists of two parts: resource declarations and operations. Resource declarations define the processor resources like registers, buses, memories, pipelines, etc. The major part of a model consists of operations. OPERATION is the basic element of the instruction set description. The binary coding, assembly syntax, behavior and timing information are distributed over a number of operations, which are organized hierarchically. One of the advantages of the operation hierarchy is that the commonality of instructions can be easily exploited. Figure 2 shows three example operations arithm, ADD and SUB. Because ADD and SUB use the same type of operands, their operand fetching behavior is modelled in the operation arithm which belongs to the higher hierarchy. Their relationship is realized through the definition of GROUPs, whose members correspond to a list of alternative operations. In the example, the information about coding, timing and syntax is omitted for simplicity.

As mentioned in section 2, the LISA language allows arbitrary C/C++ descriptions of instruction behaviors, which is shown in the example. If a pipeline is modelled, this C/C++ instruction behavior description will be distributed over different pipeline stages. In the example, the BEHAVIOR sections of only two stages are shown, and the code inside does not model any features like register bypassing, side-effects, etc. If these are modelled, the C/C++ behavior description will be much more complex than what is shown in the example. Taking this

```
OPERATION arithm IN pipe.ID{
    DECLARE{
        GROUP opcode = { ADD || SUB || ... };
        GROUP Rs1, Rs2, Rd = { reg_32 };
    }
    ...
    BEHAVIOR{
        PIPELINE_REGISTER(pipe, ID/EX).src1 = GPR[Rs1];
        PIPELINE_REGISTER(pipe, ID/EX).src2 = GPR[Rs2];
    }
}
OPERATION ADD IN pipe.EX{
    ...
    BEHAVIOR{
        int op1 = PIPELINE_REGISTER(pipe, ID/EX).src1;
        int op2 = PIPELINE_REGISTER(pipe, ID/EX).src2;
        PIPELINE_REGISTER(pipe, EX/WB).dst = op1+op2;
    }
}
OPERATION SUB IN pipe.EX{
    ...
    BEHAVIOR{
        int op1 = PIPELINE_REGISTER(pipe, ID/EX).src1;
        int op2 = PIPELINE_REGISTER(pipe, ID/EX).src2;
        PIPELINE_REGISTER(pipe, EX/WB).dst = op1-op2;
    }
}
```

**Fig. 2.** Operation Hierarchy

into account, it is nearly impossible to extract instruction semantics from the BEHAVIOR sections. For this reason we introduce the SEMANTICS section to the LISA language.

## 5   Semantics Section

The SEMANTICS section is designed under certain criteria. Firstly, because SEMANTICS sections and BEHAVIOR sections both describe the behavior of instructions but from different perspectives, the new section should be concise so that the redundancy is reduced to minimum and the legacy LISA models can be easily extended to aid the compiler generation with few additional work. Moreover, the extension should be flexible so that a broad range of instruction set architectures can be described. For the purpose of compiler generation, ambiguity should be strictly avoided.

### 5.1   Micro-operations

After the examination of the instruction set architectures of a number of modern processors, we see that the high-level behavior of most of the instructions used in these processors are normally either arithmetic calculations based on several operands or branches. The calculations carried out by the instructions can be further decomposed into one or several primitive operations, and the set of primitive operations is quite limited. Therefore, we model these primitive operations with so-called *micro-operations* in the SEMANTICS section.

```
OPERATION ADD IN pipe.EX{
    DECLARE{
        GROUP Rs1, Rs2, Rd = { reg_32 };
    }
    ...
    SEMANTICS{
        _ADD|_C|(Rs1, Rs2)<0,32>->Rd;
    }
}
```

**Fig. 3.** An Example of SEMANTICS Section

Figure 3 shows the ADD operation of figure 2 with SEMANTICS section added. One statement is used to describe the semantics of an ADD instruction. The _ADD symbol is a micro-operator representing an integer addition. The following _C specifies that the carry flag is affected by the operation. Rs1 and Rs2 in the parentheses are the operands of the addition. They are GROUPs with one member, the reg_32 operation. That means, the semantics of the operands is defined in the SEMANTICS section of reg_32. The <0,32> after the brackets explicitly specifies that the result of the addition is 32-bit wide and bit 0 is the first bit. Assignments in SEMANTICS sections are specified with -> with the source on its left hand side and the destination on the right. Compared with the BEHAVIOR sections shown in figure 2, the description in SEMANTICS section is much simpler.

Generally, a micro-operation contains four parts, micro-operator, side-effects declaration, operands and bit-field specification. The operands of the micro-operators can be terminal elements, e.g., integer constants, OPERATIONs, or other micro-operations. The constraint of the OPERATIONs used as operands is that they must contain a SEMANTICS section. Side-effects in SEMANTICS sections are all predefined to avoid ambiguity. The behavior of four commonly used flags are provided, carry, zero, negative and overflow flags. If an instruction has any of the predefined side-effects, they can be declared by putting the corresponding short-cut after the micro-operator like what is shown in figure 3. The bit-field specification provides the bit-width and offset information of the micro-operations. It is compulsory for those micro-operations whose output bit-width cannot be deduced from their operands, such as sign/zero extension. Besides, allowing the use of micro-operations as the operands of other micro-operations is very useful in modeling complex operations. The next subsection will discuss the modeling of complex operations in detail.

## 5.2   Modeling Complex Operations

Many DSP processor architectures have instructions doing combined computation, e.g. multiply and accumulate. Such behavior is captured in SEMANTICS sections with *chaining*, i.e. using a micro-operation as the operand of another micro-operation. A simple example of a MAC operation can be found in figure 4. _MULUU is the micro-operator that denotes the unsigned multiplication. Its result is used as one of the operands of the _ADD, which forms a micro-operation chain.

The chaining mechanism helps to describe some complex operations without introducing temporary variables, and keeps the statements in a tree-like structure. Such a structure is suitable for code selectors, because most of the code selection algorithms use the tree-pattern matching technique [4] [3].

```
OPERATION MAC{
    DECLARE{
        GROUP Rs1, Rs2, Rd = { reg_32 };
    }
    ...
    SEMANTICS{
        _ADD(_MULUU(Rs1, Rs2)<0,32>, Rd) -> Rd;
    }
}
```

**Fig. 4.** Micro-Operation Chaining

With *chaining*, most of the RISC instructions can be modelled with one statement, but obviously this is not enough for those instructions transferring data to multiple destinations. They are modelled with multiple statements in SEMANTICS sections. If a SEMANTICS section contains multiple statements, they are assumed to execute in parallel. That means, a preceding statement's result cannot be used as the input of the following statement. To illustrate this, an example is given in figure 5. The SWP operation swaps the content of a register by exchanging the higher and lower 16 bits. Because the execution is in parallel, the data in the register are exchanged safely without considering sequential overriding.

```
OPERATION SWP{
    DECLARE{
        GROUP Rs = { reg_32 };
    }
    ...
    SEMANTICS{
        Rs<0,16>->Rs<16,16>;
        Rs<16,16>->Rs<0,16>;
    }
}
```

**Fig. 5.** Multiple Statements

Another kind of important behaviors used in modern processors is conditional execution, i.e., an instruction is executed according to certain conditions. In order to model such instructions, IF-ELSE statements can be used. a total of 10 comparison operators can be used in SEMANTICS sections to model all kinds of conditions. Comparisons can be chained, too. In figure 6, the _EQ operator checks whether its two operands are equal or not. According to the result, the IF statement will execute the code specified in the braces.

```
OPERATION CADD{
    DECLARE{
        GROUP Rs1, Rs2, Rd = { reg_32 };
    }
    ...
    SEMANTICS{
        IF(_EQ(_CF,1)){ _ADD(Rs1, Rs2)->Rd; }
    }
}
```

**Fig. 6.** IF-ELSE statement

## 5.3   Semantics Hierarchy

In section 4 we have already illustrated the the LISA operation hierarchy. Taking advantage of hierarchical descriptions, SEMANTICS sections can be very concise. Figure 7 shows the hierarchical SEMANTICS sections of the three operations in figure 2. In the `arithm` operation, the GROUP `opcode` is used as micro-operator instead of predefined ones, which means that the concrete micro-operators can be found in the SEMANTICS sections of the GROUP members. Accordingly, the SEMANTICS sections of the ADD and SUB operation contain simply a micro-operator. The similarity of the ADD and SUB operations' semantics is well exploited here to simplify the description.

```
OPERATION arithm IN pipe.ID{
    DECLARE{
        GROUP Rs1, Rs2, Rd = { reg_32 };
        GROUP opcode = { ADD || SUB || ... };
    }
    ...
    SEMANTICS{ opcode|_C|(Rs1, Rs2)->Rd; }
}
OPERATION ADD IN pipe.EX{
    ...
    SEMANTICS{ _ADD; }
}
OPERATION SUB IN pipe.EX{
    ...
    SEMANTICS{ _SUB; }
}
```

**Fig. 7.** Hierarchical Operators

A SEMANTICS section can return not only a micro-operator but also a complete micro-operation expression. In figure 8, the SEMANTICS sections of the SHL and SHR operations do not contain a complete statement with assignment but micro-operators with operands (_LSL and _LSR are logical left and right shift micro-operators). As a result, the semantics of these two operations is not self-contained, because the data sink is missing. The use of these two operations is actually doing operand pre-processing for the ADD operation, which can be seen in its SEMANTICS section. The `opd` GROUP, which contains the previous two operations, is used as one of the operands of the _ADD micro-operation. Thereby, depending on the binary encoding of the instruction, one of the operand registers will be left or right shifted before addition.

```
OPERATION ADD IN pipe.EX{
    DECLARE{
        GROUP Rs1, Rd = { reg32 };
        GROUP opd = { SHL || SHR };
    }
    ...
    SEMANTICS{ _ADD(Rs1, opd)->Rd; }
}
OPERATION SHL IN pipe.EX{
    DECLARE{
        GROUP Rs2 = { reg_32 };
        GROUP imm = { imm8 };
    }
    ...
    SEMANTICS{ _LSL(Rs2, imm); }
}
OPERATION SHR IN pipe.EX{
    DECLARE{
        GROUP Rs2 = { reg_32 };
        GROUP imm = { imm8 };
    }
    ...
    SEMANTICS{ _LSR(Rs2, imm); }
}
```

**Fig. 8.** Hierarchical Operands

In short, the formalism in SEMANTICS sections is very flexible and well integrated into LISA 2.0. If the commonalities of instructions are fully exploited, their instruction semantics can be described with only a few lines of code.

### 5.4 Difference between SEMANTICS and BEHAVIOR

Though SEMANTICS and BEHAVIOR sections are similar in terms of describing the behavioral model of the processor, they are different in several ways:

- **Contents:** in BEHAVIOR sections, C/C++ code can be used without limitation. However, in SEMANTICS sections, only a limited set of micro-operators (31 in total) are allowed, and their usages are fully formalized.
- **Operands:** in BEHAVIOR sections, nearly all processor resources and arbitrary variables can be used. However, in SEMANTICS sections, only compiler related resources can be accessed directly, e.g. registers, memories, etc.

## 6   Case Studies

In order to prove the concept described in this paper, five architectures have been examined totally, namely ARM's ARM7 core, CoWare's LTRISC core, STMicroelectronics' ST220 VLIW multimedia processor [15], Infineon's PP32 network processing unit, and Texas Instruments' C54x digital signal processor. The LTRISC processor is a very small RISC core, which is provided with CoWare's LISATek Processor Designer. The PP32 is an evolution of [17] and comprises instructions which are able to operate on bit-fields. The existing LISA 2.0 models of these five processors have been extended with SEMANTICS sections.

Although the SEMANTICS section is not intended for the extension of already existing models, our test approach proved that the new section does not impose any particular modeling style. This is very important to keep the flexibility of LISA 2.0.

**Table 1.** Modeling Results of Five Processors

|                  | ARM7 | LTRISC | ST220 | PP32 | C54x |
|------------------|------|--------|-------|------|------|
| ISA              | RISC | RISC   | RISC  | RISC | CISC |
| No. instructions | 62   | 17     | 82    | 41   | 110  |
| Design effort    | 4d   | 2d     | 10d   | 8d   | 15d  |

The modeling result is summarized in table 1. Note that the design effort is calculated in man-days. It can be seen that the work for adding SEMANTICS sections scales with the number of instructions in the architecture. The complexity of the instructions (RISC vs. CISC) also has influence on the effort. Generally, the predefined micro-operations and the bit-field specification make the behavioral description code size in SEMANTICS sections significantly less than that of the C code in BEHAVIOR sections. Furthermore, the ambiguity of the C description is avoided, which is important for C compiler generation.

## 7   Conclusion

In this paper, we presented an approach for modeling instruction semantics based on an existing ADL with the main purpose of C compiler generation. Our approach incorporates a new SEMANTICS section into the structure of LISA 2.0 without influencing the existing flexibility, and achieves a concise formalism for instruction-set description which is important for code selector generation. Besides providing instruction semantics for C compiler generation, it is also possible to generate instruction-set simulator and documentation with the information provided by SEMANTICS sections.

A further interesting result of our approach is that both instruction- and cycle-accurate descriptions of the processor architecture are able to coexist in a single model. This allows for a very high design efficiency on different abstraction levels, while maintaining consistency through using a single model during the entire design process. Our future research activities will be in the area of processor specific code optimization based on instruction semantics.

## References

1. *EXPRESSION User Manual (version 1.0)*
   http://www.ics.uci.edu/~express/documentation.htm.
2. ACE – Associated Computer Experts bv. *The COSY Compiler Development System http://www.ace.nl.*

3. A. Aho, M. Ganapathi, and S. Tjiang. Code generation using tree matching and dynamic programming. *IEEE Transactions on Programming Languages and Systems*, 11(4):491–516, Oct. 1989.
4. A. Aho, R. Sethi, and J. Ullman. *Compilers, Principles, Techniques and Tools*. Addison-Wesley, Jan. 1986. ISBN 0-2011-0088-6.
5. S. Bashford, U. Bieker, B. Harking, R. Leupers, P. Marwedel, A. Neumann, and D. Voggenauer. The MIMOLA Language, Version 4.1. Reference Manual, Department of Computer Science 12, Embedded System Design and Didactics of Computer Science, 1994.
6. G. Braun, R. Leupers, G. Asheid, and H. Meyr. A Novel Approach for Flexible and Consistent ADL-driven ASIP Design. *Proc. of the Design Automation Conference (DAC)*, Mar. 2004.
7. CoWare Inc., http://www.coware.com. *LISATek product family*.
8. A. Fauth, J. Van Praet, and M. Freericks. Describing Instruction Set Processors Using nML. In *Proc. of the European Design and Test Conference (ED & TC)*, Mar. 1995.
9. G. Hadjiyiannis, S. Hanono, and S. Devadas. ISDL: An Instruction Set Description Language for Retargetability. In *Proc. of the Design Automation Conference (DAC)*, Jun. 1997.
10. A. Halambi, P. Grun, V. Ganesh, A. Khare, N. Dutt, and A. Nicolau. EXPRESSION: A Language for Architecture Exploration through Compiler/Simulator Retargetability. In *Proc. of the Conference on Design, Automation & Test in Europe (DATE)*, Mar. 1999.
11. Silvina Hanono and Srinivas Devadas. Instruction selection, resource allocation, and scheduling in the AVIV retargetable code generator. In *Design Automation Conference*, pages 510–515, 1998.
12. A. Hoffmann, T. Kogel, A. Nohl, G. Braun, O. Schliebusch, O. Wahlen, A. Wieferink, and H. Meyr. A Novel Methodology for the Design of Application Specific Instruction Set Processors (ASIP) Using a Machine Description Language. *IEEE Transactions on Computer-Aided Design*, 20(11):1338–1354, Nov. 2001.
13. A. Hoffmann, R. Leupers, and H. Meyr. *Architecture Exploration for Embedded Processors with LISA*. Kluwer Academic Publishers, Boston, Jan. 2003. ISBN 1-4020-7338-0.
14. M. Hohenauer, H. Scharwaechter, K. Karuri, O. Wahlen, T. Kogel, R. Leupers, G. Ascheid, and H. Meyr. A Methodology and Tool Suite for C Compiler Generation from ADL Processor Models. *Proc. of the Conference on Design, Automation & Test in Europe (DATE)*, Mar. 2004.
15. F. Homewood and P. Faraboschi. ST200: A VLIW Architecture for Media-Oriented Applications. In *Microprocessor Forum*, Oct. 2000.
16. R. Leupers and P. Marwedel. A BDD-based frontend for retargetable compilers. In *Proc. of the European Design and Test Conference (ED & TC)*, pages 239–243, 1995.
17. X. Nie, L. Gazsi, F. Engel, and G. Fettweis. A new network processor architecture for high-speed communications. In *Proc. of the IEEE Workshop on Signal Processing Systems (SIPS)*, pages 548–557, Oct. 1999.

# A Communication-Centric Design Flow
# for HIBI-Based SoCs

Tero Kangas, Jouni Riihimäki, Erno Salminen, Vesa Lahtinen, Heikki Orsila,
Kimmo Kuusilinna, and Timo D. Hämäläinen

Tampere University of Technology, Institute of Digital and Computer Systems
P.O. Box 553, FIN-33101 Tampere, Finland
tero.kangas@tut.fi

**Abstract.** This paper describes a design flow for Systems-on-Chip
(SoCs) utilizing a previously presented HIBI communication network.
The system designer is assisted with an automated two-level architecture exploration that optimizes the component allocation, task mapping
and scheduling with static application analyses, and dynamic simulations. The utilization of a system-level model of computation enables
fast analysis of the design and facilitates automated architecture exploration. Communication design is in a key role in the design flow since
it is a critical part of contemporary SoCs. The platform of the design
flow is based on the HIBI communication network that is easily scalable and parameterizable for a variety of communication requirements.
As a result, the design flow selects the computational component from
library, HIBI network instance and application mapping that optimizes
the result of cost function. The designer assists the flow by defining the
cost function and optimization control parameters as well as giving the
architecture and mapping constraints.

## 1   Introduction

To enable automation for system design, a well specified design flow with an
underlying flexible platform should be utilized. Platform-based design has been
envisioned to meet the design challenges of ever-increasing system complexity
[1]. The platform-based design approach theoretically allows rapid construction
of very large systems and their architecture exploration. However, the analysis of
such systems is very labor intensive and slow using traditional methods; partly
because many of the physical architecture evaluation tools operate on relatively
low abstraction levels and partly because of the typically huge design space.
Hence, novel methods, in the form of a design flow, are needed to fully exploit
the new possibilities.

### 1.1   Motivation

Communication design has become a critical part of SoCs for which reason
communication-centric design methodologies have been presented [2], [3]. The

A. Pimentel and S. Vassiliadis (Eds.): SAMOS 2004, LNCS 3133, pp. 474–483, 2004.
© Springer-Verlag Berlin Heidelberg 2004

communication network should provide means to separate computation from communication by hiding architectural complexity with simple interfaces and protocols. These requirements are addressed in the HIBI communication network [4]. The simple structure, parameterization, and scalability are HIBI properties that are utilized in the design flow to optimize the communication between concurrent processing elements.

In this paper, we present a high-level design flow, called Koski, which utilizes automated architecture exploration at several abstraction levels and the HIBI platform for efficient communication design. The entry point for the design flow is a UML design environment, where the application is developed and verified without over-specifying the architecture. For a described application, the automated architecture exploration tool attempts to find an architecture that meets the constraints such as performance, area, and power. Following the original HIBI principles, the design flow and the underlying communication network are targeted towards multimedia applications including dataflow intensive processing. This paper covers the system-level design phases of the flow whereas the component-level design and ASIC synthesis are left outside.

## 1.2   Related Work

High-level architecture exploration that has the characteristics of separating communication and computation, functional abstraction, library-based architecture, and a gradual refinement of the architecture and the application is a very active research area. The current research of high-level system design methodologies tackle various aspects such as developing models of computation (MoCs) [5], [6], simulation environments [3], [7], [8], architecture exploration [7], [9], and automating the model refinement [10], [11]. There are also projects trying to cover all the high-level system design phases from specification to RTL architecture [12], [13].

SpecC design methodology [3] consists of a language and tools needed for describing, exploring, refining, and synthesizing a design. For fast architecture exploration, SpecC methodology includes task estimation that analyzes design metrics such as performance and memory usage. The SpecC language is an extension to ANSI C having similar properties to describe parallel software and hardware systems to the more widely adopted SystemC language. The architecture exploration, however, has to be mainly carried out manually.

The VCC design tool [14] provides a method to automatically explore the architecture among the library components. The ideas behind VCC come from the POLIS project [15], or currently METROPOLIS, which is developing a formal methodology for SoC design. VCC offers performance estimations for different architectures and hardware/software partitions. The available hardware and software models are very limited and not suitable to synthesis with available design tools [12].

In Artemis [7], the objective is to develop a workbench for system architecture exploration and an experimental framework for reconfigurable architectures. The applications are modeled with the Kahn process network MoC. The mapping of

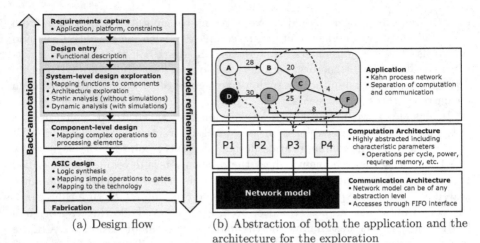

(a) Design flow

(b) Abstraction of both the application and the architecture for the exploration

**Fig. 1.** Overview of the Koski design flow and abstraction for exploration

application tasks to the multiprocessor architecture is assisted with an automatic optimization based on an evolutionary algorithm which generates a number of candidates for simulation.

Common property of the referenced design methods is the utilization of MoCs that describes functionality very accurately making them suitable for model refinement. In our approach, the aim is to constrain the design model with such an abstract MoC that it is a good fit to system-level architecture exploration.

This paper is organized as follows. The following Section presents an overview of the design flow. In Section 3, the abstractions for architecture exploration and the design entry front-end are presented. Section 4 describes the architecture exploration with emphasis on the model abstraction. In Section 5, the concluding remarks are given.

## 2   Overview of the Design Flow

With the conventional design methods, software and hardware development are already separated in the beginning of the design. The processing elements and the hardware/software partitioning are fixed or modified manually according to the intuition of the designer. In the case of improvements in algorithms or a totally new application, the previous architectures can no longer be considered as optimal. The Koski design flow tries to address this problem by enabling an architecture independent application development and an automated architecture exploration.

The outline of the design flow is depicted in Fig. 1(a). The design phases are common to contemporary design methods but the novelty is in abstraction for architecture optimization and design automation. The design flow starts with capturing the requirements for an application and a platform including implementation constraints such as the overall cost. Following the requirements, the functionality of the system is described. The design entry is predominantly functional but is extended to cover some very high-level architectural aspects. Particularly, this information can be back-annotated from the later stages of the flow, to facilitate the evaluation of design performance.

Finding an platform instance for the described application is carried out with two-phase architecture exploration consisting of static and dynamic exploration methods. The architecture exploration can be divided into *component allocation*, *task mapping*, and *scheduling*. Allocation denotes the selection of processing elements and instance of communication platform. The application tasks are then mapped onto the allocated processing elements. Scheduling is used to define the order and timing of the execution of tasks and communication. After architecture exploration, both application and architecture models are refined and optimized at the component-level. The rest of the flow covers the low-level synthesis and fabrication-related steps of the refined models. The following sections describe the system design phases, shown with gray background in Fig. 1(a), in more detail and present an overview of the model refinement.

## 3   High-Level Design Entry

System abstraction is the key for fast architecture exploration. The objective of the abstraction is to hide the details that are unnecessary in the high-level exploration phase. Arbitrary designs cannot be analyzed automatically to a degree that would allow effective automatic optimization. Constraining designs with a system-level MoC enables a better analysis of designs and, therefore, exploration of the design space.

### 3.1   System Abstraction for Architecture Exploration

The application is modeled as communicating tasks, as depicted in Fig. 1(b). The application model resembles a Kahn process network model [16] that fits well for our purposes. It is suitable for streaming applications, computation and communication are separated inherently, and the FIFO channel representation suits well the HIBI. For practical reasons the FIFO channels have to be bounded. However, with communication scheduling and optimization of the buffer sizes, blocking can be minimized during write operations.

A significant increase in the speed of architecture exploration can be achieved by abstracting the architecture model. In our static architecture exploration method, both the communication and computation architecture models are abstracted to get better exploration speed without loosing too much in accuracy.

Both in the static and the dynamic method, the abstraction of the computation architecture is accomplished by characterizing the processing element with property metrics such as performance (operations/cycle), required internal memory, area, and power. Since the static architecture exploration is based on application analysis, the model of communication architecture is highly abstracted.

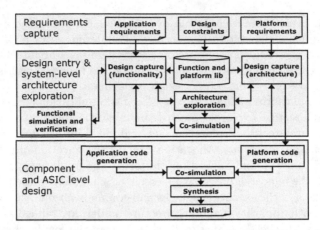

**Fig. 2.** UML as a design entry front-end in the Koski design flow

Only the bandwidth, area, and power of the communication architecture are given for static exploration. In the dynamic method, the model is then refined to cycle-accurate for more accurate performance estimation.

To assist the exploration tool in task mapping, the user can label both the application tasks and the processing elements according to their computational properties. The processing element is able to execute the task only if their labels match. The labeling reduces the possible mapping combinations and therefore increases the exploration speed.

### 3.2   UML Design Environment

Currently, the functionality is described with the Unified Modeling Language (UML) [17] and verified by functional simulations in Telelogic Tau Generation 2 design environment [18]. UML is, in general, a collection of notations for capturing a specification of a software system [19]. Even if it was originally targeted for SW engineering, it can also be employed for designing embedded systems as discussed in [19], [20]. Despite the restrictions in describing detailed architecture, UML can be utilized in high-level system design with abstract architecture notations.

Figure 2 presents the utilization of the UML design environment as a front-end to the Koski flow. The design is started by describing the application according to the requirements. In this phase, the description is purely functional and, therefore, does not include information about the computation or communication architecture. The functionality of the application is verified with simulations in the UML design tool.

Separately from the application, the system designer describes the archiecture by generating a new platform component or taking existing components from the library. Naturally, the design of the architecture depends on the functional requirements. For example, there might exist a hardware accelerator for a certain algorithm or an optimized software algorithm for a certain processor.

In addition, the designer may also decide how the processes from the functional description are mapped to the processing elements. The mapping can be either fixed or optimizable. In the latter case, the architecture exploration tool may change the mapping during the optimization.

The components in the platform are UML classes that are characterized with parameters that describe the performance and associated costs. The parameters are given as stereotypes. Therefore, all the components of the same type have the same parameters, but each component may have different parameter values. Many of the parameters, such as cycles/operations ratio, area, and power consumption, are fixed when the component is modeled in the library. The user can modify the rest of the parameters within practical limits, for instance data width, clock frequency, and memory size.

In addition, the communication architecture is modeled as a UML class and can be parameterized similarly to the processing elements. For the bus wrappers, the user can set the parameters that are unique for each agent, such as buffer size, priority, address, and the maximum time the agent can reserve the network.

The application and platform component descriptions as well as the design constraints have to be converted to the format expected by the architecture exploration tool. Since the UML design is stored in XML format [21], it is relatively easy to parse the description and generate the required intermediate formats for the architecture exploration. The laborious task is to transform the UML model to correspond to the Kahn MoC if that was not the original description style.

# 4    Architecture Exploration

Exploration attempts to find an optimal selection of platform components and mapping of the tasks that are not yet mapped to any platform component. Mapping in UML environment is not required but it can be used to guide the architecture exploration tool. The initial mapping is used as a starting point in the optimization and user fixed mappings are not changed. A detailed description of the architecture exploration is presented in the next Section. In the design flow, the architecture exploration is carried out in two phases. First, the coarse-grain exploration is performed by statically analyzing the application model. Then, the architecture is explored with iterative simulations and more accurate system models. The optimization objective is to minimize the result of the cost function that the designer defines in the UML design environment.

## 4.1    Static Method

The static part of the architecture exploration analyzes the application model to optimize the allocation, mapping, and scheduling. It is used for fast, coarse, input-independent analysis. The outline of the static method is illustrated in Fig. 3(a). The system design initializes the exploration by giving an initial candidate for allocation and mapping. The initial candidates can be labeled as fixed so that the exploration tool does not try to optimize them. The task mapping is performed for a number of processing element allocations.

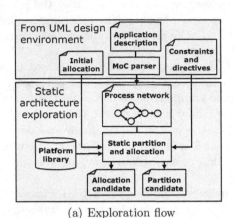

```
while k < max_k:
    S_next = move(S,T)
    E_new = objective(S_next)

    if E_new < E_best:
        E_best = E_new
        S_best = S_next

    if E_new < E_old or
            rand() < acceptor(E_new - E_old, T):
        S = S_next
        E_old = E_new
        rejects = 0
    else:
        rejects = rejects + 1
        if rejects >= max_rejects:
            break

    k = k + 1
    if k % schedule_max == 0:
        T = schedule(T, k /schedule_max)
```

(a) Exploration flow                (b) The utilized simulated annealing algorithm

**Fig. 3.** Static method of the architecture exploration

In both allocation and mapping, the utilized optimization algorithm is *simulated annealing* [22]. The implementation of the algorithm can vary remarkably depending on the application and the objectives. The implementation utilized in static architecture exploration is outlined in Fig. 3(b). The simulated annealing algorithm can avoid local minima by rejecting the locally optimized choice based on a probability. The probability for the acceptance is given by the *acceptor* function. The *objective* function is the cost function to be minimized and it can be the same for both allocation and mapping optimizations. The *move* function determines the next allocation or mapping to be examined. S is the whole design space including all the combinations of allocations and mappings. T is the portion of the architecture to be affected in the *move* function. It is modified in certain iteration intervals, defined by *schedule_max*, to decrease the size of the step in the design space during the optimization.

In the allocation optimization, S is the processing element library from which the *move* function chooses the components. The *move* functions starts with a minimum number of processing elements, defined by the designer, and utilizes heuristics in selecting the components. T denotes the portion of the architecture that is modified in *move*.

For each allocation candidate, several task mappings are examined. Because the application is modeled with a process network model, it is convenient to apply the *group migration algorithm* [23] to optimization. Since our group migration is a greedy algorithm, it is unable to escape the local minima of the cost functions. It is utilized together with simulated annealing to try to find the global minimum. The group migration algorithm is implemented as a part of the *move* function. The idea is to localize the communication by mapping the tasks into groups so that the cost function is minimized. An estimate of the timing of the task execution has to be determined to define the costs. This can be accomplished with task scheduling.

## 4.2  Dynamic Method

The static architecture exploration produces several allocation and mapping candidates. Although the static method reduces significantly the architectural space that needs exploring, many architectural parameters still remain unfixed due to the abstract model. Statically produced candidates are passed to the dynamic optimizer that examines the candidates with a more accurate model of the communication architecture and performs the fine-grain allocation and mapping optimizations. The dynamic method of the architecture exploration is based on iterative simulations of application and architecture where optimization is performed according to the results of performance analysis, as presented in Fig. 4. The model of the HIBI communication network is refined for the dynamic method to achieve better accuracy in the optimization.

Since the models for applications, processing elements, and communication architectures are at different abstraction levels, a tool that combines a model for simulation is required. This tool, called Transaction Generator [24], composes the abstract application and architecture models for simulation. It executes the communication on the network by reading and writing data. In addition, it delays the writes according to the process network description to mimic the process execution, as depicted in Fig. 1(b). Therefore, data is not transferred directly between processes inside Transaction Generator but the transfers are addressed to the network. This produces comparably accurate communication delays in the process network. Naturally, no transfers on communication network are needed, if the processes are mapped to the same processing element.

The purpose of the simulation is to execute the process network model and to produce statistics about processes and the platform instance that can later be used to determine the performance of the system. Performance information is back-annotated to the task mapping and platform component allocation phase for the following optimization iterations. If necessary, part of this information may be forwarded to the specification phase for refinement. After the mapping and allocation has been fixed, the communication architecture parameters are optimized with a similar iteration method [25].

## 5  Conclusion

In this paper, we presented a high-level design flow, called Koski, which utilizes automated architecture exploration at several abstraction levels. The computation and communication are separated both in architectural and application level to facilitate the design exploration. The design flow can be considered as communication-centric since the platform relies on HIBI communication network and the optimization focus is on efficient communication realization.

The architecture exploration utilizes both static and dynamic methods to divide the problem into a coarse-grain and fine-grain exploration. The key for fast architecture exploration is the system abstraction with a MoC which hides the unnecessary details of the functionality. In the design flow, the application

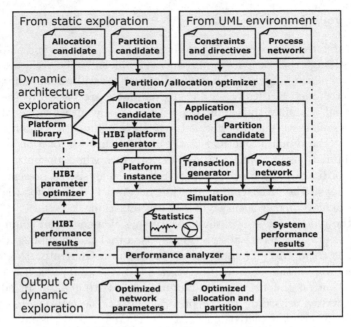

**Fig. 4.** Dynamic architecture exploration

is modeled as communicating tasks. As a result, the design flow selects the processing elements from library, HIBI network instance, and application mapping that optimizes the result of cost function.

Currently, the framework for the design flow exists and has been tested with simple application models. Different algorithms for static architecture exploration, especially variations of simulated annealing and genetic algorithms, are being evaluated. Moreover, the applied MoC and the related tools, such as Transaction Generator, are further developed to better fit the control intensive application models.

# References

1. Ferrari, A., Sangiovanni-Vincentelli, A.: System Design: Traditional Concepts and New Paradigms. In: Proceedings of IEEE International Conference on Computer Design: VLSI in Computer and Processors (1999) 2–12
2. Cesário, W., et al.: Component-Based Design Approach for Multicore SoCs. In: Proc. of 39th Design Automation Conference (2002) 789–794
3. Gerstlauer, A., et al.: System: Design: A Practical Guide with SpecC. Kluwer Academic Publishers, Boston, MA (2001)
4. Lahtinen, V., et al.: Interconnection Scheme for Continuous-Media Systems-on-a-Chip. In: Microprocessors and Microsystems, Vol. 26, No. 3. (2002) 123–138
5. Lee, E.A., Parks, T.M.: Dataflow Process Networks. In: Proc. of the IEEE, Vol. 83, No. 5 (1995) 773–801

6. Haubelt, C., *et al.*: System Design for Flexibility. In: Proc. of Design, Automation and Test in Europe (2002) 854–861
7. Pimentel, A.D. *et al.*: Exploring Embedded-Systems Architectures with Artemis. In: IEEE Computer, Vol. 34, No. 11 (2001) 57–63
8. WWW site of Ptolemy project, http://ptolemy.eecs.berkeley.edu
9. Kogel, T., *et al.*: Virtual Architecture Mapping: A SystemC based Methodology for Architectural Exploration of System-on-Chip Designs. In: Proc. of the International Workshop on Systems, Architectures, Modeling and Simulation (2003) 108–113
10. Brunel, J.-Y. *et al.*: COSY Communication IP's. In: Proceeding of 37th Design Automation Conference (2000) 406–409
11. Cesário, W., *et al.*: Component-based Design Approach for Multicore SoCs. In: Proc. of Design Automation Conference (2002) 789–794
12. Dziri, M.A. *et al.*: Combining Architecture Exploration and a Path to Implementation to Build a Complete SoC Design Flow from System Specification to RTL. In: Proc. of Asia and South Pacific Design Automation Conference (2003) 219–224
13. Cai, L., *et al.*: C/C++ Based System Design Flow Using SpecC, VCC and SystemC. Technical Report CECS-TR-02-30. Center for Embedded Computer Systems, University of California, Irvine (2002)
14. Cadence. WWW site of Cadence, www.cadence.com
15. Hsieh, H., *et al.*: Efficient Methods for Embedded System Design Space Exploration. In: Proc. of Design Automation Conference (2000) 607–612
16. Kahn, G.: The Semantics of a Simple Language for Parallel Programming. In: Proc. of IFIP Congress 74 (1974) 471–475
17. Object Management Group. WWW site of UML Resources, http://www.omg.org/uml/
18. Telelogic. WWW site of Telelogic Tau Generation 2, http://www.taug2.com/
19. Martin, G., *et al.*: Embedded UML: A Merger of Real-Time UML and Co-Design. In: Proc. of International Symposium on Hardware/Software Codesign (2001) 23–28
20. Green, P.N., Edwards, M.D.: The Modeling of Embedded Systems Using HASoC. In: Proc. of Design, Automation and Test in Europe (2002) 752–759
21. Object Management Group. XML Metadata Interchange (XMI) Specification, Version 2.0, (2003)
22. Kirkpatrick, S., *et al.*: Optimization by Simulated Annealing. In: Science, Vol. 220, No. 4598 (1983) 671–680
23. Krishnamurthy, B.: An Improved Min-Cut Algorithm for Partitioning VLSI Networks. In: IEEE Transactions on Computers, Vol. 33, No. 5 (1984) 438–446
24. Kangas, T. *et al.*: Using a Communication Generator in SoC Architecture Exploration. In: Proc. of International Symposium on System-on-Chip (2003) 105–108
25. Riihimäki, J., *et al.*: Parameter Optimization Tool for Enhancing On-chip Network Performance. In: Proc. of the IEEE International Symposium of Circuits and Systems (2002) 61–64

# Performance Analysis of SoC Communication by Application of Deterministic and Stochastic Petri Nets

Holger Blume, Thorsten von Sydow, and Tobias G. Noll

Lehrstuhl für Allgemeine Elektrotechnik und Datenverarbeitungssysteme
RWTH Aachen, Schinkelstraße 2, 52062 Aachen
{blume,sydow,tgn}@eecs.rwth-aachen.de
http://www.eecs.rwth-aachen.de

**Abstract.** Design space exploration (DSE) for heterogeneous Systems on Chip (SoCs) is a key issue as today's SoC complexity is steadily increasing. Methods for the estimation of implementation specific performance and cost features on all levels of design have to be developed. This contribution proposes an approach utilizing deterministic and stochastic Petri nets (DSPN) to analyze on-chip communication which is of increasing importance. In order to demonstrate the suitability of this approach the on-chip communication structure of two examples featuring typical SoC communication conflicts like competition for common communication resources have been studied. A modern heterogeneous DSP and a design example with an on-chip bus have been examined. The results show that sufficient modeling accuracy can be achieved with low modeling effort in terms of computation and implementation time.

## 1 Introduction

As modern heterogeneous Systems on Chip (SoCs) include a variety of different architecture blocks and different communication structures, it is mandatory to prune the design space. This so-called design space exploration (DSE) is required in order to achieve short innovation cycles for new products.

An efficient high performance SoC architecture has to include different types of architecture blocks to provide the required performance at reasonable costs (area, power dissipation) as well as ensuring sufficient flexibilit. Therefore, systems have to be partitioned into system blocks which are mapped onto appropriate architecture blocks. To meet the specifications of a system and to optimize efficiency it is important to elaborate strategies, models and tools which assist designers with performance and cost features of the inspected architecture on all levels of design [2], [5], [12].

A model based DSE concept allowing to explore the design space has been successfully demonstrated in [2]. According to this methodology a system designer is able to evaluate early in the design process different partitioning/mapping alternatives in terms of performance and costs.

For SoCs which require intensive communication between architecture blocks the performance of the complete system (throughput rate, latency, etc.) is strongly de-

A. Pimentel and S. Vassiliadis (Eds.): SAMOS 2004, LNCS 3133, pp. 484–493, 2004.

pending on the communication structure. Therefore, different approaches have been proposed in the past to model and analyze on-chip communication. Generally, these methods can be classified into simulative, stochastic and analytic approaches: For example in [8] a hybrid two-phase methodology based on simulative and analytic phases has been proposed. A pure simulative approach utilizing the SystemC library has been applied in [13].

Deterministic evaluation of communication structures in modern SoCs causes a very high amount of simulation effort since the parameter space assigned to the design of on-chip communication subsystems is getting increasingly complex. The parameter space is spanned by parameters like arbitration scheme, number of communicating participants, word lengths etc.. Furthermore, the manner in which a computational on-chip resource creates communication traffic is typically strongly data dependent. Large stimuli sets are required for comprehensive simulations. Here, the application of stochastic modeling methods seems to be a promising approach to analyze the behavior and performance of the underlying communication subsystem of SoCs. Stochastic modeling means for example that the access of a computational resource to a communication resource can be modeled by an appropriate probability distribution. Such modeling methods are implementable at reasonable costs in terms of modeling effort and require much less computational effort for the evaluation of the performance of a communication system.

This paper presents the modeling of different on-chip communication systems by application of deterministic stochastic Petri Nets (DSPNs). Examples, featuring typical communication conflicts are presented and an evaluation of the modeling accuracy is performed. In chapter 2 the basics of stochastic modeling approaches are sketched and the modeling with DSPNs is briefly described. An exemplary modeling of a DSP and an example utilizing an on-chip bus as well as a discussion of the modeling results are presented in chapter 3. Conclusions are given in chapter 4.

## 2   Stochastic Modeling Approaches

In the past, different stochastic modeling approaches have been applied to analyze the performance of distributed systems like for example a multiprocessor system. In the following three stochastic modeling approaches will be sketched. They are suited to model performance issues with the focus on the interconnect communication structure. An extensive comparison and analysis of these approaches is presented in [9].

**Markov processes** are well-known stochastic processes which represent a sequence of random values or states. The probability for the occurrence of a state depends on the previous state of the corresponding state sequence. So, conditional probabilities can be given. For example, a methodology presented in [10] and based on Markov processes yields a performance model of a multiprocessor system.

**Queuing theory** [6] is concerned with queuing systems which consist of one or more queues with waiting tasks and one or more servers which process the tasks. The arrival rate and service rate of tasks and servers are characteristics of a queuing system. Rates with negative exponential distribution are well examined and commonly used. Queuing theory is applied to estimate e.g. the throughput rate and load of computer and communication networks with interdependencies between the nodes.

**Petri nets** were introduced in 1962 by Adam Petri. He proposed a graphical modeling formalism to analyze the behavior of a system with concurrent processes. Petri nets were deduced from the theory of automata. By supplementing features like the "concept of time" the Petri net formalism has become a powerful method to analyze performance issues of distributed systems. By the introduction of deterministic transitions [9] it is also suitable for highly accurate modeling which is required e.g. for on-chip communication.

In principle, the modeling of communication structures would be possible with all mentioned stochastic approaches. We utilized Petri nets as they provide different transition schemes which can be applied advantageously to model different communication behaviors. Furthermore, the available tool support facilitates their application: Today there are a couple of commercial and non-commercial tools available to implement and analyze Petri nets [11], [3]. TimeNET [15] is the Petri net tool utilized in this contribution as it is well documented and provides all required features.

### Deterministic and Stochastic Petri Nets

The underlying principles of deterministic and stochastic Petri nets (DSPN) are deduced in [9] and extend the modeling possibilities of Petri nets. In the following, only a small subset of all possibilities provided by DSPNs are discussed.

Generally, Petri nets consist of so-called places, arcs and transitions. Places, depicted as circles in the graphical representation, are states of components of a system. E.g. a place could be named *copy word* to make clear that this place represents the state of copying a word of the belonging component. Places can be untagged or marked with one or even more tokens which illustrate that the corresponding place is actually allocated. For example this means that if a place called *copy word* is marked, the belonging component is in the state of copying a word.

In Petri nets the change of a state can be described by so-called timed transitions. Three types are differentiated in DSPNs. There are immediate transitions, transitions with a probability density function for the delay (e.g.: negative exponential) or deterministic delayed transitions.

Transitions and places are connected via arcs. Arcs can be of two types, regular or inhibitor. Inhibitor arcs are identified by a small circle instead of an arrowhead at the end of a regular arc (see Figure 1). If more than one place is connected to a transition via regular arcs, the transition will only be activated if all connected places are marked. If one or more of these arcs is an inhibitor arc the transition will not fire if the corresponding place is marked. Once a Petri net model is implemented, probability and expectation values for marking places can be acquired by:

- simulation,
- mathematical approximation,
- mathematical analysis.

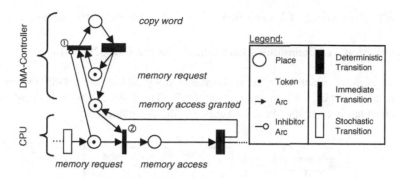

**Fig. 1.** Basic DSPN example (depicted here for a specific point of time)

Each alternative has its own advantages and disadvantages in terms of accuracy and computational effort. E.g. in the case of two immediate transitions which could be concurrently activated mathematical analysis is not possible [9].

In order to demonstrate the application of DSPNs to model communication structures a very simple DSPN is depicted in Figure 1. A simplified arbitration scheme which handles the competition of a DMA-controller and a CPU for the critical resource memory interface is modeled here. The DSPN consists of two components: CPU and DMA-Controller. The CPU component is only depicted in parts as this example should only explain the arbitration mechanism.

In the following, two aspects of the actual state and their implications for the succeeding state of this simple net will be explained. As can be seen in Figure 1 the *memory request* place of the CPU and the *memory access granted* place are connected to the immediate transition ② via regular arcs. These two places are the only places which are connected to this transition and both are marked with tokens. Thus, the transition is going to fire immediately. The mentioned places are going to be cleared and the *memory access* place of the CPU is going to be marked. This transition example describes the situation where the CPU requests the memory at a time where memory access is allowed. The CPU accesses the memory and transfers data from or to the memory. The resource memory is therefore busy. Thus, the access to the memory by another device (here the DMA-Controller) is not granted.

The upper immediate transition ① of the DSPN depicted in Figure 1 behaves differently compared to transition ②. Three marked places are connected to transition ①. This transition is not going to fire as the *memory request* place of the CPU is connected to this transition via an inhibitor arc. If the *memory request* place of the CPU were to be cleared and the *memory request* place of the DMA-controller and the *memory access granted* places remain marked, then the connected immediate transition would fire immediately. Thus, the DMA controller only gets access to copy a word if the CPU is no longer requesting memory access. Therefore, in this arbitration scheme the CPU has higher priority than the DMA-controller.

The described DSPN demands input parameters such as memory access delays etc. to calculate probabilities and expectations of previously defined places. Therefore, statements of the communication behavior and performance can be acquired.

# 3  DSPN Modeling of Exemplary On-Chip Communication

## 3.1  DSPN Model of Communication Scenarios of the TMS320C6416

One basic example which has been modeled and analyzed here is the DSPN modeling of a state-of-the-art digital signal processor (DSP). The TMS320C6416 [14] (see Figure 2) which has been studied here is based on a VLIW-architecture.

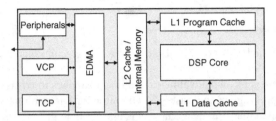

**Fig. 2.** Simplified block diagram of the TMS320C6416 DSP

This DSP includes a couple of interfaces, an Enhanced DMA-controller (EDMA) and two dedicated coprocessors (Viterbi and Turbo decoder coprocessor, VCP and TCP). Exemplary communication scenarios of this DSP have been modeled.

In Figure 3 a simplified block diagram of the C6416 and different communication paths of exemplary conflict scenarios for basic communication processes are depicted.

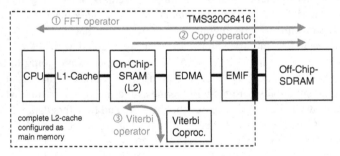

**Fig. 3.** Communication path of concurrent operators

In the first inspected scenario two operators compete against each other for one critical resource, the memory access. An FFT operator utilizes the CPU and reads and stores data from the external memory. The corresponding communication path ① of this operator is illustrated in gray above the simplified schematic of the C6416. The communication path of the copy operator ② is also depicted in Figure 3. This operator utilizes the Quick Direct Memory Access mechanism (QDMA) which is a part of the EDMA-controller. It copies data from the internal to the external memory section. Since both operators run concurrently, both aim to access the critical external memory interface resource. The arbitration is handled by the EDMA applying an arbitration scheme which is based on priority queues.

The corresponding DSPN depicted in Figure 4 represents the simplified scheme of the concurring operators and the arbitration of these two operators for the memory resource. It is separable into three subnets (see dashed boxes: Arbiter, FFT on CPU and QDMA-copy operator). The QDMA-copy operator functions similar to the DMA-controller device depicted in Figure 1. It consists of the two places *copy word* and *memory request*. The FFT on CPU operator depicted on the top left consists of a read and a write branch. The CPU writes data in the external memory or it reads data from this memory section. A more complex arbitration scheme is depicted on the bottom of Figure 4. This part of the DSPN models the queuing arbitration scheme utilized in the EDMA-Controller of the C6416.

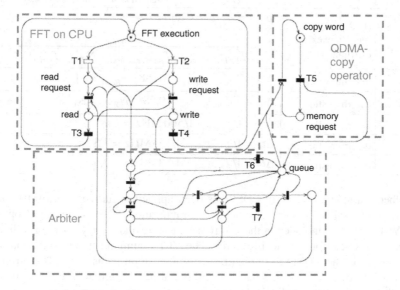

**Fig. 4.** DSPN model of concurrent FFT/copy operators

The required parameterization of the deterministic and stochastic transitions T1-T7 of this DSPN model is given in Table 1.
Here, it holds:

$$T_{FFT} = \text{duration of a single FFT operation}$$

(dependent on FFT length, without parallel copy operation)

$$N_{Read/Write} = \text{number of memory read/write accesses per FFT operation}$$

$$T_{Read/Write,ext.mem} = \text{time required to read/write a word from the external memory}$$

$$p_i(t) = \text{probability density function of the delay time of a specific transition}$$

The modeling results of the DSPN for the duration of the FFT are depicted in Figure 5a). Here the calculation time of the FFT operator computed by simulation with the DSPN model has been plotted against different FFT lengths. In order to attain a quantitative evaluation of the computed FFT's duration, reference measurements have been made on a reference DSP board. A measurement of the FFT duration without running the concurrent copy operator has also been applied to determine input parameters for the DSPN model. As can be seen from Figure 5a) the model yields a good estimation of the duration for the FFT operator. The maximum error is less than 10 % for an FFT length of 1024 points.

**Table. 1.** Transition type and transition parameters of the DSPN model of Figure 4

| Transition | Transition type | Formula and parameters |
|:---:|:---|:---|
| T1 | stochastic (negative. expon. distributed) | $p_1(t) = \lambda_1 \cdot e^{-\lambda_1 t}$ for $t > 0$ with $\lambda_1 = \dfrac{N_{Read}}{T_{FFT} - N_{Read} \cdot T_{Read,\,ext.mem} - N_{Write} \cdot T_{Write,\,ext.mem}}$ |
| T2 | stochastic (negative. expon. distributed) | $p_2(t) = \lambda_2 \cdot e^{-\lambda_2 t}$ for $t > 0$ with $\lambda_2 = \dfrac{N_{Write}}{T_{FFT} - N_{Read} \cdot T_{Read,\,ext.mem} - N_{Write} \cdot T_{Write,\,ext.mem}}$ |
| T3 | deterministic | $\Delta t_3 = T_{Read,ext.mem} = 0{,}188 \cdot N_{Read}$ [µs] |
| T4 | deterministic | $\Delta t_4 = T_{Write,ext.mem} = 0{,}088 \cdot N_{Write}$ [µs] |
| T5 | deterministic | $\Delta t_5 = 1/f_{Proc} = 1/500\,\text{MHz} = 2$ ns |
| T6 | deterministic | $\Delta t_6 = 1/f_{ext.mem} = 1/133\,\text{MHz} = 7{,}5$ ns |
| T7 | deterministic | $\Delta t_7 = 1/f_{ext.mem} = 1/133\,\text{MHz} = 7{,}5$ ns |

Another example based on this DSP has been applied to further confirm the suitability of using DSPNs in terms of on-chip communication. Here, the Viterbi Coprocessor (VCP) which is included in the C6416 architecture and a copy operator utilizing the EDMA compete for a critical resource. The VCP communicates with the internal memory also via the EDMA (see Figure 3, communication paths ① and ③). Arbitration is handled by a queuing mechanism configured here to utilize one queue by assigning the same priority to all EDMA requestors. I.e. memory access is granted to the VCP and the copy operator according to a first-come-first-serve policy.

For this experiment the VCP has been configured in the following way. The constraint length of the Viterbi decoder is 5, the number of states is 16 and the rate is 1/2. In the VCP configuration inspected here, the VCP communicates with the memory by getting 16 data packages of 32x32 bit in order to perform the decoding. Both, EDMA and VCP are clocked with a quarter of the CPU clock frequency ($f_{CPU} = 500$MHz). The results are transferred back to the memory with a package size of 32x32 bit. Performing two parallel operations (Viterbi decoding and copy operation), the two operators have to wait for their corresponding memory transfers. The EDMA mechanism of the C6416 always completes one memory block transfer before starting a new one. Hence, there is a dependency of the Viterbi decoding duration on the EDMA frame length. This situation has been modeled and the results have been compared to the measured values. The results are depicted in Figure 5b.

Performing only the Viterbi decoding, there is no dependency on the EDMA frame length (number of 64 bit words). If an EDMA frame length dependent copy operation is carried out, this significantly increases the Viterbi decoding time. In detail not the decoding process itself is concerned but the duration of data package transfers between VCP and internal memory. Again the maximum error is less than 10%.

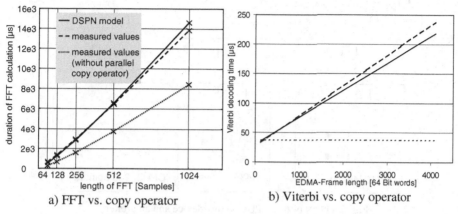

a) FFT vs. copy operator            b) Viterbi vs. copy operator

**Fig. 5.** Comparison of measured values with DSPNs

## 3.2 DSPN Model of an On-Chip Bus

On-chip busses are frequently used communication structures on today's SoCs. For example AMBA and CoreConnect bus systems are available commercial on-chip busses which are already employed in modern SoCs [1], [4]. A typical problem in designing a bus based SoC is how to fix all parameters which are associated with this on-chip bus structure (arbitration scheme, bus width, frame length etc.).

Such an exemplary communication structure featuring three components which exchange data has been modeled with a DSPN. The model demonstrates the impact of parameter variations of the connecting bus architecture on the total communication performance. Here, three components are connected to a 32 bit bus and their bus access is managed by an arbiter. The three components connected to the bus are two CPUs performing here exemplarily a 1024 point FFT (CPU 1) and a 256 point FFT (CPU 2). The third component is a DMA unit performing a copy operation within an infinite loop (copy device). This parallel access to the bus has been modeled by the DSPN in Figure 6. One aspect of this exemplary system which can be analyzed by application of DSPNs is the bus usage. For example depending on the slot length assigned to each component which can be expressed by the number of bus cycles the resulting bus usage will change.

The arbitration scheme which has been applied is a 2L-TDMA scheme [7]. This means, the bus resource is distributed evenly between the three components. But, if no bus access is demanded by a component within its time slot the next scheduled requesting participant can utilize this time slot. While the copy device always demands the bus resource, the CPUs need some time to calculate new results. Therefore, the bus usage is nearly 100% for fine granular time slots as the copy device utilizes nearly all clock cycles and the bus usage drops for larger time slots.

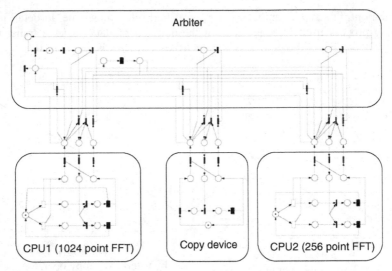

**Fig. 6.** DSPN of two CPUs, a copy device and an arbiter

Figure 7 depicts this dependency of the bus usage on the time slot length. Hence, the DSPN modeling helps to analyze which time slot length results in which bus usage. Furthermore, the computation and the corresponding memory access time of the FFT tasks can be analyzed. So for example, it can be examined, if a given specification can be fulfilled with this communication scheme. For this example the effort for developing the model (model complexity) was in the range of one hour. The required computation time took only a few seconds on a Linux based 800 MHz PC.

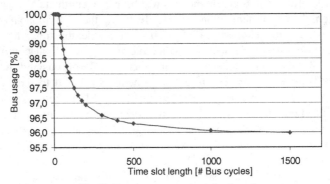

**Fig. 7.** Bus usage over time slot length

One key advantage of modeling with DSPN is the possibility to easily trade model complexity for performance estimation accuracy. For example, starting the performance analysis for SoCs with a coarse grain model and with restricted accuracy it is possible to refine the granularity and hence the accuracy stepwise. The refinement of the granularity causes an increase in model complexity and computation time. Nevertheless, even coarse grain DSPN models yield a good estimation accuracy.

# 4 Summary

Design space exploration for heterogeneous Systems on Chip (SoC) is a key issue for modern chip design. Here, the suitability of applying deterministic and stochastic Petri nets (DSPN) to model the performance behavior of on-chip communication has been demonstrated. Therefore, a state-of-the-art heterogeneous DSP featuring dedicated coprocessors has been examined. Performance parameters of two examples utilizing this platform have been measured. These measurement results have been compared to results yielded by the corresponding DSPN models. This comparison proves that modeling with DSPNs yields a sufficient performance estimation accuracy at reasonable effort.

In conclusion, DSPNs seem to be a promising candidate to analyze performance aspects of on-chip communication in an early stage of design space exploration.

# References

1. ARM AMBA; http://www.arm.com/armtech/AMBA
2. Blume, H.; Huebert, H.; Feldkämper, H.; Noll, T. G.: "Model based exploration of the design space for heterogeneous Systems on Chip", Proc. IEEE ASAP, San Jose, USA, Jul. 02
3. DSPNexpress; http://www.dspnexpress.de
4. IBM CoreConnect; http://www-3.ibm.com/chips/products/coreconnect
5. Keutzer, K.; Malik, S.; Newton, A.; Rabaey, J.; Sangiovanni-Vincentelli, A.: "System-Level-Design: Orthogonalization of Concerns and Platform-Based Design", IEEE Trans. on CAD of Integrated Circuits and Systems, Vol. 19, No. 12, Dec. 2000
6. Kleinrock, L.: "Queueing Systems – Vol. 1: Theory", JOHN WILEY AND SONS, 1975
7. Lahiri, K.; Raghunathan, A.; Dey, S.: "Evaluation of the traffic performance characteristics of system-on-chip architectures", Proc. VLSI Design, pp. 29-35, Jan. 2001
8. Lahiri, K.; Raghunathan, A.; Dey, S.: "System-Level Performance Analysis for Designing On-Chip Communication Architectures", IEEE Trans. on CAD of Integrated Circuits and Systems, Jun. 2001
9. Lindemann, C.: "Performance Modeling with Deterministic and Stochastic Petri Nets", JOHN WILEY AND SONS, Berlin, Germany, 1998
10. Mickle, M. H.: "Transient and steady-state performance modeling of parallel processors", Applied Mathematical Modelling, Vol. 22, No. 7, Jul. 1998, pp. 533-543
11. Petri net tools data base; http://www.daimi.au.dk/PetriNets
12. Pimentel, A.; Hertzberger, L.; Lieverse, P.; van der Wolf, P.; Deprettere, E.: "Exploring embedded System Architectures with Artemis", IEEE Computer, Vol. 34, Nr. 11, Nov. 01
13. Kogel, T.; Doerper, M.; Wieferink, A. et. al.: "A Modular Simulation Framework for Architectural Exploration of On-Chip Interconnection Networks", CODES+ISSS, Oct. 2003
14. Texas Instruments; http://www.ti.com
15. TimeNET; http://pdv.cs.tu-berlin.de/~timenet/

# Communication Optimization
# in Compaan Process Networks

Ioan Cimpian[1], Alexandru Turjan[1], Ed Deprettere[1], and Erwin de Kock[2]

[1] Leiden Institute of Advanced Computer Sciences (LIACS), Leiden University,
Niels Bohrweg 1, 2333 CA Leiden, The Netherlands
{icimpian,aturjan,edd}@liacs.nl
[2] Philips Research The Netherlands,
Prof. Holstlaan 4, 5656 AA Eindhoven, The Netherlands
erwin.de.kock@philips.com

**Abstract.** Compaan Process Networks (CPN) are Kahn Process Networks (KPN) that are generated by a compiler, called Compaan, that translates imperatively specified affine nested loop programs to input-output equivalent KPN - specified programs. This paper presents a method to convert a given CPN to an input-output equivalent CPN in which no redundant channels appear. The method has been implemented and applied to a large set of given affine nested loop programs that Compaan can accept.

## 1 Introduction

Over the last years there has been an increased interest in designing embedded systems that are able to solve more complex problems and that are obeying very tight constraints in terms of performance and cost. This problem consist first in designing platforms that provide the necessary hardware resources in terms of computational power and performance - these are multiprocessor platforms, and second in finding ways to efficiently use these resources by the applications - this is the mapping problem. Although such multiprocessor platforms have been already designed and developed by many companies, the mapping of applications onto them still relies on the ability of the designer to perform a manual partitioning of the application across platform processing units [1]. Therefore, a great part of the mapping effort was focused in the direction of expressing the application in such way that the inherent parallelism becomes explicit.

The Compaan compiler [2] has been developed to facilitate the mapping of imperative specified affine nested loop programs to such multiprocessor platforms by deriving for the imperative input program a functionally equivalent Process Network (PN). Indeed, this mapping is easier when the program is specified in a parallel manner instead of a sequential one. Imperative affine nested loop programs could be specified non-sequentially by using the so-called cyclo-static data-flow model of computation [3]. However, it turns out that an more appealing way of modeling is to rely on the Process Network model of computation [4], because this results in more compact specification and, moreover, it makes any further clustering for scheduling of cyclo-static data-flow model specifications superfluous.

A. Pimentel and S. Vassiliadis (Eds.): SAMOS 2004, LNCS 3133, pp. 494–506, 2004.

Compaan Process Networks (CPN) being KPNs, they consist of a finite set of processes that communicate point-to-point over unbounded FIFO channels and synchronize through *blocking-read* primitives. In a CPN the processes themselves are also imperatively specified affine nested loop programs. The inter-process communication in such CPN has some particularities. We say that communication between two processes, a producer and a consumer, is *in-order* if the order of production is the same with the order of consumption. We will call the channel involved is such communication *in-order channel* (IOC). If the order of production is not the same with the order of consumption then the communication is *out-of-order* and it is necessary to use at the consumer side a reordering controller. We will call the channel involved in such communication *out-of-order channel* (OOC) [5]. In this context our problem is to find out how can we minimize the number of IOCs in a CPN by merging IOCs between the same two processes (adjacent FIFOs), i.e. replace them with a single IOC.

This question is relevant when the CPN is to be mapped on e.g., a multiprocessor platform that consist of some processing units, a shared bus and a shared memory. In such an architecture communication and synchronization may be costly enough that redundant channels are not acceptable. Therefore, the in-order channel merging aims two important objectives: **(1)** reducing the total memory size allocated to the network FIFO channels (Fig. 1) and **(2)** reducing the control involved when communicating data over the network FIFO channels (Fig. 2).

## 2  Basic Terminology

Because a process in a CPN is an imperative specified affine nested loop program, the loop nest impose an iteration domain and an ordering of the operations called *get*, *execute*, and *put*. Fig. 3 shows two processes communicating in a CPN. The iteration domain and the lexicographic ordering are also shown. An *input port domain* IPD (*output port domain* OPD) is a subset of the iteration domain that is involved in an interprocess communication action, *put* and *get*, respectively [8]. Each FIFO uniquely relates an input port to an output port forming a *Producer/Consumer* pair. The Consumer is related to the Producer by a data-dependency function $f$ that maps an iteration from the IPD to the correspondent iteration from the OPD, that is, knowing the iteration where a token is consumed at the consumer side we can find out applying this function the iteration where the token was produced at the producer side. As shown in Fig. 3 a process port contains a *FIFO.get()* statement or a *FIFO.put(...)* statement. In order to reason about the FIFO merging we need to be able to keep track of the order of executing such *get/put* statements inside the same process.

Let $s$ be either a *get* or a *put* statement in a CPN process, and let $s(v \in D)$ be such a statement addressed in the iteration point $v$ of the domain $D$, where $D$ stands for either $IPD$ or $OPD$. Now, given $s(v_1 \in D_1)$ and $s(v_2 \in D_2)$, where $D_1$ and $D_2$ are either both IPDs or both OPDs belonging to the same process, we say that $s(v_1) \prec_l s(v_2)$ $(s(v_1) \succ_l s(v_2))$ if $v_1 \prec_l v_2$ $(v_1 \succ_l v_2)$ - **lexicographic order**. Also, given $s_1(v \in D_1)$ and $s_2(v \in D_2)$, where $D_1$ and $D_2$ are as before, we say that $s_1(v) \prec_t s_2(v)$ $(s_1(v) \succ_t s_2(v))$ if $s_1(v)$ textually precedes (succeeds) $s_2(v)$ - **textual order**.

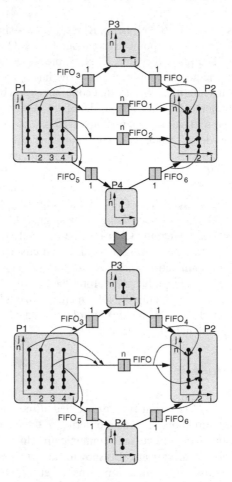

**Fig. 1.** An example that shows opportunity for memory size reduction. We observe that $FIFO_1$ needs to be filled with $n$ tokens before the process P2 can start to execute its first stage and after all tokens from $FIFO_1$ are consumed, similarly $FIFO_2$ needs to be filled with $n$ tokens before the process P2 can start to execute its second stage. On the other hand if we analyze the figure $FIFO_1$ and $FIFO_2$ can be merged. Thus we obtain an absolute memory reduction of $n$ locations.

Next, the notation $s_1(v_1) \prec s_2(v_2)$ will stand for $s_1(v_1) \prec_l s_2(v_2) \lor (v_1 =_l v_2 \land s_1(v_1) \prec_t s_2(v_2))$ - **global order**. And similar for $s_1(v_1) \succ s_2(v_2)$. For simplicity we will use the notation $v_i$ for $s_i(v_i \in D_i)$. Therefore, the relation above become: $v_1 \prec v_2 \equiv v_1 \prec_l v_2 \lor (v_1 =_l v_2 \land v_1 \prec_t v_2)$.

We observe that for operations corresponding to the same port (*IPD/OPD*) the lexicographic order represents a total order. But we need to order statements belonging to different ports, thus, we have to extend this order. This is done by introducing the textual order. Thus, we obtain the global order which is a total order relation among operations corresponding to different ports within the same process. Detailed explanations about order relation can be found in [9], therefore we will not elaborate further on it.

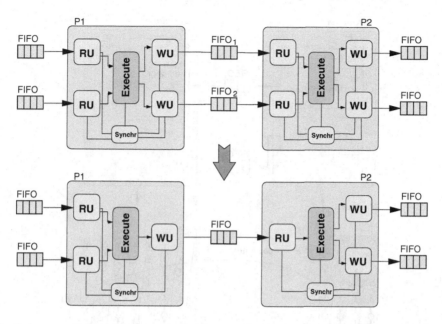

**Fig. 2.** An example that shows opportunity for control reduction. For each FIFO we have a read control unit RU and a write control unit WU. The structure of these control units depends greatly of their implementation, and, for example in a pure hardware implementation using FPGAs [6] they may contain numerators used to address the FIFO locations, and automatons used to check the status of the FIFO (empty or full). Therefore by merging the two FIFOs we reduce also the control units. However, assuming a different platform [7] we expect that by merging FIFOs the control involved in communicating data is reduced as well.

## 3   Problem Statement

Process networks generated by Compaan often contain multiple FIFO channels (adjacent FIFOs) between two nodes. In many cases these FIFOs can be merged into one FIFO. Although this may reduce concurrency, it also reduces the topological complexity of the CPN and it can reduce the cost of implementation.

The FIFO channel merging problem consist in minimizing the number of the FIFO channels in a CPN, thus in finding all the groups of adjacent FIFOs that can be merged. Therefore in order to merge a group of $k$ adjacent FIFOs: $Ch_1(OPD_1, IPD_1, f_1)$, ... $Ch_k(OPD_k, IPD_k, f_k)$, the global order of production in the domain $\cup_{i=1}^{k} OPD_i$ must be the same with the global order of consumption in the domain $\cup_{i=1}^{k} IPD_i$. If the global orders of production and consumption are not the same, it may be possible to enforce the textual order at the producer or consumer side to obtain the same global order. In this case we can merge this group of $k$ FIFOs by replace them with a single FIFO. In order to have a clear understanding of the problem we present an illustrative example that presents various situations related to the in-order channel merging problem. Fig. 4 shows two processes that are communicating data over four FIFO channels. We observe from here that the order of production is the same as the order of consump-

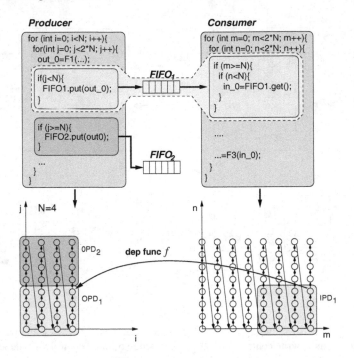

**Fig. 3.** A Producer and Consumer process. For Producer we show the output port domains (OPDs) and for Consumer, we show the input port domains (IPDs). Each OPD is uniquely connected to another IPD via a FIFO. In this example, $OPD_1$ is connected to $IPD_1$ via $FIFO_1$. The Producer/Consumer with the FIFO form an instance of the classical consumer/producer pair.

tion for each of the four channels. This means that the communication channels are in-order. We will analyze now $FIFO_3$ and $FIFO_4$. We observe that the global order of producing tokens in $OPD_3$ and $OPD_4$ is the same as the global order of consuming tokens in $IPD_3$ and $IPD_4$. This leads to the conclusion that the two FIFO channels can be replaced by a single one. We will analyze now $FIFO_2$ and $FIFO_3$. Here the global order of producing tokens in $OPD_2$ and $OPD_3$ is not the same as the global order of consuming tokens in $IPD_2$ and $IPD_3$. As it can be seen tokens are produced first in $OPD_2$ and then in $OPD_3$ but are first consumed in $IPD_3$ then in $IPD_2$. As a consequence the two FIFO channels can not be replaced by a single FIFO channel. The same situation is for the pairs: $FIFO_1$ and $FIFO_3$, $FIFO_1$ and $FIFO_4$, $FIFO_2$ and $FIFO_4$. We will analyze now $FIFO_1$ and $FIFO_2$. Here the global order of producing tokens in $OPD_1$ and $OPD_2$ is not the same as the global order of consuming tokens in $IPD_1$ and $IPD_2$. As it can be seen, tokens are produced first in $OPD_1$ and then in $OPD_2$ but are first consumed in $IPD_2$ then in $IPD_1$. After a first glance we would say that FIFO merging is not possible. However, after a close analysis we observe that at the consumer side the order of consuming tokens from channel is given only by the textual order of IPDs. Therefore we can control the order of consuming by controlling this textual order. This leads to interesting results: even if initially the merging is not possible after a simple code transformation (textual reorder) - we impose the

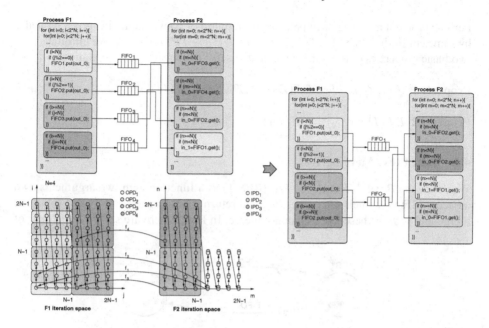

**Fig. 4.** A comprehensive example showing various situations related to the in-order channel merging problem.

order from the producer side to the consumer side - the FIFOs can be merged. This is illustrated in Figure 4 right side. The textual reorder is done in the following way: at the consumer side we change the textual order of reading the channels putting first $OPD_1$, then $OPD_2$. After this reorder we can replace the two FIFO channels by only one FIFO channel.                                                                         □

In the next section we describe in detail the proposed solution to this problem. First we describe a test function, called *Basic FIFO Merging Test*, which is used to decide if two adjacent FIFOs can or cannot be merged. Next we describe how this function can be extended to a *General FIFO Merging Test* used to find if more than two adjacent FIFOs can or cannot be merged. Last we describe the standard procedure that use this test functions above to find all the groups of adjacent FIFOs that can merge in a PN.

## 4   Solution

### 4.1   Empty Test

To help the presentation of the solution we need to introduce first a function called Empty Test (ET). This function takes as argument a *domain* and returns a boolean: *true* if there are no integer solutions in that domain or *false* if there is at least an integer solution in that domain:

$$ET(D) = \begin{cases} True, & \nexists x \in D \\ False, & \exists x \in D \end{cases}$$

For our problem a domain will be always a reunion of convex domains given typically by some constraints like $D = (x, y) \mid x \in IPD_1, y \in IPD_2, x \prec y$. We introduce now two basic properties of this function that are useful for our future presentation:

**Property 1** *If* $D_2 \subset D_3$ *then* $ET(D_2) = ET(D_2) \vee ET(D_3)$.

**Property 2** $ET(D_1 \cup D_2) = ET(D_1) \wedge ET(D_2)$.

## 4.2   Basic FIFO Merging Test

We define the *Basic FIFO Merge Test* (BFMT) as a function with two arguments, two adjacent FIFO channels $Ch_1$ and $Ch_2$, and return a boolean: *true* if these FIFOs can merge and *false* if these FIFOs can not merge. In Fig. 5 there are shown a P/C pair of

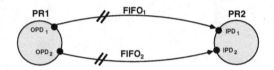

**Fig. 5.** PN showing opportunity in FIFO channels sharing.

processes connected by two FIFO channels namely $Ch_1 = (OPD_1, IPD_1, f_1)$ and $Ch_2 = (OPD_2, IPD_2, f_2)$. In order to merge $Ch_1$ and $Ch_2$ the global order of the producer iterations included in $OPD_1 \cup OPD_2$ must be the same with the global order of the consumer iterations included in $IPD_1 \cup IPD_2$. This means that there must be a common global order of producing and consuming over the two FIFO channels. Formally this statement can be verified by checking whether the domains specified by the following two sets of constraints are empty:

$$\text{PD} : \begin{cases} x \in IPD_1, & (1) \\ y \in IPD_2, & (2) \\ x \prec y, & (3') \\ f_1(x) \succ f_2(y). & (4') \end{cases} \qquad \text{DD} : \begin{cases} x \in IPD_1, & (1) \\ y \in IPD_2, & (2) \\ x \succ y, & (3'') \\ f_1(x) \prec f_2(y). & (4'') \end{cases}$$

Note that "$\prec$" is the global order and $f$ is the data-dependency function between Consumer and Producer as presented in section 2. If there are iterations $x$ and $y$ that obey one of the constraints defined above, then merging is not possible. Therefore, the Basic FIFO Merge Test BFMT can be expressed as follows:

$$BFMT(Ch_1, Ch_2) = ET(PD) \wedge ET(DD).$$

Further we investigate how BFMT is solved in the CPN context, i.e., when operating over convex input and output port domains connected via affine dependency functions. For this purpose we use Integer Linear Programming (ILP) [10, 11] in order to perform

ET on a domain with lexicographical constraints. Therefore, we decompose the global order from relations $(3')(4')$ and $(3'')(4'')$ according to section 2.

$$PD: \begin{cases} x \in IPD_1, & (1) \\ y \in IPD_2, & (2) \\ x \prec y, & (3') \\ f_1(x) \succ f_2(y). & (4') \end{cases} =$$

$$PD_1: \begin{cases} x \in IPD_1, \\ y \in IPD_2, \\ x \prec_l y, \\ f_1(x) \succ_l f_2(y). \end{cases} \cup \quad PD_2: \begin{cases} x \in IPD_1, \\ y \in IPD_2, \\ x \prec_l y, \\ f_1(x) =_l f_2(y) \wedge f_1(x) \succ_t f_2(y). \end{cases} \cup$$

$$PD_3: \begin{cases} x \in IPD_1, \\ y \in IPD_2, \\ x =_l y \wedge x \prec_t y, \\ f_1(x) \succ_l f_2(y). \end{cases} \cup \quad PD_4: \begin{cases} x \in IPD_1, \\ y \in IPD_2, \\ x =_l y \wedge x \prec_t y, \\ f_1(x) =_l f_2(y) \wedge f_1(x) \succ_t f_2(y). \end{cases}$$

Applying a similarly decomposition procedure the $DD$ domain is decomposed as follows:

$$DD: \begin{cases} x \in IPD_1, & (1) \\ y \in IPD_2, & (2) \\ x \succ y, & (3') \\ f_1(x) \prec f_2(y). & (4') \end{cases} =$$

$$DD_1: \begin{cases} x \in IPD_1, \\ y \in IPD_2, \\ x \succ_l y, \\ f_1(x) \prec_l f_2(y). \end{cases} \cup \quad DD_2: \begin{cases} x \in IPD_1, \\ y \in IPD_2, \\ x \succ_l y, \\ f_1(x) =_l f_2(y) \wedge f_1(x) \prec_t f_2(y). \end{cases} \cup$$

$$DD_3: \begin{cases} x \in IPD_1, \\ y \in IPD_2, \\ x =_l y \wedge x \succ_t y, \\ f_1(x) \prec_l f_2(y). \end{cases} \cup \quad DD_4: \begin{cases} x \in IPD_1, \\ y \in IPD_2, \\ x =_l y \wedge x \succ_t y, \\ f_1(x) =_l f_2(y) \wedge f_1(x) \prec_t f_2(y). \end{cases}$$

Therefore, we can evaluate now the Basic FIFO Merge Test as follows, according to *Prop. 2*:

$$\begin{aligned} BFMT = \; & ET(PD_1) \wedge ET(PD_2) \wedge ET(PD_3) \wedge ET(PD_4) \wedge \\ & ET(DD_1) \wedge ET(DD_2) \wedge ET(DD_3) \wedge ET(DD_4). \end{aligned}$$

However, the description of the domains $PD_2$, $PD_3$, $PD_4$, $DD_2$, $DD_3$ and $DD_4$ depends on the textual order. Hence, we further decompose those sets into two subsets:

the first set i.e., $D_i^l$ is defined purely according to the lexicographical order and therefore we can apply ILP in order to determine $ET(D_i^l)$. The second set i.e., $D_i^t$ is defined only according to the textual order: $D_i = D_i^l \cap D_i^t$, where $i = \overline{2,4}$. For example according to this decomposition the domain $PD2$ is decomposed as follows: $DD_2 = DD_2^l \cap DD_2^t$, where

$$
DD_2^l = \begin{cases} x \in IPD_1, \\ y \in IPD_2, \\ x \succ_l y, \\ f_1(x) =_l f_2(y). \end{cases} \qquad and \qquad DD_2^t = \begin{cases} x \in IPD_1, \\ y \in IPD_2, \\ f_1(x) \prec_t f_2(y). \end{cases}
$$

On the other hand because the textual order is fixed once the network is executed, that is the textual constraint $f_1(x) \prec_t f_2(y)$ is added to the constraints describing $DD_2^l$, results that $DD_2^l \subset DD_2^t$ such that by applying *Prop. 1* results that:

$$ ET(DD_2) = ET(DD_2^l) \vee ET(DD_2^t), $$

Therefore, we get the next formula for BFMT:

$$
\begin{aligned}
BFMT = \ & ET(PD_1) \wedge \\
& ( \ ET(PD_2^l) \vee ET(PD_2^t) \ ) \ \wedge \\
& ( \ ET(PD_3^l) \vee ET(PD_3^t) \ ) \ \wedge \\
& ( \ ET(PD_4^l) \vee ET(PD_4^t) \ ) \ \wedge \\
& ET(DD1) \wedge \\
& ( \ ET(DD_2^l) \vee ET(DD_2^t) \ ) \ \wedge \\
& ( \ ET(DD_3^l) \vee ET(DD_3^t) \ ) \ \wedge \\
& ( \ ET(DD_4^l) \vee ET(DD_4^t) \ ) \ \wedge
\end{aligned}
$$

As you can see we have decomposed now the Basic FIFO Merge Test into separate tests regarding the lexicographical order and regarding the textual order. Observe that the merging is possible (i.e. $BFMT = true$) iff all the component predicates are also true:

$$
\begin{aligned}
BFMT = true \ \equiv \ & ET(PD1) = true \ \wedge \\
& ( \ ET(PD_2^l) \vee ET(PD_2^t) \ ) = true \ \wedge \\
& ( \ ET(PD_3^l) \vee ET(PD_3^t) \ ) = true \ \wedge \\
& ( \ ET(PD_4^l) \vee ET(PD_4^t) \ ) = true \ \wedge \\
& ET(DD1) = true \ \wedge \\
& ( \ ET(DD_2^l) \vee ET(DD_2^t) \ ) = true \ \wedge \\
& ( \ ET(DD_3^l) \vee ET(DD_3^t) \ ) = true \ \wedge \\
& ( \ ET(DD_4^l) \vee ET(DD_4^t) \ ) = true \ \wedge
\end{aligned}
$$

Here we make the observation that while the lexicographical order is fixed such that for example we get $ET(PD_i^l) = false$, the textual order can be modified in such way that $ET(PD_3^t) = true$. Hence, $ET(PD_i^l) \vee ET(PD_3^t) = true$. *In other words although the global order does not allow to do the merging, by choosing an appropriate textual order the merging becomes possible.* Therefore, we first evaluate the predicates involving lexicographic order and then choose IPDs and OPDs textual orders to make possible the merging. However, according to these textual order requirements in the end of this evaluation procedure we get a list of textual constraints regarding the ordered OPDs and IPDs. After that we analyze whether these lists of textual constraints are logically valid and if yes we decide under what textual orders the merging is possible. We will illustrate this, using two simple examples:

*Example:* Suppose the hypothetical case where we have evaluated the Empty Domain Test on the domains regrading the lexicographic order (see section 2) getting $ET(PD_3^l) = false$ and $ET(DD_3^l) = false$. In order to make the merging possible we have to impose a textual order like this: from the first relation results that $IPD_2$ must be textually before $IPD_1$, and from the second relation results that $IPD_1$ must be textually before $IPD_2$ such that $ET(PD_3^t) = true$ and $ET(DD_3^t) = true$. But This set of textual constraints is in a logical contradiction, and the FIFO merging is not possible.                                                                          □

### 4.3   Extending the Merge Test to More Than Two FIFO Channels

So far we have analyzed only the case in which two FIFO channels are considered for merging. For this purpose we have introduced the function BFMT. However, we still have to solve the merging problem in the case when there are more than two adjacent FIFOs. For this purpose we introduce the *General FIFO Merge Test.*

**Property 3** : *Let be three FIFO channels $Ch_1, Ch_2$ and $Ch_3$ with their dependency functions $f_1, f_2$ and respectively $f_3$, that are connecting the same P/C pair of processes. Hence, $Ch_1, Ch_2$ and $Ch_3$ can be merged i.e., $GFMT(Ch_1, Ch_2, Ch_3) = true$ iff:*

$$BFMT(Ch_1, Ch_2) = true \wedge BFMT(Ch_1, Ch_3) = true \wedge$$
$$BFMT(Ch_2, Ch_3) = true.$$

**Proof:** '⇒': Let be arbitrarily $x \in IPD_1$, $y \in IPD_2$ and $z \in IPD3$. Because "≺" is a global order results that we can order $x, y$ and $z$. Suppose having the following order: $x \prec y \prec z$. On the other hand because $BFMT(Ch_1, Ch_2) = true$ results that $x \prec y \prec z \Rightarrow f_1(x) \prec f_2(y)$. Applying a similar procedure for the other two pairs results that $f_1(x) \prec f_2(y) \prec f_3(z)$. Therefore, we conclude that the three FIFO channels cam be merged: $GFMT(Ch_1, Ch_2, Ch_3) = true$.

'⇐': Because "≺" is a global order that does not get disturbed from the Consumer to the Producer process (i.e., the three FIFOs can e merged) results that also restricted to pairs of IPDs and OPDs the order does not get disturbed such that each pair of channels can be separately merged.                                                                          □

**Corollary 1** *Let be $n$ FIFO channels $Ch_i$ with $i = \overline{1, n}$ connecting the same P/C pair of processes. Hence,*

$$GFMT(Ch_1, .., Ch_n) = true \Leftrightarrow \forall\, u, v,\ such\ that\ 1 \leq u, v \leq n,$$
$$BFMT(Ch_u, Ch_v) = true.$$

**Table 1.** Experimental results.

| Algorithm name | Nb. Processes | Initial Nb. Channels | Initial Nb. FIFOs | Nb. of FIFOs after merging | FIFO reduction |
|---|---|---|---|---|---|
| SVD | 8 | 118 | 84 | 35 | 58% |
| Faddeev | 9 | 28 | 24 | 19 | 20% |
| M-JPEG | 9 | 50 | 33 | 13 | 60% |
| Motion Estim | 11 | 98 | 98 | 93 | 5% |
| DigBeamFormer | 8 | 17 | 17 | 14 | 17% |
| QR | 5 | 12 | 12 | 12 | 0% |
| Gauss-Elimin | 4 | 11 | 7 | 4 | 0% |

Based on Corollary1 we can decide whether $n$ FIFOs can be merged into a single one.

**Remark 1** The number of BFMT that has to be done to prove $GFMT(Ch_1, ..., Ch_n)$ is given by:

$$C_n^2 = \frac{n!}{(n-2)!2!} = \frac{(n-1)n}{2}.$$

In order to decide if $n$ adjacent FIFOs can merge, we have to do all $C_n^2$ BFMT. However, this does not necessarily means that all these tests will return true. Therefore, we must divide this group of n FIFOs in groups of FIFOs that can merge, i.e. for each such group $GFMT$ must be true. The problem is to find all the largest, exclusive groups of FIFOs, such that for each group $GFMT$ is true, all channels belong at least to one group, no channel belong to two groups, and each group is maximal.

We associate to this problem a graph where each FIFO represent a vertex and each $BFMT(Ch_i, Ch_j)$ that is $true$ represent an edge between vertexes $Ch_i$ and $Ch_j$. Therefore our problem is reduced to a problem of finding all the maximal and exclusive complete subgraphs (cliques) in this graph. For solving this problem we can use a recursive algorithm that explore all the possibilities of complete subgraphs in the graph or we can use a heuristic algorithm [12, 13].

## 5   Implementation and Results

In Compaan we have implemented a transformation which change the topology of a PN by merging adjacent FIFOs, thus reducing the number of in-order channels in the network. This transformation makes an extensive use of polyhedron manipulation, and integer linear programming. Instead of implementing this functionality ourselves, we have integrated already existing C libraries, such as PolyLib [14] and Pip [10] or Omega [11].

In Table 1 we present some quantitative results when applying FIFO merge over seven PN generated by Compaan. For each application we give the number of processes, the total number of channels before merging, the number of FIFOs before merging, the number of FIFOs after merging, and the reduction rate of FIFOs. We observe from this table that the reduction rate depends greatly of the original process network. The

PNs that shows the highest reduction rate (SVD and M-JPEG) initially contain a larger number of adjacent FIFOs while the PNs that have a reduction rate of 0% have none or very few adjacent FIFOs. But this is not true always: the Motion Estimation PN even if it has initially a large number of adjacent FIFOs the reduction rate is very low (only 5%). Therefore, we draw the conclusion that the reduction rate depends not only on the topology of the PN but on the algorithm implemented by this PN.

# 6 Conclusions

In this paper we describe a well structured procedure which allows us to automatically transform a PN by merging in-order channels related to the same processes. We have implemented this procedure completely in software and we have integrate it with Compaan. Our procedure analyze the internal representation of the PN in Compaan, searching for groups of adjacent FIFOs that can be merged. This is done by checking that the global order of production is the same as the global order of consumption for each such group. After this the PN is generated by replacing each group of FIFOs that can be merged with one single FIFO. As future work we plan to do other transformations on the network such as: *process splitting* in which the loop structure of a process is unrolled resulting a larger number of processes, *channel splitting* in which a channel is splitted mainly in order to enable process splitting, *process merging* in which the loop structures of a number of processes are merged resulting a smaller number of processes, and *process re-timing* in which the iteration space of a process is rescheduled by applying unimodular transformations.

# References

1. de Kock, E.: Multiprocessor Mapping of Process Networks: A JPEG Decoding Case Study. In: Proc. 15th Int. Symposium on System Synthesis (ISSS'2002), Kyoto, Japan (2002) 68–73
2. Deprettere, E.F., Rijpkema, E., Kienhuis, B.: Translating imperative affine nested loop programs into process networks. In: Springer - Lecture Notes in Computer Science, Tutorial on Embedded Processor Design Challenges, LNCS 2268,(SAMOS'01). (2002) 89–112
3. Lee, E.A., Parks, T.M.: Dataflow process networks. Proceedings of the IEEE **83** (1995) 773–799
4. Kahn, G.: The semantics of a simple language for parallel programming. In: Proc. of the IFIP Congress 74, North-Holland Publishing Co. (1974)
5. Turjan, A., Kienhuis, B., Deprettere, E.F.: A compile time based approach for solving out-of-order communication in kahn process networks. In: IEEE 13th "Int. Conf. on Application-specific Systems, Architectures and Processors (ASAP 2002). (2002)
6. Zissulescu-Ianculescu, C., Stefanov, T., Kienhuis, B., Deprettere, E.: Laura: Leiden architecture research and exploration tool. In: FPL. (2003)
7. Stravers, P., Hoogerbrugge, J.: Homogeneous multiprocessors and the future of silicon design paradigms. In: Proceedings of the Int. Symposium on VLSI Technology, Systems, and Applications. (2001)
8. Rijpkema, E.: From Piecewise Regular Algorithms to Dataflow Architectures (2001)
9. Feautrier, P.: Dataflow analysis of scalar and array references. Int. J. of Parallel Programming **20** (1991) 23–53

10. Feautrier, P.: Parametric integer programming (1988) Operations Research, 22(3):243-268.
11. Pugh, W.: The Omega Test: A Fast and Practical Integer Programming Algorithm for Dependence Analysis. Communications of the ACM **35** (1992) 102–114
12. Bron, C., Kerbosch, J.: Algorithm 457: Finding all cliques of an undirected graph. Communications of the ACM **16** (1973) 575–577
13. De Micheli, G.: Synthesis and optimization of digital circuits (1994) McGraw-Hill series in electrical and computer engineering. Electronics and VLSI circuits.
14. Wilde, D.: A library for doing polyhedral operations. In: Technical Report PI 785, IRISA, Rennes, France. (1993)

# Analysis of Dataflow Programs
# with Interval-Limited Data-Rates

Jürgen Teich[1,*] and Shuvra S. Bhattacharyya[2,**]

[1] University of Erlangen-Nuremberg, Germany
teich@cs.fau.de, http://www12.informatik.uni-erlangen.de
[2] University of Maryland, USA
ssb@eng.umd.edu, http://www.eng.umd.edu

**Abstract.** In this paper, we consider the problem of analyzing data flow programs with the property that actor production and consumption rates are not constant and fixed, but limited by intervals. Such interval ranges may result from uncertainty in the specification of an actor or as a design freedom of the model. Major questions such as *consistency* and *buffer memory requirements* for single-processor *schedules* will be analyzed here for such specifications for the first time.

## 1 Motivation

The role of data flow models of computation is becoming increasingly important for modeling and synthesis of digital processing applications. Our paper is concerned with analyzing dataflow graphs whose component data rates are not known precisely in advance. Such models are often given due to imprecise specifications or due to uncertainties in the implementation. Examples of imprecise specifications include unknown execution times of tasks, unknown data rates, unknown consumption and production behavior of modules and many more. For example, a speech compression system may have a fixed overall structure. However, the subsystem data rates are typically influenced by the size of the speech segment that is to be processed [1]. Here, we will propose a data flow model of computation that is able to model such uncertain behavior.

To understand such models, it useful to first review principles of the *synchronous data flow* (SDF) model of computation, where production and consumption rates of data flow actors, representing computational blocks, consume fixed, known amounts of data (tokens) upon each invocation. For such graph models, often represented by a graph in which actors are connected by directed arcs that transport tokens, many interesting results have been shown such as 1) *consistency*, 2) *memory bounds and memory analysis*, and 3) *scheduling algorithms*. Consistency, e.g., is a static property of an SDF-graph specification which is necessary in order to guarantee the existence of

---

* The first author was supported in this work by the Deutsche Forschungsgemeinschaft (DFG) under grant Te163/5-2.
** The second author was supported in this work by the US National Science Foundation (grant numbers 0325119 and 9734275), and the Semiconductor Research Corporation (contract number 2001-HJ-905).

A. Pimentel and S. Vassiliadis (Eds.): SAMOS 2004, LNCS 3133, pp. 507–518, 2004.

a finite sequence of actor firings, also called a *schedule*. Typically, an SDF specification is compiled by constructing a *valid schedule*, i.e., a schedule that fires each actor at least once, does not deadlock, and produces no net change in the number of tokens queued on each edge. For each actor firing, a corresponding code block is instantiated from a library to produce machine code.

In [5], efficient algorithms are presented to determine whether or not a given SDF graph is consistent or not and to determine the minimum number of firings of each actor in a valid schedule. Typically, a (sequential) schedule may be represented by a string of actor firings such as $A(2B)(6C)$ for an SDF graph with 3 actors named $A, B$, and $C$ in Fig. 1. Here, a parameterized term $(nS_1S_2\ldots S_k)$ specifies $n$ sucessive firings of the subschedule $S_1S_2\ldots S_k$, and may be translated into a loop in the target code. Each parenthesized term $(nS_1S_2\ldots S_k)$ is called *schedule loop*. A *looped schedule* is a finite sequence $V_1V_2\ldots V_k$, where each $V_i$ is either an actor or a schedule loop.

For a given SDF graph $G$, lower bounds for the amount of required program memory have been shown to correspond to so-called *single-appearance schedules*, where each actor appears exactly once in the schedule term, e.g., $A(2B(3C))$ for the graph shown in Fig. 1.

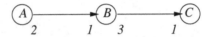

**Fig. 1.** Simple SDF graph.

Furthermore, data memory requirements, resulting from implementing each arc communication via a FIFO, are given by the sum of the maximum number of tokens, resulting on each arc during the execution of a schedule.

In [2], algorithms such as PGAN (pairwise grouping of adjacent nodes) and a complementary algorithm called RPMC (recursive partitioning by minimum cuts) have been presented to create schedules with the goal to generate single-appearance schedules in the first line with the second goal to minimize the amount of data memory needed.

With results such as these in mind, we propose a powerful intermediate representation model for a broad class of non-deterministic dataflow graphs. This model, called ILDF, standing for *interval-rate, locally-static dataflow*. In ILDF graphs, the production and consumption rates on graph edges remains constant throughout execution of the graph (*locally static*), but these constant values are not known exactly at compile time; instead it is only known what their minimum and maximum values (*interval-rate*) are.

Locally static behavior arises naturally in reconfigurable dataflow graphs, such as those arising using parameterized dataflow semantics [1]. For example, a speech compression system may have a fixed overall structure with subsystem data rates that are influenced by the size of the speech segment that is to be processed [1]. Similarly, during rapid prototyping of a filter bank application [9], one might parameterize the data rates of various filters to explore a range of different mulitirate topologies.

Figure 2 shows a compact disc to digital audio tape sample rate conversion system that is formulated as an ILDF graph. Two of the conversion stages, $B$ and $D$, are not fully specified at compile time to allow for run-time experimentation during rapid prototyping. Using ILDF parameterized schedules, different versions of these filters can be evaluated without having to re-schedule and re-compile the application.

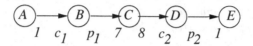

**Fig. 2.** An example of a compact disc to digital audio tape sample rate conversion system that is formulated as an ILDF graph.

Reasonable interval ranges for the unknown consumption and production values are $c_1, c_2 \in [3, 7]$, and $p_1, p_2 \in [2, 10]$. In addition, to achieve the desired overall rate conversion, the values must satisfy $(p_1 p_2)/(c_1 c_2) = 20/21$.

An ILDF representation of such applications with careful compile-time analysis can help to streamline run-time management (e.g., scheduling and memory allocation) and verification of such applications. This is the main motivation for our work on ILDF.

More precisely, in ILDF, the consumption and production rates, denoted $c(e)$ and $p(e)$ in the following for each arc $e \in E$ of a directed graph $G(V, E)$ with actor set $V$ and arc set $E$, are not constants and not statically fixed. Instead, the only information that we have is that the numbers range within intervals, e.g., $p(e) \in [p(e)_{min} \ldots p(e)_{max}] \cap \mathbf{N}$ [1], for each arc $e \in E$. Similarly, $c(e) \in [c(e)_{min} \ldots c(e)_{max}] \cap \mathbf{N}$.

The uncertainty given by the introduction of rate intervals may be the result of an unknown or activation-dependent behavior of an actor, or the freedom of the specification to later fix the parameter if possible or necessary in order to guarantee certain properties.

For ILDF graphs, we want to address similar issues as with SDF graphs:

- consistency
- memory bounds
- valid schedule

In Section 2, we define the ILDF model. In Section 3, we assume that a valid schedule is possible and given by an algorithm such as PGAN for which we investigate the problem of determining the data memory requirements. We deduce expressions and algorithms to determine the maximum required data memory requirements. If the execution time of an actor is also bounded by an interval, we finally also analyse worst-case and best-case execution times of a given schedule in Section 4. Experimental results are given in Section 5. Section 6 provides a review of related work.

---

[1] Let $\mathbf{N}$ denote the set of the natural numbers in the following.

## 2   Interval-Rate SDF

**Definition 1.** *An ILDF graph $G(V, E)$ is a locally-static dataflow graph where the production value $p(e)$, consumption value $c(e)$, and delay $d(e)$ of each edge $e \in E$ are constrained by intervals, i.e.,*

- $c(e) \in [cmin(e) \ldots cmax(e)] \cap \mathbf{N}$,
- $p(e) \in [pmin(e) \ldots pmax(e)] \cap \mathbf{N}$.
- $d(e) \in [dmin(e) \ldots dmax(e)] \cap \mathbf{N}$.

### 2.1   Consistency

Since the production and consumption values of an ILDF graph are not precisely known in advance, it is generally not possible to determine whether a particular execution of an ILDF graph will proceed in a consistent manner (i.e., with avoidance of deadlock, and with balanced data production and consumption along the graph edges). We can speak of three different levels of consistency for ILDF graphs. First, an ILDF graph is *consistent*, or *inherently consistent*, if for every valid setting of production, consumption, and delay (P-C-D) values (any setting that conforms to the production, consumption, and delay intervals associated with the graph edges), the corresponding synchronous dataflow graph is consistent. Inherent consistency occurs, for example, in chain-structured ILDF graphs, such as the ILDF application shown in Figure 2. Conversely, an ILDF graph is *inconsistent*, or *inherently inconsistent*, if for every valid setting of P-C-D values, the corresponding synchronous dataflow graph is inconsistent. An ILDF graph that contains a delay-free cycle is an example of an inherently inconsistent graph. Third, an ILDF graph is *conditionally consistent* if it is neither inherently consistent nor inherently inconsistent. In other words, an ILDF graph is conditionally consistent if there is at least one valid setting of P-C-D values that gives a consistent synchronous dataflow graph, and there is at least one valid P-C-D setting that leads to an inconsistent synchronous dataflow graph. In general, the particular form of consistency that an ILDF graph exhibits depends both on the topology of the graph, and the production, consumption, and delay intervals.

## 3   Memory Analysis

In general, for an SDF graph, the buffer memory lower bound of a delayless arc $e \in E$ is given by

$$BMLB(e) = \frac{p(e)c(e)}{\gcd(\{p(e), c(e)\})} \tag{1}$$

For example, in Fig. 1, we obtain $BMLB((A, B)) = 2$, $BMLB((B, C)) = 3^2$. A valid single-appearance schedule that achieves the total lower bound of 5 memory units,

---

[2] Note that the value $BMLB(e)$ is given as the lcm (least common multiple) of the values $p(e)$ and $c(e)$.

(sum) is $A(2B(3C))$. In this consistent SDF graph, actor $A$ thus fires 1 time, actor $B$ two times, and actor $C$ 6 times.

Let's see how the buffer memory lower bound may be computed for ILDF graphs. For example, let's look at an ILDF graph with just two actors $A$ and $B$ and one arc $e = (A, B)$. Let $p(e) = 2$, and $c(e) \in [1\ldots 3]$. The BMLB depends obviously on the value of the consumption rate. Corresponding to Eq. (1), we obtain $BMLB(e) = 3$ in case $c(e) = 1$, $BMLB(e) = 2$ if $c(e) = 2$, and $BMLB(e) = 6$ if $c(e) = 3$. Hence, if we do not know the actual rate, we must reserve at least

$$BMLB(e) = \max_{p(e),c(e)} \frac{p(e)c(e)}{\gcd(\{p(e), c(e)\})} \tag{2}$$

memory space for arc $e$.

Example: Consider the ILDF graph in Fig. 3 and the highlighted arc $e = (A, B)$. Under the implicit assumption of consistency, we would like to know the minimal memory requirements for arc $e$ if $p(e) \in [1\ldots 3]$ and $c(e) \in [2, 3]$. Obviously, the lower bound is obtained for the combination $p(e) = 3, c(e) = 2$ or for $p(e) = 2, c(e) = 3$ with 6 units.

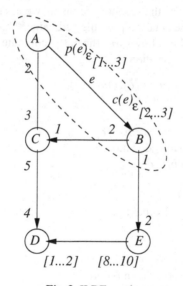

**Fig. 3.** ILDF graph.

The natural question is how one can compute the BMLBs for each arc efficiently without having to compute all combinations of $p(e)$ and $c(e)$ separately?

**Theorem 1 (BMLB computation).** *Given an ILDF graph $G(V, E)$ with a rate interval associated with each production number $p(e)$ and each consumption number $c(e)$. The maximum in Eq. (2) determining $BMLB(e)$ is determined by the largest product of $p(e)c(e)$ where $\gcd(p(e), c(e))$ reaches its minimal possible value.*

**Proof.** Let $p \in [pmin(e) \ldots pmax(e)]$ and $c \in [cmin(e) \ldots cmax(e)]$ be a combination, where $\gcd(p(e), c(e))$ reaches its minimum value and let $p, c$ satisfy the condition that there is no distinct pair $p' \geq p$, $c' \geq c$ in the above interval ranges with larger product $p'c'$ and with equal gcd according to the assumption in the theorem. Let $bmlb$ be the corresponding value of the buffer memory lower bound according to Eq. (1). We will show in the following that decreasing either $p$ or $c$ will produce lower values of the buffer memory lower bound according to Eq. (1). Hence, the maximum according to Eq. (1) cannot be determined by such pairs. Indeed, if we decrease $p$ by $\delta \in \mathbf{N_0}$ or $c$ by $\gamma \in \mathbf{N_0}$, we prove that we will obtain a BMLB value $bmlb'$ that is smaller than or equal to $bmlb$. We have

$$bmlb' = \frac{(p - \delta)(c - \gamma)}{\gcd(p - \delta, c - \gamma)} \tag{3}$$

Relating $bmlb$ and $bmlb'$ gives

$$\frac{bmlb}{bmlb'} = \frac{(pc)}{(p - \delta)(c - \gamma))} \times \frac{\gcd(p - \delta, c - \gamma)}{\gcd(p, c)} \tag{4}$$

$$\geq 1 \times 1 \tag{5}$$

The first fraction is rational and greater or equal to 1 as $delta$ and $\gamma$ are both natural numbers. The same holds for the second fraction as we assumed that the denominator of the second fraction is the smallest possible gcd value. This finishes the proof.

The following algorithm allows to efficiently compute $BMLB(e)$ according to Eq. (2) due to the above observation.

```
Input:  pmin(e), pmax(e), cmin(e), cmax(e)
Output: BMLB(e)
        bmlb = 1;
        for c = cmax(e) downto cmin(e)
                for p = pmax(e) downto pmin(e)
                bmlb' = bmlb(p, c);
                if blmb' > bmlb
                bmlb = bmlb';
                if gcd(p, c) = 1 break;
                od
        od
        for p = pmax(e) downto pmin(e)
                for c = cmax(e) downto cmin(e)
                bmlb' = bmlb(p, c);
                if blmb' > bmlb
                bmlb = bmlb';
                if gcd(p, c) = 1 break;
                od
        od
        return(bmlb);
```

Note that the two loops are not completely identical. Each loop can be quit once we obtain a combination of $p$ and $c$ where their gcd is 1 as this the minimal gcd value possible. The second loop, however, is necessary, as we need a combination of $p$ and $e$ where their product is minimal. The first loop decreases $p$ in the inner loop while the second loop decreases $c$ in the inner loop. The following two examples try to make this procedure clear.

Example: Let $p \in [1, 9]$ and $c \in [1, 5]$. Starting with $c = 5$ and $p = 9$, we obtain immediately a break of the first nested loop block for the values $c = 5, p = 9$ already because their gcd is 1. Then, the second loop nest is executed but this loop is also immediately exited. Hence, $BMLB(e) = 5 * 9 = 45$ for this example. Although enumerative, the BLMB computation is quite fast as in most cases, if the intervals are quite large, it is likely that the gcd becomes 1.

Example: Let $p \in [5, 7]$ and $c \in [3, 3]$. Starting with $c = 3$ and $p = 7$, we obtain also a break immediately. Note that although the pair $c' = 3, p' = 5$ also has the same and minimal gcd value, we do not have to care because $bmlb = 3 * 7 = 21$ whereas $bmlb' = 3 * 5 = 15$. Hence, $p$ and $c$ determine the maximum und thus $BMLB(e)$.

## 3.1 Scheduling by PGAN

Clustering [2] by pairwise grouping adjacent nodes is a frequently applied technique in order to obtain single-appearance schedules that minimize data memory require-ments. In the original algorithm, a cluster hierarchy is constructed by clustering ex-actly two adjacent actors at each step. At each clustering step, a pair of adjacent actors is chosen that maximizes the number of times this clustered subgraph may be exe-cuted subsequently. Fig. 3 and Fig. 4 show the application of PGAN. For fixed val-ues $p((A, B)) = 1, c((A, B)) = 3$, and $p((E, D)) = 10, c((E, D)) = 2$, PGAN clusters $A$ and $B$ first into cluster $\Omega$ shown in Fig. 4a), then $C$ and $\Omega$ into a clus-ter $\Omega'$ shown in Fig. 4b), and so on, until the graph condenses into a single node. By traversing the so-created hierarchy from top to bottom, the single-appearance schedule $(2(3A)B(2C))(5D)E)$ is obtained. Bhattacharyya proved that under certain conditions stated in [2], the clustering leads to a schedule satisfying for each arc the BMLB prop-erty.

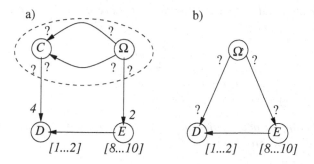

**Fig. 4.** Clustering of an ILDF graph.

In the presence of unknown data rates, the application of PGAN to construct *pa-rameterized schedules* has been explored in [1]. In general, a paramterized schedule is like a looped schedule, except that iteration counts of loops can be symbolic expressions in terms of one or more graph variables. In ILDF, we adapt this concept of parameterized schedule to incorporate intervals for iteration counts that are not known precisely at compile time, but for which lower and upper bounds are known. For example, $A([2,4]B([1,3]C))$ specifies an ILDF parameterized schedule with a nested loop, where the outer loop iteration count ranges from 2 to 4 at runtime, while the inner loop iteration count ranges from 1 to 3.

Even if we do not yet know the meaning of consistency for ILDF graphs, we want to show here how we are able to compute the minimal data memory requirements assuming that a valid schedule is given by clustering, i.e., a given clustering order of adjacent nodes.

The major question on which we want to focus here is therefore the determination of intervals of clustered nodes, see Fig. 4a), b). This problem is addressed in Fig. 5.

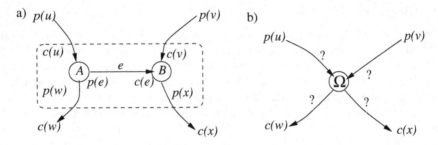

**Fig. 5.** Clustering step.

If we condense two nodes into a cluster as indicated in Fig. 5, the production and consumption numbers must be updated.

**Theorem 2 (Clustered intervals).** *Given an ILDF graph $G(V'E)$ and one arc $e \in E$ which is to be clustered into a cluster node $\Omega$. Let $src(e)$ be the source, $snk(e)$ denote the target node of $e$. Let*

- $u \in E : snk(u) = src(e) \land src(u) \neq snk(e)$,
- $v \in E : snk(v) = snk(e) \land src(v) \neq src(e)$,
- $w \in E : src(w) = src(e) \land snk(w) \neq snk(e)$,
- $x \in E : src(x) = snk(e) \land snk(x) \neq src(e)$.

*Then by clustering the nodes adjacent to $e$ into a single clustered node $\Omega$, the weights of arcs $u, v, w,$ and $x$ are changed as follows:*

- $p'(u) = p(u), c'(u) = \frac{c(u)c(e)}{\gcd(\{p(e),c(e)\})}, \, snk(u) = \Omega$,
- $p'(v) = p(v), c'(v) = \frac{c(v)p(e)}{\gcd(\{p(e),c(e)\})}, \, snk(v) = \Omega$,
- $p'(w) = \frac{p(w)c(e)}{\gcd(\{p(e),c(e)\})}, c'(w) = c(w), \, src(w) = \Omega$,
- $p'(x) = \frac{p(x)p(e)}{\gcd(\{p(e),c(e)\})}, c'(x) = c(x), \, src(x) = \Omega$.

*The rate intervals of the changed attributes of the arcs of type $u, v, w,$ and $x$ may be computed by computing the minimum and the maximum values over the given previous intervals.*

**Proof.** The first part is to prove that the clustering process leads to the above transformed values $p'(u), c'(u), p'(v), \ldots$. This part is proven in [2]. The claim of the last sentence is an obvious fact.

Example: Consider the ILDF graph in Fig. 3. Assume we cluster actors $A$ and $B$ into a clustered node $\Omega$ as shown in Fig. 4a). We have two arcs of category $x$ and one arc of category $w$. The new values $p'(w)$ and $p'(x)$ are shown in Fig. 6a) for the example values $p((A, B)) = 3, c((A, B) = 2$.

### 3.2 Local Consistency Clustering

We may observe that not any arbitrary combination of pairs $p(e)$ and $c(e)$ leads to a consistent behavior. E.g., let $p((A, B)) = 3, c((A, B)) = 2$ in Fig. 3. This leads also to the memory lower bound of 6. If we cluster now $A$ and $B$ into a clustered node $\Omega$, then the transformed weights are obtained as shown in Fig. 6a). Obviously, these fixed weights do not allow consistency because if actor $\Omega$ fires once, producing 6 tokens on the upper arc $(\Omega, C)$, and 6 tokens also on the second arc $(\Omega, C)$, whereas $C$ consumes 3 tokens on the first and only token on the second arc, definitely, there is no valid schedule.

On the other hand, if we choose $p((A, B)) = 1, c((A, B)) = 3$ in Fig. 3, we obtain the transformed graph as shown in Fig. 6b). Obviously, the parallel arcs do not provide objections against consisteny here.

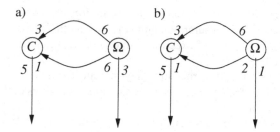

**Fig. 6.** Local consistency violation a) and satisfaction b).

If we condense two nodes into a cluster as indicated in Fig. 5, the production and consumption numbers must be updated. Therefore, in general, if a schedule generated by clustering is given, also the formula for computing the data buffer memory lower bound may be refined by restricting the search only to those pairs of values, that do not create local consistency violations after clustering.

## 4   Execution Time Analysis

In the following, we assume given an ILDF graph $G(V, E)$ with corresponding rate intervals and a given looped schedule $S$, obtained e.g., by PGAN. In order to calculate the influence of timing uncertainty, we may add another property to each actor, the so-called *latency interval*, denoted $l(v) \in [lmin(v)...lmax(v)] \cap \mathbf{N}$ for each actor $v \in V$, see Fig. 7, for instance.

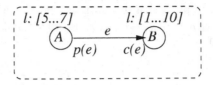

**Fig. 7.** Latency intervals associated to actors.

**Theorem 3.** *The* worst-case execution time *for a given clustering of two actors, e.g., A and B as shown in Fig. 7, and connected by the arc* $e = ((A, B))$, *is given by the following expression:*

$$WCET((A, B)) = \max_{p(e),c(e)} \{ \frac{lmax(A)c(e)}{\gcd(\{p(e), c(e)\})} + \frac{lmax(B)p(e)}{\gcd(\{p(e), c(e)\})} \} \qquad (6)$$

Explanations:

- As the number of firings of each actor $A$ and $B$ that are clustered together into a cluster node $\Omega$ is uncertain due to the rate-intervals of the production and consumption numbers, and the sequential computation time is additive in case of sequential execution, we have to calculate the maximum of the sum of the execution times of both.
- If there is no correlation given between the execution time of an actor in dependence on the production and consumption numbers, we get the worst case execution time if we take the maximum of execution time $lmax(A)$, and $lmax(B)$ in order to obtain the WCET.
- For a given clustering, the procedure may be repeated then for the next clustering step by calculating the production and consumption numbers of the clustered graph as indicated by Theorem 2.
- The best case execution time $BCET$ of a two node cluster may be obtained by replacing the max by a min and $lmax$ by $lmin$ in Eq. (6). This leads to a new latency interval $l(\Omega) \in [BCET((A, B))...WCET((A, B))]$ for the clustered node $\Omega$.

The above procedure might be used in order to define a new variant of PGAN as follows: Instead of clustering those two actors together that have the biggest common repetition factor, we could construct a clustering such to optimize the WCET instead or a combintation thereof.

## 5   Experiments

In this section, we provide the results of experiments that show that the algorithm BLMB in Section 3 performs well. For doing this, we have created a test series as follows: Let $p \in [pmin, ...pmax]$ and $c \in [cmin, ..., cmax]$ where $pmin, pmax,$ $cmin, cmax$ are random numbers in a given interval from 1 to $Z \in \mathbf{N}$. Then, for different values of $Z$, we generated $N = 1000$ times two random intervals given by $pmin, pmax, cmin, cmax$ and evaluated the number of $gcd$ evaluations performed by algorithm BMLB with respect to an exhaustive search for the maximum using any pair of values inside the random intervals. The following table provides the result of these experiments performed for 5 different values of $Z$ and for $N = 1000$ experiments each. The table lists the average number $x$ of gcd computations of BLMB over $N$ sample intervals in the given range and the average number $y$ of gcd computations in a total search for the maximum value determining the buffer memory lower bound for given two intervals.

**Table 1.** Average number of gcd computations $x$ performed over $N = 1000$ samples of random intervals in each indicated interval range using the BMLB algorithm and average number of gcd computations $y$ when using exhaustive interval search in the same interval.

| Range of intervals | x | y |
|---|---|---|
| $[1...10^1]$ | 1.42 | 15.50 |
| $[1...10^2]$ | 1.53 | 1167.00 |
| $[1...10^3]$ | 1.57 | $1.04 \times 10^4$ |
| $[1...10^4]$ | 1.52 | $1.10 \times 10^7$ |
| $[1...10^5]$ | 1.57 | $4.21 \times 10^8$ |

As can be seen, the average number of gcd computations using the BLMB algorithm is 1.5 and almost constant and independent on the interval range of the experiments. The gain when using the BLMB algorithm is biggest for large intervals. It can thus be seen that buffer memory computations can be done quite efficiently for dataflow graphs with interval firing rates.

# 6 Related Work

Various alternative dataflow modeling strategies with different objectives have been developed for more general or more precise modeling of dataflow graphs beyond synchronous dataflow; a partial review of these approaches is provided here. In cyclo-static dataflow [3], production and consumption rates can be specified as tuples of integers that correspond to distinct execution phases of the incident actors. In scalable synchronous dataflow [8], actor specifications are augmented with vectorization parameters that enable schedulers to control the degree of block processing performed by the actors. In synchronous piggybacked dataflow [7], actors access global states by passing special pointers alongside regular data tokens. In parameterized dataflow [1], dynamic reconfiguration of actor and subsystem parameters is allowed through separation of functionality into subgraphs that perform reconfiguration and subgraphs that are periodically reconfigured. Boolean [4], bounded dynamic [6], and cyclo-dynamic [10] dataflow offer dynamically varying production and consumption rates by incorporating various other data-dependent modeling constructs.

# 7  Conclusions and Future Work

We have presented a form of dataflow, called interval-rate, locally-static dataflow (ILDF). In ILDF graphs, the token production and consumption rates on graph edges remain constant throughout execution the graph, but these constants are not known exactly at compile time. We have motivated the use of ILDF as an intermediate representation for an important class of non-deterministic dataflow graphs, and have described a number of application examples. We have analyzed worst-case data memory requirements, and worst- and best-case execution time performance of schedules for ILDF graphs. Many useful directions for further work emerge from this study, including the development of algorithms for constructing efficient uniprocessor and multiprocessor schedules for ILDF graphs, and integration of ILDF concepts to work with other dataflow models of computation, particularly the more dynamic ones.

# References

1. B. Bhattacharya and S. S. Bhattacharyya. Parameterized dataflow modeling for DSP systems. *IEEE Transactions on Signal Processing*, 49(10):2408–2421, October 2001.
2. S. S. Bhattacharyya, P. K. Murthy, and E. A. Lee. *Software Synthesis from Dataflow Graphs*. Kluwer Academic Publishers, 1996.
3. G. Bilsen, M. Engels, R. Lauwereins, and J. A. Peperstraete. Cyclo-static dataflow. *IEEE Transactions on Signal Processing*, 44(2):397–408, February 1996.
4. J. T. Buck and E. A. Lee. Scheduling dynamic dataflow graphs using the token flow model. In *Proceedings of the International Conference on Acoustics, Speech, and Signal Processing*, April 1993.
5. E. A. Lee and D. G. Messerschmitt. Synchronous dataflow. *Proceedings of the IEEE*, 75(9):1235–1245, September 1987.
6. M. Pankert, O. Mauss, S. Ritz, and H. Meyr. Dynamic data flow and control flow in high level DSP code synthesis. In *Proceedings of the International Conference on Acoustics, Speech, and Signal Processing*, 1994.
7. C. Park, J. Chung, and S. Ha. Efficient dataflow representation of MPEG-1 audio (layer iii) decoder algorithm with controlled global states. In *Proceedings of the IEEE Workshop on Signal Processing Systems*, 1999.
8. S. Ritz, M. Pankert, and H. Meyr. Optimum vectorization of scalable synchronous dataflow graphs. In *Proceedings of the International Conference on Application Specific Array Processors*, October 1993.
9. P. P. Vaidyanathan. *Multirate Systems and Filter Banks*. Prentice Hall, 1993.
10. P. Wauters, M. Engels, R. Lauwereins, and J. A. Peperstraete. Cyclo-dynamic dataflow. In *EUROMICRO Workshop on Parallel and Distributed Processing*, January 1996.

# High-Speed Event-Driven RTL Compiled Simulation

Alexey Kupriyanov, Frank Hannig, and Jürgen Teich

Department of Computer Science 12, Hardware-Software-Co-Design,
University of Erlangen-Nuremberg, Germany
{kupriyanov,hannig,teich}@cs.fau.de

**Abstract.** In this paper we present a new approach for generating high-speed optimized event-driven register transfer level (RTL) compiled simulators. The generation of the simulators is part of our *BUILDABONG* [7] framework, which aims at architecture and compiler co-generation for special purpose processors. The main focus of the paper is on the transformation of a given architecture's circuit into a graph and applying on it an essential graph decomposition algorithm to transform the graph into subgraphs denoting the minimal subsets of sequential elements which have to be reevaluated during each simulation cycle. As a second optimization, we present a partitioning algorithm, which introduces intermediate registers to minimize the number of evaluations of combinational nodes during a simulation cycle. The simulator's superior performance compared to an existing commercial simulator is shown. Finally, we demonstrate the pertinence of our approach by simulating a MIPS processor.

## 1   Introduction

Today, due to the increasing complexity of processor architectures, 70-80% of the development cycle is spent in validation. Here, beside formal verification methodologies, simulation based validation plays an important role. Furthermore, cycle-accurate and bit-true simulations are necessary for the debug process when mapping applications to a not physically available architecture. Moreover, in the domain of architecture/compiler co-design for application-specific instruction set processors (ASIPs), fast estimation and simulation methodologies are essential to explore the enormous design space of possible architecture/compiler co-designs.

In the following, we list some significant approaches aiming at architecture simulation. Today's simulation techniques include the flexible but often very slow interpretive simulation and faster compiled simulation. The simulation can be performed at the different levels of abstraction starting from gate level, register transfer (RT) level, up to instruction-set (IS) level. The lower the abstraction level used, the higher simulation flexibility is achieved but at the same time the simulation speed dramatically slows down. Nowadays, the IS simulators are widely used in the domain of application specific instruction set processors because of their extremely high simulation speed.

In [4], a fast retargetable simulation technique improves traditional static compiled simulation by the utilization of the host machine resources.

FastSim [11] and Embra [14] simulators use dynamic binary translation and result caching to improve simulation performance. Embra provides a high performance but it is restricted to the simulation of only the MIPS R3000/R4000 [1] architectures.

A. Pimentel and S. Vassiliadis (Eds.): SAMOS 2004, LNCS 3133, pp. 519–529, 2004.

The architecture description language LISA [10] is the basis for a retargetable compiled approach aiming at the generation of fast simulators for microprocessors even with complex pipeline structures. LISA is also used as entry language in the MaxCore framework [3] which automatically generates fast and accurate processor simulation models.

In the BUILDABONG framework ([12], [6], [7]), a cycle-accurate model of the register transfer architecture using the formalism of Abstract State Machines (ASMs) is generated. Here, a convenient debugging environment is generated but the functional simulation is not optimized and can be performed only for relatively simple architectures. The problem of this approach is that the simulation engine is based on a library operating on bitstrings which is relatively slow.

One of the largest drawbacks in all of these approaches is that some high-level machine description language must be additionally used in order to generate highest speed simulators.

In this paper, we propose a mixed register-transfer/instruction-set level compiled simulation technique where the simulator is automatically extracted from a RTL description and the application program is compiled prior to simulator run-time. Hence, there is no need to use any particular machine description language. Furthermore, we present two new approaches to optimize the simulation speed: (a), a novel graph decomposition algorithm to transform the graph into subgraphs denoting the minimal subsets of sequential elements which have to be reevaluated during one simulation cycle, and (b), we present a partitioning algorithm to minimize the number of evaluations of combinational nodes during a simulation cycle by the introduction of intermediate registers.

The rest of the paper is structured as follows: In Section 2, the basic concepts when generating high-speed optimized event-driven bit-true and cycle-accurate compiled simulators are described. Here, a given graphical architecture description is transformed into a graph representation. Subsequently, the main focus of the paper is on the above mentioned *RTL graph decomposition* and *partitioning algorithms*. In Section 3, experiments and a case study when simulating a MIPS processor are presented and the results of our simulation approach are compared to an existing commercial simulator. Finally in Section 4, the paper is concluded with a summary of our achievements and an outlook of the future work directions.

## 2   Event-Driven Compiled Simulation

The flow of conventional compiled simulation, particularly *Levelized Compiled Code (LCC)* [13] simulation consists of circuit description, code generation, compilation, and running of the stand-alone compiled simulator, which reads input vectors and generates the circuit's output values. In our case, the circuit description is extracted from the *ArchitectureComposer* [7] tool, where the architecture is graphically entered using a library of customizable building blocks such as register files, memories, arithmetic and logic units, busses, etc. The simulator is compiled from a C++ program, which is generated automatically using the *SimulatorGenerator*, a tool built-in *ArchitectureComposer*. The structure of the generated simulator is similar to the structure of a conventional LCC simulator. It includes the *main simulation loop* in which the stimuli vectors are read from an external stimuli file, the simulation routine *sensitivity-update* (definition follows) is called to perform the current simulation cycle, and the selected tracing values are stored. In order to be able to simulate arbitrary bitwidths accurately, our simulation engine uses the GNU Multiple Precision (GMP) library [8], which performs efficient arbitrary word-length arithmetic and logic computation. The simulation engine itself is a set of nested inline functions which evaluate each output of the hardware components of the circuit. This approach allows the C++ compiler to perform an optimization of the program execution speed by reducing the number of intermediate variables in a data flow graph compared to conventional approaches, where the simulation engine uses a table of functions for each hardware element and a table of interconnections between them most of the times.

As our objective is a cycle-accurate and pipeline-accurate bit-true simulation of a given computer architecture, the architecture's behavior have to be simulated at the RTL level. Such a behavior may be described by a set of guarded register transfer patterns [9]. From a hardware-oriented point of view, register transfers (RT) take place during the execution of each machine cycle. During a RT, input values are read from a set of storage elements (registers, memory cells, etc.), a computation is performed on these values, and the result is assigned to a destination, which is again a set of storage elements.

Often, it can be seen that not all regions of the given circuit are involved in its entire functional process during any significant time interval. For example, in such architectures as FPGAs or reconfigurable arrays some inactive cells do not perform any signal changes from cycle to cycle, especially those parts which are responsible for the reconfiguration process. That is why, it is very reasonable not to recompute or *update* these regions in each simulation cycle. Hence, an event-driven simulation is applied in order to optimize the simulation speed by evaluating only those parts of the circuit whose values are affected from one to another simulation cycle. This is also called *forward event-driven simulation.*

**Definition 1 (Sensitivity-update-mapping).** *A* sensitivity-update-mapping *defines a set of sequential elements* $\{u_{r_1}, \ldots, u_{r_n}\}$ *of the circuit which must be recomputed if at least one sequential element of a set* $\{v_{r_1}, \ldots, v_{r_m}\}$ *has changed it's value compared to the previous simulation cycle. It can be represented by the following notation:* $\{v_{r_1}, \ldots, v_{r_m}\} \longmapsto \{u_{r_1}, \ldots, u_{r_n}\}.$

The RTL circuit is represented as a directed graph $G(V, E)$. In the following sections, we present two essential algorithms to enable highest speed simulations on this graph: (i) a graph decomposition algorithm whose purpose is to divide a given description of an RTL architecture into subgraphs which denote the minimal subsets of sequential elements which have to be recomputed (determination of an optimal set of sensitivity-update-mappings) during one simulation cycle, and (ii), a partitioning algorithm to minimize the computational cost of the sensitivity-update-mappings. But first, we show how a given netlist is transformed into such a graph representation.

**Definition 2 (Netlist).** *A netlist* $N = (V, F)$ *is a set* $V$ *of logic elements and a set* $F$ *of nets interconnecting the elements* $v \in V$ *with each other. It defines a circuit in terms of*

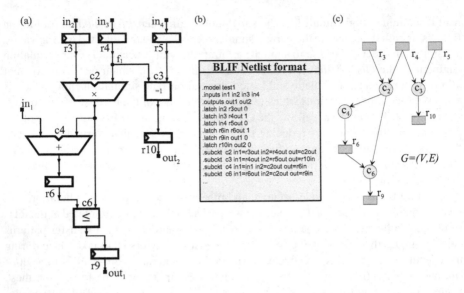

**Fig. 1.** Netlist representation. In (a), schematic graphical representation, in (b), BLIF textual representation , and in (c), netgraph representation of the given netlist.

*basic logic elements. A unidirectional[1] net $f \in F$, which interconnects $n + m$ elements will be represented through $f = (\{v_1, \ldots, v_n\}, \{u_1, \ldots, u_m\})$, where $v_1, \ldots, v_n \in V$ are source nodes and $u_1, \ldots, u_m \in V$ are target nodes of net $f$.*

*Example 1.* In Fig. 1, a netlist is shown with $|V| = 10$ elements. Net $f_1$ is given by $f_1 = (\{r_4\}, \{c_2, c_3\})$. Nodes named $r_i$ denote sequential elements whereas nodes named $c_i$ denote combinational (i.e., state free) logic elements.

A netlist can be given as a schematic graphical entry or in the form of a textual description (e.g., in BLIF [5]). A netlist can be seen as a hypergraph, where the elements and nets are vertices and edges, respectively. This hypergraph can be transformed into a graph by the introduction of a *netgraph* concept.

**Definition 3 (Netgraph).** *A netgraph $G = (V, E)$, $E \subseteq V \times V$ is a directed graph containing two disjoint sets of vertices $V = V_r \cup V_c$, representing the sequential elements or registers $V_r$ and combinational elements $V_c$ of a given netlist $N = (V, F)$. Netlist interconnections are represented by directed edges $e = (v_1, v_2) \in E$.*

*Example 2.* In Fig. 1, a netlist and its netgraph $G = (V, E)$, respectively, is shown. The subset of combinational elements $V_c = \{c_2, c_3, c_4, c_6\}$ is shown as circles and the subset of registers or sequential vertices $V_r = \{r_3, r_4, r_5, r_6, r_9, r_{10}\}$ is represented by rectangles.

In order to transform a given netlist $N$ into a netgraph $G$ all elements of the netlist must be analyzed first and, according to the element's type (combinational or sequential),

---

[1] A bidirectional net can be modeled by two unidirectional nets.

they are either included in the subset $V_c$ or in the subset $V_r$. In the generated simulator, the subset $V_c$ will be represented by a set of inline nested functions implementing the functionality of the combinational elements, and the subset $V_r$ will be represented by a set of variables of the certain data type. Furthermore, all of the nets are represented as directed edges $e \in E$ of a netgraph $G$. In case, when a net contains a $n : m$ connection, it is transformed into $n \times m$ directed edges of the netgraph, (in Example 1, for $f_1$ the case of a $1 : 2$ connection is represented which is transformed into edges $(r_4, c_2)$ and $(r_4, c_3)$ of the graph $G$ in Fig. 1 (c)).

Given such a netgraph, a simple procedure to perform a determination of the initial *sensitivity-update-mappings* could be as follows: if there exist a directed path from one register $v_{r_1}$ to an other register $v_{r_2}$ and on the path between these registers are no other sequential elements, then if the value of $v_{r_1}$ changes, $v_{r_2}$ has to be updated by evaluating the path of combinational elements in between. A set of such initial sensitivity-update-mappings and evaluation paths can be achieved by a search algorithm like *depth-first search* (DFS). For the example in Fig. 1 (c), the initial sensitivity-update-mappings are extracted in (a):

$$
\begin{array}{ll}
(a) & (b) \\
\{r_3\} \longmapsto \{r_6, r_9\} & \{r_3, r_4\} \longmapsto \{r_6\} \\
\{r_4\} \longmapsto \{r_6, r_9, r_{10}\} \qquad \longrightarrow & \{r_4, r_5\} \longmapsto \{r_{10}\} \\
\{r_5\} \longmapsto \{r_{10}\} & \{r_3, r_4, r_6\} \longmapsto \{r_9\} \\
\{r_6\} \longmapsto \{r_9\} &
\end{array}
$$

In a technical implementation, for instance, registers $r_6$ and $r_9$ would have to be updated twice if $r_3$ and $r_4$ would have changed their values compared to the previous simulation cycle.

In order to avoid multiple updates, we present a graph decomposition algorithm, which groups the sensitivity-update-mappings such that, at most one of the sequential elements will be updated during each simulation cycle. For the above example, the grouping result is than represented by the sensitivity-update-mappings in (b).

## 2.1    RTL Circuit Graph Decomposition

Now, we propose a graph decomposition into $n$ subgraphs $G_i = (V_i, E_i), i = 1, \ldots, n$. Each subgraph will consist of three regions: (i), the sequential input region is a subset of sequential nodes: $V_i^{inp} \subseteq V_i, V_i^{inp} \subseteq V_r$, (ii), the combinational region is a subset of combinational nodes: $V_i^{comb} \subseteq V_i, V_i^{comb} \subseteq V_c$, and (iii), the sequential output region is a subset of sequential nodes: $V_i^{out} \subseteq V_i, V_i^{out} \subseteq V_r$. The set $V_i^{inp}$ specifies which input sequential elements $v \in V_i^{inp}$ have to be analyzed such that, if at least one of them differs from the value in the previous simulation cycle, then only the output sequential elements $v \in V_i^{out}$ have to be updated. An *update* of a sequential element $v \in V_i^{out}$ here means (i), the evaluation of all combinational elements $v \in V_i^{comb}$, which are affected by $v$ or, in other words, the combinational elements that lie on the paths from $v$ to $u \in V_i^{inp}$ in the subgraph $G_i$, and (ii), an assignment of the newly evaluated result to the sequential element $v$. However, in practice, the sequential element $v \in V_i^{out}$ can be updated by the function call of the corresponding combinational element $c \in V_i^{comb}$, which is the unique direct predecessor of $v$, as the call of one nested function leads to the calls of all dependent functions. Finally, the conditions of the following routine can be directly extracted from the set of subgraphs and the generated simulator code will look as follows:

### Sensitivity-update routine in generated simulator

```
1    FOR all subgraphs Gᵢ DO
2       IF (∃v ∈ Vᵢⁱⁿᵖ : v(t_cur) ≠ v(t_old)) THEN
3          FOR all nodes u ∈ Vᵢᵒᵘᵗ DO
4             update(u);
5          ENDFOR
6       ENDIF
7    ENDFOR
```

In the above algorithm, $t_{cur}$ and $t_{old}$ denote the current and the previous simulation step, respectively.

We propose a novel decomposition algorithm, which (i) guarantees that each register is updated at most once during each simulation cycle and (ii) minimizes the number of input registers $v \in V_i^{inp}$ which have to be analyzed (see line 2 of the above algorithm), whether a register has changed with respect to the previous simulation cycle as a secondary goal. In Fig. 2, the decomposition algorithm to derive the set of subgraphs $G_i(V_i, E_i)$ is given as pseudo-code. The worst-case running time of the decomposition algorithm is $O(|V|^2 + |E||V|)$. First, the algorithm performs DFS[2] in order to extract the unique set of *sensitivity-update-mappings* such that, each left hand side of them has only one register. Then, the set of sensitivity-update-mappings is represented by an adjacency matrix $M(|V_r| \times |V_r|)$. Each row of it represents a register on the left hand side of a sensitivity-update-mapping and each column represents the registers on the right hand side of a sensitivity-update-mapping. Afterwards, the rows and columns of this matrix are sorted in descending order. The sorting in the adjacency matrix allows to group the input registers together which have to be analyzed, whether a register has changed with respect to the previous simulation cycle. By this a heuristical minimization of input registers in each subgraph is performed. And finally, the subgraphs $G_i$ are generated.

**Theorem 1.** *The algorithm DECOMP in Fig. 2 satisfies the condition that during each simulation cycle, the set of registers that have to be recomputed will be updated at most once.*

*Proof.* Each column of the adjacency matrix $M$ represents exactly one register that must be updated. Furthermore, according to the lines 20–32 of DECOMP, each column will be uniquely assigned to one sensitivity-update-mapping with index $l$.            □

*Example 3.* For the netgraph shown in Fig. 3 (a), the result of the decomposition is shown in Fig. 3 (d). Three subgraphs have been extracted:

---

[2] The DFS is modified such that, if a sequential node $v$ is found no outgoing edges of $v$ traversed anymore.

<u>DECOMP</u>

```
 1  IN:     G(V, E)
 2  OUT:   Set of subgraphs G_i(V_i, E_i)
 3  BEGIN
 4  //Find the sensitivity-update-mappings list L_i = (v_{r_i} ↦ {u_{r_1},...,u_{r_n}})
 5      integer i ← 0;
 6      FOR all sequential elements v ∈ V_r DO
 7          i ← i + 1; v_{r_i} ← v;
 8          {u_{r_1},...,u_{r_n}} ← DFS(G, v);
 9          L_i ← (v_{r_i}, {u_{r_1},...,u_{r_n}});
10      ENDFOR
11  //Build adjacency matrix M(|V_r| × |V_r|)
12      m_{ij} ← { 1, if ∃L_i : (v_{r_i} ↦ u_{r_j}),
                  { 0, otherwise;
13  //Sorting the rows of M in descending order (criteria is a sum of the elements in each row)
14      sum_in_rows[1..|V_r|] ← get_sum_in_rows(M);
15      sort_rows(M, sum_in_rows);
16  //Sorting the columns of M in descending order (criteria is a sum in each column)
17      sum_in_columns[1..|V_r|] ← get_sum_in_columns(M);
18      sort_columns(M, sum_in_columns);
19  //Clustering graph G into subgraphs
20      integer j ← |V_r|; l ← 0;
21      WHILE (j > 1) DO
22          l ← l + 1; V_l^{inp} ← ∅; V_l^{out} ← ∅;
23          WHILE (columns[j] = columns[j − 1])&&(j > 1) DO
24              V_l^{out} ← V_l^{out} ∪ {v_{r_j}};
25              j ← j − 1;
26          ENDWHILE
27          V_l^{out} ← V_l^{out} ∪ {v_{r_j}};
28          FOR i = 1 TO |V_r| DO
29              IF (m_{ij} > 0) THEN V_l^{inp} ← V_l^{inp} ∪ {v_{r_i}};
30          ENDFOR
31          j ← j − 1;
32      ENDWHILE
33  END
```

**Fig. 2.** RTL circuit graph decomposition algorithm.

$G_1 : (V_1^{inp} = \{r_1, r_2, r_3, r_4\}, \ V_1^{comb} = \{c_1, c_2, c_4, c_5\}, \ V_1^{out} = \{r_6, r_7, r_8\}),$
$G_2 : (V_2^{inp} = \{r_3, r_4, r_6\}, \ V_2^{comb} = \{c_2, c_6\}, \ V_2^{out} = \{r_9\}),$ and
$G_3 : (V_3^{inp} = \{r_4, r_5\}, \ V_3^{comb} = \{c_3\}, \ V_3^{out} = \{r_{10}\}).$

Here, the corresponding set of sensitivity-update-mappings is:
$\{r_1, r_2, r_3, r_4\} \longmapsto \{r_6, r_7, r_8\}, \{r_3, r_4, r_6\} \longmapsto \{r_9\},$ and $\{r_4, r_5\} \longmapsto \{r_{10}\}.$

## 2.2 RTL Circuit Graph Partitioning

As a result of the decomposition algorithm we obtain a set of subgraphs from which the *sensitivity-update* routine can be directly extracted and the compiled simulator code can be generated as shown in the previous section. Considering one subgraph $G_i$, an update of each output register $v \in V_i^{out}$ can lead to multiple evaluations of the corre-

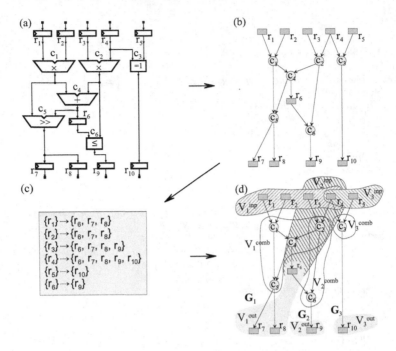

**Fig. 3.** RTL circuit graph decomposition. In (a), a netlist is shown, in (b) the corresponding graph $G$. In (c), the set of initial sensitivity-update-mappings for the sequential elements of the graph $G$ is depicted. Finally, in (d), the decomposition into subgraphs $G_1$, $G_2$ and $G_3$ is shown.

sponding combinational elements $c \in V_i^{comb}$ in the same simulation cycle. Obviously, this dramatically slows down the simulation speed.

*Example 4.* In Fig. 4 (a), if the value of register $r_1$ is changed compared to it's value in the previous simulation cycle then the RT update for registers $\{r_2, r_3, r_4\}$ must be performed. Namely, for $r_2$ the set of combinational elements $\{c_1, c_2, c_3, c_4\}$, for $r_3$ the set $\{c_1, c_2, c_4\}$, and for $r_4$ the set $\{c_1, c_2, c_4, c_5\}$ must be reevaluated. The sets overlap each other which implies multiple evaluations of the combinational elements $c_1, c_2, c_4$ during the same simulation cycle.

To avoid this effect and to minimize the subset of combinational elements which have to be evaluated during the simulation cycle, a graph partitioning algorithm is presented in the following. The algorithm inserts so called *virtual intermediate registers* (VIR) at certain places of the graph. The function of a VIR is to store the required intermediate circuit value (assignment operation), reducing by this the overall number of function calls during the register transfer updates (see Fig. 4). In the following, we consider only the subgraph $G_i = (V_i^{inp}, V_i^{comb}, V_i^{out}, E_i)$, particularly, only the subset of combinational elements $V_i^{comb}$. Let $n = |V_i^{comb}|$ be the number of nodes in $V_i^{comb}$. Let $W = (w_{c_1}, w_{c_2}, \ldots, w_{c_n})$ be the vector of the weights of the corresponding combinational elements denoting the simulation time in milliseconds of each combinational element. In the vector $L = (l_{c_1}, l_{c_2}, \ldots, l_{c_n})$ each element $l_{c_i}$ denotes, how often each

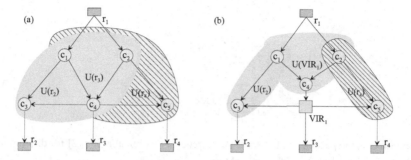

**Fig. 4.** RTL circuit graph partitioning. In (a), before partitioning, if the value of $r_1$ is changed compared to it's value in the previous simulation cycle then the RT update for $\{r_2, r_3, r_4\}$ must be performed. The overlapping subsets $U(r_2)$, $U(r_3)$, and $U(r_4)$ include the combinational nodes which must be reevaluated for each output register respectively during RT. In (b), after a first step of partitioning the virtual register $VIR_1$ is inserted and, as a result, the common subsets include only two combinational elements $c_1$ and $c_2$.

combinational element $c_i$ is called. Let $w_{vir}$ be the a constant weight denoting the simulation time of one VIR assuming that all VIRs have the same bitwidth. Then, the total simulation time depends on the number $m$ of inserted VIRs: $S(m) = W \cdot L + w_{vir} \cdot m$.

Assume the case when $m = n$; $w_{c_{min}} = \min\limits_{\forall j=1,\dots,n} \{w_{c_i}\}$; $l_{c_i} = 2$ (i.e., each combinational element is called at least twice). Then, only one case is possible, when $w_{c_{min}} \geq w_{vir}$, then $w_{vir} = w_{c_{min}} - \delta$, where $\delta \to 0$, $\delta > 0$. The insertion of the maximal possible number of VIRs (i.e., in all places, where the output degree of combinational node is $> 1$) results in the minimal simulation time. This case is dominant, since the simulation time of one assignment operation (VIR) is always less or equal then the simulation time of any other combinational element. It could be theoretically possible to have the case when $w_{c_{min}} < w_{vir}$ for instance in a system with hard memory restrictions, where each additional insertion of VIR could be very expensive considering memory constraints. But practically, the insertion of a VIR is nothing else as one assignment function and, from other hand, the implementation of any combinational element includes already the assignment as well, which means a VIR will never consume more memory compared to a combinational element. Moreover, as far as our simulation engine is a set of inline functions, insertion of a VIR will reduce the calls of the same function in the same simulation cycle, which, as consequence, also will reduce the program code size of the generated simulator.

## 3    Experimental Results and Case Study

First, we performed a number of tests to measure the speedup which can be obtained by using the proposed graph partitioning algorithm. Here, the simulation times were reduced by 7-12%.

Secondly, we present simulation results for various architectures of different complexity using different simulation engine libraries at link-time. Performance results of

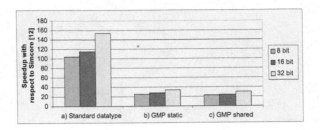

**Fig. 5.** Simulation speedups with respect to the generated simulators in [12] for different linked libraries: a) integer, b) GMP static and c) GMP shared library.

**Table 1.** MIPS processor simulation speed. The simulation speed in machine cycles per second is compared to the existing commercial RTL Scirocco simulator in event-driven mode.

| MIPS R3000 | SUN (GMP) | SUN (Integer) | SUN Scirocco (VHDL) | Linux (GMP) | Linux (Integer) |
|---|---|---|---|---|---|
| Simulation speed, CPS | 253 807 | 3 448 280 | 9 940 | 540 541 | 9 090 920 |

different generated simulators were obtained using a Pentium IV at 2.5GHz with 1GB RAM running Linux SuSe 8.0. In Fig. 5, different linked libraries have been used and compared in the generated simulator versions. The speedup is shown with respect to the *Simcore* library [12] which is based on bitstrings. The use of the GNU Multiple Precision (GMP) arithmetic library showed simulation speedups of a factor of 24 higher for 8-bit architectures, of a factor of 27 for 16-bit architectures, and of a factor of 34 for 32-bit architectures. The use of standard data structures such as, for instance, *integer* (without linking of any library) showed even better results with simulation speeds of a factor of 4 faster than using the GMP arithmetic library. But in this case, we are able to simulate only the architectures with standard fixed bitwidths (8, 16, 32 bit) as standard data types operate only on the values of these bitwidths. As far as such architectures are widespread, this approach is not unimportant for us and can be considered during the simulator generation.

Third, as a realistic case study, a simulator for the MIPS R3000 32-bit processor has been generated and evaluated, too. Table 1 shows the simulation performance of the MIPS processor using our approach compared to the existing commercial RTL Scirocco simulator (in event-driven mode) (Synopsys)[2]. In the table, the performance results were obtained using a Sun workstation running Solaris 2.9 with a 900 MHz UltraSPARC-III processor. Furthermore, the simulation speed, reported in the last two columns, was achieved by using the described Linux environment. A notable improvement in simulation speed of almost two magnitudes compared to Scirocco is shown. Up to 9 mill. machine cycles per second were demonstrated here at RTL which is equally fast or faster than most compiled instruction-level simulators.

Additionally, the binary code size of the generated simulators is about factor 50 less compared to the commercial one.

# 4  Conclusions and Future Work

In this paper, we proposed a new mixed register-transfer/instruction-set level compiled simulation technique where the simulator is automatically extracted from a RTL architecture description and the application program is compiled prior to simulator run-time. Furthermore, several optimization techniques to accelerate the simulation speed have been introduced: *Event-driven simulation, efficient generation of simulator code* by use of inlining to allow highest compiler optimizations, a *graph decomposition algorithm* that divides a netgraph description into subgraphs which denote optimal sets of update rules, and a *partitioning algorithm* to minimize the subset of combinational elements which have to be evaluated during one simulation cycle. The results show a high simulation speed with flexibility, cycle-accuracy, and bit-truth of entirely RT level simulation.

In the future, we would like to work on the visualization of the simulation process and/or results. Further optimizations can be done by using a combination of different data types (arbitrary- and fixed-width) in one generated simulator.

# References

1. Mips homepage. http://mips.com/.
2. Synopsys homepage. http://synopsys.com/.
3. Axys design automation. http://www.axysdesign.com.
4. J. Z. Daniel. A retargetable, ultra-fast instruction set simulator. In *Proceedings on the European Design and Test Conference*, 1999.
5. K. S. E. Sentovich et al. Sis: A system for sequential circuit synthesis. In *Technical Report UCB/ERL M92/41*. University of California, Berkeley, May 1992.
6. D. Fischer, J. Teich, M. Thies, and R. Weper. Efficient architecture/compiler co-exploration for asips. In *ACM SIG Proceedings International Conference on Compilers, Architectures and Synthesis for Embedded Systems (CASES 2002)*, pages 27–34, Grenoble, France, 2002.
7. D. Fischer, J. Teich, M. Thies, and R. Weper. BUILDABONG: A framework for architecture/compiler co-exploration for ASIPs. *Journal for Circuits, Systems, and Computers, Special Issue: Application Specific Hardware Design*, pages 353–375, 2003.
8. T. Granlund. The GNU multiple precision library, edition 2.0.2. Technical report, TMG Datakonsult, Sodermannagatan 5, 11623 Stockholm, Sweden, 1996.
9. R. Leupers. *Retargetable Code Generation for Digital Signal Processors*. Kluwer Academic Publishers, Dordrecht, The Netherlands, 1997.
10. S. Pees, A. Hoffmann, and H. Meyr. Retargeting of compiled simulators for digital signal processors using a machine description language. In *Proceedings Design Automation and Test in Europe (DATE'2000)*, Paris, March 2000.
11. E. Schnarr and J. R. Larus. Fast out-of-order processor simulation using memorization. In *Proceedings of the eighth international conference on Architectural support for programming languages and operating systems*, pages 283–294, 1998.
12. J. Teich, P. Kutter, and R. Weper. Description and simulation of microprocessor instruction sets using asms. In *International Workshop on Abstract State Machines*, Lecture Notes on Computer Science (LNCS), pages 266–286. Springer, 2000.
13. L.-T. Wang, N. E. Hoover, E. H. Porter, and J. J. Zasio. SSIM: A software levelized compiled-code simulator. pages 2–8.
14. E. Witchel and M. Rosenblum. Embra: Fast and flexible machine simulation. In *Measurement and Modeling of Computer Systems*, pages 68–79, 1996.

# A High-Level Programming Paradigm for SystemC

Mark Thompson and Andy D. Pimentel

Department of Computer Science, University of Amsterdam
Kruislaan 403, 1098 SJ Amsterdam, The Netherlands
{mthompsn,andy}@science.uva.nl

**Abstract.** The SystemC language plays an increasingly important role in the
system-level design domain, facilitating designers to start with modeling and simulating system components and their interactions in the very early design stages.
This paper presents the SCPEx language which is built on top of SystemC and
which extends SystemC's programming model with a message-passing paradigm.
SCPEx's message-passing paradigm raises the abstraction level of SystemC models even further, thereby reducing the modeling effort required for developing
the (transaction-level) system models applied in the early design stages as well
as making the modeling process less prone to programming errors. Moreover,
SCPEx allows for performing automatic and transparent gathering of various simulation statistics, such as statistics on communication between components.

## 1 Introduction

The heterogeneity of modern embedded systems and the varying demands of their target applications greatly complicate the system design. It is widely agreed upon that
traditional design methods fall short for the design of these systems as such methods
cannot deal with the systems' complexity and flexibility. This has led to the notion
of *system-level design* in which designers already start with modeling and simulating
system components and their interactions in the very early design stages (e.g., [5, 8]).
More specifically, system-level models typically represent application behavior, architecture characteristics, and the relation (e.g., mapping, hardware-software partitioning)
between application(s) and architecture. These models do so at a high level of abstraction, thereby minimizing the modeling effort and optimizing simulation speed that is
needed for targeting the early design stages. This high-level modeling – of which the
class of *transaction-level models* [2] is especially gaining interest – allows for early
verification of a design and can provide estimations on the performance, power consumption or cost of the design.

The SystemC language [1] plays an increasingly important role in the system-level
design domain. This language allows for modeling systems at a relatively high (behavioral) level of abstraction, after which the models can be gradually refined towards a
level of abstraction at which synthesis of the modeled design is possible.

In this paper, we present the SCPEx (SystemC Pearl Extension) language that is
built on top of SystemC v2.0, and which extends SystemC's programming model with
a message-passing paradigm – based on the Pearl simulation language [7] – raising the
abstraction level of SystemC models even further. This increase of abstraction level reduces the modeling effort required for developing the (transaction-level) system models

A. Pimentel and S. Vassiliadis (Eds.): SAMOS 2004, LNCS 3133, pp. 530–539, 2004.

applied in the early design stages, and makes the modeling process less prone to programming errors. Moreover, SCPEx also allows for automatic and transparent gathering of various statistics on, for example, communications between components.

The paper is organized as follows. In Section 2, we motivate the development of SCPEx. Section 3 provides an overview of SCPEx's simulation primitives with their semantics. To illustrate SCPEx's programming paradigm and demonstrate its modeling power, Section 4 presents SCPEx code samples taken from a realistic case study. This section also illustrates SCPEx's support for YML (Y-chart Modeling Language) [3] which provides an explicit description of the structure of SCPEx models (i.e., how components are connected and parameterized). Finally, Section 5 concludes the paper.

## 2   Raising the Abstraction Level of SystemC

To cope with the growing complexity of (embedded) systems, system-level design has been increasing the level of abstraction at which systems are modeled and simulated. A clear example of this trend is the emergence of the high-level modeling and simulation language SystemC [1]. Hardware description languages (HDLs) such as VHDL and Verilog are slowly being replaced by languages such as SystemC (and related variants like SpecC [6]) in especially the early stages of design. The rationale behind this transition to higher-level languages is that they allow for more efficient exploration of system-level design tradeoffs and enable earlier verification of the entire system, thereby reducing risks. In addition, software is playing an increasingly important role in systems design, where traditional HDLs typically are hardware oriented. By building the new modeling and simulation languages on existing high-level languages such as C/C++, existing code can easily be (re-)used during system design. Applying these high-level design languages usually means that a system initially is modeled at a high (behavioral) level of abstraction, after which the model is gradually refined towards a level of abstraction at which synthesis of the modeled design is possible.

In the past decade, we have gained a lot of experience with our own high-level architecture modeling and simulation language called Pearl [7, 4]. This object-based discrete-event simulation language has proven to be highly efficient for abstract performance modeling and simulation of computer architectures, both in terms of modeling effort as well as simulation speed. Pearl's modeling efficiency is mainly due to the message-passing programming paradigm it adheres to. A Pearl program consists of a collection of objects running concurrently, where each object executes ordinary sequential code and has its own data space which cannot directly be modified by other objects. When an object wants to modify some remote data, it sends a message to the object with a request to change the data. Subsequently, the remote object will only change the data after explicitly accepting the request.

Comparing Pearl's programming paradigm and associated primitives to those of SystemC v2.0, one can observe a number of areas where Pearl adopts a higher level of abstraction. Pearl, for example, abstracts from the concept of ports and explicit channels between ports as applied in SystemC. Pearl objects only contain a single "link" with each neighboring object and can communicate with these objects using *remote method calling* implemented via the aforementioned message-passing mechanism. Implementing remote method calling by means of message passing implies that objects remain autonomous in their execution: an object decides itself when to process an incoming remote method call. This also means that in Pearl buffering of messages at objects is taken care of by the run-time system, rather than having to implement explicit buffering as one would have to do in SystemC. As we will show later on, this message-passing programming paradigm nicely fits the modeling of transactions in transaction-level models. In addition, Pearl's message passing primitives (performing a remote method call) transparently incorporate inter-object synchronization, while this is done by separate and explicit event notifications in SystemC. The latter may be more prone to programming errors. Another valuable benefit of Pearl's message-passing paradigm is that the run-time system can automatically gather statistics on communications between objects, utilization of objects, critical paths between objects, and so on. Such automatic feedback may be a significant help to recognize early bottlenecks in the modeled system.

This paper presents SCPEx (SystemC Pearl Extension), which is a software-library on top of SystemC v2.0 (see Figure 1) that provides SystemC modelers with Pearl's message-passing programming paradigm. Hence, it allows for raising the abstraction level of SystemC models, which can be especially beneficial for the efficient development of initial system-level models. As illustrated in Figure 1, modelers have the choice of *i)* using a so-called Model of Computation (MoC) – like process networks, dataflow networks, CSP, and so on – that has been implemented on top of SystemC/SCPEx, *ii)* using SCPEx to start the modeling after which models can be refined towards SystemC v2.0 in a later stadium, or *iii)* immediately start modeling in SystemC v2.0.

As will be explained later on, SCPEx also features support for the Y-chart Modeling Language (YML) [3] that is used in our Sesame system-level modeling and simulation framework [4] to describe the structure of models, i.e., how model components are connected and parameterized. YML support for SCPEx gives us the choice of using either Pearl or SCPEx architecture models in Sesame, where the translation of Pearl models to SCPEx models (and vice versa) is relatively straightforward. The latter will facilitate exporting Pearl models to SystemC-based environments as well as importing SystemC (IP) models in Sesame.

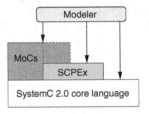

**Fig. 1.** SCPEx: Adding a layer on top of SystemC v2.0.

## 3   SCPEx

The SCPEx library extends SystemC's sc_module class with an scpex_module class to provide the modeler with all the required functionality to use the Pearl programming paradigm in SystemC. Whereas SystemC modules can contain many (different types of) processes, SCPEx only allows one process in a module in order to maintain a strict message-passing paradigm for exchanging data between processes/modules. The process in an SCPEx module is managed by the simulation scheduler as a non-preemptive user-level thread. As there is a one-to-one mapping of execution threads to modules, we speak of the "execution of a module". The simulation scheduler schedules a module when it is ready to run. If – at some point in simulated time – there is more than one module ready to run, the scheduler will select them in turn. The modeler should assume that the scheduling is non-deterministic as to prevent that the correct working of the simulation depends on the order in which modules are scheduled.

An SCPEx module consists of C++ code with any number of functions, methods and SCPEx primitives. Functions and methods differ only in that execution of methods may be requested by other modules, whereas functions are only used internally by a module. There are two types of SCPEx primitives: block and call primitives. A call primitive performs a remote method call, merely being a *request* to another module to execute one of its methods. A block primitive specifies that a module is going to wait for the simulation clock, for one or more method(s) to be called by a remote module, or a combination of these two. As mentioned before, the remote method calling is performed via a message passing mechanism of which the implementation details are hidden from the modeler by means of the call/block primitives. In the remainder of this section, we present the semantics of these primitives and explain the message passing mechanism.

There are two types of call primitives: synchronous and asynchronous. They have the following abstract syntax:

| abstract syntax | `{a}synch_call( remote_module,`<br>`             method,`<br>`             argument_1, ..., argument_n )` |
|---|---|
| examples | `int res = synch_call(alu, add, 2, 4);`<br><br>`asynch_call(alu, add, 2, 4);` |

A `call` statement sends a request to `remote_module` to execute `method` with the associated arguments. Here, `remote_module` is a pointer to the remote module and `method` is the name of the method that should be executed in the other module where the `argument_x` variables have to match the argument types of that method. The `synch_call` statement does not return until it receives an acknowledgment from the remote module. To illustrate this, let us assume that the calling module is named `module1`. A `synch_call` will halt the thread of `module1` and yield control to the scheduler. The scheduler will then select one of the other modules to resume execution. At some point, the remote module (`remote_module`) may accept and execute the requested `method`. Doing so, `method` will send an acknowledgment back to `module1`. After receiving this acknowledgment, the scheduler knows that `module1` is runnable again and may be scheduled for execution. The `synch_call` statement in `module1` then evaluates to the value of the acknowledgment with which the method of `remote_module` has replied. Replies are sent using a special reply primitive:

| abstract syntax | `reply( reply_data )` |
|---|---|
| example of a<br>reply in a<br>synchronous<br>method | `void add(int a, int b) {`<br>`    /* model, e.g., computation time */`<br>`    reply(a+b);`<br>`}` |

The asynchronous call statement has a similar syntax to `synch_call`. This asynchronous version of the call primitive also sends a request to execute a method with the given arguments to `remote_module`. However, this statement does not wait for `remote_module` to handle the request, but returns immediately. It is not necessary for the remote method to issue an acknowledgment using the reply primitive. This explains why `asynch_call` has no reply value. We note that methods that issue a reply may be called synchronously as well as asynchronously (the reply-value is then ignored), while synchronously calling a method without a reply causes the caller to block indefinitely.

On the implementation side, a remote method call made by `synch_call` and `asynch_call` results in a message being sent from the calling module to the remote module. This message contains all the information a remote module requires to handle the request. This includes a method identifier and the actual parameters of the method as well as the reply data and pointer to the calling module required to notify the calling module upon completion of the method.

A module may receive more method-call requests (i.e., messages) than it can process at any given time. Therefore, there is a need to store unprocessed messages. Any two communicating modules are connected using a *message queue* that accepts writing of messages by the calling module and reading by the receiving module. This is totally transparent to the modeler as the call and block primitives handle the queuing and dequeuing of messages.

| abstract syntax | `block ( method1, method2, ..., methodN )` |
| | `blockt( time )` |
| | `blockt( time-out, method1, method2, ..., methodN )` |
| examples | `block (add, sub, mult, div);` |
| | `blockt(20);` |
| | `blockt(10, read, write);` |

Semantically, the block primitive – being similar but not identical to SystemC's `wait` primitive – indicates what behavior of a module will be simulated in the following simulation time-steps. One instance of this primitive – the `blockt` statement – is identical to SystemC's `wait(time-units)` as it simulates that a module is busy for a fixed number of time-steps after which the module resumes execution.

To model that a module is ready to process a request (i.e., an incoming remote method call), the `block` statement is used. It allows for specifying a selection of methods in the argument list in order to accept only requests for these particular methods. Applying the special keyword `any` as an argument, the `block` statement will accept any incoming request. The implementation of the `block` statement first checks whether or not an acceptable request is already stored in the module's inbound message queue. If present, then the first message for `methodX` (being one of the arguments of the `block` statement) is dequeued and `methodX` is called in the local module with the parameters stored in the message. If there is no request stored in the message queue, then the module halts execution and yields control to the scheduler. The module will be rescheduled whenever a matching request arrives. A `block` statement does not return control to the next statement until one of the specified methods has been executed. The last form of the block primitive is a combination of the previous two: it waits for one or more methods to be called with a specified time-out. So, if no incoming method call was received during this time-out period, then control is returned after `time-out` time-steps (thus operating like a `blockt` statement).

Figure 2 illustrates the semantics of the aforementioned primitives using a simple simulation model of a processor, cache and memory. We note that, for the purpose of brevity, we slightly simplified the code (e.g., we omitted instantiations and initializations). The next section will present real SCPEx code samples. In the code of Figure 2, the processor reads a word, prefetches another, and reads the two words again. The prefetch is simulated by calling the fetch method asynchronously: the processor does not wait for the result. The cache implements the fetch method. If the requested data is in the cache, it takes only 2 time-steps to complete the request, otherwise it takes 4 time-steps plus the time needed to fetch the data from memory. The memory implements a fetch that always takes 15 time-steps. The graph in Figure 2 shows the activity of the different modules during the time of the simulation: solid lines indicate that the module is busy, dashed lines indicate that the module is waiting for the results of a synchronous method call, while blanks imply that the module is idle and waiting for a method call. The scheduler terminates the simulation when all modules are blocking and no new requests are made. In this case, the simulation is stopped at $t = 50$.

It is not difficult to see that SCPEx nicely aligns with the modeling support needed for implementing transaction-level models. The transactions in transaction-level models – being atomic transfers of high-level data and/or control – perfectly map onto SCPEx's communication primitives.

```
class processor: scpex_module {
    void main() {
        synch_call(cache, fetch, 0x0000);
        blockt(4); /* model some computation */
        asynch_call(cache, fetch, 0x0020);
        blockt(9);
        synch_call(cache, fetch, 0x0000);
        blockt(4);
        synch_call(cache, fetch, 0x0020);
    }
}
```

```
class memory: scpex_module {
    void main() {
        while (1)
            block(fetch)
    }
    void fetch(int addr) {
        blockt(15);
        reply(lookup(addr));
    }
    /* module functions: */
    int lookup(int addr) {...}
}
```

```
class cache: scpex_module {
    void main() {
        while (1) /* main loop of module */
            block(fetch)
    }
    void fetch(int addr) {
        blockt(2);
        if (present(addr))
            reply(lookup(addr));
        else {
            int data =
                synch_call(memory, fetch, addr);
            blockt(2);
            store(data);
            reply(data);
        }
    }
    /* module functions: */
    int present(int addr) {...}
    int lookup(int addr) {...}
    int store(int data) {...}
}
```

**Fig. 2.** Illustrating SCPEx's primitives.

## 4    Illustrating SCPEx: A Case Study

To show SCPEx in action, we present several code snippets from a case study that was performed earlier with our Sesame system-level modeling and simulation framework [4] (using Pearl), and that we have repeated using SCPEx. In this case study, we mapped a Motion-JPEG encoder application – modeled as a Process Network – onto an architecture model that models a bus-based shared-memory multiprocessor architecture. This mapping is performed via trace-driven co-simulation in which the M-JPEG application model generates *application events* representing the workload imposed on the architecture, while the (transaction-level) architecture model simulates the performance consequences of these application events. Architecture models in Sesame usually account for performance constraints (i.e., timing behavior) only and do not model functional behavior since the latter is already captured in the application model. For a comprehensive description of Sesame, the reader is referred to [3, 4].

In Sesame, YML (Y-chart Modeling Language) [3] is used to describe the structure of simulation models and their parameterization. YML is based on XML so as to be simple and flexible and was developed to allow for rapid creation and modification of simulation models. Sesame applies YML to describe both application and architecture models as well as the mapping between these models. Besides statically describing model components and their connections, YML also features support for dynamic descriptions using *scripting*. This scripting allows, for example, for rapidly defining models that consist of many similar components (such as a large lattice of switches in a network). Moreover, as library support is inherent to XML, it is possible to make libraries of (parameterized) model component descriptions. Since YML supports hierarchy, this means that it is easy to reuse model components together with their descriptions as part of different models. To simplify the use of YML even further, a YML editor has been developed to compose model descriptions using a graphical interface. As the properties of YML can also be very beneficial for SystemC-based models, we added YML support to SCPEx. An additional advantage to adding YML support is that Sesame architecture models can either use the Pearl simulation language or SCPEx.

To illustrate YML, the code in Figure 3 shows a part of the architecture model description for the M-JPEG case study. Each `node` represents a simulation module, which in our example are a processor (`mp`) and a `bus` component. The value of the `class` property describes which SCPEx class needs to be instantiated for this object. The `port` objects together with the `link` element describe the connection between the processor and the bus. The `init` property describes the initialization values of variables of a module. In SCPEx, the initialization values can be integers, port names, or arrays of one of the two types. Before port names are assigned to the corresponding variable, they are transformed to module references (which are used by the call primitives). To do so, the YML interface of SCPEx traces the links of the port (possibly crossing several levels of hierarchy in YML) until it reaches the node it is connected to.

Figure 4 shows (most of) the real SCPEx code of the processor and bus modules from the M-JPEG case study. We only omitted the inclusion of header files and the `store` method in the processor module since the `store` is almost identical to the `load` method. Modules have to implement a constructor with a fixed prototype, as shown in the declaration of the proc and bus classes (two top boxes in Figure 4). This

```
<network xmlns=".../YML" name="MJPEG-arch" class="net">
...
<node name="mp" class="scpex_object">
    <property name="class" value="proc"/>
    <property name="init" value="net,10,[359,0,0,0,154,1,45,0,4,154]"/>
    <port name="net" dir="out"/>
    <port name="vp" dir="in"/>
</node>
...
<node name="bus" class="scpex_object">
    <property name="class" value="bus"/>
    <property name="init" value="mem,1,8"/>
    <port name="input" dir="in"/>
    <port name="mem" dir="out"/>
</node>
...
<link innode="mp" inport="net" outnode="bus" outport="input"/>
```

**Fig. 3.** Example YML code for processor and bus modules.

constructor is used by the YML interface to instantiate a module. The INIT macro is used to initialize module variables with values given in the YML specification file.

A processor module may be requested – by means of an application event from the application model – to model the timing consequences of a computation (`compute` method) or a communication (`load` and `store` methods). The `opers` array in the `compute` method contains the latencies of the different computational operations that can be performed by the processor, while the `operindx` argument specifies which operation is performed by the application at some moment in time. In Figure 3, it can be seen how the `opers` latency-array is passed to the processor module as part of a YML `init` property. The `load` and `store` methods – modeling the processor's communication – simply are synchronous calls to the communication network which in this case is a bus. This implies that the bus, and subsequently the memory that is attached to the bus, will account for the timing consequences of the communication. The bus module accounts for a `setup` latency which models the overhead to gain access to the bus without contention (pure arbitration overhead, etc.). Communication latency due to bus contention (one request waiting for another) is implicitly modeled – so without an explicit arbiter – which is straightforward because of SCPEx's message-passing paradigm. While the bus module services a communication from one processor module, a request for communication from another processor module will simply be stored in the SCPEx message queue of the bus module until the bus is available again. Bus arbitration is thus performed using SCPEx's FCFS message-queue policy, which may be especially useful in early design stages for rapidly obtaining an initial system model. Naturally, an explicit arbiter can be added to realize different arbitration policies.

Explicit references to target modules with which is communicated – such as the processor module in Figure 4 that directly communicates with the bus module – may limit the reusability of SCPEx modules. To avoid such problems, SCPEx models can apply the concept of subtyping. For example, in Figure 4 we can write "interconnect *net" instead of "bus *net", where interconnect is an abstract class (merely being an interface). In addition, the first argument of the synch_calls, containing the class of the remote module, should also be adapted accordingly. Subsequently, using the YML description, we can map a bus module, which is a subtype of the

```
struct proc: public scpex_module {        struct bus: public scpex_module {
    bus *net;                                 memory *mem;
    int nopers;                               int setup;
    int *opers;                               int width;

    void main();                              void main();
    void compute(int operindx);              void load(int nbytes, int addr);
    void load(int nbytes, int addr);         void store(int nbytes, int addr);
    void store(int nbytes, int addr);

                                              bus(sc_module_name name,
    proc(sc_module_name name,                     (init_values **) is):
         (init_values **) is):                    scpex_module(name) {
        scpex_module(name) {                          INIT(mem);
            INIT(net);                                INIT(setup);
            INIT(nopers);                             INIT(width);
            INIT(opers);                          }
    }                                         };
};
```

```
void proc::main() {                        void bus::main() {
    while (1)                                  while (1)
        block(any);                                block(any);
}                                          }

void proc::compute(int operindx) {         void bus::load(int nbytes, int addr) {
    blockt(opers[operindx]);                   blockt(setup);
    reply();                                   synch_call(memory, mem, load,
}                                                          nbytes, addr, width);
                                               reply();
void proc::load(int nbytes,                }
              int addr) {
    synch_call(bus, net, load,             void bus::store(int nbytes, int addr) {
               nbytes, addr);                  blockt(setup);
    reply();                                   synch_call(memory, mem, store,
}                                                          nbytes, addr, width);
                                               reply();
// store method has been omitted           }
```

**Fig. 4.** The SCPEx code of processor and bus modules of the M-JPEG case study. The top code boxes show the declaration of the modules, while the bottom boxes show their implementation.

interconnect class and which provides the implementation of interconnect's methods, onto the net variable. Doing so, we can, for example, substitute the bus in our architecture model by alternative interconnects (such as a crossbar, point-to-point links, etc.) in a plug-and-play fashion.

It should be clear from the code samples presented so far that SCPEx reduces the channel connections needed between modules in comparison to plain SystemC. For any two connected modules, SCPEx uses only a single predefined channel for communication of all data, and this data can be of any type. In SystemC, either a port and associated channel per data type, or channels that communicate composite data (structs or classes) would be needed. The first solution may result in a considerable number of ports/channels and associated read/write statements, while the latter solution requires to explicitly pack and unpack data elements before respectively writing and reading them. Moreover, SCPEx's communication primitives, which can provide synchronization in a transparent manner, make the manual creation and use of SystemC-events redundant. As a result, the errors that are typically caused by complicated event notification schemes are avoided.

Another benefit of SCPEx is that simulation statistics can be gathered automatically at runtime. This is possible since the two mechanisms that are responsible for SCPEx's semantics (message passing and synchronization) are accessible exclusively through the call/block primitives. For example, the utilization of a module – indicating the amount of time a module is busy or idle – can be computed because the simulation scheduler exits or enters the single thread of a module only on a `call` or `block` statement. Utilization can be computed if the primitives record whether the module was busy or idle in the period between being halted and rescheduled. We are currently working on the implementation of more advanced statistics such as contention and bandwidth analysis as well as profiling and call-graph analysis. Of course, a modeler can add his own statistics, either directly in the simulation code or by modifying the SCPEx primitives.

## 5    Conclusions

In this paper, we have presented the SCPEx language which is built on top of SystemC v2.0 and which raises SystemC's abstraction level by extending its programming model with a message-passing paradigm. Connections and synchronizations between modules in SCPEx do not have to be explicitly programmed, reducing the modeling effort required for implementing transaction-level models as well as reducing the probability of programming errors. To demonstrate SCPEx's modeling power, a case study was presented that uses SCPEx combined with our Sesame system-level modeling and simulation environment. Future research will focus on methods for refining SCPEx models to plain SystemC and mixed SystemC/SCPEx models.

## Acknowledgment

We thank Pieter van der Wolf for his valuable comments on a draft version of this paper.

## References

1. SystemC initiative. http://www.systemc.org/.
2. L. Cai and D. Gajski. Transaction level modeling: An overview. In *Proc. of CODES-ISSS*, pages 19–24, Oct. 2003.
3. J. E. Coffland and A. D. Pimentel. A software framework for efficient system-level performance evaluation of embedded systems. In *Proc. of the ACM Symposium on Applied Computing (SAC '03)*, pages 666–671, March 2003.
4. A. D. Pimentel et al. Towards efficient design space exploration of heterogeneous embedded media systems. In *Embedded Processor Design Challenges: Systems, Architectures, Modeling, and Simulation*, pages 57–73. Springer, LNCS 2268, 2002.
5. F. Balarin et al. Metropolis: An integrated electronic system design environment. *IEEE Computer*, 36(4), April 2003.
6. D. D. Gajski, J. Zhu, R. Dömer, A. Gerstlauer, and S. Zhao. *SpecC: Specification Language and Methodology*. Kluwer Academic Publishers, Dordrecht, The Netherlands, 2000.
7. H.L. Muller. *Simulating computer architectures*. PhD thesis, Dept. of Computer Science, Univ. of Amsterdam, Feb. 1993.
8. A.D. Pimentel, P. Lieverse, P. van der Wolf, L.O. Hertzberger, and E.F. Deprettere. Exploring embedded-systems architectures with Artemis. *IEEE Computer*, 34(11):57–63, Nov. 2001.

# Power, Performance and Area Exploration for Data Memory Assignment of Multimedia Applications

Minas Dasygenis[1,*], Erik Brockmeyer[2], Bart Durinck[2],
Francky Catthoor[2], Dimitrios Soudris[1], and Antonios Thanailakis[1]

[1] VLSI Design and Testing Center,
Department of Electrical and Computer Engineering,
Democritus University of Thrace, 67 100 Xanthi, Greece
{mdasyg,dsoudris,thanail}@ee.duth.gr
[2] DESICS, IMEC, Kapeldreef 75,
Leuven, Belgium
{Erik.Brockmeyer,Bart.Durinck,Francky.Catthoor}@imec.be

**Abstract.** New embedded systems will feature more and more multimedia applications. In most multimedia applications, the dominant cost factor is related to organization of the memory architecture. One of the primary challenges in embedded system design is designing the memory hierarchy and restructuring the application to take advantage of it. Although in the past there has been extensive prior research on optimizing a system in terms of power or performance, this is, perhaps, the first technique that takes into consideration data reuse and limited lifetime of the arrays of a data dominated application, and performs a thorough exploration for different on-chip memory sizes, presenting not a single optimum, but a number of optimum implementations. We have developed a prototype tool that performs an automatic exploration and discovers all the performance, power consumption and on-chip memory size tradeoffs, which has been tested successfully on five applications.

## 1 Introduction

The number of multimedia systems used for exchanging information is rapidly increasing nowadays. In multimedia and other applications that make use of large multidimensional array type data structures, energy consumption related to memory transfer and storage dominates over the total system energy [1]. Furthermore, there is an increasing gap between the access frequency of modern CPU cores and memory modules. This gap results in significant delays during the execution of an application, which has many off-chip memory accesses. Hence, memory optimization should have top priority, starting from system specification

---

* This work was partially sponsored by a scholarship from Public Benefit Foundation of Alexander S. Onassis and from Marie Curie Host Fellowship project HPMT-CT-2000-00031

A. Pimentel and S. Vassiliadis (Eds.): SAMOS 2004, LNCS 3133, pp. 540–549, 2004.
© Springer-Verlag Berlin Heidelberg 2004

and moving down the design flow. As it was demonstrated in recent studies [1], the memory system is the main power consuming unit and performance bottleneck in multimedia systems, which is justified by the following reasons: (*i*) the data dominated nature of multimedia applications, as it was stated before, and (*ii*) the power consumed and high access latency in accessing off-chip memories, which is significant more than normal arithmetic or logical operations.

It is widely accepted that architectures that have more than one layer in their memory subsystem, operate more efficient than others that lack this. For this reason, existing platforms, nearly always, have more than one layer in their memory hierarchy. The idea of using a number of memory layers to increase the performance and minimize the power consumption of an application, is based on the fact that both of them depend primarily on the access frequency and the size of memory. Thus, by exploiting the memory hierarchy, power and performance savings can be obtained by accessing heavily used off-chip data from smaller on-chip memories.

Existing techniques [2–4] only incorporate part of the available reuse search space though, and many of the "partitioning and assignment" approaches even ignore this issue totally. Memory hierarchy layers can thus contain normal (software controlled) memories or caches. An application has to be mapped efficiently on this memory hierarchy, which is a time consuming task if done manually. Researchers have also suggested the use of hardware caching schemes as a solution of system optimization in terms of performance and power. Hardware caches [3, 5] are transparent to the application since they are accessed through the same address space as the larger off-chip memory storage. They often improve overall software performance and reduce power consumption, but they are unpredictable. Although the cache replacement hardware is known, predicting its performance depends on accurately predicting past and future reference patterns.

The problem of the memory management and optimization in the embedded systems as well as the fundamental research contributions in that field is described extensively by Panda *et al* [6]. A methodology to systematically explore the design space for finding the optimal data cache and register configuration, according to specific time and power constrains, is introduced by Wen-Tsong Shiue *et al* [2], but their model is based on solving linear equations of the manually extracted dependence graph of the data elements, making it very time consuming for the designer in real-life applications. Bennini *et all* [7] present an interesting trace based analysis technique, but the optimization capabilities that are presented are few and data reuse or in-place possibilities are not exploited and only one point is selected in the search space.

Hardware caches have been proposed as a viable way to optimize performance and power requirements. Chiou *et al* [3] proposed some modifications to existing hardware caches, called column caching, which enables dynamic cache partitioning by mapping data regions to a specified sets of cache columns or ways. Their conclusion is that it is worthwhile to provide finer software control of the hardware cache so the cache can be used more efficiently. Our selection

of software controlled on-chip memories is in accord with this claim. Givargis
*et al* [5] propose a methodology for a cache and performance power exploration
for embedded systems, varying cache parameters. In their exploration flow they
use an instruction-set simulator (IIS) to generate a trace file, which is piped to
a cache simulator. Incorporating an IIS in the exploration flow, constitutes the
whole process cumbersome and very slow.

At IMEC, extensive research has been performed in array-oriented custom
memory organizations. A complete methodology for custom background memory management (or Data Transfer and Storage Exploration (DTSE)) has been
proposed in the ATOMIUM [1] script. The technique that we present in this
paper is a sub-step in this methodology, which has not been described fully until
now.

In this paper we present a technique, called Memory Hierarchical Layer Assignment (MHLA), which addresses the problem of optimizing the data assignments into memory layers. It has a global view of the data reuse search space
and selects the appropriate data copy candidates. This technique takes into consideration the limited lifetime of data arrays and temporal locality and finds
a number of Pareto-optimal implementation points in terms of on-chip area,
performance, and power consumption. Specifically, many different and implementable solutions are reported and not a single point, giving to the engineer an
increased flexibility for his design. This technique is based on the analysis and
efficient manipulation of memory accesses, and thus it is applicable to applications, which have large working sets, like multimedia or image processing. This
technique has been implemented into a prototype tool, which has been tested on
five multimedia applications of industrial relevance. The fast exploration that
this tool provides enables us to quickly discover, from the early stages of design,
all possible tradeoffs between performance, power and on-chip memory size.

## 2   On-Chip Memory Size, Performance, and Power Tradeoffs

Performance, power consumption and on-chip memory size are three very important characteristics that need to be analyzed, explored and implemented in a
very efficient way. While embedded systems range from simple micro-controller-
based solutions to high-end mixed hardware/software solutions, embedded systems designers need to pay particular attention to these three issues: minimizing
memory requirements, improving system performance and reducing the power
dissipated by the embedded system. Improving one of these issues does not mean
the other two may be unaffected.

The idea of using a memory hierarchy to minimize the power consumption
and increase the performance, is based on the fact that both of these characteristics depend primarily on the access frequency and the size of the memory.
Thus, by exploiting a hierarchy data reuse, savings can be obtained by accessing heavily used data from smaller memories instead of from large background
memories. Such optimizations require architectural transformations that consist

of adding layers of smaller and smaller memories to which frequently used data will be copied.

Usually, arrays have more than one opportunity to make a copy. These are called copy candidates (CC) for this array. Only when we decide that a candidate will be implemented, we call it "copy". A relation exists between the size of a CC and the number of transfers from the higher layer, typically called misses (Figure 1). This figure shows a simple loop nest with one reference to an array $A$ with size 250. The array has 10000 accesses. Several CCs for array $A$ are possible. For example we could add a copy $A''$ of size 10 which is made in front of the $k$-loop by adding the statement "for $(z=0;z_i10;z++)$ $A''[z]=A[j*10+z];$". This statement is executed 100 times, resulting in 1000 misses to the $A$ array. This CC point is shown in Figure 1(b). Note that the good spatial locality in this example does not influence the amount of misses to the next level. In theory, any CC size ranging from one element to the full array size is a potential candidate. However, in practice only a limited set of CCs leads to efficient solutions. Obviously, a larger CC can retain the data longer and can therefore avoid more misses. All possible CCs for this very simple case are shown in Figure 1(b). The most promising CC sizes and miss counts are kept and put into a data reuse chain as shown in Figure 1(c). The above example considers only a single array with one reference. In practice multiple arrays exist, each with one or more references. To each read access on the algorithm corresponds a reuse chain.

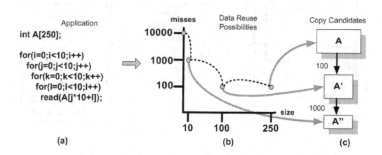

**Fig. 1.** Usually, there are more than one copy candidates for an array. This results in many different implementations different characteristics.

The lifetime of copy candidates plays a very important role also in performance and power. Proper in-place mapping guides to efficient utilization of on-chip memory space. We define life time of a CC, as the period of time that this array is live and carries useful data that is required in a future reference. If the data that an array carries is not needed any more, then it can be overwritten by another CC in a subsequent loop. Therefore, the size of the memory on a given layer is determined by the amount of data that has to be copied to this memory within this time frame. A time frame is usually the time of a nested loop. If a CC carries data that will be used in a future loop, then this array has to remain alive, which means that this memory space cannot be used to store other data of another loop. Our technique considers lifetime information of every array and copy candidate, and thus can use effectively the same memory space to assign copy candidates that have non-overlapping life time information. IMEC has presented in the past the principles of in-place mapping [8]. These principles have been incorporated into the MHLA technique.

## 3    Architecture Template

A programmable processor environment is the selected platform in this proposed work (Figure 2). Of course MHLA technique can support other processing cores like hardware functional units, application specific cores or data paths. Our target architecture model is a generic platform and consists of: (*i*) a single embedded programmable processing core, (*ii*) on-chip memory layers and (*iii*) off-chip memory layers. Each layer contains multiple memory modules. All memory modules within a partition are of the same type but can have different sizes and number of ports. Typical types are software controlled SRAM or DRAM (typically called scratchpad memories) off-chip (S)DRAM and caches.

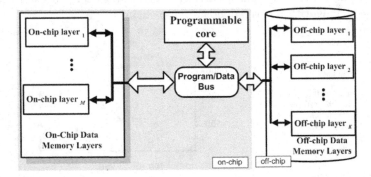

**Fig. 2.** Our selected platform consists of one processor and a multi layered on-chip and off-chip memory architecture.

## 4    Demonstrators and Experimental Results

The objective of our technique is to discover all possible tradeoffs in terms of power consumption, performance and on-chip memory size, of assignments of arrays and copies to different memory layers. In order to investigate the effectiveness of the MHLA technique we use the prototype MHLA tool to perform a thorough exploration of five multimedia applications of industrial relevance. First, we give a brief description of the real life applications that we used as test vehicles, and then we present and interpret the estimations of the different optimum assignments, that our tool found.

Our demonstrator applications are selected to be five well known real-life motion estimation (ME) variants of industrial relevance: (*i*) Full Search (FS)[9], (*ii*) Hierarchical Search (HS)[10], (*iii*) Parallel Hierarchical One Dimensional Search (PHODS)[9], (*iv*) 3-Step Logarithmic Search (3SLOG)[11] and (*v*) Quadtree Structured Difference Pulse Code Modulation (QSDPCM)[12].

The ME algorithms that we have selected, are fundamental multimedia algorithmic cores used in many embedded systems. Indeed, the motion estimation complexity stands for 60% to 80% of the total computational complexity of video encoding [13]. All the ME algorithms are block based: to compute the motion vectors between two successive frames, they divide the previous frame and the current frame into blocks, of a fixed number of pixels. They compare every block from the current frame with blocks from the previous frame that are located near the coordinates of the first block. They determine the best match between a previous and a current block frame by minimizing a given cost function. The five ME kernels differ mainly in the number of blocks of the previous frames that are examined and in the implementation of the cost function.

### 4.1  Experimental Results

Our experiments for the motion estimation algorithms are carried out using the luminance component of QCIF frames (144x176 pixels) of a sequence of two successive frames with the name 'Akiyo'. A reference window is selected to include 15x15 pixels $(2p+1 \times 2p+1)$, where $p = 7$ is the search space. Without loss of general applicability we have selected a two layered architecture. One layer (L1) is located on-chip and the other (L2) off-chip. Given the proper layer descriptions, MHLA can easily handle more than two memory layers. Also, for our experiments we consider an I/O profile with 1 cycle for a single access in on-chip memory and 10 cycles in a single off-chip memory access.

The evolution of the estimated execution time for some of the the five applications by varying on-chip memory sizes, is shown in Figure 3. The sudden drops that are noticed in this figure are caused by the insertion of copy candidates with high data reuse grade that are executed in the innermost loops. For this reason, it is crucial to have a fast and accurate exploration of different on-chip memory sizes, in order for the designer to select a specific tradeoff point between performance, power and on-chip memory size.

QSDPCM is an application that has many different possibilities for copy candidates. This is caused by the fact that there are many arrays that can be exploited by data-reuse. In total, 22 different copy candidates can be defined for all the arrays. Exploring all of the different selections and assignments manually is a very tedious task for the designer. MHLA has performed an exhaustive design space exploration and presents a number of different tradeoff points (Figure 3(*i*)). The performance of this application can be improved from 33% (by using a small on-chip memory of 128 bytes) to 88% (by using an on-chip memory of 3680 Kbytes). Figure 3(*ii*) shows that using an on-chip memory of 1304 bytes or 3864 bytes, the new implementation of PHOD will have 82% or 90% respectively, less execution cycles that the implementation without any on-chip memory. It is

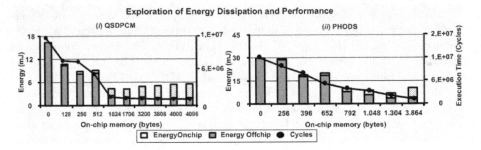

**Fig. 3.** While the increase of on-chip memory reduces overall power consumption, after some application-dependent memory size, the power consumption starts to increase without performance gain.

up to the designer to decide whether this performance improvement worth the cost of the additional on-chip memory size. Further increase of the L1 size does not improve performance, since all important arrays and copy candidates have been assigned in the on-chip layer.

### 4.2 Power Consumption Estimations

MHLA tool can also provide estimations for power consumption (Figure 3). The energy models that we used in this paper, are based on real memory models from vendor data sheets. The energy model is slightly super-logarithmic so a memory which is 256 times larger consumes 8.6x more energy per access. The energy consumption is obtained using the memory activity (read and write accesses) as input to the energy model that ATOMIUM scripts [1] are using.

Our exploration of the five ME applications shows that increasing the on-chip memory space, the power consumption on off-chip is decreased with a simultaneous increase in L1 memory consumption. Even though the increase of on-chip memory reduces power consumption, and increases performance, there is a limit. The law of diminishing returns applies here as well, since a very large on-chip memory usually returns the same benefits as smaller ones. Every application has a limit on the on-chip memory size, which, once exceeded, the total memory power consumption increases, without any simultaneous performance increase (Figure 3(i)). After exceeding 3300 bytes of on-chip memory there is no performance gain in the execution of QSDPCM, while an increase in power consumption is noticeable. Note that there are a few different optimum implementations before reaching that point. For example, 128 bytes of on-chip memory have a performance improvement of 33%. Until 256 bytes of on-chip memory the performance improvement stays the same (33%). If the designer selects 200 bytes of on-chip memory the performance improvement is the same with 128 bytes of memory, because the same arrays are assigned, because they are the most efficient ones.

Finally, the estimations of MHLA show in some cases that performance can improve significantly, which will cost in terms of power consumption. For example we found out that in PHODS (Figure 3($ii$)) the increase of on-chip memory is beneficial both to power and performance, until 1304 bytes of on-chip memory. After 1304 bytes, performance continues to improve while power consumption start increasing. For 3864 bytes of on-chip memory the performance has 8% less execution cycles and 10% more power consumption, than the implementation that has 1304 bytes on-chip memory. Thus, there is a limit in the on-chip memory size, after which the performance will increase but the power consumption will start increasing.

## 4.3   Energy vs. Performance for Fixed On-Chip Memory Size

The exhaustive search reveals that different implementations are feasible for a fixed on-chip memory size, too. In other words, there are different data assignments not only between different on-chip memory sizes, but also different copy candidates in a fixed on-chip memory size. The results show that energy and performance can vary significantly; up to 2.5 times higher energy consumption within a fixed memory size, for example for 3SLOG on 512 bytes memory (Figure 4 ($i$), points A and B), or up to 4 times more execution cycles, for example on FS with 512 bytes ( Figure 4($ii$), points A and B). For very low memory sizes, almost no copy candidates can fit into on-chip memory. Thus, no tradeoff points exist and only one solution is Pareto-optimal.

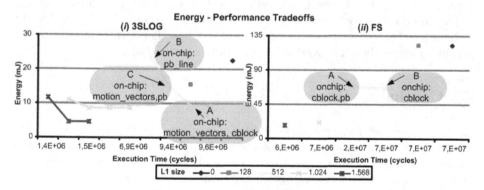

**Fig. 4.** MHLA estimates tradeoffs between performance and power consumption for fixed on-chip memory sizes for the 3SLOG ($i$) and FS ($ii$).

Tradeoffs are also possible for 3SLOG (Figure4($i$)). For 0 bytes on-chip memory only a single Pareto point is present. 128 bytes of on-chip memory are enough only for one copy candidate to fit, while 512 bytes allow three different implementations to be achieved: ($i$) high energy consumption (23.4 mJ) and low execution time ($8, 9 \times 10^5$ cycles), assigning only one copy candidate at on-chip (pb_line),

($ii$) an intermediate solution with execution time $9.3 \times 10^5$ cycles and power consumption 14.7 mJ, assigning one copy candidate and an array (motion_vectors, pb), and ($iii$) a very low power solution of 9.3 mJ and $9.6 \times 10^5$ execution cycles, which requires an array and a different copy candidate to be placed in on-chip memory (motion_vectors, cblock). The copy candidate tree for the ME kernels is illustrated at Soudris $et$ $all$ [14].

The results of full search (Figure 4($ii$)) are very interesting, too. For 512 bytes the best performance can be achieved using two copy candidates (cblock, pb). This results in $160 \times 10^5$ cycles with energy consumption of 68.15 mJ. For the same fixed memory, another solution is to use just one copy candidate (cblock). The power consumption reduces to 66.7 mJ (2% improvement) and performance gets worst: $740 \times 10^5$ cycles (460% slower). This shows again that power and performance are not two metrics that behave inversely proportional. Power reduction can change negligible, but this may impact performance heavily.

Tradeoffs exist for hierarchical search, too. For 256 bytes on-chip memory, one solution is to use one copy candidate of current block. This implementation requires $125 \times 10^5$ cycles and has a power consumption of 17.22 mJ. MHLA estimates that another tradeoff solution is not to use any copy candidate at all. The off-chip only solution requires only $124 \times 10^5$ cycles but has a power consumption of 19.72 mJ. Thus, using a copy candidate the energy is improved, while the performance deteriorates. This is explained by the fact that the copy candidate is small and has a small reuse ratio. Therefore, with the use of that copy candidate some off-chip accesses are transferred to on-chip memory. This improves energy. The addition of this CC poses an extra overhead to the system, which is shown by the estimated worse performance. As a reminder, all the copies are done under CPU control, and not in parallel, in order to simplify the estimations. If the copies could be scheduled in parallel with computationally intensive loops, then this overhead would not be noticed at all.

## 5   Concluding Remarks

In this paper, we have presented a high-level design technique for a fast exploration of the three major tradeoffs (on-chip memory area, performance, and power consumption) that a designer of embedded devices is asked to decide on. The usefulness of such an exhaustive exploration before the system design begins, is evident from the experiments presented. Our findings are that: ($i$) large savings can occur from the temporal locality (data-reuse) and the exploitation of lifetime of copies, ($ii$) optimum solutions are found using algorithmic transformations together with a careful selected memory hierarchy, ($iii$) the assignment of arrays and copies into memory layers is impractical to be done manually due to the number of different assignment possibilities and the high complexity of modern applications, thus a tool is required to perform this automatic and ($iv$) no single optimum implementation exists, but instead a great number of opportunities for performance, data memory power and on-chip data memory area trade-off exists.

# References

1. Catthoor, F., Wuytack, S., Greef, E.D., Balasa, F., Nachtergaele, L., Vandecappelle, A.: Custom Memory Management Methodology, Exploration of memory organization for embedded multimedia system design. Kluwer Academic Publishers, Boston, MA (1998)
2. Shiue, W., Chakrabarti, C.: Memory design and exploration for low power, embedded systems. IEEE Workshop on Signal Processing Systems (SiPS) (1999) 281–290
3. Chiou, D., Jain, P., Rudolph, L., Devadas, S.: Application-specific memory management for embedded systems using software-controlled caches. Proc. of Design Automation Conference (DAC) (2000)
4. Benini, L., Macii, A., Poncino, M.: Increasing energy efficiency of embedded systems by application-specific memory hierarchy generation. IEEE Design and Test of Computers **17** (2000) 74–85
5. Givargis, T.D., Henkel, J., Vahid, F.: Interface and cache power exploration for core-based embedded system design. International Conference on Computer Aided Design (ICCAD) (1999) 270–273
6. Panda, P., Catthoor, F., Dutt, N., Danckaert, K., Brockmeyer, E., Kulkarni, C., Vandecappelle, A., Kjeldsberg, P.: Data and memory optimizations for embedded systems. ACM Trans. on Design Automation for Embedded Systems (TODAES) **6** (2001) 142–206
7. Benini, L., Macchiarulo, L., Macii, A., Poncino, M.: Layout-driven memory synthesis for embedded systems-on-chip. IEEE Trans on Very Large Scale Integration (VLSI) Systems **10** (2002) 96–105
8. Troncon, R., Bruynooghe, M., Janssens, G., Catthoor, F.: Storage size reduction by in-place mapping of arrays. Third International Workshop on Verification, Model Checking, and Abstract Interpretation (2002) 167–181
9. Bhaskaran, V., Konstantinides, K.: Image and Video Compression Standards. Kluwer Academic Publishers, . (1998)
10. Nam, M., Kim, J.S., Park, R.H., Shim, Y.S.: A fast hierarchical motion vector estimation algorithm using mean pyramid. IEEE Trans on Circuits and Systems for Video Technology **54** (1995) 344–351
11. J, J., A., J.: Displacement measurement and its applications in intraframe image coding. IEEE Trans on Communications **29** (1981) 98–106
12. Strobach, P.: A new technique in scene adaptive coding. Proc. 4th Eur. Signal Processing Conf (1988) 1141–1144
13. Peter, K.: Complexity Analysis and VLSI Architectures for MPEG-4 Motion Estimation. Kluwer Academic Publishers, Boston (1999)
14. Soudris, D., Zervas, N.D., Argyriou, A., Dasygenis, M., Tatas, K., Goutis, C., Thanailakis, A.: Data-reuse and parallel embedded architectures for low-power, real-time multimedia applications. Proc. of 10th Int. Workshop Power And Timing Modeling, Optimization And Simulation (PATMOS) (2000) 243–254

# Constraints Derivation and Propagation for Large-Scale Embedded Systems Exploration

Laurenţiu Nicolae and Ed Deprettere

Leiden Institute for Advanced Computer Science
Niels Bohrweg 1, 2333 CA Leiden, Netherlands
{nld,edd}@liacs.nl

**Abstract.** The translation of user requirements to system constraints and parameters during an exploration exercise is a hard problem, especially in the context of large scale embedded systems. This process is almost never simple and straightforward, and it often requires multidisciplinary skills. The user requirements are not fixed during the exploration stage. Furthermore, the system constraints may vary according to the design choices made in the course of the exploration and development process.

In this context, a need for hot-linking the constraints of the architecture to the top-level requirements of the application becomes apparent. We consider the system model as separate hierarchies of application and architecture components, coupled by a mapping layer. We aim towards an automatic derivation of these constraints downwards to all the levels of the hierarchy. Furthermore, we employ a procedure of validation and adjustment of these constraints in the lowest levels, to eliminate possible inconsistencies.

## 1 Introduction

The design of a large scale system is usually multidisciplinary, and a great deal of effort is invested into translating abstract user requirements into hard numbers that can be used in the design cycle. These requirements become thus design objectives, such as the need for a nominal throughput, latency, power consumption, cost etc. The objectives are usually expressed in terms of constraints associated with the system building blocks. This is usually done by experts that evaluate different concepts and baseline systems at a very high level of abstraction.

Once one or more system concepts are selected, they are taken through a system-level exploration. This stage takes as an input the translated top-level requirements and baseline systems and tries to evaluate different design decisions while remaining at a reasonably high level of abstraction. If critical components are detected in this stage, they can be taken out of the system and evaluated separately in a component-level exploration exercise [1]. This exploration process is illustrated in figure 1.

The paradigm we are employing when designing large scale digital signal processing systems requires the partitioning of the system into three views: application, architecture and mapping. We use this separation of concerns as a way to master the complexity inherent to such systems. Each of these views is further decomposed into

A. Pimentel and S. Vassiliadis (Eds.): SAMOS 2004, LNCS 3133, pp. 550–559, 2004.

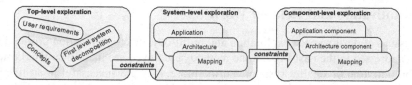

**Fig. 1.** Exploration can be performed at different levels of abstraction

hierarchies of interconnected components. Our goal is to compare different implementation concepts for a set of given requirements and answer "what-if" questions at the system level as early in the design cycle as possible.

A system exploration exercise consists of several stages. The first stage is dealing with the qualitative or functional requirements and constraints dictated by the top-level, such as the choice of algorithms, the signal quality etc. It first establishes a fixed set of top-level requirements. A hierarchical topology of an application, an architecture and the mapping relations between the two are then specified by the designer.

The second stage introduces the quantitative requirements and constraints, such as the number of bits used for the digitization of the signal, the required throughput of the system, the maximum power dissipation and so on. The result of the second stage is an executable specification of the system which fulfills the top-level requirements, both quantitative and qualitative. This specification can be evaluated and compared with previous results. A more detailed description of the methodology is given in [2].

Ideally, the constraints of the system would be orthogonal. However, for real designs this is hardly the case. The constraints of the application are related via the mapping step to the constraints of the architecture. Thus the modifications of the model in one domain are related to the choices made in the other domain in a two way traceable manner. For instance, if a complex filtering algorithm has been selected as an application and a new quantitative requirement for this algorithm is a very high throughput, the designer may choose to select a different algorithm with a different set of parameters. Another alternative is to adjust the architecture, by either adding more filtering blocks or by selecting a different component from the library.

When the model structure and user requirements are fixed, the system constraints are seldom modified, if at all, and this is the reason why in a normal development cycle the managing and automatic derivation of constraints is not a priority. However, this changes dramatically when one has to deal with evaluating different system realizations under alternative user requirements, which leads to ever changing constraints on the model. We argue that an automatic constraint derivation system is a crucial part of a successful exploration framework, as it allows for fast design space exploration by minimizing the amount of user interaction. Furthermore, our approach facilitates a tracing of the steps taken from requirements to specification over the whole project life cycle.

In this paper we are describing the methods and tools we apply for the manipulation of constraints for large scale systems exploration. The mathematical constraint derivation model and the constraint propagation methods are described in detail. We present a constraint validation scheme we use to assert and adjust the system constraints. Then we conclude with a real-life example of constraints derivation.

## 2   Motivation and Related Work

The issues of design space exploration and multi-objective optimization problem have been addressed in the past [3], but the methods employed are mainly targeted towards the optimization of smaller systems. Furthermore, they are successful in an fixed and well organized design space. Our goal is to provide methods and tools that help a designer to explore alternatives not only in terms of design choices, but also in terms of requirements.

The orthogonalization of concerns by separating the system model into multiple views has been successfully employed in other tools, such as Polis[4] for System-on-a-Chip designs. For larger, more heterogeneous systems, assigning constraints across models for verification becomes an issue that is addressed in the successor of Polis, namely the Metropolis[5] project. The model they employ is designed for co-simulation of the application and the architecture, and consists of a formal specification of the application behavior connected to the architecture layer via executable traces, together with a formal model for performance constraints.

It is indeed possible to derive the system constraints from a detailed behavior specification; however, creating this specification is both tedious and time-consuming. Therefore we argue that this approach is less suitable for high level design space exploration. Our goal is to quickly explore several alternatives and gain a certain degree of confidence before delving into lower-level modeling and final implementation.

Since we are examining different, and sometime even unrelated solutions, we need to be able to rapidly specify the system alternatives we want to explore. Therefore this exploration framework is currently based on a library of system components. The performance evaluation of the system is obtained by using stochastic models[6], also based on information taken from the library.

We propose here a formalization of the constraints model which we use to automate the derivation of constraints from user requirements. This supports our rapid specification approach, and allows us to trace the requirements across the system model.

## 3   Constraints Derivation

The main role of the constraints of a given system is to express quantitatively the user requirements set for the system in all the system components. Usually the constraints are obtained from the user requirements by quantification, refinement and decomposition over the system, as shown in figure 2. The system is considered a viable design solution if and only if all the constraints are met.

Let us consider again our filtering example. Given a number of sensors and a sampling rate as top-level requirements, they are translated into a throughput for the filter block. This throughput is then distributed into I/O rates for all the filter processes on the lowest level.

In the course of an exploration exercise, the goal is to evaluate system alternatives as early in the design process as possible. The best of them are then selected and studied in-depth. Another goal is to evaluate if an alternative is flexible enough to easily accommodate more demanding requirements. This is especially important for large scale infrastructures, which are deployed and operated for long periods of time.

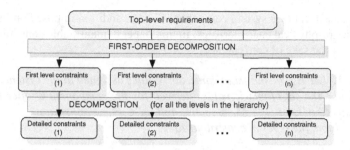

**Fig. 2.** Converting user requirements to system constraints

## 3.1   Constraints Dependencies

In this context, the need for an automatic derivation of constraints from requirements becomes apparent. The first step in creating such a system is identifying the dependencies of the constraints at both local and system level. After careful consideration, we concluded that the constraints have the following dependencies, as shown in figure 3:

- *The user requirements* are obviously the main driver for the constraint derivation. However, for automatic derivation we may only use quantifiable requirements. For instance "we want a fast system" is a requirement that may be quantified by a throughput constraint.
- *The system topology*, which includes by definition the partitioning and connections of our system, is playing an important role in constraint refinement. If, for instance, we choose to split one of the components in two smaller pieces that may work in parallel, the constraints for the original component will be redistributed accordingly.
- *The instantiations* of various system components are defining parameters that may also influence constraints. If we have an algorithm that requires a certain amount of data to start, such as a matrix inversion, this requirement is translated to a input constraint.
- Various other *local parameters* that do not fit in the above categories may be defined at any level in the system hierarchy.

**Fig. 3.** System constraints do not depend only on user requirements

If we want to capture the system constraints and to derive them in an automatic fashion, all these parameters must be encompassed in a formal constraint model.

## 3.2   The Mathematical Constraint Model

The formalism that we employ to describe the system constraints is based on the quantifiable user requirements obtained after the first level translation, as shown in figure 4.

A general constraint of a system component $C$ is a condition imposed on its behavior, performance or physical characteristics. In this paper a quantifiable constraint is called constraint for the sake of convenience.

**Definition 1.** *Let $K_C$ be the set of constraint values assigned to the system component $C$. Let $M_C$ be the set of metric values derived for the component $C$ after the performance evaluation. Let $m_x \in M_C$ a metric and $\kappa_x \in K_C$ a constraint.*

*By definition, the types of constraints are:*

1. *Equality (E): $m_x = \kappa_x$*
2. *Upper-bound (UB): $m_x \leq \kappa_x$*
3. *Lower-bound(LB): $m_x \geq \kappa_x$*
4. *Range (R): $m_x \in [\kappa_x(inf), \kappa_x(sup)]$*

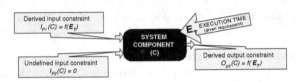

**Fig. 4.** A simple constraints derivation example: the I/O constraints depend on the execution time requirement of the given system component

**Definition 2.** *Let $P_C$ be the set of parameters that defines an instance of a system component $C$. Let $R_C$ be a set of requirements associated with $C$. Let $LP_C$ be the set of local parameters also associated with $C$.*

*A constraint of a system component $C$ is expressed as a function $\kappa_x = f_x(r_1, ..., r_m, p_1, ..., p_n, lp_1, ..., lp_o)$, where $r_i \in R$, $p_j \in P_C$ and $lp_k \in LP_C$.*

If we compare this definition with the relations expressed in figure 3, we notice that the formula does not capture explicitly the relation between a component topology and its constraints. However, we are to consider that the I/O constraints are defined on the ports of a given component, which are topological properties. Based on definition 2 we can conclude that we can define a superset of the requirements for the whole model:

**Definition 3.** *The union of all component requirement sets for a given system model $S$, $\bigcup_{C \in S} R_C$, $\forall C \in S$, is called a **requirement set**, and is denoted with $R_S$.*

The set $R_S$ defines all the requirements needed to instantiate the constraints of a model. Therefore the definition of a "what-if" scenario is essentially reduced to the creation of a new requirement set for the current model. We can define in the same fashion a superset of the local parameters:

**Definition 4.** *The union of all local component parameter sets for a given model, $\bigcup_{C \in S} LP_C$, $\forall C \in S$, is called a **parameter set**, and is denoted with $LP_S$.*

Together, $R_S$, $LP_S$ and the instantiation of the components in the current system completely determine the constraints. Therefore this formalism allows us to define a coherent way of deriving the constraints from the user requirements. Furthermore, by redefining $R_S$, $LP_S$ or both, the designer can automatically rederive the constraints of the model, thus being able to check flexibility, scalability and system tolerance issues.

Our constraint model is is essentially a simplified subset [7]and it is mainly designed to accompany existing library components and to provide an accessible way of specifying constraints. The simplifications derive mainly from the fact that we are evaluating the systems in their stable working state, and we neglect the transitional periods, which enables us to have static constraints that are valid during the whole life time of the system. However, we do enable the evaluation of the same system with different sets of constraints, which enable us to test the system also in border conditions and transitional states.

## 4  Constraint Propagation

In the ideal case, after the constraint derivation we would have instantiated all the constraints in the model. However, there may be situations where the requirement set is incomplete, and some of the constraints cannot be derived. In such cases we can take advantage of the topological information encompassed in the model and use it to propagate the I/O constraints over the communication lines, as shown in figure 5.

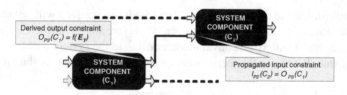

**Fig. 5.** The constraints are propagated over the connections between the system components

The non-I/O related constraints may only be propagated through the levels of the hierarchy, by using aggregation rules for all the components in a given container. For instance, an aggregation rule for the processing constraints of a container $\Omega$ may be written as $P_\Omega = \sum_{C_i \in \Omega} P_{C_i} * w_i$ where $w_i$ is a predefined weight associated with the component $C_i$.

If there are multiple connections on a given port, the behavior of the port may vary, and so the I/O constraint derivation will not be always consistent. That is why we have to impose certain restrictions on these topology patterns. Therefore, if an input port is writing on multiple output ports, we consider that the output is *duplicated*. If an output port reads from multiple input ports, we consider that the reading of data is simultaneous, and therefore the data streams are *summed*. The same operations will reflect upon the constraints on these ports.

The true value of constraint propagation is shown when we make use of the mapping layer to propagate constraints from the application model to the architecture model. The mapping layer describes the relations between the components in the two models, as

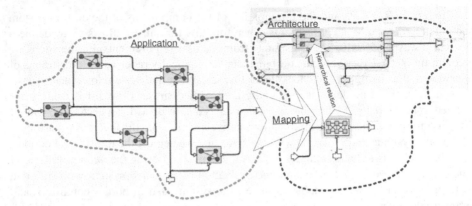

**Fig. 6.** The application constraints are pushed through the mapping layer into the architecture components and then further up in the architecture layer hierarchy

shown in figure 6. By treating the application components as being part of the bottom-most architecture layer, we are able to apply the same methods and aggregation rules as described above.

## 5   Constraint Validation and Adjustment

The compatibility of the derived constraints cannot be guaranteed without severely limiting the freedom of choices for the designer. Therefore we have to create a procedure that would validate the derived constraints according to the system topology, and adjust them if possible. We currently operate only on the I/O constraints, as shown in figure 7.

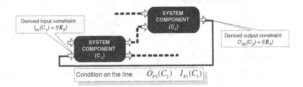

**Fig. 7.** If two I/O constraints are specified on a topology connection, we can verify if they are compatible

The example depicted in figure 7 takes into account only the case where we have two lower-bound constraints on the edges of a connection. However, there are many more cases to be considered. We are describing these cases with the use of three tables, which represent all the possible cases that we may encounter when we connect an output port $O$ with an associated constraint $\kappa_O$ to an input port $I$ with its respective constraint $\kappa_I$.

Table 1 and 2 describe the error and warning conditions for the constraints on the two given ports. Table 3 shows the adjustments that may be performed automatically if a warning condition is encountered. The adjustment procedure may change one or both constraints in order to make them compatible. The procedure is reliable in most cases; however, the constraints thus obtained are flagged in the model for later review. If necessary, the designer may choose to skip the adjustment procedure and manually fix the errors and warnings that may occur.

**Table 1.** Error conditions for constraints on a given connection

| Output/Input | $E_I : m = a$ | $UB_I : m \leq a$ | $LB_I : m \geq a$ | $R_I : m \in [a_1, a_2]$ |
|---|---|---|---|---|
| $E_O : m = b$ | $a \neq b$ | $a < b$ | $a > b$ | $b \notin [a_1, a_2]$ |
| $UB_O : m \leq b$ | $a > b$ | – | $a > b$ | $a_1 > b$ |
| $LB_O : m \geq b$ | $a < b$ | $a < b$ | – | $a_2 < b$ |
| $R_O : m \in [b_1, b_2]$ | $a \notin [b_1, b_2]$ | $a < b_1$ | $a > b_2$ | $(a_1 > b_2) \lor (a_2 < b_1)$ |

**Table 2.** Warning conditions for constraints on a given connection

| Output/Input | $E_I : m = a$ | $UB_I : m \leq a$ | $LB_I : m \geq a$ | $R_I : m \in [a_1, a_2]$ |
|---|---|---|---|---|
| $E_O : m = b$ | – | – | – | – |
| $UB_O : m \leq b$ | $a \leq b$ | $a < b$ | $a \leq b$ | $a_1 \leq b$ |
| $LB_O : m \geq b$ | $a \geq b$ | $a > b$ | $a \geq b$ | $a_2 \geq b$ |
| $R_O : m \in [b_1, b_2]$ | $a \in [b_1, b_2]$ | $a \in [b_1, b_2]$ | $a \in [b_1, b_2]$ | $(a_1 < b_1 \leq a_2 \leq b_2) \lor$ $(a_1 \leq b_1 \leq a_2 < b_2) \lor$ $(b_1 < a_1 \leq b_2 \leq a_2) \lor$ $(b_1 \leq a_1 \leq b_2 < a_2)$ |

**Table 3.** Adjustment of the constraints on a given connection

| Output/Input | $E_I : m = a$ | $UB_I : m \leq a$ | $LB_I : m \geq a$ | $R_I : m \in [a_1, a_2]$ |
|---|---|---|---|---|
| $E_O : m = b$ | – | $a = b$ | $a = b$ | $a_1 = b$ $a_2 = b$ |
| $UB_O : m \leq b$ | $b = a$ | $a = \min(a, b)$ $a = \min(a, b)$ | $a_1 = a, b_1 = a$ $a_2 = b, b_2 = b$ | $b_1 = a_1$ $b_2 = \min(a_2, b)$ $a_2 = \min(a_2, b)$ |
| $LB_O : m \geq b$ | $b = a$ | $a_1 = b, b_1 = b$ $a_2 = a, b_2 = a$ | $a = \max(a, b)$ $b = \max(a, b)$ | $b_1 = \max(a_1, b)$ $b_2 = a_2$ $a_1 = \max(a_1, b)$ |
| $R_O : m \in [b_1, b_2]$ | $a_1 = b_1$ $a_2 = \min(a, b_2)$ $b_2 = a$ | $a_1 = \max(a, b_1)$ $a_2 = b_2$ $b_2 = \min(a, b_2)$ | $a_1 = \max(a, b_1)$ $a_2 = b_2$ $b_1 = \max(a, b_1)$ | $a_1 = \max(a_1, b_1)$ $a_2 = \min(a_2, b_2)$ $b_1 = \max(a_1, b_1)$ $b_2 = \min(a_2, b_2)$ |

# 6   Implementation

We have implemented the constraint derivation and validation procedures in the *Massive Exploration Tool*[8], a framework that facilitates design space exploration for large scale embedded systems. The implementation integrates a mathematical expression evaluator for the constraint model, and defines requirement sets using a database core. The derived constraints may be reviewed by the designer and adjusted manually if necessary.

During an exploration exercise the automatic constraint derivation is playing a very important role. By defining ten alternative architectures and five different requirement sets, for instance, we are able to evaluate up to fifty different scenarios with ease. These scenarios may include "what-if" questions, scalability tests for future extensions, flexibility and stress conditions etc. The power of the constraint derivation is such that if

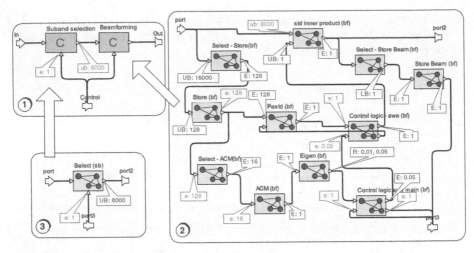

**Fig. 8.** A real-life example of the constraint derivation: the beam-forming subsystem of the LOFAR digital signal processing station. The application containers(1) partition the process network into a sub-band selection cluster(2) and a beam-forming cluster(3)

a requirement set for one of these conditions is defined, it can be reused to generate constraints for all the defined alternatives of the system.

As a driver application for our tool set we used the LOFAR radiotelescope, which is a good example of a large-scale distributed embedded system. The tool has been used to explore different realizations for the digital signal processing station of LOFAR[9].

The figure 8 depicts the constraint derivation and propagation for the beam-forming application of the DSP station. The application is specified as a Kahn process network[10], which is partitioned by the use of containers, shown in the first section of the picture. Initially the constraints were only derived on the components of the beam-forming cluster (shown in the second section), but after propagation they were propagated through the hierarchy all the way up to the containers.

During the exploration we did not encounter errors in the validation procedure - which is normal, if we are to consider that this is a real-life application. However, the error detection and adjustment were verified using small artificial examples during the development of the tool.

## 7   Conclusions

The translation of requirements into constraints is a crucial step in the design of any system. When fixed requirements are given, the translation usually has to be performed only once before the optimization stage. However, when the requirements are constantly changing, a need for automating the translation process becomes apparent. This is especially true for large scale embedded systems, which undergo extensive exploration in the initial development stages.

In this paper we have presented structured methods of automatically deriving constraints from user requirements and propagating these constraints through a hierarchical system topology. The derived constraints are also checked for inconsistencies and adjusted where possible.

We have implemented these methods in a software platform called the *Massive Exploration Tool*. This tool has been successfully used during a real-life exploration exercise for the digital signal processing station of the LOFAR radiotelescope.

# References

1. Nicolae, L., Alliot, S., Deprettere, E.: Component-level design space exploration for large scale embedded systems. In: In Proc. Advanced School for Computing and Imaging (ASCI'03). (2003) 68–73
2. Alliot, S.: Architecture Exploration For Large Scale Array Signal Processing Systems. PhD thesis, Leiden University (2003)
3. Taguchi, G.: System of Experimental Design. Volume 1,2. UNIPUB/Krass International Publications, New York (1987)
4. Balarin, F., Sentovich, E., Chiodo, M., Hsieh, H., Tabbara, B., Jurecska, A., Lavagno, L., Passerone, C., Suzuki, K., Sangiovanni-Vincentelli, A.: Hardware-Software Co-design of Embedded Systems - The POLIS Approach. Kluwer Academic Publishers (1997)
5. Balarin, F., Watanabe, Y., Hsieh, H., Lavagno, L., Passerone, C., Sangiovanni-Vincentelli, A.L.: Metropolis: An integrated electronic system design environment. In: IEEE Computer. Number 1 in 36 (2003) 45–52
6. Alliot, S.: A performance/cost estimation model for the large distributed array signal processing system and specification. In: In Proc. Workshop on Synthesis, Architectures, Modeling, and Simulation (SAMOS03). (2003) 154–160
7. Balarin, F., Burch, J., Lavagno, L., Passerone, R., Sangiovanni-Vincentelli, A., Watanabe, Y.: Constraints specification at higher levels of abstraction. In: In Proceedings of IEEE International High Level Design Validation and Test Workshop (HLDVT2001). (2001)
8. Alliot, S., van Veelen, M., Nicolae, L., Coolen, A.: The MASSIVE Exploration Tool. University Booth Demonstration, Design Automation and Test in Europe (DATE'03) (2003)
9. Alliot, S.: LOFAR station digital processing, architectural design description. Technical Report LOFAR-ASTRON-ADD-007, ASTRON (2002) www.lofar.org.
10. Kahn, G.: The semantics of a simple language for parallel programming. In: Proc. of the IFIP Congress 74, North-Holland Publishing Co. (1974)

# Author Index

# Lecture Notes in Computer Science

For information about Vols. 1–3025

please contact your bookseller or Springer-Verlag

Vol. 3068: E. André, L. Dybkj{\}ae r, W. Minker, P. Heisterkamp (Eds.), Affective Dialogue Systems. XII, 324 pages. 2004. (Subseries LNAI).

Vol. 3067: M. Dastani, J. Dix, A. El Fallah-Seghrouchni (Eds.), Programming Multi-Agent Systems. X, 221 pages. 2004. (Subseries LNAI).

Vol. 3066: S. Tsumoto, R. S lowiński, J. Komorowski, J.W. Grzymala-Busse (Eds.), Rough Sets and Current Trends in Computing. XX, 853 pages. 2004. (Subseries LNAI).

Vol. 3065: A. Lomuscio, D. Nute (Eds.), Deontic Logic in Computer Science. X, 275 pages. 2004. (Subseries LNAI).

Vol. 3064: D. Bienstock, G. Nemhauser (Eds.), Integer Programming and Combinatorial Optimization. XI, 445 pages. 2004.

Vol. 3063: A. Llamosí, A. Strohmeier (Eds.), Reliable Software Technologies - Ada-Europe 2004. XIII, 333 pages. 2004.

Vol. 3062: J.L. Pfaltz, M. Nagl, B. Böhlen (Eds.), Applications of Graph Transformations with Industrial Relevance. XV, 500 pages. 2004.

Vol. 3061: F.F. Ramos, H. Unger, V. Larios (Eds.), Advanced Distributed Systems. VIII, 285 pages. 2004.

Vol. 3060: A.Y. Tawfik, S.D. Goodwin (Eds.), Advances in Artificial Intelligence. XIII, 582 pages. 2004. (Subseries LNAI).

Vol. 3059: C.C. Ribeiro, S.L. Martins (Eds.), Experimental and Efficient Algorithms. X, 586 pages. 2004.

Vol. 3058: N. Sebe, M.S. Lew, T.S. Huang (Eds.), Computer Vision in Human-Computer Interaction. X, 233 pages. 2004.

Vol. 3057: B. Jayaraman (Ed.), Practical Aspects of Declarative Languages. VIII, 255 pages. 2004.

Vol. 3056: H. Dai, R. Srikant, C. Zhang (Eds.), Advances in Knowledge Discovery and Data Mining. XIX, 713 pages. 2004. (Subseries LNAI).

Vol. 3055: H. Christiansen, M.-S. Hacid, T. Andreasen, H.L. Larsen (Eds.), Flexible Query Answering Systems. X, 500 pages. 2004. (Subseries LNAI).

Vol. 3054: I. Crnkovic, J.A. Stafford, H.W. Schmidt, K. Wallnau (Eds.), Component-Based Software Engineering. XI, 311 pages. 2004.

Vol. 3053: C. Bussler, J. Davies, D. Fensel, R. Studer (Eds.), The Semantic Web: Research and Applications. XIII, 490 pages. 2004.

Vol. 3052: W. Zimmermann, B. Thalheim (Eds.), Abstract State Machines 2004. Advances in Theory and Practice. XII, 235 pages. 2004.

Vol. 3051: R. Berghammer, B. Möller, G. Struth (Eds.), Relational and Kleene-Algebraic Methods in Computer Science. X, 279 pages. 2004.

Vol. 3050: J. Domingo-Ferrer, V. Torra (Eds.), Privacy in Statistical Databases. IX, 367 pages. 2004.

Vol. 3049: M. Bruynooghe, K.-K. Lau (Eds.), Program Development in Computational Logic. VIII, 539 pages. 2004.

Vol. 3047: F. Oquendo, B. Warboys, R. Morrison (Eds.), Software Architecture. X, 279 pages. 2004.

Vol. 3046: A. Laganà, M.L. Gavrilova, V. Kumar, Y. Mun, C.J.K. Tan, O. Gervasi (Eds.), Computational Science and Its Applications – ICCSA 2004. LIII, 1016 pages. 2004.

Vol. 3045: A. Laganà, M.L. Gavrilova, V. Kumar, Y. Mun, C.J.K. Tan, O. Gervasi (Eds.), Computational Science and Its Applications – ICCSA 2004. LIII, 1040 pages. 2004.

Vol. 3044: A. Laganà, M.L. Gavrilova, V. Kumar, Y. Mun, C.J.K. Tan, O. Gervasi (Eds.), Computational Science and Its Applications – ICCSA 2004. LIII, 1140 pages. 2004.

Vol. 3043: A. Laganà, M.L. Gavrilova, V. Kumar, Y. Mun, C.J.K. Tan, O. Gervasi (Eds.), Computational Science and Its Applications – ICCSA 2004. LIII, 1180 pages. 2004.

Vol. 3042: N. Mitrou, K. Kontovasilis, G.N. Rouskas, I. Iliadis, L. Merakos (Eds.), NETWORKING 2004, Networking Technologies, Services, and Protocols; Performance of Computer and Communication Networks; Mobile and Wireless Communications. XXXIII, 1519 pages. 2004.

Vol. 3040: R. Conejo, M. Urretavizcaya, J.-L. Pérez-de-la-Cruz (Eds.), Current Topics in Artificial Intelligence. XIV, 689 pages. 2004. (Subseries LNAI).

Vol. 3039: M. Bubak, G.D.v. Albada, P.M.A. Sloot, J.J. Dongarra (Eds.), Computational Science - ICCS 2004. LXVI, 1271 pages. 2004.

Vol. 3038: M. Bubak, G.D.v. Albada, P.M.A. Sloot, J.J. Dongarra (Eds.), Computational Science - ICCS 2004. LXVI, 1311 pages. 2004.

Vol. 3037: M. Bubak, G.D.v. Albada, P.M.A. Sloot, J.J. Dongarra (Eds.), Computational Science - ICCS 2004. LXVI, 745 pages. 2004.

Vol. 3036: M. Bubak, G.D.v. Albada, P.M.A. Sloot, J.J. Dongarra (Eds.), Computational Science - ICCS 2004. LXVI, 713 pages. 2004.

Vol. 3035: M.A. Wimmer (Ed.), Knowledge Management in Electronic Government. XII, 326 pages. 2004. (Subseries LNAI).

Vol. 3034: J. Favela, E. Menasalvas, E. Chávez (Eds.), Advances in Web Intelligence. XIII, 227 pages. 2004. (Subseries LNAI).

Vol. 3033: M. Li, X.-H. Sun, Q. Deng, J. Ni (Eds.), Grid and Cooperative Computing. XXXVIII, 1076 pages. 2004.

Vol. 3032: M. Li, X.-H. Sun, Q. Deng, J. Ni (Eds.), Grid and Cooperative Computing. XXXVII, 1112 pages. 2004.

Vol. 3031: A. Butz, A. Krüger, P. Olivier (Eds.), Smart Graphics. X, 165 pages. 2004.

Vol. 3030: P. Giorgini, B. Henderson-Sellers, M. Winikoff (Eds.), Agent-Oriented Information Systems. XIV, 207 pages. 2004. (Subseries LNAI).

Vol. 3029: B. Orchard, C. Yang, M. Ali (Eds.), Innovations in Applied Artificial Intelligence. XXI, 1272 pages. 2004. (Subseries LNAI).

Vol. 3028: D. Neuenschwander, Probabilistic and Statistical Methods in Cryptology. X, 158 pages. 2004.

Vol. 3027: C. Cachin, J. Camenisch (Eds.), Advances in Cryptology - EUROCRYPT 2004. XI, 628 pages. 2004.

Vol. 3026: C.V. Ramamoorthy, R. Lee, K.W. Lee (Eds.), Software Engineering Research and Applications. XV, 377 pages. 2004.